CW01496819

On Sacred Grounds

Culture, Society, Politics, and the Formation of the Cult of Confucius

Harvard East Asian Monographs 217

像之王宣文聖至成大

"The Great Consummation, Supreme Sage, Exalted King of Culture." Seated Image of Confucius wearing the royal twelve-tassled head gear and robe bearing the twelve insignias of the sovereign.

On Sacred Grounds

Culture, Society, Politics, and the Formation of the Cult of Confucius

Thomas A. Wilson, editor

Published by the Harvard University Asia Center
and distributed by Harvard University Press
Cambridge (Massachusetts) and London 2002

Printed in the United States of America

The Harvard University Asia Center publishes a monograph series and, in coordination with the Fairbank Center for East Asian Research, the Korea Institute, the Reischauer Institute of Japanese Studies, and other faculties and institutes, administers research projects designed to further scholarly understanding of China, Japan, Vietnam, Korea, and other Asian countries. The Center also sponsors projects addressing multidisciplinary and regional issues in Asia.

Library of Congress Cataloging-in-Publication Data
On sacred grounds : culture, society, politics, and the formation of the cult of Confucius / Thomas A. Wilson, editor.
    p. cm -- (Harvard East Asian monographs ; 217)
    Includes bibliographical references and index.
    ISBN 0-674-00961-4 (alk. paper)
       1. Confucianism--Rituals. I. Wilson, Thomas A., 1954– II. Series
    BL.1858.O5 2002
    299'.512--dc21   2002027570

Index by the editor and authors

☧   Printed on acid-free paper

Last figure below indicates year of this printing
12 11 10 09 08 07 06 05 04 03 02

Contents

Table, Maps, Music Examples, and Figures   vii

Preface   xi

Contributors   xiii

Maps   xv

Introduction: Culture, Society, Politics, and the Cult of Confucius   1
Thomas A. Wilson

PART I   RITES AND MUSIC

1   Ritualizing Confucius/Kongzi: The Family and State Cults of
the Sage of Culture in Imperial China   43
Thomas A. Wilson

2   Destroying Confucius: Iconoclasm in the Confucian Temple   95
Deborah Sommer

3   Musical Confucianism: The Case of 'Jikong yuewu'   134
Joseph S. C. Lam

PART II   IMAGINING CONFUCIUS

4   The Genesis of Kongzi in Ancient Narrative: The Figurative
As Historical   175
Lionel M. Jensen

5   Varied Views of the Sage: Illustrated Narratives of the
Life of Confucius   222
Julia K. Murray

PART III   POLITICS AND SOCIETY

6   *The Cultural Politics of Autocracy: The Confucius Temple
     and Ming Despotism, 1368–1530*   267
     Huang Chin-shing

7   *The Kongs of Qufu: Power and Privilege in Late Imperial China*   297
     Abigail Lamberton

PART IV   THE PAST IN THE PRESENT

8   *Knowledge, Organization, and Symbolic Capital: Two Temples
     to Confucius in Gansu*   335
     Jun Jing

9   *The Confucius Temple Tragedy of the Cultural Revolution*   376
     Wang Liang

     Index   401

Table, Maps, Music Examples, and Figures

TABLE

5.1 Major versions of the *Shengji tu*   234

MAPS

1   Ming China   xv
2   Qufu area around the time of Confucius   xvi

MUSIC EXAMPLES

1   Song of welcome, Ming *jikong yuewu*   149
2   Li Zhizao's version of the Ming dynasty song of welcome   153
3   Qiu Zhilu's version of the song of welcome in the
    Qing *jikong yuewu*   162
4   Song of welcome in the Qufu *jikong yuewu* (1990)   167

FIGURES

The Confucius Temple in Modern China (following p. 94)

   Hall of Great Completion, Confucius Temple, Beijing
   Principal consecration officer, Beijing
   Principal offerings to the spirit of Confucius, Beijing

Confucius Temple, Quzhou, Zhejiang

Ceremonial dancers, Beijing

Confucius's altar, Confucius Temple, Qufu, Shandong

Confucius's spirit tablet, Confucius Temple, Beijing

Conficius's spirit table, and altar, Confucius Temple, Tainan, Taiwan

3.1   Choreographic poses for the first phrase of the first offering song in the Ming *jikong yuewu*, 1544   158

3.2   Choreographic poses for the first phrase of the first offering song in the Ming *jikong yuewu*, 1618   159

3.3   Choreographic poses for the first phrase of the first offering song in the Qing *jikong yuewu*, 1719   160

3.4   Choreographic poses for the first phrase of the first offering song in the Qing *jikong yuewu*, 1749   163

Images of the Sage (following p. 254)

5.1   Confucius plays the chimes stones, Eastern Han

5.2   Confucius meets Laozi, Eastern Han

5.3   Confucius's mother prays on Mount Ni, Ming

5.4   Confucius plays at performing rites, Ming

5.5   Confucius visiting Laozi, Ming

5.6   Confucius leaves the state of Qi, Ming

5.7   Confucius plays the chime stones, Ming

5.8   Confucius mourns the dead *qilin*, Ming

5.9   A feeble Confucius stands in the gate and talks with Zi Gong, Ming

5.10 The disciples mourn at Confucius's grave, 1548

5.11 Han Gaozu's sacrifice, late sixteenth century

5.12 Scenes from the life of the Buddha, 543

5.13 Confucius's mother receives the tablet from the *qilin*, 1599

5.14 Confucius is born with a five-character inscription on his chest, 1589

5.15   Confucius kneels to acknowledge the rainbow from
       the Big Dipper, 1548

5.16   The birth of Confucius's son and gift of a carp, Ming

5.17   Confucius at the ancestral temple of Duke Huan of Lu, Ming

5.18   Disciples mourn at Confucius's grave, 1598

5.19   Confucius's parents pray in temple to deity of Mount Ni, Ming

5.20   Confucius entertaining his parents at a feast, Ming

5.21   Confucius's father receives the tablet from the *qilin*, Ming

5.22   Birth of Confucius's grandson, Ming

5.23   Qin Shihuangdi desecrates Confucius's grave, Ming/Qing

5.24   Discovery of old texts in the wall of Confucius's house, Ming/Qing

5.25   Confucius's parents pray on Mount Ni, Ming/Qing

5.26   Burying his parents in the same mound, 1592

5.27   Respect and yielding: Duke Jing, 1592

5.28   Receiving favor and requesting punishment, Qing

5.29   The birth of Confucius, Qing

5.30   Birth of Confucius's son, 1934/1984

5.31   Confucius sets his heart on study, 1989

5.32   Page from *Recorded Matters Concerning Divine Beauties*, 1602

Preface

Widely regarded as China's most influential thinker, Confucius (551–479 BCE) is known around the world by the humanist philosophy advanced in the *Analects*. Yet, Confucius was more than a philosopher, and the teachings associated with him are not limited to this book. Confucius was, indeed, many things throughout the ages. He was an object of cult veneration in temples, where his spirit received sacrifices from officers of the court and from the emperor himself. These rites were elaborate ceremonies based on ancient ritual canons that prescribed the foods offered to the spirit, the hymns to be chanted, and music to be played. The statue of Confucius placed in the temple was exactingly fashioned to facilitate his spirit's access to the offerings.

Confucius was China's premier exemplar of a code of ethical and political ideals. He was also a mythic figure surrounded by lore of sacred pedigree and miraculous birth and life. Stories about his descent from a divine lineage of kings can be found in ancient writings. Other fabulous stories about him are found in Sima Qian's (ca. 145–ca. 86 BCE) history of China and in the noncanonical, apocryphal works that proliferated in the Han dynasty (206 BCE–220 CE). It is said that he was born of a mage who encountered a dark god in the wilds where she prayed for a son. The figure of Confucius as moral paragon dominates the first pictorial biographies of his life, yet the ever-changing status of Confucius as cultural icon was soon evident with the addition, in later versions of this pictorial biography, of miraculous stories of his birth, life, and encounter with a fabulous beast in his final year of life.

As the consummate embodiment of the ritual and canonical traditions called "Confucianism" in the West, Confucius symbolized the classically trained men who served the emperor at the imperial court in the capital and in the bureaucracy throughout the empire. During the Ming, more autocratically inclined emperors sought to exalt their standing at court and in the imperial cult by demoting the gods of the pantheon and even briefly suspending sacrifices to Confucius, which provoked strident resistance from court ministers, who risked their lives in their defense of these sacred rites.

Confucius was the progenitor of China's oldest hereditary noble family; a family that maintained its own ancestral cult and held a vast estate in Confucius's ancestral homeland. Many descendants migrated to other parts of China, even to distant Gansu province in the northwest. The noble title of Duke held by the senior lineage heir since the tenth century was abolished in the twentieth century, but many of the hereditary privileges of this household continued until the advent of socialist revolution, when the fortune of China's "first family" reversed dramatically. In the Cultural Revolution (1966–76), the statue of Confucius and the temple in which it was housed were objects of political desecration by Red Guards who came to Confucius's birthplace to "topple the Confucius family shop." In the decades since then, Confucius's descendants have pooled their cultural and economic resources to gradually recapture at least a glimmer of an ancient brilliance through the restoration of the temple.

The chapters in this volume examine Confucianism from the varied perspectives of ritual cults, music, myth, material culture, politics, and genealogy, and in so doing complicate our understanding of it as an ethical philosophy adhered to exclusively by China's social and cultural elite. Several of the essays began as conference papers presented on panels at two successive meetings of the Association for Asian Studies. Two other pieces originally written in Chinese were translated into English with support by a grant from the China and Inner Asia Council of the Association for Asian Studies funded by the Chiang Ching-kuo Foundation of Taiwan.

T.A.W.

Contributors

Huang Chin-shing is head of the History Section of the Institute of History and Philology, Academia Sinica. He recently published *Business as a Vocation: The Autobiography of Wu Ho-su* (2002).

Lionel M. Jensen, Associate Professor of East Asian Languages & Literatures and Concurrent Associate Professor of History at the University of Notre Dame, is the author of *Manufacturing Confucianism: Chinese Traditions and Universal Civilization* (1997).

Jun Jing is Professor of Anthropology in the School of Humanities and Social Sciences at Tsinghua University in the People's Republic of China and the author of *Temple of Memories: History, Power, and Morality in a Chinese Village* (1996) and of many articles on Chinese popular religion and environmental issues.

Joseph S. C. Lam is Professor of Music at the University of Michigan and author of *State Sacrifices and Music in Ming China* (1998). His current projects include a book manuscript on Southern Song dynasty music and articles on music and musicians of the Northern Song and Ming dynasties.

Abigail Lamberton is visiting Instructor at Gustavus Adolphus College in St. Peter, Minnesota. She is writing a Ph.D. dissertation on a social history of the descendants of Confucius in Qufu, Shandong.

Julia K. Murray is Professor of Chinese Art History at the University of Wisconsin-Madison. Her publications include *Ma Hezhi and the Illustration of the Book of Odes* (1993), *Last of the Mandarins* (1987), and numerous articles on Chinese art, particularly narrative illustration, including pictorial biographies of Confucius.

Deborah A. Sommer is Assistant Professor of Religion at Gettysburg College. She is writing a book on the subject of spirit and images in the cult of Confucius and the religious significance of the body of Confucius.

Curtis Dean Smith, Assistant Professor of Chinese at Grand Valley State University, received his Ph.D. in Chinese Literature from National Taiwan Normal University. He has published articles on the literature and thought of Su Shi (1037–1101) and is currently working on a book on the intellectual life of Su Shi.

Wang Liang is the editor of a newspaper published by the Qufu Cultural Center and the author (under the pseudonym Yazi) of *Kongfu da jienan* 孔府大劫難 (The great Confucius Mansion disaster; 1991).

Thomas A. Wilson, Professor of History and Chair of Asian Studies at Hamilton College, is the author *Genealogy of the Way: The Construction and Uses of the Confucian Tradition in Late Imperial China* (1995).

Map 1 Ming Dynasty China

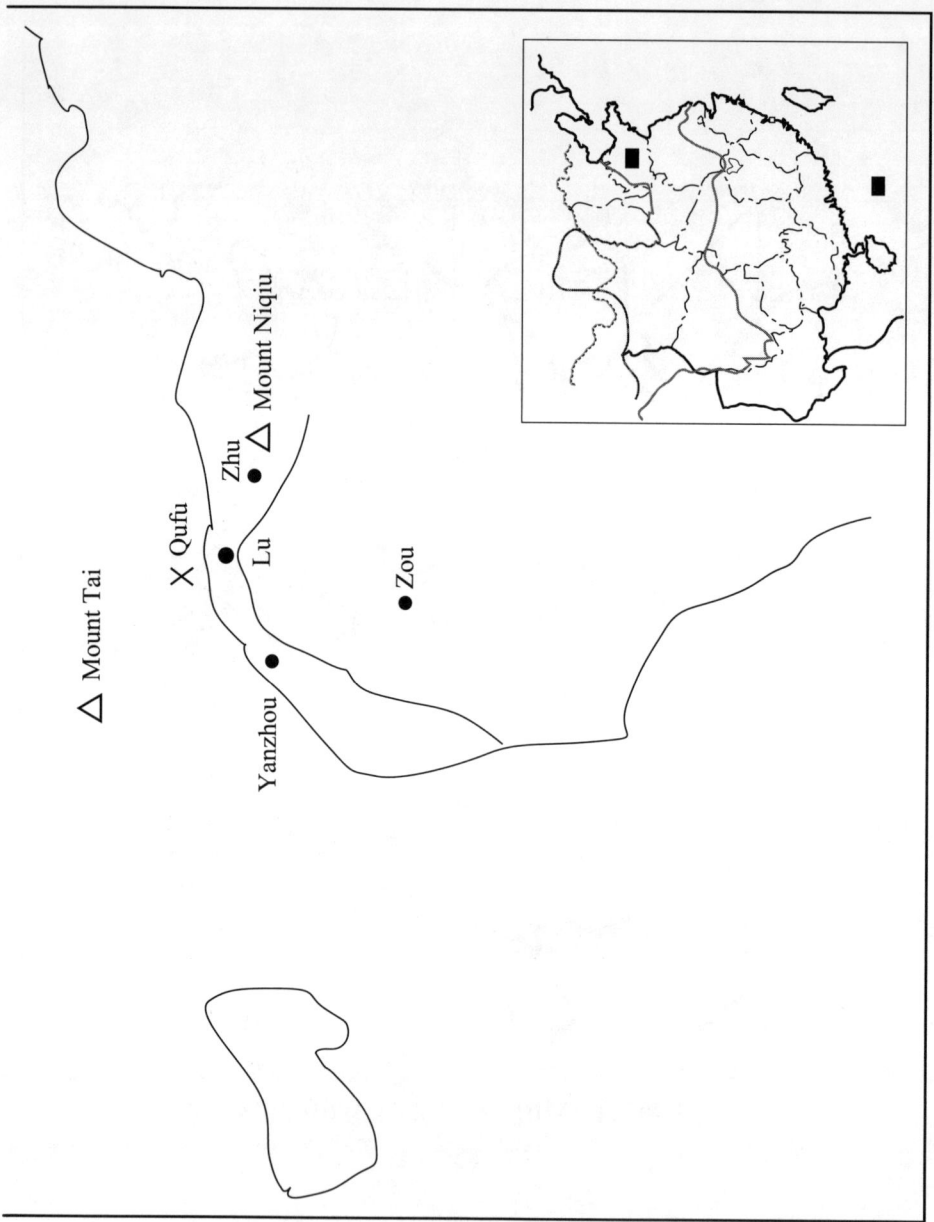

Map 2 Qufu Area Around the Time of Confucius

On Sacred Grounds

Culture, Society, Politics, and the Formation
of the Cult of Confucius

INTRODUCTION

Culture, Society, Politics, and

the Cult of Confucius

Thomas A. Wilson

LOCATING THE TEMPLE

The map of the sacred landscape of imperial China found in local gazetteers is dotted with temples and shrines scattered throughout town and country. To the untutored eye, this profusion of Buddhist monasteries, Daoist temples, shrines devoted to local deities, and the temples and altars of the mandarinate must appear random. Indeed, many worshippers on the ground (as opposed to those viewing the map) may not have discerned any order at all, for it was possible not to be aware of the hierarchy superimposed on this sacred landscape by the officials in the Ministry of Rites. At the pinnacle of the imperial pantheon of gods and spirits propitiated by these temple cults was the Supreme Emperor of Mysterious Heaven (Xuan Tian shangdi 玄天上帝), who received the great sacrifice from the emperor at the open round altar of Heaven (tiantan 天壇) south of the imperial city.[1] Heaven was

I thank Buzzy Teiser for his thorough comments on this essay and my student Brooks Jessup for his work on nineteenth-century missionary writings on Chinese religion.

1. The names of the deities and spirits in the pantheon and the locations where sacrifices were offered changed somewhat over time. Sacrifices to Hao Tian Shangdi 昊天上帝 (the name used in Zhouli zhengyi 18.119 [757]) at one altar in the southern suburbs with imperial ancestors as correlates tended to prevail throughout imperial times (e.g., Xin Tang shu 11.314; Ming shi 47.1230). There are, however, occasional references to separate sacrifices to Heaven at the southern suburban altar with Lord Millet as correlate, and to Shangdi in the Mingtang with King Wen 文王 as correlate. Tang commentaries on Liji zhengyi (24.211 [1439]) and

followed by other deities in the official pantheon: August Earth (*huangdiqi* 皇地祇) received sacrifices at an open square altar north of the capital, and the spirits of the dynastic ancestors and the gods of soils and grains received offerings in temples located inside the imperial city walls. These were followed by mid-level sacrifices to deities of the sun and moon, of agriculture and sericulture, spirits of the culture heroes of remote antiquity, and the sovereigns of past dynasties, among others.[2]

In the middle of this hierarchy was the temple devoted to the veneration of the sage of culture known in the West by the latinate name Confucius (Kong Fuzi 孔夫子 or Kongzi 孔子).[3] Inside the Temples to Confucius (*Kongmiao* 孔廟) located in the capital and in every provincial capital and county seat of the empire were two corridors (or cloisters) running the full length of both sides of the inner temple grounds. In the center, toward the

---

Chunqiu Zuozhuan zhengyi (30.236 [1938]) refer to such sacrifices offered by the Duke of Zhou 周公 as described in *Xiaojing zhushu* (5.15 [2553]). The Han court followed this precedent at least twice: in 89 BCE (Wudi zhenghe 4/3/18; *Hanshu* 6.207) and 4 CE (Pingdi yuanshi 4/1; *Hanshu* 12.356) and the Tang court followed it at least once, in 656 (*Jiu Tang shu* 21.821–22). The identity of Shangdi as the recipient of sacrifice was subject to disagreement. Wang Su 王肅 (195?–256) made the simple equation that Shangdi is Heaven; Ma Rong 馬融 (79–166) held that Heaven is the spirit of Taiyi 太一 and is what is most revered in Heaven; Du You 杜佑 (735–812) believed that when primal *qi* 元氣 expands, it is called Hao Tian, and that nothing is more revered by people than Di, which rests in Heaven and thus is called Shangdi (*Zizhi tongjian* 36.1144).

2. The system of cults described here is based on late imperial sources. For descriptions of these ritual sites in the capital, see Meyer, *The Dragons of Tiananmen*, chaps. 2–3. The emperor was the first to plow the land at the beginning of each planting season (*huangdi gengjing* 皇帝躬耕), and the empress personally offered the first incense to the sericulture god (*huanghou qinxiang* 皇后親饗) on the event of its birthday (*Qing huidian tu* 12.114, 14.140). The culture heroes were Fuxi 伏羲, Shennong 神農, the Yellow Emperor 黃帝, Yao 堯, Shun 舜, Yu 禹, Tang 湯, King Wen 文王, and King Wu 武王. The Duke of Zhou 周公 and Confucius 孔子 were correlates (ibid., 15.145–46). The sovereigns included the Three August Ones 三皇, the Five Emperors 五帝, and the emperors of seventeen dynasties from the Xia through the Ming (ibid., 15.153–54).

3. The name "Confucius" was coined by Jesuits in the seventeenth century, purportedly based on the colloquial Chinese name Kong Fuzi. The man is referred to in formal writing as Kongzi (Master Kong) and the Master (Fuzi). See Chapter 1 of this book for other official titles conferred on Confucius. I refer to temples that honored the major Confucian thinkers as "Confucius temples" or "Kong temples" (*Kongmiao*) because the Chinese term refers to Confucius's surname (Kong 孔), not to the literati tradition (*ru* 儒), which, since at least as early as the 1830s, English-speaking missionaries have rendered as Confucianism.

north end of the complex, opposite the entrance, was an elevated square hall that housed Confucius's spirit tablet, which bore the inscription "Supreme sage, first master, Master Kong." Twice a year members of the local educated elite and the highest officials in the area gathered before dawn to offer a feast of wine, animal sacrifices, vegetables, grains, soups, and cakes to the spirit of Confucius, his disciples, and the eminent scholars of the Confucian tradition (the latter were housed in the two corridors). Drums, bronze bells, jade chimes, and string and wind instruments were played, promising youth from the local school danced in a slow, deliberate sequence of prescribed bodily dispositions, and celebrants sang prayers extolling Confucius as without peer in human history, equal to Heaven and Earth.

CHRISTIAN MISSIONARIES AND CONFUCIAN RELIGIOUSNESS

The worship of Confucius is probably one of the least understood aspects of Confucianism, even though the temple was one of the most visible signs of Confucianism's existence on the cultural landscape of imperial China. To many Western observers in China over the past several centuries, the temple cult has proved difficult to reconcile with the dominant image of Confucius as the consummate ethical humanist, who, the *Analects* tells us, urged his followers to keep the spirits at a distance. The tendency of not confronting the messy ramifications of the religious worship of a philosopher began at least as early as the seventeenth century when Jesuit missionaries sought to convince Rome that the Confucian literati—the principal target of their proselytizing efforts—need not renounce their creed before converting to Christianity since Confucianism was merely a system of ethics. Jesuits attributed to Confucianism a separation between society and the divine as early as the writings of Matteo Ricci (1552–1610), who declaimed, "Although the literati do not set out to speak of supernatural things, in morals they are almost completely in accord with us."[4] At times, however, Ricci seemed ambivalent toward Confucius: he admired Confucius as a "pagan philosopher," much as he admired Plato and Aristotle, yet he referred to Confucius as a saint and spoke of him as a prophet of a Chinese monotheism that had perished in the

---

4. Quoted in Jensen, *Manufacturing Confucianism*, p. 93.

cataclysmic burning of the Confucian classics in the Qin dynasty (246–207 BCE), although vestiges of it remained in some of the older books.[5]

The Jesuits' image of the Confucius temple in their construction of this pagan philosopher is especially germane to this volume. The Jesuits were at pains to convince Rome that the temple sacrifices to Confucius were "purely civil respect" that did not pay him "divine honors."[6] The major scholarly Jesuit project, entitled *Confucius, Chinese Philosopher* (*Confucius sinarum philosophus*), completed in 1687, included translations of the *Analects*, *Great Learning*, *Doctrine of the Mean*, and a biography of Confucius. The frontispiece of this work bears an engraving of Confucius that could be a full frontal version of the Tang (618–907) painter Wu Daozi's 吳道子 (ca. 689–ca. 755) famous portrait of Confucius, except that he is holding one of the jade tablets used to designate court or feudal rank, much like the sitting statue of him in the temple located in his birthplace in Qufu, Shandong.[7] In the Jesuit rendering, Confucius is standing before what appears to be a temple—the lower portion of the building's interior is lined with spirit tablets—or a library—the upper portion is lined with books. The composite of temple and library, David Mungello suggests, is almost certainly an intentional conflation, for the "Jesuits were doubtless aware that associating a temple with a library would dull the religious import of the temple."[8]

---

5. Ricci and Trigault, *China in the Sixteenth Century*, p. 30; Mungello, *Curious Land*, pp. 57, 266; Jensen, *Manufacturing Confucianism*, p. 94. Athanasius Kircher (1601–80), among other Jesuits, refuted this accommodationist stance toward Confucianism (Mungello, *Curious Land*, pp. 157–64). The Congregation for the Propagation of the Faith rejected this approach when, in 1645, it condemned official rites to Confucius and Confucian ancestral sacrifices as pagan rites incompatible with Christianity. Ricci's view prevailed in Rome from 1656 until 1704, at which point the ban on these rites was restored. It was not lifted until 1939. For two studies on Jesuit accommodation and Confucianism, see Mungello, *Curious Land* (esp. pp. 247–99); and Jensen, *Manufacturing Confucianism*, chap. 1.

6. Mungello, *Curious Land*, p. 291; Jensen, *Manufacturing Confucianism*, p. 64.

7. Murray, "Illustrations of the Life of Confucius," p. 75. See the frontispiece to this book.

8. Mungello, *Curious Land*, pp. 271–77; Jensen, *Manufacturing Confucianism*, pp. 130–32. The frontispiece is reproduced in Mungello (p. 274) and Jensen (p. 82). Ricci's journals mention the temple, which he is quick to locate "in that part of the city which has been described as the center of learning." He describes the ritual as a series of "bowing and of bending knees, of the lighting of candles, and the burning of incense. . . . they offer him dishes of food elaborately prepared and assert their thanks for the doctrines contained in his writings." He assures the reader that "they do not recite prayers to Confucius nor do they ask for favors of him or expect help from him" (Ricci and Trigault, *China in the Sixteenth Century*, pp. 96–97).

Papal authorities in Rome did not fully endorse the Jesuit image of Confucius as a pagan philosopher, although many elements of this view can be found in Western discussions of Confucius in the following centuries. The Protestant missionary James Legge's (1815–97) understanding of China was largely a product of the community of Protestant missionary-sinophiles, including Robert Morrison (1782–1834), William Milne (1785–1822), and Walter Medhurst (1796–1857), who, among them, had produced an impressive body of scholarship and travel accounts that played an important role in training Legge and several generations of Protestant missionaries that followed.[9] In *A Dictionary of the Chinese Language*, Robert Morrison summarized Chinese discussions of the concept of Heaven: "The philosophers of China have groped as men in the dark, in their reasonings respecting the Diety, but they can scarcely be said to have found *Him*."[10] Legge was convinced that Confucius "was unreligious rather than irreligious." He said that by identifying "God with a principle of reason and the course of nature," Confucius had led his disciples "to deny, like the Sadducees of old, the existence of any spirit at all."[11] Legge drew from the *Analects* to support this view: in response to a query on how to serve the spirits of the dead, Confucius said, "While you are not able to serve man, how can you serve their spirits?"[12] And Legge translated Confucius's answer to a query on wisdom as "To give oneself earnestly to the duties due to men, and, while respecting spiritual beings, to keep aloof from them, may be called wisdom."[13] Legge found Confucius wanting in the sincere faith in God evident in such ancient books as the *Odes* and *Documents*, in which references to *shangdi* 上帝 are frequent. Instead,

---

9. See Rubinstein, *The Origins of the Anglo-American Missionary Enterprise in China*, chap. 3. There were some important differences among them. They differed, for example, over the critical issue of how to translate the term "God" into Chinese. Morrison and Milne favored the generic term *shen*, and Medhurst and Legge favored *Shangdi* (Couling, *Encyclopaedia Sinica*, p. 554).

10. Morrison, *A Dictionary of the Chinese Language*, 1: 578. Italics in original.

11. Legge, *Confucian Analects*, pp. 99–100.

12. Ibid., 99 (11.11). Soothill (*Analects of Confucius*, pp. 520–22) notes that "Confucius evaded a difficult question" but does not infer skepticism from this remark; rather, he cross-references this to passages that affirm the importance of sacrificing to spirits (e.g., *Analects* 3.12) and quotes Zhu Xi's comment, "Someone has said that though Confucius did not inform Tzu Lu, who did not understand, yet he gave him a profound answer" (*Lunyu jizhu* 6.2b–3a). Ōtsuki Nobuyoshi (*Shushi "Shi sho shūchū" tenkyo kō*, 178) points out that the preceding passage attributed to Cheng Yi ends just before the passage beginning "Someone has said."

13. Legge, *Confucian Analects*, p. 100 (6.20).

Confucius nearly always used the impersonal term "Heaven," which Legge regarded as a colder, harsher god.[14] In debates with other missionaries, Legge maintained that the two terms were ultimately synonymous but granted higher status to Shangdi as the "one Being" that rules supreme above all else.[15]

Like the Jesuits before him, Legge regarded Confucius himself as a religious skeptic, but he was at the same time deeply impressed by what he saw as the vestiges of an underlying monotheism in the state religion. Legge maintained that imperial worship of Heaven preserved an ancient monotheism expressed in the term "Shangdi," which he translates "God," and argued against the position taken by many, perhaps most other Protestants in China, that because of the polytheism evidenced in the Chinese emperor's worship of both Heaven and Earth at the altars outside the capital, the "Chinese do not know any being who may truly and properly be called God." After a meeting held in Hong Kong in 1843 to standardize translations of the Bible, Protestant missionaries debated the question of how to translate the word "God" into Chinese. William J. Boone (1811–64), missionary bishop of the Protestant Episcopal Church, argued that since Shangdi was a "heathen Deity," to use this word to refer to the true God "would be derogatory to the glory and honor of Jehovah." Like the "Apostles who preached the gospel to the [polytheist] Greek and Romans," Boone reasoned, Protestant missionaries must use the generic word in Chinese for spirit—which he determined was "shin" or *shen* 神—in missionary tracts.[16] Legge, however, was emphatic:

I hold that the Shang-te [Shangdi] of the Chinese—the Being of whom their classical works speak, and whom as a nation they have worshipped for 4000 years—is the true God, and have endeavored to meet the various objections which have been exhibited, the religion of China cannot be called a polytheism, strictly speaking. It ac-

---

14. Ibid., pp. 98–99.

15. Legge, *Religions of China*, pp. 24–34, 51. Historians generally agree that Shangdi was the spirit of the Shang royal clan's founding ancestor, who had been elevated to the status of supreme deity in the Shang pantheon, and that Tian was superimposed on and/or elevated above Shangdi by the Zhou after its conquest of the Shang. For an earlier response to Legge's equating of Heaven and Shangdi, see Nelson, "*Confucianism in Relation to Christianity*," p. 3. See Hall and Ames (*Thinking Through Confucius*, pp. 204–8) for the problems with attributing transcendence to Tian or Shangdi.

16. Boone, *An Essay on the Proper Rendering*, pp. 3–6. Legge surveys other terms used for God in *The Notions of the Chinese Concerning God and Spirits*, pp. 140–62.

knowledges one perfect Being, who is above all, the maker and ruler of the universe. It does not give His glory—His great name—to another, nor His praise to graven images.[17]

Legge demonstrated his conviction that the object of imperial veneration was indeed the true God just prior to his final departure from China. During a visit to the altar of Heaven, he took off his shoes, ascended the steps, and "sang the (Christian) doxology, 'recognizing there the worship of God, as handed down for 4,000 years.'"[18]

MODERNITY AND
CONFUCIUS'S AGNOSTICISM

The secularization of Confucius in the first half of the twentieth century was often motivated by a different desire: to find in China's ancient past a rational mode of thinking that would gain China entry into the narrative of modernity. Hu Shi 胡適 (1891–1962), scholar, modernist reformer, and major cultural intermediary between China and the West, juxtaposed the "agnostic humanism of Confucius" to the amalgamation of the "vast number of popular beliefs and occult superstitions of the various races and localities which had been brought together by migration of peoples, by military conquests and, finally, by the formation of the empires of Ts'in [Qin] and Han [206 BCE–220 CE]."[19] The Han court, Hu says, was "full of ignorant and superstitious persons who gave great prestige and popularity to a number of

---

17. Legge, *The Notions of the Chinese Concerning Gods and Spirits*, p. 53.

18. Nelson, "*Confucianism in Relation to Christianity*," p. 8. The Jesuit Philippe Couplet (1622–93) singled out the sage-king Shun for special praise because he honored Shangdi as the supreme emperor of the Heavens (Mungello, *Curious Land*, p. 264), whereas Legge argued that Shun was the first to corrupt this ancient monotheism when, upon ascending the throne, he sacrificed to a host of other deities besides Heaven ("Shun dian" 舜典, *Shangshu zhengyi* 3.14). Legge concludes his note on this passage by saying that this sacrifice "was offered in B.C. 2283, so soon had men departed from the truth of God, and added to His worship of their own inventions" (Legge, *The Shoo King*, p. 34n6).

19. Hu, "The Establishment of Confucianism as a State Religion," pp. 29, 39. Hu based his account of the multiethnic regional cults absorbed into the state religions of the first empires, accurately I think, on *Han shu* 25A, especially pp. 1210–12. For discussion of Hu Shi's education in the United States, his studies with John Dewey, and his role as a liberal pragmatist in China's cultural modernization, see Grieder, *Hu Shih and the Chinese Renaissance*. For an analysis of Hu Shi's reconstruction of Chinese antiquity and his uses of it in his modernism, see Jensen, *Manufacturing Confucianism*, chap. 4.

primitive worships." The "moral and social teachings" of Confucianism, Hu continued, could not "escape from the contagious influence of this tremendously powerful atmosphere of the popular superstitions." What was ultimately produced during the Han was "a great conglomeration of popular beliefs and practices of the time through a thin and feeble process of rationalization." The "religious and intellectual atmosphere, even in the highest quarters of the nobility and royalty, was primitive and crudely superstitious. . . . It frankly rejected the agnosticism of Confucius himself and openly took a theistic position similar to that of the school of Mo Ti whom earlier Confucius philosophers had condemned."[20]

Legge's and Hu's views of Confucius coincide in intriguing ways. Both regarded him as an agnostic. To Legge, Confucius's skepticism began the erosion of an ancient monotheism, until then regarded as the only true form of religion and only imperfectly preserved in imperial worship of Heaven. To Hu Shi, Confucius's agnosticism posed an important but ultimately feeble spirit of rationalism that never eradicated the primitive religions of the Chinese people. The critical difference between the two, however, is that for Legge Confucius marks man's fall from his Edenic origins in the one True God's embrace, whereas for Hu Confucius begins man's ascent toward the freedom of modernity. The rational humanist that Confucius became in the evangelical and modernization narratives was seen as somehow opposed to the state cult, as if he had at some point dissociated himself from the sovereign's worship of Heaven (and/or Shangdi). Writing in 1913, E. T. Williams responded to such views: "We often hear it said that Confucianism is 'not a religion but merely a system of ethics.' What the original author of this statement could have meant by it I do not pretend to know." Williams goes on to point out that this view has "misled" many people to believe that Confucianism "is no religion at all."[21]

In an essay written in 1935 entitled "Was Confucius Agnostic?," Herrlee Creel refuted the idea that Confucius was unreligious by analyzing the pas-

---

20. Hu, "The Establishment of Confucianism as a State Religion," pp. 31, 28, 34–35, 40. In a later essay on the *Ru*/literati class, Hu argued that Confucius was a descendant of the hereditary ritualist class of the Shang dynasty that was conquered and subjugated by the less civilized tribal people who ruled the Zhou dynasty (see Jensen, *Manufacturing Confucianism*, pp. 225–33).

21. Williams, "The State Religion of China," p. 11. Christian Jochim ("Imperial Audience Ceremonies of the Ch'ing Dynasty," p. 3) cites this passage to preface his argument that Confucianism constitutes a religious system.

sages in the *Analects* that are often adduced to support this view. These passages not only are "totally lacking in that agnosticism . . . but include the most affirmatory references to the directive power of Heaven and to the spirits, the sacrifices, etc."[22] Creel showed that agnostic ideas had been insinuated into the text through mistranslation. Creel's analysis of *Analects* 6.22, which Legge renders "while respecting spiritual beings, to keep aloof from them, may be called wisdom," is especially pertinent. Legge's choice of "aloof" for *yuan* 遠 implies a subjective attitude of disdain toward the spirits, whereas the more literal rendering of keeping the spirits at a "distance" implies something quite different. According to Creel, even this literal translation does not capture Confucius's implication. One should maintain an attitude of "austere respect" amounting to awe toward the spirits who are the recipients of one's offerings.[23] This reading, I might add, avoids the obvious incongruity in being aloof toward the spirits one is supposed to respect and is more consistent with the first part of the passage, in which Confucius encourages reverence (*jing* 敬) toward the spirits. Confucius is advocating not the adoption of an agnostic attitude toward the spirits, but the preservation of "the correct degree of respectful distance between himself and the superior power or powers." He is dissociating himself from the "mystic [who] desires to be with his deity."[24]

Another passage in the *Analects* often adduced as proof of Confucius's secularism is his remark on sacrificing to the spirits (3.12). Legge translated the first part of the passage as "He sacrificed *to the dead*, as if they were present. He sacrificed to the spirits, as if the spirits were present."[25] In his translation of Fung Yu-lan's (1895–1990) *History of Chinese Philosophy*, Derk Bodde

---

22. Creel, "Was Confucius Agnostic?," p. 67.

23. Ibid., pp. 83–85; Waley, *The Analects of Confucius*, p. 120. Creel also compares this instance of the term *yuan* in the text with others, such as *Analects* 9.22, which Legge translates as "I have heard that the superior man maintains a distant reserve (*yuan*) toward his son," which does not suggest aloofness in the sense of disdain.

24. Creel, "Was Confucius Agnostic?," p. 84. Waley (*The Analects of Confucius*, p. 120n2) construes Confucius's sense of "distance" in this passage as a warning against the dangers of the spirits' not receiving their proper share of sacrificial offerings, for "they do not keep their distance, but 'possess' humans, causing madness, sickness, pestilence, etc." One might also juxtapose the ritualist's respectful distance from the spirits to the shaman priest's sensual yearning to be with the god he or she pursues, found in the ritual songs of the ancient state of Chu. See especially the third song on the Goddess of the Xiang River in "The Nine Songs" (*The Songs of the South*, pp. 100–118).

25. Legge, *Confucian Analects*, p. 159 (3.12). Original emphasis used to indicate interpolation.

italicized the words "as if," thereby implicitly ascribing to Confucius a rational skepticism about the existence of spirits.[26] (Hu Shi also read this passage as evidence of Confucius's secular tendencies.)[27] Fung then posed the question of why Confucius might be skeptical toward the existence of spirits that he admonished people to revere in the passage discussed above (*Analects* 6.22). The contradiction is important, however, for the rest of this section of the *Analects* reads, "The Master said, 'I consider my not being present at the sacrifice, as if I did not sacrifice.'" Legge construed this remark as evidence of Confucius's sincerity in performing the rites, which is consistent with the views of earlier commentators such as Kong Anguo 孔安國 (fl. 156–ca. 174), who explains that the first part of the chapter "says to serve [or 'sacrifice to'] the dead as one serves the living" (*shi si ru shi sheng* 事死如事生).[28] Thus, in Kong Anguo's reading of this passage, offerings to the spirits are efficacious if one serve the spirits in the same way (*ru*) that one serves a living person, thereby expressing the sincerity of one's heart, and that one does so personally rather than assigning the task to a surrogate. Fung's (and Bodde's) hypothetical presence or existence (*ru zai* 如在) of the spirits encourages a distinctively modernistic understanding of sacrifice.[29] Deborah Sommer's discussion in this volume (pp. 101–2) of the use in ancient times of personators, who "marked exactly that contiguity between the living and the dead and between representation, substitution, and actuality," adds another possible meaning: make the sacrifice as though the person receiving the offering were present.

---

26. Fung, *A History of Chinese Philosophy*, 1: 58. Fung does not underscore the word *ru* (as if) in the Chinese version of his book (*Zhongguo zhexue shi*, p. 84), although the point of Fung's analysis of these passages in the *Analects* is to assert that Confucius "did not believe in many of the superstitions of his day." Patricia Ebrey also underscores these italics as evidence of Confucius's secularism; for her discussion of secularism in ancient China, see *Confucianism and Family Rituals*, pp. 28–31.

27. Jensen, *Manufacturing Confucianism*, p. 255.

28. *Lunyu zhengyi* 3.53–54; Legge, *Confucian Analects*, p. 159n12. Instead of attributing to Confucius the view that spirits may not exist, William Soothill (*The Analects of Confucius*, pp. 195–97) also emphasized Confucius's concern about the efficacy of a sacrifice in which he did not personally participate.

29. Kong Anguo's reading of the word *zai* 在 as *living*, rather than *present*, is consistent with other passages in the *Analects*, such as "While a man's father is alive (*fu zai* 父在), look at the bent of his will; when his father is dead, look at his conduct" (Legge, *Confucian Analects*, p. 142, 1.11); and "While his parents are alive (*fumu zai* 父母在), *the son* may not go abroad to a distance" (Legge, *Confucian Analects*, p. 171, 4.19; italics in original).

In his later, perhaps more rationalistic, years Herrlee Creel modified his stance on Confucius's religiousness. Although in his 1949 book *Confucius, the Man and the Myth* he acknowledged the central place of religion in Confucius's day, Creel no longer seemed so sure if Confucius believed sacrificial ritual was efficacious or valued it "merely as a social act." He cautioned that "what we call 'religious' and 'secular' activities were not widely separated in ancient China; in fact they were almost inextricably mingled."[30] Yet Confucius is portrayed in Creel's later work as standing "wholly apart" from the ritual tradition extending back to the Shang; Confucius emphasized only the ethical lessons that could be derived from this tradition and thus marks the "transition from ritual to ethical thinking."[31] With this "transition," we return to the rational, agnostic Confucius of the seventeenth century. Yet it is not clear whether this transition occurred in Confucius's day, or whether it is the effect of a much later, modernist Cartesian separation between, on the one hand, ritual, religion, and the corporeal and, on the other hand, ethics, rational philosophy, and the mental. The scholarly separation between ritual and ethics is not merely analytical: it presupposes a teleological history in which all human cultures eventually pass from a religious stage to a rational one. It severs us from our own liturgicized pasts so that we no longer understand practices that differ from our own. Talal Asad locates a rupture between a medieval Christian conception of ritual as a disciplinary means of cultivating virtue to a modern, ethnographic reading of ritual as symbolic, surface gesture, a type of practice that is interpretable as standing *for* something else.[32] Although it may differ from Legge's claim that the "Shang-te of the Chinese . . . is the true God . . . the maker and ruler of the universe," Creel's understanding of Confucian religiousness as premised on the "directive power of Heaven" inadvertently posits a Christian transcendent god as a standard of religiousness as such. Rather than focusing on questions of Confucian ritual practice and theories of sacrifice, Creel's earlier "recognition" of

---

30. Creel, *Confucius*, pp. 82, 114–20.

31. Ibid., pp. 118, 120. Ebrey (*Confucianism and Family Rituals*, p. 30) also sees this transition in "late Chou and early Han punctilious, political, and rationalistic approaches to ritual [which] all worked to give weight to the moral side of ritual at the expense of the sacred or religious side." For the secularization of ancient Confucianism in early twentieth-century scholarship, see Jensen, *Manufacturing Confucianism*, pp. 222–24; for Creel's praise of Jesuit scholarship on Confucius, see Creel, *Confucius*, pp. 142–43.

32. Asad, "Toward a Genealogy of the Concept of Ritual."

Confucian religiousness hinges on finding in it ideas of the sacred familiar to a modern audience.

Part of the problem of ascertaining the nature of Confucian religiousness may be due to the nearly exclusive reliance among many Western scholars of early Confucianism on the *Analects*.[33] It is, at best, an elliptical record of conversations on a range of topics whose unifying themes are not explicitly stated in the text but have been asserted by later commentators and canonized by later sects of Confucianism. Scholars have long noted that the text is an accumulation of passages and fragments compiled by contending factions among Confucius's followers—not necessarily in chronological sequence—in the centuries after his death. These factions often disagreed on what Confucius said or meant; nor did they necessarily gain ascendancy—and thus the prerogative of adding to "the text"—on the basis of the merits of their views.[34] Although the *Analects* remains a repository of important philosophical fragments, the accretion theory of its composition raises doubts that it is in any sense a comprehensive account of, or a reliable guide to, what concerned Confucius and his followers.

That the received *Analects* is a contested and partial document underscores the need to read it in the context of the larger corpus of Confucian books. It also enables us to reconsider the direction of Western scholarship on Confucianism, which has bestowed privileged status on the *Analects* and produced an image of Confucius—particularly that of the agnostic—that is incongruous with the richly textured world of liturgical song and ritual sacrifice found in such works as the *Record of Rites* and *Book of Odes*.[35] The insight into this world offered by the *Rites* and *Odes* deepens our understanding of Confucius's acute sense of the breakdown of the cosmic (as well as the social) order of things as he witnessed the degradation of the rites that he lamented

---

33. Elman (*Classicism, Politics, and Kinship*, pp. 205–13, esp. p. 211) points to the tendency among sinologists—Creel in particular—to follow the Ancient Text tradition that emphasized the *Analects* in its construction of a Confucius who was disinclined to speculate on matters that were not immediately perceptible.

34. For the accretion of the *Analects* and other early texts, see Van Zoeren, *Poetry and Personality*, pp. 19–28, 32–44; Lewis, *Writing and Authority in Ancient China*, pp. 54–63, 383n9. For the views of translators, see Legge, "Prolegomena," in idem, *Confucian Analects*, pp. 14–18; Waley, *The Analects of Confucius*, p. 21; Lau, *Analects*, appendix 3; Brooks and Brooks, *The Original Analects*, pp. 201–49.

35. I examine the role of sacrifice in the cult of Confucius in "Sacrifice and the Imperial Cult of Confucius."

in Book 3 of the *Analects*. By returning to the *Analects* after reading other canonical works in this way, it is possible to realize that the problem of ascertaining the nature of Confucian religiousness might not be with the *Analects*
as such but with how it has been read in the service of Western philosophical and theological agendas.

CONFUCIAN RITUAL THEORY

Missionaries introduced into Western discourses on Chinese religion a conception of all religion as irrevocably evolving toward its most perfect expression, monotheism. The god of monotheism is a transcendent creator who is
ultimately separate from the universe he created *ex nihilo* and who possesses an
intelligence that is gradually, if imperfectly, revealed to the creatures that in-
habit the cosmos. The Jesuits and many later Protestants agreed that the ancient Chinese had possessed knowledge of this god but had since lost it because of polytheism, idolatry, and materialism. Although avoiding the
theological controversies that enveloped Christian missionaries in the previous three centuries, twentieth-century scholars generally concurred with the
missionaries' assessment of the secular tendencies of Confucianism: philosophers concentrated on ethics and metaphysics, and social scientists on the role
of the Confucian gentry in the maintenance of social control at the local
level.[36] In a trend that oddly reproduces the dichotomy between literati secularism and popular superstition, social science research on popular cults has
thrived in the past thirty years, whereas the cultic dimension of literati life has
been ignored. This inclination in twentieth-century sinology to elide the cult
of Confucius was not shared by nineteenth-century Protestants; although
they may have found Confucius personally lacking in full knowledge of the
one true God, they nonetheless devoted considerable attention to the imperial
cults of Heaven, Confucius, and others in their voluminous and detailed descriptions of Chinese society. An avid nineteenth-century reader of books on
China may well have been better informed about Confucian religiousness,
even though it was adjudged to be "pagan"—and thus not truly monotheistic
in the Christian sense—than a well-informed reader of the past fifty years.

---

36. For gentry-bureaucratic participation in local control, see Hsiao, *Rural China*. Hsiao
discusses the imperial government's use of religion as an instrument of ideological control in
ibid., pp. 220–29. For more recent research on local control, see Wakeman and Grant, *Conflict
and Control*.

To take seriously the religious dimension of Confucian sacrifices to the gods and spirits of the imperial pantheon does not require us to accept the terms and theological framework, let alone the evangelical aspirations, of Christian missionaries in China, nor does it obligate us to accept uncritically their firsthand descriptions of Chinese religious life. To the contrary, confronting missiological discourses on Chinese religion helps alert us to the manifold ways that they have subtly shaped our understanding of the nature of religious life. For centuries Christian missionaries attempted to reconcile Chinese ritual practice with Christian readings of the Confucian classics, in part by positing an originary monotheism in China's remote past. China, much like ancient Greece and Rome, had numerous gods, none of which was all-powerful, or even powerful enough, to expiate sin. The sacred landscape of China's religions accommodated a range of primordial gods, nature deities, spirits of extraordinary personages, minor tutelary gods, and others in ways that, by the standards of monotheism, might appear contradictory. Any attempt to find theological coherence in Confucian sacrifice of the kind found in Christian conceptions of the crucifixion or the host must in the end be thwarted by the multiplicity of deities in the Confucian canon.

Rodney Taylor points out that the study of Confucianism in the West has been "dominated by historical and philosophical approaches" to the neglect of "religion and spirituality." Because early Confucianism "has long been defined in intellectual, or at most ethical terms," he continues, "anything that fell outside that frame has been left out to gather dust in outer darkness." More recently, scholars have begun to approach Confucianism as "a lived and living faith rather than a philosophy or an ethic."[37] Tu Weiming, for example, counters the Judeo-Christian tendency to posit an "ontological gap between Heaven and man" with the observation that, in Confucianism, this relationship is "not that of creator and creature but one of mutual fidelity."[38] Writing very much as a Mencian theological exegete of the Confucian canon—here looking at the *Doctrine of the Mean*—Tu argues that Confucian religiousness "means being engaged in the process of learning to be fully human," a process aimed at "ultimate self-transformation." This process hinges on the realization that "although we are not what we ought to be, we can reach the highest state of humanity through personal cultivation.

---

37. Taylor and Arbuckle, "Confucianism," p. 347.
38. Tu, *Centrality and Commonality*, pp. 9–10.

Learning to be fully human is to learn to become a sage (an authentic manifestation of our nature, indeed our essence as ordained by Heaven)."[39] What Heaven has ordained, Tu says, is humanity (ren 仁), an innate predisposition toward compassion and love for others that is universally and most convincingly expressed in one's love for one's parents.[40] The capacity to be good is innate, but it must be nourished through moral self-cultivation, which, as Rodney Taylor argues, takes on a soteriological dimension.[41] The quest for human perfection and the cultivation of sagehood are not solitary undertakings because the self as an inherently ethical agent is not construed as an isolable individual in Confucianism. The Confucian sage is not sequestered from society; rather, as Tu and Taylor make clear, the domain in which this sacred quest is pursued includes the family (children, parents, ancestors), the court in service to the Son of Heaven, and all of society as the fiduciary community.[42]

If Taylor is correct that the spirit has been neglected in Western studies of Confucianism, most of the body has virtually disappeared as well. One's everyday corporeal existence, whether in social intercourse with other people or in worship of one's ancestors, was central to being Confucian and was an underlying concern in Confucian discourses on li 禮, or "ritual," from ancient times to the present. The word li has a broad range of meanings that tends not to distinguish between sacred and secular contexts. Etymologically it consists of two parts: the left-hand radical shi 示, which the first-century CE dictionary Shuowen glosses as "Heaven's omens that inform the living of impending good or ill," and which, by extension, came to signify the spirits generally. The right-hand phonetic means a sacrificial vessel. Thus, the Shuowen explains, li is "the way to serve the spirits and secure blessings" (suoyi shi shen zhi fu 所以事神致福).[43] The earliest meaning of li as sacrifice to, or ritual feasting of, ancestral spirits specified a stratified relationship between the living and the spirits of their ancestors that carried over into its later meaning of the proper form of one's disposition vis-à-vis other living persons, each of whom occupies a definite place in a hierarchy in the family, the community, and the empire.

---

39. Ibid., pp. 95–96.
40. Ibid., pp. 50–51.
41. Rodney Taylor, *The Cultivation of Sagehood*, pp. 4–12, 101–5.
42. Tu, *Centrality and Commonality*, pp. 107–16; Taylor, *The Cultivation of Sagehood*, chap. 1.
43. *Shuowen jiezi* 1A.4b.

In Benjamin Schwartz's words, *li* is the "cement of the entire normative sociopolitical order"; it establishes "the behavior of persons related to each other in terms of role, status, rank, and position within a structured society." In an analysis of ritual theory in the late Zhou and early Han, Patricia Ebrey argues that ritual served as external standards that restrained people from impulses toward lawlessness and licentiousness.[44] Schwartz, however, emphasizes the structural parallels between society and family, both of which involve hierarchies, authority, and power. To someone like Confucius, he says, "who associated the family with the transfiguring rites of ancestral worship, . . . the ideal family is the ultimate source of all those values which harmonize the relations of authority and hierarchy which must exist in any civilized society." For Confucius, "the family is precisely the domain within which authority comes to be accepted and exercised not through reliance on physical coercion, but through the binding power of religious, moral sentiments based on kinship ties."[45]

The importance of the concept of *li* in Confucius's thought has been disputed throughout the history of Confucianism. At least as early as Mencius 孟子 (372–289 BCE), *li*, along with humanity, righteousness, and wisdom, was regarded as one of the cardinal virtues. However, Mencius gave priority to humanity, which produced feelings of commiseration, and to righteousness, which was an internal predisposition toward loving what is proper and abhorring evil (6A.4).[46] Xunzi 荀子 (d. 238 BCE), Mencius's most important Confucian critic in ancient times, countered that the basic nature of human desire is selfish, which produces evil. People do not, by nature, possess the virtues enumerated by Mencius, he said, but they have the capacity to overcome this original evil through conscious effort and by learning the rites devised by the ancient sages.[47] This tension between humanity and rites proved enormously productive in Confucianism for thousands of years and continues to be compelling in more recent scholarship. For example, Herbert Fingarette argues that humanity is the "uncarved . . . raw impulses

---

44. Ebrey, *Confucianism and Family Rituals*, pp. 25–28. Ebrey does not distinguish between *li* as a rationalizing ideology that perpetuates a stratified status quo—which virtually all organized conservative religions do—and a secularized reading of ritual, which elides cosmological and metaphysical implications of ritual while preserving ritual's rationalizing effects.

45. Schwartz, *The World of Thought in Ancient China*, pp. 67–70.

46. Ibid., 263–68. Humanity is elucidated as a cardinal virtue in Book 4 of the *Analects*.

47. Xunzi's argument that we possess the innate capacity to learn goodness and his critique of Mencius can be found in the chapter "Nature Is Evil" (*Xunzi jijie* 23).

and potential which can be fashioned into a mature person," but its meaning is obscure and does not operate on the level of conscious will.[48] Thus "humanity" as used in the *Analects* should not be construed as an innately good conscience. According to Fingarette, Confucius never considered ethics a matter of internal moral choice, for the very notion of an inner moral self is not even a rejected possibility in the *Analects*.[49] Fingarette argues that in the *Analects* the self as a moral agent is constituted through the magic of "Holy Rite"; that is, through the seemingly effortless mastery of "ritual, gesture and incantation" without resorting to strategies or physical force. The efficacy of ritual power does not emanate from the self conceived as an atomic individual defined by definite boundaries in the human community. This community is created through its members' submission to *li*, understood as a process of fulfilling a human impulse rather than as "mechanically carrying out prescribed routines."[50]

Fingarette's thesis produced a number of responses that shed light on the meaning of ritual in ancient Confucianism. Tu Wei-ming, for example, reaffirms the innate goodness of humanity and its propensity to manifest itself spontaneously in compassion through ritual.[51] Benjamin Schwartz disagrees with Fingarette's claim that the meaning of ritual must be located in the external act itself rather than in an inner subjectivity.[52] Contrary to Fingarette's claim that the *Analects* is disinclined to speak of an inner subjective life, Schwartz contends that this is precisely the concern of a number of passages in the text. For example, Confucius's indignation over the usurpation of royal rituals by local hegemonic clans in *Analects* 3.1–2 was directed not at their technical ignorance of ritual forms or their inept performance of the sacrifices but at their moral degradation of the rituals because of their lack of the proper inner subjective state: "A person who is not humane," Confucius declared in the next passage (*Analects* 3.3), has nothing to do with rites and music. Later in the same book, Confucius said that he could not bear to watch someone who "performs rites without reverence or who observes mourning without grief" (3.26). Humanity—"the true inner virtue"— reverence, and grief, Schwartz points out, are the subjective state, the inter-

---

48. Fingarette, *Confucius*, p. 48.
49. Ibid., pp. 19–24.
50. Ibid., p. 7.
51. Tu, "*Jen* as a Living Metaphor."
52. Fingarette, *Confucius*, chap. 3.

nal source of the sacred meaning of rites.[53] He suggests that Fingarette's disinclination to attribute to Confucius a concept of an inner moral life in order
not to psychologize the *Analects* "reflects Fingarette's own involvement with
the modern Western psychology/sociology antithesis rather than anything
found in the *Analects*. The notion that the person's involvement in various
self-subsisting 'systems of action' 'out there' means that he has no 'inner'
autonomous life as an individual or that this inner life can have no effect on
behavior is a notion which Fingarette brings to the *Analects*."[54]

Schwartz's emphasis on inner virtue may not be as far from Fingarette's position as he supposes. The subjective qualities Schwartz cites—
particularly humanity and righteousness—are nearly always spoken of and
authenticated in the *Analects* on the basis of external traces—observable
situations that occasioned outward expressions of inner dispositions. One
rarely finds in these ancient sources metaphysical expositions of humanity,
righteousness, and reverence as localizable ontological entities like mind or
nature. (Later Confucians of the Song and Ming culled passages from ancient sources to develop intricate metaphysical structures that situated affective states in specific sources said to have definite ontological status.) Fingarette is concerned not so much with rejecting an inner side of external
conduct as with questioning preconceptions of an internal subject understood as an entity that is prior to and independent of relations with others.
Like Tu Wei-ming, Fingarette conceptualizes the self as the effect of a nexus
of ever-changing relationships, but, unlike Tu, he is disinclined to attribute *a
priori* predispositions to humanity before it is shaped by experience.

RITUAL PERFORMANCE,
RITUAL BELIEF

Fingarette's claim that Confucius located the meaning of the rites in the act
itself rather than in an inner subjectivity and Schwartz's rebuttal parallel a
debate over the performance of ritual and the beliefs that rituals express.[55] A

---

53. Schwartz, *The World of Thought in Ancient China*, pp. 72–73.

54. Ibid., p. 74.

55. Beginning in the 1870s, anthropologists investigating the religious origins of primitive
cultures argued that myths about the dead established the foundation of human culture.
Other anthropologists maintained that religion began as a form of ritual worship of divine
representations of the existing social order. See Bell, *Ritual*, chap. 1; and Jochim, "Imperial
Audience Ceremonies of the Ch'ing Dynasty," chap. 1.

number of scholars have noted the considerable differences in the understanding of rituals and objects of veneration by various segments of Chinese society. James Watson found, for example, that in two geographically proximate villages the cult of Tianhou 天后 (Empress of Heaven) was viewed quite differently depending on such variables as literacy, clan status (that is, whether one's clan dominated local society), and gender.[56] The Chinese empire succeeded in effecting cultural integration across class and geographic boundaries, Watson argues, by standardizing the rituals rather than the ideological content of the various local and regional cults; the state promoted and regulated *orthopraxy*—correct performance of rites—rather than *orthodoxy*—correct belief in a specific meaning of the rites. "Performance," he says, "took precedence over belief—it mattered little what one believed" about a particular ritual "as long as the rites were performed properly."[57]

Evelyn Rawski responds that at least since the Song (960–1279), the imperial bureaucracy not only was greatly concerned about propagating orthodox beliefs to the nonliterate populace but was quite successful in doing so. She cites as evidence of this the spread of such notions as the "continuity of kinship links between the living and the dead," the belief that "ancestors could intercede with deities on behalf of their living descendants," and the values associated with filial piety, particularly as expressed in proper observance of mourning. Rawski contends that Confucians did not assume belief preceded performance; rather, they believed that performances could lead to the inculcation of belief, and thus officials and local elites were trying to promote orthodoxy by imposing orthopraxy.[58] For many members of the literati, the temple cult of Confucius constituted a veritable sanctum for ritualized life in an otherwise corrupt world. This point is vividly demonstrated in Wu Jingzi's 吳敬梓 (1701–54) novel about the literati class titled the *Unofficial History of the Scholars* (*Rulin waishi* 儒林外史). Much of the

---

56. Watson, "Standardizing the Gods."

57. Watson, "The Structure of Chinese Funerary Rites," p. 4.

58. Rawski, "A Historian's Approach to Chinese Death Ritual," pp. 23–24, 26, 28. This approach to ritual as performance, Angela Zito adds, perpetuates the Cartesian mind-body dualism by separating the knowing mind from the acting, docile body. Watson's assertion that performance is more important than belief may seem to reverse Descartes's prioritization of mind, as that which can be known with certainty, over body, as that which cannot. But by construing ritual as a performance by actors as if on a stage, the observing mind of the anthropologist nonetheless claims the position of the one who properly interprets the meaning of the ritual performance (Zito, *Of Body and Brush*, pp. 52–60).

novel satirizes official corruption and the degradation of Confucian values with biting irony; the only exception is the description of the earnest work of a group of gentrymen as they endeavor to build a temple to honor Taibo, who, according to legend, yielded the throne of the Zhou kingdom to his younger brother.[59] Shang Wei poses the question of why Wu did not examine the inner thoughts of these men in his description of their sacrifices to Taibo. Rather, the ceremony described in the novel is, as Shang shows, a vernacular rendering of the sacrifices to Confucius as prescribed by imperial ritual manuals.[60] Shang maintains that Wu Jingzi's scholars—and the Confucian literati in general—did not separate the meaning of this cult from the ritual enactment of it: "Moral truth was immanent in the institutions of ritual that the sage-kings had designed in high antiquity. It could be manifested in the present not through abstract speculation on theoretical formulation, but through the thorough study of Confucian classics of ritual, and it could be finally achieved in reality only through the practice of ritual."[61]

Analyzing a process similar to that studied by James Watson, Prasenjit Duara describes the transformation of Guan Yu 關羽 as a protector deity of Buddhist temples in the eighth century to Guandi 關帝, the imperially sanctioned god of war by the seventeenth century. Duara emphasizes the continual overlay of new interpretations of this late Han military general as new groups—Buddhists, Daoists, imperial officials, the populace at large—inscribed symbols that articulated their own interests and values. At times they reiterated existing symbols; at other times they invested Guandi with new meanings. But, in a process he calls "superscribing," rarely if ever did they erase what came before. The Guandi cult was thus an interpretive arena in which competing groups negotiated the meaning of the cult with other groups.[62]

The cult of Confucius, like the Guandi and other cults in the imperial pantheon, was itself an interpretive arena in which Confucian literati disputed matters of correct practice and belief. The results of these disputes were enshrined in the imperial liturgy and codified in the official statutes so

---

59. For the history of the cult of Taibo, see Shang, "The Collapse of the Taibo Temple," pp. 102–15.

60. Ibid., pp. 134–49.

61. Ibid., p. 155.

62. Duara, "Superscribing Symbols." See also Jing (pp. 357–58) in this volume for instances of multivocality.

that ritual meaning and ritual practice would be uniform throughout the empire. This was the intention, but, as with other temple cults, the results often fell short of the imperium's desires. Because of the court's continual scrutiny and institutionalization of the ritual texts of the literati cult, however, sacrifices to Confucius were more uniform across the empire than liturgies at most other temples on the sacred landscape of imperial China. Yet, as the chapters in this book show, Confucians disputed the meaning and form of the cult of Confucius throughout the imperial era.

CONFUCIUS/KONGZI, CONFUCIANISM/RU 儒

Before describing the essays in this volume and how they address the concerns raised above, I should explain some key terms used in this book. By "*cult* of Confucius" is meant the regular sacrifices to his spirit offered by imperial officers at temples in the capital and throughout the empire as part of a larger pantheon of gods and their cults. The imperial pantheon comprised dozens of cults, and there was no single managerial body with exclusive authority to oversee them. The Ministry of Rites was charged with regulating the cults, but important liturgical issues were debated by all court officials. Indeed, local officials often provoked court debates by presenting memorials to the throne about various details of the sacrifices. A separate body, the Court of Imperial Sacrifice, oversaw the implementation of the liturgies promulgated by the Ministry of Rites. The ritual practices associated with the cult of Confucius and all other cults of the imperial pantheon were distributed throughout the bureaucracy in complex ways that cannot always be charted along formal lines of administrative authority. To further complicate matters, as a cult of people schooled in Confucian principles, texts, and liturgies, the worship or simple veneration of Confucius took place outside the purview of the imperial bureaucracy in temples at private academies, at altars in private residences, and in ancestral shrines of Confucius's descendants. No single deity—not even Heaven—held such supreme status that it could stand for the whole imperial pantheon; the whole comprised many parts that intersected and overlapped but did not converge, except in the sense that each cult was subservient, though not assimilable, to Heaven. In a sacred landscape populated by many gods and spirits, each cult was necessarily partial. What distinguishes a cult from a religion is just this partial status in a larger whole that has no single god that embodies all of the others.[63]

Several authors in this volume follow the long-standing convention of using the term "Confucius," which is a Latin name Christian missionaries gave to the man referred to in Chinese as Fuzi 夫子 (master), Kongzi 孔子 (Master Kong), Kong Qiu 孔丘, Zhongni 仲尼 (Second son Ni), and occasionally Kong fuzi 孔夫子 (Master Kong), among several other terms.[64] In references to the flesh-and-blood man and his biological descendants, the transliteration "Kongzi" helps make explicit the family connection between the Sage and the Kong clan of later times. The temple in which sacrifices were offered to Confucius also poses problems of translation because Chinese sources virtually never refer to it as a *"Confucian* temple" (I have found only one instance of the term *Rumiao* 儒廟). The most frequent names used are the Kongzi Temple (Kongzi miao 孔子廟) and Temple of Culture (Wenmiao 文廟).[65]

The term "Confucianism" poses yet another level of problems because it is not a translation of any Chinese term, although it appears to be one. It *seems* to correspond to the Chinese term *Ru* 儒, literally "scholar" or "literatus," but this term did not come into frequent use to refer to a distinct school of ritual and textual experts and court advisors until the fourth century BCE. These Ru and their court competitors were not explicitly named as a distinct school until relatively late, but most of them claimed traditions extending back to the sage-kings of high antiquity. To translate the word *ru* with generic terms such as "literatus," "scholar," or "classicist" belies its specific meaning of a specialist of the Ru/Confucian canon called the Five Classics (*wujing* 五經)—*Change, Documents, Odes, Rites,* and *Spring and Autumn*

---

63. This sense of "cult" differs from the term's popular usage as an idiosyncratic fringe group led by a charismatic leader that separates itself from an established church and the rest of society (see Bell, *Ritual*, pp. 205–9).

64. Jensen (*Manufacturing Confucianism*, chap. 2) contends that Jesuit missionaries invented the term "Kongfuzi," which they transliterated as Confucius. Kongfuzi is a colloquial expression that is virtually never used in canonical sources and official documents composed in the classical language, although it appears in vernacular sources as early as the twelfth century (see e.g., *Zhuzi yulei* 119.2874 and 137.3255–55). Jensen dissociates himself from the missionary origins of the terms "Confucius" and "Confucianism" on grounds that their formulation was inextricably tied to Jesuit strategies of conversion.

65. Most official documents refer to the temple by whatever official posthumous title was conferred upon Kongzi at the time; see the chapter by Wilson in this book, pp. 50–57.

Annals—and thus inadvertently implies a lack of classically educated scholars in the Daoist and Buddhist canons. In late imperial times, the problem of
meaning was further complicated by the emergence of other ancient books
such as the Four Books competing for primary status and, by Ming times,
nonexegetical methods of defining Confucian truth that explicitly rejected
the privileged authority of any written text.

Some scholars avoid this confounding proliferation of unintended meanings by retaining the transliteration *ru*, which, on the surface, maintains a
certain quiet on the question of what to call this tradition. But the conun-
drum does not disappear, it merely shifts location. Consider what has been
gained and what has been lost by drawing from the Chinese lexicon to speak
about this tradition. Most important one gains "the loss" of a term that refers inaccurately, even misleadingly, to a person's name. The Chinese terms
for what has been called "Confucianism" usually refer not to the man we call
Confucius, but to a tradition that antedates him and includes him as one of
its followers; it is an older tradition comprising liturgists of ancient rituals,
teachers of earlier wisdom, and exegetes of archaic records. And yet, for at
least the past millennium, the compilation, editorship, and, in some cases,
authorship of the canon was attributed to Confucius, who was regarded as
the central figure of this tradition. Therefore it would be appropriate to
think of this tradition since at least the seventh century as "Confucian"—as
centered on the teachings and texts attributed to this man—even though it
would not be accurate to presume there is a Chinese term for this tradition
that explicitly invokes his name.

Even though there was broad agreement in the last 1,200 years of the imperial era on the centrality of Confucius, doctrinal, liturgical, and exegetical issues divided this tradition. By Song times, Confucians began to privilege doctrines and books not among the Five Classics as the repository of a more
fundamental truth they called the Dao. These proponents of the learning of
the Dao (*Daoxue* 道學) maintained that the truth was not apprehended by all
canonical exegetes and dissociated themselves from some of the latter by constructing genealogies of the Dao (*daotong* 道統) in lineages of sages who correctly understood and transmitted the Dao. Those outside these lineages
were seen as common Ru who did not fully understand the true teachings that
lay behind the literal meaning of the canon. Although by Ming times (1368–
1644) the Dao School came to dominate the various sites of Confucian culture—its educational institutions, school curricula, the temple of Confu-

cius—the Ru literati tradition was divided into contending sects. Thus, beginning in Song times, the learning of what we call Confucianism was believed to transcend Ru scholarship, which was often seen as a hindrance to the full realization of the Confucian Dao. The Yuan court formally elevated Dao Learning over Ru Learning in its official history of the Song dynasty.[66] Here we begin to incur losses in our appeal to native terms, for they are no more stable or uncontested than the Western ones. There is no certainty inherent in the word *ru* because it has been used to signify different conceptions of the tradition and was at times not even viewed positively by those whom we are predisposed to call Ru. It appears, then, that our appeal to native terms is not wholehearted; we evidently do not desire to pronounce the original Chinese terms as they were historically spoken by those in the tradition because our ecumenicalism—our disinclination to exclude on ideological grounds—is often incommensurate with the exclusionary discourses that served to define and legitimate one school over the others. One might then conclude that there was not just one Ru tradition, but many. There were ecumenical scholars in the tradition, of course, but the framework of their inclusiveness rarely accommodated all Ru literati on equal terms. Rather, they constructed hierarchical lineages and situated scholars of different orientations on different, unequal planes. The aim of such attempts, moreover, was to mediate the controversies that divided scholars, to dissolve contention through philosophical synthesis, rather than to give full voice to the fractious multiplicity of conflicting schools, each in its own terms. An important exception to the tendency of ecumenical Confucianism to synthesize rather than illuminate the contention over the truth is Huang Zongxi's anthology of Ming Confucian writings, which consciously restored the category of Ru to a status of the common ground upon which doctrinal disputes took place.[67] The term *ru* certainly comes closest to our naively inclusive term "Confucianism," but the two words are not commensurate or equivalent.

The contributors to this volume have not followed a single set of translations for these important terms because we are not as a group convinced that any one of them is inherently better than the others. By conjuring a tradition that was seemingly always devoted to one man, "Confucianism" is an invented signifier that bears a problematic relationship to the thing it signifies.

---

66. Wilson, "Confucian Sectarianism and the Compilation of the *Ming History*."
67. For Confucian constructions of their traditions, see Wilson, *Genealogy of the Way*, chap. 2.

Nevertheless, using it does not, in itself, irrevocably ensnare one in a Jesuit accommodationist discourse or a missionary's quest to convert the Chinese to Christianity. In using it, however, one must be vigilant since the terms we use can evoke unintended meanings in the reader's mind and even unwittingly in the rhetorical choices of the author. The Chinese term *ru* is no less problematic, although it seems to be a more felicitous name for what we have called "Confucianism." The problem lies not so much in the name itself, since it does not insinuate foreign meanings into native discourses, but rather in how we use it: when *ru* is uttered to evoke something other than the exclusionary senses that have historically informed its use, then one must be aware of a dissonance that separates our catholicity as outsiders from an indigenous discourse of power. In the following summary of each chapter in this book, I use the same terms used by its author.

RITES AND MUSIC

My chapter surveys the formation of the Kongzi cult during the imperial era and in the early Republic to show that its status in the imperial pantheon of deities and spirits was not stable in several respects. In the absence of a classical precedent, the liturgy for the sacrifices to Kongzi had to be fashioned through ritual analogies with other cults. Successive courts did not always agree on Kongzi's posthumous ranking, which further complicated the question of how and where to locate this cult in the hierarchy of the pantheon. The protean quality of the figure of Kongzi as the object of cult verneration was due in part to the absence of any singular conception of who Kongzi was: beginning with the earliest written sources that speak of him, there were nearly always more than one figure of Kongzi. Distinguishing between the canonical Kongzi that tended to prevail in later scholarly writings about the sage and the noncanonical uncrowned king that suggested godly descent from the Shang kings, I examine the tension in discourses on Kongzi's ritual status that persisted throughout the late imperial era. Neither a dualism nor a split personality, the canonical and noncanonical figures rarely, if ever, overtly confronted one another in Confucian writings. Rather, they tended to be invoked or alluded to indirectly in court debates over his ritual status in order to determine the level of sacrificial offerings and the kind of music and dance to be performed at the sacrificial ceremonies. The virtual feasting of Kongzi was at once an imperial cult uneasily situated in the official pantheon of gods propitiated by the throne and an ancestral cult observed by Kongzi's biological heirs in closed ceremonies that honored eminent ancestors of the Kong lineage.

The basic question of how Confucius as the central figure of the literati cult was to be physically represented in the temple was subject to controversy during much of the imperial era. Since the official worship of Confucius began only in the post-classical era, there was no canonical liturgy of sacrifices to the reputed author of the canon. Imperial sacrifices to Confucius from the eighth century until 1530 were, for the most part, offered to a painting or statue, but, as Deborah Sommer shows, many ritualists criticized the practice of imaging the Sage with three-dimensional statues made of painted clay by querying how the spirit could reach down and imbibe in the sacrificial feast without appearing to creep and crawl about groping for food. Some scholars advocated using seated statues on grounds that the standing image constrained the movement of the spirit during the ceremony. Others maintained that since sacrifices of this kind during the Zhou used spirit tablets with names inscribed on them rather than visual images, post-classical rituals must also be aniconic. This view was not implemented until the tumultuous reforms of the Jiajing era (1521–66) described in Huang Ching-Shing's chapter in this volume, but as Sommer shows, this view marked the culmination of a centuries-long debate on how Confucius's body was to be represented.

Imaging the physical body whose ethereal spirit imbibed the offerings was important to the efficacy of sacrifices to ancestors and the spirits of once-human deities in the imperial pantheon, such as Confucius. It is significant that arguments against the use of images were not based on doubts that the spirits were present at the sacrifices, much less that they existed. To the contrary, some iconoclasts like Song Na 宋訥 (1310–90) preferred to shroud the sanctity of the spirit world in mystery because graphic images of the Sage groping for food not only robbed the spirit of its dignity but also bordered on blasphemy. Other iconoclasts were clearly awestruck by the power that animated the statues and feared that such power might be dangerous if the portrait of the physical body was "even a whisker off": inaccurate images not only lacked authenticity but risked invoking the wrong spirits and inviting the spirit of another personage to the ceremony. Drawing from the *Zuo Commentary on the Spring and Autumn Annals* and other classical sources, Qiu Jun 丘濬 (1421–95) articulated an iconoclastic conception of the spirit world that cannot be adequately represented by physical images because the spirits are formless and unfathomable. But even Qiu Jun was ambivalent about the status of these sacrificial images, as Sommer points out, for he objected to the emperor's bowing before statues of Confucius's followers on grounds that they were commoners but consented to his bowing before their spirit tablets.

Rituals performed in the temple were complex liturgical and richly choreographed ceremonies that included offerings of a sacrificial feast, dance, and music. Joseph Lam draws from standardized liturgies of rites and music prescribed by the imperial court and treatises authored by music masters who arranged the choreography of ceremonies performed at local temples to explore the Confucian "ideology of proper music." The standardized liturgy emanates from court discussion on what is correct based on the canon; the local traditions are expressions of "individual hearts" as manifested in specific and often personal contexts.[68] The mechanisms used to effect these localized and perhaps subtle adjustments often entailed minute variations in musical pitch, harmonics, and technical manipulation of the bodies of the dancers. Lam contends that this substratum of musical expression reveals the essential "humanism" of musical Confucianism.

Lam's essay also addresses the question of ritual performance and belief discussed above, for it provides excellent examples of regional variations within the framework of imperial standardization of orthopraxy precisely where we expect none: in the imperial cult of Confucius. Lam substantiates Rawski's observation that Confucians believed that correct practice leads to proper belief in, for example, his discussion of Li Zhizao's 李之藻 (1565–1630) counterpointing of musical instruments played in the *yang* 陽 pitch to voices sung in the *yin* 陰 pitch in order to balance the *qi* 氣 of the ceremony and to better facilitate communication between the officiants and the spirits in the temple. Li's concern for communication between the living and the spirits of the dead also corroborates the position that these sacrifices were not merely figurative offerings to a spirit "as if" it were really present. A number of intriguing questions are raised by the fact that Li Zhizao was a friend of Matteo Ricci and a Christian convert (baptized as Leo in 1610), not the least of which is how Ricci could downplay the religious, albeit "pagan," implications of the temple sacrifices while his friend thought so carefully about how to facilitate the spiritual aspects of the liturgy.

---

68. Ebrey (*Confucianism and Family Rituals*, pp. 31–34, chap. 3) discusses adjustments in canonical procedures to conform to individual feelings.

IMAGINING CONFUCIUS

Lionel Jensen scrutinizes the lore about Kongzi's ancestry, conception, and birth to produce an overtly skeptical reading of the received canonical and noncanonical imaginings of the Sage. Fragments of the Kongzi story dispersed throughout early commentaries on the *Spring and Autumn Annals* and a variety of other sources converged in what became the standard normative biography, compiled by Sima Qian 司馬遷 soon after 127 BCE. The account of Kongzi in Sima Qian's *Historical Records* parallels certain details about his descent from Shang royalty and the extraordinary events surrounding his birth found in Kong family sources, such as the *Family Sayings of Kongzi* (*Kongzi jiayu* 孔子家語), which scholars have long regarded as apocryphal. Like much of the history of ancient China, Kongzi's life first came into sharp narrative focus in Sima Qian's history, which was one critical part of the formation of a unified political and religious empire forged by the Han emperors out of fragments that remained from the ruins of the Zhou. The protean status of the figure of Kongzi in Chinese culture, the vitality of regional cults that honored him, is attested by the appearance of new and fabulous tales of uncertain provenance. Jensen speculates on clues that Kongzi's mother was seen as a mage of an ancient fertility cult and the rare references to a mortal father, which, Jensen argues, suggests that Kongzi was imagined as the offspring of his mother's intercourse with a god or possibly a mythical bird. It is not necessary to concur with Jensen's inferences from this long and artful history of cultic imaginings of Kongzi that he was "a symbolic rather than historic artifact" or that he died without an heir. The value of this chapter lies in its implicit argument against the habit of thinking of an icon like Kongzi in specific, overly familiarized ways. Clearly Kongzi signified many things that were not always consistent and that often conflicted with the familiar canonical master found in the *Analects*. The complex and diverse figures of the noncanonical Kongzi were largely dissipated again during the imperial era when sectarian orthodoxies were canonized in books, examination curricula, and sacrifices to the sages and worthies in the temple, but they never entirely disappeared. Pieces of this ancient lore were transmitted in sources produced by Kongzi's descendants and in the vernacular "strange tales" genre, and thus were always accessible for later uses. The fifteenth-century pictures of Confucius's biography discussed by Julia Murray in this volume allude to anecdotes that come from the apocryphal texts, and nineteenth-century missionaries included some of these stories in English-language biographies of Confucius.

The practice of narrating the lives of sages in pictorial biographies had existed for centuries in Buddhism and Daoism before the *Pictures of the Sage's Traces* was compiled in the mid-fifteenth century. Zhang Kai's 張楷 (1398–1460) annotated illustrations of the life of Confucius analyzed by Julia Murray in this volume established a genre in Confucian discourses on the Sage. Over the centuries, dozens of different versions expressed different conceptions of Confucius and served a variety of aims. The original version of the *Pictures* focused largely on a couple dozen anecdotes associated with Confucius's career as itinerant teacher and official that attested to his exemplary moral character. These pictures were evidently intended as a pedagogical device to promulgate some basic tenets of state orthodoxy rather than as artwork. But why, Murray asks, did Zhang Kai select a visual medium for teaching the values of the literati class rather than the principal means of Confucian expression: the classical written language? The appeal to the visual senses as a means to prescribe proper conduct is perfectly consonant with the corporeality of literati lives discussed in a number of contexts so far.

That pictures were used to articulate ideas that might be expressed more precisely in words—which is not to say more vividly or even more effectively—however, suggests a certain breach of the imaginary boundaries that separated literati from popular culture. The *Pictures*, indeed, became a vehicle for the diffusion of Confucian values as embodied in the life of Confucius into the popular culture of late imperial times. Publication of some of the later versions of the *Pictures* was underwritten by non-degree-holding patrons of Confucian culture, such as imperial princes and wealthy men. Moreover, as Murray shows, the *Pictures of the Sage's Traces* genre unmistakably facilitated the diffusion of specific anecdotes and images of Confucius in such popular media as Ming opera, which transported the birth and life of Confucius into a distinctively Ming setting of a well-appointed garden villa of a wealthy gentry family. This contrasts with the desperate circumstances attributed to Confucius by Sima Qian. The illustrations that accompany the opera script move the original solitary worship at Mount Ni of Confucius's mother to a suspiciously Daoist-looking temple, where she is joined by her husband (a late appearance that Murray examines). The first version of the *Pictures* portrayed the canonical master of the Ancient Text tradition, where-as some later versions helped disseminate Confucius throughout popular culture by depicting the miraculous stories of the noncanonical moments, such as the appearance of supernatural omens and Heaven's expression of its approval of Confucius's writing by issuing a red rainbow from the Big Dipper. For centuries, therefore, the *Pictures* genre embodied the tension between canonical and noncanonical conceptions of Confucius, even while it did not resolve it. Nor did it attempt to do so. Even the 1934 version, published just before the Nationalist government launched the conservative New Life movement and revived the state worship of Confucius, retained pictures of the miraculous events surrounding Confucius's life. The modernization of the *Pictures* genre (as opposed to the ultra-modernist annihilation of Confucian culture under Mao discussed by Jun Jing and Wang Liang in this volume) occurred fairly recently, in the late 1980s, with the production of the black limestone version rendered in the post–Socialist Realist mode of the post-Mao era in which the supernatural episodes were ("finally") excised and Confucius was rehabilitated as, in Murray's words, "a model citizen of secular society."

POLITICS AND SOCIETY

Huang Chin-shing examines the role that imperial worship of Confucius played in the formation of Ming autocracy. Engaging long-standing views of imperial historians, he maintains that the temple reforms during the reigns of Taizu (1368–98), the dynastic founder, and Shizong (1521–66) were orchestrated by autocratic rulers mindful of the import of the reforms and knowledgeable of the long history of the ritual precedents used to justify the changes. Huang urges us to think of the actions of these two emperors as motivated by their own autocratic aims rather than by those of calculating ministers purportedly manipulating the rulers behind the scenes. The effect of both these reforms was to merge the tradition of the Confucian Dao (*Daotong*) with the tradition of proper imperial governance (*zhitong* 治統). In a Weberian mode, he argues that in so doing, the Dao became subservient to the power of the throne as represented by the lineage of proper rulers. Against the background of changing attitudes of rulers toward the temple, Huang analyzes how the 1530 temple reforms exemplify attempts by

Ming rulers to use sacrificial rituals to oppress the Confucian officials at court.

Although the two rulers may have been similarly motivated by the goal of using the Confucius temple rites as a means of increasing their political power, the particular circumstances of the reforms they promoted differed, with somewhat different consequences for the liturgy that was produced. Taizu suspended sacrifices to Confucius in 1369 on the pretext that Confucius condemned sacrifices that were not offered to one's own ancestors (*Analects* 2.24). Not coincidentally, the suspension of imperial sacrifices occurred just after Confucius's fifty-fifth generation ducal descendant declined to travel to the capital on grounds of illness; Taizu would later pass over this duke and confer a lucrative sinecure on the duke's successor on the grounds that added responsibilities might overburden the frail man. When the sacrifices were reinstated in 1382, Taizu was still laboring to rebuild bureaucratic support in the aftermath of the bloody purges surrounding his execution of his prime minister Hu Weiyong 胡惟庸 (d. 1380). In contrast, many of the reforms during the Shizong reign grew out of the need to legitimate that emperor's refusal to be adopted into the imperial line of his cousin and predecessor, who had died without an heir. In both cases, the temple reforms resulted in changes that elevated the emperor's status relative to the imperial bureaucracy and the political legacy of the imperial throne vis-à-vis the Confucian tradition.

Before imperial temples honoring Confucius were constructed in the capital and government schools throughout the empire, the temple in Qufu, Shandong, was the center of an ancestral cult supervised by Confucius's descendants, who performed sacrifices to his spirit as the progenitor of the Kong lineage. The Qufu Kongs were headed by a senior lineage heir who had received a hereditary title from the throne since the first century BCE and had been known as the Duke for Propagating Culture since the eighth century. Addressing questions raised by social historians, Abigail Lamberton examines the social organization of the Kong lineage, which ruled over one of the largest (and certainly the oldest) feudal manors in the empire, its relationship with the imperial court, particularly during the Qing dynasty (1644–1911), and its privileged status. The Qufu Kongs' peculiar status is perhaps best illustrated in the relative absence of their use of social strategies common among other powerful lineages in the late imperial era, such as forming marriage alliances with other elite families. Lamberton suggests that the daughters of the Kongs were the objects of such strategies, as evidenced by the impressive marriages in the Ming and Qing. Lamberton also argues that the Kongs did not need high examination degrees—those Kongs who did gain regular degrees tended not to have distinguished bureaucratic careers. The more prominent public servants in the Kong clan attained high positions through recommendation by the Duke or other high-ranking kin. The Kongs' land was protected from taxation and almost immune from government investigation, due largely to the Kongs' control of the local magistracy from the Ming to the mid-eighteenth century. The Kongs received gifts of land and serfs from the throne; by the middle of the eighteenth century, they reputedly owned 164,000 acres of land and more than 100,000 households. The Qufu Kongs, she argues, maintained their exalted status by means of a strategy of descent that hinged upon the cultural memory of their most prestigious ancestor. Yet, the very source of the Kongs' wealth and power, imperial patronage, was also the source of their vulnerability. When the incumbent duke fled north China with the Song emperor Gaozong (r. 1127–62) during the Jurchen invasion, the new rulers of the north appointed his younger brother as the new duke of Qufu, establishing two main lineages, a division that exists to the present. The Kong clan thus paid a certain price for its exalted status and local hegemony, for it was always potentially susceptible to the throne's intervention. The Kongs were ever-loyal servants of the throne rather than potential dynasts.

THE PAST IN THE PRESENT

Jun Jing draws from Pierre Bourdieu to describe distant relations of Confucius's descendants in Qufu. This branch of the family left Qufu for south China in the tenth century and then settled in Lanzhou, Gansu province after the Mongol conquest. Four brothers of the Lanzhou Kongs settled in the nearby village of Dachuan in present-day Yongjing county in the seventeenth century; the third brother later established a branch in the neighboring village of Xiaochuan. Soon after their arrival in Dachuan, the Kongs built a temple that functioned as the county's Kong family ancestral shrine and as a temple for local worship of Confucius and the literati tradition; the Xiaochuan Kongs built a temple around the turn of the twentieth century. Both temples were destroyed after the founding of the People's Republic— the Xiaochuan temple was demolished in 1960 to make way for a hydraulic plant, and the Dachuan temple was dismantled in the throes of the anti–Lin Biao / anti–Confucius campaign of 1974. Both temples were being rebuilt when Jing did fieldwork in Dachuan. Jing describes a lineage that lives at the cultural frontier of Confucian China, far removed from the sacred ancestral grounds of Confucius's birthplace, without access to the books that contained liturgies for the sacrifices, which have had to be reconstructed from memory. He recounts how the details of the ritual were recalled from the fading memories of those who had participated in the rites forty years earlier; it was the corporeal memory of the body that acted out these initially nameless gestures and allowed them to be rendered into liturgical words on paper. The meeting at which the ceremony was reconstituted brought into play the symbolic capital wielded by the Dachuan Kongs, who claimed dominant ritual authority on grounds of senior descent and superior cultural knowledge: only Dachuan had members who had received the education necessary to write the ritual manual in the classical language, and Dachuan had always been the sole site for the worship of the four brothers who established the Kongs of Yongjing county. The less educated junior kin of Xiaochuan commanded their own forms of capital: they were wealthier and possessed the political savvy to take advantage of Party contacts in the post-Mao era to gain state support and other advantages when they rebuilt their temple a year after the Dachuan Kongs.

Despite its remoteness and the destructive effects of modernization, the Kong temple cult of Yongjing county encountered a number of the same problems as other temples. Although this was a Kong family ancestral shrine, the post-1991 reconstructed temple also served as a temple to honor the great scholars of the Confucian tradition: unlike other ancestral shrines, the temples operated by Confucius's descendants have spirit tablets of persons who were not his flesh and blood descendants. The distinction between ancestral and literati cult is blurred by the merging of these two kinds of worship (see also Chapter 1). But the tension was not erased in Dachuan, where two ceremonies are held: a daytime festival open to the public and a midnight sacrifice in which only male members of the Yongjing Kongs participated. Members of the public were encouraged to bow before the spirit tablets of Confucius and his disciples, but they were prohibited from such acts of obeisance in the presence of the founders of the Yongjing Kongs. Qiu Jun's aniconic ambivalence toward the spiritual efficacy of the icons he sought to remove from the temples in the Ming (see Deborah Sommer's chapter) evidently persists in the Dachuan Kongs' taboo against outsiders praying to their direct lineal ancestors. This is yet another example of Evelyn Rawski's

argument (discussed above) about the widespread beliefs concerning ancestor worship that transcend locality.

The final chapter, a report on the Red Guard assault on the temple in
Confucius's hometown from August to December of 1966, is dramatically told
by Wang Liang, a journalist who lives in Qufu. Drawing from interviews, interrogation testimony, and contemporary Red Guard sources, Wang Liang
gives a blow-by-blow account of militant cultural iconoclasm in an early phase
of the Cultural Revolution, just as the Communist Party was about to lose
control of the course of revolutionary action. The Cultural Revolution, at
this point, was still quite literally a war over cultural icons that inhabited
parts of the superstructure that had not yet conformed to the dictates of the
socialist transformation of the economic base. On June 8, 1966, the Party
proclaimed itself the enemy of the old order and called for the destruction of
the Four Olds ("old ideology and culture, and old customs and habits which
imperialism and all exploiting classes use to poison the minds of the working
people"). What the *People's Daily* editorial writers apparently had in mind,
however, was the destruction of the "remnants of feudal ideology" through
"reasoned criticism," which they regarded as the principal "weapon against all
the evils left over by imperialism and the landlord and bourgeois classes" in
the period *after* the Revolution.[69] Thus the mainstream party apparatus advocated what would later seem like a rather mild post-revolutionary mop-
ping-up operation, whereas the Maoists and the Red Guards were intent on
a more destructive campaign. By the summer of 1966, Mao Zedong (1893–
1976) had re-emerged from the isolation imposed on him by the Party and
eliminated many of his more powerful opponents. By early August, Mao had
taken charge of the Central Committee and urged broader participation in
the revolutionary activities that began at Beijing University that spring. The
campaign against the Four Olds was officially launched on August 8, when
the Central Committee adopted a series of decisions that set forth some basic principles of the Cultural Revolution. "Although the bourgeoisie has
been overthrown," the Central Committee proclamation states, "it is still trying to use the old ideas, culture, customs, and habits of the exploiting classes
to corrupt the masses, capture their minds and endeavor to stage a come-
back." The document calls for the working classes to "criticize and repudiate
the reactionary bourgeois academic 'authorities' and . . . to transform educa-

---

69. "We Are Critics of the Old World" (from the *People's Daily*, June 8, 1966), in *People's
China*, pp. 257–61.

tion, literature and art and all other parts of the superstructure not in correspondence with the socialist economic base."[70]

The ideological campaign against the Four Olds reached Qufu at the end
of August. When the Red Guards prepared to enter the Kong temple with
the intention of destroying it, however, they encountered stiff resistance
from the workers whose families had maintained the temple for many generations and who possessed proletarian credentials superior to those of the
students in the Red Guard. The students' retreat in the face of the power-
fully symbolic State Council plaque that protected the temple, mansion, and
cemetery from destruction was temporary. In November, Tan Houlan, one
of the main leaders of the movement, led a Beijing contingent of the Red
Guards to Qufu, which ceremoniously smashed the State Council's plaque
to pieces, then plundered the temple grounds, destroying Qing dynasty stelae (pre-Qing stelae were to be preserved, but earlier ones were destroyed in
the melee that followed), and slit the throats of the temple statues of Confucius's major disciples and disemboweled the canonical texts and bronze mirrors placed in them. Confucius's statue was labeled "number one hooligan"
and paraded through the streets and thrown into a bonfire. Local Confucian
scholars were publicly humiliated. When the Red Guard arrived at the
Kong cemetery to disinter Confucius's corpse they—anticlimactically, but
not surprisingly—found the grave empty. Plans were later drawn up to
"renovate" the temple and cemetery, which called for the removal of the
temple's exterior walls and the installation of an exhibition hall extolling
Mao's thought. The cemetery was to be plowed over and used as agricultural
land. In the end, political and economic factors forced these plans to be
shelved, barely averting what Wang calls "a great tragedy in the history of
human civilization."

"FROM ETHICS TO RITUAL"

This collection of studies is not a comprehensive account of the cult of Confucius. Rather, it endeavors to reconsider the judgment of modern scholars
that Confucianism marks a "transition from ritual to ethical thinking"; it
aims to return ritual (as theory and practice) to our thinking about Confucianism. The academic disciplines represented here raise a variety of ques-

---

70. "Decision Concerning the Great Proletarian Cultural Revolution" by the Central
Committee of the Chinese Communist Party (Aug. 8, 1966) in *People's China*, pp. 272–73.

tions and employ diverse modes of analysis in the scrutiny of different kinds
of sources. Without downplaying the importance of the wealth of research
on Confucian ethics and metaphysics, these essays draw attention to Confucianism's corporeality and religiousness, its myths and cultic practices, and
the continual disputation over these issues among Confucian scholars and
those who have observed them; this applies equally to the chapters on the
political and social contexts of imperial worship of Confucius and to the vicissitudes of his descendants from imperial times through the post-Mao era.
As such, the essays in this volume run counter to the habit of modern studies that have gathered the disparate parts of Confucian life in a box labeled
"world's great philosophies," a habit that fretted little about what to do with
the round pieces of the cult that could not be pushed through the square
hole at the top of the philosophy box.

The reader will discern numerous methodological and interpretive differences in the chapters of this book. As editor, I have not endeavored to conceal or reconcile these disparities. Rather, I have strived to refrain from imposing my views upon the other authors too much, although my comments
on earlier drafts of these essays might suggest otherwise. I can honestly say
that the authors have proved admirably resistant to suggestions that ran
contrary to what they considered important. The multidisciplinarity of these
essays is necessary in a collective effort such as this to examine the complex
issues posed by the literati cult of the Sage of culture. It is my hope that
this diversity of approaches presents the reader with choices of where and
how to enter the study of dimensions of Confucian life that have not been
adequately studied in modern research on Confucianism. Perhaps the book
may be likened to "a barrel of water on the highway," to borrow Huang
Zongxi's characterization of his anthology of Ming Confucianism, from
which travelers "may use either a pottery cup or a wooden ladle to drink
their fill." The choices of what to take away and how to take it are left for the
reader to decide.

WORKS CITED

Asad, Talal. "Toward a Genealogy of the Concept of Ritual." In idem, *Genealogies of Religion: Discipline and Reasons of Power in Christianity and Islam*, pp. 55–79. Baltimore: Johns Hopkins University Press, 1993.

Bell, Catherine. *Ritual: Perspectives and Dimensions*. New York: Oxford University Press, 1997.

Boone, William J. *An Essay on the Proper Rendering of the Words Elohim and Theos into the Chinese Language*. Canton: Office of the Chinese Repository, 1848.

Brooks, E. Bruce, and A. Taeko Brooks. *The Original Analects: Sayings of Confucius and His Successors*. New York: Columbia University Press, 1998.

Chunqiu Zuozhuan chengyi 春秋左傳正義. Comp. Zuoqiu Ming 左丘明; commentary by Du Yu 杜預; annot. Kong Yingda 孔穎達. In *Shisanjing zhushu* (q.v.).

Couling, Samuel. *The Encyclopaedia Sinica*. London: Oxford University Press, 1917.

Creel, Herrlee G. *Confucius, the Man and the Myth*. New York: John Day, 1949.

———. "Was Confucius Agnostic?" *T'oung Pao* 29 (1935): 55–99.

Duara, Prasenjit. "Superscribing Symbols: The Myth of Guandi, Chinese God of War." *Journal of Asian Studies* 47 (1988) 4: 778–95.

Ebrey, Patricia Buckley. *Confucianism and Family Rituals in Imperial China: A Social History of Writing About Rites*. Princeton: Princeton University Press, 1991.

Elman, Benjamin A. *Classicism, Politics, and Kinship: The Ch'ang-chou School of New Text Confucianism in Late Imperial China*. Berkeley: University of California Press, 1990.

Fingarette, Herbert. *Confucius: The Secular as Sacred*. New York: Harper & Row, 1972.

Fung Yu-lan (Feng Youlan) 馮友蘭. *A History of Chinese Philosophy*. 2 vols. Trans. Derk Bodde. Princeton: Princeton University Press, 1952.

———. *Zhongguo zhexue shi* 中國哲學史. Shanghai: Shangwu yinshuguan, 1934.

Grieder, Jerome B. *Hu Shih and the Chinese Renaissance: Liberalism in the Chinese Revolution, 1917–1937*. Cambridge, Mass.: Harvard University Press, 1970.

Hall, David L., and Roger T. Ames. *Thinking Through Confucius*. Albany: State University of New York Press, 1987.

Han shu 漢書. 12 vols. 76 BCE. Ban Gu 班固. Beijing: Zhonghua shuju, 1962.

Hsiao Kung-chuan. *Rural China: Imperial Control in the Nineteenth Century*. Seattle: University of Washington Press, 1960.

Hu Shih. "The Establishment of Confucianism as a State Religion During the Han Dynasty." *Journal of the North China Branch of the Royal Asiatic Society* 60 (1929): 20–41.

Jensen, Lionel M. *Manufacturing Confucianism: Chinese Traditions and Universal Civilization*. Durham: Duke University Press, 1997.

Jiu Tang shu 舊唐書. 16 vols. Comp. Liu Xu 劉昫. Beijing: Zhonghua shuju, 1975.

Jochim, Christian. *Chinese Religions: A Cultural Perspective*. Englewood Cliffs, N.J.: Prentice Hall, 1986.

———. "Imperial Audience Ceremonies of the Ch'ing Dynasty: A Study of the Ethico-Religious Dimension of the Confucian State." Ph.D. diss., University of Southern California, 1980.

Lau, D. C., trans. *Analects*. Middlesex, Eng.: Penguin, 1979.

Legge, James. *The Notions of the Chinese Concerning Gods and Spirits: with an Examination and Defense of "An Essay on the Proper Rendering of the Words Elohim and Theos into the Chinese Language," by William J. Boone, D.D.* Hongkong: Hongkong Register, 1852.

———. *The Religions of China: Confucianism and Taoism Described and Compared with Christianity*. London: Hodder and Stroughton, 1880.

Legge, James, trans. *Confucian Analects*. The Chinese Classics, vol. 1. Oxford: Clarendon Press, 1893.

———. *The Shoo King or the Book of Historical Documents*. The Chinese Classics, vol. 3. London: Trübner and Co., 1865.

Lewis, Mark Edward. *Writing and Authority in Early China*. Albany: State University of New York Press, 1999.

Liji zhengyi 禮記正義. Commentary by Zheng Xuan 鄭玄; annot. Kong Yingda 孔穎達. In *Shisanjing zhushu* (q.v.).

Lunyu zhengyi 論語正義. 1866. Comp. Liu Baonan 劉寶楠. *Zhuzi jicheng* 諸子集成 ed. Beijing: Zhonghua shuju, 1954.

Meyer, Jeffrey F. *The Dragons of Tiananmen: Beijing as a Sacred City*. Columbia: University of South Carolina Press, 1991.

Ming shi 明史. 14 vols. 1739. Comp Zhang Tingyu 張廷玉 et al. Beijing: Zhonghua shuju, 1974.

Morrison, Robert. *A Dictionary of the Chinese Language, in Three Parts*. Macao: East India Company Press, 1815–23.

Mungello, D. E. *Curious Land: Jesuit Accommodation and the Origins of Sinology*. Honolulu: University of Hawai'i Press, 1985.

Murray, Julia K. "Illustrations of the Life of Confucius: Their Evolution, Function, and Significance in Late Ming China." *Artibus Asiae* 57 (1997) 1/2: 73–134.

Nelson, R. *"Confucianism in Relation to Christianity* by Rev. James Legge." Pamphlet. Shanghai: Presbyterian Mission Press, 1877.

Ōtsuki Nobuyoshi 大槻信良. *Shushi "Shisho shūchū" tenkyo kō* 朱子四書集注典據考. Kyoto: Chūbun shuppansha, 1976.

People's China: Social Experimentation, Politics, Entry onto the World Scene, 1966 Through 1972. Ed. David Milton, Nancy Milton, and Franz Schurmann. The China Reader, vol. 4. New York: Vintage Books, 1974.

Qing huidian tu 清會典圖. Comp. Kun'gang 崑岡 et al. Guangxu (1899) ed.

Rawski, Evelyn S. "A Historian's Approach to Chinese Death Ritual." In *Death Ritual in Late Imperial China*, ed. James L. Watson and Evelyn Rawski, pp. 20–34. Berkeley: University of California Press, 1988.

Ricci, Matteo, and Nicolá Trigault. *China in the Sixteenth Century: The Journals of Matthew Ricci, 1583–1610.* Trans. Louis J. Gallagher. New York: Random House, 1953.

Rubinstein, Murray A. *The Origins of the Anglo-American Missionary Enterprise in China, 1807–1840.* Lanham, Md.: Scarecrow Press, 1996.

Schwartz, Benjamin I. *The World of Thought in Ancient China.* Cambridge, Mass.: Harvard University Press, Belknap Press, 1985.

Shang shu zhengyi 尚書正義. Comp. Kong Anguo 孔安國; annot. Kong Yingda 孔穎達. In *Shisanjing zhushu* (q.v.).

Shang Wei. "The Collapse of the Taibo Temple: A Study of *The Unofficial History of the Scholars*." Ph.D. diss., Harvard University, 1995.

Shaughnessy, Edward L. *Before Confucius: Studies in the Creation of the Chinese Classics.* Albany: State University of New York Press, 1997.

Shisanjing zhushu 十三經注疏. 3 vols. 1816. Ed. Ruan Yuan 阮元. Beijing: Zhonghua shuju, 1980.

Shuowen jiezi 說文解字. 100 CE. Xu Shen 許慎. Annot. Duan Yucai 段玉裁, 1815. Jingyun lou cangban 經韻樓藏版 ed.

Songs of the South: An Anthology of Ancient Chinese Poems by Qu Yuan and Other Poets. Trans. David Hawkes. Middlesex, Eng.: Penguin, 1985.

Soothill, William E. *The Analects of Confucius.* Shanghai: Presbyterian Mission Press; London: Messrs. Oliphant, Anderson & Ferrier, 1910.

Taylor, Rodney L. *The Cultivation of Sagehood as a Religious Goal in Neo-Confucianism: A Study of Selected Writings of Kao P'an-lung.* Missoula: American Academy of Religion, 1978; Ph.D. diss., Columbia University, 1974.

Taylor, Rodney L., and Gary Arbuckle. "Confucianism." Part II of the series "Chinese Religions: The State of the Field." *Journal of Asian Studies* 54 (1995) 2: 347–54.

Tu Wei-ming. *Centrality and Commonality: An Essay on Confucian Religiousness.* Albany: State University of New York Press, 1989.

———. "*Jen* as a Living Metaphor in the Confucian *Analects*." In idem, *Confucian Thought: Selfhood as Creative Transformation*, pp. 81–92. Albany: State University of New York Press, 1985.

Van Zoeren, Steven. *Poetry and Personality: Reading, Exegesis and Hermeneutics in Traditional China.* Stanford: Stanford University Press, 1991.

Wakeman, Frederic, and Carolyn Grant, eds. *Conflict and Control in Late Imperial China.* Berkeley: University of California Press, 1975.

Waley, Arthur, trans. *The Analects of Confucius.* New York: Vintage Books, 1938.

Watson, James. "Standardizing the Gods: The Promotion of the T'ien Hou ('Empress of Heaven') Along the South Coast, 960–1960." In *Popular Culture in Late*

Imperial China, ed. David Johnson, Andrew J. Nathan, and Evelyn S. Rawski, pp. 292–324. Berkeley: University of California Press, 1985.

———. "The Structure of Chinese Funerary Rites: Elementary Forms, Ritual Sequence, and the Primacy of Performance." In *Death Ritual in Late Imperial China*, ed. James L. Watson and Evelyn Rawski, pp. 3–19. Berkeley: University of California Press, 1988.

Williams, E. T. "The State Religion of China During the Manchu Dynasty." *Journal of the North Branch of the Royal Asiatic Society* 44 (1913): 11–45.

Wilson, Thomas A. "Confucian Sectarianism and the Compilation of the *Ming History*." *Late Imperial China* 15 (Dec. 1994) 2: 53–84.

———. *Genealogy of the Way: The Construction and Uses of the Confucian Tradition in Late Imperial China*. Stanford: Stanford University Press, 1995.

———. "Sacrifice and the Imperial Cult of Confucius." *History of Religions* 43, no. 3 (Feb. 2002): 251–87.

Xiaojing zhushu 孝經注疏. Comp. Xing Bing 邢昺. In *Shisanjing zhushu* (q.v.).

Xin Tang shu 新唐書. 20 vols. 1060. Ouyang Xiu 歐陽修. Beijing: Zhonghua shuju, 1975.

Xunzi jijie 荀子集解. 1891. Ed. Wang Xianqian 王先謙. Zhuzi jicheng 諸子集成 ed. Beijing: Zhonghua shuju, 1954.

Zhu Xi 朱熹. *Sishu jizhu* 四書集注. Sibu beiyao 四部備要 ed. Shanghai: Zhonghua shuju, 1935.

Zhuzi yulei 朱子語類. 8 vols. Ed. Li Jingde 李靖德. Beijing: Zhonghua shuju, 1986.

Zito, Angela. *Of Body and Brush: Grand Sacrifice as Text/Performance in Eighteenth-Century China*. Chicago: University of Chicago Press, 1997.

Rites and Music

ONE

Ritualizing Confucius/Kongzi
The Family and State Cults of the Sage of
Culture in Imperial China
Thomas A. Wilson

THE CANONICAL AND THE
NONCANONICAL SAGE

It is said that he transcribed the sagely traditions of the ancients in sacred books that would be transmitted for ten thousand generations. The imperial courts of the last thousand years worshipped him as the "supreme sage" of state orthodoxy in temples devoted to him. To Confucian scholars of the same era, he played a pivotal role in the transmission of the Dao 道統; indeed, without him it would have been lost forever.[1] To common folk, he was

Research in China was supported by the American Philosophical Society and the Couper faculty research fund of Hamilton College. The author wishes to acknowledge the assistance of Zhu Weizheng 朱維錚 (Fudan University), Kong Xianglin 孔祥林 and Luo Chenglie 駱承烈 of Qufu, Kong Xiangkai 孔祥楷 and Kong Liuxian 孔柳先 of Quzhou, He Jun 何俊 (Hangzhou University), Huang Chin-shing (Academia Sinica, Taiwan), and Jun Jing (CCNY) during his research travels in China and Taiwan, and Sue Naquin, Michael Nylan, Benjamin Elman, and participants in a colloquium at the Institute for Advanced Study in November 1999 for their comments on earlier drafts of this piece. The writing was funded by the National Endowment for the Humanities.

1. Consider, e.g., Zhu Xi's statement: "If Kongzi had never been born after Yao and Shun, where could anyone go to understand [the Dao]?" He then goes on to say the same thing about Mengzi and the Cheng brothers (*Zhuzi yulei* 93.2350).

the inventor of the written language and the rituals that governed their conduct in everyday life.[2] Statues of him found their way into Buddhist and Daoist temples, where he was worshipped as a god in the pantheon of deities and culture heroes, despite the throne's periodic proscriptions of such activities.[3] To conservative reformers at the end of the imperial era, his teachings were tantamount to the spirit of Chinese culture.[4] To many in the West, he was "Confucius," the founder of a humanistic ethical philosophy called Confucianism.[5]

Here, I call him Kongzi 孔子 (Master Kong), although he has had many names through the ages. His surname was Kong 孔. His parents named him Qiu 丘 (literally, "hill"), and he took the style name (zi 字) Zhongni 仲尼, second son Ni. These names allude to the mountain southeast of his residence in the Watchtower district (Queli)[6] in present-day Qufu, Shandong, where his mother prayed for a son and later gave birth to him.[7] Duke Ai of Lu 魯哀公 eulogized him with the name of Venerable Ni (Nifu 尼父) in 478 BCE and his disciples simply called him Master (Zi 子 and Fuzi 夫子). Later generations would call him the Supreme Sage (zhi sheng 至聖), although it is not clear that he considered himself one. Indeed, he said he had never seen one (Lunyu 論語 7.26). His "canonical" persona—that found in the Analects (Lunyu)—was concerned principally with the Dao of the true

---

2. Gu Jiegang, "Chunqiu shidai de Kongzi he Handai de Kongzi," 2: 494. Fuxi 伏羲 is usually credited with inventing a writing system after seeing the eight trigrams on a tortoise, and the four-eyed Cang Jie 倉頡 (a contemporary of the Yellow Emperor) is regarded as the inventor of Chinese characters (see *Sancai tuhui*, "Renwu," 4.3a–b).

3. The court proscribed popular worship of Kongzi in 1438 (Zhengtong 3/3) (*Ming tongjian* 22.905) and 1836 (*Qing shi gao* 84.2536).

4. For Kang Youwei's identification of Kongzi and Chinese culture, see Qian Mu, *Zhongguo jinsanbainian xueshu shi*, p. 689.

5. Modern scholars tend to view Confucius as a rationalist (Creel, *Confucius, the Man and the Myth*, pp. 82–84, 113–22, 169) and Confucianism as an ethical philosophy (e.g., Shryock, *The Origin and Development of the State Cult of Confucius*). See the Introduction to this volume, pp. 7–13.

6. On the meaning of Queli, see Gu Yanwu, *Rizhi lu jishi* 31.38a–b.

7. It was also said that his forehead protruded in a manner resembling Mount Ni, inviting the names Qiu and Zhongni (*Analects*, pp. 181–82). For fuller treatment of the significance of this, see the chapter by Lionel Jensen in this volume, pp. 196–97. Traditional sources date his birth to the twenty-first day of the tenth lunar month of King Ling's twenty-first year (551 BCE). He died at 74 *sui* 歲, on the ninth day of the sixth lunar month of King Jing's forty-first year (479 BCE). See Kong Shangren, *Kongzi shijia pu* 2.2a, 33b; and Kong Jifen, *Queli wenxian kao* 2.1a.

gentleman (*junzi* 君子), which, in his day, generally referred to the son of a nobleman. For Kongzi, the gentleman was a paragon that all people should emulate. In the *Analects*, the gentleman is said to "attend to the fundamentals" (1.2) and never "depart from humanity" (4.5), a quality that enables one to discern right and wrong (4.3). "There are three [attributes] of the gentleman's Way," Kongzi said, of which he "himself was incapable of achieving. To be humane without reserve, knowing without deception, and brave without fear."[8] To this disclaimer, a disciple replied: "This is the Master's own way" (14.28).

SAGELY LUMINARY AND DARK SAGE

Kongzi was a member of an emerging group of learned men who served several functions at the courts of late Eastern Zhou (770–221 BCE) noblemen. As ritualists versed in the liturgical traditions, they advised and supervised sacrifices to the gods and royal ancestors. They also advised the royal Zhou court and lesser nobles on matters of proper government.[9] Kongzi is widely regarded as China's first teacher because he was the first to assemble a large group of pupils drawn from diverse social classes and to formulate a philosophy of virtuous governance that would enable all subjects to perfect their Heaven-conferred natural capacity to be humane. These various orientations help explain how Kongzi's two greatest followers (who lived after his death) developed schools of interpretation based on conflicting presuppositions. Mengzi 孟子 (Mencius, 372–289 BCE) argued that human nature is originally good; thus, perfection of the self and the social order are possible by drawing from and cultivating an innate humanity (*ren* 仁) that could not endure the suffering of others. Xunzi 荀子 (d. 238 BCE), in contrast, maintained that we are naturally inclined to satisfy our own selfish desires, but that we are perfectible through education in the wisdom of the sages and moral disciplining in the rituals they formulated.[10]

For the most part, the Kongzi of the *Analects* thought of himself as a tireless teacher (7.2), a follower of the wisdom of earlier sages, and a lover of

---

8. All translations are my own unless otherwise noted. D. C. Lau (*Analects*, p. 128) translates this passage as: "A man of benevolence never worries; a man of wisdom is never in two minds; a man of courage is never afraid."

9. See Hsu, *Ancient China in Transition*, pp. 34–37, 96–105.

10. For more on this tension in Confucianism, see the Introduction to this volume, pp. 1–40.

antiquity (7.1). Although not formally included in the official canon until relatively late in Chinese history, the *Analects* has been regarded as the most reliable source on the thought of the canonical Kongzi since as early as the first century BCE.[11] Yet even in the *Analects* there are occasional traces of another, noncanonical persona, such as the beleaguered Master who, surrounded by the soldiers of Kuang, fearlessly proclaimed, "Once King Wen died, wasn't Culture invested in me? If Heaven was going to destroy This Culture (*si wen* 斯文), a mortal such as me would not be able to obtain it. Since Heaven has not destroyed This Culture, what can the people of Kuang do to me" (9.5)?[12] This remark is striking not because Kongzi believes that Heaven would protect him from harm—for that does not seem to be what he was thinking here—but because, all other humble disclaimers of sagehood notwithstanding, Kongzi seems sure that Heaven has invested This Culture in him (alone). The startling revelation of this statement is not adequately captured by this prosaic rendering of *wen* 文 as "culture." James Legge's translation provides another insight; after King Wen's death, he says, "Was not the cause of truth lodged in me?"[13] *Wen* here signifies the culmination of the cultural patterns of the Three Dynasties. Kongzi does not humbly say he follows the sagely patterns of yore, but that he embodies them—a claim that would elevate him to the status of a sage. At the time, this was a status reserved only for a limited number of sage-kings of high antiquity.[14] After his death, his disciples and their disciples, and also his descendants, began to ascribe extraordinary qualities to him.[15] In the *Mengzi*, a disciple of Kongzi proclaimed him a much greater worthy than the sage-kings Yao 堯

---

11. The earliest extant biography of Kongzi, based largely on the *Analects*, is the account in the *Shiji* 史記. For a more recent study based on these sources, see Creel, *Confucius, the Man and the Myth.*

12. Although his son founded the Zhou dynasty, King Wen initiated the overthrow of the tyrannical last Shang king and was said to have obtained the mandate of Heaven. Kongzi was apparently ambivalent over the Zhou's use of force, for he says that unlike the music of Shun, the music of King Wen was beautiful but not perfectly good (*Lunyu* 3.25). King Wen is also credited with composing the commentaries on the sixty-four hexagrams in the *Book of Change* (*Shiji* 4.117–19).

13. Legge, *Confucian Analects*, pp. 217–18.

14. The *Baihu tong shuzheng* (7.335) cites this passage as evidence that Kongzi recognized himself as a sage. This sentiment is also expressed in the statement, "Heaven produced virtue in me, what can Huan Tui do to me?" (*Lunyu* 7.22).

15. Gu Jiegang, "Chunqiu shidai de Kongzi he Handai de Kongzi," 2: 489.

and Shun 舜. Mengzi elaborated: "Since the birth of the people, no one has surpassed Kongzi"自生民來誰底其盛 (2A.2).

He was born when the once-brilliant Dao of the Zhou kings had declined. In the absence of a virtuous sovereign, Kongzi withdrew from the world and wrote the *Spring and Autumn Annals* to rectify the usurpers who expropriated royal privileges by honoring themselves and their ancestors with the sacred rituals meant for the Son of Heaven and to illuminate the Dao of the uncrowned king (*su wang* 素王).[16] According to early non-canonical commentaries on the Classics (sometimes called *wei* 緯, or apocrypha), which survive in fragments, Kongzi was conceived when his mother went to Mount Ni and prayed for a son, whereupon she "felt the seminal spirit of a black god" (*hei di* 黑帝), sometimes depicted as a black dragon or water god.[17] (One member of Lord Amherst's embassy reported seeing a black-faced statue of Kongzi at a temple in the White Deer Academy in Nan-kang, Jiangxi, in 1816, and a black-faced statue still exists in a temple in Ping-yao, Shanxi.)[18] Kongzi prophesied the end of the Zhou dynasty when he found a fatally wounded one-horned animal with the body of a deer and the tail of an ox (a *lin* 麟, translated here as "unicorn"). This miraculous event is recorded in the last line of the *Spring and Autumn Annals*, which says simply, "In the spring of the fourteenth year of Duke Ai's reign [481 BCE], hunters in the west caught a unicorn." The *Zuo Commentary* adds little to this brief entry: the "hunters took this [animal's appearance] as an ill omen. When he saw it, Kongzi understood that it was a unicorn and took it away."[19]

This is an ambiguous note on which to conclude such a monumental book, although the economy of this passage is exemplary of the text as a whole. What could this mean? According to the *Gongyang Commentary* on the *Spring and Autumn Annals*—which often concurs with apocryphal ver-

---

16. *Mengzi* 3B.9; Dong Zhongshu (ca. 179–104 BCE), quoted in *Han shu* 56.2509; Liu Xiang (77–6 BCE), *Shuo yuan jiaozheng*, 5.95; Wang Su, *Kongzi jiayu* 40.64. Lewis (*Writing and Authority in Early China*, pp. 233–38) argues that Kongzi's legacy was that of "textual kingship" and that his judgments were construed as tantamount to those of a sovereign.

17. Quoted in Zhou Yutong, "Weichan zhong de Kongsheng yu tade mentu," pp. 293, 311n5; *Chunqiu wei yan Kong tu* 4a (56.50a); and Jensen, "Wise Man of the Wilds," p. 428. Lewis (*Writing and Authority in Early China*, pp. 447–48n117) notes that stories of this kind are common in myths about sages.

18. Davis, *The Chinese*, 2: 72; *Da zai Kongzi*, 334; see also Morrison, *A Dictionary of the Chinese Language* 1: 714.

19. "Ai gong" 哀公, *Chunqiu Zuozhuan zhengyi* 59.470–71 (pp. 2172–73).

sions of the dark sage (*xuansheng* 玄聖)—Kongzi wept when he saw the strange animal and anxiously asked, "For whom has it come?" He understood that its appearance augured the demise of his Dao.[20] This exhausts the official canonical explanation of the significance of the unicorn's appearance, which raises as many questions as it answers. According to the noncanonical commentaries, the appearance of the unicorn presages the end of the ruling house of Zhou and the imminent arrival of an enlightened ruler. The Kongzi found in the apocrypha fully understands the deeper significance of the unicorn and says that the Zhou house will soon end: "Today the unicorn has come out, but it has been killed. My Dao is lost."[21] Why? As the son of the black god, Kongzi must rule with the power (*de* 德) of water (as did the Shang). The Zhou ruled with the power of wood, a natural successor to water, but, according to the logic of five phases cosmology, water produces wood and thus cannot succeed it, and the son of the black god cannot succeed the Zhou.[22] In another noncanonical commentary, Kongzi sees not only that it will not be he who will succeed the Zhou but also that it will be a man named Liu, who will rule with the power of fire. In this anticipation of Liu Bang's 劉邦 founding of the Han dynasty some 275 years later, the unicorn spits out a book that confirms this prognostication and "mandates the dark Qiu to set the regulations" for the coming new order. Thus Kongzi sets about the task of writing the *Spring and Autumn Annals*, known as the "Vermillion Regulations" (*chizhi* 赤制) in the Gongyang tradition. The Han would rule with the power of fire, whose color is vermillion.[23]

These tales of a noncanonical master were rarely evident in the official discourse that determined orthodoxy in later times. Yet even long after the waning of the Modern Text (*jinwen* 今文) tradition,[24] which upheld the extra-

---

20. *Chunqiu Gongyang zhuan zhushu* 28.158–59.

21. Zhou Yutong, "Weichan zhong de Kongsheng yu tade mentu," p. 294.

22. Ibid., p. 293.

23. Ibid., pp. 296–97, 312n22; *Chunqiu wei yan Kong tu* 5a (56.51a); Fu Qian, *Chunqiu Zuoshizhuan jieyi* 4.49b–50a; *Chunqiu Gongyang zhuan zhushu* 1.1 (p. 2195). For discussion of Modern Text interpretations of these apocrypha in the Qing, see Elman, *Classicism, Politics, and Kinship*, pp. 205–13, 238–42.

24. The Modern Text versions of the canon, which revolved around the *Gongyang Commentary* on the *Spring and Autumn Annals*, were accepted by the court from the third century BCE to about the fifth century CE. The Ancient Text versions, which centered on the *Rites of Zhou* (*Zhou li*), effectively replaced the Modern Text versions from the fifth century to the eighteenth century. See Elman, *Classicism, Politics, and Kinship*; and Wilson, *Genealogy of the Way*, pp. 29–32.

ordinary lore surrounding the uncrowned king, Kongzi's noncanonical persona endured in the culture. The Modern Text proponent Kang Youwei's 康有爲 (1858–1927) resurrection of the radical reformer in the late nineteenth century is probably the most familiar noncanonical Kongzi, but the dark figure of this other sage was also present in the imperial temple, where signs proclaim him the equal of Heaven and Earth (*yu tian di can* 與天地參)[25] and perhaps most graphically in the *Pictures of the Sage's Traces* (*Shengji tu* 聖迹圖), which proliferated beginning in the fifteenth century (see the chapter by Julia Murray in this volume, pp. 222–64). A unicorn appears before Kongzi's mother with a jade book announcing the imminent birth of the "water spirit's son, who will succeed the Zhou ruling house as the uncrowned king." Regarding the animal as extraordinary, she ties an embroidered cord of the type used for government documents around its horn. On the evening of Kongzi's birth, two dragons circled around the family's house and five elderly beings descended from heaven to its courtyard. Harmonious music came from the heavens. He was born with the forty-nine birthmarks of a sage and the words "mandate [or omen] to create the regulations to order the world" (*zhizuo dingshi fu* 制作定世符) inscribed on his breast; a prognostication of his authorship of the *Spring and Autumn Annals*, which was believed to have established the regulations of the Han dynasty.[26] This bodily inscription is used to explain the reference to Kongzi as a wooden-tongued bell in *Lunyu* 3.24: "Heaven mandates that Kongzi will create the regulations to order the world." When Kongzi announced completion of the work to Heaven, a red rainbow descended from above and transformed into a jade tablet that stated that Kong had written the vermillion regulations in fulfillment of this mandate.[27]

---

25. Allusion to the description of the way of the sage in *Doctrine of the Mean* (*Liji zhengyi* 53.44 [p. 1632]; *Zhongyong zhangju* 6b–17a; see also "Liyun" 禮運, *Liji zhengyi* 22.194 [p. 1422]). References to Kongzi as equal to Heaven and Earth made their way into the temple vocabulary as early as 1310 (Zhida 3), when Emperor Wuzong of the Yuan used slightly different wording: *yu tian di bing* 與天地並 (Kong Jifen, *Queli wenxian kao* 33.21a). In an edict dated 1132 appointing a Kong to a post, Emperor Gaozong of the Song said that the "Master's Dao was equal to Heaven and Earth" (Chen Hao, *Queli zhi* 7.20b). The Yongle emperor of the Ming also had words to the same effect: *Kongzi can tian di* 孔子參天地 (Kong Jifen, *Queli wenxian kao* 33.28a).

26. These events are recorded in Wang Su, *Kongzi jiayu*; Kong Chuan, *Dongjia zaji* 1.2a–3a; and Kong Yuancuo, *Kongshi zuting guangji* 8.1b–4a.

27. *Lunyu zhushu* 3. 2469; *Lunyu zhengyi* 3.72. See, e.g., *Chunqiu weiyan Kong tu* 5a (p. 56.51a) and Fig. 5.15 of this volume.

NAMES AND TITLES OF THE SAGE

Centuries after Kongzi's death, and throughout the imperial era, the court conferred posthumous titles (*shi* 諡) upon him as a means of expressing its respect. In the Western Han (206 BCE–8 BCE), he was given the title Exalted Ni, Duke of Consummate Perfection (*baocheng xuan Ni gong* 褒成宣尼公).[28] During the Northern Wei dynasty, which controlled northern China during the North-South era (420–589), Kongzi was given the title of Sage of Culture, Venerable Ni (*wensheng Nifu* 文聖尼父),[29] and in the Latter Zhou, which briefly controlled western China just before the unification under the Sui (589–618), he was designated Duke of the State of Zou (*Zouguo gong* 鄒國公).[30] Yet, since China was divided into separate, and usually warring, countries, it is difficult to ascertain the significance of these honors. The lack of a single, unified register of sacrifices (*sidian* 祀典) and system of titles of nobility (*fengjue* 封爵) during the four hundred years that followed the Han (206 BCE–220 CE) raises basic questions of the geographic extent and efficacy of court homage. *How* and on *whom* were these posthumous titles of homage conferred? In *what form* were they manifested in the world, besides as imperial decrees recorded in the archives? *Where*, in what ritual and institutional settings, were they given? *Who* were the beneficiaries of the cultural capital produced by such praise? The Northern Wei dynasty (which called him Sage of Culture) controlled Qufu, Kongzi's birthplace, whereas the Latter Zhou (which called him Duke of Zou) ruled over western China where few if any of Kongzi's descendants lived to benefit

---

28. The date of this posthumous honor is given as Han Pingdi Yuanshi 1/6 (9/1 CE); see *Han shu* 12.351. I give Chinese dates as the ruler's reign year/month/day, followed by the equivalent Western date in parentheses, given as (month/day/year). The word *xuan* 宣 in Kongzi's title is typically translated as "propagator." Here, I follow the standard explanation of *xuan* as "sagely goodness that is widely known," i.e., eminent or exalted (*Tang huiyao* 99.1723). Qiu Jun (*Daxue yanyi bu* 65.14b–15a) encourages such a reading, which is endorsed by Li Zhizao (*Pan'gong liyue shu* 1.3b).

29. Dated Wei Xiaowendi Taihe 16/2/21 (3/4/492); see *Wei shu* 7B.169; *Zizhi tongjian* 147.4320; Kong Chuan, *Dongjia zaji* 1.2a; and Kong Yuancuo, *Kongshi zuting guangji* 1.4a. According to the *Tang huiyao* (99.1721), *wen* means a model that crisscrosses Heaven and Earth; thus "paragon" more aptly translates the meaning of the term as it applied to posthumous titles generally.

30. Dated Zhou Jingdi Daxiang 2/3/1 (4/1/580); see *Zhou shu* 7.123; Kong Chuan, *Dongjia zaji* 1.2a; and Kong Yuancuo, *Kongshi zuting guangji* 1.4a.

from such honors. There are no records of new titles conferred on Kongzi in the Liu-Song (420–79), which was located south of the Yangtze river, but this court was possibly the first to construct a state temple outside Qufu. Modeled on the original structure in Kongzi's hometown, the Liu-Song built this temple four years after being forced to retreat from the area around Qufu in the face of the Northern Wei's onslaught. The location of this temple is not given in the sources, but it was possibly built in Kuaiji (modern Shaoxing, Zhejiang), where a prominent branch of Kongzi's descendants had settled in the fifth century.[31] Kongzi's doctrinal heirs certainly benefited from the court's elevation of him, but his biological descendants were also heirs to his cultural legacy.

One of the most significant changes in Kongzi's official posthumous status was the Tang (618–907) court's promotion of him to king in 739,[32] when he was given the title of Exalted King of Culture (*wenxuan wang* 文宣 王).[33] During the Song (960–1279), the noncanonical Master made a brief appearance, when, in 1008, the words "Dark Sage" were added to his title King of Exalted Culture (*xuansheng wenxuan wang* 玄聖文宣王), in an allusion, as some ritualists later pointed out, to the union between Kongzi's mother and the Black God.[34] The official chronicles maintain that "dark" was replaced by the more canonical Supreme Sage (*zhisheng* 至聖) in 1013 to avoid an imperial taboo,[35] although Ming ritualists later upheld the correct-

---

31. *Nan shi* 2.47; Li Zhizao, *Pan'gong liyue shu* 1.6a. There are biographies of at least a dozen Kongs from Kuaiji in the standard histories of the southern dynasties (see, e.g., *Nan shi* 71.1740 and 1743–44, 75.1864–65 and 1881–82, 76.1889, 77.1941–42; *Liang shu* 48.677; and *Nan Qi shu* 48.835–40, 53.922), several of whom were prominent scholars and government officials. In 454 (Wudi Xiaojian 1/10/15; 11/20/454), the Liu-Song emperor ordered the construction of a Zhongni temple; the liturgy followed was that used for feudal lords; see *Nan shi* 2.58; and Li Zhizao, *Pan'gong liyue shu* 1.6b.

32. "Prince" is administratively more appropriate, since *wang* no longer designated the supreme political authority after the Qin. As with my translation of *wen* as "culture" in the title *wengong* 文公, I employ terms that mark Kongzi's status as partly outside the conventional nomenclature on which posthumous titles was determined. Moreover, his ritual statue was moved in 739 from the minister's position facing west to the imperial position facing south.

33. *Jiu Tang shu* 24.920–21; *Xin Tang shu* 15.375; *Zizhi tongjian* 214.6838; Li Zhizao, *Pan'gong liyue shu* 1.17b. Dated Tang Xuanzong Kaiyuan 27/8/23 (10/1/739).

34. *Song shi* 7.139; *Xu zizhi tongjian* 27.619; Qiu Jun, *Daxue yanyi bu* 66.1b; Li Zhizao, *Pan'gong liyue shu* 1.18b–19a. Dated Song Zhenzong Dazhong xiangfu 1/11/1 (12/1/1008).

35. *Song shi* 8.152; *Xu zizhi tongjian* 27.680; dated Song Zhenzong Dazhong xiangfu 5/12/9 (1/23/1013). Kong Chuan (*Dongjia zaji*, part A.5b) and the *Wenxian tongkao* cite two sources for Kongzi's title of *xuansheng*: the *Chunqiu wei yan Kong tu*, which calls Kongzi the Dark Sage

ness of this change on the grounds that the dark rendezvous was apocryphal and not corroborated by canonical sources; some Ming ritualists regarded it as heresy.[36] Contrary to the situation in the preceding several centuries, China was unified under a single court and imperial bureaucracy for extended periods of time during the Tang and Song. Beginning largely in the seventh century, the imperial courts institutionalized Confucian learning in government schools from the metropolis down to the county level and greatly expanded the imperial cult[37] of Kongzi through the construction of temples at government schools and the formation of liturgies that honored and fed the spirits of the great figures of the Confucian tradition. During this period there were two parallel and not always consistently deployed procedures of expressing imperial reverence toward Kongzi and his followers. The first was the practice of conferring posthumous titles of respect (*zhuizun* 追尊) on deceased meritorious persons. Such appellations usually included titles of nobility (duke, marquis, earl) or, on extraordinary occasions, royalty (emperor and king or prince) and were given to accomplished military men, government officials, culture heroes, and masters of Daoism as well as Confucianism. As such, this system extended well beyond the Confucian tradition and the imperial cult of Kongzi into a vast pantheon of gods propitiated in local religious festivals and worshipped at countless sites from the imperial altar of Heaven to the temples of city gods. This religious order was at least nominally regulated by the Ministry of Rites. The second procedure began later as an integral part of the Kongzi temple cult, exemplified by the distinction between Kongzi as Sage (*sheng* 聖) and his greatest disciple Yan Hui 顏回 as correlate (*pei* 配), who shared in the offerings given primarily

---

because of his mother's impregnation by the Black God, and the "Heavenly Way" chapter of *Zhuangzi*, which refers to the "Way of the Dark Sage and the Uncrowned King" (*xuansheng suwang zhi dao* 玄聖素王之道). Later commentaries on the *Zhuangzi* gloss this passage as a reference to Laozi as Dark Sage and Kongzi as uncrowned king (*Zhuangzi jishi* 13.205). Sima Qian (*Shiji* 47.1947) refers to Kongzi as a Supreme Sage (*zhi sheng*), whereas the official histories of the Han (*Hou Han shu* 40B.1376, 49.1660) and Tang (*Jiu Tang shu* 24.921) also refer to him as the Dark Sage, although he was not formally canonized as such.

36. Qiu Jun, *Daxue yanyi bu* 66.1b–2a.

37. "Imperial cult" refers to the sacrifices to feed the deities and spirits of the pantheon as enumerated in the imperial register of sacrifices (*sidian*). Imperial cults of particular spirits often existed alongside unofficial liturgies that the imperium typically sought to bring into the official register of sacrifices, though with uneven and inconsistent results. See "Temple Cult," pp. 72–89, in this volume; and Wilson, "Sacrifice and the Imperial Cult of Confucius," pp. 253–59.

to Kongzi.[38] Both effected an explicit hierarchy in the Confucian tradition, although the practice of conferring posthumous titles existed independently of particular temple cults and implied an overlapping intersection among all cults within a larger imperial system of sacrifices.[39]

Some ritualists sought to elevate Kongzi's posthumous status higher than king. There was an effort in 1001 to promote him to emperor, to no avail, although he was briefly elevated to emperor in the court sacrifices of the Tangut kingdom of Xia (1032–1227) in northwestern China.[40] A debate on the proper status of the Kongzi cult persisted throughout the Ming (1368–1644), precipitated largely by its founder, Taizu (r. 1368–98), who, in 1369, suspended sacrifices to Kongzi in imperial temples throughout the empire and allowed them to continue only at the Qufu temple in Kongzi's hometown. In response to Taizu's call in 1371 (Hongwu 4/9) for a court debate on Kongzi's ritual status, Wu Chen 吳沈 (d. 1386) argued that Kongzi had attained the position of minister but had never been "invested with an inch of land"; nor had he ever been a king. Although it is "unfortunate that he never sat on the throne, it is not permissible to call such a man a king" for the same reason that Kongzi himself took "the brush that wrote the 'unicorn classic'" (i.e., *Spring and Autumn Annals*) and rebuked the feudal lords of his day who had arrogated to themselves the title of king. Names must be rectified according to actual circumstances; Wu said that "names without the actuality are immoral." He concluded by saying that Kongzi had held the title of king for some time and ministers did not dare to question the practice, because of their "fearful reverence for the sage." But this is not fearful reverence for the sage, Wu retorted, it is merely "fear of incurring the wrath of all under heaven." "How should we revere the sage?" asked Wu. "By illuminating his Dao, not by making kings out of commoners."[41]

---

38. See "Enshrinement and the Ritualization of Orthodoxy," pp. 79–85, in this volume.

39. See Taylor, "Official and Popular Religion," pp. 126–57; Wilson, *Genealogy of the Way*, chap. 1.

40. *Wenxian tongkao* 43.409; Qiu Jun, *Daxue yanyi bu* 66.1b–2a; Li Zhizao, *Pan'gong liyue shu* 1.18b; Tao Shiyou, *Kongzi sheng dasi kao* 30b.

41. Wu Chen, "Kongzi feng wang bian," 12.32a–34a. Also in response to Ming Taizu's call for discussion of the rites, Song Lian 宋濂 (1310–81), director of studies in the Directorate of Education, recommended that Kongzi's statue in the temple be seated facing east, as appropriate for a court minister, rather than facing south, the direction reserved for the son of Heaven; see Song Lian, "Kongzi miaotang yi," *Wenxian ji* 28.9a–13a; Huang Xun, *Huang Ming mingchen jingji lu* 12.29a–32a; *Ming tongjian* 4.279–281; *Ming huiyao* 11.174–75; and the chapter by Huang Chin-shing in this volume, pp. 283–89.

This inclination to protect the sanctity of the throne from the encroachment of commoners should come as no surprise at the court of Ming Taizu, who would subsequently accumulate ever greater imperial powers by eliminating the institution of prime minister. Yet disputes over Kongzi's ritual status, and its political implications, were not unique to the Ming, even if the concentration of unchecked power in the hands of an autocratic ruler was unprecedented. As early as the fifth century, court ministers had argued that sacrifices to Kongzi should be limited to a liturgy appropriate for a lord because he was not himself a king. In 445, for example, the Liu-Song court used six rows of dancers (*liu yi* 六佾) and three racks of hanging jade chimes and bronze bells (*xuanxuan* 軒懸) in its sacrifices to Kongzi, the number appropriate for a higher-level lord, rather than the eight rows of dancers and four racks of hanging instruments (*gongxuan* 宮懸) customary for royalty.[42]

These debates on Kongzi's ritual status should not be reduced to questions of political power understood in its conventional, juridical sense as state apparatuses that the sovereign deploys over the populace; rather, these debates need to be understood as a mode of negotiation that had implications for social relations within literati culture and for Chinese society as a whole, as well as relations between scholar-officials and the sovereign. Indeed, even Taizu was ambivalent: in 1382, when Taizu was about to enter the recently reopened Imperial University to sacrifice to Kongzi, an official urged him to reconsider because, "even though he was a sage, Kongzi was [merely] an official." The emperor replied that he dare not refrain from paying homage to Kongzi because he was the "teacher of hundreds of generations of rulers." Wittingly or not, the emperor repeated precisely the same point made by the Jin classicist Fan Xuan 范宣 a thousand years earlier.[43]

Ming ritualists found other means to elevate Kongzi's ritual status in the temple liturgy to equal that of the Son of Heaven without explicitly conferring the imperial title. Beginning in 1476 (Chenghua 12/9), Zhou Hongmo 周洪謨 (1419–91), secretary of the Ministry of Rites, repeatedly argued that ever since Kongzi had been elevated to king in the Tang (739 BCE), his statue in the temple had worn the imperial cap with twelve tassels and the imperial robes with twelve embroidered insignia, and that the emperor's music had

---

42. *Nan Qishu* 9.143–44. Three ranks emulate the lord's three-sided chariot; four ranks, the enclosed wall of the royal court.

43. *Ming huiyao* 13.218 (dated Hongwu 15/5/11). For Fan Xuan, see *Nan Qi shu* 9.144.

been played during state sacrifices to his spirit.[44] "Our own Sagely Dynasty has continued these ritual regulations; thus Kongzi's cap and robe already follow the ritual appropriate to an emperor, but the number of ritual dancers used corresponds to that of a feudal lord. Viewed from the perspective of rites, the music is presently incomplete; viewed from the perspective of music, the rites amount to usurpation" (because the use of royal music in sacrifices to a feudal lord was improper). In 1477 (Chenghua 13/2/8), the court finally agreed to Zhou's request to increase the number of sacrificial vessels from ten to twelve and the rows of ritual dancers from six to eight.[45]

Yang Shouchen 楊守陳 (1425–89) responded to opponents of the elevation of Kongzi's status by saying the court already treated Kongzi as a sovereign in the liturgy by seating him in the temple facing south and using the number of ritual vessels and dancers appropriate for an emperor, while declining to actually call him one. He pointed out that the Duke of Zhou had been the first to promote his ancestors posthumously to royalty even though they were commoners. Kongzi's virtue surpassed that of Yao and Shun; thus later sovereigns took him as their teacher. Calling him the "first master" (*xianshi* 先師) was perfectly appropriate. The duty between master and disciple is the same as that between father and son; just as a son may posthumously treat his father as a king, so may a disciple. As the "one man of ten thousand generations," Kongzi was certainly deserving of such honors.[46]

Much of the disagreement on Kongzi's ritual status hinged on questions of how and where to locate him in history. Should Kongzi be honored with titles, caps, and liturgies appropriate to someone of his station in his own day, or should these signs of honor be conferred within the context of his august status as teacher of the ten thousand generations? Wu Chen and others opposed Kongzi's elevation to king on the grounds that it conflicted with

---

44. The locus classicus of the imperial cap with twelve tassels is the *Record of Rites*, which says, "With twelve long hanging tassels of colored jade dangling from his cap front and back, and with dragon-embroidered garb, the son of Heaven offered sacrifice [to his royal ancestors]" ("Yuzao" 玉藻, *Liji zhengyi* 29.245 [p. 1473]). The twelve embroidered insignia are the sun, the moon, the stars, a mountain, dragon, colored pheasant, two temple cups, pond weed that grows in a pattern (*wen*), fire, grain, a hatchet, and a *fu* 黻 symbol of two opposing bows (*gong* 弓), the one on the right written backwards. See "Yi ji" 益稷, *Shang shu zhengyi* 5.29 (p. 141).

45. *Ming tongjian* 33.1270; *Ming huiyao* 11.178; Li Zhizao, *Pan'gong liyue shu* 1.40b; Zhang Chaorui, *Kongmen chuandao lu* 4.5b–6a.

46. Yang Shouchen, "Lun zun Kongzi di hao," 12.34a–36b.

Kongzi's own practice of the rectification of names: to call him king could not be reconciled with his actual life circumstances. Moreover, had he not written the *Spring and Autumn Annals* to rebuke such misuse of the rites? Conversely, Yang Shouchen stressed that Kongzi was the teacher of the sovereigns of all ages, not just those of the Zhou; thus he argued that posthumous noble titles must change with the times and correspond to present circumstances rather than retain their original meaning. He refuted the argument suggested by Wu Chen that since Kongzi was a man of the Zhou, the Zhou regulations should be applied to him in temple sacrifices. This would mean that he could be called only a minister of justice from Lu (Lu da sikou 魯大司寇), since this was the title Kongzi actually held in his lifetime. The title of king that Kongzi held in the Ming was a posthumous honor bestowed by later generations, Yang continued, not an application of Zhou regulations. In the Ming, the status of those who held the title of king was equivalent to that of a minister in Kongzi's day, and the emperor was equivalent to the king of old. By ranking him as a king, later dynasties had made this teacher of all sovereigns equivalent to a minister of one dynasty, a practice that did not extend posthumous honors to their fullest extent. In fact, he said, those "narrow scholars" who would prefer to seat Kongzi facing east, in the position of a court minister, were betraying "not only their ignorance of the rites but the heart that cannot distinguish right from wrong."[47] Although Yang Shouchen failed in his attempt to have Kongzi's titular status elevated to that of emperor, he shared with many scholar-officials of his day the view that conferring posthumous titles was an appropriate means of articulating the court's reverence for Kongzi and that such titles should reflect the court's true sentiments unhampered by antiquated historical precedent. One is tempted to discern in the ritualized elevation of Kongzi resonances of the apotheosis of the Sage often associated with the Modern Text tradition, although it is not evident that Yang Shouchen and others explicitly drew from *jinwen* sources. Rather, it would appear that the then-dominant Ancient Text tradition had long since absorbed elements of these, and certainly other, Modern Text sentiments, which occasionally surfaced in disputes over Kongzi's meaning within the tradition.

By the sixteenth century, however, the view that Kongzi transcended history no longer prevailed at the Ming court. In 1530 the Jiajing emperor (r. 1521–66) and his grand secretary Zhang Cong 張璁 (1475–1539) changed

---

47. Ibid., 12.35a–37a.

Kongzi's title, over considerable opposition, from Supreme Sage, King of Exalted Culture to Supreme Sage, First Master Master Kong (*zhisheng xianshi Kongzi* 至聖先師孔子), effectively demoting him to non-noble status by removing his royal title.[48] Zhang Cong's memorial advocating these changes drew thoroughly and directly from the arguments presented over the preceding two and a half centuries. He reproduced Wu Chen's essay in full and reiterated Qiu Jun's 丘濬 (1421–95) basic principle that the proper way to revere Kongzi was to revere his Dao, not to confer noble titles on him. He quoted Qiu's warning against the use of hypothetical (*jiashe zhi ci* 假設之辭) metaphors (*biyu* 比喻) in posthumous titles by arguing that it was important to describe the actual, concrete virtues (*zhenshi zhi de* 真實之德) of the Sage.[49] In a defense of the 1530 changes written somewhat later, Zhang Cong refuted the claim made by Yang Shouchen and others that Taizu intended to continue the Mongol precedent of Kongzi's royal title. Although he conceded that Taizu did not remove Kongzi's royal appellation when he eliminated the "exaggerated titles" of other figures, Zhang Cong maintained that Taizu referred to Kongzi as the "teacher of all under Heaven."[50] In other words, he revered Kongzi as a teacher not as a king. Clearly there was considerable precedent for these changes in the writings of early Ming ritualists, but Huang Chin-shing argues in this volume that the authority to sweep aside the centuries-old tradition of Kongzi's royal status over strident opposition was possible only in the context of an increasingly autocratic sovereign able to use ritual precedents to his advantage.[51] In the early Qing, there were a few, less exceptional changes in Kongzi's posthumous title: in 1645 it was changed to Great Completer, Supreme Sage, Exalted First Master of Culture (*dacheng zhisheng wenxuan xianshi* 大成至聖文宣先師) and in 1657 to the simpler Supreme Sage, First Master (*zhisheng xianshi* 至聖先師),[52] the title still in use today.

---

48. Kongzi's demotion necessitated reductions in the number of the ritual vessels used in the imperial sacrifices from twelve to ten (eight in local school temples) and in the number of rows of ritual dancers from eight to six; see *Da Ming huidian* 91.28b.

49. Qiu Jun, *Daxue yanyi bu*, 65.14b, 66.5a–b; Zhang Chaorui, *Kongmen chuandao lu* 4.14b–15a; Sommer, "Images into Words." Zhang also quoted from the writings of Yao Sui 姚燧 (1238–1313) and Xia Yin 夏寅 (*jinshi* 1448).

50. Zhang Cong, "Xian shi Kongzi sidian huowen," 178.20b–22a.

51. See the chapter by Huang Chin-shing in this volume, pp. 270–82.

52. *Qing shi gao* 84.2533f. These changes are dated Shunzhi 2/1/23 (2/19/1645) and Shunzhi 14/3/13 (4/26/1657), respectively.

GENEALOGY

Sacred Pedigree

According to most reconstructions of Kongzi's genealogy, his ancestors were almost as intimately intertwined with the sage-kings of high antiquity as his teachings would become with the civil administration of imperial China. It is said in sources of the Kong clan that the surname (*shi* 氏) of Zi 子 was granted to Kongzi's early ancestor Xie 契, who was enfeoffed in the state of Shang (in modern-day eastern Henan province) after he assisted the sage-ruler Yu 禹 (r. 2205–2198 BCE)—founder of the Xia dynasty (2205–1766 BCE)—in controlling the great deluge. The Zi clan eventually established the Shang ruling house (1766–1123 BCE).[53] Kongzi's ancestral lineage branched off from the royal Shang line with Zhongsi Yan 仲思衍, son of Di Yi 帝乙 (r. 1209–1175 BCE), the second to last ruler of the Shang dynasty.[54] Yan and his older brother Weizi Qi 微子啓 were born of Di Yi's consort before the empress bore Xin 辛 (King Zhou), a licentious sibling who, as the authentic heir, succeeded his father to the throne.[55] After the Zhou conquest of the Shang, King Zhou's son was enfeoffed in the state of Song in order to maintain sacrifices to the Shang founder and his descendants, but he was soon executed for fomenting unrest and was replaced by Weizi Qi.[56] When Qi died without an heir, Zhongsi Yan replaced him, and Yan's descendants

---

53. As early as Han times, the ancestry of the Shang royal house was traced to the Yellow Emperor (trad. reign dates: 2697–2597 BCE), who followed Divine Farmer (Shennong 神農) as the Son of Heaven and ruled with the power of earth (one of the five phases). He was said to have had twenty-five sons, fourteen of whom were given surnames (*xing* 姓). His son Xuanxiao 玄囂 followed him as the Son of Heaven and ruled with the power of metal. (According to Sima Qian, *Shiji* 1.13, Xuanxiao did not rule. Rather, his brother assumed the throne and was succeeded by his son.) The sources agree that Xuanxiao's grandson Diku 帝嚳 then succeeded to the throne and ruled with the power of water. Diku's son Qi was minister of education during the reigns of Yao and Shun. See Kong Shangren, *Kongzi shijia pu* 1.1b–2a; Kong Jifen, *Queli wenxian kao* 1.1a; Kong Decheng, "Xing yuan," in idem, *Kongzi shijia pu* 1a.

54. Zhongsi Yan is also often called Weizhong 微仲, or Wei the Second.

55. This is Sima Qian's version (*Shiji* 3.105). Another early account states that Diyi's three sons were born of the same mother, but Xin was born after she was established as empress (*Lüshi chunqiu* 11.110–11).

56. "Weizi zhi ming" 微子之命, in *Shang shu zhengyi* 13.88–89 (pp. 200–201). The *Shiji* provides a detailed account of King Zhou's intransigence in the face of Weizi Qi's repeated admonitions to cease his licentious ways (see "Song Weizi shijia" 宋微子世家, in *Shiji* 38.1607–10).

ruled as dukes of Song for four generations until Fu He 父何. Fu He yielded the ducal title to his younger brother and founded a line of hereditary high officers (*qing* 卿) that lasted for five generations until Kongfu Jia 孔父嘉. According to the ancient regulations governing surnames, in the fifth generation after the senior heir of a hereditary noble lineage, a separate cadet line is formed. Kongfu Jia was the fifth-generation descendant of Fu He and thus was granted the surname Kong[57] and given the rank of Grand Master (*dafu* 大夫). In 710 BCE, Kongfu Jia was killed by the grand steward of Song,[58] and his son fled Song and relocated the lineage in the neighboring state of Lu. After another four generations Shuliang He 叔梁纥, Kongzi's father, was appointed grand master of Zou township, near Kongzi's birthplace of Qufu.[59]

The significance of these genealogical claims is quite extraordinary. It gives Kongzi a pedigree that places him within the ranks of one of the most prestigious ancient lineages—that of the Shang kings—yet removes him from the line of descent extending from one of China's most infamous personages, King Zhou, the archetypal evil last ruler of the Shang.[60] It is as if his ancestral line inherited only what was virtuous from the Shang royalty

---

57. "Sang fu xiaoji" 喪服小記, *Liji zhengyi* 32.267 (p. 1495). Such new lineages were often named after the founder's style name or *zi* ("Yin Gong" 殷公, *Chunqiu Zuozhuan zhengyi* 4.31–32 [pp. 1733–34]). The sources refer to this surname variously as a *shi* and a *xing* (see Gu Yanwu, *Rizhi lu jishi* 27.6a–b). According to the regulations in effect during the Zhou, conferral of a new surname and enfeoffment of hereditary land was called a *shi*. According to Allen Chun ("Conceptions of Kinship," pp. 16–48), a *shi* was a sign of nobility that was a reward for outstanding service to the throne; it was changeable within a *xing* group and tied to a fiefdom, whereas a *xing* tended to have greater biological fixity through a closer tie with its *zong* 宗, or common descent group.

58. According to the *Spring and Autumn Annals*, Grand Steward Hua Du 華督 killed his lord Yuyi 與夷 and Grand Master Kongfu Jia in the spring of Duke Huan's second year (710 BCE). The *Zuozhuan* elaborates that Hua Du "attacked the Kong family, killed Kongfu [Jia], and took his wife" ("Huan gong" 桓公, *Chunqiu Zuozhuan zhengyi* 5.38 [p. 1740]). The *Shiji* (38.1623) reports that Hua Du coveted Kongfu Jia's wife after a chance encounter on the road and spread rumors that Kongfu Jia was responsible for the state's frequent wars and its people's misery; he then killed Kongfu Jia the following year.

59. Kong Shangren, *Kongzi shijia pu* 1.3b–4b; Kong Jifen, *Queli wenxian kao* 1.1a–3a; Kong Decheng, "Xing yuan," in idem, *Kongzi shijia pu* 1a–4b.

60. Standard genealogies trace this lineage through the line of Shang rulers that reputedly constituted an unbroken lineage; i.e., the founder, the fourth, sixth, ninth, twelfth, thirteenth, fourteenth, sixteenth, twenty-first, twenty-second, twenty-fourth, twenty-sixth, twenty-seventh, twenty-eighth, and twenty-ninth rulers. See Qian Mu, *Guoshi dagang* 1: 15–16.

and was destined to produce the Middle Kingdom's Supreme Sage. It is not entirely clear when Kongzi first became associated with the Shang royal house. Although Kongzi and his immediate disciples never made such a claim, the *Zuo Commentary* identifies Kongzi as a descendant of the ducal house that ruled the state of Song when the descendants of the Shang royal house were enfeoffed after the Zhou conquest, a passage that is repeated nearly verbatim in the *Historical Records*: "I have heard that a seer named Kong Qiu will come. [He] is a descendant of the sage who perished in Song" (吾聞 將有達者曰孔丘聖人之後也而滅於宋). This is an intriguing passage because it not only names Kong Qiu as a descendant of the Song dukes but also presages his arrival as a seer and suggests that he is predestined to have such comprehending insight because his ancestor, Fu He, was a "sage with brilliant virtue" who "did not assume his rightful position in the world" (聖人 之有明德者若不當世其後必有達者).[61] This passage, which resonates with noncanonical prognostications of Kongzi's imminent arrival and penetrating insight, is unexpected in such a solidly canonical source as the *Zuo Commentary* and would probably have been dismissed as a later corruption had Sima Qian not quoted it in the *Historical Records*.[62]

Kongzi's descent from the Shang kings is also mentioned in the *Guliang Commentary* on the *Annals*, which dates to the early Han era.[63] The commentary on Kongfu Jia's death concludes with an explanation of the origin of the Kong surname, which simply remarks that "Kongzi was originally of Song" (*Kongzi gu Song ye* 孔子故宋也).[64] According to the *Record of Rites*, Kongzi realized he was a man of Yin (Shang) when he dreamed he was sitting with sacrificial offerings between two pillars, as is the custom in the funeral rites of the Shang.[65] A clear delineation of Kongzi's ancestry is out-

---

61. "Zhao gong" 昭公, *Chunqiu Zuozhuan zhengyi* 44.349 (p. 2051), dated Duke Zhao 7/9; *Shiji* 47.1907–8. Cf. Jenson (p. 191) in this volume.

62. Some commentators question its placement in Duke Zhao's seventh year, or 535 BCE, because Kongzi would, at the age of thirty-five *sui* (e.g., "Zhao gong," *Chunqiu Zuozhuan zhengyi* 44.349 [p. 2051]), have already been well known.

63. The *Guliang Commentary* was purportedly written by a Guliang Shu 穀梁叔 (or Chi 赤) after receiving instruction from Kongzi's disciple Bushang 卜商 (Zixia 子夏), but was not formally recognized until the court of Han Gaozu (206–195 BCE), when Lu Jia 陸賈 was made erudite of the *Guliang Commentary*. See Gan Pengyun, *Jingxue yuanliu kao* 6.14b; and Pi Xirui, *Jingxue tonglun* 4.15–17.

64. *Chunqiu Guliang zhuan zhushu* 3.9 (2373), dated Duke Huan 2/1/15.

65. "Tangong" 檀弓, *Liji zhengyi* 7.55 (p. 1283); see also *Shiji* 47.1944.

lined in the third century BCE text *Family Sayings of Kongzi* (*Kongzi jia yu* 孔子
家語),[66] which recounts the circumstances of Zhongsi Yan's rise to duke of
Song in the early years after the Zhou conquest. The same lineage of ancestors is found in later Kong family genealogies, such as Kong Yuancuo's 孔元
措 (b. 1181) *Expanded Record of the Kong Family's Ancestral Court* (*Kongshi zuting
guangji* 孔氏祖族庭廣記) and Kong Shangren's 孔尚任 (1648–1718) *Gene-
alogy of Kongzi's Hereditary Household* (*Kongzi shijia pu* 孔子世家譜).[67]

By the late Western Han, there was enough of a consensus at the court
on Kongzi's descent from the Shang kings to establish his senior living descendant as the heir to the Shang rulers in order to maintain sacrifices to
Tang 湯, founder of the Shang, and his descendants. During Yuandi's reign
(49–33 BCE), the Han court began to search for descendants of earlier ruling
houses in order to establish and maintain ancestral temples for earlier kings.
Court minister Mei Fu 梅福 lamented that since Tang's descendants could
not be found, one of Kongzi's descendants should be established because,
according to the *Guliang Commentary*, he was a descendant of the house of
Yin. The court finally agreed to this in 8 BCE (Han Chengdi Suihe 1/2/20)
and invested Kong Heqi 孔何齊 as Continuing Auspicious Marquis of Yin
(*Yin shaojia hou* 殷紹嘉侯) and enfeoffed him with 1,670 households to
support the costs of maintaining the sacrifices.[68] Since Heqi was the most
direct descendant of Kongzi, his separation from the Kongs effectively seg-
mented the senior line from the Kong lineage. The descendants of his
younger brother, Kong Fang 孔房, continued the lineage of Kongzi's

---

66. The approximate date of this book's compilation is subject to some speculation. The
text was possibly handed down from Xunzi and/or compiled by Kong Anguo 孔安國,
Kongzi's eleventh-generation descendant who lived in the second century BCE, on the basis of
miscellaneous manuscripts passed down among the Master's disciples, and then eventually
edited by Wang Su 王肅 (195–256 CE). See Kramers, *K'ung Tzŭ Chia Yü*, pp. 17, 108–14.

67. Kong Yuancuo begins his version of the lineage with Kongfu Jia (*Kongshi zuting guangji*
1.12); Kong Shangren begins with the Yellow Emperor (*Kongzi shijia pu* 1.4a–5a). Cf. Jensen,
"Wise Man of the Wilds," pp. 424–33.

68. In 2 CE this title was changed to Duke of Song (*Song gong* 宋公); see *Han shu* 10.328,
18.709, 67.2924–27; Cheng Minzheng, *Huangdun wenji*, "shiyi," 1b; and Shryock, *The Origin and
Development of the State Cult of Confucius*, p. 98. The impetus for this search is canonical. The
Liji implores the ruler to maintain the temple and the descendants of the kings of the previous
two dynasties, just as one honors the worthy ("Jiao tesheng" 郊特牲, *Liji zhengyi* 25.220 [p.
1448]).

descendants; the revived lineage of the Shang kings disappeared some time in the early decades of the Eastern Han era (25–220).[69] Even the descendants of the original Son of Heaven could not perpetuate their line with greater surety than those of the Supreme Sage.

Descendants and Their Controversies

The discussion of the court's involvement in the lineage of Kongzi's ancestors has led, rather abruptly, fifteen generations deep into the line of his descendants. Kongzi's early descendants played a prominent role in the scholarly tradition we call Confucianism. A chapter in the *Record of Rites* titled "Doctrine of the Mean" is attributed to his grandson, Kong Ji 孔伋, who was sought after by high officials during the Warring States period (480–222 BCE) and who nearly brought about his own demise by greatly offending one of them.[70] Kongzi's ninth-generation descendant, Kong Fu 孔鮒 (264–208 BCE), mastered the six arts, and, with his younger brother, Kong Teng 孔騰 (aka Rang 襄), hid the family copies of the *Odes* and *Documents* in a wall of the house when the Qin undertook to burn the texts of the Confucian canon. Kong Fu also authored *The Kong Masters' Anthology*,[71] and Kong Sheng was an erudite at the court of Emperor Huidi (r. 195–188 BCE). Kong Anguo 孔安國 (156–74 BCE), younger brother of the eleventh-generation heir, was court erudite in the *Documents* and wrote commentaries on the *Analects*, *Filial Piety*, and the *Documents*, using both the Ancient and the Modern Text versions.[72] These commentaries were considered as authoritative well into the Qing era. Kongzi's thirteenth-generation descendant, Kong Ba 孔霸, was an erudite during the reign of Emperor Zhao (r. 87–74 BCE), later served as Superior Grand Master of the Palace (*taizhong dafu* 太中大夫),

---

69. The last reference to the lineage in the Han is dated 37 CE, when the title of Heqi's son, Kong An 孔安, was set as Duke of Song (*Hou Han shu* 1B.61). The sources refer to these lords of Shang by the surname (*xing*) Kong rather than by the Shang royal name because Kong was one of several surnames granted to descendants of the Shang royal house (Zhang Chaorui, *Kongmen chuan dao lu* 1.11a–12b).

70. Chen Hao, *Queli zhi* 1.15b–16a.

71. For assessment of this book and Kong Fu's authorship, see Ariel, *K'ung-ts'ung-tzu*, pp. 20–22, 56–69.

72. *Han shu* 81.3352, 88.3607; see also Chen Hao, *Queli zhi* 3.58a; and Kong Shangren, *Kongzi shijia pu* 3.8a–b.

and then was ennobled as the Marquis (*hou* 侯) of Guannei and invested with 800 households.[73]

The marquisate was inherited by a series of for the most part unremarkable descendants until 739 (Tang Xuanzong kaiyuan 27/8), when Kong Suizhi 孔璲之 (thirty-fifth generation) was promoted to Duke of Exalted Culture (*wenxuan gong* 文宣公).[74] The Kongs' status probably began to change over a century earlier when, in 608, Kong Sizhe 孔嗣悊 (thirty-second generation) passed the civil examination and served under the Sui court in a number of administrative positions.[75] In 626 the title of Sizhe's son was changed to Marquis of the Consummate Sage (*bao sheng hou* 襃聖侯), and in 637 this title was elevated to the equivalent of the third rank. Kong Sizhe's younger brother, Kong Yingda 孔穎達 (574–648), rose to post of Libationer and headed a panel of eminent classicists that compiled the official edition of the Five Classics used from the seventh to about the fourteenth century.[76] Thus, meritorious service and scholarly contribution were probably two factors in the Kong family's gradual rise through the imperial government's noble hierarchy. With some notable exceptions, few Kongs were very prominent or scholarly between Kong Ba (thirteenth generation) in the Eastern Han and Kong Sizhe, who was the first Kong to receive the *jinshi* 進士 degree in the civil service examinations.[77] Kong Sizhe was followed by several generations of descendants who received honorary titles or played a role in government. The promotion of the head of the family to duke in 739 was nonetheless more likely a result of the growing importance of Confucianism because of the expansion of the civil examinations and the formation of an imperial temple cult of Kongzi under the Tang.[78]

---

73. *Han shu* 81.3353. Another prominent Kong of the early imperial era was Kong Rong 孔融 (153–208), who excelled in learning and served Cao Cao 曹操 until his execution (*Hou Han shu* 70.2261–80).

74. *Jiu Tang shu* 24.920–21.

75. *Sui shu* 3.72; Chen Hao, *Queli zhi* 2.37b–38a.

76. *Jiu Tang shu* 5.90, 7.140, Chen Hao, *Queli zhi* 2.38a–b (for the text of 739 edict, see 7.17b).

77. *Jiu Tang shu* 15.373. Twenty-six Kongs attained the highest degree during the Tang (including five *zhuangyuan*), twenty-six in the Song (one *zhuangyuan*), four in the Jin, and just five in the Ming (Chen Hao, *Queli zhi* 2.76b–88a; Lü Yuanshan, *Shengmen zhi* 3B.217–28).

78. See McMullen, *State and Scholars in Tang China*, chap. 2.

The fate of the Kongs reversed rather decisively under the forty-second generation descendant, Kong Guangsi 孔光嗣 (869–912). The hereditary dukedom vanished during the chaos that followed the end of the Tang dynasty, and in 912 Guangsi was murdered by a member of a serf household (exempted from corvée obligations and attached to the Kong lineage since 443 to attend to the Kong cemetery) who assumed the name Kong Mo 孔末 as well as the post of magistrate.[79] The story passed down is that Guangsi's nine-month-old son Renyu 孔任玉 (912–56) was secretly spirited away by his mother, née Zhang, to her natal home, where he was raised. When Kong Mo came in search of Renyu, another child from the Zhang household was surrendered and killed in his stead. All other members of the Kong clan were reportedly killed, and only Renyu survived. Upon seeing Renyu some years later, the "people of Lu" reported Kong Mo's misdeeds to the local authorities, and Renyu was established as the rightful heir to the Sage in 930.[80] According to clan records, all subsequent authentic descendants of Kongzi come from the lineage established by Renyu, who is appropriately referred to as the Progenitor of the Revived Lineage (*zhongxing zu* 中興祖).[81] The details and allegations connected with Kong Mo are far from certain, due largely to the paucity of contemporary sources and to the silence on the matter in official histories and clan genealogies before the Ming. The Kong Mansion archive contains two early pertinent documents: Kong Duanchao's 孔端朝 preface to a now-lost clan genealogy dated 1132 (Shaoxing 2/5) refers to the near-extermination of the Kongs during the Five Dynasties era, without implicating anyone by name; Duke Kong Sihui 孔思晦 (1267–1333) identifies Kong Mo as the culprit, describes his ancestors, and then attributes a number of other crimes and attempted encroachments to

---

79. Kong Jing and his descendants were attached to the Kong household as hereditary grave sweepers in 443 (Wendi yuanjia 19/12/24); see *Song shu* 5.89–90.

80. Abby Lamberton suggests that the court restored Renyu because Kong Mo was unable to collect taxes (see p. 312 in this volume).

81. Kong Sihui, "Queli zongzhi tu ji," pp. 349–50; Chen Hao, *Queli zhi* 2.39a–40b; *Qufu xianzhi* 60.4b–5a. The woman who carried Renyu to safety is referred to in most accounts as *mu* 母, which could mean either a natal mother or a wetnurse. Some recent accounts refer to Ms. Zhang as Renyu's wetnurse, using the affectionate term of *laolao* 姥姥, which can also be interpreted as a natal mother or wetnurse. I follow Luo Chenglie's (*Qufu shiji baiti*, pp. 82–83) identification of her as Guangsi's wife (*qizi* 妻子). She is buried in Zhangyang village just north of Qufu, where stone tablets erected by successive dukes commemorate her kindness (Kong Fanyin, *Yansheng gongfu jianwen*, pp. 342–43).

Kong Mo's descendants in his "Record of the Queli Genealogy" 闕里宗枝圖記 dated 1329 (Tianli 2/8). The details of this incident had cohered as a story and taken on legendary proportions at least as early as Chen Hao's 陳鎬 (*jinshi* 1487) widely read history of Queli and the Kong family, completed in 1505, which includes Renyu's dramatic escape in his mother's arms.[82]

Kong Mo's descendants continued to use the Kong surname and live in the area. Clan genealogies refer to his descendants as "Kongs of the outer court" (*wai yuan* 外園) or simply as "outer Kongs" (*wai Kong* 外孔) and contrast them to Renyu's descendants, the "inner Kongs" (*nei Kong* 內孔). According to clan accounts, Kong Mo's descendants continued to cause trouble for centuries. In 1192, for example, an outer Kong sued the Kong clan in the Ministry of Rites after his son had been prevented from entering the clan school. Another outer Kong murdered a member of the inner Kongs and his family when the former's attempts to become the clan head were thwarted. A genealogy of the main lineage and collateral branches, carved in stone in 1097, was used to investigate this and other cases. An inscription on this stone genealogy states that the Kongs of the outer court did not originally reside with those of the inner court and that this genealogy was set in stone so that "after the passage of many years, later generations would not confuse the main lineage with the collateral branches and the outer Kongs." To prevent any confusion with the Sage's authentic heirs, the outer Kongs were forbidden to bury their dead in the Kong cemetery, and a wall was constructed in the late thirteenth century to separate the Kong cemetery from a nearby burial site where Kong Mo's descendants were interred.[83]

The ducal title was restored to Kong Renyu under the Latter Zhou (951–60), but the re-establishment of central authority under the Song court began a long period of uninterrupted imperial support of Kongzi's descendants, which would endure until the twentieth century. This coincided with the

---

82. Kong Duanchao, "Kongzi shi jiapu jiu xu" 1: 312; Kong Sihui, "Queli zongzhi tu ji," pp. 349–50; Chen Hao, *Queli zhi* 2.39b. As products of the Yuan, these sources authored by Duanchao and Sihui are evidence of relatively early circulation of certain details of the Kong Mo story, but one must consider the effect that the split between the two Kong lineages of the 1120s (see the discussion of Kong Duanyou below, p. 66) may have had as a motivation for such a poignant story and perhaps even for the addition of new details that are now impossible to substantiate. The issue of this story's accuracy is not as important or interesting as the fact that it was accepted as such.

83. Kong Sihui, "Queli zongzhi tu ji," pp. 349–50; Kong Honghao, "Wei Kong bian," 34a–35b.

growing dominance of Confucianism in state orthodoxy, in elite circles, and throughout Chinese society generally. The Kongs themselves produced twenty-six *jinshi* degree holders during the Song, including one optimus (*zhuangyuan* 狀元) and twelve others who passed the examination in the next highest tier (*jinshi jidi* 進士及第) of candidates.[84] Renyu's son served the Song in a series of military posts, and, after his grandson was appointed duke and magistrate of Qufu county, the emperor exempted the latter from all other administrative responsibilities to concentrate on managing the temple sacrifices to Kongzi.[85]

Due to the Jurchen invasion, however, not all was harmonious among the Sage's descendants in Song times. When the Emperor Gaozong (r. 1127–62) fled the invading Jurchens and established the Southern Song (1127–1279) in Lin'an (Hangzhou), Duke Kong Duanyou 孔端友 (d. 1132; forty-eighth generation) followed him with some of his kin and relocated the main Kong lineage in Quzhou, Zhejiang. Duanyou's younger brother, Kong Duancao 孔端操, remained in Qufu and, after the Jurchen formally proclaimed the Jin dynasty (1115–1234) in 1128, was appointed duke. This began a period of two ducal households, one under the Song court in Lin'an and the other under the Jin and Yuan courts in the north. When the Mongols reunited the empire in 1282, the Yuan emperor asked the southern duke, Kong Zhu 孔 洙 (d. 1316; fifty-third generation), to return north and become duke of the Kongs in Qufu. Kong Zhu declined on the grounds that he could not abandon his parents' grave. The emperor reportedly sighed, "He would rather give up emoluments than give up the Dao! This is truly the Sage's descendant." The emperor gave him the titles Libationer of the Nation's Sons and Education Intendant of Eastern Zhe Schools and then allowed Kong Zhu to return south to maintain the temple and cemetery in Quzhou.[86] After Kong Zhu ceded the ducal title to the northern lineage, the southern Kongs fell into near oblivion until the late fifteenth century (see discussion of Kong Yansheng on pp. 69–70 below).

---

84. Chen Hao, *Queli zhi* 2.76b–88a; Lü Yuanshan, *Shengmen zhi* 3B.222–26.

85. Chen Hao, *Queli zhi* 2.40a–42a.

86. Chen Hao, *Queli zhi* 2.42a–46b; *Quzhou fuzhi* (1711 ed.) 7.1a–12a; Wilson, "The Ritual Formation of Confucian Orthodoxy," pp. 571–72. Given the Qufu Kong's forty-plus-year working relationship with the Yuan court (witness Kong Yuancuo's contribution to the compilation of court rituals below), it is difficult to ascertain whether the court's offer to Kong Zhu was altogether genuine.

The junior branch of the Kongs in the north fared quite well under the Jin and Yuan ruling houses. Indeed, the Jin conferred honorary titles on the northern Kongs that ranked them higher in its civil bureaucracy than their southern kin ranked under the Song. Most northern dukes under the Jin and Yuan were given the title Grand Master (*dafu*), which carried a rank of between 2a and 4a, whereas the southern dukes were given the title Gentleman for Attendance (8b), if they received any honorary titles at all. One of the most eminent northern dukes, Kong Yuancuo 孔元措 (b. 1181) of the fifty-first generation, achieved great prominence under the Jin as a minister in the Court of Imperial Sacrifices, among other appointments, in addition to serving as duke. He also played a prominent role during the early years of Mongol rule in the north when he headed efforts to reconstruct court and sacrificial music. The Yuan emperor commissioned Kong Yuancuo to gather surviving ritual and music masters to compile new regulations. The group was brought to Qufu in 1240 to oversee rehearsals at the Kongzi temple there. Kong Yuancuo later retired to Qufu to serve out his days as Duke for Fulfilling the Sage (*yansheng gong* 衍聖公).[87]

Duke Yuancuo is perhaps best known for his history of the Kong family titled *Expanded Record of the Kong Family's Ancestral Court* (1227), which includes a genealogy of Kongzi's descendants down to his own (i.e., fifty-first) generation. This book expands on a similar text, *Miscellaneous Record of the Eastern Household*, completed a hundred years earlier by Kong Chuan 孔傳 in 1134, after he fled south along with the Song emperor and Duke Kong Duanyou. These books contain similar information on the founders of the Kong lineage, the descent of spiritual beings from the heavens and other miraculous circumstances surrounding Kongzi's birth, and details of the unicorn, as well as descriptions of his descendants down to the Song dynasty.[88] Although Yuancuo detailed Duke Duanyou's service to the Northern Song

---

87. *Yuan shi* 68.1691; Chen Hao, *Queli zhi* 2.42b–48a. In 1055 (Renzong zhihe 2/3/13), the ducal title was changed from Duke of Propagating Culture on the grounds that it was improper for descendants to inherit an ancestor's posthumous title (*shi* 諡). This change was initiated by Zu Wuze 祖無擇 (1006–85); see *Xu zizhi tongjian* 55.1337. See also Chen Hao, *Queli zhi* 7.18b–19a, for the text of the imperial edict.

88. Kong Chuan, *Dongjia zaji* A2a–b; Kong Yuancuo, *Kongshi zuting guangji* 8.3a–b. Kong Chuan's book does not include a formal genealogy—organized by generational sequence— rather, Kongzi's descendants are taken up in the form of an annals based on imperial announcements of appointments of new dukes organized by emperors' reign dates. The *Song shi* (203.5122) also lists a *Queli zuting ji* 闕里祖庭記 by Kong Chuan.

(960–1127), he was silent about the southern lineage and matters concerning Duanyou's service after 1127, and indeed about all matters related to the Southern Song dynasty. He listed his own grandfather as Duanyou's immediate ducal successor, which leaves the distinct impression that he, Yuancuo, was the uncontested duke of all the Kongs.[89]

Although the Mongols succeeded in temporarily settling the differences between the northern and the southern Kong lineages, all did not go smoothly for the ducal household of the Qufu Kongs during the Yuan. The ducal title of Kong Zhu's northern cousin, Duke Zhen 孔滇, was revoked in 1259 on the grounds that "he was not serving with learning and refinement," but since he had no sons, his cousin, Kong Zhi 孔治, was given the ducal post in 1295. When it was discovered that Kong Zhi had been succeeded by his son by a concubine (shuzi 庶子), the dukedom was revoked and was not conferred on anyone until 1316, when Kong Sihui was ennobled.[90] In the following year, a man claiming to be a descendant of Kong Jingjin 孔景進 (twenty-eighth generation) of Northern Wei times (386–543) attempted, unsuccessfully, to enter the Kong ancestral temple to pay homage to the ancestors. An investigation determined that he was a descendant of Kong Jing 孔景, the serf attached to the Kong cemetery in the fifth century who founded the line that produced the villainous Kong Mo. Duke Kong Sihui remarked that the outer Kongs "are not known by members of our clan. Is it possible for just anyone to make sacrifices together with us in the ancestral temple?" He gathered clan members to examine the records and expel from the clan all Kongs living in the area who were not regarded as the Sage's authentic descendants. Duke Sihui had another genealogy of the main lineage and collateral branches engraved in stone. This genealogy organized the Qufu Kongs into twenty branches (*pai*), based on the number of scions in his parents' generation (i.e., the fifty-third). Duke Sihui's efforts at identifying false Kongs, preventing them from entering the ancestral temple, and expelling them from the ranks of the Sage's true descendants served to bring stability to a household that had been on the verge of chaos when he began his tenure. His deeds were valued by his kin, who reported that on the day he died, "a flock of cranes on his roof cried out and a southeasterly numinous

---

89. Kong Yuancuo, *Kongshi zuting guangji* 1.13b–14a. After Yuancuo died without an heir, the ducal title was passed to a distant nephew related through his great-great-grandfather's younger brother.

90. Chen Hao, *Queli zhi* 2.46a–b.

light pierced through to the northern side of the house." He was posthumously ennobled Duke of Lu and given the title Cultured and Dignified (*wensu* 文肅).[91]

The meticulous compilation of the clan genealogy remained one of the most important means of protecting the Qufu Kongs from infiltration by would-be claimants to membership in the hereditary Kong household. Beginning in the fifteenth century, genealogies were regularly compiled, revised, and updated,[92] but few are easily accessible today. It is often difficult, therefore, to ascertain when certain genealogical claims were first made or even put into writing. As early as 1498, the southern Kongs in Quzhou submitted a genealogy to the Ducal Mansion in the north listing Kong Zhu's descendants to Yansheng 孔延繩 of the fifty-ninth generation. In a memorial to the throne in 1495, the new Quzhou prefect, Shen Jie (*jinshi* 1484), successfully requested that the throne confer the hereditary title of Hanlin Erudite of the Five Classics (*Hanlin wujing boshi* 翰林五經博士) on the eldest male descendant of the southern Kong lineage, who at the time was Kong Yansheng. This title elevated the southern Kongs to a status equal to that of a duke's second son and the descendants of Kongzi's major disciples,[93] although it ranked them below the northern branch. The Kongs in Qufu nonetheless objected to this proposal for at least two reasons. First, they maintained that Yansheng was not a true descendant of the last southern duke, who had yielded his title to the northern Kongs in 1282.[94] Kong

---

91. Kong Sihui, "Queli zongzhi tu ji," pp. 349–50; Kong Honghao, "Wei Kong bian," 34a–35b; Chen Hao, *Queli zhi* 2.47a–48a.

92. Only charts of the lineage were kept before the Song. The first full genealogy with biographical data was compiled by Kong Zonghan 孔宗翰 in 1085. Handwritten copies were maintained in several key households. The genealogy was revised in 1489 by Kong Honggan 孔弘幹; at that point, it was decided that it should undergo major revision every sixty years and minor revisions every thirty years. The first published version of the Kong genealogy is Kong Honghao, *Kongshi zupu*, dated 1622. A partial copy of a handscroll version of this text is in the possession of the Kong Mansion Archive in Qufu, but I was not able to consult it. Ninety-eight copies were printed and stored in the Kong mansion and temple and distributed throughout other locations in Qufu (Kong Jifen, *Queli wenxian kao* 30.1a–2b; *Shandong shengzhi*, pp. 178–79). The next edition of the Kong genealogy was Kong Shangren's *Kongzi shijia pu* of 1684, which is widely available.

93. See the chapter by Abigail Lamberton in this volume, pp. 315–17; and Wilson, "The Ritual Formation of Confucian Orthodoxy," pp. 571–72.

94. Kong Jifen (*Queli wenxian kao* 30.5b) maintains that Kong Zhu (fifty-third generation) died without an heir and that Yansheng is Kong Chuan's descendant, although he confuses some members of this line. Song Ji and Qing Chang (*Queli guangzhi* 9.13b–14a) and the *Xi'an*

Gonghuang 孔公璜 of the Qufu Kongs wrote that Kong Yansheng's 1498 genealogy had "arbitrarily switched the genuine with the collateral (*shanyi zongtiao* 擅移宗祧) and inserted himself" into the "line of descendants of the patriarchal lineage that went south [with Song Gaozong] as successors to Kong Zhu" by claiming descent from Kong Duanyou rather than his uncle Kong Chuan of a junior line. The descendants of Ruoyu's 若愚 northern lineage that assumed the ducal title under the Jin "constitute the genuine heads of the lineage." Nonetheless, Kong Chuan's descendants "no longer take Kong Chuan as their progenitor and have arrogated Duanyou's heritage." This, in effect, uses "the collateral to take over the genuine."[95]

Second, the Qufu Kongs also opposed the southern Kongs' request for a hereditary title because it was simply the latest in the continuing assault on the Sage's descendants, who have "carefully attended to the sacrifices and have loyally and piously revered this culture."[96] Gonghuang wrote that "lineage regulations are an ancient rite" and that few clans from ancient times were preserved after the Three Dynasties. "Only we Kongs of Queli have been invested with noble rank for generations and supervised the performance of sacrifices." He then described the lineage of Kongzi's descendants and its near-extinction at the hands of Kong Mo and suggested that the southern lineage's request for a hereditary title was at least in some sense comparable. "There is nothing they will not do." Gonghuang continued, "They have concocted a new appointment for a hereditary title to add to

---

xianzhi (28.2a) list Kong Zhu's son as Sixu 思許, succeeded by Yansheng five generations later. The *Lishi xingchuan* (23b) in Kong Zhaozhen's genealogy specifies that Sixu was Kong Lü's 孔律 son who "continued" (*ji* 繼) Zhu's line, presumably through adoption. Kong Shangren does not mention any Kongs who live outside Qufu. Adoption of nephews to continue the ducal line was practiced by both the northern and the southern lineages: several accounts agree that the man who succeeded Duanyou as the second southern duke, Jie 玠, was adopted from Duancao, the first northern duke (see, e.g., Kong Shangren, *Kongzi shijia pu* 4.11a; *Quzhou fuzhi* [1711 ed.] 12.13a–b; *Lishi xingchuan* 19a–b). The court acknowledged that Jie was not Duanyou's natural son when it appointed him duke in 1132 (Gaozong Shaoxing 2/6); see Kong Chuan, *Dongjia zaji* A.32a–b. Chen Hao (*Queli zhi* 2.6b–7a) lists Jie as Duanyou's son. When a duke died without an heir, the hereditary title was more typically passed on to a nephew (e.g., in the twentieth, thirty-second, fiftieth, fifty-first, sixty-fourth, and seventy-second generations).

95. Kong Gonghuang, "Diyi kao," 30a. A similar argument is made in Kong Zhendong, "Sheng yi kao bian," 2.37a–39a. See also the chapter by Lamberton, pp. 316–17, in this volume.

96. Kong Gonghuang, "Donglu dacheng dian xingtan qian zongfa beiwen chao song duidian."

their glory and riches. Having gained this, they are already eyeing further concessions. Their inner thoughts are reprehensible. Of old, when the Sage patriarch [Kongzi] served in government, the rectification of names was primary."[97] The southern Kongs' pretense of legitimate succession to a hereditary title, according to this argument, was simply false and an affront to the principal teachings of their ancestor.

By the late seventeenth century, the number of Kongzi's descendants living in Qufu was approaching 11,000.[98] As Abby Lamberton writes in her chapter in this volume (pp. 317–20), the wealth and power of the Kong lineage in Qufu continued to grow throughout the late imperial era, largely as a result of gifts of money, land, and peasant households conferred by successive ruling houses. Imperial support of the Qufu Kongs benefited the emperor, because it demonstrated his pious devotion to Kongzi and his Dao. As Lamberton points out, the power of the Qufu Kongs was both extensive and local. The Kongs lived in a ducal mansion virtually impervious to seizure by the state or anyone else; they owned 164,000 acres of tax-exempt farmland and benefited from the labor of thousands of households. During the Ming and Qing, the duke was given the privilege of selecting the county magistrate, who was thus beholden to the Kongs. This further enabled them to take advantage of opportunities to profit from their tax-exempt status. Yet, as Evelyn Rawski has suggested, the localized nature of the Kongs' entrenched power—based largely on land rather than access to instruments of imperial power—limited their ability to influence the court on national matters, let alone pose a threat to the legitimacy of an emperor or dynasty. That the Kongs could dominate Qufu county for centuries—that they were China's oldest feudal household—yet never pose a threat to any dynasty suggests that the court's material investment in the Kongs' local dominance was calculated to restrict their power at the national level.[99] Many Kongs pursued scholarly endeavors, although few sat for the imperial examinations

---

97. Kong Gonghuang, "Diyi kao," 30b–31b.

98. Kong Shangren, *Kongzi shijia pu*, "shou juan," 33b.

99. Comments made at the AAS panel "The Cult of the Supreme Sage: Social, Ritual/Music, and Political Aspects of the Temple of Confucius," Hawai'i. Han Yuandi invested the Kongs with 800 households, and Pingdi (r. 1 BCE–5 CE) with 2,000 households. Tang Taizong (r. 626–49) invested them with 2,000 households in 637 (Zhenguan 11/7/13); at the same time he invested the descendants of Laozi with an equal number of households (*Xin Tang shu* 2.37; Li Zhizao, *Pan'gong liyue shu* 1.1a–9a). It is not clear whether the households given in the Tang added to those given in the Han or restored them.

and only a handful achieved great eminence as classicists. In Ming-Qing times they often married well, even though social mobility or consolidation of alliances with prestigious families probably rarely figured into marriage considerations.

The high social standing of the Qufu Kongs was secure during the remainder of the imperial era and, indeed, beyond. In the early years of the Republic, the new constitutional government took steps to maintain the ducal status of the Kongs in the same feudal arrangement in place for centuries. On March 16, 1914 (Minguo 3/2/20), the president's office issued the Worshipping the Sage Code (*chong sheng dianli* 崇聖典禮), which reaffirmed the status of Kongzi's senior living heir as the Yansheng Duke.[100] In the aftermath of the May Fourth Movement, however, modernist intellectuals such as Cai Yuanpei 蔡元培 (1868–1940) increasingly agitated for the dismantling of remnants of feudalism. On February 20, 1935 (Minguo 24/1/18), the ducal title was changed to Sacrificing Official for the Supreme Sage and First Master of Great Completion (*dacheng zhisheng xianshi fengsi guan* 大成至聖先師封祀官). The southern Kongs' hereditary title was changed to Southern Lineage Sacrificing Official for the Supreme Sage and First Master (*zhisheng xianshi nanzong fengsi guan* 至聖先師南宗封祀官) in the following year.[101]

TEMPLE CULT

Formation of the Liturgy

If the imperial cult of Kongzi is understood as the regular worship of Kongzi through rituals performed by the emperor (or his surrogate) in the capital and by officials in temples throughout the empire that honored and fed Kongzi's spirit, then it is possible to date it to the late sixth or seventh century. The Tang court initially gave a higher place of honor in the imperial temple to the Duke of Zhou, who was called a sage, and relegated Kongzi to a position as his correlate. The Duke of Zhou, younger brother of the man who established the Zhou dynasty, is credited with building the institutions of the Zhou and loyally serving his nephew, the second Zhou king,

---

100. *Ji Tian si Kong*, 3–4. This code also changed the southern Kong hereditary title of Erudite of the Five Classics to Sacrificing Official (*fengsi guan* 封祀官).

101. *Kongfu dang'an xuanbian* 1: 4; Xu Yingpu, *Kongshi nanzong kaolüe*, p. 89.

was still an infant when the founder died. Several important chapters of the *Book of Documents*, as well as the *Rites of Zhou* 周禮 (one of three ritual books of the canon), are attributed to him. Kongzi was said to have revered him and assisted in the sacrifices to him at the Great Temple in the state of Lu. Joint sacrifices to the Duke of Zhou and Confucius were performed at the state schools as early as the Han, although apparently the Duke of Zhou seldom received offerings between the Han and his brief elevation to sage in the Tang. In the mid-seventh century, the Duke of Zhou was given the status of correlate in the Temple of Kings, and Kongzi was restored to the position of sage in the Temple of Culture, where his disciple Yan Hui was also made a correlate.[102]

Because there was no classical precedent for a Kongzi cult, Tang ritualists devised a liturgy by gradually combining rites from ancient books with ritual precedents from later periods. The issue of what rites to use in paying obeisance to Kongzi evidently vexed his followers from the very beginning. Kongzi's disciples were initially uncertain what form of mourning to observe when he died. They decided to treat Kongzi as their father in ritual terms, without actually wearing mourning dress, on the grounds that Kongzi had earlier mourned the deaths of two of his disciples as if they were his sons. They observed these rites for three years, after which they dispersed. One disciple was said to have built a hut near the burial site and lived in it for another six years, and other disciples built a temple near the Apricot Altar— where Kongzi lectured—to honor his spirit and store his belongings, such as his books, clothing, and even his chariot. Four hundred years later, Sima Qian reported witnessing a cult that venerated relics associated with Kongzi at the Zhongni temple where sacrifices had been performed since Kongzi's death.[103] Most sources date the first imperial sacrifice as early as 195 BCE, when Emperor Gaozu (r. 206–195 BCE) of the Han offered a "large beast" sacrifice (*tailao* 太牢) of an ox, goat, and pig to Kongzi's spirit at his tomb in Queli.[104] Other emperors of the Han and most successive dynasties traveled

---

102. *Xin Tang shu* 15.373–74; Wilson, *Genealogy of the Way*, p. 33. For Kongzi's sacrifices to the Duke of Zhou, see *Lunyu* 3.15 (*Lunyu zhengyi* 3.56). The joint sacrifices in the Han took place in 59 CE (Zhang Chaorui, *Kongmen chuandao lu* 1.13b; and Li Zhizao, *Pan'gong liyue shu* 1.4a). The Tang court ordered the construction of Kongzi temples in all prefectural and county schools in 630 (*Xin Tangshu* 15.373).

103. *Shiji* 47.1945–47; Chen Hao, *Queli zhi* 4.3b.

104. *Shiji* 47.1945–46, *Han shu* 1B.76 (Gaozu 12/11).

to Queli to repeat this rite. The music and dance described in the *Rites of Zhou* as used in sacrifices to the ancient sage-kings accompanied the offerings as early as 85 BCE, and portraits of Kongzi and his disciples were added in 178 CE. Several years earlier, in 170, the court ordered that the sacrifices at Queli were to be performed twice a year, in the spring and autumn.[105]

The performance of sacrifices in the imperial capital was an important factor in the gradual merging of the local Kongzi cult with the imperial state cult. Due to the continuing importance of imperial sacrifices at the Qufu temple, however, as well as the prominence of Kongzi's descendants, the imperial cult was always closely intertwined with the Kong family ancestral cult. Sacrifices to Kongzi in state schools were performed as early as the third century CE, when, on several occasions, the Wei court (220–65) presented a large beast sacrifice to Kongzi and his disciple Yan Hui as correlate at the Imperial University (Biyong 辟雍).[106] Basing its practices on the *Record of Rites*, the Jin (265–316) offered an ox, goat, and pig (*san sheng* 三牲) to Kongzi and his seventy-two disciples, and in 271, the heir apparent presented offerings in the Imperial University, a precedent that would be repeated, eventually by the emperor personally, at least six times during the Jin.[107]

State worship of Kongzi in early imperial times was formed through an accumulation of ritual practices. The result would be difficult to characterize as neatly linear because the evidence suggests that ritual experts at court were not always cognizant of their predecessors' decisions. The editor of the *Collected Statutes of the Eastern Han* complained that some emperors did not know of the sacrifices and that when they were performed, they were not always performed correctly.[108] Toward the end of the Eastern Han, it was decided that the ceremony would follow the regulations of the imperial sacrifices at the Altar of Soils and Grains 社稷, which did have classical prece-

---

105. The music and dance used in 85 CE (Zhangdi Yuanhe 2/3/27) is referred to in the *Hou Han shu* (3.150, 79A.2562) as the music of the six reigns (i.e., Huangdi, Yao, Shun, Yu, Tang, and Wu), which is described in detail in the *Zhouli zhushu* (22.149 [p. 787]). For the portraits of 178 and the regular performance of these rites, see Chen Hao, *Queli zhi* 6.4b; and Li Zhizao, *Pan'gong liyue shu* 1.5a.

106. *Sanguo zhi*: *Wei shu* (4.119ff) and *Jin shu* (19.599) date these sacrifices to 241 (Qiwang zhengshi 2/2), 244 (5/5/30), and late 246 or early 247 (7/12). Qiu Jun (*Daxue yanyi bu* 65.7a) and Li Zhizao (*Pan'gong liyue shu* 1.5a–b) list only the last of these sacrifices.

107. *Jin shu* 19.599; *Wenxian tongkao* 43.405; Li Zhizao, *Pan'gong liyue shu* 1.5b–6a. For the *san sheng* sacrifice, see "Ji tong" 祭統, *Liji zhengyi* 49.375 (1603).

108. Xu Tianlin, *Dong Han huiyao* 5.43. This book was compiled in the thirteenth century.

dents.[109] After the Han and before the Tang, Kongzi's rank in the court sacrifices was that of upper lord (*shang hou* 上侯), which required six rows of dancers (*liu yi*) and three racks of hanging bells and jade chimes. In 723, not long before Kongzi's elevation to king (in 739), sacrifices to him in the capital were accompanied by the four racks of bells and chimes (*gongxuan*) accorded a king.[110]

By the seventh century the classical precedent for sacrifices to Kongzi most often cited was the "When King Wen Was Heir Apparent" chapter of the *Record of Rites*, which describes the education of the eldest sons of the royal family and the nobility, who, in ancient times, were the heirs to the family's hereditary titles. The text says:

> In all schools, the officers in spring present libations (*shidian* 釋奠) to the late masters [or teachers]. This is also done in the autumn and winter. Whenever a school is established, offerings were always presented to the former sages and masters. Silk was always used when performing these rites. There was always [music] accompaniment with the presentation of offerings, except when there were pressing matters of state.[111]

In ancient times the term "former masters" did not refer to a fixed group and did not include Kongzi. By the Han dynasty, they tended to be construed as the founding masters of the canonical traditions of the *Rites, Music, Odes,* and *Documents.* The "former sages" were also not fixed in early times. They were

109. The use of the liturgy for the sacrifices at the Altar of Soils and Grains was implicit in Han Gaozu's use of the *tailao* sacrifice, which, according to the *Record of Rites* ("Jiao tesheng," *Liji zhengyi* 25.216 [p. 1444]), is to be offered at this altar. This connection was made explicit in 169. See Chen Hao, *Queli zhi* 6.4a–5b; and Li Zhizao, *Pan'gong liyue shu* 1.5a. This is not recorded in the *Hou Han shu* (*Gujin tushu jicheng* 198.48a).

110. *Nan Qi shu* 9.143–44; *Tang huiyao* 35.745, 750. The number of ritual vessels called baskets and jars (*bian dou* 籩豆) was not, however, increased to ten each until 1371 (*Ming shi* 50.1296) and not increased to the royal twelve until 1477 (Chenghua 13/2/8), when Kongzi's ritual statue was also dressed with imperial cap and robe (*Ming shi* 50.1297–98). Kongzi's royal title was removed in 1530 (Jiajing 9/11/15) when the number of baskets and bowls was decreased to ten each and the rows of dancers to six (*Ming shi* 55.2068). The issue of imperial garb became moot since statues were also replaced with spirit tablets at this time.

111. "Wenwang shizi" 文王世子, *Liji zhengyi* 20.177–78 (pp. 1405–6). This passage was probably first used as the basis of the Kongzi liturgy in the Tang (e.g., *Jiu Tang shu* 15.374). Fang Xuanling's (578–648) seventh-century history of the Jin uses the term *shidian* for sacrifices in the Wei (*Jin shu* 19.599), whereas Chen Shou's third-century history of the Three Kingdoms refers to the same sacrifices as *tailao* (*Sanguo zhi* 4.121); see Wilson, "Sacrifice and the Imperial Cult of Confucius," pp. 259–66.

typically thought of as the founding rulers of the ancient dynasties.[112] The imperial cult of Kongzi was thus formed through a continual appropriation of classical precedents that in effect retroactively inserted Kongzi into a hierarchy of deities, spirit cults, and temple liturgies. Since he had never been part of the canonical pantheon of antiquity,[113] Kongzi's status was repeatedly subject to revision, as we have seen in the discussion on his names in the first part of this chapter.

It is not entirely clear when the imperial court began to observe a regular, codified liturgy in temples specifically devoted to Kongzi—a "Confucius" temple—but early official chronicles describe an imperial cult in the capital that was undergoing gradual formation at various courts in the era of the North-South division. The first temples devoted to Kongzi outside Qufu were probably built in the mid-fifth century, although the sources differ on their locations.[114] The *Sui History* describes a full liturgy for a Venerable Kong Temple (Kongfu miao 孔父廟), at the court of the Latter Qi (550–77), consisting of prescribed clothing for the emperor, three offerings presented to Venerable Kong and Yan Hui, music appropriate for an upper lord, and six rows of dancers.[115] As early as 445, the Liu-Song court set the number of rows of dancers at six, based on the number used in ceremonies honoring dukes as described in the *Spring and Autumn Annals*.[116] The impe-

---

112. "Wenwang shizi," *Liji zhengyi* 20.177–78 (pp. 1405–6); Qin Huitian, *Wuli tong kao* 117.4a–6b.

113. The three-tiered division of the pantheon (i.e., great, middle, and minor sacrifices) is adumbrated in the *Zhouli zhushu* 18.119 (757), 19.130 (768). In the Ming, recipients of great sacrifices included Heaven and Earth, the imperial ancestors, the gods of Soils and Grains, and the spirits of the sun, moon, and harvest. Recipients of middle sacrifices included the Great Star (i.e., Jupiter) and the stars, wind and clouds, thunder and rain, the sacred peaks, seas and lakes, mountains and streams, the sovereigns of the successive dynasties, the first teacher (Kongzi), etc. See *Ming shi* 47.1225.

114. The *Nan shi* (2.47, 2.58), the earliest of these sources, Li Zhizao (*Pan'gong liyue shu* 1.6a), and Lan Zhongrui (*Wenmiao dingji pu* 2A.4b–5a) cite the construction of a Kongzi miao in 443 (Wendi Yuanjia 19/12/24) and a Zhongni miao in 454 (Wudi Xiaojian 1/10/15) during the Liu-Song dynasty in south China, whereas the *Wenxian tongkao* (43.406) and Qiu Jun (*Daxue yanyi bu* 65.7b) date the earliest such temple, called Exalted Ni (Xuan Ni miao), to the time of Emperor Wencheng (r. 452–65) of the Northern Wei (386–534).

115. *Sui shu* 9.180.

116. *Nan Qi shu* 9.143–44; *Wenxian tongkao* 43.405; Qiu Jun, *Daxue yanyi bu* 65.7b; Li Zhizao, *Pan'gong liyue shu* 1.6a–b. For precedent in the *Chunqiu*, see "Yin gong" 隱公, fifth year, in *Chunqiu Zuozhuan zhengyi* 3.25–26 (pp. 1727–28); *Chunqiu Gongyang zhuan zhushu* 3.13 (p. 2207); and *Chunqiu Guliang zhuan zhushu* 2.5 (p. 2369).

rial cult expanded during the period of political unity under the Sui and Tang dynasties. Magistrates and school officials at local state schools were ordered to perform sacrifices as early as the Sui dynasty, although an empire-wide local cult based in schools probably began no earlier than 630, when the Tang court ordered the construction of state schools and temples in all prefectures and counties.[117] From then on, the cult of Kongzi based on ritual offerings in temples became an integral part of the upbringing and training of most educated men, particularly those who attended state schools in preparation for service in the civil bureaucracy.

Based on canonical texts on ritual, the detailed Tang codes for sacrifices to Kongzi established much of the basic liturgy subsequently used throughout imperial times. Kongzi and the other spirits in the main hall received three offerings (*san xian* 三獻) presented by different consecration officials: the first offering 初獻 was presented by the crown prince, and the second (*yaxian* 亞獻) and final offerings (*zhongxian* 終獻) by the two top officials of the Directorate of Education, the Libationer and Director of Studies, respectively. Li Zhizao 李之藻 (fl. 1598–1630) pointed out that the "Single Victim Feast" (*tesheng kuishi* 特牲饋食) chapter of the canonical book the *Ceremonial Rituals*, which outlines the ceremony of three offerings to the ancestral spirits, was used as the basis of this imperial liturgy. The amount of offerings to each spirit was determined by its location in the temple hierarchy, which was headed by Kongzi, who, by the mid-eighth century, held the posthumous title of King of Exalted Culture. He was followed by Yan Hui as correlate, who was ennobled as a duke, and then other major disciples called the savants (*zhe* 哲), who were ennobled as marquises (*hou* 侯). Seventy other personal disciples were enshrined as earls (*bo* 伯), followed by twenty-two exegetes of the canon, who were enshrined as masters (*xianshi* 先師).[118]

The precise details of the offerings and the ritual procedures by which they were presented changed somewhat during the imperial era. In the Ming dynasty, sacrifices at the temple were offered twice a year on the first *ding* 丁 day (the fourth day of the ten-day cycle) of the second and eighth lunar months in spring and autumn.[119] The ceremonies in the capital were super-

---

117. *Jiu Tang shu* 15.373; *Wenxian tongkao* 43.406; Chen Hao, *Queli zhi* 6.5b; Li Zhizao, *Pan'gong liyue shu* 1.10b–11a.

118. *Xin Tang shu* 15.373–76; *Wenxian tongkao* 44.407–8.

119. *Da Ming huidian* 91.28a. According to the Chen Hao, *Queli zhi* (6.4a), regular spring and autumn sacrifices, based on the liturgy for Soils and Grains, began as early as 169 (Jian-

vised by members of the Court of Imperial Sacrifices, the Director of Studies of the Directorate of Education, and senior officials from the Ministry of Rites.[120] For the three days before the ceremony, they abstained from meat, contact with wives and concubines, funerals, criminal cases, punishments, and music.[121] The day before the ceremony, they supervised the rehearsals and inspected the sacrificial offerings. The feast included wine, simple beef broth and mixed soup, dried meats and fish, nuts, herbs, sauces, sweet breads, pork blades, cakes, millet and sorghum, white silk damask, and incense. Behind these offerings was placed the principal sacrifice of an ox, goat, and pig called the large beast sacrifice (*tailao*) which had been part of the imperial sacrifices since the Han. Each of the correlates was offered a small beast sacrifice (*shaolao* 少牢) of a goat and pig and the same libations and foods except they received less grain; the savants shared a pig, silk, and wine, and each received a reduced amount of grain. The remaining spirits collectively shared a pig, silk, and three goblets of wine, and each received a reduced amount of other foods.[122]

According to the Ming liturgy, the ceremony begins well before dawn. The blood and fur of the sacrificed animals are buried outside the main gate, Kongzi's spiritis escorted into the inner temple grounds (*yingshen* 迎神), musical verses praising Kongzi are sung, and the principal consecration official offers silk, wine, incense, and the feast to Kongzi's spirit. Secondary consecration officials perform these same rites to the spirits of correlates, then to the savants, the remaining disciples, and the canonical exegetes. The whole ceremony is repeated in the second and final offerings, accompanied by other verses. The consecration official then drinks some of the libation and receives a portion of the meat. This completes the sacrifice. The spirits

---

ning 2/3). The selection of the tenth day of the second month of the spring and autumn was first made in 739 (Kaiyuan 27/8); see *Jiu Tang shu* 24.921; Li Zhizao, *Pan'gong liyue shu* 1.17b.

120. Since the third century CE, the emperor and heir apparent periodically presented the first offering during sacrifices in the Imperial University (*Sanguo zhi* 4.119).

121. Participants in the sacrifices normally observed a two-day working abstinence (*san zhai* 散齋/齊), when most routine duties not related to the sacrifices were still performed, followed by a one-day strict abstinence (*zhi zhai* 致齋/齊), when they resided at the temple and attended to these preparations exclusively. See *Ming shi* 50.1296; and Lü Yuanshan, *Shengmen zhi* 4.280. I analyze the aims of abstinence in "Sacrifice and the Imperial Cult of Confucius," pp. 268–77.

122. *Da Ming huidian* 91.20a–21b, 30a–b; Qu Jiusi, *Kongmiao liyue kao* 3.20a–24b; Lü Yuanshan, *Shengmen zhi* 4.280–84; Jin Zhizhi and Song Hong, *Wenmiao liyue kao*, "Libu," 36a.

are bidden farewell, and all parade out of the temple through the main gate following Kongzi's spirit.[123]

Enshrinement and the Ritualization of Orthodoxy

The Kongzi temple's function as a ritual training ground for men who would hold great power was one way that it served in the formation of state orthodoxy. It also provided a venue for the court[124] to assert its interpretation of the Confucian tradition by formally enshrining the Confucian scholars and exegetes who it believed truly understood the Way and ranking them in a temple hierarchy. During the early years of the imperial temple in the seventh century, the court concerned itself with enshrining Kongzi's immediate disciples and the later exegetes of the Five Classics. These were not simple or unprejudicial matters. The identity of several disciples was obscure since nothing but their name was known, and the early sources do not always agree even on this. Kongzi's other disciples named in the *Analects*, *Historical Records*, and *Family Sayings of Kongzi* (*Kongzi jiayu*) occasionally received imperial sacrifices in Queli beginning in the Han dynasty and were formally enshrined in the imperial temple in the Tang.[125] The mechanism for stratifying those enshrined in the temple was established as early as the Wei dynasty when Yan Hui, whom Kongzi regarded as his greatest disciple, was named a correlate in the Imperial University to distinguish him from

---

123. *Da Ming huidian* 91.21b–24a; Jin Zhizhi and Song Hong, *Wenmiao liyue kao*, "Libu," 30a–33b.

124. The "court" includes members of the upper metropolitan bureaucracy as well as the emperor. The views of other members of the imperial bureaucracy were also represented in formal memorials addressed to the throne. Even though lower-ranking officials could not directly participate in final decisions, debates at court served as a means to address matters that were of concern to all levels of the bureaucracy throughout the empire. Thus decisions of the court required considerable consensus building and were rarely the result of imperial fiat. Even the more autocratic Ming emperors, discussed by Huang Chin-shing in this volume (see pp. 270–82), worked through court ministers to enact their visions in the temple.

125. The emperor sacrificed to Kongzi and seventy-two of his disciples in 72 CE (Mingdi Yongping 15/3); see *Hou Han shu* 2.118; and Chen Hao, *Queli zhi* 6.3b (Li Zhizao dates this to the preceding month; *Pan'gong liyue shu* 1.4a). Sixty-seven disciples received sacrifices with the ten savants in the imperial temple in 739 (Xuanzong Kaiyuan 27/8/24); see *Xin Tang shu* 15.375–76; and *Zizhi tongjian* 214.6838–39.

Kongzi's other followers.[126] Although he was also included among the ten savants—who were in turn elevated above the others as Kongzi's major disciples—Yan Hui alone was honored as the Master's correlate and ennobled as duke, one rank higher than the other savants, who were given the title of marquis. This distinction became a major point of contention when the Duke of Zhou was elevated to sage and Kongzi demoted to correlate in the temple during the seventh century.

The enshrinement of twenty-two exegetical masters might appear to be simply a bestowal of honors on those who transmitted the canon. Yet it belied an older controversy over conflicting versions of the canonical books transmitted by different schools in the Han dynasty. In the Eastern Han there was more than one exegetical school for each book: five schools transmitted different versions of the *Book of Odes*, for example, and four schools transmitted the *Book of Documents*. This excess of exegesis is further complicated by differences between texts written in "scribe characters," or the modern script (*jinwen*), and older versions written in "seal characters," or the ancient script (*guwen* 古文). Scribe characters were promulgated by the Qin state after its conquest of China in 221 BCE, whereas books transcribed before the conquest and purportedly rediscovered after the Qin fell in 206, were written in seal characters. The differences between modern and ancient script versions of the canon ranged from variations in content (e.g., passages that appeared in one version were not present in the other) to contrasts in underlying philosophy (the ancient texts tended to portray Kongzi as a follower of earlier wisdom, whereas the modern texts tended to view him as a prophet). The Han canonical masters usually labored to reconcile some of these differences—many, in fact, specialized in both versions of a book—although on occasion these textual discrepancies escalated into confrontations, particularly when the court took sides by formally canonizing one version over another. In 175 CE the Eastern Han court sanctified the Modern Text canon, which was engraved in stone and placed outside the Imperial University, but in 653 the Tang court promulgated the Ancient Text version (used with rare misgivings for the next eleven centuries) in the *Correct Meaning of the Five Classics*. The ostensible purpose of these imperial projects was

---

126. Dated 241 (Qiwang zhengshi 2/2); see *Sanguo zhi: Wei shu* 4.119. This section on enshrinement and the formation of orthodoxy is based on a longer treatment of this issue in Wilson, *Genealogy of the Way*, chap. 1. See also Neskar, "The Cult of Worthies," chaps. 6–7.

to provide a standard authoritative edition of these books, not to intervene into sectarian polemics, yet the practical effect of imperial editions of the classics was to set limits on what constituted legitimate classical scholarship. The Tang court's enshrinement of the twenty-two masters in 647 did not include such important Modern Text exegetes as Dong Zhongshu 董仲舒 (ca. 179–ca. 104 BCE; who would not be enshrined until 1330), even though other Han exegetes were admitted to the temple.[127]

Although they served the ideological aims of the Tang court by exalting the masters of the Ancient Text tradition, the enshrinements of 647 were not exactly at the forefront of ideological controversy, for the shift away from the Modern Text version of the canon had begun centuries earlier. There was evidently no dispute over the exclusion of Dong Zhongshu since his commentaries had already been largely superseded by those of the Ancient Text masters. That temple enshrinement often reflected a well-established consensus long after the controversy ended tended to be the norm in the Tang (with the important exception of the Duke of Zhou's brief rise to sage in the seventh century), but by the Song dynasty enshrinement and the temple generally played a more prominent role in controversies over the nature of the Confucian tradition and the content of its doctrines. The Tang differed from the Song in that local society and the metropolitan bureaucracy were largely controlled by a nobility that had access to power and high political station through hereditary privilege. After the mid-eighth-century rebellion that all but destroyed the hereditary nobility, the Confucian gentry, a social and political elite determined by its success in civil examinations through mastery of classical learning, gradually came to fill the political vacuum. By the twelfth century, the classically educated literati formed the majority of officeholders in the metropolitan and local bureaucracies; Confucian education had become a prerequisite for gaining power.[128]

The content and nature of Confucian learning also changed in fundamental ways during the post-classical era. The difference between the Modern and Ancient Text traditions is an example of these changes in the early

---

127. Wilson, *Genealogy of the Way*, pp. 29–36; Nylan, "The Chin Wen / Ku Wen Controversy in Han Times." Doubts about the authenticity of some Ancient Text versions gave new currency to the Modern Text tradition in the late Ming; see Elman, *Classicism, Politics, and Kinship*.

128. For changes in Confucianism between the eighth and eleventh centuries, see Bol, *"This Culture of Ours,"* chap. 2.

imperial era. Although certain ideas once associated with Modern Text exegesis persisted from the Tang to the early Qing, classical scholarship in this period was concerned with the Ancient Text canon. But even within the Ancient Text tradition, there were many important changes, particularly the emergence of the Dao School (Daoxue 道學) from a persecuted intellectual minority in the twelfth century to its establishment as the basis of state orthodoxy by the fifteenth century. An in-depth discussion of the teachings of this school is outside the purview of this chapter; suffice it to say that much of the doctrinal controversy that enveloped the Dao School and its adversaries concerned the personal realization of sagehood through the apprehension of the Dao. The belief that it is possible to achieve sagehood distinguishes the Confucianism of this later period (sometimes called Neo-Confucianism) from that of the ancient period. This difference makes sense within the context of the extended philosophical encounter between the Confucian literati and Buddhist thinkers since the Tang. The silence of the Five Classics on how one becomes a sage was one important reason for a shift to a new set of canonical texts called the Four Books: the *Analects*, *Mengzi* (or *Mencius*), *Great Learning*, and *Doctrine of the Mean* (the last two are chapters from the *Record of Rites*). Although not the first time these books were emphasized, Zhu Xi's 朱熹 (1130–1200) collection of commentaries on the Four Books, completed in 1190, eclipsed all others in Confucian exegesis for the next eight hundred years. The Four Books were introduced into the civil examinations as early as the Yuan dynasty and became the basis of the examination curriculum in the Ming, which effectively gave them canonical status.[129]

The shift from the Five Classics—and their exegetes—to the Four Books was marked in the temple by the enshrinement of the authors of the Four Books in the upper echelons of the Kongzi temple hierarchy. Mengzi had received increasing attention from Confucian thinkers since the Tang dynasty but was not enshrined in the temple until 1083, when he joined Yan Hui as the second correlate. Mengzi's rise to the near-summit of the temple was due largely to his book's importance in the thought of Wang Anshi 王安石 (1021–86), whose controversial reforms were based on a model of

---

129. Wilson, *Genealogy of the Way*, pp. 47–59. The Five Classics never lost their canonical status but were de-emphasized in the Ming and Qing examinations.

landownership described in the *Mengzi* and rocked the empire in the eleventh and early twelfth centuries.[130] Less spectacular but no less significant was the promotion of Kongzi's grandson Kong Ji 孔伋 and disciple Zeng Sen 曾參 to correlates in 1267: Kong Ji, reputed author of the *Doctrine of the Mean*, was enshrined in the early twelfth century when he was ranked among the other disciples.[131] Zeng Sen, who was believed to have authored the *Great Learning*, received sacrifices as early as 668 and was ranked among the later exegetes during much of the Tang. By the end of the Song dynasty, therefore, the Dao School's notion of the true sages of antiquity was reflected in the enshrinement, with the highest honors, of these four masters, who in this school's view alone understood the Dao. This judgment is expressed in the oft-quoted view, common from the Song on, that "after Kongzi died, Zengzi [Zeng Sen] alone received this transmission of the Dao, which he transmitted to Zisi [Kong Ji], who then transmitted it to Mengzi. After Mengzi died, there was no transmission."[132]

A few decades earlier, in 1241, five Dao School masters of the Song dynasty had been enshrined in the temple, not because they had authored commentaries on canonical books, but because they had transmitted Kongzi's Dao, which had ceased to be transmitted after the death of the last sage of antiquity. At the time of the Dao School masters' enshrinement, Emperor Lizong (r. 1225–65) said:

We believe that Kongzi's Dao was not received by anyone after Mengzi. Only in our own dynasty, with the authentic insight, concrete practice, and profound search into the Sage's domain by Zhou Dunyi 周敦頤 [1017–73], Zhang Zai 張載 [1020–77], Cheng Hao 程顥 [1032–85], and Cheng Yi 程頤 [1033–1107], did the learning that was terminated long ago finally have a point of convergence. After this revival, Zhu Xi's subtle thought and brilliant analysis harmonized form and content, thoroughly

---

130. Even more unprecedented was the enshrinement of Wang Anshi himself as a correlate in 1104, although he was demoted in 1126 and removed from the temple altogether in 1241; see Neskar, "The Cult of Worthies," chap. 6; Wilson, *Genealogy of the Way*, pp. 41–42, 280n79.

131. *Song shi* 105.2549. Enshrinement dated to the Chongning era (1102–7) of Huizong (r. 1100–1125).

132. This is the Yuan emperor's paraphrase in 1313 of Cheng Yi's account of the transmission of the Dao (Wilson, *Genealogy of the Way*, pp. 68, 91). After the seventh century, Yan Hui's status as correlate in the temple was inviolable, even though he never authored any works that were canonized.

illuminating the *Great Learning, Analects, Mengzi,* and *Doctrine of the Mean* from beginning to end and greatly manifesting Kongzi's Dao in the world.[133]

This concern for the transmission of the Dao itself constituted a new criterion for enshrinement. Before the Song, the two criteria for enshrinement
into the temple were discipleship to the Sage and authorship of canonical
books and their commentaries. The notion that the Dao was transmitted in
doctrines and that it had ceased to be transmitted after Mengzi was new in
the Song. It was used to legitimate Dao School teachings and to delegitimate
opponents of the Dao School and other books that were at variance with
them. Not only were scholars who were not exegetes enshrined, but canonical masters who had been enshrined centuries earlier were increasingly re-
evaluated in terms of this genealogical logic of transmission. By the sixteenth
century, several men had been removed from the temple on grounds that
their commentaries transmitted heretical teachings.[134]

The Four Books and the teachings of the Dao School masters were integrated into the institutions that produced state orthodoxy from the thirteenth to the fifteenth centuries. No single act or proclamation could effect
orthodoxy because the pertinent institutions were dispersed throughout the
imperial bureaucracy. Enshrinement in the temple was a necessary but not
sufficient means of canonizing orthodoxy. The court's prescription of the
civil examination curriculum was also critical. The Mongols had given primacy to the Four Books over the Five Classics beginning in 1313, but due to
stringent quotas that discriminated against the Han Chinese who passed
these examinations, it is difficult to gage the extent to which the Dao School
curriculum had affected the values and thinking of the men who held
power.[135] It was only during the Ming that the civil examinations produced a
Confucian gentry schooled in a Dao School curriculum. By 1415 the court
had promulgated Dao School teachings in imperial editions of the canon
based on Dao School exegesis that were the versions used in the examinations.[136]

---

133. *Song shi* 42.807; Wilson, *Genealogy of the Way,* pp. 43–44; Neskar, "The Cult of Worthies," pp. 293–94.

134. I describe the nature and ideological uses of this genealogical discourse in Wilson,
Genealogy of the Way, chap. 2.

135. Ibid., pp. 47–51.

136. The texts are the *Great Collection on the Five Classics and Four Books (Wujing sishu daquan*
五經四書大全) and the *Great Collection on Nature and Principle (Xingli daquan* 性理

The Ming dynasty was a critical period in which several disparate imperial acts together articulated a cogent statement on the orthodoxy of the Dao School. The living descendants of the authors of the Four Books and the Dao School masters were given hereditary positions in the fifteenth century, and the fathers of these authors were honored in a shrine located in the primary position just north of the main hall of the Kongzi temple in the sixteenth century.[137] In the final years of the dynasty, the Dao School masters of the Song were elevated to a status that was essentially equal to that of Kongzi's immediate disciples. The final apotheosis of the Dao School in the temple hierarchy came under the Qing, in 1712, when Zhu Xi was promoted from worthy to the eleventh savant housed in the main hall of the temple complex.[138]

The Cult Under the Republic

Classical learning was closely associated with the throne at least as early as the second century BCE, but by the Song it had become a dominant force throughout the imperial bureaucracy. It is important, however, not to reduce Confucianism to its ideological function as a legitimating rationale for state power, particularly if state power is construed in conventional terms as a sovereign's overt manipulation of the formal instruments of a controlling governing apparatus. Although Confucianism was ineluctably affected by its intimate relations with imperial power and was by no means an innocent bystander in the service of imperial power, there was more to Confucianism than its function as state ideology. This can be seen in a paradoxical way after the demise of the imperial order in 1911. Contrary to what one might expect, state worship of Kongzi continued under the Republic (1912–). This cult had a deeper significance for many educated people who claimed intellectual descent from the literati traditions of imperial China than an expression of respect for the authors of the official canon. In March 1914, after the fall of the Qing dynasty, Yuan Shikai 袁世凱 (1859–1916), president of the Republic and aspiring emperor, revived the official cult and established the tenth day of the second lunar month in spring and autumn to worship Kongzi as an "equal to Heaven," in accordance with the statutes of the great

大全). The Dao School masters were promoted to worthies in 1642. See Wilson, *Genealogy of the Way*, pp. 58–59.

137. Wilson, "The Ritual Formation of Confucian Orthodoxy," pp. 567–68. The construction of this shrine was ordered in 1530.

138. Wilson, *Genealogy of the Way*, pp. 62–63.

sacrifice. The president was to preside over the ceremony in the capital.[139] In a proclamation of November 12, 1914 (Minguo 3/9/25), the president claimed that there was not one political, social, or moral "institution that did not flow out of the teachings of the First Sage. Throughout the order and chaos of Chinese history, only Kongzi's Dao remained eternally constant."[140] Although sacrifices to Kongzi's spirit continued into the Republican era, the status of the emerging Kongzi cult (*Kong jiao* 孔教) was certainly institutionally more tentative than it had been when the temple housed the sages and worthies of a state orthodoxy that was regulated and propagated through the civil examination system.

Yuan Shikai's resurrection of the state cult was not a unilateral act, for he was tapping into a movement that was not atypical of the pre–May Fourth period of Republican China. Drawing from Kang Youwei's Modern Text apotheosis of Kongzi, the Shanghai-based Confucian Society (Kong jiao hui 孔教會) had already been agitating for the establishment of Confucianism as the Republic's official religion. The debate over whether to establish formal sacrifices to Kongzi continued during the first decade of the Republic. Proponents, such as Chen Huanzhang 陳煥章 (1881–1931) of the Confucian Society, argued that China should emulate the example of Christianity in the West as a means of preserving traditional Chinese values in the process of technological modernization.[141] This religious reading of Kongzi was opposed by conservative modernizers such as Hu Shi 胡適 (1891–1962) and Zhang Binglin 章炳麟 (1868–1936), who construed him as a rationalist whose thought was antithetical to the religious superstitions that China's modernizers were seeking to eradicate from society.[142] The nature of the

---

139. *Ji Tian si Kong*, 3; *Shandong sheng zhi: Kongzi guli zhi*, p. 48. September 28 was eventually designated as a national day of commemoration when sacrifices to Kongzi were to be performed by officials in each locality.

140. *Ji Tian si Kong*, 6; Young, "The Hung-hsien Emperor as a Modernizing Conservative," pp. 174–77.

141. Chen Huanzhang, "Si tian yi Kongzi peiyi"; Gu Zhenfu, "Lun Kongzi pei tian wei jiaozhu zhi zheng." Zhang Ertian ("Si tian fei tianzi zhi si ji kao") further argues that worship of Heaven should not be limited to the son of Heaven. The ancient statutes, he argues, gave sole responsibility of sacrifice to Heaven to the king because he also offered sacrifice to his ancestors at the altar of Heaven.

142. For disputes on Kongzi's cult status in the first decade of the Republic, see Furth, "Culture and Politics in Modern Chinese Conservatism," pp. 31–38; and Jensen, *Manufacturing Confucianism*, chap. 3. For Hu Shi's opposition to the revival of the sacrifices in 1934 during

Kongzi cult under the Republic is subject to some speculation, although given the history of ever-changing posthumous titles, there is compelling testimony in support of Gu Jiegang's 顧頡剛 (1893–1980) remark that "Each age has its own Kongzi; it's just that in any one era there are a number of different Kongzis."[143]

---

the New Life movement, see Hu Shi, "Xie zai Kongzi danchen ji'nian zhi hou"; and Grieder, *Hu Shih and the Chinese Renaissance*, pp. 282–83.

143. Gu Jiegang, "Chunqiu shidai de Kongzi he Handai de Kongzi," 2: 487

88 Thomas A. Wilson

WORKS CITED

For early Chinese sources, the original date of completion or publication follows the book title, which is followed by the edition used, and the date of that edition.

Analects. Trans. D. C. Lau. Middlesex, Eng.: Penguin Books, 1979.

Ariel, Yoav. *K'ung-ts'ung-tzu: The K'ung Family Masters' Anthology.* Princeton: Princeton University Press, 1989.

Baihu tong shuzheng 白虎通疏證. Ed. Chen Li 陳立. Beijing: Zhonghua shuju, 1994.

Chen Hao 陳鎬. *Queli zhi* 闕里誌. 1505. Kangxi (ca. 1700) ed.

Chen Huanzhang 陳煥章. "Si tian yi Kongzi pei yi" 祀天以孔子配議. *Kongjiao hui zazhi* 孔教會雜誌 (Shanghai) 1 (May 1913): 4.1–8.

Cheng Minzheng 程敏政. *Huangdun wenji* 篁墩文集. Wenyuange Siku quanshu 文淵閣司庫全書, 1779.

Chun, Allen. "Conceptions of Kinship and Kingship in Classical Chou China." *T'oung Pao* 76 (1990): 16–48.

Chunqiu Gongyang zhuan zhushu 春秋公羊傳注疏. Comp. Gongyang Shou 公羊壽 (AKA Gao 高). Commentary He Xiu 何休. Annot. Xu Yan 徐彥. In *Shisan jing zhushu* (q.v.).

Chunqiu Guliang zhuan zhushu 春秋穀梁傳注疏. Comp. Guliang Chu 穀梁俶 (AKA Chi 赤). Commentary Fan Ning 范甯. Annotated Yang Shixun 楊士勛. In *Shisan jing zhushu* (q.v.).

Chunqiu wei yan Kong tu 春秋緯演孔圖. Ca. 100 BCE. Commentary Song Jun 宋均. In *Yuhan shanfang ji yishu* 玉函山房輯佚書. Comp. Ma Guohan 馬國翰.

Chunqiu Zuozhuan zhengyi 春秋左傳正義. Comp. Zuoqiu Ming 左丘明. Commentary Du Yu 杜預. Annotated Kong Yingda 孔穎達. In *Shisan jing zhushu* (q.v.).

Creel, Herlee. *Confucius, the Man and the Myth.* New York: John Day, 1949.

Da Ming huidian 大明會典. 5 vols. Wanli (1587) ed. Comp. Li Dongyang 李東陽 and Shen Shixing 申時行. Taibei: Xinwen feng chuban, 1976.

Davis, John F. *The Chinese: A General Description of the Empire of China and Its Inhabitants.* New York: Harper and Brothers, 1839.

Da zai Kongzi 大哉孔子. Ed. Zhang Zuoyao 張作耀 et al. Hong Kong: Heping tushu, 1991.

Elman, Benjamin A. *Classicism, Politics, and Kinship: The Ch'ang-chou School of New Text Confucianism in Late Imperial China.* Berkeley: University of California Press, 1990.

Fu Qian 服虔. *Chunqiu Zuoshizhuan jieyi* 春秋左氏傳解誼. In *Yuhan shanfang ji yishu* 玉函山房輯佚書. Comp. Ma Guohan 馬國翰.

Furth, Charlotte. "Culture and Politics in Modern Chinese Conservatism." In *The Limits of Change: Essays on Conservative Alternatives in Republican China*, ed. idem, pp. 22–53. Cambridge, Mass.: Harvard University Press, 1976.

Gan Pengyun 甘鵬雲. *Jingxue yuanliu kao* 經學源流考. 1938. Taibei: Guangwen shuju, 1977.

Grieder, Jerome B. *Hu Shih and the Chinese Renaissance: Liberalism in the Chinese Revolution, 1917–1937*. Cambridge, Mass.: Harvard University Press, 1970.

Gu Jiegang 顧頡剛. "Chunqiu shidai de Kongzi he Handai de Kongzi" 春秋時代孔子和漢代的孔子. In *Gu Jiegang gushi lunwen ji* 顧頡剛古史論文集, 2: 487–95. Beijing: Zhonghua shuju, 1988.

Gujin tushu jicheng 古今圖書集成. Shanghai: Zhonghua shuju, 1934.

Gu Yanwu 顧炎武. *Rizhi lu jishi* 日知錄集釋. 1695. Sibu beiyao 四部備要 ed.

Gu Zhenfu 顧震福. "Lun Kongzi pei tian wei jiaozhu zhi zheng" 論孔子配天爲教主之徵. *Kongjiao hui zazhi* 孔教會雜誌 (Shanghai) 1 (May 1913): 4.9–23.

Han shu 漢書. 12 vols. 76 CE. Ban Gu 班固. Beijing: Zhonghua shuju, 1962.

Hou Han shu 後漢書. 12 vols. Ca. 430–445. Fan Ye 范曄. Beijing: Zhonghua shuju, 1965.

Hsu, Cho-yun. *Ancient China in Transition: An Analysis of Social Mobility, 722–222 B.C.* Stanford: Stanford University Press, 1965.

Hu Shi 胡適. "Xie zai Kongzi danchen ji'nian zhi hou" 寫在孔子誕辰紀年之後. *Duli pinglun* 獨立評論 111 (Sept. 1934): 2–6.

Huang Xun 黃訓. *Huang Ming mingchen jingji lu* 皇明名臣經濟錄. 2 vols. Jiajing (1521–66) ed. Taibei: Xuehai chubanshe, 1984.

Jensen, Lionel M. *Manufacturing Confucianism: Chinese Traditions and Universal Civilization*. Durham: Duke University Press, 1987.

——. "Wise Man of the Wilds: Fatherlessness, Fertility, and the Mythic Exemplar, Kongzi." *Early China* 20 (1995): 408–37.

Ji Tian si Kong 祭天祀孔. *Zhengfu gongbao fenlei huibian* 政府公報分類會編, vol. 21. Shanghai: Saoye shanfang, 1915.

Jin shu 晉書. 10 vols. 648. Comp. Fang Xuanling 房玄齡. Beijing: Zhonghua shuju, 1974.

Jin Zhizhi 金之植 and Song Hong 宋鈜. *Wenmiao liyue kao* 文廟禮樂考. 1691. Kongzi wenhua daquan 孔子文化大全. Ji'nan: Shandong youyi chubanshe.

Jiu Tang shu 舊唐書. 16 vols. 995. Comp. Liu Xu 劉昫. Beijing: Zhonghua shuju, 1975.

Kong Chuan 孔傳. *Dongjia zaji* 東家雜記. 1134. Kongzi wenhua daquan 孔子文化大全. Ji'nan: Shandong youyi chubanshe, 1990.

Kong Decheng 孔德成. *Kongzi shijia pu* 孔子世家譜. 1937. Kongzi wenhua daquan 孔子文化大全. Ji'nan: Shandong youyi chubanshe.

Kong Duanchao 孔端朝. "Kongzi shi jiapu jiu xu" 孔子世家譜舊序. In *Qingdai dang'an shiliao* 1 (file case 1000), p. 312 (q.v.).

Kong Fanyin 孔繁银. *Yansheng gongfu jianwen* 衍圣公府见闻. Ji'nan: Ji Lu shushe, 1992.

Kongfu dang'an xuanbian 孔府檔案選編. 2 vols. Zhongguo shehui kexue yuan 中國社會科學院 and Qufu wenwu guanli weiyuanhui 曲阜文物管理委員會. Beijing: Zhonghua shuju, 1982.

Kong Gonghuang 孔公璜. "Diyi kao" 嫡裔考. 1501. In Kong Shangren (q.v.).

———. "Donglu dacheng dian xingtan qian zongfa beiwen chao song duidian" 東魯大成殿杏壇前宗法碑文抄送對電. 1495. Kong Mansion Archive 衍聖公府檔案 file case no. 104. Qufu, Shandong.

Kong Honghao 孔弘顥. "Wei Kong bian" 僞孔辨. In idem, *Kongshi zupu* 孔氏族譜, 1622; reprinted in Kong Shangren (q.v.).

———. "Zongpai zong lun" 宗派總論. In idem, *Kongshi zupu* 孔氏族譜, 1622; reprinted in Kong Shangren (q.v.).

Kong Jifen 孔繼汾. *Kongshi jiayi* 孔氏家儀. 1765. Kongzi wenhua daquan 孔子文化大全. Ji'nan: Shandong youyi chubanshe, 1989.

———. *Queli wenxian kao* 闕里文獻考. 1762. Taibei: Zhongding wenhua, 1967.

Kong Shangren 孔尚任. *Kongzi shijia pu* 孔子世家譜. 1684. Taibei: Guoli zhongyang tushuguan, 1969.

Kong Sihui 孔思晦. "Queli zongzhi tu ji" 闕里宗枝圖記. In *Qingdai dang'an shiliao* 1 (file case 1000), pp. 349–50 (q.v.).

Kong Yuancuo 孔元措. *Kongshi zuting guangji* 孔氏祖庭廣記. 1227. Sibu congkan 四倍叢刊 ed.

Kong Zhaozhen 孔昭槙. *Kongshi zongpu: nanzong shipu* 孔氏宗譜南宗世譜. Shili tang 詩禮堂 ed., 1918.

Kong Zhendong 孔貞棟. "Shang yi kao bian" 聖裔考辨. In *Queli zhi* 闕里誌, ed. Kong Zhencong 孔貞叢. Wanli (1609) ed.

Kramers, Robert. *K'ung Tzû Chia Yü: The School Sayings of Confucius*. Leiden: E. J. Brill, 1950.

Lan Zhongrui 藍種瑞. *Wenmiao dingji pu* 文廟丁祭譜. 1845. Kongzi wenhua daquan 孔子文化大全. Ji'nan: Shandong youyi chubanshe, 1989.

Legge, James, trans. *Confucian Analects*. The Chinese Classics, vol. 1. Oxford: Clarendon Press, 1893.

Lewis, Mark E. *Writing and Authority in Early China*. Albany: State University of New York Press, 1999.

Li Zhizao 李之藻. *Pan'gong liyue shu* 頖宮禮樂疏. 2 vols. 1618. Taibei: Guoli zhongyang tushuguan, 1970.

Liang shu 梁書. 2 vols. 635. Yao Silian 姚思廉. Beijing: Zhonghua shuju, 1973.

Liji zhengyi 禮記正義. Commentary Zheng Xuan 鄭玄. Annot. Kong Yingda 孔 達. In *Shisan jing zhushu* (q.v.).

Lishi xingchuan 歷世行傳. 1876. In Kong Zhaozhen (q.v.).

Liu Xiang 劉向. *Shuo yuan jiaozheng* 說苑校證. Beijing: Zhonghua shuju, 1987.

Lü Yuanshan 呂元善. *Shengmen zhi* 聖門志. 1613. Congshu jicheng 叢書集成 ed., 1937.

Lüshi chunqiu 呂氏春秋. Gao Buwei 高不韋 and Gao You 高誘. Ed. Bi Yuan 畢 沅 (1789). Zhuzi jicheng 諸子集成 ed. Beijing: Zhonghua shuju, 1954.

Lunyu zhengyi 論語正義. 1866. Comp. Liu Baonan 劉寶楠. Zhuzi jicheng 諸子集 成 ed. Beijing: Zhonghua shuju, 1954.

Lunyu zhushu 論語注疏. Ed. He Yan 何晏 and Xing Bing 邢昺. In *Shisan jing zhushu* (q.v.).

Luo Chenglie 骆承烈. *Qufu shi ji baiti* 曲阜史迹百題. Ji'nan: Ji Lu shushe, 1987.

McMullen, David. *State and Scholars in Tang China*. New York: Cambridge University Press, 1988.

Mengzi zhengyi 孟子正義. Ed. Jiao Xun 焦徇. Zhuzi jicheng 諸子集成 ed. Beijing: Zhonghua shuju, 1954.

Ming huiyao 明會要. 2 vols. Nineteenth century. Comp. Long Wenbin 龍文彬. Taibei: Shijie shuju, 1956.

Ming shi 明史. 14 vols. 1739. Ed. Zhang Tingyu 張廷玉 et al. Beijing: Zhonghua shuju, 1974.

Ming tongjian 明通鑑. 1897. Comp. Xia Xie 夏燮. Beijing: Zhonghua shuju, 1959.

Morrison, Robert. *A Dictionary of the Chinese Language in Three Parts*. 6 vols. Macao: East India Company, 1815–23.

Nan Qi shu 南齊書. 3 vols. Comp. Xiao Zixian 蕭子顯. Beijing: Zhonghua shuju, 1972.

Nan shi 南史. 6 vols. Comp. Li Yanshou 李延壽. Beijing: Zhonghua shuju, 1975.

Neskar, Ellen G. "The Cult of Worthies: A Study of Shrines Honoring Local Confucian Worthies in the Sung Dynasty (960–1279)." Ph.D. diss., Columbia University, 1993.

Nylan, Michael. "The Chin wen / Ku wen Controversy in Han Times." *T'oung Pao* 80 (1994): 83–145.

Pi Xirui 皮錫瑞. *Jingxue tonglun* 經學通論. 1907. Taibei: Shangwu yinshu guan, 1969.

Qian Mu 錢穆. *Guoshi dagang* 國史大綱. 2 vols. Shanghai: Shangwu yinshu guan, 1940.

———. *Zhongguo jinsanbainian xueshu shi* 中國近三百年學術史. 2 vols. Shanghai: Shangwu yinshu guan, 1937.

Qin Huitian 秦蕙田. *Wuli tongkao* 五禮通考. Wenyuange Siku quanshu 文淵閣 四庫全書, 1779.

Qingdai dang'an shiliao 清代檔案史料. Ed. Luo Chenglie 駱承烈 et al. Qufu Kongfu dang'an shiliao xuanbian 曲阜孔府檔案史料選編. Ser. 3. Ji'nan: Ji Lu shushe, 1980.

Qing shi gao 清史稿. 48 vols. 1927. Zhao Erxun 趙爾巽 et al. Beijing: Zhonghua shuju, 1985.

Qiu Jun 邱濬. *Daxue yanyi bu* 大學衍義補. 1487. Wenyuange Siku quanshu 文淵閣四庫全書, 1779.

Qu Jiusi 瞿九思. *Kongmiao liyue kao* 孔廟禮樂考. 1609. Naikaku Bunko 內閣文庫 ed.

Qufu xianzhi 曲阜縣志. 1774. Comp. Pan Xian 潘相. Taibei: Xuesheng shuju, 1968.

Quzhou fuzhi 衢州府志. 1564. Zhao Tang 趙鐺. Library of Congress microfilm of Beiping tushuguan Rare Book collection.

Quzhou fuzhi 衢州府志. 1711. Yang Jingru 楊兢如. Rev. ed. Liu Guoguang 劉國光, 1882.

Sancai tuhui 三才圖會. 1609. Wang Qi 王圻 and Wang Siyi 王思義. Shanghai: Shanghai guji chubanshe, 1985.

Sanguo zhi 三國誌. 5 vols. 297. Comp. Chen Shou 陳壽. Ed. Pei Songzhi 裴松之. Beijing: Zhonghua shuju, 1959.

Shandong shengzhi: Kongzi guli zhi 山東省志孔子故里志. Beijing: Zhonghua shuju, 1994.

Shang shu zhengyi 尚書正義. Comp. Kong Anguo 孔安國. Annotated Kong Yingda 孔穎達. In *Shisan jing zhushu* (q.v.).

Shiji 史記. 10 vols. 87 BCE. Sima Qian 司馬遷. Beijing: Zhonghua shuju, 1962.

Shisan jing zhushu 十三經注疏. 3 vols. 1816. Ed. Ruan Yuan 阮元. Beijing: Zhonghua shuju, 1980.

Shryock, John K. *The Origin and Development of the State Cult of Confucius*. New York: American Historical Association, 1932. Reprinted—New York: Paragon Book, 1966.

Sommer, Deborah. "Images into Words: Ming Confucian Iconoclasm." *National Palace Museum Bulletin* 14 (1994): 1-24.

Song Ji 宋際 and Qing Chang 慶長. *Queli guangzhi* 闕里廣誌. Tongzhi (1870) ed.

Song Lian 宋濂. "Kongzi miaotang yi" 孔子廟堂議. In idem, *Wenxian ji* 文憲集, 28.9a-13a. 1781. Wenyuange Siku quanshu 文淵閣四庫全書.

Song shi 宋史. 20 vols. 1345. Ed. Toghto [Tuotuo 脫脫] et al. Beijing: Zhonghua shuju, 1977.

Song shu 宋書. 8 vols. 493. Ed. Shen Yue 沈約. Beijing: Zhonghua shuju, 1974.

Sui shu 隋書. 6 vols. 636. Ed. Wei Zheng 魏徵. Beijing: Zhonghua shuju, 1973.

Tang huiyao 唐會要. 2 vols. 961. Ed. Wang Bo 王溥 et al. Shanghai: Shanghai guji chubanshe, 1992.

Tao Shiyou 陶士橾. *Kongzi sheng dasi kao* 孔子升大祀考. Yiwen zhai Yang Zi-gang pai 藝文齋楊子岡排, 1911.

Taylor, Romeyn. "Official and Popular Religion and the Political Organization of Chinese Society in the Ming." In *Orthodoxy in Late Imperial China*, ed. Kwang-ching Liu, pp. 126–57. Berkeley: University of California Press, 1990.

Wang Su 王肅. *Kongzi jiayu* 孔子家語. Shanghai: Xin wenhua shushe, 1933.

Wei shu 魏書. 8 vols. 554. Comp. Wei Shou 魏收. Beijing: Zhonghua shuju, 1974.

Wenxian tongkao 文獻通考. 1322. Comp. Ma Duanlin 馬端臨. Shitong 十通 ed. Shanghai: Shangwu yinshu guan, 1936.

Wilson, Thomas A. *Genealogy of the Way: The Construction and Uses of the Confucian Tradition in Late Imperial China*. Stanford: Stanford University Press, 1995.

———. "The Ritual Formation of Confucian Orthodoxy and the Descendants of the Sage." *Journal of Asian Studies* 55 (1996): 559–84.

———. "Sacrifice and the Imperial Cult of Confucius." *History of Religions* 41 (Feb. 2002): 251–87.

Wu Chen 吳沈. "Kongzi feng wang bian" 孔子封王辯. In Huang Xun (q.v.), 12.32a–34a.

Xi'an xianzhi 西安縣志. Comp. Yao Baokui 姚寶煃. 1811 ed.

Xin Tang shu 新唐書. 20 vols. 1060. Ouyang Xiu 歐陽修. Beijing: Zhonghua shuju, 1975.

Xu Tianlin 徐天麟. *Dong Han huiyao* 東漢會要. 1226. Taibei: Shijie shuju, 1980.

Xu Yingpu 徐映璞. *Kongzhi nanzong kaolüe* 孔氏南宗考略. 1946. In *Nanzong shengdi: Quzhou Kongshi jiamiao* 南宗聖地衢州孔氏家廟, 1989. Quzhou: Internal documents 內部資料.

Xu zizhi tongjian 續資治通鑑. 1801. Bi Yuan 畢沅. Beijing: Zhonghua shuju, 1957.

Yang Shouchen 楊守陳. "Lun zun Kongzi di hao" 論尊孔子帝號. In Huang Xun (q.v.), 12.34a–37a.

Young, Ernest P. "The Hung-hsien Emperor as a Modernizing Conservative." In *The Limits of Change: Essays on Conservative Alternatives in Republican China*, ed. Charlotte Furth, pp. 171–90. Cambridge, Mass.: Harvard University Press, 1976.

Yuan shi 元史. 15 vols. 1370. Ed. Song Lian 宋濂. Beijing: Zhonghua shuju, 1976.

Zhang Chaorui 張朝瑞. *Kongmen chuandao lu* 孔門傳道錄. 1594. Ed. Yao Lixuan 姚履旋 et al., 1598. University of Chicago Library.

Zhang Cong 張璁 (Fujing 孚敬). "Xian shi Kongzi sidian huowen" 先師孔子祀典或問. In *Huang Ming jingshi bian* 皇明經世編, comp. Xu Fuyuan 徐浮遠, Chen Zilong 陳子龍, Song Zhengbi 宋徵壁, 178.20a–24b. Chongzhen (1628–44) Pinglu tang 平露堂 ed.

Zhang Ertian 張爾田. "Si tian fei tianzi zhi si ji kao" 祀天非天子之私祭考. *Kongjiao hui zazhi* 孔教會雜誌 (Shanghai) 1 (Apr. 1913): 5.11–19.

Zhongyong zhangju 中庸章句. 1189. Comp. Zhu Xi 朱熹. Sibu beiyao 四部備要 ed.

Zhouli zhushu 周禮注疏. Comp. Jia Gongyan 賈公顏. In *Shisan jing zhushu* (q.v.).

Zhou shu 周書. 4 vols. 635. Ed. Linghu Defen 令狐德棻. Beijing: Zhonghua shuju, 1971.

Zhou Yutong 周予同. "Weichan zhong de Kongsheng yu tade mentu" 緯讖中的孔聖與他的門徒. In *Zhou Yutong jingxue shi lunzhu xuanji* 周予同經史學論著選集, ed. Zhu Weizheng 朱維錚, pp. 292–321. Shanghai: Renmin chubanshe, 1983.

Zhuangzi jishi 莊子集釋. 4 vols. 1894. Commentary Guo Qingfan 郭慶蕃. Zhuzi jicheng 諸子集成 ed. Beijing: Zhonghua shuju, 1954.

Zhuzi yulei 朱子語類. 8 vols. 1270. Ed. Li Jingde 黎靖德. Beijing: Zhonghua shuju, 1986.

Zizhi tongjian 資治通鑑. 10 vols. 1067. Comp. Sima Guang 司馬光. Beijing: Zhonghua shuju, 1966.

Hall of Great Completion (Dacheng dian), Confucius Temple, Beijing (photograph by Thomas A. Wilson, 1993)

Principal consecration officer kneels before the spirit of Confucius during the sacrifice, Confucius Temple, Beijing (photograph by Thomas A. Wilson, 1993)

Principal libation offerings
to the spirit of Confucius,
Confucius Temple, Beijing
(photograph by Thomas
A. Wilson, 1993)

Confucius Temple, Quzhou, Zhejiang (photograph by Thomas A. Wilson, 1995)

Ceremonial dancers at
the sacrifice to Confucius,
Confucius Temple, Qufu,
Shandong (photograph by
Thomas A. Wilson, 1993)

Confucius's altar and spirit
image in the Confucius Temple,
Qufu, Shandong (photograph
by Thomas A. Wilson, 1995)

Confucius's spirit tablet,
Confucius Temple, Beijing
(photograph by Thomas
A. Wilson, 1995)

Confucius's spirit tablet and offerings in the Confucius Temple,
Tainan, Taiwan (photograph by Thomas A. Wilson, 1998)

Offerings to Confucius of leeks, reed grass, celery grass, bamboo shoots,
wheat-honey white cakes, Confucius Temple, Tainan, Taiwan
(photograph by Thomas A. Wilson, 1998)

Altar and spirit tablets of former sages and worthies, with offering vessels and
candlestick holder in the foreground, Confucius Temple, Tainan,
Taiwan (photograph by Brooks Jessup, 1998)

Offerings to savants including wine tripods, covered bowl of unsalted
broth, and eight containers of salt, dried foods, nuts, and
edible grasses, Confucius Temple, Tainan, Taiwan
(photographs by Thomas A. Wilson, 1998)

Main altar for Confucius's ancestors through five generations in the
Shrine for Adoring the Sage (Chongsheng ci), Confucius Temple, Tainan, Taiwan
(photographs by Brooks Jessup, 1998)

Main altar for Confucius's ancestors through five generations in the
Shrine for Adoring the Sage (Chongsheng ci), Confucius Temple, Tainan, Taiwan
(photograph by Brooks Jessup, 1998)

Altar of the fathers who gave birth to sages, Confucius Temple, Tainan, Taiwan
(photograph by Thomas A. Wilson, 1998)

TWO

Destroying Confucius

Iconoclasm in the Confucian Temple

Deborah Sommer

Confucius was liquidated in 1530. Clay images of the Sage that had once stood on the altars of temples to his memory were dissolved in water, and mud that had once given form to the sculpted bodies of Confucius was turned into landscape paintings. In a movement that in some ways paralleled contemporary European efforts to clean Christian altars of three-dimensional cultic images, clay images used in the sacrificial offerings to Confucius were dissolved in water and transformed into paste for painting murals of clouds and mountains on the temple walls. Wooden spirit tablets inscribed with the names and titles of the deceased replaced anthropomorphic depictions of the worthies of the classical tradition. But why destroy Confucius? What motivated this movement to destroy anthropomorphic depictions of the sages of the literati tradition? What made these three-dimensional images dangerous or undesirable? What was to be accomplished by replacing figural art with written inscriptions?

The images of Confucius's body were not perceived as inanimate masses of clay and color; instead, they were seen as somehow animated or charged with the presence of their human prototype, a presence that merited an appropriate visual display (or that merited being hidden, veiled, or rendered invisible). Literati attitudes toward images of Confucius were premised on

The author expresses her appreciation to Butler University and the National Endowment for the Humanities for supporting research on this project.

beliefs about the relationships between the body of a living person and the spirit-existence of that person in the post-death state. The religious significance of such images, which emerged from the liminal realms of ritual time and space in commemorative sacrificial offerings and which visually marked the resonances between body and spirit, is the focus of this essay.

More specifically, I focus on the visual depictions of one particular figure—Confucius. Here I consider the religious and philosophical premises underlying the relationships of body, spirit, and image that shaped literati responses to the iconography of Confucius, particularly during the early Ming in the period predating the Jiajing reforms of 1530. I am concerned primarily with the religious aspects of this phenomenon rather than with the political dimensions of iconographic disputes (which are assessed by Huang Chin-shing in his chapter in this volume, pp. 267–96) or by their aesthetic dimensions (which are addressed by Julia Murray in this volume, pp. 222–64, and elsewhere).[1] Confucius's *thought* has been the subject of sustained inquiry in modern times; more recently, the religious aspects of his cult have been examined.[2] But almost nothing is known of the *visual* and *somatic* significance of the person of Confucius in his various apotheoses. The literati's reactions to figural depictions of Confucius were grounded on their conceptualization of how the post-mortem human body might be apprehended or depicted (or

---

1. See Huang Chin-shing, *You ru sheng yu*; Murray, "The Hangzhou Portraits"; idem, "Illustrations of the Life of Confucius"; and idem, "The Temple of Confucius." For collections of images of Confucius, see Laufer, "Confucius and His Portraits," which draws on the large collection of rubbings of images of Confucius gathered by Laufer and housed at the Field Museum of Natural History in Chicago. A much larger collection of rubbings is reproduced in the multivolume *Beijing tushuguan cang huaxiang*. For portraits of the Kong clan housed at Qufu, see Shandongsheng Qufushi wenwu guanli weiyuanhui, *Kongzi xiang*; for the history of these images, see Gong and Wang, *Kongmiao zhushen kao*. Reproductions of extant images are included in Zhang, *Da zai Kongzi*; Shandongsheng Qufushi wenwu guanli weiyuanhui, *Qufu: Kongzi de guxiang*; and Wang and Kong, *Tianxia di yi jia*. A series of woodblock prints of Confucius and his disciples (which exist in dozens of variant forms) is reproduced in Lü Weiqi, *Shengxian xiangzan*; see also Huang Yongquan, *Li Gonglin*. For modern secondary studies of images of Confucius, see Huang Shaozu, "Kongmiao muzhu hu"; and Liu Ningyan, "Tan Kongzi xiang."

2. One of the earliest such studies in English is Shryock, *Origin and Development*. For more recent secondary studies, see Huang Chin-shing, *You ru sheng yu*; Jing, *Temple of Memories*; Wilson, *Genealogy of the Way*; and idem, "Ritual Formation." Song rites to other literati are described in Neskar, "Cult of Worthies." Selected documents on the rites to Confucius are collected in Du You, *Tong dian, juan* 53; Ma Duanlin, *Wenxian tongkao, juan* 43–44; Qiu Jun, *Daxue yanyibu, juan* 65–66; and Qin Huitian, *Wuli tongkao, juan* 117–21.

remain unseen). My understanding of these reactions has been informed by cross-cultural studies of icons and by modern studies of the body.[3] Literati understood images of Confucius not as autonomous objects of "art" but as phenomena that still embodied the identity of their once-living prototype, and their arguments about the merits and perils of representation were profoundly shaped by mortuary practices that dated to high antiquity. Controversies over the visual apprehension of the body of Confucius were as complex as those of Byzantine or Reformation debates about the body of Christ or of Buddhist discussions of the bodies of the Buddha. Over the centuries, responses to figural images of Confucius encompassed an entire range of sentiments, from iconolatry (love of images) to iconomachy (hatred of images) to iconoclasm (destruction of images). Images that marked the presence of human bodies in ritual contexts variously invoked hatred, fear, or reverence from their beholders.

IMAGINED BODIES AND
INCARNATED IMAGES

To understand responses to images of Confucius, we must first explore the interrelationships of the visible world of the living human body, the invisible world of spiritual beings, and the liminal status of images (both imagined and concrete) that mark the intersections of the visible and invisible realms. Images of various kinds—envisioned, personated (as by the shi 尸, the personators of the dead), or created in such media as paint, wood, or clay— instantiated the presence of the spirit world in the mortuary and commemorative rituals of the literati tradition. The boundaries between the worlds of the living and the departed were remarkably fluid: the realms of the quick and the dead, the visible and the invisible, and the material and the nonmaterial were coeval and contiguous. As parallel, overlapping worlds, their boundaries were subtle, fluid, and indeterminate, just beyond the range of ordinary comprehension. The invisible spirits of the deceased were themselves once-living bodies, physical forms that disintegrated (despite the best

---

3. For icons and iconoclasm, see Belting, *Likeness and Presence*; Camille, *Gothic Idol*; Gutmann, *The Image and the Word*; Kuryluk, *Veronica and Her Cloth*; Sahas, *Icon and Logos*; and Sommer, "Images into Words." For body studies, see Bynum, *Resurrection of the Body*; idem, *Fragmentation and Redemption*; Feher, *Fragments for a History of the Human Body*; and Law, *Religious Reflections on the Human Body*.

intentions of their handlers) in their interment underground. Spirits could not be seen under ordinary circumstances: they were formless and invisible, undetectable to the senses. But the spirit never quite forgot its previous abode—the mortal shell of its physical frame. The spirit carried the qualities of its once-living body into its post-death state, for there existed a continuum between the living body of flesh and bones and the body transformed by the passage into death and beyond, into the spirit world. The presence of the once-living frame cloaked, as it were, the invisible spirit with its memory. A temple to Confucius was, as Jun Jing has noted, a "temple of memories."[4]

Pious sacrificers apprehended the subtleties of these boundaries and communicated between the worlds, invoking the invisible and the dead to become manifest in the realms of the visible and the living. A dead body might not actually be revivified (a possibility not unheard of),[5] but the visual and emotional *experience* of a remembered or imagined encounter with a once-living person could be invoked through regularized ritual processes. Moreover, duplicate, parallel, or counterpart bodies (envisioned, incarnated, personated, painted, sculpted, and so on) were employed to facilitate the manifestation of the invisible world of spirits of the deceased in this world. Confucius could not be brought back from the dead, but a simulacrum of his body, whether a sculpted likeness or a textualized spirit tablet, could be installed in the spirit places of the Confucian temple and be present there for tens of generations even though his original, physical body was hidden underground in the world below or had disintegrated completely.

Sacrificial offerings (*ji si* 祭祀) allowed communication between the unknown worlds of the mysterious vastness of the heavens; what was distant and unknowable could be brought into one's immediate presence. They permitted communications between two aspects of the Chinese cosmos: between the dark, invisible, hidden realm (*you* 幽) inhabited by the unseen spirits of the dead and other numinous powers, on the one hand, and the bright, visible aspect (*ming* 明) inhabited by living human beings and physical forms, on the other. Ritual passages regularly sustained the transformations from life into death, from the manifest to the unmanifest and back again, and facilitated commerce between the hidden and visible. Mourning rites, funerary rites, pre-sacrificial vigils, and commemorative sacrificial

---

4. Jing, *Temple of Memories.*
5. On the resurrection of the dead in antiquity, see Harper, "Resurrection." Song inscriptions on revivification are described in Morgan, "Inscribed Stones."

offerings for the deceased marked passages between the worlds where the living and the dead could meet and become contemporaneous, if only for a time.

It was here, in the in-between world of ritual performance on the sacred spaces marked by the spirit places (*shen wei* 神位) of temple altars, that the invisible could be apprehended; the unseen spirits, envisioned and rendered visible. Images of various kinds—envisioned and incarnated, spontaneously emerging and consciously created by painters and sculptors—marked this liminal realm where the bodies of the living resonated with those of the dead, and where two realms commingled. Startlingly lifelike visions of deceased ancestors appeared during pre-sacrificial vigils; visions of ancestors appeared in dreams during mourning rites; personators of the dead acted as living "images" of the ancestors at commemorative rites; painted and sculpted portraits of the dead reflected the faces and bodies of their once-living prototypes. No longer enjoying the fullness of life yet clearly not perceived as inanimate objects, such images visually marked interstices between two parallel worlds. Those who apprehended the manifestations of the invisible did not respond to what they saw as mere arrangements of color, shape, and form but as entities with lives of their own.

Envisioning mental images of the deceased was a long-established custom, documented as early as the *Record of Rites* (*Li ji* 禮記), which dates to at least Han times and contains materials from much earlier periods. Filial descendants of a deceased person experienced such mental images or visions in the pre-sacrificial vigils observed prior to the performance of commemorative sacrificial offerings. According to the *Rites*, filial children could "see" their ancestors in eidetic visions (vivid moving images of perfect similitude) of the deceased induced by vigils that lasted several days and required abstention or occlusion of the senses. In order to focus the will, or attention, the sacrificer was not permitted to listen to music or indulge any sensual desires. Observance of the rite entailed thinking for three days about the person for whom one was conducting the vigil; during this time one would actually see and hear that person. The *Record of Rites* describes the experience of the officiant.

One thinks of how they lived, thinks of how they smiled and spoke, thinks of their views and intentions, and thinks of what they enjoyed. On the third day, one will see those for whom one is conducting the vigil. On the day of sacrifice, when one enters the chamber, one will indeed seem to see them at the [spirit] place. After one has made one's rounds and is about to go out, with a sense of awe one will hear their voices. When one has gone out into the hall, softly one will hear the sounds of their sighs.[6]

The sacrificer seemed to see and hear the ancestors themselves at their spirit places, and visionary images thus became, in a sense, enlivened. Through emotive remembrances evoked in the focused memory of the filial child, the dead became present in the eidetic images of sacrifice. The sage-rulers of antiquity themselves were reported to have experienced such visions. When King Wen sacrificed, he served the dead as he had served the living; on the anniversaries of his ancestors' deaths, "when he called out their posthumous names, it was as if he saw them personally."[7]

The liminal period of mourning allowed communication between the realms of the living and the dead not available under ordinary circumstances. The instantiation of death within the bodies of descendants who voluntarily immolated themselves through afflictions of occlusion, sensory deprivation, isolation, and starvation allowed unusual visual entree into things otherwise not visible. The phenomena seen in that world could be introduced to the realm of the living through the creation of images. The *Book of Documents*, for example, records that a king, during an extended, silent period of mourning, apprehended in a dream an image (*xiang* 象) of an unknown man who was to be his prime minister—a substitute or double who was to speak for the king during the enforced period of silence. The king wrote down a description of the man he had seen in the dream, ordered that a form or shape (*xing* 形) of him be made, and dispatched the image throughout the realm; a man resembling (*xiao* 肖) the person depicted by the form was located and established as prime minister.[8] In another instance of the appearance of spontaneous visions of the deceased during mourning, Han apocryphal traditions about the mythic sage-rulers of antiquity record that the legendary ruler Shun 舜 so revered his predecessor and father-in-law, Yao 堯, that for three years after Yao died (the customary mourning period for parents), Shun saw

----

6. *Li ji*, "Ji yi." See also Legge, *Li Ki*, 28: 211. All translations are my own unless otherwise noted. For translations from the *Li ji*, I have consulted the *Shisanjing zhushu* edition; Wang Meng'ou, ed., *Li ji jin zhu*; Chen Hao, *Li ji jishuo*, and so on.

7. *Li ji*, "Ji yi." See also Legge, *Li Ki*, 28: 212.

8. *Shang Shu*, "Yue ming shang." See also Legge, *Shoo King*, pp. 248–53. On the significance of substitute or duplicate bodies, see Dupont, "The Emperor-God's Other Body"; Faure, "Substitute Bodies"; Freedberg, *The Power of Images*; and Foulk and Sharf, "On the Ritual Use of Ch'an Portraiture."

Yao on the wall whenever he sat down and saw him in his soup whenever he took his meals.[9]

Shun had no biological connection with Yao, but in other cases it was the blood relationship and connection of vital energy, or qi 氣, between parent and child that determined what the child perceived in a sacrificial vision. Chen Chun 陳淳 (1159–1223), for example, recorded a Han dynasty story of a son from a well-off family who sacrificed to what he thought was his ancestor, only to have a vision of a butcher receiving the offerings. The son later found out that he had been adopted from a butcher's family; the vital energy connecting parent and offspring operated independently of the son's misperceptions of his ancestry and invoked the spirit of the biological parent.[10] These examples from Han and pre-Han texts document the emergence of images, both envisioned and created, in the liminal realm of mortuary rites.

Yet another kind of image, an incarnated image, occupied the space between the living and the dead: the personator of the dead, a young descendant of the deceased who temporarily adopted the identity of the recently departed and participated as a guest of honor in a commemorative funerary meal. Personators bore a great physical resemblance to their "prototypes," their parents and grandparents. A similitude shaped by consanguineous ties stretched from the personator's deceased ancestors to his or her as yet unborn descendants. When alive, a person's physical body formed a continuity with the bodies of the members of his or her clan, all of whom stemmed from a common ancestor and shared the same kind of flesh, bones, marrow, blood, and qi, or vital energy. In the visible world, this similitude of consanguinity was manifested in physical resemblance; in the hidden world, the continuity of blood and vital energy allowed one to communicate with the spirits of one's ancestors in the eidetic visions of pre-sacrificial vigils. Personators were literally considered to image (xiang 象) the dead, and in fact many later scholars believed the custom of personation was the forerunner to the custom of using painted and sculpted images of the deceased at sacrificial offerings.[11] Whether the personator metaphorically represented or lit-

---

9. *Ershiwu shi, Hou Han shu*, 93.984, biography of Li Gu. The saying was also quoted by Zhu Xi in a critique on Buddhist views of the mind and the sense faculties (Chan, *Source Book*, p. 652). On the religious significance of self-immolation, see Camporesi, *Incorruptible Flesh*.

10. Chen Chun, *Beixi ziyi*, B36. Chan, *Neo-Confucian Terms Explained*, p. 151.

11. *Li ji*, "Jiao tesheng." See also Legge, *Li Ki*, 27: 446, where the word "imaged" disappears and is translated as "personated." For scholars who believed the custom of personation was the forerunner to the custom of setting up images, see, e.g., Du You, *Tong dian*, 48.1353; and

erally substituted for the deceased or temporarily *was* the deceased is a difficult and perhaps ultimately unnecessary distinction to make, since the body
of the personator marked exactly that contiguity between the living and the
dead and between representation, substitution, and actuality. The personator had one foot in the realms of both past and present and both spirit and
living flesh. Since the personators were living descendants of the deceased,
such "images" would bear strong physical resemblances to their prototypes.

Parent and child are of the same essential substance and are of the same
class and kind (*lei* 類). According to the principles of sacrificial offerings, it is
precisely the quality of being of the same class and kind that allows for
communication between the visible world of ritual performance and the invisible world of spiritual beings. The establishment of categories of resemblance, similarity, and correlation permeated discussions of correct sacrificial
offerings: one might properly sacrifice only to spirits with whom one had a
proper relationship and with whom one was of the same class and kind.
Since ancient times, sacrifices to spirits with whom one had no proper relationship (*Analects* 2.24) were considered wanton sacrifices, which brought no
blessings.[12] Notions of "class" and "kind" were subject to varying interpretations over the centuries, but thinkers often asserted that ancestral sacrifices
should be offered only to the spirits of one's own direct patriline five generations back; public sacrifices to natural powers, such as mountains and rivers,
could be performed only by officials of appropriately high rank. Being of the
same class and kind was not, then, just an aesthetic concern; similitude allowed one to communicate with spiritual beings and thus was a kind of
spiritual empowerment. Consanguineous resemblance, the surface manifestation of the similitude of class and kind, was associated with the ability to
interact with the invisible world of spirits.

When a painted or sculpted image depicts a human body, the degree of
resemblance between image and prototype can range from almost photographic verisimilitude to highly stylized figuration; what actually constitutes
"resemblance" is somewhat arbitrary, and the satisfactoriness of correlation
between image and prototype is culturally determined. In the context of an-

---

Chen Chun's disciple Wang Jun, in Chan, *Neo-Confucian Terms Explained*, p. 158. For secondary studies of personators, see Carr, "Personation of the Dead"; Hu Xinsheng, "Zhoudai
jisi"; and Zheng Xianren, "Gudai jizu." On the religious significance of blood, see Camporesi,
Juice of Life; and Kuryluk, *Veronica and Her Cloth*.

12. *Li ji*, "Qu li." See also Legge, *Li Ki*, 27: 116.

cient China, the body of the personator represented another human body not by correlation but by incarnation; it shared the same bone, marrow, flesh, and blood and the same vital energy; it bore a physical resemblance to its prototype. The reverence toward ancestors in China reflected not an appreciation of a unique incarnation of the divine—a notion that was to engage iconophiles and iconoclasts in the West for centuries—but an appreciation of the continual regeneration of human life from one generation to the next. One's own "incarnation," one's own bodily existence, was a boon granted by one's parents, not by a divinity; one's body belonged to one's parents.

Such, in brief, is the significance of resemblance in the relationships of spirit, body, and image as described in the classical texts that informed the views of Ming scholars who argued that statues of Confucius be liquidated.

THE SPIRIT UNFIGURED

Their iconoclastic sentiments are all the more surprising since images of Confucius had been placed in shrines commemorating sages and worthies since at least the Tang and had been set up in the Kong mansion in Qufu in the Six Dynasties, if not much earlier.[13] Scholars such as Zhu Xi 朱熹 (1130–1200) even believed that images had been used in sacrificial rites to the sage as early as the Han official and educator Wen Weng 文翁 (fl. second century BCE). A master of the *Spring and Autumn Annals*, Wen Weng was known for fostering education and building academies in Sichuan. Zhu Xi claimed that Wen Weng set up a carved stone image of Confucius in a regional academy in Chengdu; the image was kneeling and sat on a mat on the floor.[14] Wen Weng's biography in the *History of the Former Han*, however, has no record of this image,[15] and hence the Chengdu statue is most likely a creation of later folklore—a folkloric tradition, nonetheless, that had much currency in the Song. That bas-relief images of Confucius did exist in the Han is not in question, as many are still extant.[16] As Audrey Spiro has noted,

---

13. Yang Shoujing, ed., *Shuijing zhushu*, 25.2095–III. The Qufu region had temples, with images, to Confucius, his mother, his wife, and so on.

14. Zhu Xi, *Zhuzi daquan* 68.2a, "Gui zuo bai shuo" 跪坐拜說 (On kneeling and sitting when worshipping).

15. *Ershiwu shi, Qian Han shu*, 89.700.

16. For reproductions, see, e.g., Zhu Xilu, *Jiaxiang Han hua*, pp. 32, 42, 44, 65, 70, 86–88; and Spiro, *Contemplating the Ancients*, pp. 24–26. On the content of these early depictions of Confucius, see Soymié, "L'Entrevue de Confucius."

the *History of the Former Han* lists a lost work titled *The Method for Picturing Confucius and His Disciples* (*Kongzi turen tufa* 孔子徒人圖法),[17] although it is not known whether these images were intended as recipients of sacrificial offerings.

By at least Tang times, however, painted and sculpted images of Confucius and the scholars of the classical tradition had become widely accepted in the imperially sponsored rites to the sages and worthies. The presence of such images was seldom a matter of contention; in fact, in 720, Vice Director of Education Li Yuanguan 李元瓘 remarked, "How could a state academy have no such paintings?"[18] The focus was instead on who should be included in the official sacrifices, how they should be ranked, and how they should be depicted—on wood panels, in paintings, in sculpture, as standing images, or as sitting images. Iconodules (those who revere images) such as Li Yuanguan, for example, petitioned that greater respect be shown Yan Hui, Confucius's favorite disciple, by depicting him sitting down.

Li's primary concern was to establish new criteria of authority within the literati tradition, for he believed the spirits of Confucius's closest disciples, the "Ten Wise Ones," should be given food sacrifices at least on a par with those already offered to the "Twenty-two Worthies," who were mostly Han scholars of the Classics. The images of the Ten Wise Ones, which probably were paintings (they were most often described with the verb *hui* 繪, "to paint," rather than *su* 塑, "to sculpt"), were set up in the temple hall, but the figures were depicted standing and they received inadequate food offerings. Li successfully petitioned for change; some disciples were shown seated, and their food offerings were increased. Li obviously did not perceive himself as engaging in idolatry. He implied that reverence of such images promoted filial piety and other values; the written encomia that hung near the images encouraged the scholarly tradition and paid homage to the accomplishments of the sages.[19]

But in the early Ming, some scholars questioned the validity of the painted and sculpted images prescribed for centuries by the various dynasties' ritual canons. These individuals, however, did not necessarily share the same motivations or goals, nor were such proposals without precedent. For example, memorials requesting the destruction of *particular* images had been

---

17. Spiro, *Contemplating the Ancients*, p. 22; see also *Ershiwu shi*, *Qian Han shu*, 30.528.
18. Ma Duanlin, *Wenxian tongkao*, 43.407.
19. Ibid.

composed in earlier centuries. In 1126, Zhu Xi's pupil Yang Shi 楊時 (1053–1135) petitioned the throne seeking the destruction of the image of Wang Anshi 王安石 (1021–86) in the temple to Confucius.[20] This request was most likely related to Wang's perceived responsibility for the fall of northern China and hence was a posthumous personal attack (a vicarious desecration of the corpse?) rather than a broader-based iconoclastic movement against images of literati in general.

But the attempt to destroy entire *genres* of images—statues of city gods and of literati—gained impetus in the early Ming. Persecutions of Buddhism in the Tang had resulted in the wholesale destruction of Buddhist art, but Ming iconoclasts did not claim these earlier movements as historical antecedents for their own programs. They rarely drew on Tang antecedents at all and preferred instead to hark back directly to antiquity as they constructed histories of the use of painted and sculpted images in the ritual traditions of classical times. Many argued that in ancient times sacrificers had not availed themselves of anthropomorphic painted or sculpted images; hence, they argued, such images, including those of Confucius, should be removed from altars. The textual tradition on which they based their argument could be interpreted to support this view, as could the archeological record as they then understood it.

One thinker who drew on this tradition was Song Lian 宋濂 (1310–81), a longtime advisor to the court of Ming Taizu (r. 1368–98). Song expressed no concerns about the inherent validity of images in general or about images used in contexts other than the rites to Confucius. In fact, Song's collected writings include dozens of eulogies for images of bodhisattvas, Chan masters, lohans, and immortals. Moreover, he believed that these paintings and statues had didactic value; for example, in his "Encomium for a Painting of the Bodhisattva Guanyin," he stated that "this image could help one draw near the Way."[21] He perceived no inconsistency between praising Buddhist images and questioning the appropriateness of statues of Confucius. This is not to suggest hypocrisy on Song's part; it does indicate, rather, that he believed the images of Confucius and other scholars belonged to a different category from Buddhist images and were subject to other religious, historical, and aesthetic standards.

---

20. Ibid., 44.415.
21. Song Lian, *Song Wenxiangong quanji*, 9.9b–10a.

Song Lian's appreciation of Buddhist images did not extend to three-dimensional images of Confucius. In his 1371 memorial "On the Confucian Temple" ("Kongzi miaotang yi" 孔子廟堂議), Song argued that certain aspects of the sacrifices to Confucius were irreverent because they were not based on ancient precedents: in antiquity, sacrifices were performed with tablets (*zhu* 主) of wood, not with images, which were introduced to those rites only in 720, he claimed. Moreover, he asked, did this introduction of images in the eighth century not profane the "spiritual and numinous"?[22]

Most later scholars who, like Song Lian, asserted the existence of an ancient aniconic tradition ("aniconic" is used here to refer specifically to nonanthropomorphic representation) in sacrificial offerings believed that such rites were performed with *zhu*, a term that in modern usage refers to spirit tablets. The perception that the ancient sages used spirit tablets made that practice authoritative, and that precedent was frequently invoked to support attempts to replace images with tablets. The appearance of the *zhu* in antiquity, however, is unknown, and it was not necessarily understood strictly as a physical object. When Confucius, for example, was asked by his disciples how people sacrificed when away from home on military maneuvers and the regular *zhu* were unavailable, he replied that they should take the mandate, or charge (*ming* 命), to be their *zhu*.[23] The tablet in this instance was understood metaphorically as an internalized point of focus, concentration, and remembrance. But in the Ming, the tablets were upright wooden planks, usually painted red, that displayed the name and title of the deceased in gold script.

The debate between images and tablets was not new to the Ming. Su Shi 蘇軾 (1036–1101), for example, in his "Temples Should Have Tablets, and Sacrifices Should Have Personators," noted how contemporary sacrificial offerings to Confucius (and to other spirits) contained embarrassing incongruities and inconvenienced the spirits: images of spirits sat on high altars, but the food offerings presented in sacrificial offerings were placed far down on the ground.

In antiquity, people sat on mats, and so the size of the food stands and casseroles and the height of the serving dishes and food baskets were all made according to human proportions. But nowadays the images of wood and clay are way up high, but the trays and platters are set out on the ground, such that the ghosts and spirits

---

22. Ibid., 35.1a–2a.
23. *Li ji*, "Zengzi wen." See also Legge, *Li Ki*, 27: 326.

cannot partake of them. Who knows how they would eat them. The situation being what it is, they would have to creep and crawl (*fufu pufu* 俯伏匍匐) to get them.[24]

It would be better, he added, to use spirit tablets instead. The imagery of Su Shi's alliterative *fufu pufu*, or creeping and crawling, articulated widely felt sentiments, for it was quoted for centuries thereafter.[25] In Su Shi's time, the placement of the food offerings to the spirits followed classical precedents: the dishes were set on mats on the floor. But the images of the deceased were now set on altars, a tradition that had developed some time after antiquity. Those who unwittingly and infelicitously combined the two traditions, he implied, had not completely thought out the consequences for the spirits being honored.

Implicit in Su's allusion to creeping and crawling is the notion that spirits have bodies: for a spirit to stoop and prostrate itself on the floor to accept food offerings, it must be assumed to have arms and legs, not to mention an appetite and a stomach. (The notion that spirits consumed the aromas, although not the actual substance, of food offerings dated to earliest times). Su Shi implied that the physical appearance and posture of the image somehow contained and limited the presence of the spiritual being it represented. The image was not considered just a token reminder of the spirit, with an existence independent of the statue and the ability to float about at will. For Su Shi, the behavior of a spirit is circumscribed, or limited, by the iconography of its painted or sculpted representation. Image and spirit were not separate entities; they were expressions of the same identity.

Su Shi would not, then, have agreed that images are symbolic or metaphoric representations of prototypes that are not circumscribed by the image itself. He would not have concurred with the comments of the iconophile Nicephorus the Patriarch (806–15, d. 828):

In truth, he who constructs the image of a man—by which I mean the painter, since it is of him we must now speak—he in no way circumscribes the true identity of the person he paints. It is wrong to believe that by determining someone's limits we imprison him within a space that contains him, when in fact he is absent from it. . . . We commonly say that a man is figured in such and such a space, whether on a wall or on a canvas, but in fact no soberly intelligent being would ever assert that a painted space puts us in the presence of the actual circumscription and delimitation

---

24. Su Shi, *Su Shi wenji*, 1: 203, "Miao yu you zhu, ji yu you shi" 廟欲有主, 祭欲有尸.
25. See, e.g., Ma Duanlin, *Wenxian tongkao*, 44.414; and Qiu Jun, *Daxue yanyibu*, 66.7b–8a.

of the model. A man is inscribed in the image that represents him, but he is not circumscribed by it.[26]

Nicephorus's arguments would have been unconvincing to literati such as Su
Shi, for whom images *did* limit the spirit and force it to crawl upon the
ground to receive its offerings.

Su Shi's writings on images influenced Zhu Xi, who was also concerned
with the question of images versus tablets; Zhu invoked Su's passage on images when he installed representations of Confucius in his White Deer Hollow Academy.[27] Zhu's preferred form of representation was a spirit tablet,
but he was required to make concessions. Zhu Xi outlined his views on appropriate depictions of Confucius in his "Treatise on Kneeling and Sitting in
the Context of Worship," which was usually better known as "Treatise on
the Sculpted Images in the White Deer Hall." In this document, Zhu Xi es-
chewed the installation of sculpted images in the ritual hall, citing as precedent the Tang *Rites of the Kaiyuan Era* (*Kaiyuan li* 開元禮), which specified
tablets instead of images, he claimed. (The *Kaiyuan li*, however, uses the generic terms *shen wei*, "spirit place," or *shen zuo* 神坐, "spirit seat," terms that
in themselves do not preclude the possibility that images were placed on
them). He attempted to do this just as he was leaving his official post in the
region in 1181, however, and his successor installed a standing image instead.
Zhu Xi implored (to no avail) that the image at least sit on the floor lest the
spirit of Confucius be forced to crawl to reach his food offerings.[28]

Failing in his efforts to set up tablets rather than images, Zhu tried at
least to eliminate Buddhist influences from figural depictions of Confucius.
He took careful pains to clarify what he meant by "sit" (*zuo*), since Confucius
would now be seated on the floor: in antiquity people sat on the upturned
soles of their feet with their knees folded under them. Ancient sitting, then,
was much more like kneeling and, one might infer, not at all like the Buddhist practice of sitting cross-legged with one's knees in front of one's body.
In fact, the commentary to the "Treatise" states that one of Zhu Xi's main
points was to show that "sitting in meditation" (*zuo chan* 坐 禪) is wrong, in
the sense that it has no classical antecedents.[29]

---

26. Baudinet, "Face of Christ," p. 158.

27. Zhu Xi, *Zhuzi daquan*, 46.7b.

28. Ibid., 68.1a–b, "Gui zuo bai shuo"; and Ma Duanlin, *Wenxian tongkao*, 44.414,
"Bailudian suxiang shuo" 白鹿殿塑像說. See also Chan, *Chu Hsi: Life and Thought*, p. 179.

29. Chan, *Chu Hsi: Life and Thought*, p. 179.

Zhu Xi's views on images in a ritual context are complex, for he did not always insist on tablets and was not against the use of figural images in all contexts. He believed that installing sculpted images on high altars when food offerings were placed on the ground was "without righteousness or principle" and voiced concern that the spirit in the public space of an academy altar thus be treated with respect.[30] But images in private contexts were another matter. Zhu Xi's son-in-law Huang Gan 黃幹 (1152–1221) in his biographical account of Zhu noted, for example, that his father-in-law made daily obeisance to a statue of Confucius. "In his quiet life," Huang wrote, "he would get up before dawn, put on a loose robe, a cloth cap, and square headed shoes. He would then worship in the family temple and also bowed before the image of Confucius."[31] Since this passage describes daily life, the image must have been installed in or near Zhu Xi's home. Zhu also planned to set up images of other figures in different contexts: after finding a sculpted image of the culture hero Fuxi 伏羲, the mythic figure to whom is attributed the trigrams of the *Book of Change*, he wanted to install it in his retreat at Wuyi Mountain in Fujian province.[32] Moreover, he once performed rites with a group of his disciples before a portrait of Zhou Dunyi 周敦頤 (1017–73), an indication that he was not averse to using images, presumably painted ones, in ritual contexts.[33]

Song Lian, then, who also exhibited different degrees of tolerance for different kinds of images, advocated nothing new in his request to use tablets instead of images. Ming Taizu planned a similar substitution in his formulations for renovating the temples of the city gods, or the spirits of the walls and moats. These powers oversaw activities in the spirit world within the space of a particular walled city and could be supplicated for protection from malevolent forces.[34] Taizu dispatched a directive to destroy the images of the spirits of the walls and moats throughout the realm and replace them with spirit tablets. Foreshadowing the fate that the images of Confucius were to experience over a hundred years later, the images were ordered ground into a paste that would then be used to plaster the walls of the temple, which in turn would be painted over with clouds and mountains. Taizu was not con-

30. Zhu Xi, *Zhuzi yulei*, 3.83.
31. Chan, *Chu Hsi: Life and Thought*, p. 18.
32. Zhu Xi, *Zhuzi daquan*, "Supplement," 6.19b; Chan, *Chu Hsi: Life and Thought*, p. 166.
33. Zhu Xi, *Zhuzi daquan*, 34.9b; Chan, *Chu Hsi: Life and Thought*, p. 145.
34. Qiu Jun, *Daxue yanyibu*, 61.12a.

tent merely to retire the images to storage or to disempower them by defacing them or by breaking off their limbs; instead he transformed them into another medium entirely.

Although Taizu's decrees offer little insight into his motivations for these actions, stele inscriptions by Song Na 宋訥 (1310–90), a libationer at the Imperial University, indicate the religious premises on which such decisions were justified: anthropomorphic images profaned the ineffable realm of invisible spirits. Song personally oversaw the renovation of at least one city-god temple, which he described in his stele inscription "On the Renovation of the Temple to the Walls and Moats in Yangcheng County,"[35] which recorded the renovations at the temple three years after Taizu's decree. Song Na established Taizu's relationship with the spirit world in the opening lines of the inscription. "As a dynasty arises," Song began, "so its institutional canons are established. The August Ming has received the mandate of heaven and pacified the ten thousand regions; in cherishing the myriad spirits, it has the Way."[36] Song thus demonstrated Taizu's reverence for the spirit world and the importance of that reverence for securing religious authority. Further praising Taizu, Song asserted that the temple's physical appearance was markedly improved by the renovations accompanying the shift from images to tablets. The old temple building, Song claimed, had a weak, cracked foundation that could no longer support the structure; after almost a year's work, however, the temple was in splendid condition and now had spirit tablets in place of the images. If the renovations at Yangcheng are representative of the activities in other cities, Taizu's directive to destroy the images of the city gods resulted in the wide-scale renewal of temple buildings.

When the construction was complete, Song Na was invited to compose a text to commemorate the occasion: a sacrificial report to the spirit world also recorded in stone for a human audience. His report was an apologia, based on historical precedent, for the use of spirit tablets. Song, unlike most scholars, presumed that ancient formulations regarding the use of either tablets or images were no longer known; he turned instead to Han and Tang precedents. When in the Han people revered such worthies as the Four Graybeards (four famous recluses from the early Han), they did so with spirit tablets, he claimed. Moreover, the Tang *Comprehensive Statutes* (*Tong dian* 通典) had also recorded that over the centuries, ancestral temples always had

---

35. Song Na, *Xiyin ji*, 7.1a–3a.
36. Ibid., 7.1a.

wooden tablets. It is known from the *Northern Histories*, he continued, that those who created people of clay (*ni ren* 泥人) or people of copper (*tong ren* 銅人) were severely punished. Thus, clay people were not used for sacrificial offerings in China proper.

Moving beyond these arguments from historical precedent, Song Na raised the issues of the uniformity of the iconographic representations and their resemblance to one another, the process by which the image is created, the relationship of the image to its creator, the skill of the artisan, the relationship of the image to the spirit represented, and the nature of spiritual beings. Spiritual beings are at the mercy of the skills of artisans, who are not, he implied, of the same class and kind as the spirits they depict and who in any case cannot convey the ineffable virtues of spirits in wood and clay.

Of the clay and wooden dummy-images (*ou xiang* 偶像) of the myriad spirits throughout the land, some are short in appearance, and some are tall; they are old or young, plump or thin, or beautiful or ugly, depending on the artisan's skill. But consider the very virtue (*de* 德) of spirits: what is "soundless and without smell" does not have [visible] traces. How could an artisan's handiwork depict this in clay or wood?[37]

The phrase "soundless and without smell" (*wusheng wuxiu* 無聲無臭), or "soundless and imperceptible," was an often-quoted passage recorded in both the "Decade of King Wen" of the *Odes* (Mao 235) and the last verse of the *Doctrine of the Mean* (33.6). The expression contained an implicit moral agenda, for its locus classicus in the *Odes* is a narrative that exhorts the ruler to model himself after the sage-kings of the past. It is the very intangibility of spirits that evidences the mysterious workings of Heaven, and a correlation is made between the intangible on the one hand and the charge of the moral imperative, or mandate (*ming*), on the other. The "Decade of King Wen," a narrative traditionally attributed to the Duke of Zhou (*Ode* no. 235), lauds the virtues of King Wen and exhorts the king's descendants and their officials to model themselves on him.

> The mandate is not easy.
> Do not bring ruin upon yourselves.
> Promulgate your righteousness and reputation widely,
> And consider how the [fallen] Yin dynasty fared with heaven.
> The workings of heaven on high

---

37. Ibid., 7.2a–b.

Have neither sound nor smell.
Comport yourselves and model yourselves upon King Wen,
And the ten thousand regions will trust you.

Holding on to the mandate was a precarious enterprise, and heaven provided no visible guidelines for maintaining it. To counter the uncertainty of heaven's ways, however, one could pattern oneself inwardly after the virtuous King Wen. This internal iconography is expressed outwardly through comportment or demeanor.

Intangibility and integrity are conjoined in the expression "soundless and without smell" in the concluding verse of the *Doctrine of the Mean* (33.6). Here Confucius belittles the superficiality of mere physical appearances and outward show and contrasts these with the subtlety of invisible integrity.

The *Odes* says, "I esteem your illustrious integrity, which boasts neither loud sounds nor colors" [Mao 241]. The master said, "Sounds and colors are of secondary importance for transforming the people. The *Odes* [Mao 260] says, 'Integrity is as light as a feather'; a hair, nevertheless, may be gauged in size. 'The workings of heaven on high have neither sound nor smell'—that is perfect."

Genuine values and transformative powers are found not in the sensible world but in the intangible quality of integrity, and a correlation is established between virtue and invisibility on the one hand and superficiality and appearance on the other. Here is one source of Song Na's uneasiness with sculpted images: they profane the invisible realm, and hence they profane the efficacy of integrity, which is finer and subtler than a strand of hair.

Moreover, Song Na was troubled by the contradictory images of the spirits: some were fat, some thin; some tall, some short. The dissimilarities were presumably evidence that the artisans never intended any of them to resemble a prototype. Resemblance was of crucial importance to Song, and to support his insistence on similitude he cited Cheng Yi's 程頤 (1033–1107) brief but extremely influential comments on the proper use of "shades"—*ying* 影, literally "reflections" or "shadows," a term used in the Song for ancestral portraits. These two-dimensional paintings of the deceased were displayed in shade halls (*ying tang* 影堂) or hung during rites performed for ancestral spirits. The term *ying* appeared in the *Book of Documents* in the expression *ying xiang* 影響 (the modern compound "to influence"); *ying* were the "echoes" or traces of visual phenomena, and *xiang* of sounds.[38] Conceptu-

---

38. *Book of Documents*, "Da Yu mo." See also Legge, *Shoo King*, p. 54.

ally, *ying* eventually encompassed the notions of shadow, reflection, and the soul-like visual emanations or doubles of human bodies projected effortlessly by the physical frame. The shade existed at the threshold between the visible and unseen worlds; it occupied this liminal space as early as the *Zhuangzi* in the famous conversation between Penumbra and Shade and also figured in Tao Yuanming's 陶淵明 (365–427) "Form, Shade, and Spirit" ("Xing ying shen" 形影神); in Ming popular culture, Bridal Du's shade was the protagonist in Tang Xianzu's 湯顯祖 (1550–1616) *The Peony Pavilion* (*Mudan ting* 牡丹庭).[39]

When or why ancestral portraits called *ying*, or shades, came into use in mourning rites is unknown, but they were definitely in use by Cheng Yi's time. Cheng Yi was ambivalent about the use of shades himself: he stated that wealthy families and gentry could establish halls for the shades; he nevertheless cautioned against using them in sacrificial offerings but gave no reason to support his admonition. Cheng Yi conceded that shades might be acceptable provided the portraits were literally not even a hair's breadth off. "If there is even one whisker too many," he asserted, "then it is not that person"[40]—such were Cheng's exacting requirements of similitude to a prototype. The created portrait had to be a precise replica of the physical body and face. Cheng Yi's close attention even to the placement of hairs on the face was not necessarily hyperbole; many extant ancestral portraits do in fact depict every single whisker of their subject. Moreover, in discussions of shades, the term "hair" (*mao* 毛) was often paired with its homonym "appearance" (*mao* 貌), which referred to surface appearance, particularly facial surfaces or the surface of other facades; the radical for "hair" appears in the character for "shade" itself. Confucius himself used the fineness of hair as a comparison with the even finer subtlety of integrity, as Song Na recalled in the passage quoted above. Song Na, then, by citing Cheng Yi, applied these exacting criteria of verisimilitude to the images of the city gods and trans-

---

39. For the passage in the *Zhuangzi*, see Mair, *Wandering on the Way*, pp. 24, 281–82; for Tao Yuanming, see Watson, *Columbia Book of Chinese Poetry*, pp. 126–28; for *The Peony Pavilion*, see Birch, trans., *The Peony Pavilion*. On the significance of the shadow in European art, see Baxandall, *Shadows*; and Stoichita, *A Short History*.

40. Cheng Yi, *Yi shu*, 22A.7a. For collections of reproductions of ancestral portraits, see Ma and Bao, *Zhonghua gexing zuxianxiang*; and Xiong, *Ming Qing guanxianghua*; for secondary studies, see Siggstedt, "Forms of Fate"; and *Zhongguo minjian xiaoxiang hua*, which includes a reproduction of a nineteenth-century painter's handbook.

ferred the standards of resemblance observed in ancestral portraits to statues of historical figures, the city gods.

Song Na lauded Taizu's removal of the images of the city gods, claiming that he thus washed away several hundred years of deluded customs. Rejoicing in the renewal of a sense of awe and mystery toward the spirit world, he remarked approvingly that now the approaches of the spirits are, in the words of the *Odes*, "unfathomable" (*bu ke du si* 不可度思).[41] Unfathomability had since classical times been one of the hallmarks of spiritual beings (*shen* 神), ethereal entities that abide in an invisible realm just beyond the periphery of ordinary understanding; their presence is not seen but is sensed when they are evoked to descend to the visible world of rites and music. These two worlds were separated not by distance but by the limits of apprehension, for participants in a sacrifice may unexpectedly experience spirits floating close by, just above their heads. As described in classical texts, spirits are elusive and ineffable (*nan ming* 難明) and are undetectable by the senses. Their contours are circumscribed primarily with negatives: they are without form (*wuxing* 無形), sound (*wusheng* 無聲), or smell (*wuxiu* 無臭); they are subtle and mysterious and are neither there (*wei you* 爲有) nor not there (*wei wu* 爲無). Although bodiless, they are possessed of moral character, and their distinguishing marks, as the *Zuo Commentary* states, are the (invisible) qualities of intelligence, moral uprightness, and consistency or oneness.[42] The spirits' invisibility nevertheless belied their presence, for during sacrificial offerings, "from the vastness, it is as if they are floating above one, as if they are on one's left and right"[43] (*Mean* 16.3). This unfathomable hierophany, or manifestation of the sacred, occurred during sacrificial offerings and was directly apprehended by the sacrificer. Rejecting concrete depiction of undepictable phenomena, Song Na thus advocated the non-figural spirit tablets over anthropomorphic images.

Invisibility and non-figuration were powers in themselves. In a poem Song Na wrote especially for the temple, he associated the presence of the new tablets with the unlimited powers of protection that now encircled the city with virtual walls of metal and moats of boiling water and that rid the city of troublesome manifestations of unidentified forces: "Tablets of wood / Walls of metal / Moats of boiling water / Protect the clouds and moun-

---

41. *Odes*, Mao 256; *Doctrine of the Mean*, 16.4.
42. *Zuo Commentary*, Duke Zhuang 32.
43. *Doctrine of the Mean*, 16.3.

tains."[44] Here Song evoked the powers of the Five Phases of wood, metal, water, fire, and earth: the wood of the tablets, the walls of metal, the water of the moats, the fire to boil the water, and the earth of the mountains. Water overcame earth as the images were dissolved into mud and re-emerged as clouds and mountains.

Tablets were also preferred over images in the Confucian temple. Several years after the images of the city gods were destroyed, spirit tablets were installed in the temple to Confucius in the Imperial University (Guozijian 國子監) completed in 1382 in Nanjing. Since the university was a new structure, no statues of Confucius were destroyed to make way for the tablets. Song Na performed ritual libations at the temple of the Imperial University when it opened in the summer of 1382 and described the ritual activities there in his stele inscription "The Imperial University Constructed by Order of the Great Ming."[45] This document provides insights into the ideology behind the construction of the temple and illustrates how Taizu drew upon the values of the classical literary tradition, used them to bolster his self-styled image as a purveyor of the *daotong* 道統, or the "transmission of the Way," and incorporated these values into the physical space of the building. By claiming to transmit the Way, or Dao, of traditional culture and mores, Taizu accrued to himself the power and legitimacy of those ideals.

Song Na approved of the aniconic tenor of the Imperial University, noting that "from the Master [Confucius] on down, there were no images in either clay or pigment; for sacrifices, spirit tablets were used. Several hundred years of old formulations were thus eliminated."[46] By eliminating tablets, Taizu created a new aniconic dynastic style for the rites to the premier sages and teachers. Both Song Na and Song Lian asserted that the sacrificial tradition of antiquity used tablets rather than images; Taizu, by re-establishing that perceived tradition, could claim credibility as a transmitter of the norms of ancient times. Taizu might have found earlier aniconic precedents in the *Rites of Zhou*, a text that greatly influenced his model of governance; the *Rites'* descriptions of commemorative rites to teachers at the Zhou academies made no mention of the use of images.

In the new Imperial University at Nanjing, written inscriptions with the names and titles of spirits replaced the images on the altars. The "textuality"

---

44. Song Na, *Xiyin ji*, 7.3a.
45. Ibid., 7.8a–10b.
46. Ibid., 7.9a.

of the new university did not end there, however. The structure of the building itself and the rituals enacted there emphasized the visual display and performance of the written word—specifically, the words of the classical texts of the literati tradition. Each of the university's 801 ornate pillars bore lines from the Classics. Moreover, erudites held copies of the Classics when they made ritual presentations, and other officials lectured on them after the proceedings. Taizu used the display of classical learning to promote his image as a modern-day counterpart to the sage-rulers of the Three Dynasties. Song Na's inscription intertwines the vocabulary of the transmission of the Way of Confucius with the vocabulary of the rule of emperors and kings; such concepts as heavenly principle, the mind of humankind, and the transmission of the Way were associated with the august axial standard (*huang ji* 皇極) of the "Great Plan" in the *Documents*. Song wrote:

The Way of Confucius has been transmitted for ten thousand generations, and when emperors and kings arise, they first build an imperial university. Through study, one supports heavenly principle and purifies the mind of humankind; through it, the august axial standard effects great transformations, conveys the Way, and clarifies mores. . . . The Sage Son of Heaven presides as sovereign, continuing the transmission of the way from Yao, Shun, and Yu, Tang, Wen, and Wu. He has built the university and established standards from high antiquity.[47]

Song drew a parallel between the transmission of learning from Confucius and the transmission of rule from the emperors and kings of antiquity. These two modes of transmitted authority merged in the space of the Imperial University, the place where the imperium shaped students who, Song Na claimed, would quite literally become pillars of the state (*zhen gan* 楨幹). By the time they completed their studies, they would have internalized the classical inscriptions on the wooden pillars of the university.

Song Na's approbation of the aniconic arrangement of the new university building did not stem from a hatred of images; he was in fact a noted connoisseur of art, and his funerary inscriptions state that his sole enjoyment was admiring famous works of painting and calligraphy.[48] Temple statues were not, however, judged by the same aesthetic criteria as works on paper and silk, and it is extremely unlikely that Song Na would have conceived of temple images and fine ink paintings as occupying a common artistic ground.

---

47. Ibid., 7.10b.
48. Ibid., *Supplement*, 7a, 11b.

Nor did his support for the absence of images of Confucius stem from bias against the literati tradition, for he was said to be "intoxicated by the Six Classics of the Duke of Zhou and Confucius."[49] Song Na perceived the new aniconicity of the university as a return to an earlier age that adhered more closely to the practices of the sages themselves.

Unlike Taizu, his successors did not promote aniconism in either temples to the city god or temples to Confucius. In 1410, when the temple to Confucius in the Imperial University was renovated, the painting and sculpting of the costumes of the sages was ordered to conform to "older formulations."[50] The phrasing of the passage suggests that older images (perhaps dating to the Yuan) were repainted and reworked, not that new sculptures were created. Not all images, then, had been destroyed.

The expression "old formulations" presumably refers to Yuan iconolatry. The writings of Yuan literati indicate that the use of statues of the Sage in sacrificial contexts was widely accepted and even encouraged. Such images were often described as capable of leading the beholder closer to the virtues propounded by Confucius. For example, Wang Yun 王惲 (1227–1304), in describing the renovation of the temple to Confucius temple in Taiping county in 1271, noted with approval the artistry of the "newly painted portraits (xiao xiang 肖像) of the seventy masters on the wall."[51] His descriptions in another essay of the elegant attire and composed demeanor of the sages and worthies are immediately followed by exhortations to teach people the ways of the Three Dynasties to prevent them from being lost to perdition; the implication is that the images themselves were a medium for accomplishing precisely that.[52]

The "Yuan ways" were not easily eradicated. In the 1470s, Zou Gan 鄒幹 (fl. Chenghua era, 1465–88) attempted to resurrect Taizu's aniconic precedent in the Imperial University in Nanjing and advocated applying it to the temple to Confucius at the newer university in the new northern capital of Beijing, where Chengzu (r. 1403–24) had relocated the capital in the early 1420s. People there still could not bear, he said, to rid themselves completely of Yuan ways.[53] Zou equated "Yuan ways" with iconolatry, yet neither he

49. Ibid., 7a.
50. Qin Huitian, Wuli tongkao, 120.7276.
51. Wang Yun, Qiujian ji, 36.15a.
52. Ibid., 52.15b.
53. Qin Huitian, Wuli tongkao, 120.7279–81.

nor other Ming scholars pointed out that the practice of revering images of Confucius, far from being a Mongol Yuan innovation, was clearly documented in Tang and Song histories.

So in the 1480s, Yuan ways were still in effect in the temple to Confucius in the Imperial University in Beijing. The scholar and later grand secretary Qiu Jun 邱濬 (1421–95) attacked the use of images there in his *Supplement to the Extended Meaning of the Great Learning (Daxue yanyibu 大學衍義補)*, an encyclopedic handbook for formulating and interpreting governmental policy.[54] The *Supplement* was widely distributed in the fifteenth and sixteenth centuries and was consulted by those preparing for the imperial examinations, and Qiu's proposals to reformulate the sacrificial offerings to the sages of the literati tradition were influential as far as Korea and Japan. Building on ideas expressed earlier by Cheng Yi, Song Na, Song Lian, and Ming Taizu, Qiu Jun focused on promoting the destruction of the images of Confucius in the Imperial University.[55] The essay provided much of the text for the 1530 memorial, described by Huang Chin-shing in his chapter in this volume (pp. 267–96), that officially prohibited the use of images and florid posthumous titles in the temple to Confucius.

Qiu Jun, like Song Na and Song Lian, believed the sacrifices of antiquity were aniconic rituals; in ancient times, he asserted, the worship of the Chinese sages was conducted with spirit tablets, not images. He recounted the history of the worship of the sages and worthies from Zhou times until Taizu's reign; in his view, the evidence showed that the Ming rites had departed from Zhou precedents. The rites should be reformulated in the light of ancient usages. Qiu also appealed to a xenophobic argument: the practice of using images in sacrificial rites, he claimed, had been introduced to China by Buddhists. This association of iconism with Buddhism was something of an innovation, and here Qiu differed from Song Lian, who both espoused aniconic sacrifices to Confucius and admired Buddhist images.

Qiu's vision of a golden aniconic past might not be unrelated to his aversion to the foreign culture of Buddhism. David Freedberg's studies of the "myth of aniconism" in the historiography of Western art may have some relevance here. Freedberg describes a "deep and persistent historiographic

---

54. For Qiu Jun's writings on the principles of sacrificial offerings, see Sommer, "Ch'iu Chun's *On the Conduct of Sacrificial Offerings*."

55. Qiu Jun, *Daxue yanyibu*, 65.12a–14a.

myth" in the modern study of art history (a myth aided by the histo-
riographical traditions of particular religious traditions themselves) that
"certain cultures, usually monotheistic or primitively pure cultures, have no
images at all, or no figurative imagery, or no images of the deity."[56] Freedberg
shows that many purportedly aniconic traditions do in fact employ figural
art and asks why the notion of aniconism persists in the historiography of
Western art. Claims of aniconism and abstention from the use of images,
Freedberg states, "are always based on belief in the moral and ethical superiority of spirituality and divinity that is abstracted from matter rather than
presented in or represented by it."[57] Freedberg also associates arguments for
aniconism in part with claims for cultural superiority over other traditions:
"If we can show that our culture at least began by being aniconic," he writes,
"then our sense of superiority over purportedly less spiritualized cultures is
affirmed."[58]

This observation might well be applied to literati such as Qiu Jun who
asserted that the aniconic, golden days of Chinese antiquity were spiritually
superior to the foreign tradition of Buddhism. "Setting up sculpted images
was unknown in antiquity and began only with the coming of Buddhism to
the Middle Kingdom," wrote Qiu Jun. "It is not surprising that the heterodox teachings use them."[59] The popularity of such arguments in the early
Ming is perhaps associated with attempts by some scholars to remove
northern and Central Asian influences, largely Buddhist and especially Tibetan Buddhist influences, introduced during the Yuan from the Chinese
cultural mainstream and to return to a culturally "purer" tradition. Qiu in
fact stated that he sought to turn away from the old ways of the Yuan people.
He decried the end-of-the-year exorcisms conducted by monks from the
western regions who resided in the capital. These rites entailed carrying a
white canopy around the city and were most likely invocations of the Tibetan Buddhist divinity Ushnishashitatapattra, a divinity who extirpates
baleful influences and whose iconographic emblem is a white parasol. Qiu
Jun had reason to worry about Buddhist influences in the capital. Some
early Ming emperors were indeed enamored of Tibetan Buddhism: they invited Tibetan Buddhist masters to court, participated in initiation rites, and

---

56. Freedberg, *Power of Images*, p. 54.
57. Ibid., p. 65.
58. Ibid., p. 60.
59. Qiu Jun, *Daxue yanyibu*, 65.12a.

sponsored the production of mandalas, paintings of Tibetan Buddhist deities, and other ritual art.[60]

Qiu Jun expressed his distaste for Buddhism in other essays. Besides the Imperial University, Qiu attempted to eliminate Buddhist images from a temple that he believed manipulated folk piety with graphic scenes of hell. People were being misled by accounts that the followers of Shakyamuni gave of hell, Qiu stated, and the frightening images on Buddhist altars should be removed for the sake of the common people. For these followers "say that when people die, their ethereal souls must pass through a temple of hell and undergo torture. There [in the temple] you will find twenty-four altars full of images. These accounts are not the least bit canonical. I beg that the officials concerned get rid of them [the images], so that they do not delude the world and deceive the people."[61] Qiu rejected the Buddhist cosmology of heavens and hells, and he castigated the followers of the foreign-born Shakyamuni for deceiving people with visions of physical suffering and retribution. In contrast, the literati cosmology provided few descriptions of an afterlife, much less graphic scenes of carnal torment, and espoused self-cultivation rather than fear as a method of inner development. Qiu's exhortation to remove the images, images that must have been calculated to frighten pilgrims into pious repentance, reflected his concern for the undue suffering and mental torment the statues instilled in the unsophisticated observer. In his view, then, Buddhism was an ethically and spiritually inferior culture, and this inferiority was clearly manifested in its temple art.

This critique of Buddhist images was part of Qiu Jun's overall project of reinstituting the "glorious rites of antiquity" and eradicating the "evil arts of heterodoxy" that he believed imperiled the realm.[62] In his imagination, the "evil arts" encompassed a diverse and vaguely defined array of cultic practices and folkways that had over the centuries attached themselves to the classical tradition and obscured it, such as conducting spirit writing sessions, performing incantations, sculpting images, and even burning incense. He believed many of these practices had originally been promulgated by the followers of Shakyamuni and then appropriated by the adherents of Laozi. To

---

60. Ibid., 64.13b–14a. I thank Nima Dorje for his explanation of the probable significance of the white canopy in this rite. For the popularity of Tibetan Buddhism in the early Ming court, see Sperling, "Early Ming Policy."

61. Qiu Jun, *Daxue yanyibu*, 61.9b–10a.

62. Ibid., 63.18a.

his mind, these charlatans "exploited the spirits to wreak havoc"; they were people who made offerings of "vulgar comestibles and unholy flavorings" to spirits they should not worship.[63] His proposals to destroy the clay images of Confucius in the Imperial University in Beijing stemmed from this same agenda. Using sculpted images of Confucius in sacrificial offerings, he believed, had become so widespread by Ming times that the numinous way of spiritual beings had become obscured. Taking Taizu's decree ordering the destruction of images of the spirits of the walls and moats as a precedent, Qiu advocated the destruction of the images of the sages in the Confucian temple at the Imperial University, "whereby their clay would be used to plaster the walls, which would then be painted with scenes of clouds and mountains."[64]

The motivations for Qiu's iconoclasm become clearer when we explore his understanding of the nature of spiritual beings that the images purportedly represented. His dislike of images stemmed from the premise that a superficial perspective on the material world inhibited a greater understanding of the invisible powers of integrity; the physical form of a concrete figure impeded an effective apprehension of its spirit prototype. In the performance of sacrificial offerings, Qiu Jun focused on the development of internal moral qualities, not on external physical objects. Although he conceded, for example, that ritual objects such as bronzes, silks, and animals were necessary accompaniments to the rites for communicating with spiritual beings, he asserted that these were primarily outward expressions of inner qualities of the mind. "The Way of sacrificial offerings," he claimed, "is called humanity, filiality, sincerity, and reverence; that is all."[65] Qiu's unfiguring and disembodiment of the spirit of Confucius from its profane entrapment in clay forms was thus paralleled by his program to encourage people to embody these values within themselves. Perhaps he was influenced by Xunzi's assertion that the learning of petty people enters their ears but exits quickly through their mouths; the short space between ears and mouth prevents that learning from affecting the rest of the body significantly. The learning of noble people, however, enters their ears and minds and spreads throughout their four limbs, transforming them completely and manifesting itself in their actions.[66]

---

63. Ibid., 54.10a and 55.13b, respectively.

64. Ibid., 65.13a.

65. Ibid., 55.17a.

66. *Xunzi*, "Quan xue"; Wang Xianqian, *Xunzi jijie*, pp. 12–13.

Qiu's vision of the spirit world, like Song Na's, was drawn from the *Doctrine of the Mean*, the *Book of Odes*, and the *Zuo Commentary*, and it incorporated virtually nothing of popular devotional beliefs in the gods and goddesses of temples and shrines. Unlike folk temple deities, the spirits of Qiu's cosmology are ineffable and unfathomable. "The principles of ghosts and spirits are subtle and mysterious," Qiu stated; "they are difficult to describe in words. One may think they are there—one looks for them, but they are formless; one listens for them, but they give no sound."[67] They have no distinguishing signs comparable to the Buddha's long earlobes or the temple goddess's regalia. For Qiu the operations of heaven are the source of all sacred power, and he contrasts heaven's invisible, mysterious ways with the coarse visibility of crafted images of temple gods and goddesses. The worship of these images, he states, is "most certainly not the way of the 'spiritual and numinous' and the 'soundless and without smell.'"[68]

Qiu Jun did not believe that images had power or life and stated that even those who revered sculpted images knew the figures were merely inanimate composites of earthly dross. "Suppose that someone has already taken up some clay and made an image," Qiu posited. "They treat it as if it were a sage or worthy, but as soon as it breaks they consider it just dust and dregs." Even quality workmanship could not enliven images. For "even if they should be superbly done," he continued, "how can they convey the sense of the fullness of life?"[69] His insistence that an image completely mirror a living prototype indicates his unwillingness to accord an image any metaphoric or symbolic value. Images of the same spiritual being vary considerably, he stated, building on a phrase from Song Na, for "from one place to another, none are the same. Their appearance—whether they are tall or short, fat or thin, old or young, handsome or ugly—depends entirely on the quality or lack thereof of the workmanship."[70] If the images resembled their prototype, he implied, then all of them would resemble one another. Their dissimilarity belies any such relationship and indicates that they are merely the arbitrarily shaped works of human hands.

Again building on the arguments of Song Na, Qiu applied Cheng Yi's criteria for judging ancestral portraits to the sculpted images of the Confu-

---

67. Qiu Jun, *Daxue yanyibu*, 55.16a.
68. Ibid., 65.12b.
69. Ibid., 65.12b–13a.
70. Ibid., 65.12b.

cian sages: "If a likeness (*mao*) made by someone who has seen the subject in person does not resemble (*xiao*) that person, and if it can thus be considered not to be that person if it is only a hair's breadth off, then how much more is this true for one made by an artisan whose handiwork relies only on his own imagination!" Given this line of thinking, the possibility of creating valid likenesses of the sages of antiquity disappears. If someone should attempt to model the sages, he continued, then "what are sculpted are only human shapes (*ren xing* 人形), that is all. How could these be the bequeathed likenesses (*yi mao* 遺貌) of the true sages and worthies?"[71] The expression "bequeathed likenesses" usually referred to portraits of the deceased made at or near the time of death; the Ming statues of Confucius were clearly not this type of image. Such shapes modeled in human form are then arbitrary creations that have no prototype, and every image of a spirit, Qiu Jun implied, must have a prototype: the physical body of the spirit represented. The lack of a connection between the images of the sages in the Imperial University and the actual bodies of their prototypes thus rendered them invalid. The image of Confucius was not a representation of Confucius's body; it was an entirely artificial body, a representation of no body, an arbitrary creation that, in Qiu's words, was nothing more than the product of an artisan's imagination. Such arbitrary images, unlike visions seen in pre-sacrificial vigils or personators, provided no access to the spirit world.

Qiu's iconoclasm did not extend to all religious images indiscriminately; it was directed primarily at the images of the sages in the Imperial University and not at the statues in the temples to Confucius in the commanderies and cities of the realm. Qiu feared that eliminating the images in local temples would disturb the common people. Many literati perceived the folkways of the common people as misguided but innocent; Qiu held popular piety and state-level rites to different standards.

His own protestations to the contrary, however, Qiu did implicitly believe anthropomorphic images possessed identities of their own. Qiu professed concern that in bowing before three-dimensional images of Confucian sages at the temple in the Imperial University, the sovereign was doing obeisance to images of men who, no matter how worthy, had nevertheless been commoners in their own time. It was acceptable for the emperor to bow to the sage Confucius, but bowing to lesser luminaries was a breach of title and

---

71. Ibid., 65.13b.

rank. Moreover, Qiu Jun feared, the spirits of the sages and worthies in heaven would themselves be somewhat uneasy about the emperor's actions. His objection implies that he did consider these images to be more than just dust and mud: they were in some sense physical bodies, bodies representative enough of their originals that they were tainted by the commoner status of their once-living prototypes. Even if these statues were replaced by spirit tablets, as Qiu Jun wanted, then the emperor would be bowing before the tablets of commoners. How, one might ask, is that less objectionable than bowing before their images? That Qiu considered bowing before figural art objectionable indicates that he himself ultimately considered the figures somehow enlivened or imbued with the presence of their prototypes.

To further his own iconoclastic arguments, Qiu Jun reminded the reigning Ming ruler of the filial imperative of following the injunctions of his own founding ancestor, Taizu. In Qiu's opinion, Taizu "brilliantly saw through the mistakes that had been perpetuated for a thousand years. Under his rule, from Confucius on down, there were neither sculpted nor painted images, and spirit tablets were used in sacrificing. . . . Ah! Wonderful!"[72] In addition, Qiu also cited Taizu's edict on the destruction of images of the spirits of the walls and moats. The destruction of the images of these spirits (who represented powerful natural forces) more than warranted a similar destruction at the Imperial University, where the images were sculptures of ordinary human beings. Qiu regretted that Taizu's edict had not been implemented in the Beijing temple, which was apparently full of images. This practice Qiu attributed to the old ways of the Yuan people. He believed, nevertheless, that had Taizu's edicts been made known in the Zhengtong era (1436–49) when the temple and university were being restored, they would have been followed. In conclusion, Qiu implored the emperor to follow his ancestor's decree and reform the "vulgar practices" that had been perpetuated for a thousand years.

Qiu wanted not only to replace images with spirit tablets but also to change the content of the inscriptions on the tablets themselves, for he was no more tolerant of textual metaphors than visual ones. He proposed replacing the exaggerated posthumous titles and ennoblements that had been granted to Confucius and others over the centuries with simpler titles that bespoke their actual accomplishments. He attributed the practice of bequeathing fanciful posthumous titles to the "usurper" Wang Mang 王莽

---

72. Ibid., 65.12b.

(r. CE 9–23) and opined that "of course the spirit of the Sage [Confucius] in heaven did not accept this [title]."[73] Qiu Jun disagreed with the Yuan decision of 1307 to add the two characters "great accomplishment" (da cheng 大成) to Confucius's list of honorifics; in this Qiu criticized even Mencius, who first used the term to describe Confucius (Mencius 5B.2.6). This was the language of rhetoric and metaphor, he stated, and "in antiquity, when using posthumous names, one had to use genuinely appropriate words, and metaphorical expressions were not employed." He continued, "Mencius took the commencing and terminating of musical performances and placed them parallel to the perfection of sagacity and wisdom, and he used this as a metaphor for Confucius's sagacity. Now this is rhetorical language, not genuine accomplishment. Adding these two characters . . . adds nothing significant in terms of his sagelike accomplishments."[74] Qiu Jun preferred the complete elimination of superficial honorifics in favor of a genuine return to the Way. How, then, would he address the Sage? "It is said that after a million generations have passed, he will just be called 'the first master, Confucius' [xianshi Kongzi 先師孔子]. This is because the reason a person is revered and worshipped for a thousand generations lies in the Way, not in noble rank or appellations."[75] The basic principle underlying Qiu's views on both images and honorifics is that they are obstacles to a direct personal understanding of the subtleties of the Way. Arbitrarily shaped images and imaginary titles obscure and obfuscate. To circumscribe the Way or the ineffable nature of spiritual beings with images is to circumscribe the incircumscribable, to borrow the language of the Byzantine iconoclasts. Metaphor and allusion distort; verisimilitude perfects. What was important was to shape oneself after ancient models and embody filiality, humanity, and righteousness within, not to worship them as "idols" from without.

Qiu Jun's views on sculpted images were well known and were incorporated, either in full or in part, into such later works as the Chunmingmeng yulu 春明夢餘錄 by Sun Chengze 孫承澤 (1593–1675) and the Wuli tongkao 五禮通考 by Qin Huitian 秦蕙田 (1702–64).[76] Qiu's proposals for the elimination of both sculpted images and florid posthumous names were not im-

---

73. Ibid., 66.6b.

74. Ibid., 66.5a–b.

75. Ibid., 65.6b.

76. See Sun Chengze, Chunmingmeng yulu, 21.13b–14a; and Qin Huitian, Wuli tongkao, 120.7089, respectively.

plemented in his own lifetime, but they surfaced again and were adopted during the reign of the Jiajing emperor (r. 1521–66) following a memorial of 1530 by Grand Secretary Zhang Fujing 張孚敬 (also known as Zhang Cong 張璁, 1475–1539), who incorporated large segments of Qiu's arguments wholesale into his text.[77] The Jiajing arguments add nothing new to earlier Ming opposition to images of Confucius, although the actual implementation of them was novel. The Jiajing emperor changed Confucius's title to "Perfected Sage, Premier Teacher, Confucius" (*zhisheng xianshi Kongzi* 致聖 先師孔子), which is still somewhat longer than Qiu's recommended "Premier Teacher, Confucius." It is significant that the images of Confucius at the ancestral shrines at Qufu were exempted from this decree, for in Confucius's ancestral home there existed a genuine connection between spirit and sacrificer.

VULGAR ICONOCLASM?

The decree to destroy the images was officially promulgated in 1530, but its legacy in the Qing is difficult to assess. Some scholars, such as Gu Yanwu 顧炎武 (1613–82), approved of the movement to unfigure Confucius and restore the ineffable realms of the spiritual and numinous. Others, however, held on secretly to the concrete forms of clay and wood. Gu recounted with disapproval one of the ingenious ways people devised to circumvent the decree. "In the ninth year of the Jiajing era [1530], it was decreed that the posthumous ennoblements and sculpted images of the Premier Teacher, Confucius, be eliminated. Some authorities disregarded this and in many cases built walls in the main halls of the temples, placed the images within them, and hid them from view. Truly, such vulgar customs are difficult to fathom!"[78]

Hence it is with no small irony that iconodules who entered the hall were thus compelled to pay obeisance to what was invisible, as the new barrier walls concealed images they could no longer see; iconoclasts who entered, however, unwittingly revered images they thought no longer existed. Gu's account of this phenomena was so well known that it found its way into the eighteenth-century *Encyclopedia of Illustrations and Documents from Ancient and*

---

77. Gu Yingtai, *Mingshi jishi benmo*, 51.70–83. See also the discussion of this issue by Huang Chin-shing in his chapter in this volume, pp. 270–77.

78. Gu Yanwu, *Yuanchaoben Rizhi lu*, 18.429.

Modern Times (*Gujin tushu jicheng* 古今圖書集成), where it was included with tales of strange and bizarre images.[79] The relegation of images of Confucius to the category of the strange and the bizarre by the early eighteenth century, when the encyclopedia was compiled, suggests that the removal of images had been quite thorough.

In private academies and temples to Confucius in twentieth-century Taiwan, however, iconolatry is far from dead—although official temples to Confucius are another matter. The active private Confucian Temple in Ilan City, for example, contains two carved statues of Confucius that receive regular offerings of incense from the many students in attendance. (The official temple to Confucius in that city still uses tablets and is, by comparison, an inactive historical relic.) In an innovative modern conjunction of text, image, and body, the spirit tablets of Confucius at the private Ilan temple— and even at official Confucian temples throughout the island—are covered with photocopies of the student identification cards necessary for taking college entrance examinations. The duplicate faces on these photocopies (*ying yin* 影印, literally "shade prints," the common term for photocopies) continually implore the Sage for academic help on behalf of their human prototypes. And iconolatry still survives in the literature of popular apologetic Confucianism: in a modern journal dedicated to the study of Confucius and Mencius, an essay on images of Confucius written by a latter-day iconophile labels the iconoclasts Song Lian and Qiu Jun as pernicious and vulgar scholars.[80]

The Ming destruction of images of Confucius still influences the current iconography of official Confucian temples in modern Taiwan, however. There the transformation from images into words that took place in the Ming is still visible. In the main building and east and west halls of the Confucian temple in Tainan, for example, the only visual distractions from the "spiritual and numinous" are the names of the sages and scholars on the spirit tablets that range the temple halls. In an auxiliary shrine room to the east, the entire north wall is taken up by a calligraphic inscription of the *Great Learning*, which is now the main icon of that chamber. The spirit tablets in the main hall are devoid of iconographic clues that might directly identify the spirit represented. Buddhist images, by comparison, are covered with iconographic symbols that communicate the identity of the image even

---

79. *Gujin tushu jicheng, ce* 493, *juan* 47.36b.
80. Huang Shaozu, "Kongmiao muzhu hu," p. 42.

to the illiterate. Even the most literate visitor to the temple to Confucius, however, would be unable to identify the spirits there without the considerable number of written texts that give a meaningful historical context to the names inscribed on the tablets. What is signified by the names is not so much the particular identities of the sages and worthies themselves, but the canon of learning they transmitted. The textual inscriptions, unlike the images, did not limit or circumscribe their prototypes to the statues that represented them; rather, they signified the larger warp and weft (*jing* 經) of values contained within the Classics.

WORKS CITED

Baudinet, Marie-José. "The Face of Christ, the Form of the Church." In *Fragments for a History of the Human Body*, ed. Michel Feher, 1: 149–59. New York: Zone Books, 1989.

Baxandall, Michael. *Shadows and Enlightenment*. New Haven: Yale University Press, 1995.

Beijing tushuguan cang huaxiang tapen huibian 北京圖書館藏畫像拓本匯編 (Rubbings from the collections of the Beijing Library). 10 vols. Beijing: Shumu wenxian chubanshe, 1993.

Belting, Hans. *Likeness and Presence: A History of the Image Before the Era of Art*. Chicago: University of Chicago Press, 1994.

Birch, Cyril, trans. *The Peony Pavilion*. Bloomington: Indiana University Press, 1980.

Bynum, Caroline Walker. *Fragmentation and Redemption: Essays on Gender and the Human Body in Medieval Religion*. New York: Zone Books, 1991.

———. *The Resurrection of the Body in Western Christianity, 200–1336*. New York: Columbia University Press, 1995.

Camille, Michael. *The Gothic Idol: Ideology and Image-making in Medieval Art*. Cambridge, Eng.: Cambridge University Press, 1989.

Camporesi, Piero. *The Incorruptible Flesh: Bodily Mutation and Mortification in Religion and Folklore*. Cambridge, Eng.: Cambridge University Press, 1988.

———. *Juice of Life: The Symbolic and Magic Significance of Blood*. New York: Continuum, 1995.

Carr, Michael. "Personation of the Dead in Ancient China." *Computational Analysis of Asian and African Languages* 24 (1985): 1–107.

Chan, Wing-tsit. *Chu Hsi: Life and Thought*. Hong Kong: Chinese University Press, 1987.

Chan, Wing-tsit, trans. *Neo-Confucian Terms Explained: Ch'en Ch'un's "Pei-hsi tzu-i."* New York: Columbia University Press, 1986.

———. *A Source Book in Chinese Philosophy*. Princeton: Princeton University Press, 1963.

Chen Chun 陳淳. *Beixi ziyi* 北溪字義 (Neo-Confucian terms explained). Wenyuange siku quanshu 文淵閣四庫全書 ed.

Chen Hao 陳澔. *Li ji ji shuo* 禮記集說 (Collected commentaries on the *Record of Rites*). Shanghai: Guji chubanshe, 1987.

Cheng Yi 程頤. *Yi shu* 遺書 (Surviving works). Sibu beiyao 四部備要 ed.

Du You 杜佑. *Tong dian* 通典 (Encyclopedic history of institutions). 5 vols. Beijing: Zhonghua shuju, 1988.

Dupont, Florence. "The Emperor-God's Other Body." In Michel Feher, ed., *Fragments for a History of the Human Body*, ed. Michel Feher, 3: 396–419. New York: Zone Books, 1989.

Ershiwu shi 二十五史 (Twenty-five dynastic histories). 12 vols. Shanghai: Guji chubanshe, 1994.

Faure, Bernard. "Substitute Bodies in Chan/Zen Buddhism." In *Religious Reflections on the Human Body*, ed. Jane Marie Law, pp. 211–29. Bloomington: Indiana University Press, 1995.

Feher, Michel, ed. *Fragments for a History of the Human Body*. 3 vols. New York: Zone Books, 1989.

Foulk, T. Griffith, and Robert H. Sharf. "On the Ritual Use of Ch'an Portraiture in Medieval China." *Cahiers d'Extrême-Asie* 7 (1993–94): 149–219.

Freedberg, David. *The Power of Images: Studies in the History and Theory of Response*. Chicago: University of Chicago Press, 1989.

Gong Yanxing 宮衍興 and Wang Zhiyu 王致玉. *Kongmiao zhushen kao* 孔廟諸神考 (On the spirits in the temple to Confucius). Ji'nan: Shandong youyi chubanshe, 1994.

Gu Yanwu 顧炎武. *Yuanchaoben Rizhilu* 原抄本日知錄 (A manuscript copy of the *Record of Things Learned Day by Day*). Taipei: Wenshizhe chubanshe, 1979.

Gu Yingtai 谷應泰. *Mingshi jishi benmo* 明史紀事本末 (The *Ming History* topically arranged). Wanyou wenku huiyao 萬有文庫薈要 ed. Taipei: Taiwan Shangwu yinshuguan, 1965.

Gujin tushu jicheng 古今圖書集成 (Encyclopedia of illustrations and documents from ancient and modern times). Shanghai: Zhonghua shuju, 1934.

Gutmann, Joseph. *The Image and the Word: Confrontations in Judaism, Christianity and Islam*. Missoula, Mont.: Scholars Press, 1977.

Harper, Donald. "Resurrection in Warring States Popular Religion." *Taoist Resources* 5, no. 2 (1994): 13–28.

Hu Xinsheng 胡新生. "Zhoudai jisizhong de lishi li ji qi zongjiao yiyi" 周代祭祀中的立尸禮及其宗教意義 (Rites of personation in Zhou sacrificial offerings and their religious significance). *Shijie zongjiao yanjiu* 4 (1990): 14–25.

Huang Chin-shing 黃進興. *You ru sheng yu: quanli, xinyang, yu zhengdangxing* 優入聖域: 權力, 信仰, 與正當性 (Entering the master's sanctuary: power, belief, and legitimacy in traditional China). Taipei: Yunchen wenhua chubanshe, 1994.

Huang Shaozu 黃紹祖. "Kongmiao muzhu hu? Suxiang hu?" 孔廟木主乎? 塑像乎? (Tablets or sculpted images for the Confucian temple?). *Kong Meng yuekan* 22, no. 9 (1984): 39–45.

Huang Yongquan 黃涌泉. *Li Gonglin shengxiantu shiko* 李公麟聖賢圖石刻 (The stone carvings of Li Gonglin's "Portraits of Sages and Worthies"). Beijing: Renmin chubanshe, 1963.

Jing, Jun. *The Temple of Memories: History, Power, and Morality in a Chinese Village.* Stanford: Stanford University Press, 1996.

Kuryluk, Ewa. *Veronica and Her Cloth.* Cambridge, Mass.: Basil Blackwell, 1991.

Laufer, Berthold. "Confucius and His Portraits." *Open Court* 26, no. 3 (1912): 147–68, 202–18.

Law, Jane Marie, ed. *Religious Reflections on the Human Body.* Bloomington: Indiana University Press, 1995.

Legge, James, trans. *The Li Ki.* Sacred Books of the East, vols. 27–28. Delhi: Motilal Banarsidass, 1964.

———. *The Shoo King.* Taipei: Southern Materials Center, 1985.

Liu Ningyan 劉寧顏. 1994. "Tan Kongzi xiang" 談孔子像 (A discussion of images of Confucius). *Taibei wenxian* 37 (1976): 177–94.

Lü Weiqi 呂維琪. *Shengxian xiangzan* 聖賢像讚 (Portraits of the sages and worthies, with encomia). Shandong: Youyi shushe, n.d.

Ma Duanlin 馬端臨. *Wenxian tongkao* 文獻通考 (Conspectus of documentary records). 3 vols. Taipei: Xinxing shuju, 1965.

Ma Xiaolin 馬小林 and Bao Guoqiang 鮑國強, eds. *Zhonghua gexing zuxianxiang chuanji* 中華各姓祖先像傳集 (Collection of ancestral portraits of divers Chinese surnames). 10 vols. Beijing: Minzu chubanshe, 1999.

Mair, Victor H. *Wandering on the Way: Early Taoist Tales and Parables of Chuang Tzu.* Honolulu: University of Hawai'i Press, 1994.

Morgan, Carole. "Inscribed Stones: A Note on a Tang and Song Burial Rite." *T'oung Pao* 82 (1996): 317–48.

Murray, Julia K. "The Hangzhou *Portraits of Confucius and Seventy-two Disciples* (*Sheng xian tu*): Art in the Service of Politics." *Art Bulletin* 74 (1992): 7–18.

———. "Illustrations of the Life of Confucius: Their Evolution, Functions, and Significance in Late Ming China." *Artibus Asiae* 57, no. 2 (1997): 73–134.

———. "The Temple of Confucius and Pictorial Biographies of the Sage." *Journal of Asian Studies* 55, no. 2 (1996): 269–300.

Neskar, Ellen G. "The Cult of Worthies: A Study of Shrines Honoring Local Confucian Worthies in the Sung Dynasty (960–1279)." Ph.D. diss., Columbia University, 1993.

Qin Huitian 秦蕙田. *Wuli tongkao* 五禮通考 (Conspectus of the five rites). Taipei: Geda shuju, 1970.

Qiu Jun 邱濬. *Daxue yanyi bu* 大學衍義補 (Supplement to *Extended Meaning of the Great Learning*). Wenyuange siku quanshu 文淵閣四庫全書 ed.

Sahas, Daniel J. *Icon and Logos: Sources in Eighth-Century Iconoclasm.* Toronto: University of Toronto Press, 1986.

Shandongsheng Qufushi wenwu guanli weiyuanhui 山東省曲阜市文物管理委員會 (Cultural Services Committee of Qufu, Shandong). *Kongzi xiang, Yansheng gong ji furen xiaoxiang* 孔子像, 衍聖公及夫人肖像 (Portraits of Confucius, portraits of the Dukes of Yansheng and their wives). Shandong: Youyi shushe, 1987.

———. *Qufu: Kongzi de guxiang* 曲阜: 孔子的故鄉 (Qufu, Confucius's hometown). Beijing: Wenwu chubanshe, 1990.

Shisanjing zhushu 十三經注疏. [Beijing]: Zhonghuashuju, 1979.

Shryock, John K. *The Origin and Development of the State Cult of Confucius*. New York: Paragon, 1966.

Siggstedt, Mette. "Forms of Fate: An Investigation of the Relationship Between Formal Portraiture, Especially Ancestral Portraits, and Physiognomy (*xiangshu*) in China." In *International Colloquium on Chinese Art History*, pp. 714–48. Taipei: National Palace Museum, 1991.

Sommer, Deborah. "Ch'iu Chün's *On the Conduct of Sacrificial Offerings*." Ph.D. diss., Columbia University, 1993.

———. "Images into Words: Ming Confucian Iconoclasm." *National Palace Museum Bulletin* 29 (Mar.–June 1994).

Song Lian 宋濂. *Song Wenxiangong quanji* 宋文獻公全集 (Complete works of Master Song). Sibu beiyao 四部備要 ed.

Song Na 宋訥. *Xiyin ji* 西隱集 (includes a *Supplement* 續). Siku quanshu zhenben 四庫全書珍本 ed.

Soymié, Michel. "L'Entrevue de Confucius et de Hiang T'o." *Journal Asiatique* 242 (1954): 311–92.

Sperling, Elliot. "Early Ming Policy Toward Tibet." Ph.D. diss., Indiana University, 1983.

Spiro, Audrey. *Contemplating the Ancients: Aesthetic and Social Issues in Early Chinese Portraiture*. Berkeley: University of California Press, 1990.

Stoichita, Victor I. *A Short History of the Shadow*. London: Reaktion Books, 1997.

Su Shi 蘇軾. *Su Shi wenji* 蘇軾文集. 5 vols. Beijing: Zhonghua shuju, 1986.

Sun Chengze 孫承澤. *Chunmingmeng yulu* 春明夢餘錄. Siku quanshu zhenben 四庫全書珍本 ed.

Wang Meng'ou 王夢鷗, ed. *Li ji jin zhu jin yi* 禮記今註今譯 (Record of Rites, with modern annotations and translation). Taipei: Shangwu yinshuguan, 1971.

Wang Xianqian 王先謙. *Xunzi jijie* 荀子集解 (Collected commentaries on the *Xunzi*). 2 vols. Beijing: Zhonghua shuju, 1988.

Wang Yongji 汪永基 and Kong Xiangmin 孔祥民. *Tianxia di yi jia* 天下第一家 (The number-one clan of the realm). Beijing: Xinhua chubanshe, 1995.

Wang Yun 王惲. *Qiujian xiansheng daquanji* 秋簡先生大全集. Sibu congkan 四部叢刊 ed.

Watson, Burton. *The Columbia Book of Chinese Poetry from Early Times to the Thirteenth Century*. New York: Columbia University Press, 1984.

Wilson, Thomas A. *Genealogy of the Way: The Construction and Uses of the Confucian Tradition in Late Imperial China.* Stanford: Stanford University Press, 1995.

———. "The Ritual Formation of Confucian Orthodoxy and the Descendants of the Sage." *Journal of Asian Studies* 55 (1996): 559–84.

Xiong Yizhong 熊宜中, ed. *Ming Qing guanxianghua tulu* 明清官像畫圖錄 (Catalogue of Ming and Qing ancestral portraits of sitters in official court attire). Taipei: Yishuguan, 1998.

Yang Shoujing 楊守敬. *Shuijing zhushu* 水經注疏 (*The Water Classic*, with commentaries and subcommentaries). 3 vols. Jiangsu guji chubanshe, 1989.

Zhang Zuoyao 張作耀, ed. *Da zai Kongzi* 大哉孔子 (Great Confucius). Hong Kong: Heping tushu, 1991.

Zheng Xianren 鄭憲仁. "Gudai jizu lishi zhidu qiantan" 古代祭祖立尸制度淺探 (Personation and ancestral sacrifices in antiquity). *Kong Meng yuekan* 33, no. 7 (1995): 11–18.

Zhongguo minjian xiaoxiang hua 中國民間肖像畫 (Chinese folk portraiture). *Hansheng zazhi* 漢聲雜誌 (Taipei: special issue) 63–64 (1994).

Zhu Xi. *Zhuzi daquan* 朱子大全 (Complete works of Master Zhu). Sibu beiyao 四部備要 ed.

———. *Zhuzi yulei* 朱子語類 (Collated sayings of Master Zhu). Taipei: Zhengzhong shuju.

Zhu Xilu 朱錫祿. *Jiaxiang Han hua xiang shi* 嘉祥漢畫像石 (Han stone carvings from Jiaxiang). Ji'nan: Shandong meishu chubanshe, 1992.

THREE

Musical Confucianism
The Case of 'Jikong yuewu'

Joseph S. C. Lam

Confucius was musical. He practiced music diligently and listened to it criti-cally; indeed, he left many insightful comments on Shao 韶, Wu 武, and other ancient musical works.[1] Drawing attention to the essential nature of music in human existence, the philosopher once asked: "Music! O music! Does it mean no more than bells and drums?"[2] Confucius left no definitive answer behind, but he made it clear that "music" (*yue, yuewu* 樂/樂舞) is much more than aesthetic and autonomous sounds.[3] Music is not only a counterpart of ritual (*li* 禮) but also a sonic embodiment of human heart/minds (*xin*). Thus, music should be properly produced (composed, trans-mitted, and performed) and consumed (heard and interpreted) as a means of governance and self-cultivation. As a philosophical and cultural concept,

---

1. There are many descriptions of Confucius's musical activities and comments. For ex-amples of classical descriptions, see *The Analects*, pp. 45–47, 67, 71, 87, 93–94, 133–34, 143–47; and *Kongzi jiayu*. For modern studies, see Zhang Dainian, *Kongzi da cidian*; and Yang Yinliu, *Zhongguo gudai yinyue shigao*, pp. 45–92.

2. *The Analects*, p. 145.

3. Understanding music as aesthetic and autonomous expressions of sounds is essentially a Western and modern practice. In this essay, the word "music" is used as an equivalent of *yue*, a traditional Chinese term that refers to expressions of sounds in the contexts of multimedia performance arts that communicate sonic and non-sonic messages. "*Yue*" is oftentimes an abridged form of "*yuewu*" (music and dance); traditional Chinese discussions of "*wu*" (dance) always involved music.

this Confucian ideology of proper music (*yayue* 雅樂) is widely known. However, musical Confucianism—musical theories, practices, and products derived from the ideology—has been largely ignored in modern Chinese studies. To illustrate musical Confucianism, this chapter presents a case study of *jikong yuewu* (祭孔樂舞), the repertory of fixed songs and dances performed in Confucian temples (*wenmiao* 文廟, *kongmiao* 孔廟) and during the Confucian Ceremonial—the ceremonial and presentational worship of Confucius (*jikong* 祭孔, *shidian* 釋奠). Through this case study, I hope to show that musical Confucianism is much more than philosophical ideals and sounds: it sonically embodies individual Confucians and their diverse understandings and realizations of Confucianism.[4]

This nature of musical Confucianism becomes apparent when it is viewed historically. Once Confucianism became the official ideology in the Han dynasty, the idea of proper music generated a tradition of theories, practices, and products that permeated Chinese history and culture. Among the many historical genres of Confucian proper music, the most elaborate was the state sacrificial music that Chinese courts performed to honor imperial ancestors, deified natural forces, and historical personages during large-scale rites. Other, less elaborate but no less vivid, demonstrations of musical Confucianism emerged in the playing of the seven-string zither (*qin* 琴), the singing of classical poems (*shiyue* 詩樂), and the performing of other refined music by Confucian scholars and officials.[5] When imperial China ended in 1911, state sacrificial music lost its raison d'être. The genre still survives, however, as the *jikong yuewu* performed during public worship of Confucius inside and outside China.[6] Similarly, music for the seven-string zither is still played and is now recognized as the representative music of the traditional Chinese elite. Musical Confucianism no longer enjoys official sanction, but its theories and practices still affect Chinese music, including avant-garde genres produced and consumed by westernized and modernized Chinese

---

4. In this paper, I use technical data on various historical versions of *jikong yuewu* to discuss structure and performance. Suffice it to say such data are no substitute for the music itself, which is now irretrievable.

5. For a survey of these musical genres, see Yang Yinliu, *Zhongguo gudai yinyue shigao*. For a discussion of music for the seven-string zither and the Chinese elite, see Gulik, *The Lore of the Chinese Lute*.

6. *Jikong yuewu* is regularly performed in Korea and occasionally in North America. See Cultural and Educational Foundation of Confucius Institute, U.S.A., *Recordation of International Confucius Worship Movement*.

throughout the world.[7] Musical Confucianism still thrives because it has adjusted to fit the changing world of Confucians.

Musical Confucianism is usually discussed in broad generalizations that are more intellectual than musical and more prescriptive than descriptive.[8] Broad generalizations cannot, however, explain musical Confucianism. First, they gloss over the diversity of Confucian music over the course of Chinese history. Even within the rigidly controlled genre of state sacrificial music, there were different manifestations of the ideology of proper music.[9] Second, their disregard for personal expression undermines the humanist nature of musical Confucianism. Unless Confucian music is produced and consumed as a form of personal expression, it cannot reveal the heart/minds of individual Confucians. Unless music reveals the heart/minds of individuals, it cannot serve as a means of governance or self-cultivation, two human processes that occur only in the specific contexts of time, place, thought, and person. If music were no more than sounds produced according to philosophical ideals, neither the diversity of Confucian music nor the numerous debates about proper music would have occurred in historical and contemporary China.

A historically objective, theoretically informed, and musically meaningful understanding of musical Confucianism must explain, with musical evidence, the ways Confucian music simultaneously operates with two contradictory forces, namely, the Confucian ideology (standard) of proper music and the individualistic heart/minds of musical Confucians. Philosophical ideals are abstract and universal; they generate prescriptive theories and normative performance practices, producing music that is structurally standardized and expressively generalized. Individualistic heart/minds are, however, personal and contextually specific; they adjust prescriptive theories and normative practices to match personal needs and specific contexts, producing music that is structurally distinctive and expressively localized.

The Confucian production and consumption of music is both sonic and humanist. This is vividly captured in the famous story of Confucius learning to play a piece of seven-string zither music from Shi Xiang 師襄, a music

---

7. In the present age, the Confucian ideology of proper music often appears as a concern for serious and refined music that promotes social and artistic values.

8. See, e.g., Fung, *A History of Chinese Philosophy*, 1: 341–44.

9. A comparison of state sacrificial music from the Southern Song and the Ming would be illustrative. See Lam, *State Sacrifices and Music in Ming China*; idem, "Musical Relics"; and Yang Yinliu, *Zhongguo gudai yinyue shigao*, pp. 380–405, 1005–8.

master of the state of Lu.[10] After learning the notes of the piece, Confucius practiced it for a period of time. When Shi Xiang told Confucius that he had learned the piece well and could move on to other works, Confucius refused, claiming that he had mastered only its sounds (*qu* 曲) and that he had to continue to practice. A while later, the music teacher commented that Confucius had comprehended the structure (*shu* 數) of the piece. Again, the philosopher kept on practicing, explaining that he had understood only the intention (*zhi* 志) of the piece. He practiced until he realized that the piece sonically embodied King Wen. Shi Xiang was very impressed because the piece he taught Confucius was "Wenwang cao" 文王操 (King Wen's tune).[11] Whatever the truth of the story, it pinpoints the sonic and humanist nature of musical Confucianism. Music cannot be produced and consumed without reference to sounds and people. Music exists as distinctive works, whose meanings are decoded through identification and interpretation of particular structural features that reference specific ideas and people. Such a process of music making and decoding is empirically grounded. Only through people can music be produced and consumed; only with reference to prescriptive theories and normative practices can music become intelligible (or unintelligible); only with distinctive features, however subtle, can music exist as separate works. A piece of music that cannot be distinguished from another piece cannot have a distinctive meaning.

This sonic and humanist operation of musical Confucianism can be hypothesized as follows. Confucian music is the sonic embodiment of the Confucian world, and musical works (performances) constitute sonic products and processes through which Confucians communicate their intellectual and practical understandings of Confucianism. The production and consumption of music are complex processes that involve diverse elements from the past and the present. From the past, we inherit musical works, their established meanings, prescriptive theories, normative performance practices, historical models for musical interpretation, and so forth. The present gives us a subjective and selective understanding of the musical past, personal and creative choices in the application of prescriptive theories and normative practices, adjustments to cope with contextual constraints and current needs, and so forth.

---

10. *Kongzi jiayu* 35.210.

11. A piece of seven-string zither music still bears the same title. The reliability of *Kongzi jiayu* has been challenged. See Wilson (p. 61*n*66) and Jensen (pp. 193–94) for more on this text.

In other words, music is produced and consumed in specific contexts of time, place, ideas, and persons, and individual pieces (performances) of music always include unique combinations of various standard (orthodox) and distinctive (creative) elements. Confucian musicians manipulate and appropriate such elements to express their understanding of Confucian ideals and their individualistic heart/minds. Their expressions are understood by audiences who identify the manipulated and appropriated elements and decipher the encoded meanings in specific terms. Thus, as produced and consumed, Confucian music is much more than aesthetic and autonomous sounds. It embodies not only a philosophical tradition called Confucianism but also a diversity of people who call themselves Confucians.

THE RITUAL AND MUSICAL FEATURES
OF 'JIKONG YUEWU'

There are many examples of the musical embodiment of Confucians, but none is more illustrative than *jikong yuewu*, the ritual and musical features of which vary with the different versions of the Confucian Ceremonial. The current versions practiced in Mainland China and Taiwan follow a basic structure first standardized by the founding emperor of the Ming, Taizu, in 1393.[12] It is a sequence of ritual activities that include, for example, the formal announcement of a ritual schedule, the breeding and inspection of the sacrificial animals, and the *sacrificial offering* (*ji* 祭), which is the climax of the Confucian Ceremonial.[13] Presented inside Confucian temples, the ceremony of sacrificial offering is ritually and musically performed in six stages:

1. Welcoming the deities (*yingshen* 迎神);
2–4. Three offerings of silk, wine, and food to the deities (*chu* 初, *ya* 亞, and *zhong xian* 終獻); the first round includes the reading of a prayer addressed to the deified Confucius and a selection of meritorious Confucians; the third round features the acceptance of the consecrated wine and meat, a gesture that symbolizes contact between the deified and the celebrants;
5. Clearing the sacrificial offerings (*chezhuan* 撤饌); and

---

12. *Taichang xukao* 5.17a–37b.
13. For further descriptions of Ming dynasty state sacrifices, see Lam, *State Sacrifices and Music in Ming China*, pp. 13–56. On the historical formation of the liturgy, see Wilson (pp. 72–79) in this volume.

6. Bidding farewell to the deified (*songshen* 送神) and burning the sacrificial articles (*wangliao* 望燎).

Every detail in the sacrificial offering is precisely planned. For example, the offerings of silk, wine, and food honor, in addition to Confucius, a sizable number of deified and ranked Confucians. Thus, the three rounds of offerings consist of a series of coordinated actions performed by a combination of primary and secondary celebrants. The primary celebrant presents offerings to Confucius and four main followers (*sizhe* 四哲), whose altars (*tan* 壇), and thus spiritual presence, are inside the main hall of the Confucian temple. The secondary celebrants present the subordinate offerings to Confucius's other disciples and to meritorious Confucians whose altars are located in the western and eastern halls of the temple.[14] Other details of the sacrificial offering, such as the identity of the celebrants, the types of silk, the number of dishes of prepared food (*biandou* 邊豆), the roster of the meritorious disciples and Confucians, are similarly and meticulously controlled. No changes in these details were made without careful analysis and extensive debate. It is these details that define localized and personalized meanings of different versions of the Confucian Ceremonial.

Music is performed in all six stages of the ceremony. Dance is restricted to the three rounds of offerings. Since the Ming, *jikong yuewu* has included six fixed songs, one for each stage of the ceremony; three of these accompany dances. In addition to this selective itemization of music and dance, the Confucian Ceremonial incorporates many sounds, sights, and physical movements during the course of the ceremonial, such as the music that accompanies the procession of the celebrants to and from the temple, the chanting of the prayer, and ritual gestures like the stylized bodily movements used to offer wine, and the music and dance performed to celebrate the completion of the ceremony of sacrificial offering.[15] Confucians have adopted a selective itemization and focused on the six fixed songs and three dances because they understand these as sonic and choreographic embodiment of specific ritual and semantic meanings in the worshipping of Confucius—each tone and each gesture of the music and dance correspond to a particular word in the song texts. *Jikong yuewu* is not a sonic and kinetic

---

14. For a discussion of the spirit in the ceremony, see Sommer (pp. 95–133) in this volume.

15. These controlled and performed sounds, sights, and bodily movements are included in late twentieth-century descriptions of ritual, music, and dance.

means through which ritual participants enter into a trance state, which is fundamental to many participatory rituals. Rather, *jikong yuewu* is presentational: it is performed by musician-dancers (*yuewu sheng* 樂舞生) for celebrants and ritual staff, who neither sing nor dance but perform the ritual gestures, and for members of the audience, who observe the ritual and musical actions.

A HISTORICAL OUTLINE OF

THE CONFUCIAN CEREMONIAL AND

'JIKONG YUEWU'

As a subgenre of state sacrificial music that originated in ancient China, as music of a ceremonial constructed right after Confucius's death in 478 BCE, and as music that can still be heard in Qufu and Taipei, *jikong yuewu* is the product of a complex and centuries-long development of theories and practices. Although this development has always been described as a continuously practiced and monolithic tradition of ritual and music, it really operates as a conglomerate of many distinctive and yet closely related local traditions in Confucius's hometown of Qufu, the national capital(s), and centers of local governments.[16]

Soon after Confucius's death, his descendants and disciples in Qufu began the practice of worshipping him with sacrificial offerings, and possibly with music and dance—Qufu was also the capital of the state of Lu and had an indigenous tradition of state sacrificial music and dance. This local and "family" tradition of ritual and music received imperial recognition in 195 BCE, when Han emperor Gaozu (r. 206–195) passed through Qufu and worshipped Confucius with the most exalted type of state sacrifices, which featured the sacrifice of a bull, a pig, and a goat (*tailao* 太牢).[17] Then Han emperor Yuandi (r. 48–33 BCE) began the practice of ennobling direct descendants of Confucius and giving them the financial and human resources to support their worship of Confucius. In 1 CE, Han emperor Pingdi (r. 1–5 CE) ennobled Confucius as the Duke Xuanni of Baocheng 襃成宣尼公 and thereby legitimated the philosopher as a sage who deserved to be

---

16. This historical outline is based on Qin Huitian, *Wuli tongkao*, juan 117–21; and Kong Jifen, *Queli wenxian kao*, juan 23–25.

17. See pp. 73–75 of this volume.

honored with state sacrifices. These imperial endorsements and allotments of financial as well as human resources allowed Confucius's direct descendants to transform the worship of their ancestor into a practice of national importance. Soon Chinese emperors and scholar-official began to visit Qufu regularly to offer state and personal sacrifices to Confucius and to demonstrate that they were Confucian rulers and officials. As a result, the Qufu tradition of worshipping Confucius became established in imperial China.

The tradition of worshipping Confucius in national capitals formally began, in 241 CE, when King Qi of Wei 魏齊王 (r. 240–54) ordered the most exalted type of state sacrifices to honor Confucius in the imperial university (biyong 辟雝).[18] This was more a revival of an ancient practice than an invention, however. As described in the Record of Rites, ancient rulers and scholar-officials worshipped sages and teachers (xiansheng xianshi 先聖先師) in national universities through the performances of ceremonials. King Qi's order simply established Confucius as a member of this group of deified sages and teachers. Being the teacher of Confucianism, however, Confucius was always worshipped with the most elaborate of the three types of ceremonials honoring sages and teachers, the shidian, which employs music.[19] In 489, the tradition of worshipping Confucius in the capital acquired its own ritual space. In that year, Emperor Xiaowen 孝文 (r. 471–99) of Wei had a Confucian temple built in his capital, Datong, and thus established the practice of erecting Confucian temples in national capitals and of worshipping Confucius in that ritual space. Since then, Confucian temples in national capitals have been the sites where new versions of the Confucian Ceremonial would regularly appear. A history of these rites, especially those introduced by the emperors and scholar-officials who founded new dynasties (or reigns) would more or less outline the development of Chinese court ritual and music over the past fifteen centuries.

The traditions of worshipping Confucius in centers of local government began, in 59 CE, with the Han emperor Mingdi's (r. 58–75) edict to worship the philosopher in local schools. Almost six centuries later, these practices found their own ritual sites when the Tang emperor Taizong (r. 627–49) ordered, in 630, local schools to build Confucian temples. This edict is symbolic of the imperial control over the Confucian Ceremonial. Throughout

---

18. Qin Huitian, Wuli tongkao 117.9b.

19. The other two types of ceremonials are shibi 釋幣 and shicai 釋菜, both of which are irregular rituals performed on special occasions or to inform the deities of specific messages.

Chinese history, Chinese dynasties instituted elaborate systems of ritual and music as their administrations became established. Then in subsequent years, they would revise the ritual and music as needed. To codify and to standardize complex practices, comprehensive manuals and/or treatises would be compiled. Many of these court documents have been preserved, including, for example, *Tang Kaiyuan li* 唐開元禮 (Ceremonials of the Tang Kaiyuan era), Ouyang Xiu's 歐陽修 (1007–72) *Taichang yin'ge li* 太常因革禮 (History of the rites of the Court of Imperial Sacrifice), the *Jin jili* 金集禮 (Collected ceremonials of the Jin), *Zhongxing lishu* 中興禮書 (Compilation of ceremonials and music of the Southern Song), *Taichang zonglan* 太常總覽 (General record of the Court of Imperial Sacrifice) of the Ming, *Qing huidian* 清會典 (Collected statues of the Qing), and Yunlu's 允祿 *Lülü zhengyi houbian* 律呂正義後編 (Correct music theories, final compilation) of the Qing. Once compiled and deposited in imperial and personal libraries, these court documents became references for subsequent generations of emperors and scholar-officials, who would rely on the authority of historical documents to support their ritual and musical revisions. The *Tang Kaiyuan li*, for example, was a particularly influential reference: its comprehensive descriptions of national and local versions of the Confucian Ceremonial were often cited by Ming and Qing scholar-officials as a historical model.

In addition to court documents, there are many other descriptions of the Confucian Ceremonial music and dance. Local scholars and officials compiled many treatises and manuals to specify local practices of worshipping Confucius and to promote an individualistic understanding of the ideology of proper music.[20] Through *jikong yuewu*, local scholars and officials found an avenue for discussing the theories and practices of musical Confucianism and state sacrificial music. The Confucian Ceremonial was the only state sacrifice that scholar-officials could freely discuss and practice among themselves: other state sacrifices, as well as the music that accompanied them, were imperial privileges and not to be discussed without imperial permission.[21] For this reason, scholar-officials' ritual and musical discussions

20. For a distinctive collection of Ming and Qing manuals on the Confucian Ceremonial and *jikong yuewu*, see *Zhongguo yinyue shupuzhi*, pp. 46–47.

21. Scholar-officials could, however, freely discuss historical versions of state sacrifices and music.

concentrated on the Confucian Ceremonial and led to many comprehensive treatises. Many of these treatises are extant, from Zhang E's 張鶚 (fl. 1520s–30s) *Dacheng yuewu tupu* 大成樂舞圖譜 (Musical scores and dance illustrations for the Confucian Ceremonial) of 1520 to Yang Shusen's 楊樹森 *Zhenxing yayueyi* 振興雅樂議 (Proposal to revitalize proper music) written in the 1930s(?). Through their positive and negative discussions of historical models, detailed explanations of theories and practices, and comprehensive descriptions of ritual-musical procedures (*yizhu* 儀注), these documents provide historical and cultural references (and a standardizing mechanism) with which practitioners could merge the past and the present, the standard and the distinctive, into their versions of Confucian Ceremonial music and dance.

Such a merger was furthered by the constant interactions among the traditions of the Confucian Ceremonial in Qufu, in the capitals, and in local centers. To enforce the standardized versions of the Confucian Ceremonial, Chinese courts periodically bestowed sets of musical scores and instruments on Qufu and other local centers. For example, in 1719, the Kangxi emperor (r. 1662–1721) sent a set of musical instruments of state sacrificial music (*zhonghe shaoyue* 中和韶樂) to Qufu. And in 1747, the Qianlong emperor (r. 1736–95) sent Zhang Yuesheng 張樂盛, an officer of music and dance (*xielü lang* 協律郎) of the Court of Imperial Sacrifice (*taichangsi* 太常寺), to Qufu to teach a new version of *jikong yuewu*. Furthermore, as Confucian scholar-officials moved among the capitals and local centers to perform their official duties, they exchanged views on the ceremonial with local teachers and music masters. The arrival of musical scholar-officials always energized the practice of *jikong yuewu* in local centers.

Local traditions could, however, develop independently. Few local leaders and music masters hesitated to adjust ritual and musical details to incorporate their own ideas. For example, Kong Jifen 孔繼汾 (1721–86) Qufu did not agree with the music and dance taught by Zhang Yuesheng; Kong consulted Yunlu's *Lülü zhengyi houbian* and constructed a version that he considered an accurate reading of the imperial instructions.[22] Similarly, Qiu Zhilu 邱之稑 of nineteenth-century Liuyang broke with the practice of syllabic singing by introducing ornamental notes into his *jikong yuewu*. Even today, local traditions still thrive. A representative example can be found in Tainan

---

22. Kong Jifen, *Queli wenxian kao* 24 *xubian*.1a–3a.

in Taiwan. Nominally this locality performs the ceremonial as prescribed by the Qing court. However, its current performances include the use of local music and other distinctive features.[23]

As an integral part of the Confucian Ceremonial, the musical and choreographic features of *jikong yuewu* evolved as the rite changed over time. The first imperial effort to standardize music and dance came in 485, when the Emperor Wu (r. 479–502) of the Southern Qi ordered a performance of the Confucian Ceremonial and asked imperial clansmen and scholar-officials to participate as the audience.[24] This imperial order generated a discussion on the required music and dance when the court realized that ritual and musical procedures were unclear. Various proposals compared the use of music and dance in the Confucian Ceremonial to that in the state sacrifices offered to imperial ancestors and deified natural forces. Eventually a proposal whose use of music and dance was practical and reflected an appropriate ranking for the ceremonial was accepted. Thus standardization of music and dance in the Confucian Ceremonial began: *jikong yuewu* would henceforth use the "noble" type of orchestra (*xuanxuan* 軒懸), and choreograph the dances in the six-row-format (*liuyi* 六佾) performed by thirty-six dancers arranged in six rows.

Tang and Song emperors further developed ceremonial music and dance and produced many distinctive versions, many of which only survive as song texts. Among these versions, the Song emperor Huizong's (r. 1101–26) set of fourteen tunes of 1115 is particularly influential. The lyrics of these tunes have been preserved and were the direct exemplar of *jikong yuewu* of the Yuan and Ming times—the music of the tunes is now lost. Fourteen of the sixteen songs in the Yuan dynasty liturgy of 1306 derive from Huizong's version; all six songs in the Ming dynasty liturgy of 1393 came from the same source. Judging from the labels of the musical modes used, the number of set songs, and the ritual functions they served, Huizong's version is, however, substantively different from the Yuan and Ming versions.[25] Nevertheless, it demonstrates many standardized features of *jikong yuewu* as we know it today. These features include, for example, the classical style of four-word phrases in the song texts, the syllabic style of singing, and the use of drum calls (*sangu*

---

23. See Chen Fu-Yen, "Confucian Ceremonial Music in Taiwan"; the music performed at this ceremony is available on Laade's CD, *The Confucius Temple Ceremony.*

24. Qin Huitian, *Wuli tongkao* 117.10b–11a.

25. *Songshi* 129.3001–12, 137.3236–38; *Yuanshi* 69.200; *Mingshi* 62.1552–53.

三鼓) to mark the beginning of the ceremony of sacrificial offering. The Ming dynasty version, as proclaimed and standardized by Taizu in 1393, is also influential. It is the direct model of the Qing dynasty *jikong yuewu*. Both the capital and local versions of the Qing, which were proclaimed in 1711 and 1749, respectively, followed the Ming practice of six fixed songs and three dances. In 1968, when Taiwanese authorities revived the Confucian Ceremonial in Taipei, they reconstructed the music and dance according to the Ming version. In 1984, when local authorities in Qufu revived the Confucian Ceremonial there, however, they emulated the local version of the Qing.

PRESCRIPTIVE THEORIES
AND NORMATIVE PRACTICES OF MUSICAL
CONFUCIANISM AND 'JIKONG YUEWU'

The neo-Ming and neo-Qing versions of the *jikong yuewu* in Taipei and Qufu are distinctive, but they also share many features drawn from musical and choreographic theories and practices described in the Confucian classics and ritual manuals. Above all, they subscribe to the Confucian ideology of proper music, which is succinctly described in the *Record of Music* 樂記.[26] When people are moved by external stimuli, they make sounds. When such sounds are shaped into particular patterns and are performed with dance, they become music (*yue* or *yuewu*), which communicates human feelings. Since music elicits correspondences between human and nonhuman beings, it deeply affects people's heart/minds and is thus an effective means of governance and self-cultivation. In other words, proper music, which is produced by people of benevolence (*ren* 仁), should be promoted, and vulgar music (*suyue* 俗樂), which corrupts human heart/minds, should be banned. Music is an integral aspect of human efforts to excel. Confucius once asked: "Wha can a man do with music who is not benevolent?"[27]

To convince themselves of the truth of this ideology, Confucians needed only to refer to their master's words and deeds, which illustrate the fundamental thinking of Confucianism on music.[28] Confucius reported that he

---

26. This summary is based largely on *Yueji*, "Yueben," pp. 1262–63.
27. *The Analects*, p. 67.
28. The following summary of Confucius's utterances and actions is developed from *The Analects*, pp. 67, 71, 87, 93–94, 143–47.

once forgot the taste of meat for three months after listening to a performance of the perfectly beautiful and good (*jinmei, jinshan* 盡美盡善) Shao, a work of dance and music that originated from the ancient court of the sage-king Shun 舜. Confucius not only was overwhelmed by the harmonious, clear, and unbroken sounds of the work but also was mesmerized by the sonic embodiment of a benevolent ruler and the ideal society he launched. In other words, proper music and the ideal society it promoted had once been achieved. Confucians hence believed that they needed to revive proper music and could do so in their own times: by doing so, they would develop their innate goodness, learn the institutions of the sage-kings, and emulate their proper music, remnants of which could be found in the Classics. And to ensure the success of that revival, they had to suppress vulgar music, which leads to licentious behavior that disrupts social order. Confucius noted that vulgar music muddles proper music just as the color purple confuses the appeal of the vermilion, and glib talkers overturn states and families. Those who lack virtuous heart/minds, Confucians argued, are so affected by improper music that they act licentiously and disrupt the world order.

Proper music, benevolent heart/minds, and human efforts to excel are thus inseparable. This is perhaps why Confucius discussed music as a counterpart of ritual. Indeed, both are means through which people cultivate themselves, communicate among themselves and with the supernatural, and teach their subordinates proper behavior. Both manifest the orderly hierarchies that Confucians strove to achieve: in a piece of music, tones and rhythms perform their assigned roles, just as emperors, officials, fathers, and sons carry out their social duties. In a ceremonial, the offerings, acts of obeisance, and other ritual particulars correspond to one another; uncoordinated music and disorderly ritual project chaos and degeneration. And above all, both need to be authentic: proper music can be created only with genuine feelings by benevolent people, and legitimate rites can be respectfully performed only by the appropriate celebrants. Otherwise, the music will be licentious, and the ritual, sacrilegious.

Given the significance of proper music, Confucians theorized its elements meticulously. Thus, all musical instruments should be constructed of the eight types of materials (*bayin* 八音)—metal, stone, silk, bamboo, gourd, earth, leather, and wood—from the appropriate locales. Stone-chimes, for example, should be made with stones from Sizhouling. Musical tuning has to be accurate: the twelve absolute pitches (*shi'er lü* 十二律), which represent all the sounds for music making, should possess the right physical, *yin* and *yang*, and other cosmological attributes. For example, *huangzhong* 黃鐘, the primordial sound and the fundamental of the twelve absolute pitches, should match the *qi* 氣 of the winter solstice; the *huangzhong* pitch pipe should have a length of nine *cun* 寸 and a radius of three *fen* 分. When used in actual music, the twelve absolute pitches should appear as appropriate musical modes—categories of absolute pitches and transposable tones that are manipulated according to specified and hierarchical functions. For example, the pitches in the music honoring heavenly deities should be in the *huangzhong* mode; the *huangzhong* pitch—the fundamental tone of that musical mode—should "rule" the other tones like a sovereign.[29]

In state sacrificial music, proper music should have proper texts, shaped into classical phrases of four words each, written by the appropriate authorities—emperors and scholar-officials. These texts would then be set to tunes and dances composed by court masters of music and dance and reflecting the semantic meanings of the texts. The tunes should be composed in modes chosen according to a number of considerations: the season and the location of the sacrifices; the type and rank of the deities being honored—gods (*shen* 神) and imperial ancestors are, for example, more important than spirits (*gui* 鬼). A proper performance has to have the right number of singers, instrumentalists, and dancers. The dances have to be choreographed as a series of poses. The singers sing harmonious and moderate melodies that follow classical prescriptions on singing and melodic shapes (*juge* 句格); the orchestra should be arranged in patterns appropriate to the deities being honored, providing "metallic sounds" and "jade vibrations" (*jinsheng yuzhen* 金聲玉振), which are in turn marked by drumbeats and cadences of the wooden-tiger (*yu* 敔) and the wooden-crate (*zhu* 柷).

The prescriptive theories and normative practices surrounding state sacrificial music, the highest realization of the Confucian ideology of proper music, are repeatedly described in the Confucian classics and in numerous musical and historical references studied by Chinese scholar-officials.[30]

---

29. A comprehensive discussion of musical modes is beyond the scope of this essay. For current studies on modes, see the *New Grove Dictionary of Music and Musicians*, 6th ed., s.v. "China IV, 4: Theory-Modes," and "Modes."

30. The constant discussions of rites and music in Chinese courts demanded that scholar-officials consult these music references and have at least a familiarity with these ideas; see Lam, "Ritual and Musical Politics."

Works like Chen Yang's 陳暘 *Yueshu* 樂書 (Treatise on music) of 1104, Ma Duanlin's 馬端臨 (1254–1325) *Wenxian tongkao* 文獻通考 (Comprehensive investigation of documents and traditions) of 1370, and Qin Huitian's 秦蕙 田 (1702–64) *Wuli tongkao* 五禮通考 (Comprehensive study of the five rites) of 1753 are representative. Encyclopedic in nature, these works are de facto summaries of the musical Confucianism of their respective times. Ma's work is a general reference, and Qin's is a chronological history of the five categories of Chinese state ceremonials. The presence of detailed descriptions of musical theories and practices in such general reference works as these attests to the prevalence of musical Confucianism among scholar-officials.

As realized in ceremonial music, the theories and practices of musical Confucianism are, however, much more specific than the preceding description might imply. *Jikong yuewu* is music and dance for a very specific rite. Besides embodying the meanings of the Confucian Ceremonial sonically and visually, *jikong yuewu* is employed to mark the structural points of the ceremony of sacrificial offering. The drum calls announce the beginning of the ceremony; the songs mark its six ritual stages and accompany all the important ritual gestures; the dances draw attention to the three rounds of offerings, which are performed in various halls and terraces inside Confucian temples and thus cannot comprehensively be experienced by any one participant. Because of its special functions, *jikong yuewu* is perceived as a very special set of fixed songs and dance. All its features, including the song texts, the tunes, the choreography, the musical instruments, the number of musician-dancers, and so forth, were meticulously prescribed by the court. The orchestra, for example, includes seven-string zithers, twenty-five-string zithers (*se* 瑟), bell-chimes (*bianzhong* 編鍾), stone-chimes (*bianqing* 編磬), ocarinas (*xun* 壎), horizontal flutes (*chi* 箎 and *di* 笛), panpipes (*feng xiao* 風簫), vertical flutes (*xiao* 簫), mouth-organs (*sheng* 笙), wooden-tiger, and wooden-crate.

As described in the *Taichang zonglan* of 1470 and in Huang Zuo's 黃佐 (1490–1566) *Nanyong zhi* 南雝志 (Account of the southern Imperial University) of 1544, the Ming version of *jikong yuewu* has the following standardized features. The tunes are composed in the *zhonglü* 仲呂 mode, a mode that is reserved for Confucius and that is not used in any other state sacrificial music (see Music Example 1). Each song begins with the sound of the wooden-crate and ends with that of the wooden-tiger. Similarly, each phrase of the

Music example 1. Song of welcome in the Ming *jikong yuewu* (Taipei, 1995). The text reads:

1 Great is the sage, Confucius!	大哉孔聖
2 He promotes virtue.	道德尊崇
3 Maintaining the way of imperial governance,	維持王法
4 He is the teacher of our people.	斯民是宗
5 We worship you with regular sacrifices,	典祀有常
6 And offer to you elaborate but pure offerings.	精純並隆
7 Please come to this temple,	神其來格
8 And show your holy appearance.	於昭聖容

songs begins with the sounds of the bell-chimes and ends with those of the stone-chimes. The songs are sung syllabically and "harmoniously" (*he, xiehe* 和/諧和): each word of the text is set (and sung) to a specific pitch as a long and sustained sound, rhythmically punctuated by specific drum patterns. The dances are performed by two groups of performers, respectively positioned on the eastern and western sides of the terraces in front of the main hall of the Confucian temple. The dancers carry a flute in their left hand and a staff topped with feathers in their right hand and perform a series of "poses," each of which involves stylized and categorized bodily movements. There are, for example, eleven patterns for manipulating the feather and the flute; five for relating the eastern and western groups of the dancers; three for the directions in which the dancers look; and five for positioning their torsos.[31]

---

31. Li Zhouwang and Xie Lüzhong, *Guoxue liyue lu* 16.1–3a.

These standardized and categorized movements render the Ming dynasty *jikong yuewu* an objectifiable and analyzable set of songs and dances. In performances, however, these features can be adjusted by the interpretations and preferences of the music masters. This is clearly indicated in the descriptions in Zhang E's *Dacheng yuewu tupu*, a well-known treatise on *jikong yuewu*. Zhang was the music master summoned to court to help Emperor Shizong (r. 1522–66) revise the state sacrifices and music in the 1530s. Zhang made such an impressive entry into the court that the *Mingshi* 明史 (Ming history) summarizes his theories and cites the titles of his musical treatises.[32] Zhang's treatise was prefaced by Lü Nan 呂楠 (1479–1542), the noted Ming Confucian. Lü praised Zhang as a music master who had aspired to benevolence (*ren*) for a long time and who practiced music with a skillful hand and a critical ear.

Zhang's treatise reflects the understanding of *jikong yuewu* common among Ming scholar-officials, but it also reveals the author's individualistic practices.[33] To make the *jikong yuewu* proper and harmonious, Zhang asked performers to produce resonant, sustained, and accurate tones—the sounds required for proper music. Zhang's instructions for producing such sounds are, however, distinctive and personal. For example, he instructed that the strings of the seven-string zither should only be plucked (*santan* 散彈) and that the ocarinas should be blown forcefully with tightened lips. Zhang also gave specific instructions to the dancers. The bodily movements of the eastern group of dancers should mirror that of the western group. All the dance gestures should conform to the stylized gestures of greeting (*yi* 揖), jumping (*dao* 蹈), and other formal bodily movements.

In 1618, Yue Hesheng 岳和聲, a surveillance vice commissioner (*anchasi fushi* 按察司副使) for Fujian, prepared an edition of Zhang's treatise; his notes on the performance of this rite reveal the personal touches he added to the *jikong yuewu* within his jurisdiction. Yue devised a unique scheme of singing and musical dynamics to show the semantic meaning and structure of the fixed songs—the text of each song consists of thirty-two words/syllables that are divided into four 8-syllable couplets. Yue divided each song text into a sequence of four cycles and had each cycle sung in the following manner. The first two notes of the cycle were to be sung calmly (*you* 幽), softly (*wei* 微), slowly (*huan* 緩), and steadily (*chang* 長); the third and

---

32. *Mingshi* 61.1510–16.
33. Zhang E, *Dacheng yuewu tupu* ff. 7, 10, 15–16.

fourth notes with a gradual crescendo (*hong* 宏) and accelerando (*shao cu* 少促); the fifth and sixth notes without restraint (*fang* 放); and the seventh and eight notes with a gradual decrescendo.[34]

The performances supervised by Zhang and Yue were distinctive and personalized, but they did not alter the fundamental structure of the Ming dynasty *jikong yuewu*. They were no more than variants of the official Ming version, which continued in use into the early decades of the Qing dynasty when the official Qing versions appeared. That the Qing versions owed much to Ming ritual is clearly acknowledged in many Qing documents. Pang Zhonglu's 龐鍾路 (*jinshi* 1847) *Wenmiao sidian kao* 文廟祀典考 (Study of thesacrifical statutes of the culture temple) of 1875, for example, faithfully describes the history, the text, and the fixed songs and dances of the Confucian Ceremonial and reveals the direct connections between the *jikong yuewu* of the Ming and of the Qing.

'JIKONG YUEWU' AS SONIC EMBODIMENTS OF CONFUCIAN IDEALS AND CONFUCIANS

Such direct connections highlight the continuity of ceremonial music of different times and give the impression that it is standardized and projects universal ideals. Indeed, if one understands a performance of *jikong yuewu* in terms of preserved texts, notated music, codified performance practices, and established cultural and philosophical meanings, one gets a picture of timeless musical Confucianism. The Confucian ideology of proper music and its appropriation by Chinese emperors, scholar-officials, and their contemporary counterparts permeate every visual, auditory, and intellectual stimuli of *jikong yuewu*. However, statements of the ritual and music participants and actual performances give a very different picture. In addition to their historical, cultural, and ideological understanding of the ceremonial, the participants hear the music as a personal expression. By identifying what is normative and what is distinctive in the performances, the participants interpret the identified features in specific contexts. In the following, I survey seven examples of Ming, Qing, and contemporary *jikong yuewu* to illustrate

---

34. Ibid., f. 26.

the sonic embodiment of individual Confucians. I focus on distinctive features that embody their heart/minds and gloss over the prescriptive theories and normative practices described above. I use technical and contextualized data to discuss *jikong yuewu* as performed music.[35]

Li Zhizao

In *Pangong liyue shu* 頖宮禮樂疏 (Proposal on the rites and music in schools; 1618), Li Zhizao 李之藻 (1565–1630) revealed his understanding and practice of musical Confucianism with a unique set of six instrumental tunes. The tunes are composed in the *huangzhong* mode and are meant to be instrumental counterparts of the vocal songs of the Ming dynasty liturgy (see Music Example 2). Except for the difference in musical mode, the instrumental tunes are structurally and performatively no different from the vocal ones. When the instrumental tunes and vocal songs are performed together, the result is a music that sonically embodies Li's creative heart/ mind.

Li, a noted Ming scholar famous for his scholarship and his interest in Western science, compiled *Pangong liyue shu* as an "accurate" history of and manual for the Confucian Ceremonial. His intentions were Confucian and practical: he wanted students to worship Confucius and to use the ritual and music as a means of governance. To ensure proper performance of the *jikong yuewu*, he included notated scores and choreographic pictograms (see Fig. 3.2). His explanations are comprehensive and reveal a technical, historical, and cosmological understanding of Confucian theories and practices of music. Among other things, Li clarified musical modes and performance practices, noted the physical dimensions of the musical instruments, and correlated aspects of the rite with the trigrams (*bagua* 八卦) and *yin* and *yang*. Li's explanations appear conventional but include many unique details. He commented, for example, that documents originating in Qufu were devoted to matters of the Kong clan and did not concern issues of ritual and music.[36]

---

35. Suffice it to say, such data are no substitute for the actual sounds of historical *jikong yuewu*. Unfortunately these have been lost with the passage of time and can be studied, in the present, only through verbal and preserved data. My fieldwork experiences of current performances of *jikong yuewu* have, however, provided me a basis to discuss historical performances.

36. Li Zhizao, *Pangong liyue shu*, p. 65.

Music example 2. Li Zhizao's (*Pangong liyue shu*, 1618) version of the Ming dynasty song of welcome; the whole notes show the vocal line, the quarter notes the instrumental line. For the text, see Music example 1, p. 147.

Li was wrong, but his comments are indicative of his understanding of Confucius and the Confucian Ceremonial. For Li, the ceremonial honored Confucius as the sage of an empire not as the ancestor of a clan.

Li composed his instrumental tunes for a specific reason. He accepted the official status of the Ming dynasty ceremonial, but he believed that its use of the *zhonglü* mode for both the vocal and the instrumental parts was erroneous. Basing his views on the *Rites of Zhou*, he explained that to harmonize the *yin* and *yang* elements in the world, the instrumental music used in state sacrifices should play *yang* pitches and the vocal melodies should use *yin* ones. This "correct" understanding was disputed by Han dynasty scholars, who correlated *yin* and *yang* pitches with various elements of the cosmos. After studying the *Rites of Zhou*, Zhu Zaiyu's 朱載堉 (1536–1610) *Lülü jingyi* 律呂精義 (Fundamental theories of music), and conducting his own experiments, Li concluded that the instrumental counterparts of vocal melodies sung in the *zhonglü* mode should be played in the *huangzhong* mode. In other words, the Ming use of the *zhonglü* mode for both the instrumental and the vocal parts was erroneous: the music had only *yin* and no *yang* and contradicted ancient teachings. As a remedy, Li composed instrumental tunes in the *huangzhong* mode to provide the missing *yang* element and to make the music harmonious. When music was harmonious, Li theorized, *qi* would be harmonious; then, Heaven and Earth would be in harmony, and people and the deities would communicate.[37] Li realized that the *huangzhong* mode was traditionally reserved to honor heavenly deities and that its use in *jikong yuewu* would be challenged. He argued that Confucius was unique in the human world and that honoring him with a heavenly mode would not be excessive. Li, however, acknowledged imperial authority and did not dare to implement his instrumental tunes. He did nothing more than make them available to his fellow Confucians. Li's instrumental tunes never found wide acceptance, but a performance of their distinctive sounds would reveal Li's creative heart/mind, which operated within the orthodox and imperial boundaries of a collapsing Ming world.

Shi Jishi

In 1622, Shi Jishi 史記事 (*jinshi* 1595), a Confucian scholar and music master of Weinan county in Shanxi, published *Dacheng liyue ji* 大成禮樂集 (Manual for and collection of documents on the Confucian Ceremonial), a work that reveals localized meanings in *jikong yuewu*. Superficially, Shi's *jikong yuewu* is orthodox: the ideological, historical, ritual, musical, and choreographic aspects of Shi's Confucian Ceremonial seem to follow established theories and practices. Shi's descriptions relied on the authority of the *Rites of Zhou*, the *Book of Odes*, the *Yueji*, Chen Yang's *Yueshu*, Zhang E's *Dacheng yuewu tupu*, the *Ming huidian* (Collected statues of the Ming), and other standard references. Fascicle 2, for example, describes such standard topics as the seasonal timing of the rite, the three days of fasting, the inspection of the sacrificial victims, the preparation of the sacrificial food, the arrangement of the altars, the ritual procedures (*yizhu*), and so forth. Fascicle 3 and the first part of fascicle 4 describe the music (its history, the musical instruments used in it, and their cosmological meanings) and performance techniques and include notated scores of the six fixed songs of the Ming dynasty ceremonial. The second half of fascicle 4 describes the history and meaning of the dances and describes the poses. Shi's verbal descriptions of the dances are almost identical to those found in Zhang E's *Dacheng yuewu tupu*.

---

37. Ibid., pp. 786–87. See also Sommer (pp. 99–102) in this volume.

There are, however, many subtle signs that Shi Jishi's performance of the Confucian Ceremonial was personalized and localized. For example, Shi claimed that the drum call that began the ceremony of sacrificial offering should include 360 strokes, corresponding to the number of days in the lunar year. Shi also declared that the first string of the seven-string zither should be stopped only by the middle finger; Shi compared this performance practice to the scholar-officials' loyal service to the emperor.[38] These instructions affect the structure and performance of *jikong yuewu* and produce distinctive sounds.

Participants and members of the audience in Weinan county listened to these distinctive sounds critically and proudly, a fact that is clearly demonstrated by the prefaces, letters, and colophon published in Shi's manual. The first preface, written by Li Weizhen 李維楨, a local scholar, explains the historical contexts of Shi's music. Weinan county had always been a land of ritual and music: Shanxi was the land where the Zhou dynasty rose and created a comprehensive system of ritual and music. The Ming court followed the Zhou system and worshipped teachers and sages throughout the empire. However, the Ming court did not specify music to be used in the worship of Confucius in the county schools. Shi found fault with this lack of music and introduced *jikong yuewu* in Weinan county. Once performed, the ceremonial touched the benevolent hearts (*shanxin* 善心) of the people. During the performances, the rhythms, the dances, the five colors, and the eight winds corresponded to one another, projecting a spectacle that reminded Weinan people of the ritual and music heard in schools in the Zhou capital.[39]

The other prefaces in the manual describe various aspects of the music, but the focus of description is on Shi. For example, the second preface, written by Xu Ji 徐吉 (*jinshi* 1616), an investigating censor (*jiancha yushi* 監察御使), commented on a general decline of ritual and music and then commended Shi for implementing Confucius's ideology of proper music in such a time. The third preface, written by Chen Yingyuan 陳應元, an education intendant (*duxue* 督學), commented on Shi's scholarly refutation of the argument that county schools should not use music in their worship of Confucius. Chen compared Shi's manual to a classic in Chinese music theory, the *Lülü xinshu* 律呂新書 (New treatise of music theory) of the pre-

---

38. Shi Jishi, *Dacheng liyue ji* 3.21a.
39. Ibid., preface by Li.

eminent Song scholar–music master, Cai Yuanding 蔡元定 (1135–98). The fourth preface, by Chen Yaofei 陳耀非, the county magistrate, outlined Shi's study of proper music, his introduction of *jikong yuewu* to Weinan county, and his construction of the musical instruments needed for the rite.

In the colophon, Wang Sishun 王思舜, a Confucian scholar and connoisseur of ceremonial music, described Shi as a scholar–music master totally devoted to ritual and music. Rather than wasting efforts on trivial things such as food, clothing, and interactions with fellow scholars, Wang reported, Shi chose to devote his energies to ritual and music, claiming that a Confucian scholar should never forget such matters. In response to Wang's questions about syllabic singing and the use of repeated notes in the instrumental parts of the music, Shi gave a classic answer: one sings to sustain (*yong* 詠) the words; thus, each word of the text has its own note, and the instruments should not play repeated notes. In his concluding remarks, Wang claimed that Weinan county had produced many great advocates of Confucian ritual and music: the Duke of Zhou in the Zhou dynasty, Zhang Zai 張載 (1020–77) in the Song dynasty, Lü Nan and Han Bangqi 韓邦奇 in the Ming, and now Shi in Wang's own time. Wang's claim makes it clear that Shi's *jikong yuewu* was much more than the sounds of bell-chimes and drums. The performed music not only intellectually realized Confucian ideals but also sonically embodied the pride and identity of Weinan Confucians.

Li Zhouwang and Xie Lüzhong

In 1719, Li Zhouwang 李周望 and Xie Lüzhong 謝履忠 compiled *Guoxue liyue lu* 國學禮樂錄 (Record of rites and music at the Imperial University) and described a version of *jikong yuewu* that reflects the transition between the Ming and the Qing. Writing as the libationer of the Imperial University (*guozi jijiu* 國子祭酒), Li presented a scholarly explanation of *jikong yuewu* in his preface to the volume. Then, in the text of the volume, Li and his co-editor offered a historical and analytical report.[40] According to Li and Xie, the *jikong yuewu* performed and heard at the Imperial University derived from the Ming version of 1393. The composer of the fixed songs was Leng Qian 冷謙 (fl. 1360s), the legendary music master summoned to the Ming court to establish proper music. The songs used

---

40. Li Zhouwang and Xie Lüzhong, *Guoxue liyue lu* 16.3a.

only five pitches: two *yang* pitches and three *yin* pitches, and involved sounds articulated by the throat, the front teeth (*chi* 齒), the tongue, and the lips; there were no sounds articulated against the inner teeth (*ya* 牙). The modal features of the songs were probably Ming adjustments: the Yuan version of the songs, a direct precursor of the Ming version, used ten pitches. As vocal melodies with instrumental accompaniment, the songs sounded quite harmonious (*xiehe*). However, the linguistic tones of the song texts and the musical pitches of the melodies did not match too well (*gege bu ru* 格格不入). In actual performances, this problem had to be solved by the singers' skillful adjustments.[41]

The editors provided illustrations of the poses of the dances, which were choreographically identical with those depicted in representative Ming sources, such as Huang Zuo's *Nanyong zhi*. The dancers are, however, dressed in Qing costumes (see Figs. 3.1–3.3). Instead of the long and flowing sleeves of the Ming, the sleeves of the Qing costume are closed at the wrist. Also prominently displayed are the queues protruding from under the hats of the Qing dancers. Such detailed pictures reveal the uniqueness of the *jikong yuewu* performed at Li's Imperial University: costumes are an integral part of dances, and even when the Ming and Qing dancers strike identical poses, their costumes make the dances look different. Such differences are meaningful because they help to demonstrate the ways the performance embodied the Confucian scholars. As revealed in the *Guoxue liyue lu*, Li and his fellow Confucian scholars produced and consumed *jikong yuewu* through all its details. They constructed histories of the music, analyzed its structure, and solved practical problems in actual performances. They did not comment explicitly on the unmistakable mix of Ming and Qing elements, because it did not render their music any less Confucian and proper. The amalgam of elements only underscored who they were: Confucian scholar-officials living in the early Qing era when memories of the Ming court were still fresh.

---

41. The singers have to make certain adjustments, or otherwise they would not be able to sing the words.

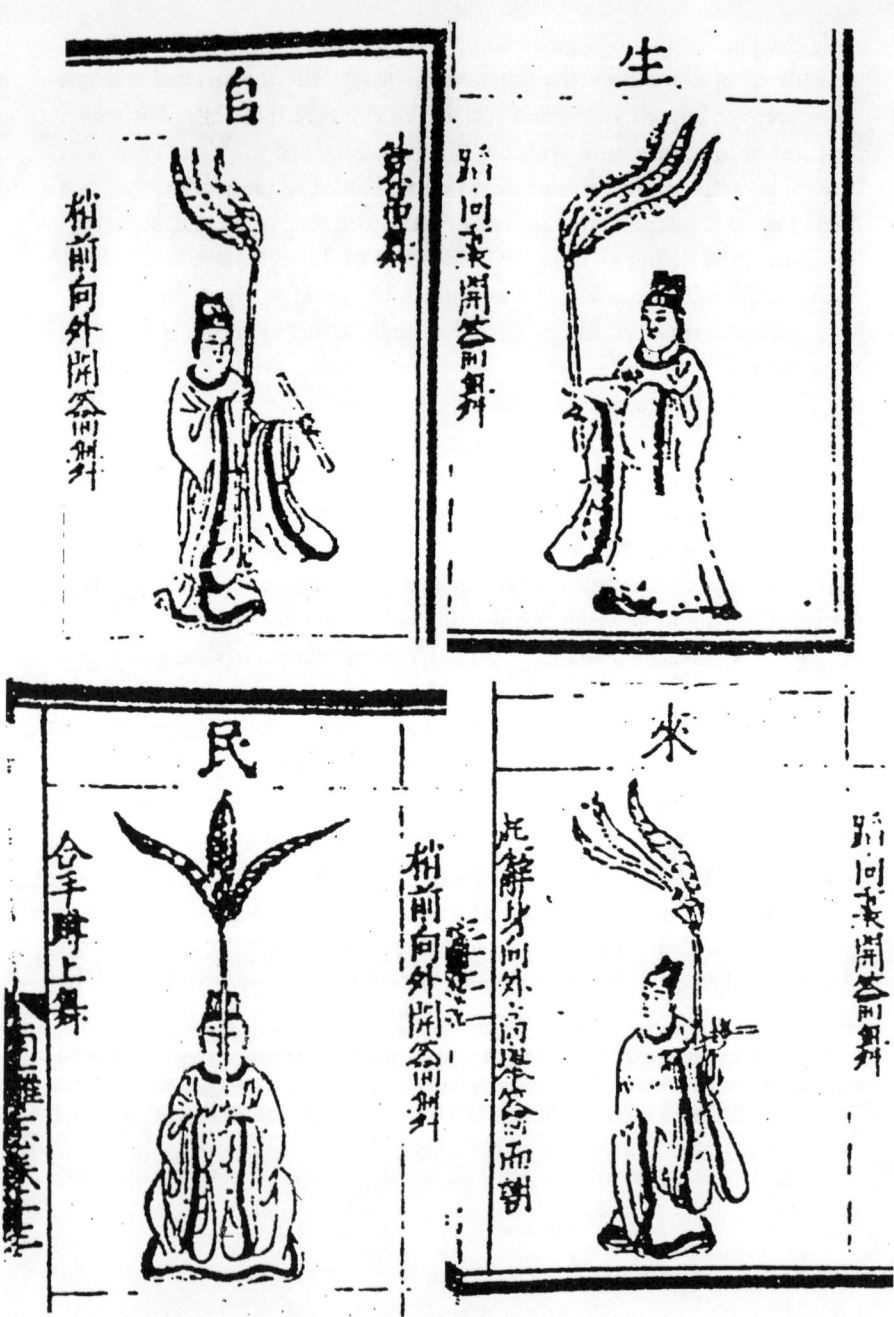

Fig. 3.1. Choreographic poses for the first phrase of the first offering song in the Ming *jikong yuewu* (Huang Zuo, *Nanyong zhi*, 1544, 13.32a). In this and the following figures, the four panels are to be read in the order: top left, top right, bottom left, bottom right.

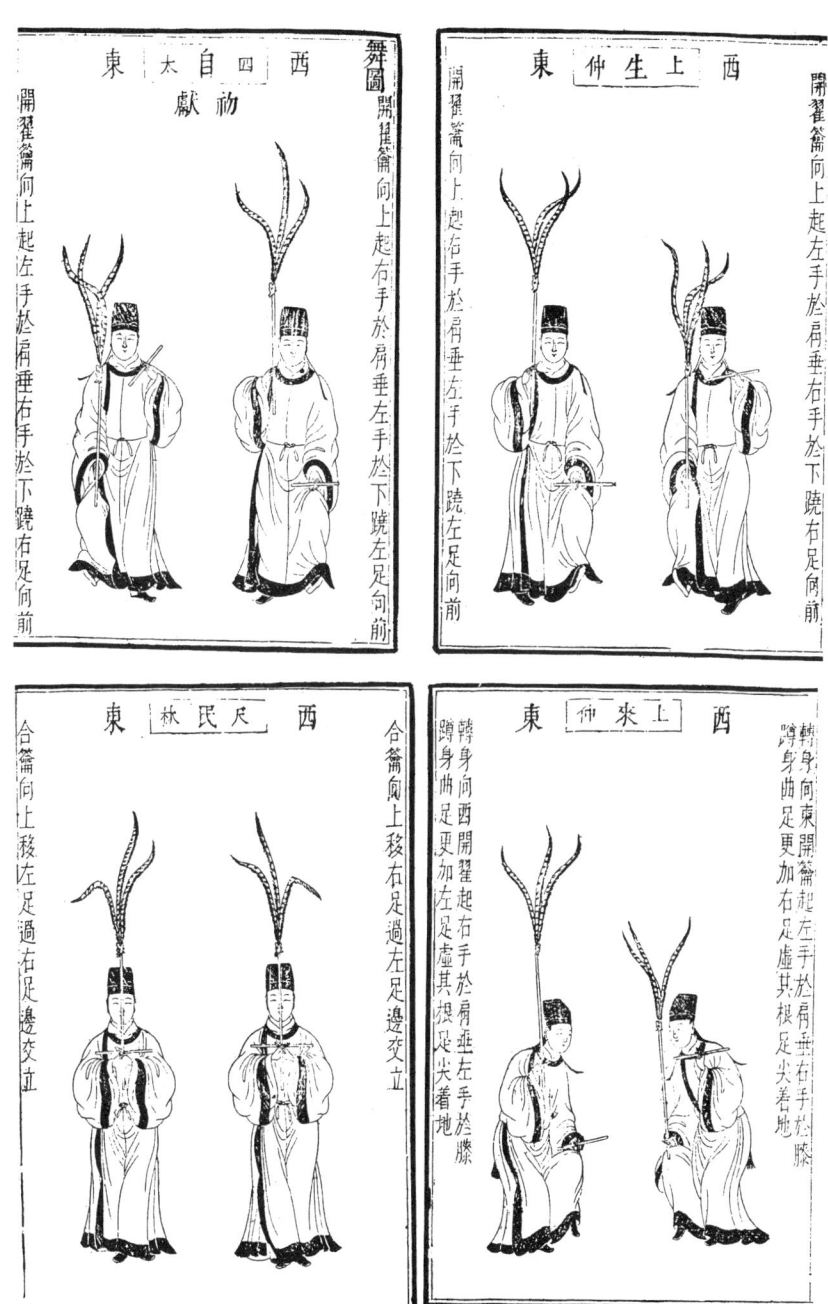

Fig. 3.2. Choreographic poses for the first phrase of the first offering song in the Ming *jikong yuewu* (Li Zhizao, *Pangong liyue shu*, 1618, 8.13–14)

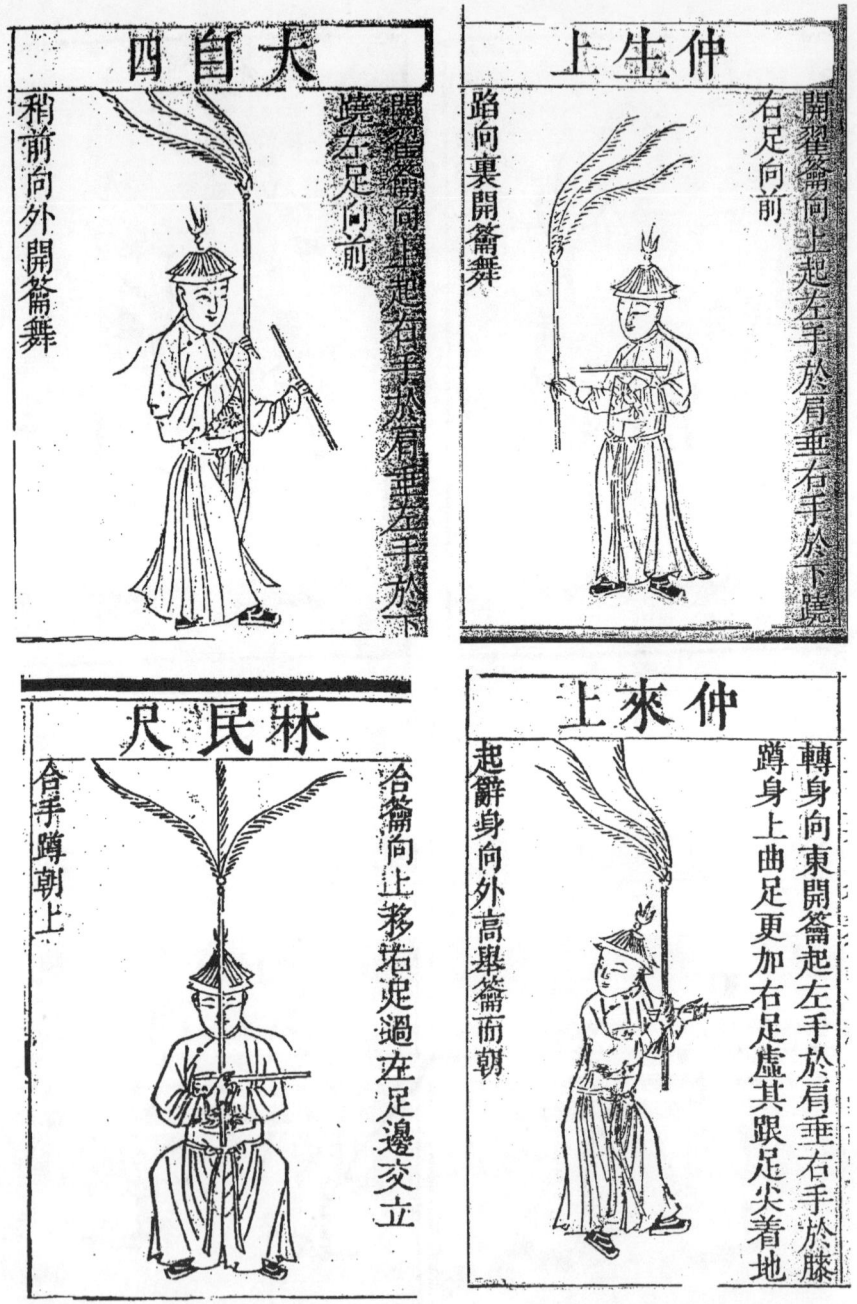

Fig. 3.3. Choreographic poses for the first phrase of the first offering song in the Qing *jikong yuewu* (Li Zhouwang and Xie Lüzhong, *Guoxue liyue lu*, 1719, 16.2a)

Qiu Zhilu

In 1840, Qiu Zhilu of Liuyang county compiled *Dingji liyue beikao* 丁祭禮樂備考 (Complete study of the rites and music of the Confucian sacrifices), revealing a personal and local version of the Qing dynasty ceremony. The distinctive features of Qiu's *jikong yuewu* are clearly described in the specialized scores for the musicians and in choreographic instructions for the dancers. In the singers' musical score, Qiu instructed them to control their vocal organs so that they could accurately and intelligibly sing the words of the song text.[42] For example, "da zai Kongzi" 大哉孔子 (Great is Confucius), the first four words of the first song of the local version of the Qing dynasty ceremony, should be sung, respectively, with (1) an open mouth and the tip of the tongue; (2) an open mouth and the top of the front teeth; (3) closed mouth and the inner teeth; (4) and an open mouth and the front teeth. In the score for the wind players, Qiu instructed them to play detailed rhythmic and ornamental notes, two musical features not sanctioned by normative theories of *jikong yuewu* (see Music Example 3). Qiu realized the radical nature of his ornamental notes and supported them with the authority of Zhu Xi 朱熹 (1130–1200). Thus, he argued that the ornamental notes were the natural outcomes of the playing of string and wind instruments and that they were comparable to what Zhu Xi had called the free sounds (*sansheng* 散聲) of the seven-string zither and accompanying notes (*chenqiang* 襯腔) of the flutes.[43]

Qiu's verbal descriptions of the dances are more detailed than the official descriptions and demonstrate that a variety of movements can be choreographed creatively between the standardized poses. A comparison of Qiu's poses with those prescribed by the Qing court is illustrative (see Fig. 3.4).[44] As described in Yunlu's *Lülü zhengyi houbian*, the eastern dancers performed the following poses to the words *yuhuai mingde* 予懷明德 (you have brilliance and virtue):[45] (1) stand up straight and face forward, and hold the feather and the flute straight; (2) tilt the torso to the east, bend the right foot, turn the face toward the west, stand up straight, point the flute to the east,

---

42. Qiu Zhilu, *Dingji liyue beikao* 2.3a.

43. Ibid., 3.12b.

44. Ibid., 2.9b; Yunlu et al., *Lülü zhengyi houbian* 32.1b–2a.

45. The dancers were divided into eastern and western groups; their movements were mirror images. Here only the movements of the eastern group (i.e., the right-hand side of the double pictograms in Fig. 3.4) are described.

Music example 3. Qiu Zhilu's (*Dingji liyue beikao*, 1840) version of the song of welcome in the Qing *jikong yuewu*. For the text, see Music example 1. p. 149.

and make a cross with the feather; (3) stand up straight, hold the flute straight and close to the left shoulder, hold the feather horizontal and make a cross with the flute; (4) stand up straight, cup the hands, and make a cross with the feather and the flute. In Qiu's description, the same four poses are danced as follows: (1) lift (*qiao* 蹺) the left foot to the front, hop (*dao* 蹈) on the right foot, slightly bend the torso, raise the right arm about to the shoulder, and drop the left arm below; (2) lift the right foot to the front, hop on the left foot, slightly bend the torso, raise the left arm above the shoulder, and drop the right arm below the shoulder; (3) touch the floor with the left foot, move the right foot to the left foot, "close" the flute, wait until the third beat of the drums, and then squat (*dun* 蹲); (4) move the right foot toward the east, squat, raise the left arm above the shoulder, drop the right arm below the shoulder, turn the torso, and move the right foot onto the left foot, direct the torso to the east, and look up.

Qiu was a prominent scholar-musician in his time, and his *jikong yuewu* became the pride of Liuyang county.[46] According to Xu Ke's 徐珂 *Qingbai*

----

46. *Liuyang xianzhi*, pp. 829–30.

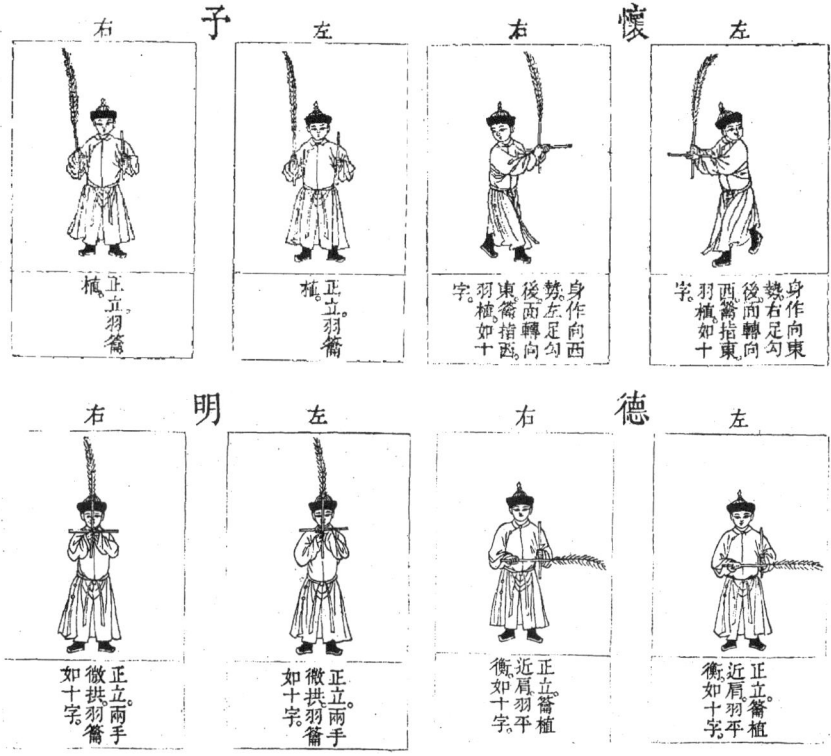

Fig. 3.4. Choreographic poses for the first phrase of the first offering song in the Qing *jikong yuewue* (Yunlu, *Lülü zhengyi houbian*, 1749, 32.1b–2a)

leichao 清稗類鈔 (Classified collection of anecdotes from the Qing),[47] Qiu was known for his special gifts and earnest pursuit of filial piety and civility (*you* 友). He studied extensively and understood theories of music. Claiming that music originated from the *qi* of the natural world, Qiu employed the ancient method of watching the ether (*houqi* 候氣) to find the accurate pitches of proper music. Qiu then correlated the pitches with the 64 hexagrams (*gua* 卦). When Qiu was hired to teach *jikong yuewu* in Liuyang, he made the required musical instruments and rehearsed with students. To publicize his musical theories and practices of proper music, Qiu produced two treatises, the *Lüyin huikao* 律音彙考 (Comprehensive examination of music theories) of 1838 and the *Dingji liyue beikao*.

47. Xu Ke, *Qingbai leichao*, p. 4923.

Qiu provided an autobiography in the *Lüyin huikao*. He received a classical training from his father, studying the *Book of Odes* and theories of music. In Zhu Xi's *Yili jingzhuan tongjie* 儀禮經傳通解 (Explanations of the *Yili* and its commentaries), Qiu found the musical scores for twelve ancient poems. He tried to perform them but failed because he found that the notated melodies and the song texts did not complement one another. In 1818, Qiu studied an official score of *jikong yuewu* and began to understand the use of musical pitches. Then he was hired to teach the ceremony and launched a lifelong research on music. Qiu was successful, and his *jikong yuewu* became famous. His success was, however, not just a matter of academic and musical excellence; in addition to official sponsorship, he enjoyed the support of the audience. Qiu was familiar with the popular musical and theatrical worlds of mid-nineteenth-century China. Widely sung among the cultural elite, Kun arias of the time were famous for their ornamental notes and the perfect match between the musical tones of the melodies and the linguistic tones of the libretti.[48] By introducing ornamental notes to ceremonial music, Qiu made it a sonic embodiment of contemporary musical trends.

Yang Shusen

Qiu's music made a deep impression on the people of Liuyang. In the 1930s, it was incorporated into Yang Shusen's *Zhenxing yayue yi*. Yang, a native of Liuyang, adopted Qiu's music because he found it musical.[49] As Yang explained, the official Qing *jikong yuewu* scores specified the syllabic style of singing. However, without the use of ornamental tones (*yuyun* 餘韻), the syllabic style led to sudden beginnings and endings in musical performances and this caused a sense of being rushed. Since all chanting of poems and texts featured the use of lingering tones and accompanying notes, Yang argued, ceremonial songs should not be sung as syllabic music and Qiu's use of ornamental notes should be followed faithfully.

Yang, however, did not follow Qiu's dances faithfully. The first dance in Yang's version of the ceremony was performed as a military dance. Instead of feathers and flutes, the dancers held axes (*qi* 戚) and shields (*gan* 干). And contrary to the Ming and Qing tradition of performing the dance in the six-row format, Yang presented the dances in the eight-row format (*bayi* 八

---

48. Yang Yinliu, "Kongmiao dingji yinyue di chubu yanjiu."
49. Yang Shusen, *Zhenxing yayue yi, juan 2*, "Sidian yuezhang gaiyin" 1a.

佾).⁵⁰ Yang's *jikong yuewu* was distinctive because he wanted to promote Confucianism as a means to counteract the forces of westernization and modernization. In his treatise, he gave elaborate descriptions of all the orthodox theories and practices of ritual and music and discussed the history of ritual and music in China, the technical and cosmological attributes of the pitches, the symbolism of the musical instruments, and so forth.

Yang gave five reasons why the Chinese tradition of proper music should be revitalized.⁵¹ First, proper music would help the government manage the nation and cultivate the populace. In the past, once a government became established, it instituted proper music to nurture the heart/minds of universal love (*bo'ai* 博愛) among the populace. Second, proper music would show respect to Confucius. Historically, the Chinese people had always worshipped Confucius. The Qing court had raised the Confucian Ceremonial to the rank of a great state sacrifice (*dasi* 大祀) to emphasize education, to show respect to the Sage, and to cultivate the character of the populace. Third, proper music would dispel villainous habits. In the past, proper music touched the heart/minds of people. After listening to proper music, even ruthless and disagreeable people would control their behavior. Westerners (*wairen* 外人) emphasized music because they realized that there was no better way to change the bad habits of the people. By comparison, the Chinese of Yang's time did not emphasize their own music, and thus they compared unfavorably with the Westerners. Fourth, proper music would inspire the populace. People did not just listen to the sounds of music. They felt and understood musical messages: when they listened to a musical play about loyalty, filial piety, integrity, and morals (*zhongxiao jieyi* 忠孝節義), they cried and laughed with the sad and happy scenes. Improved (*gailiang* 改良) dramatic music could guide the stupid and stubborn, but proper music would enlighten the talented and the intelligent. Fifth, proper music would preserve the essence of China. Young students of Yang's time cherished westernization, but they were not taught the legacies of Chinese sages and rulers. Yang claimed that if proper music were revitalized and taught in the schools, it would favorably compare with Western music. Yang ended his analysis with optimism and warning: it was fortunate that proper music could still be learned and preserved in his time; otherwise, China would have the name but not the substance of a great and proud country.

---

50. Ibid., 3, "Wupu" 6a.
51. Ibid., 1, "Yayue" 4b–6a.

'JIKONG YUEWU' AND
MUSICAL CONFUCIANISM IN THE 1990S

Yang Shusan's optimism was not misplaced. Musical Confucianism still thrives in China, and *jikong yuewu* is now performed annually in Qufu, Taipei, and other centers of Confucian learning. After a hiatus of thirty or more years, the citizens of Qufu began to reconstruct the ceremony in the early 1980s. As cultural, if not blood, descendants of Confucius, they want to promote a local sage and spread his teachings. As inhabitants of a great historical town that needs to revive its economy, they also need to build industries. Qufu has no big factories, but it has a magnificent Confucian temple, a grand mansion of the Kong clan, and many memories of *jikong yuewu*. As local pride, cultural memories, and economic needs merged, and as local officials, leading musicians, and artists collaborated, Qufu once again became a center of Confucian Ceremonial music.[52] The celebrants are, however, no longer emperors, scholar-officials, and descendants of Confucius, but actors from a local theatrical arts troupe. The audience consists mostly of tourists from China, Japan, and North America. The admission fees pay for the expenses of mounting costly ritual and musical performances on the terrace in front of the hallowed Hall of Great Completion (Dacheng dian 大成殿).

Because the Qufu performance features sacrificial offerings in which the ritual victims are made of plaster and lively renditions of the fixed songs and dances, many critics would reject the ceremony of contemporary Qufu as touristy (see Music Example 4). The critics are both right and wrong. The music has been tailored to meet the expectations of tourists, and it has been a success in attracting visitors from all over the world. However, the music is as "humanistic" as any other version of *jikong yuewu* performed throughout Chinese history. The current version follows the political and economic agenda set by the central authorities in Beijing. It was, however, reconstructed by officials, artists, and musicians in Qufu. They consulted historical sources, and their reconstruction realizes many firmly established prescriptive theories and normative practices. For example, it features drum calls and syllabic singing, and the dances observe the six-row format. Above

---

52. This description is based on my 1990 fieldwork in Qufu. See Lam, "The Yin and Yang of Chinese Music Historiography."

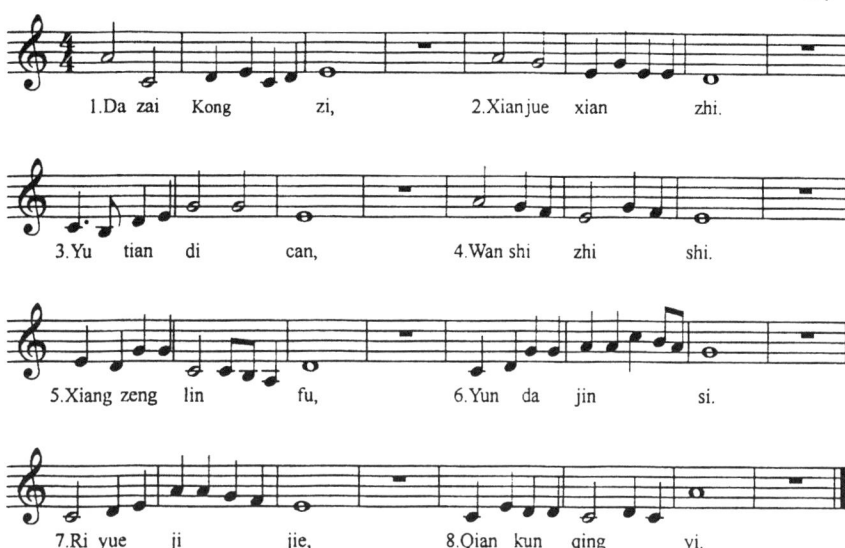

Music example 4. Song of welcome in Qufu *jikong yuewu* (1990). The text reads:

1 Great is Confucius! 大哉孔子
2 He perceives and knows in advance. 先覺先知
3 Between Heaven and Earth, 與天地參
4 He is the teacher of all generations. 萬世之師
5 This propitious sacrifice is marked by blessed silk. 祥徵麟紱
6. And its music played by instruments of metal and silk. 韻答金絲
7 Now that the Sun and Moon are unveiled to us, 日月既揭
8 The universe is clear and peaceful. 乾坤清夷

all, it embodies the heart/minds of Qufu officials, artists, and citizens. The Qufu *jikong yuewu* is more than reconstructed musical sounds and choreographic poses; it rebuilds Qufu as a significant place in China. The lively sounds of the music are not touristy but contemporary and professional: the accented rhythms and melodic twists come from professional musicians trained in the westernized Chinese music that is now heard all over China; the professional, and thus appealing, performance of the music results from regular rehearsals and from artistic and current interpretations of Confucian Ceremonial and proper music of the past. The fluid choreography comes from an artistic director who was once an opera actor and who understands the art of choreographing Chinese movements and bodies.[53] As performed,

---

53. Wang, "Jikong yuewu yanjiu."

the Qufu *jikong yuewu* blends the Confucian past and the socialist present in Qufu, revealing both continuity and change.

Compared to the flamboyant performance in Qufu, the *jikong yuewu* performed in the Confucian temple in Taipei is solemn.[54] The drum calls, the "metallic sounds" and "jade vibrations" performed by the orchestra, the syllabic singing, the local dignitaries' participation as celebrants, the hair and blood of the sacrificial animals, and other orthodox features combine to project a sense of an authentic Chinese ceremonial. There is absolutely no doubt that the Taipei authorities and the Confucius Temple of Taipei are teaching a lesson in Confucianism through *jikong yuewu*.[55] This is why there is a didactic quality to the Taipei version, and why local and international students are invited to attend the performances. The Taipei *jikong yuewu* is not only about the Confucian ideology of proper music, however. It is also part of a local festival. Even as the music is being solemnly performed, a bazaar awaits the audience outside the temple compound. Stalls sell real estate, paintings, candies, karaoke tapes, and many other refined and not so refined items. Just like its counterpart in Qufu, the *jikong yuewu* in Taipei is also a sonic embodiment of scholars, musicians, and Taipei citizens. The pure and accurate tuning of the stone-chimes and bell-chimes reflects cutting-edge research and technology in Taiwan. The short and staccato instrumental prelude to the fixed songs preserves the legacy of a former music master. The dances by students from a neighborhood primary school display dedication and many hours of rehearsals. As the current music director says, the Taipei *jikong yuewu* may be simple, but it is still a physical and musical challenge for the young boys and girls. Their amateurish performance serves to show their human nature.

What the young students learn from their participation in the Taipei *jikong yuewu* remains to be seen. What the tourists in Qufu may take away with them is questionable. However, the *jikong yuewu* in Qufu and Taipei clearly illustrate the theories, practices, and products of musical Confucianism of the past and of the present. Musical Confucianism thrives because it has adjusted to changing times and needs. Musical Confucianism is much more than philosophical concepts and the sounds of bells and drums.

---

54. This description is based on my 1995 fieldwork in Taipei.
55. This is clear from the booklets distributed by the Taipei Confucius Temple. See, e.g., Dong Jinyu, *Zhisheng xianshi Kongzi shidian jieshuo.*

It is a sonic embodiment of individual Confucians and their changing understandings and realizations of Confucianism. To understand this embodiment, one needs only to follow Confucius's example of practicing music diligently and listening to it critically. Through the sounds, one hears the people and their heart/minds.

WORKS CITED

The Analects (*Lunyu* 論語). Trans. D. C. Lau. London: Penguin Books, 1979.

Cai Yuanding 蔡元定. *Lülü xinshu* 律呂新書 (New treatise of music theory). Siku quanshu 四庫全書 ed.

Chen Fu-Yen. "Confucian Ceremonial Music in Taiwan with Comparative References to Its Sources." Ph.D. diss.: Wesleyan University, 1976.

Chen Yang 陳暘. *Yueshu* 樂書 (Treatise on music). 1104. Siku quanshu 四庫全書 ed.

Cultural and Educational Foundation of Confucius Institute, USA, comp. *Recordation of International Confucius Worship Movement*, vol. 1. San Francisco: International Confucius University, U.S.A., 1984.

Dong Jinyu 董金裕. *Zhisheng xianshi Kongzi shidian jieshuo* 至聖先師孔子釋奠解說 (A guide to the Confucius ceremony). Taipei: Taibeishi Kongmiao guanli weiyuanhui, 1995.

Fung Yu-lan. *A History of Chinese Philosophy*, vol. 1. Trans. Derk Bodde. Princeton: Princeton University Press, 1952.

Gulik, Robert Hans van. *The Lore of the Chinese Lute: An Essay in the Ideology of the Ch'in*. New ed. Tokyo: Tuttle, 1969.

Huang Zuo 黃佐. *Nanyong zhi* 南雝誌 (Account of the southern Imperial University). 1544. Copy held at the Harvard-Yenching Library, Cambridge, Mass.

Jin jili 金集禮 (Collected ceremonials of the Jin). Siku quanshu 四庫全書 ed.

Kong Jifen 孔繼汾. *Queli wenxian kao* 闕里文獻考 (An investigation of documents and traditions in Qufu). Kongzi wenhua daquan 孔子文化大全 ed.

Kongzi jiayu 孔子家語 (Family sayings of Confucius). Beijing: Yanshan chubanshe, 1995.

Laade, Wolfgang. *The Confucius Temple Ceremony: Taiwan Republic of China*. CD. Zurich: Jecklin and Co., 1991. JD 652-2.

Lam, Joseph S. C. "Musical Relics and Cultural Expressions: State Sacrificial Songs from the Southern Song Court." *Journal of Sung-Yuan Studies* 25 (1995): 1–27.

———. "Ritual and Musical Politics in the Court of Ming Shizong." In *Harmony and Counterpoint: Ritual Music in Chinese Context*, ed. Bell Yung, Evelyn Rawski, and Rubie Watson, pp. 35–53. Stanford: Stanford University Press, 1996.

———. *State Sacrifices and Music in Ming China: Creativity, Orthodoxy, and Expressiveness*. Albany: State University of New York Press, 1998.

———. "The Yin and Yang of Chinese Music Historiography: The Case of Confucian Ceremonial Music." *Yearbook for Traditional Music* 27 (1995): 34–51.

Li Zhizao 李之藻. *Pangong liyue shu* 頖宮禮樂疏 (Proposal on rites and music in schools). 1618. Facsimile reprint—Taipei: Guoli zhongyang tushuguan, 1970.

Li Zhouwang 李周望 and Xie Lüzhong 謝履忠. *Guoxue liyue lu* 國學禮樂錄 (Record of rites and music at the Imperial University). 1719. Copy held at the Beijing tushuguan.

Liuyang xianzhi 瀏陽縣誌. Zhonghua renmin gongheguo difangzhi congshu 中華人民共和國地方誌叢書 ed. Beijing: Zhongguo chengshi chubanshe, 1994.

Ma Duanlin 馬端臨. *Wenxian tongkao* 文獻通考 (A comprehensive investigation of documents and traditions). Siku quanshu 四庫全書 ed.

Ming huidian 明會典 (Collected statutes of the Ming). Beijing: Zhonghua shuju, 1989.

Mingshi 明史 (Ming history). Beijing: Zhonghua shuju, 1974.

New Grove Dictionary of Music and Musicians. 6th ed. London: Macmillan, 1980.

Ouyang Xiu 歐陽修. *Taichang yin'geli* 太常因革禮 (History of the rites of the Court of Imperial Sacrifice). Siku quanshu 四庫全書 ed.

Pang Zhonglu 龐鍾璐. *Wenmiao sidian kao* 文廟祀典考 (Study of the sacrifical statutes of the culture temple). 1875. Copy held at the Library of the University of Michigan.

Qin Huitian 秦蕙田. *Wuli tongkao* 五禮通考 (Comprehensive study of the five rites). Siku quanshu 四庫全書 ed.

Qing huidian 清會典 (Collected statues of the Qing). Beijing: Zhonghua shuju, 1991.

Qiu Zhilu 邱之稑. *Dingji liyue beikao* 丁祭禮樂備考 (Complete study of the rites and music of the Confucian sacrifices). 1840. Copy held at the Library of the Chinese University of Hong Kong.

———. *Lüyin huikao* 律音彙考 (Comprehensive examination of music theory). 1835. Copy held at the Library of the Chinese University of Hong Kong.

Shi Jishi 史記事. *Dacheng liyue ji* 大成禮樂集 (Manual for and collection of documents on the Confucian Ceremonial). 1622. Copy held at the Beijing tushuguan.

Songshi 宋史 (Song history). 1345. Beijing: Zhonghua shuju, 1977.

Taichang xukao 太常續考 (Extended monograph on the Court of Imperial Sacrifice). 1640s. Siku quanshu 四庫全書 ed.

Taichang zonglan 太常總覽 (General record of the Court of Imperial Sacrifice). 1470s. Copy held at the Gugong bowuguan tushuguan, Taipei.

Tang Kaiyuan li 大唐開元禮 (Ceremonials of the Tang Kaiyuan [713–41] era). Siku quanshu 四庫全書 ed.

Wang Mingxing 王明星. "Jikong yuewu yanjiu" 祭孔樂舞研究 (A study of the music and dance in the Confucian Ceremonial). *Wudao yishu*, no. 3 (1988): 17–36.

Xu Ke 徐珂. *Qingbai leichao* 清稗類鈔 (Classified collection of ancedotes from the Qing). Beijing: Zhonghua shuju, 1986.

Yang Shusen 楊樹森. *Zhenxing yayue yi* 振興雅樂議 (Proposal for revitalizing proper music). N.p.: Sichuan guoxue, Zhuanxiuguang yayue ke, 1930?.

Yang Yinliu 楊蔭瀏. *Zhongguo gudai yinyue shigao* 中國古代音樂史稿 (Draft history of ancient Chinese music). Beijing: Remin yinyue chubanshe, 1981.

———. "Kongmiao dingji yinyue de chubu yanjiu" 孔廟丁祭音樂的初步研究. In *Yang Yinliu yinyue lunwen xuanji* 楊蔭瀏音樂論文選集 (Selected anthology of the musicological studies of Yan Yinliu), pp. 276–97. Shanghia: Wenyi chubanshe, 1986.

Yuanshi 元史. Ershiwushi 二十五史 ed. Shanghai: Shanghai guji chubanshe, 1986.

Yueji 樂記 (Record of music). In *Baihua shisanjing* 白話十三經, ed. Qian Bocheng 錢伯城. Beijing: Guoji wenhua chubanshe, 1996.

Yunlu 允祿 et al., comps. *Lülü zhengyi houbian* 律呂正義後編 (Correct music theories, final compilation). 1746. Guoxue jiben congshu 國學基本叢書 ed. Changsha: Shangwu yinshuguan, n.d.

Zhang Dainian 張岱年, ed. *Kongzi dacidian* 孔子大詞典 (A dictionary of Confucius). Shanghai: Shanghai cishu chubanshe, 1993.

Zhang E 張鶚. *Dacheng yuewu tupu* 大成樂舞圖譜 (Musical scores and dance illustrations for the Confucian Ceremonial). Copy held at the Naikaku Bunko.

Zhongxing lishu 中興禮書 (Compilation of ceremonials and music of the Southern Song). 1184. Copy held at the Library of Zhongshan daxue, Guangzhou.

Zhongguo yinyue shupuzhi 中國音樂書譜誌 (Bibliography of Chinese music books and notated sources). Beijing: Renmin yinyue chubanshe, 1984.

Zhu Zaiyu 朱載堉. *Lülü jingyi* 律呂精義 (Fundamental theories of music). 1590s. In *Yuelü quanshu* 樂律全書. Guoxue jiben congshu 國學基本叢書 ed. Changsha: Shangwu yinshuguan, n.d.

PART II
Imagining Confucius

Previous page: Confucius is born with a five-character inscription on his chest. *Kongsheng jiayu tu*, scene 5. Original 1589 edition of Wu Jiamo. See legend to Fig. 5.14 for more details.

FOUR

The Genesis of Kongzi in Ancient Narrative

The Figurative as Historical

Lionel M. Jensen

> Stories never live alone: they are the branches of a
> family we have yet to trace backward and forward.
> —Roberto Calasso

For many centuries considerable pomp has marked the circumstance of the genealogical continuity of the Kong 孔 clan of Qufu 曲阜, Shandong. The scions of this particular house have extolled themselves and been extolled from imperial times (ca. 100 BCE) until the present for their status as direct descendants of the Warring States figure and "first sage" (*xiansheng* 先聖) of the "Weakling" (*ru* 儒) fellowship, Kongzi 孔子 (ca. 551–479 BCE), since 1687 better known in the Western world by the Latin nomination "Confucius."[1] The stories within which this genealogy was embedded, the many other stories through which Kongzi was brought to life, and the guarding of

I thank Tom Wilson for his gentle, persuasive, and perspicacious reading of this chapter and Julia Murray for her rigorous criticisms of its early form and content. In rewriting this essay, I was spared many conceptual errors by the spirited intervention and wonderfully inspired suggestions of E. Bruce Brooks, the consummate colleague and tireless teacher. Through insightful readings and recommendations, Hoyt Tillman, David Keightley, Ed Shaughnessy, Haun Saussy, and Susan Blum offered guidance essential to the chapter's final form.

1. On the history of the local Jesuit invention of the term "Confucius" in China and its subsequent wider dissemination in Europe in the seventeenth century, see Jensen, *Manufacturing Confucianism*, pp. 7–11, 33–34, 70–96, 111–33.

these stories by non-kin textual communities are the subjects of this chapter. It is conceived as a study of the multiple, sometimes contested meanings of a single figure produced by competitive systems of representation.

The branches of the extended family of stories that have left us Kongzi as a corporate product are here traced backward and forward to disclose competing forms of narrative invention among elites in the interval between 400 BCE and 150 CE.[2] The Kong estate narrative, historically recognized more as a living biological testament than a story, represents but one of these branches. As we shall see, other storied inventions sprouted from the same roots, such as the transmission of Kongzi's disciples found in the *Analects* (*Lunyu* 論語) and the *Historical Records* (*Shi ji* 史記), borne forward apostolically by the Weakling fellowship; the biblio-tradition of Liu Xiang 劉向 (77–6 BCE) and Liu Xin 劉歆 (46 BCE–23 CE) bequeathed by the "ancestral teacher" (*zongshi* 宗師), Kongzi, and elaborately inventoried in the "Yiwenzhi" 藝文志 chapter of the *History of the Former Han* (*Hanshu* 漢書); the normative biographic tradition of the *Historical Records* and the *Family Sayings of Kongzi* (*Kongzi jiayu* 孔子家語), and the elite lore of ancient fertility rite and astral genesis myth (contained in certain apocryphal texts [*weishu* 緯書] of the Latter Han).

Whether ancestor, teacher, or god, Kongzi has long acted as a point of both mimetic and generative fiction, but it has been the biological brief of the Kong clan that has enjoyed superiority and endurance. In fact, as recently as 1984 in conjunction with the 2,535th anniversary of the putative birth of Kongzi, this hallowed, millennial propagation was the subject of an "oral transmission" (*koushu* 口述) produced by a self-proclaimed seventy-seventh-generation descendant, Kong Demao 孔德懋. This work, *Anecdotes from the Inner Quarters of the Kong Residence—The Reminiscences of Kongzi's Descendant* (*Kongfu neizhai yishi–Kongzi houyi de huiyi* 孔府內宅軼事—孔子後裔的回憶),[3] is largely devoted to a retelling of the daily life of young and old inside the legendary family compound in Qufu, Shandong, imagined as the still-point of the turning world of China past and present.

The author dwells so on the magical properties of "flesh and blood descent" from Kongzi and its concomitant imperial perquisites that the real

---

2. The dates of this interval mark: (1) the approximate beginning of the Qufu Kong clan's claim of unbroken descent from Kongzi, and (2) the first appearance in a text (*Yan Kong tu* 演孔圖) of the myth of Kongzi's divine birth.

3. New World Publishers of Beijing brought out an English translation that same year under the title *In the Mansion of Confucius's Descendants*.

chronology of her narrative (1890s–1940s) seems incidental. Astonishingly, this oral history, culled from the political debris of China's explosive twentieth century, sustains a memory that recalls the earliest imperial recognition of the clan under the Han emperor Yuandi (ca. 40 BCE), the tenth-century (952) conferring of the title "Duke of Accomplished Propagation" (*wenxuan gong* 文宣公)[4] upon the forty-third-generation descendant, Kong Renyu 孔仁玉 (912–56), and of the enfeoffment in perpetuity of Kong descendants by the Emperor Renzong (r. 1023–63) of the Northern Song symbolized in the nobiliary investiture of "Duke of Overflowing Sageliness" (*yansheng gong* 衍聖公), a title held through the twentieth century.

The conferring of this official title and its privileges represented one of several irregular episodes of imperial enfeoffment of the Kong clan between the Han and the Song (ca. 150 BCE–1200 CE), which would become more frequent in the Ming and Qing (1368–1911 CE) periods.[5] This investiture was the sole province of the blood descendants of the Kong house and conveyed public recognition of its unbroken ancestral line. Moreover, because this Shandong locus was considered the reliquary of the ritual objects (*liqi* 禮器) and remains of Kongzi and was later celebrated as the location of the *san Kong* 三孔: Kongfu 孔府 (Kong Mansion), Konglin 孔林 (Kong Cemetery), and Kongmiao 孔廟 (Kong Temple), the Qufu Kongs enjoyed pride of place among imperial China's hereditary nobility and within the increasingly extended Kong clan. Thus, as branches of the Kongs were established in the south and as far away as the northwestern province of Gansu, their collective relations were conceived in vague imitation of the Zhou era "ritual chamber charter" (*zongfa* 宗法) with the Qufu clan representing the trunk

---

4. In translating *Wenxuan gong* in this manner, I break with the customary "Duke of Propagating Culture." Ancestral inscriptions since the Zhou era record the use of *wen* as a posthumous honorific, the meaning of which is peculiar to the formulaic language of the bronze inscriptions. It is clear, however, as Lothar von Falkenhausen ("The Concept of *Wen*," pp. 1–18) has pointed out, that although the "exact meaning of *wen* in ancestral designations may be unknowable," it is certainly not a reference to literary attainment. Falkenhausen explains that *wen* is an emphatic epithet and offers "accomplishment" or "accomplished" as a default equivalent. At the same time, my emphasis on the archaic translation of *wen* must yield to the conventional translation of the common later imperial uses of Duke of Propagating Culture (*Wenxuan gong*) and King of Propagating Culture (*Wenxuan wang*).

5. Some of the history of imperial recognition through the conferral of hereditary title and appanage has been retold by Thomas Wilson in "The Ritual Formation of Confucian Orthodoxy," pp. 565–68; and pp. 50–57 of this volume..

and the others the branches of the Kong's arboreal symmetry. At Qufu, the numinous cult reliquary, ritual artifacts, texts, carriage, and the Kong clan lore were all preserved. This collection of stories documented the long history of Kong descent and resembled the serial recognition of Kongzi's ancestors that opens Chapter 39 of the *Kongzi jiayu* (ca. 200 CE):

> Kongzi's ancestors were descendants of [the kingdom of] Song 宋. Weizi Qi 微子啓 and Di Yi 帝乙 being the forebears. . . . Xi 熙 begot Fu Fu He 弗父何 and Li Gong Fang Si 厲公方祀. From Fang Si on down, subsequent generations were Song officials. Fu Fu He begot Songfu Zhou 宋父周. Zhou begot Shizi Sheng 世子勝. Sheng begot Zheng Kaobu 正考甫. Kaobu begot Kongfu Jia 孔父嘉. After five generations their kin waned and so did not form a lineage as "*gong*" 公. Therefore, later they used [the name] Kong to form a clan.[6]

Such fantastic lineage reconstruction through male progenitors operated as a narrative device that lent scope and dimension to the clan's genealogical citations. Qufu, as the genealogical reliquary and the site for the reiterative re-enactment of ancestral rites to Kongzi, was a topos of narrative invention. In this way the ritual complex at Qufu worked in conjunction with the Kong estate conception to reinforce the legitimacy of the lineage claims advanced by "flesh and blood" descendants.

However, the continuity of the Kong blood line was not so seamless. The Kongs' privileged descent claim, although later honored as "true" by the unknowing apparatus of the imperial state, was contested numerous times over the centuries, especially following the Kong clan's division into northern and southern branches when Kong Duanyou 孔端友 (d. 1130) of the forty-eighth generation fled the Jurchen invasion in the company of the Song Emperor Gaozong (r. 1127–62), taking with him the Kong ancestral shrine. His younger brother, Kong Duancao 孔端操, remained at the Qufu compound and was recognized as Yansheng Duke by the Jin dynasty. The Kong clan, although divided, endured. From this juncture forward, the definitive ambiguity of immemorial descent was made evident in a succession of stentorian debates over the greater authenticity of either the northern or southern lineage in the Ming and Qing.[7]

---

6. Wang Su, ed., *Kongzi jiayu*, 99.2–100.1.

7. On the recurring disputation between the *dazong* 大宗 and *xiaozong* 小宗 branches of the Kong clan in late imperial times, see the chapter by Thomas Wilson in this volume, pp. 66–72. Immemoriality here refers to the presumptive quality of a tradition that emphasizes the timeless continuity of transmission rather than descent from a known origin. Immemorial

With this politically expedient breach, space thus opened within the Kong legacy, threatening the estate narrative's cogency and demonstrating the rhetorical limitations of its plot of immemorial transmission. I recommend that, for the sake of clarifying the many ways by which Kongzi has been rivalrously transmitted to the present, this plot of the Kong estate narrative must be taken literally and its ironies not passed over. Imperial recognition and investiture aside, the Kong genealogy functioned as a strategy of inclusion that covered up the ruptures in its transmission by emphasizing the presumptive continuity of sacrifice to Kongzi at the clan temple. In light of the disruptive Song era history of the Kongs, we must query the biological connotation of descent and consider lineage in this instance to be, like the filiation of master and disciples described in the formative texts of the Weaklings, a figurative gesture.

At such a rhetorical juncture, we can glimpse how a lineage community and its tradition were made, and what we see compels us to reconsider the common conception of the latter as immemorial. In their abiding opacity, traditions such as the Kongs' "flesh and blood" descent encourage us to take them as immemorial rather than situational, and as records of thought rather than of thinking. The evidence arrives with an order of sorts, because traditions—genealogical, intellectual, religious, cultural—come to us fully formed, as they should if they intend to command our assent. Or so, this is one way of understanding the persistence of so definitive a tradition as the one invented and purveyed by the Kong estate.

But another way of understanding tradition is to look beyond the explicit memorial presentation and recognize it as a process of selection and judgment of what will be handed down and what will be received. The content of any transmission is contested, and its longevity as tradition is a reflection of the vitality of the contest. Tradition, instead of being an uninterrupted transmission of value through successive generations of undeviating practices, is more like a flexible frame within which invention occurs and where the past serves as cultural stock that informs present invention. In this way, every cultural reproduction is a transformation where the contents of memory are shaped in dialogue with forgetting, something that has been especially true of the Kong legacy from its beginnings in the Warring States and

---

traditions are by nature ahistorical and obtain their authority from a reiterative unknowing transmission.

its many subsequent creative reinventions down to its contemporary embodiment in Gansu.[8] Moreover, the scattered record of the earliest cultural
reproduction surrounding Kongzi points to two competitive traditions of
remembrance diverging at the site of his succession.

KONGZI: THE CONTESTED LEGACY

It is precisely this understanding of tradition as transformation (particularly
evident in the chapters in this volume by Thomas Wilson, Deborah Sommer,
Abigail Lamberton, and Julia Murray) that is precluded by the narrative
within which the serial citation of Kong descent is explained. However, seeing
this tradition as a construction, as I am advocating here, permits us to recognize the Kong estate narrative as a distinct artifact of a rhetorical context that
may be drawn from the question Who mourned Kongzi? At his death it is alleged that he had more than seventy disciples and one infant grandson, but it
would be a generation before the Kong clan prominently asserted its dual
roles of doctrine and lineage arbiter. Hence, raising the question of Kongzi's
succession permits us to consider the most striking anomaly found in some of
the narratives of the Kong legacy—that he appeared to have died ritually intestate, bereft of eligible male heirs who could conduct cult to him.

Kongzi is bathed in legend, and so the claim of Kong clan descent from
him is no less awash in the fabulous; however, this particular lacuna is significant for it constitutes an exception that disallows the authenticating rule
of continuity of the Kong transmission narrative. Of course with a carefully
choreographed, imperially subsidized celebration of this inspired, and inspirational, descent, it is easy to overlook the pre-Qin and early Han evidence
of the clan's contested posterity found in the *Analects*, *Historical Records*, the
Li ji 禮記 (Record of rites), and the *Family Sayings of Kongzi*.

---

8. On the contemporary dynamics of the Kong tradition as reproduced in Gansu's
Dachuan village, see Jing, *The Temple of Memories*, pp. 23–44, 144–62. The Kongs' association
with Gansu has an even longer history than that discussed in Jing's work. Wolfram Eberhard
("The Leading Families of Ancient Tunhuang") identified a "Kong" among 29 clan names on
a Dunhuang register of noble families dating to 634 CE. According to the list, these Kongs
were originally from the ancient state of Lu and had been registered as a gentry family prior to
the Tang. Eberhard, betraying the influence of Gu Jiegang 顧頡剛, further speculated that
this clan was not of "Chinese" origin and had lived in this region of western China since before the Han dynasty.

In an intentional sequence of passages from the *Analects* having to do with the death of Yan Hui 顏回 and hinting at the mortal illness of Kongzi (Book 11, Chapters 8, 9, 10, 11) the disciples are salient as mourners, and first mention is made of the premature death of Kongzi's son, Boyu 伯魚:

When Yan Yuan 顏淵 died, Yan Lu 顏路 asked for his (Kongzi's) carriage so he could make an outer coffin [for his son]. He said, Talented or not talented, let each of us speak of sons. When Li 鯉 (Boyu) died, he had an inner but not an outer coffin. I did not go on foot to make him an outer coffin. . . . [9]

When Yan Yuan died, he said, Oh! The sky is destroying me (*tian sang yu* 天喪予)! The sky is destroying me (*tian sang yu*)! [10]

When Yan Hui died, he grieved for him poignantly. The followers said, he is moved! To which, he replied, Am I moved? If I am not moved by grief for him, then for whom? [11]

When Yan Yuan died, the disciples wanted to bury him lavishly. He said, it can't be done. [Nonetheless] they buried him lavishly. He said, Yan regarded me as a father, but I was not able (*yu bude* 予不得) to regard him as a son. [12]

A disciple mourning complex stands out, but the implication that Yan Hui was the son that Kongzi had lost confounds the succession twice over: his legacy will be left for followers less well esteemed who are non-kin. E. Bruce Brooks and Taeko Brooks have argued that the recurring use of the contrastive pronoun *yu* 予 rather than *wu* 吾 for "I/me" conveys "the presence of death," and so it is that these passages strung together with the litany "When Yan Yuan died" (*Yan Yuan si* 顏淵死) announce the "loss of intellectual and physical heirs." [13] Such circumstance at the time of death would suggest that Kongzi was fated to be a wandering ghost, rather than an ancestor trapped by the veneration of kin in an ancestral temple.

Additional evidence of an early tradition of Kongzi's ambiguous legacy is also found in Book 7, Chapter 35, and Book 9, Chapter 12, of the *Analects* where the Master's waning moments are poignantly recalled. As with the passing of Yan Hui, the disciples supervise Kongzi's final rites:

---

9. *Lunyu zhushu*, 95.2–96.1 (11.42). Brooks and Brooks, *The Original Analects*, p. 71.
10. *Lunyu zhushu*, 96.1 (11.42–43). Brooks and Brooks, *The Original Analects*, p. 71.
11. *Lunyu zhushu*, 96.1 (11.43). Brooks and Brooks, *The Original Analects*, p. 71.
12. *Lunyu zhushu*, 96.2 (11.43). Brooks and Brooks, *The Original Analects*, p. 71.
13. Brooks and Brooks, *The Original Analects*, p. 71.

He was very ill. Zilu 子路 deputed the disciples to serve as attendants. When the illness had subsided, he (Kongzi) said, Of long standing indeed are You's 由 dissemblings. I (*yu*) have no attendants, yet you pretend as though I (*yu*) had them. Who will I deceive? Will I deceive heaven? Besides, for my own part (*yu*), rather than die in the arms of attendants wouldn't I (*yu*) rather die in the arms of disciples? Even though I (*yu*) do not get a grand funeral, will I (*yu*) die by the roadside?[14]

Once again the emblematic contrast: disciples rather than blood descendants, a contrast left as narrative legacy for the compilers of the *Historical Records*.

Near the close of Chapter 47 of the *Historical Records* (Hereditary House of Kongzi, "Kongzi shijia" 孔子世家) an inventory of Kongzi's immediate legacy appears. Here we learn that following the burial of Kongzi north of the ancient city of Lu 魯 above the Si 泗 River, each of his disciples wore mourning clothes for three years.[15] These passages, like those from the *Analects*, offer no mention of descendants attending to the master in his final moments.

The closing sentences of Chapter 47 provide the genealogical information necessary for explaining the curious absence of Kong family members at the time of Kongzi's death and at his funeral, as Sima Qian 司馬遷 (ca. 145–ca. 86 BCE) recounts: "Kongzi begot Li, whose style name was Boyu. Boyu, at age 50, died before Kongzi. Boyu begot Si, style name Zisi 子思 and who reached 62 years. [They] experienced hardship in Song. Zisi wrote the *Doctrine of the Mean* (*Zhongyong* 中庸)."[16] The *Family Sayings of Kongzi* also notes Boyu's premature death at age 50, but it does not gesture to fill the lacuna.[17]

---

14. *Lunyu zhushu*, 78.1. In this instance I have followed very closely the translation of this passage in Brooks and Brooks, *The Original Analects*, p. 53.

15. Sima Qian, *Shi ji*, 6: 1945. "Kongzi zang Lu cheng bei Si shang, dizi jie fu sannian" 孔子葬魯城北泗上, 弟子皆服三年.

16. Ibid., p. 1946. The official list of the disciples appears in the "Biographies of Zhongni's (Kongzi's) Disciples" ("Zhongni dizi liezhuan" 仲尼弟子列傳) of the *Shi ji*. See ibid., 7: 2185-227. That list, barring several modifications, is very similar, if not identical to that associated with the Kong clan's transmission narrative, which is found in chap. 38 of the *Kongzi jiayu* and is called "The Explanation of the 72 Disciples" ("Qishi'er dizi jie" 七十二弟子解). On the filiative links between the *Shi ji* and the *Kongzi jiayu* disciple lists, see Brooks and Brooks, *The Original Analects*, pp. 274–83. According to the Brookses, a prototype of the "Explanation of the 72 Disciples" served as the genealogical template for Sima Qian's "Register of Disciples" ("Dizi ji" 弟子籍).

17. Wang Su, *Kongzi jiayu*, 100.2.

His son having predeceased him, Kongzi was without descendants, a condition lamented in his putative final words to Zigong 子弓, cited later in the same chapter of the *Historical Records*:

The universe is without legacy; no one can ancestor me (*tianxia wudao jiu yi*; *mo neng zong yu* 天下無道久矣; 莫能宗予). The Xia people encoffined their corpses on the east step; the Zhou people encoffined on the western step; the Yin people encoffined in the space between two pillars. Last night I (*yu*) dreamt that I sat with the offerings for the dead in the space between two pillars; I am descended from the Yin people. Seven days later he expired.[18]

The first sentence can, as well, be taken less literally as a sorrowful proclamation by Kongzi that the universe has no moral compass and consequently no one will revere him. Similar poignant phrasing appears in the passages from the "Tan gong" 檀弓 chapter of the *Record of Rites* that tell of Kongzi's portentous dreams in the days before his death; in each case death arrives without descendants in attendance.[19] Even in a broader sense, *zong's* 宗 meanings do not stray far from the literal: ancestral temple; clan; lineage; royal clan; high ancestor; to honor; to venerate as if a high ancestor. In the context of death, mourning, and remembrance, honor and veneration are not exuded so much as performed. This is not to argue for the exclusivity of a single reading of *zong* in the passage in question, but to emphasize the distinct persistence of Kongzi's uncertain legacy.

Yet, I have mentioned above, we need not rely solely on Sima Qian's fanciful reiteration of Kongzi's lamentation to recognize that the matter of Kong posterity was already contested before the *Historical Records* was composed. Indeed, for all the strident claims made later in the Han by clan members residing in Qufu, a contradictory elite lore of posthumous disciple

---

18. Sima Qian, *Shi ji*, 6: 1944. The term *wudao* 無道 may be taken on the analogy of several passages from the *Zuo zhuan* as a comment on the violation of the norms of primogeniture. The expressions *wei budao* 爲不道 and *budao* 不道 refer to actions performed in contravention of patrimonial custom. I consider this to be a linguistic warrant for the reading of *dao* as "legacy." For several instances of this use of *wei budao*, see Yang Bojun, *Chunqiu Zuo zhuan zhu*, 2: 632, 2: 714, 4: 1614. See also the interpretation of these passages in Savage, "In the Tradition of Kings." I am indebted to Bill Savage for calling my attention to this reading of *weibu dao*.

19. *Li ji zhengyi*, vol. 1, 130.1–2. The following words are uttered by Kongzi as lamentation: "Enlightened kings do not rise, and which one in the universe can ancestor/venerate me? For my own part, I fear that I am about to die" (*Fu mingwang buxing, er tianxia qishu neng zong yu. Yu dai jiang si ye* 夫明王不興而天下其孰能宗予. 予殆將死也).

care was the earliest attested account of Kongzi's death, an account upheld by the *Historical Records*' recollection of Kongzi's last words and the even later passages from the *Record of Rites*.

Kongzi, then, was at first survived only by his disciples, who, as his proxy legatees, assumed the roles of sons in mourning. In fact a vestigial symbolic re-enactment of orphanhood marked filial instruction at the side of Kongzi and is stated in the very names of his followers. The principal share of these followers (*menren* 門人) is distinguished by their possession of the Zi 子 agnomen—Zisi 子思, Zilu 子路, Zigong 子貢, Ziyou 子游, and so on. The names are normally taken as emblematic of the aristocratic status of the holder, and although this interpretation has merit, it is more reasonable in light of the earlier *Analects* evidence to read this class convention as symbolic, specifically signaling a state of mourning (*sang* 喪).

The later Han text *White Tiger Hall Disquisitions* (*Baihu tong* 白虎通) offers a warrant for such a reading in a section on the posthumous granting of ranks in stating: "When the father has died, the son calls himself, 'Eldest Son so-and-so' (*zi mou* 子某) because he is still in the presence of the encoffined corpse and so humbles himself."[20] The portrait of the Weakling fellowship during the period of Zengzi's illness and death in Book Eight of the *Analects* conveys a poignancy in the care of this community for one of its members. Warring States compilations that follow the *Analects* in the textual chronology such as the *Book of Mencius* (*Mengzi* 孟子) preserve a memory of such devotion to Kongzi.

This phenomenon, characterized by E. Bruce Brooks and A. Taeko Brooks as the "Confucius successor movement," is undisturbed until about 400 BCE during the reign in Lu of Mu Gong 穆公 (410–378 BCE), when the Kong clan obtains possession of the transmission.[21] This possession, the Brookses claim, is definitively asserted in Book 11 of the *Analects*, which they have dated to 360 BCE. In subsequent centuries, as the Kong estate narrative took shape, the original dearth of Kong legatees and the decades of cult paid to Kongzi by his followers and preserved in the *passiones* of the *Analects* were superseded by an amnesiac agnation bent upon rewriting the legacy of Kongzi. The textual consequences of this genealogical invention are still evident in the *Family Sayings of Kongzi* and, especially, the *Kong Clan Anthology*

---

20. *Baihu tong*, 11; Tjan, *Po Hu T'ung*, 1: 225.
21. Brooks and Brooks, *The Original Analects*, pp. 278–87, esp. pp. 285–87.

(*Kong congzi* 孔叢子) where one finds purely incredible "dialogues" between Kongzi and Zisi.[22]

Although scholars have long accepted the genealogical and apostolic nexus of descent through Kong Ji (Zisi), there is very good reason to question, if not reject, it even on the grounds of its own chronology. Indeed, given the evidence of the recently discovered Zisi story from the Guodian 郭店 texts (ca. 300 BCE), which depicts Zisi as discoursing with Mu Gong (lore previously stated in *Mengzi*), the received tradition of lineal and doctrinal descent through Zisi is untenable.[23] For conversations, however fantastic, to have occurred between Kongzi and Zisi, the latter would have to have been alive in the reign of Ai Gong 哀公 (494–468 BCE). Only the Latter Han hagiographic text, the *Kong Clan Anthology*, which adheres to the standard 551–479 BCE chronology for Kongzi, insists that Zisi was born in the fifteenth year of the reign of Ai Gong, 479 BCE. As Bruce Brooks has shown, given that traditional accounts state that Zisi lived 62 years, a birth in 479 BCE would preclude fundamentally his having served Mu Gong.[24] Nevertheless, because Sima Qian's "Register of Disciples" begins with Zisi, it thus contains both strands of the contentious fabric of kin and disciple lore bearing claims of descent from Kongzi.

The awkward mechanics of a "linearization" that cannot be accommodated by the facts of Kongzi's posterity is overcome by the successor movement, but it does not close debate on the matter, as the ex post facto Kong clan assertion of legitimate succession attests. However, although the thorny

---

22. *Kong congzi*, 15.2–16.2. The chronology of Boyu's life and that of Zisi are worked in a most astounding manner: Boyu dies in 483 BCE and not 480 BCE as the *Shi ji* and the *Kongzi jiayu* assert; Zisi is born, quite preternaturally, four years after his father's death. Thus Zisi is born in 479 BCE, the same year as Kongzi's purported demise, permitting grandfather and grandson to engage in an impossible conversation. Of course, making Zisi the contemporary of Kongzi, in turn, wreaks havoc on the normative tradition, which held that Mengzi learned at the side of Zisi and so both were alive in the time of Mu Gong.

23. I am indebted to Bruce Brooks for this observation. Reviewing all the evidence for lineal succession among the Kong and finding it both contradictory and "self-refutatory," Brooks has gone so far as to conclude that Zisi "was neither the grandson of Confucius nor his direct successor"; see Brooks and Brooks, *The Original Analects*, p. 285, and the entry for "Dz-sz's Dates" on the Warring States Working Group Website, <http://www.umass.edu/wsp/>.

24. Brooks and Brooks, *The Original Analects*, p. 285. See also "The Death of Confucius," Warring States Working Group Website, <http://www.umass.edu/wsp/method/confucius. html>, pp. 1–2, as well as Brooks, "The Life and Mentorship of Confucius."

legacy problem may have been solved by subsequent generations of Kongs through a genealogical reflex, it was raised again from another direction in the Han, when apocryphal accounts of Kongzi's divine birth are advanced. The inadequately veiled uncertainty of lineal descent would, in time, give way to the ambiguity of the progenitor's birth and claims that his legacy could more immediately be obtained through reading Kongzi's birth story in the map of the heavens.

In other words there were a number of ways to construct a narrative of descent from Kongzi, all figurative and some more credible than others. In the genealogical trafficking of the Kongs of Qufu, the figurative Kongzi was made historical, and this historicity was, in turn, reinforced by imperial recognition (as is evidenced in the descriptions and analyses of the Kongmiao in many of the chapters in this volume). Complementing this conscious choreography of lineal descent were ritual objects and the narrative lore of the Kong clan itself carefully maintained in Qufu, as noted by Sima Qian following his visit there in 127 BCE: "[I] read Kongzi's books [and] saw the carriage, clothes, and ritual vessels of Zhongni's 仲尼 temple."[25] And, handed down through inspired successors and their followers was the accretionally assembled *Analects* of Kongzi.[26] Both formed contiguous traditions of remembrance, the narratives of which might overlap as in the disciple inventories in Chapters 47 and 67 of the *Historical Records*.

KONGZI'S AMBIGUOUS BEGINNINGS

Insofar as we understand or imagine Kongzi as the locus of a tradition, the making of which is documented in the *Analects*, or of the progenitor of an illustrious clan, the mystery of his identity is banished to the edge of our consciousness. Our remembering him as sage, teacher, uncrowned king, redactor of the Classics, even reformer, is made possible by the forgetting of the ambiguity of his identity. This is why in an archaeology of Chinese antiquity, it is crucial to read beyond the conscious limit. Assuming a habit of mind more akin to the pluralism of the Warring States, it becomes possible

---

25. Sima Qian, *Shi ji*, 6: 1947.

26. The allusion here is to the reconstruction of the *Lunyu* in historical sequence by Bruce and Taeko Brooks according to an accretional theory of its reiterative elaboration; see Brooks and Brooks, *The Original Analects*, pp. vii–viii, 1–11, 201–48.

to read the early imperial interlaced accounts of Kongzi's life and to uncover the plural strands of narrative codes, each spun from a particular forgetting enshrined in mythology.

As with so many of the culture heroes, sages, and kings of Chinese antiquity, much can be explained by a theory of Kongzi's invention by mythologization, for his historicity, as I have recently argued, is uncertain.[27] The earliest text bearing stories of his birth, to wit the *Historical Records*, appears quite late in the chronology (ca. 90 BCE)—indeed barely a half-century before a hereditary title was conferred on Kong Ba 孔霸 by Han Yuandi. That official biography, most likely the hybrid product of Sima Qian and Sima Tan 司馬譚 (ca. 160–110 BCE), was fashioned from numerous transmissions, including the estate narrative of the Kongs and a heterogeneous elite lore that took shape in the interval between the composition of the *Historical Records* and the adoption of a new imperial calendar in the first century of the Later Han. Such mythologization is under way in the Kong estate narrative, the *Historical Records'* official biography of Kongzi, as well as an even more ideologically invested elite lore relating Kongzi's god-like generation from the heavens.

The *Gongyang* 公羊 (ca. 150 BCE) and *Guliang* 穀粱 (ca. 90 BCE) commentaries on the *Spring and Autumn Annals* (*Chunqiu* 春秋) provide the first citations of his birth and appear to have no relation to a distinguishable narrative context. They are citationally appended to the elliptical annals of the *Spring and Autumn*. In a beguiling terseness, this hallowed text records a sequence of startling astrological phenomena in the ninth and tenth months of the twenty-first year (552 BCE) of Xiang Gong 襄公 (r. 571–541 BCE) of Lu: the occurrence of two visible solar eclipses. Yet, as astonishing as these planetary movements are, the record for the eleventh and succeeding month nonchalantly states, "Cao Bo came to court,"[28] and makes clear that the significance of this entry for the compiler was as unremarkable as the two previous ones. However, for readers like ourselves, and certainly for commentators of the late Warring States, the sequential eclipses are exceptional, strange, miraculous.

However, it was this very preternatural phenomenon, the impossibility of which was likely unknown to later commentators on the *Spring and Autumn*

---

27. Jensen, "Wise Man of the Wilds."
28. Yang Bojun, *Chunqiu Zuo zhuan zhu*, 3: 1056.

Annals, that made the twenty-first year of Xiang Gong so suitable to mark the birth of a hero, for Kongzi had already attained mythical significance by the time the commentaries were composed. To be sure, eclipses were always portentous, usually baleful, and so their occurrence in sequence should have been special cause for alarm. Nevertheless, for the Gongyang and Guliang compilers such troubling movements of the firmament signified instead a miraculous beginning; both quote the Spring and Autumn Annals double eclipse entries (but for different months) and state: "on the gengzi 更子 day, Kongzi was born."[29]

Nearly fifty years ago, Homer Dubs accounted for the discrepancies in the two texts' dating of the birth of Kongzi by establishing that only the Guliang record was correct, given that there was no gengzi day in the eleventh month, twenty-first year of the reign of Xiang Gong, as the Gongyang claimed.[30] A copyist's error in the Spring and Autumn Annals, Dubs concluded, was the reason for the erroneous successive eclipse record, and so it was that the accidental became legendary. Across several centuries and texts there is a striking consistency in the citation of the gengzi day and the autumn of the twenty-first year of Xiang Gong. Although there would seem very little of narrative value in the Guliang and Gongyang accounts of nine characters each, their identification of Kongzi's birth with this miraculous mistake provided a site from which to anchor an evolving story cycle that attained definitive form in Sima Qian's Historical Records biography.[31] At the same time this beginning of Kongzi's biographical history was bound for eternity to the occurrence of extraordinary astral phenomena.

---

29. Chunqiu Guliang zhuan zhushu, 156.1; Chunqiu Gongyang zhuan zhushu, 256.1.

30. Dubs, "The Date of Confucius's Birth," pp. 142–44. One immediate difficulty with Dubs's conclusive dating is that the text he prefers, the Guliang, is more recent than the Gongyang.

31. In subsequent centuries the legend contained within this sacred mound of narrative was handed down with little modification, and when modifications were made, it was usually with respect to the story of conception and/or sacrifice. So, in reading Jiang Yong's (1681–1762) Kongzi nianpu, as well as Di Ziqi's (nineteenth century) Kongzi biannian, it is hardly surprising to find that the Shi ji birth story, without the serial citation of Song descent pedigree, provides the foundation of their chronologies.

THE MAKING OF
A NORMATIVE BIOGRAPHY

Although a moment of his birth was fixed, and this in texts centuries subsequent to his death, Kongzi begins as a figure of ambiguous ancestry. The only reference to his parentage in the *Analects* is a rather elliptical one from Book 3, Chapter 15, where it is reported that his father had been a man from Zou. The entire passage reads: "He [Kongzi], entering the grand temple, questioned everything. Someone said, 'Don't tell me that this son of a man from Zou knows the rites. Entering the grand temple, [he] inquired about everything.' He, hearing of this said, 'Yes! Such are the rites.'"[32] What is immediately evident in this passage is that Kongzi does not assert that he is the son of a man from Zou; the relationship is simply stated by a putative skeptical observer of Kongzi's behavior in the grand temple. In fact this equivocal assertion seems not to have been made in the presence of Kongzi nor did he assent to it.

Nonetheless, with this shard of evidence it was established many centuries ago that his father was a certain He 紇, who, it turns out, is the only man from Zou mentioned in the *Zuo Commentary on the Spring and Autumn Annals (Zuo zhuan)*. The Zuo commentary on events in the tenth year of Xiang Gong (562 BCE) tells of a man, perhaps a warrior, named Zou He 陬紇 who was possessed of great courage and superlative strength. It is said that He lifted the portcullis of the gate of the capital of Biyang 偪陽 to allow for the escape of a collaborative contingent of soldiers from Lu, Zou, and Song who were trapped inside the city's walls. The prodigious feat proved critical to the success of the attack, and Biyang was ceded, following a prolonged siege, to the Duke of Song.[33] Only the commentary of Du Yu 杜預 (222–84) and the subcommentary of Kong Yingda 孔穎達 (574–648) on the Zuo transmission, however, identify He as Kongzi's father: "Minister of He, Zou settlement, Father of Zhongni, Shuliang He" 叔粱紇 (He Zouyi dafu Zhongni fu Shuliang He 紇郰邑大夫仲尼父叔粱紇).[34]

---

32. *Lunyu*, 27.2; Waley, *The Analects*, p. 6.

33. Yang Bojun, *Chunqiu Zuo zhuan zhu*, 3: 974–75. The *Gongyang* and *Guliang* commentaries, incidentally, make no mention of He, Shu He, or Shuliang He.

34. Yang Bojun, *Chunqiu Zuo zhuan zhu*, 3: 975. The two forms of the character *zou* have long been presumed to be graphic variants of the same word. The latter *zou* 郰, used as a loan for *zou* 鄒, the capital of the Zhulou kingdom south of Luoyang, has signaled the liminal cul-

The commentators cite no authority for this assertion; they are merely recording what is for them the obvious: Shuliang He was the progenitor of Kongzi.

The *Zuo Commentary* lacks direct evidence of a relationship between the two figures, but it does proffer other suggestive associations. There is an oblique reference to Zhongni halfway through the narrative of the tenth year of Xiang Gong, the same one where Zou He is first mentioned. After the capture of Biyang and its acquisition by Song, we encounter Zhongni: "[When] the military officers returned home, Meng Xianzi 孟獻子 took Qin Jinfu 秦堇父 as the [guardian of the] right [of his chariot?]. [Qin Jinfu] had [a son] Qin Pici 秦丕茲, who served Zhongni."[35] In a text where discussion is devoted to the logistics of extinguishing Biyang and who should be honored by its possession, the comment about Qin Pici being a follower of Zhongni seems especially gratuitous. Certainly it adds nothing to the narrative, unless all that was remembered of Qin Jinfu at the time of the Zuo compilation was his son's service to Kongzi.

Of course, one cannot overlook that this same Meng Xianzi was the brother of Meng Xizi 孟僖子, who, moments before his death in the seventh year of the reign of Zhao Gong 照公 (r. 540–509 BCE), expresses the wish that his sons learn of the rites from Kong Qiu 孔丘, for "without rites one cannot stand,"[36] but this linkage of Kongzi and Shuliang He is strained at best. And yet another layer of this rather incomplete biography is added by Meng Xizi when he confesses to his sons that "Kong Qiu is the descendant of a sage who was slaughtered at Song."[37] Du Yu's commentary on the passage informs us that Kongzi was the sixth-generation descendant of Kongfu Jia 孔父嘉. This genealogical reconstruction is fully consistent with the lineage account of the *Family Sayings of Kongzi*[38] and stands in conscious parallel with earlier *Zuo zhuan* anecdotal material from the third year in the reign of Yin Gong 隱公 (r. 721–711 BCE), where Duke Mu of Song's final request is that his son and heir become the ward of Kongfu Jia.

---

tural status of Kongzi's ancestry in relation to Zhou cultural ecumene. See Eno, "The Social Background of the Kong Family of Lu."

35. Yang Bojun, *Chunqiu Zuo zhuan zhu*, 3: 978.

36. Ibid., 4: 1294.

37. Ibid.

38. Wang Su, *Kongzi jiayu*, 99.2–100.1.

The young duke and his foster parent are later killed by the tyrant Hua Du 華督 at Song in 710 BCE, leading to a feud between the Kong and Hua clans that culminates in the voluntary exile of the Kongs to Lu.[39] The proper name "He" also appears as a place-name in the commentary on events in the seventeenth year of Xiang Gong's reign. Here a certain Zou Shu He now commands a regiment of 300 men and in the fall of 556 BCE directs a retaliatory attack on invading troops from Qi 齊.[40] Beyond these sparse references, there are, however, no other mentions of this warrior commander, no other links to Kongzi, and not the slightest suggestion that Shu He was his father. Moreover, the little we learn of Kongzi's noble paternity in these fragments would appear to contradict the *Analects* assertion of his humble beginnings.

A little more than a century later we find only symbolic evidence of the paternal connection between Shu He and Kongzi in Chapter 15 of *Mr. Lü's Springs and Autumns Chronicle* (*Lüshi chunqiu* 呂氏春秋). Here it is reported that Kongzi, in a manner reminiscent of the heroism of his father, "raised the barrier of a kingdom's gate."[41] Although the descriptive language is not the same, the feat of father and son certainly is. Thus, the Zou warrior He and the future sage Kongzi are joined as identical characters in a morphology of fable. The story in *Mr. Lü's Springs and Autumns Chronicle* distinguishes the work of the son by stating that the muscular Kongzi accomplished his heroic task with the use of one hand! In this instance, Kongzi's feat of prowess was probably derived from the earlier Shu He narrative and attributed to him on the presumption that the two men were father and son—post hoc, ergo propter hoc.

From this rather intentional legendary link, the conclusion one may draw is that in some northern regions by the close of the third century before the common era, it was believed that Shu He was Kongzi's father. Yet, to this juncture of the reconstruction, he has no mother. The task of recollecting what has been forgotten relies upon careful scrutiny of his parentage, particularly his mother, for as one turns from the protean pre-Qin texts in favor of the richer imperial era accounts, the father becomes inconsequential. To

---

39. Yang Bojun, *Chunqiu Zuo zhuan zhu*, 1: 28–29.

40. Ibid., 3: 1031. An identical command of 300 troops poised against invaders—these from Wu—is entrusted to You Ruo, a putative follower of Kongzi, in the seventh year of Ai Gong (487 BCE). See ibid., 4: 1249.

41. *Lüshi chunqiu*, p. 162.

learn of the mother from whom his descent was commonly traced,[42] one must turn to the *Historical Records*.

Among Sima Qian's accounts of the princely houses, "The Hereditary House of Kongzi" is also the first text in which the identities and fates of the two male figures, the father, Shuliang He, and the son, Kong Qiu, are forged as a lineal pair. The *Historical Records* account is the first, genuine birth story. Rendered in a brief seven sentences of text, it is the only source in the official literature that refers to his mother or father. Indeed, should we restrict ourselves to the canonical texts of the Warring States and Han alone, virtually everything we learn about Kongzi's birth comes from Sima Qian, but what we do learn is wondrous. The terse, tantalizing account of his conception threatens to exceed the narrative frame:

Kongzi was born in Changping village, Zou district, Lu kingdom. His ancestor was a man of Song known as Kong Fangshu 孔防叔. Fangshu begot Boxia 伯夏, and Boxia begot Shuliang He. [Shuliang] He and a woman of the Yan clan were joined in the wilds and gave birth to Kongzi; [it was] through sacrifice at the numinous hillock [that she] became pregnant with Kongzi. In the twenty-second year of Xiang Gong, Kongzi was born. He was born with a protuberance on the top of his head, and so he was given the name "mound." His style was Zhongni and his surname, Kong. When Qiu was born, Shuliang He died and was buried at Fang Shan 防山. Fang Shan is in eastern Lu, and so it was that Kongzi had doubts about the place of his father's tomb; his mother concealed it [from him].[43]

A normative narration of his beginnings, one befitting the auspicious birth of the legatee of a hereditary noble clan, was herewith joined to

---

42. As late as the twelfth century, we find Kongzi identified with his mother's and not his father's clan. In December 1194, Zhu Xi 朱熹 marked the founding of the Cangzhou jingshe 滄州精舍 with a sacrifice to Kongzi in which he addressed him as "original teacher, Duke of Zou kingdom, of the Yan clan": see *Zhu wengong wenji, juan* 86, p. 1548.1.

43. Sima Qian, *Shi ji*, 6: 1905–6. There are several discrepancies in this account when compared with that of the *Kongzi jiayu*. For example Kongzi's ancestry should begin seven generations earlier with Fu Fu He, not with Kong Fangshu; moreover, in the *Kongzi jiayu* there was no Kong Fangshu, but rather a Fangshu; see Wang Su, *Kongzi jiayu*, 99.2. A more contemporary vantage on Kongzi's beginnings offers no greater distance from these normative narrations. A glance at the birth story section of the recently published *Kongzi wenhua da dian* 孔子文化大典 (Great compendium of Kongzi culture) reveals that there is no more authoritative account of the birth of Kongzi than that provided in the *Historical Records*. Moreover, the illicit quality of his parents' union is abridged by quotation of the *Family Sayings of Kongzi* passage.

the pre-existent mythic parallelism of Kongzi and the legendary hero Shu-liang He.

Sima Qian knew the date of Kongzi's birth from the *Gongyang* and *Guliang* commentaries on the two passages from the *Spring and Autumn Annals*. The improbability of the sequential eclipses was surely known to him and perhaps explains why his narrative offers only a year and not a day and month—as would be common—for the birth of Kongzi. Given the prominent concern with the movement of heavenly bodies evinced by both the Shang and Zhou, the occurrence of double eclipses would have betokened something magical.[44]

It is difficult to ascertain sources for Sima's tale of an unlikely hero beyond the *Spring and Autumn Annals* and its commentaries, but there are clues in the timing of the chapter's composition. We can glean from the summation of Chapter 47 that the "Hereditary House of Kongzi" was composed sometime after the Grand Astrologer's visit to the Kong shrine in Qufu in the spring of 127 BCE as noted previously. Certainly there are no parallel story traditions attested in the *Discourses of the Kingdoms* (*Guo yu* 國語), or the *Zuo Commentary*, although both works do contain fairly random information concerning Kongzi's early life and later career. As a result, we may presume that some of the story material for Sima Qian's Kongzi narrative was imparted to him by his hosts at Qufu, who, it is very likely, passed on the ancestral narrative of the Kong clan.

A similar account from the *Family Sayings of Kongzi* of the lineage history prior to Shuliang He confirms the role of Sima Qian's visit in providing information for his narrative. With no evidence from other earlier texts, one must presume either that older source texts have been lost or that Sima Qian's account was drawn from some undocumented popular legend. The many similarities in the *Family Sayings* and *Historical Records* versions of the circumstances of Kongzi's birth indicate, I believe, that the Grand Astrologer simply adopted, then abridged, independent lore surrounding this event, some of which was later gathered up in the *Family Sayings of Kongzi* and which may have constituted part of the Qufu ancestral transmission. Another possibility explored by E. Bruce and A. Taeko Brooks in their com-

---

44. For evidence of the exacting and exhaustive charting of the parallel relations between astronomical and terrestrial phenomena during the Three Eras (*sandai* 三代—Xia 夏, Shang 商, and Zhou 周), see Pankenier, "The Cosmo-political Background."

parative analysis of the Kongzi disciple lists as they appear in the *Family Sayings of Kongzi* and the *Historical Records* affirms the filiation of the two texts' accounts of Kongzi's life while demonstrating the chronological priority of the *Kongzi jiayu*.[45]

The *Family Sayings of Kongzi* contains a far more comprehensive account of Kongzi's antecedents, a not entirely surprising determination given the Brookses' contention that the text antedates the *Historical Records*. The thirty-ninth chapter of the *Family Sayings of Kongzi* charts the Kongs' emergence from more than ten generations of apocryphal ancestors beginning with Weizi Qi, the first son of the legendary late Shang king, Di Yi.[46] Many lines of text are devoted to reconstructing the Kong family tree, and all are curiously devoid of reference to a woman until we reach Shuliang He, where we encounter a marriage narrative to complement and counter the more risqué *Historical Records* story. It is as though with Kongzi's father, the story of descent moves from myth into history. In this lineage citation each male ancestor, quite fantastically, begets his own heir, giving birth (*sheng* 生) to him, and as the story is retold in the words of Wang Su 王肅 in the *Family Sayings*, we learn more about events preceding the wilderness union of Shu He and Zhengzai 徵在. Wang Su's version of the fateful events leading to the birth of Kongzi is without chronology and commentary:

Meng Pi 孟皮, called Boni 伯尼, had a foot disease. Thereupon [Shu] sought marriage in the Yan clan. The Yan clan had three daughters, the youngest being called Zhengzai. Father Yan inquired of his three daughters saying, "[This is] the minister of Zou, although his father and grandfather were but knights, his ancestors were the descendants of sages and kings. Today he has a height of ten feet and [because of] his unparalleled martial prowess, I eagerly seek [to establish a bond with] him. Although he is advanced in age and curmudgeonly, I doubt you would be unsatisfied. Of the three of you, who is able to be his wife?" Two of the daughters did not respond. Zhengzai approached, saying, "Since it is from you, Father, that it is arranged, how will there be any question about it?" The father said, "Very well then, you can." It followed that [Shu He] took her [Zhengzai] as his wife. Zhengzai traveled to a temple to worship, fearing that there would be no opportunity to bear a son due to her husband's advanced age. She herself beseeched Mount Niqiu 尼丘

---

45. See the analysis of the discrepancies in the members and wording of the disciple lists in Brooks and Brooks, *The Original Analects*, p. 275.

46. Wang Su, *Kongzi jiayu*, 99.2.

之山 and offered sacrifice there. [She] gave birth to Kongzi, and thus called him "Mound," giving him the style, Zhongni. When Kongzi was three years old, Shu-liang He was buried at Fang.[47]

The difficulty with Kongzi's origins in the normative traditions lies in the presumption of ancient commentators that the story of his life should conform to the emerging conventions of an official, distinguished biography—a long lineage, noble birth / aristocratic pedigree, conventional marriage. It is not the raw material but the form of the story that undermines it from within. The *Historical Records* and the *Family Sayings of Kongzi* represent commentaries on a tradition already made yet requiring additional adjustment to reconcile the miraculous of its cultic incarnation with the mundane of its emergent normative status. These Kongzi stories are, in Claude Lévi-Strauss's terminology, "pre-constrained" to tell a followable story in a didactic narrative form, although they still bear graphic intimations of other elite lore involving Kongzi. The contradictions in the *Historical Records* and the *Family Sayings of Kongzi* may well be part of an effort at later systematization of the anecdotes and apocrypha surrounding Kongzi, but the problem for us at this juncture is to understand better the larger generative fictional lore that produced the anecdote and apocrypha that lay vestigial and scattered among the comparatively "historical" biographies assembled by Sima Qian and Wang Su.

PHYSIOGNOMY, FERTILITY CULT, AND THE ILLICIT TRANSMISSION

It is as if in questioning certain ambiguous terms in the normative accounts one is cast beyond the frame of the official imagination, beyond the walls of aristocratic towns to the borders of the civilized. This is where we will discover Kongzi in another mode of existence. Most of the suggestive fragments of other lore about the divine prayerful petitioning of Kongzi's parents and the consequent magical birth are present in the birth stories of the *Historical Records* and the *Family Sayings of Kongzi*, and we confront again at the beginning of Kongzi's life the very problem that bedeviled him in his final hours—the absence of male heirs.

---

47. Ibid., 99.2–100.1.

Both texts do agree on one matter in particular—the acquisition of Kongzi's personal name, perhaps the most intriguing, because inexplicable, aspect of the birth story. Wang Su, taking the name as a reference to the raised site of his mother's intercession with the god of fertility, thereby avoids the matter of physical deformity through a gesture of symbolism. According to Sima Qian, the given name, *Qiu* 丘, was a synecdoche, representing the mound of his parents' prayer for a male heir and the bizarre, but definitive, growth on his head: the protuberance (*yuding* 圩頂) conjuring an image of a hollowed dike. The Later Han etymology *Explanation of Pattern, Elucidation of Graphs* (*Shuowen jiezi* 說文解字) gloss for *qiu* offers: "elevated earth that is not man made; it is graphically derived from *bei* 北 (north), *er* 二 (two), [and] *tu* 土 (soil)."[48] An ancient graphic version, according to Gustave Schlegel, is also pronounced "*qiu*" 坴 and means a northern mound.[49] The *White Tiger Hall Disquisitions* returns us to the curious image of an object both raised and recessed in stating that Kongzi's head resembled an inverted eaves (*fanyu* 反宇).[50] But there is additional philological evidence of Kongzi's association with a natural object that is both concave and convex in a homophonous cognate of *ni* 尼. This cognate, a compound (*xiesheng* 諧聲) graph pronounced *ni* 屁, has *qiu* as the semantic classifier and is glossed by the Han classicist and author of the *Shuowen jiezi*, Xu Shen 許慎 (55–149 CE), as: "an inverted hillock crest that collects water" (*fanding shoushui* 反頂受水).[51]

Han era mystics considered this head defect to be an augury, an outward mark of Kongzi's inner sageliness hazarding a fabulous anatomical parallel of *Qiu* and the unicorn (*lin* 麟), whose arrival in the state of Lu closes the chronicle of the *Spring and Autumn Annals*. Yet it is difficult to conceive of the magical, prophetic quality of a face that was, according to *Han's Illustration of the Didactic Use of the Book of Odes* (*Hanshi waizhuan* 韓氏外傳), "sunken," or "hollowed out" (*wa* 汚), and that, for Xunzi, resembled the animal mask of an exorcist.[52] Further still, given that the abandonment of deformed children was tolerated under Han law, why would Kongzi or his more explicitly misshapen elder half-brother, Meng Bo, have been spared in a des-

---

48. Xu Shen, *Shuowen*, 169.1.
49. Schlegel, *Uranographie chinoise*, p. 217.
50. *Baihu tong*, p. 179.
51. Xu Shen, *Shuowen*, 169.1.
52. Han Ying, *Hanshi waizhuan*, 9.9a; *Xunzi*, 3.2b.

perately bellicose era such as the Warring States?[53] Perhaps there was no
cranial abnormality, only a natural formation in the wilds appropriated to
the person of the sage.

In the reliefs of the Wu Liang Shrine in Shandong,[54] Kongzi sports a
headdress, thus preserving the ambiguity, yet the deformity of his head, to
my knowledge, is rarely represented.[55] Sartorial splendor does not always
conceal the features of his head as in the woodcuts from the late Ming reproduced in Julia Murray's contribution to this volume—the forehead is in
evidence, but it is impossible to discern the telltale cranial outlines for which
he was given the name. In fact, according to Murray, "there's also no cranial
abnormality in ANY of the many, many illustrated biographies that I have
seen, as well as not in any of the portraits except for the so-called 'Ma
Yuan.'"[56]

Although the deformity is physically negated, it is nonetheless linguisti-
cally preserved in the given name, qiu, by which after the Han he was
less frequently known. Even in Warring States texts, particularly the Zuo
Commentary, he is most commonly called Zhongni, the name marking his
lineal rank among the sons of the father. Thus the account of the conferral
of his name, qiu, represented one way of coherently construing a folkloristic
fragment and most likely did not stand for a physical trait of Kongzi's. Instead it was, rather, a sympathetic marker of the link between the long-
awaited heir and the sacred mound at which his arrival was sought and
where he was conceived. The greater significance of this qiu and of the wilds
where Kong Qiu was conceived carry our inquiry closer to the Kongzi of the
fertility cult.

The normative birth stories are consistent in maintaining that Kongzi
was the product of a union in the wilds (yehe 野合), and thus ye 野 need not
be taken as a moral reflex castigating Shuliang He for the impropriety of his
alliance with Zhengzai. The term is a common one in the literary strata of
the Book of Odes and usually refers to an unsettled, wilderness region

---

53. See Kinney, "Infant Abandonment in Early China."

54. Chavannes, Mission archéologique dans la Chine septentrionale, vol. 2, pl. 71, no. 137.

55. Ma Yuan (fl. thirteenth century) executed an imaginary portrait of Kongzi in which
the forehead is enlarged and the brow knitted, suggesting the protuberance of legend; however, I know of no other such depiction. I thank Julia Murray for calling my attention to this
exception.

56. Julia Murray, pers. corr., Sept. 16, 1999, p. 2.

where marvelous happenings transpire. It was in her wanderings in the *ye* that the mythic matriarch Jiang Yuan 姜嫄 was overcome by the footprint of a god and gave birth to Hou Ji 后稷, the primal ancestor of the Zhou. Beginning in the early Zhou, *ye* is associated as well with the native inhabitants, largely cultivators, of the territory enfeoffed to high-ranking allies of the Zhou royal house. "Wild People" (*yeren* 野人) was a term used to refer to these cultivators—people living outside the walls of the settlement, *yi* 邑—by aristocrats, who, in contrast, designated themselves people of the kingdom (*guoren* 國人).[57] The *Explanation of Pattern, Elucidation of Graphs* gloss of *ye* has "outside the suburbs" (*jiao wai ye* 郊外也),[58] while the *Literary Expositor* (*Erya* 爾雅), the earliest Chinese source for etymology, is more specific, stating: "Outside the settlement it is called the suburb; outside the suburb it is called the pasturage; outside the pasturage it is called the wilds; and outside the wilds it is called the woods" (*yiwai wei zhi jiao; jiaowai wei zhi mu; muwai wei zhi ye; yewai wei zhi lin* 邑外謂之郊; 郊外謂之牧; 牧外謂之野; 野外謂之林).[59]

In addition to symbolizing the magical and revealing something of the class architecture of Zhou society, the contrast of kingdom/settlement (*guo/yi*) and wilds (*ye*) also demarcates the limit of an ancient imagining of culture and nature, respectively. This distinction was a reflection of a dual symbolic classification registered in the religious geography of the Zhou wherein the *si* 祀 sacrifice was performed inside the temple within the settlement walls, and the *yin* 禋 was conducted in the open on an earthen mound (*yin* 堙) at a "crossroads where spirits dwelled."[60] The *yin* was also known as a *jiao* 郊 sacrifice, using the same graph as that for suburb. When considered in terms of its gloss as "beyond the *jiao*" and the recurring mention in the normative accounts of his parents' worship at an outdoor altar, *ye* opens a window onto a much larger space, a space in the kingdom of Lu. Ac-

----

57. On the stratigraphy of relations between *guo* and *ye* in what might be considered a form of military colonization, see Yang Kuan, *Gushi xintan*, pp. 145–65; and Du Zhengsheng, *Zhoudai chengbang*, pp. 22–59.

58. Xu Shen, *Shuowen*, 290.2.

59. *Erya*, 2.11a.

60. Bilsky, *The State Religion of Ancient China*, p. 41. In several odes of the *Shi jing*, the *yin* and *si* rites are paired. Both the *yin* and *si* sacrifices were seasonal and usually conducted in conjunction, the former at the crossroads altar (*jiao*), the latter inside the ancestral temple (*miao* 廟). Also both ceremonies often involved the invocation of Hou Ji.

cording to the *Literary Expositor*, "Lu has a great wild," *Lu you daye* 魯有
大野,[61] where, amid the marshes and hills, sacrifice to a divine intermediary
(*jiaomei* 郊禖 / *gaomei* 高禖) was regularly conducted. This intermediary
was a matchmaker swallow, a black bird whose intercession was sought by
the infertile or by those seeking continuance of their agnatic line.

The Shirakawa Shizuka's recent short work, *The Life of Kongzi* (*Kōshi den*
孔子伝), assembles much of this evidential variety into a more complex and
intriguing account.[62] Perhaps owing to his years of study of Shang oracle-
bone script, Shirakawa displays a religious musicality that gives breadth to
the mantic implications of the official narratives as he reconstructs the Zhou
fertility rite, enclosing within it the relevant pieces of the Kongzi birth story.
In response to the denunciation of the "illegitimate union" of Shuliang He
and Zhengzai, Shirakawa writes that, according to the nuptial conventions
of the late Zhou, a marriage such as theirs would be considered proper, and
"if a marriage is proper [by custom], it is never deemed illicit, even if it is the
second wife."[63]

He makes much of the fact that Kongzi's birth was the result of fertility
sacrifice, and he believes that Kongzi's mother, Zhengzai, must have been a
mage.[64] Furthermore, according to Shirakawa, it was the custom in Lu that
"prayer for a child was done by a *jiaomei*; their [Kongzi's parents] having
prayed at Nishan 尼山 [*sic*] probably means that there was a shamanic temple there and that the woman named Zhengzai was his [Shuliang He's]
mage."[65] He proceeds to unfold his theory that the Yan 顏 (meaning "pow-
der") were a clan of shamans and that Zhengzai, being the youngest of three

---

61. *Erya*, 2.9b. According to Tan Qixiang's *Zhongguo lishi ditu ji*, 1: 39, *daye* is also the name
of a large lake abutting the Ji River in Shandong.

62. Shirakawa Shizuka, *Kōshi den*.

63. Ibid., p. 17.

64. *Wu* 巫 is customarily rendered as "shaman," presuming that this shaman was male.
However, in the *Guo yu*, "Chu yu" (2: 559), it is said that the spirits of ancient people when
embodied in males are called *xian* 覡, and when possessed by females are known as *wu*. I follow this distinction in my translation of *wu* as "mage," one consistent with Shirakawa's emphasis on the femininity of the shaman. On the non-indigenous (Indo-Iranian) roots of the
term *wu* rendered as "mage," see Victor Mair, "Old Sinitic MyAG, Old Persian Magus and
English 'Magician.'" For a cogent defense of an alternative translation of *wu* as "shamanka,"
see Schafer, *The Divine Woman*, pp. 11–14.

65. Shirakawa, *Kōshi den*, p. 18. In his account, *jiaomei* bears a triple significance, being the
name of the divinity responsible for delivery of a descendant, of the rite performed by suppli-
cants seeking an heir, and of the mage capable of conducting the sacrifice.

daughters, was alone responsible for the family's ancestral sacrifices and consequently had to remain at home. Zhengzai, then, was the mage of the fertility shrine at Niqiu, and it was here and not at the home of her husband that she dwelt.[66] Thus, in Shirakawa's reconstruction, Zhengzai petitioned the divine intermediary, *jiaomei*, through sacrifice at a suburban altar, and where Shuliang had intercourse with her, *en plein aire*. This interpretation, on the whole, agrees with one previously put forward by Marcel Granet who first argued that *qiu* was a site for fertility and rain sacrifice. Working from the account of Kongzi's birth in the *Historical Records*, the glosses of *qiu* and *ni* found in the *Explanation of Pattern, Elucidation of Graphs*, and with knowledge of the sympathetic links of word magic, he, too, concluded that Kongzi was conceived while his mother was offering petitional sacrifice for fertility at a numinous hillock.[67]

The events leading to the conception of Kongzi, all dutifully reported in the *Historical Records* and the *Family Sayings of Kongzi* accounts, then, were those of the *jiaomei* rite, a fertility cult well-documented in pre-Han literature and one conducted by Han Wudi (r. 141–87 BCE) following the birth of his first son.[68] Wang Su's narrative employs the term *qi* 祈 to describe the sacrifice performed by Zhengzai. *Qi* specifically refers to petitional sacrifice in the spring and is a cognate homophone of *qi* 圻 meaning "border," recalling the suburban site of Zhou fertility rite. Sima Qian's retelling instead offers *dao* 禱 "to pray" but, without explanation, preserves the context of fertility sacrifice. The *jiaomei* rite is celebrated in the second month of the lunar year, according to the *Calendric Etymology of Customs and Festivals* (*Yueri jigu* 月日紀古). Its performance marks the beginning of spring, the imminence of which, it was believed, was signaled by the arrival of the "black bird"

---

66. This theory would account for the otherwise curious identification of Kongzi with the clan of his mother. The links with shamanism and fertility are not forged by Shirakawa alone; as Schafer pointed out in *The Divine Woman*, p. 11:

Linguistic facts reveal the intimate relationships between the word *wu* (*myu) "shamanka" and such words as "mother," "dance," "fertility," "egg," and "receptacle." The ancient shamanka, then, was closely related to the fecund mother, to the fertile soil, to the receptive earth. The textual evidence supports these philological associations. In Shang and Chou [Zhou] times, shamankas were regularly employed in the interests of human and natural fertility, above all in bringing rain to parched farmlands—a responsibility they shared with ancient kings. They were musicians and dancers and oracles.

67. Granet, *Danses et légendes de la Chine ancienne*, 2: 431–33.
68. Wang Xianqian, *Hanshu buzhu*, 51.7b, 63.1a.

(*yuanniao* 元鳥) at the juncture of the vernal equinox. Here citing the *Monthly Ordinances* (*Yue ling* 月令), it reads: "The day of the Spring Equinox the black bird arrives and the wild goose comes. . . . According to the *Record of the Rites*, the day the black bird arrives, the *tailao* 太牢 sacrifice is performed to *gaomei*."[69]

Placing Kongzi in this thicker mythic context, we can recognize that his appearance even in the conventional biographies was linked to petition of the principal northern deity of the solstice and the ornithological totem of both the Shang and the Zhou. Indeed, in these narratives he is magically delivered by the divine intermediary (*jiaomei/gaomei*) which is otherwise known as "swallow" (*ya* 乙) and "dark bird" (*xuanniao* 玄鳥). Furthermore, a cursory consideration of cognates and homophones of *jiao* and *mei* allows us to understand why seeking intercession from the "dark bird" usually involved intercourse in the wild of the sort described by Granet and Shirakawa. The *jiao* of *jiaomei* meaning "suburb" is cognate with *jiao* 交 "intercourse." *Mei* 禖, translated as "matchmaker" or "intermediary," is cognate with *mei* 脢, written with the "flesh" semantic classifier and meaning the "quickening of a fetus." Intercourse on the sacred mound brings life to the womb and calls up an association only adumbrated in the received accounts—the connection between funeral mounds and fertility—which is taken up below.

Working the bare bones texts of this mythology to assimilate Kongzi to the Chinese pantheon of euhemerized heroes of antiquity, Shirakawa says, "He was, as it were, a heaven-sent child; he never even knew his father's name, even less the location of his grave."[70] Here he draws on the practice in Chinese spirit possession of referring to the medium when possessed as "child of the god." In his suggestion that Kongzi began as a spirit and was made into a man, not unlike Gong Gong 共工 or Chi You 蚩尤, Shirakawa anticipates the direction of our inquiry.[71] He contends that Kongzi has a genealogy only as a consequence of the inclusion of his birth story in the biog-

---

69. Xiao Zhihan, *Yueri jigu*, 2.3a–b. The *tailao* sacrifice was also performed in memory of Kongzi in the centuries following his death; see *Shi ji*, 6: 1945–46. This ritual phenomenon is well documented in later imperial manifestations in the chapter by Thomas Wilson in this volume, pp. 72–79.

70. Shirakawa, *Kōshi den*, p. 19.

71. See Boltz, "Kung Kung and the Flood," for a much needed rectification of misunderstanding of the manner in which the culture heroes of ancient China were "made" by making them human. For the child personator's spirit possession, see Sommer (pp. 99–102) in this volume.

raphies of the feudal princes in the *Historical Records*. In other words, the vague and scattered information that constitutes this story, juxtaposed contiguously with genealogically distinct biographies of noble clans, acquired a similar narrative structure. Otherwise, Shirakawa implies, there was no structure; instead, the story was a mythic amalgam accumulated over the course of three centuries and given narrative form, but not much sense, by Sima Qian. And in stressing the distinct lack of fit between the Kongzi tale and the larger hereditary noble families collection, he reasserts the persistent figural properties of the normative transmission that in the Latter Han emerged as an independent apocryphal narrative.

APOCRYPHA AND THE
ICONIC REPRESENTATION OF KONGZI

One of the many persistent legends surrounding Kongzi, and one that has been repeated in the canonical literature, concerns his descent from the Shang. The evidence for the presumption of his links to the royal line of the Zi 子 clan comes from several sources: the story that while in Song Kongzi wore the *zhangfu* 章甫, a distinctive Shang headdress, his death dream as recounted in the "Tan Gong" chapter of the *Record of the Rites*,[72] the cognate ornithological symbolism of Kongzi's name and the founding legends of the Shang, and the alleged residence of his ancestors in Song, the kingdom to which the Shang were relegated following the Zhou conquest. A millenarian offshoot of this lore found in the Han apocryphal texts and borne forward in the *Book of Mencius* was the myth that Kongzi was a savior of the Shang people, a redeemer whose arrival had been prophesied five hundred years earlier.[73] Nothing of these tales appears in the *Historical Records* account; in fact there is no obvious effort to make him out to be a descendant of the Shang. When one considers the Modern Text (*jinwen* 今文) numerological teachings Sima Qian must have heard from fellow imperial erudites and followers of Dong Zhongshu 董仲舒 (179–104 BCE), it is strange that he does not indulge the prophetic reading of Kongzi so favored by them. The first line of Chapter 39 of the *Family Sayings of Kongzi*, however, does make an effort to

---

72. *Er qiu ye, Yinren ye* 而丘也, 殷人也 (I, Qiu, am a man of Yin). *Li ji zhengyi* 7.55, 129.2.

73. *Mengzi zhushu*, 86.1.

link the fates of Kongzi and the Shang by beginning the genealogical citation with Di Yi "Lord Swallow," the second-to-last king of the Zi clan. But in tracing these vague lines of mythic descent from the Shang beyond the settlement of the normative account, one encounters not clan ancestors but magical birds in the wilds bearing the promise of fertility.

In the components of the graph comprising the name Kong, we may find allusion to a mythology common among the Shang and recorded in several odes of the *Book of Odes*. The *Explanation of Pattern, Elucidation of Graphs* offers the following as a gloss of *kong*:

To pass through. It is graphically derived from "swallow" (*ya*) and "son" (*zi*). The swallow is a bird to which those waiting for sons appeal. When the swallow arrives, one is with child and commends the beauty of it. In antiquity people with the name Jia ["happiness"] had the courtesy name Zi Kong ["Son Passed Through"].[74]

The very explanation of the graph is a partial account of the *jiaomei* rite. The *ya* of swallow is pronounced "*yi*" 乙 when referring to the number one as with the *yi* of Di Yi, and Xu Shen tells us that "the dark bird . . . in Qi and Lu it is called *ya*, as this resembles the sound and form of its cry."[75] *Xuanniao*, or dark bird is also the eponymous title of the founding myth of the Shang's Zi 子 (literally "son") clan, as described in the *Book of Odes* (Mao 303), the first stanza of which states: "The ascendant commanded the dark bird to descend and beget the Shang. [The dark bird] dwelt in the vast land of the Yin. The ancient Lord commanded Wu Tang 武湯 [Martial Tang] to regulate the boundaries of the four quarters."[76] Mao Heng's Warring States commentary on this ode reiterates the importance of the *jiaomei* in visiting fecundity upon the womb while serving as the midwife of a new order, delivering the firstborn of the ruling clan. He writes: "The Lord [Gao Xin 高辛] went with her [Jian Di 簡狄] and prayed to the *jiaomei*; thus, Xie 契 [the founder] was born."[77]

This inaugural significance is further corroborated by the term "originary bird" (*yuanniao* 元鳥), the other name by which the black bird is known, and *yuannian* 元年, the designation for the first year of a reign in royal chro-

---

74. Xu Shen, *Shuowen*, 246.2.
75. Ibid. See also Chow Tse-tsung, "The Childbirth Myth and Ancient Chinese Medicine," p. 79.
76. *Maoshi zhengjian*, 20.11a–12b, modifying Karlgren, *The Book of Odes*, pp. 262–63.
77. *Maoshi zhengjian*, 20.11a.

nology. Another filiative link in this chain of graphic association of fertility rite, the Shang's charter myth, and the ornithological significance of the graph *kong* may be added by considering the gloss of *ru* 乳 from the *Explanation of Pattern, Elucidation of Graphs*—"to suckle," "to give birth to," and "mother's milk"—a character that figures prominently in each of the apocryphal tales of Kongzi's birth. According to Xu Shen:

Human and bird parturition is called *ru*. In quadrupeds it is called *chan* 產. It is graphically derived from *fu* 孚 [to brood over eggs near hatching; to hatch] and *ya* 乙. *Ya* is the dark bird. In the monthly ordinances of the *Mingtang* 明堂, the day the dark bird arrives, [one] performs the sacrifice to *gaomei* to appeal for sons. Thus "to suckle" (*ru*) is graphically derived from "swallow" (*ya*). Seeking the dark bird's intercession [for a son] must occur on the day that it arrives. The dark bird comes with the spring equinox and departs with the autumn equinox. It is a migrant bird that causes birth; it is the officer of Lord Shao Hao 少昊, whose duty it is to regulate the equinoxes.[78]

There is, then, a cognate complex of graphs bearing ornithological and fertility significance all associated with the Kongzi legends that compels our recognition, recalling as it does the sacrifice and intercession at Niqiu that punctuates both the mythic and the normative syntax. The officer of Shao Hao referred to in the gloss is described in the *Zuo* commentary on the seventeenth year of Zhao Gong's reign (524 BCE). He comes from the "dark bird clan" (*xuanniao shi* 玄鳥氏) and is charged with the "regulation of the equinoxes" (*sifen zhe ye* 司分者也).[79] In some legends Shao Hao is mentioned as the descendant of Huang Di, one of the legendary Five Sovereigns (*Wudi* 五帝) celebrated for his regulation of the kingdom by imitation of the order of birds. Shao Hao is also associated with the Kongzi legend: he was the deified ancestor of Eastern clans whose home and tomb, "the cavern of Shao Hao" (*Shao Hao zhi xu* 少皞之虛), were located in Lu;[80] his clan ruled through 500 years; he was the offspring of the White Lord (Bai Di 白帝) and Supreme Beauty (Huang E 皇娥) and was called "exhausted

---

78. Xu Shen, *Shuowen*, 246.2. The Shang totemic cult of the swallow is well attested in the earliest literature. The "dark bird" is variously identified as the swallow (*yan* 燕) or the phoenix (*feng* 鳳) and is symbolically linked to fertility, with *xuan niao*, as Chen Zhi ("A Study of the Bird Cult of the Shang People," pp. 134–35) has pointed out, understood as a scribal surrogate for male genitalia.

79. Yang Bojun, *Chunqiu Zuo zhuan zhu*, 4.1387.

80. Ibid., 4.1537.

mulberry" (*qiongsang* 窮桑) and "mulberry mound" (*sangqiu* 桑丘) by his mother in recognition of the site of her union with the White Lord.[81]

With such fragmentary evidence as well as several parallel stories and variants of the birth of Kongzi, the myths from which the contradictory pieces of the *Historical Records* and the *Family Sayings of Kongzi* narratives may have come can be reconstructed. The sources for this evidence are heterogeneous, unsystematic, and non-canonical and are found in medieval encyclopedias like the *Imperial Survey of the Taiping Era* (*Taiping yulan* 太平禦覽, 983 CE), *Collected Anecdotes of the Taiping Era* (*Taiping guangji* 太平廣記, 978 CE), and *Literary Writings Grouped According to Categories* (*Yiwen leiju* 藝文類聚, ca. 600 CE), all of which contain excerpts of works no longer extant, but whose accounts of Kongzi's birth reveal an impressive consistency.

In turning to these sources as a way of fleshing out a skeleton of vague assertions about fertility cult and elite lore involving Kongzi, I certainly do not mean to give the impression that I consider these alternative texts more true, *ipso facto*, than the normative accounts discussed above. Indeed, the records gathered in these apocryphal collections are normative, too: first in the manner in which they are consciously anthologized, second in the manner that they may have been ordered by specific rites, and third in the curious timing of their appearance. The late appearance of the Kongzi apocrypha in the chronology affirms that is a text subsequent to the normative *Historical Records*; yet I would caution the reader to resist the urge to conclude that such material is worked up to a different effect, perhaps to explain rather than explain away. The material one encounters in the apocrypha may appear fantastic or improbable; however, it is accounted for with respect to the contours of the geography of the local imagination. Consequently, as we move across discursive terrain—official and apocryphal—commonly thought incommensurable, we will discover more satisfying accounts of the Kongzi legend by reading against the grain of centuries of scholarly sectarianism and discovering how the ambiguity of his legacy elicited the plural inventive instincts of myth, history, folklore, and cosmography.

---

81. Most all the elements of this myth can be found in Wang Jia, *Shiyi ji*, 1.4b–5b. Wolfram Eberhard (*Local Cultures of South and East China*, p. 327) finds a confluence of southern and northern traditions in the tales of Shao Hao and places them in the Thai culture chain. He also contributes to the ethnobotanical links between Kongzi and Shao Hao by noting that the latter is sometimes associated with Di Zhi who "wept as a child in a hollow mulberry." See also Henricks, "The Hero Pattern and the Life of Confucius."

TOWARD AN ASTROLOGICAL
NARRATIVE OF KONGZI

Among the apocryphal books on the *Spring and Autumn Annals* collected by
Ma Guohan (1794–1857) in his *The Jade Box Collection of Lost Books* (*Yuhan
shanfang jiyishu* 玉函山房輯佚書), there can be found the *Springs and Autumns Apocrypha Explanatory Kong Chart* (*Chunqiuwei Yan Kong tu* 春秋緯演
孔圖). It is a curious text not attested in Han records before 150 CE but in
centuries thereafter frequently cited as a source for its narrative of Kongzi's
genesis. It is a birth story far more marvelous than we could have imagined
from the accounts examined above and reads:

Kongzi's mother Zhengzai wandered onto the slope of a large mound and fell
asleep. She dreamt of the Black Lord, whose envoy invited her to go to the marsh on
the *yisi* day to copulate (*qing yisi wang meng jiao* 請已已往夢交). He said to her:
"You will give birth in the center of a hollow mulberry." After she awoke she felt
pregnant and gave birth to Qiu ("the mound") in the center of a hollow mulberry.
For this reason he was called dark sage; when he was born his head resembled a dirt
mound (*niqiu* 尼邱), thus [he was given] the name.[82]

The version in *Literary Writings Grouped According to Category* closely parallels
this one with only a few graphic variations, most notably "invited her on the
ji day to copulate" (*qing yu ji jiao* 請與已交) instead of "invited her to go to
the marsh on the *yisi* day to copulate." The account from the *Imperial Survey
of the Taiping Era* contains virtually the same anecdote, though in this one
Zhengzai walks near the edge of an equally liminal marsh:

According to the *Kong Yan tu*: Kongzi's mother, Zhengzai, wandered along the edge
of a large marsh, and fell asleep. She dreamt of the Black Lord, who invited her to go
with him on the *yisi* day to the marsh to copulate. He said to her: "You will give
birth in the center of a hollow mulberry." After she awoke she felt pregnant and gave
birth to Qiu in the center of a hollow mulberry.[83]

---

82. *Chunqiuwei Yan Kong tu*, 4a–b. See also *Yiwen leiju*, 2.1519.

83. Li Fang, *Taiping yulan*, 321.6a. Note that the source text is mistakenly identified as the
Kong Yan Tu. On the mythic reverberations of *fusang* 扶桑 "mulberry tree" in ancient China
and its particular association with the Shang, see Allan, *The Shape of the Turtle*, pp. 27–46; and
Henricks, "On the Whereabouts and Identity of the Place Called 'K'ung-Sang' (Hollow Mulberry) in Early Chinese Mythology," pp. 69–79, 87–90. One cannot help but wonder

The second of these stories appears in a section of the *Imperial Survey of the Taiping Era* devoted to "parturition" (*chan*) and contains fables about childbirth as well as hatching. If we compare these accounts and those of the normative biography of Kongzi, it is apparent that we have entered a very different territory of the fabulous, one where the cosmic hieroglyphs of Kongzi's sageliness are overcome by the mystery of the landscape. He is no longer a man but a god, a state of being reinforced by the seamless merging of dream time and real time in the interval of his fashioning. Certain marvelous features stand out in each of these stories: divine visitation (apparition), miraculous insemination (heirogamy), the marsh (*meng* 夢), the hollow mulberry (*kongsang* 空桑), and the Black Lord (Hei di 黑帝); others were already visible in the normative narration: Zhengzai and the mound (*qiu*). At once these explicit godlike traits of Kongzi, those of singular transformation, make one suspicious of these accounts because Kongzi was never included in the mythic pantheon of culture heroes.

One aspect of the language of these texts is especially worthy of note— the graph *gan* 感 (sympathy, concinnity, fecund arousal)—for its function here illuminates the matter of fatherlessness. In the ancestral rite, "concinnity" (*gan*) refers to the harmony of sentiment binding the dead and the worshipper; it is the affective and effective grease of agnation. However, in the stories of miraculous insemination and birth, it is used to convey a feeling of human incipience brought by a divine force into the womb of the petitioner in the fertility cult or the female dreamer. Similar phraseology occurs in the birth stories of Yu 禹, Hou Ji, and Xie, as if to show that these extraordinary conceptions may be understood in the language of the everyday.[84] In each case, although the mothers are joined to a celebrated suitor or mate, the progenitor is not a man but a deity. Each tale, as well, is laden with the ponderous weight of infertility and infant abandonment, as with so many of the stories of redemptive heroes in Western mythology—Cyrus, Romulus, Hercules, Moses, and Oedipus.[85]

---

whether *kongsang* might also operate in phonetic sympathy with *zigong* 子宮, meaning "pregnant womb."

84. On the meaning and function of *gan* in the cult of the dead, see Allen J. Chun, "Kinship and Kingship in Classical Chou China." For the use of *gan* in an exemplary birth story, see the account of Yu's birth in *Wu Yue chunqiu*, 6.1a.

85. On the symbolic function and greater cultural significance of these universal heroes, see Rank, *The Myth of the Birth of the Hero*; and Raglan, *The Hero*. Anne Birrell's *Chinese My-*

Here a father is absent—indeed, superfluous. Indeed, the recurring hollow mulberry image invites further consideration on fatherlessness that threatens to invalidate any claim of normative descent whether by genealogy or textual transmission. In Wang Su's retelling of the birth story, Zhengzai alone performs the fertility sacrifice at Niqiu, and a father is a mere shadow. In the account from the *Historical Records*, Shuliang He expires coincidentally with the birth of Kongzi. In the fertility cult accounts, he is never born as "Kongzi," as is the case with the Han era stories. With notable consistency, these myths record that Zhengzai "gives birth to the mound in the center of the hollow mulberry" (*sheng qiu yu kongsang zhi zhong* 生邱於空桑之中). Kongzi is the earth itself, as his mother's womb is the center of the mulberry tree. In this light the apocrypha read like coded recitations of the bounty of what the earth and the winds coursing over it can yield, something explicitly borne out in the physical composition of the white mulberry, *morus alba*. The mulberry, as is characteristic of plants in the nettle order, has small, clustered unisexual flowers, but differs from this order in its possession of a milky sap. The unisexual flower is wind pollinated, and each female flower produces a single seed. A dicotyledon, the mulberry embryo sprouts two cotyledons. The seed leaves of one, instead of becoming foliage, provide food for the new seedling, which is enclosed in an ovary that later becomes a fruit. Its vascular tissue is arrayed in a ring and so is conducive to hollowing. The sexual sympathy explicit in the plant explains its usefulness as analogy for conception and birth; however, the manner of its pollination and reproductive mechanism reiterates male superfluity.

It is also evident that the basic story is less meaningful as biography, but very significant within the ebb and flow of the seasons and the soil of the agricultural cycle. The coincidence of paternal superfluity and the agricultural cycle, in addition, recalls the Han symbology of the emperor's two fathers—his biologic progenitor and the baleful heavens to which he must answer—as in the early imperial rite known as "worship of the heavenly universe,"[86] and

---

thology explores the synoptic parallels between such Chinese and Western mythologies, thus situating local Chinese heroes in the context of world mythology.

86. According to Michael Dalby ("The King's Two Fathers in Medieval China"), this was perhaps one of the most elaborate of early imperial rites. The worship of the heavenly universe was an eight-day ceremony requiring seven days of preparation, with the performance on the final day (the winter solstice) conducted from dawn until mid-morning on an altar atop a circular mount. In the course of the ceremony, the emperor would submit himself to the authority of a dual genealogy, that of an ancestral deity and that of heaven.

in this way draws our interpretive attention away from "popular" to "elite" considerations. The recognition of agricultural cycles and the charting of the heavens do not necessarily imply a larger popular lore from which the Kongzi apocrypha was derived. In fact the astrological significance surrounding the birth of Kongzi is more likely an aspect of the Qin and Han elite almanac-based practice that Marc Kalinowski has termed "calendérologie" and that is independent of heavenly observation.[87]

In China's southwest region, *qiu* 丘, meaning raised earth or a mound, refers to a knoll and is also a name for a village market or settlement. Wolfram Eberhard has argued that *qiu* has a particular significance within the cultic and mythological chains of the Thai people, being associated with the fertility rite. He concurs with Marcel Granet that it was a locus of human fertility, and that perhaps owing to the fecundity of the fields surrounding a *qiu*, it came to be regarded as a site of magical power.[88] Considering that, during the Zhou, the open air *yin* sacrifice performed at a *jiao* altar entailed both prayer for bountiful harvest and petition to relieve infertility,[89] participants in the cult presumed a magical sympathy between agricultural and human productivity, according to which infertile couples might obtain something of a knoll's productive power and thus be able to conceive. Although I do not claim a Thai connection for the Kongzi stories, the overtones suggested may add a hint of the richness and geographical expanse of this lore.

This same homeopathic presumption is attested to in the north, in the millennially controversial phrases of Dong Zhongshu's *Luxuriant Dew of the Spring and Autumn* (*Chunqiu fanlu* 春秋繁露): "In each of the four seasons on the day *gengzi* 庚子, it is commanded that all husbands and wives among officials and commoners dwell in pairs."[90] And, furthermore, it is most likely the word magic produced by the instinctive homophonic associations of the *gengzi* day classification with *gengzi*, meaning "again to propagate" 更孶,[91] that was responsible for the consistency of the *Chunqiu* commentators in re-

---

87. Kalinowski, "Les traités de Shuihudi et l'hémérologie chinoise a la fin des Royaumes-Combattants," esp. p. 176.

88. Granet, *Danses et légendes*, pp. 428–34.

89. Bilsky, *The State Religion of Ancient China*, pp. 40–44.

90. Su Yu, *Chunqiu fanlu yizheng*, 16.12a, and modifying Derk Bodde's translation in "Sexual Sympathetic Magic in Han China," p. 374.

91. On this particular example of sound correspondence and paronomasia, see Bodde, *Festivals in Classical China*, pp. 39–41.

cording the birth of Kongzi on the *gengzi* day. It was an especially propitious moment for both petition and conception.

Seeking intercession for the power to conceive or to ensure that such conception produced male heirs was performed by women at an altar made from a mound of earth, *qiu*, although this graph pronounced *qiu* is written as *xu* 虛, "vacuity." Indeed this practice was witnessed in this century by Hu Pu'an 胡樸安, whose ethnography of southern Chinese customs includes the observation that in Guangxi province *qiu/xu* are market sites attended almost exclusively by women and not merely for the purpose of bartering for comestibles.[92] Indeed, the Han dynasty scholar Xu Shen's definition of *xu* confirms the equivalence as well as the regional linguistic habit: "*xu* is a large mound. Kunlun mound [*qiu*] is called Kunlun *xu*."[93] They petition for progeny at mounds of earth on the northern plain as well, but here the mound is called *yin* and is both cognate and homophone of *yin* of the royal Zhou *yin* sacrifice that was conducted at the *jiao* or suburban altar in the spring.[94] Indeed the charter myth of the Ji clan, rulers of the Zhou, which is preserved in the *Book of Odes* (Mao 245), "Birth of the Tribe" (*Sheng min* 生民), offers the best evidence of this practice while returning us to the recurrent theme of miraculous insemination and birth, as well as infant abandonment:

The one who first begot the tribe was Jiang Yuan. How did she beget the tribe? [She] performed the *yin* and the *si* sacrifices so that she be no longer childless. Treading on the big toe of the lord's footprint, she was enthralled and she became pregnant. [Her time] came quickly and she gave birth and nourished [her offspring]. This was Hou Ji. She fulfilled her months, and the first born arrived—there was no bursting, nor rending, no injury, nor harm. This displayed his divinity. Did the lord not grant her ease? Did he not enjoy the *yin* and *si* sacrifices? [Thus] she serenely begot [her] son. They laid him in a narrow lane; the oxen and sheep nurtured him between their legs. They laid him in a forest of the plain; the woodcutters found him. They laid him on cold ice; birds covered and protected him with their wings. The

---

92. Hu Pu'an, *Zhongguo quanguo fengsu zhi*, 1: 8–9.

93. Xu Shen, *Shuowen*, 169.1.

94. Medical literature preserved on silk manuscripts and excavated from Tomb no. 3 at Mawangdui 馬王堆 in Hunan also confirms this association of earthen mounds and fertility. The *Taichan shu* (Fetus and parturition manual) recommends that "when the child is about to come out, first take moist and clean earth and [form] it into a square of three to four feet and a height of three to four inches. When the child is born, place [it] atop the earth. . . . After its body is entirely covered with earth, then cleanse it. Thus it will be vigorous and have strength." See *Mawangdui Hanmu boshu*, 4: 139; and Harper, *Early Chinese Medical Literature*, p. 383.

birds departed, and [then] Hou Ji wailed; his cry was strong and carried far and long.[95]

In his annotation of the Odes (Mao 303), Zheng Xuan 鄭玄 reprises the observations of Mao Heng while contributing more evidence in support of the mythic chain of man/bird parturition linking the firstborn royalty of the Shang and Zhou with Kongzi. Zheng states: "How did the birth of Hou Ji by Jiang Yuan occur? She performed the *yin* and *si* sacrifices to the Ascendant Lord (*Tian Di* 天帝) at the [place of the] *jiaomei* and thus purged her fault of childlessness and gained happiness."[96]

The parallels with the tales of miraculous birth of China's culture heroes and the founding of the Shang and Zhou houses are remarkable. These tales may well have served as a narrative skeleton for the Kongzi legend. Indeed the graphic evidence of the *gaomei* rite in Kongzi's name, combined with his well-known cranial deformity suggests that a process of symbolic abduction occurred alongside the normative transmission preserved in the *Historical Records* and *Family Sayings of Kongzi*. The physical, or rather physiognomic, emblem of fertility cult borne forward in the official accounts of Kongzi's appearance may represent a conscious appropriation of the legend of Jiang Yuan's generation of the Ji tribe from the misbegotten Hou Ji, wherein the depression of Di's footprint is now repolarized as the frontal depression of Kongzi's head.

Especially evident in the recurrence of the mulberry hollow is a mythic parallelism of Kongzi and Yi Yin 伊尹, the trustworthy and esteemed cook of the founder of the Shang house, Cheng Tang 成湯.[97] There are many more legends that could be cited in this same vein: the birth of Yu, the creation of the Yao people, the birth of Xie, the tale of Yan Wang of Xu and the egg, all attesting to a mythic parallelism, but I would like to turn back in closing to the image of Kongzi as orphan, the mulberry tree, the ubiquitous mound, *qiu*, Zhengzai, and the Black Lord and urge us to consider the contentious semiotic sovereignties governing the normative and apocryphal traditions.

When one considers Kongzi's curious fatherlessness, the salient lack of reference to his origins appears less fortuitous and more motivated. As noted

----

95. *Maoshi zhengjian*, 17.1a–2a, modifying Karlgren, *The Book of Odes*, pp. 199–201.
96. *Maoshi zhengjian*, 17.1a.
97. *Lüshi chunqiu*, p. 139.

above, in Guangxi the graph for *qiu* was written as *xu* "vacuity," which in the *Shuowen* is glossed as "*daqiu* 大丘 [a large mound]."[98] *Xu*, "funeral mound [tumulus]," according to Gustave Schlegel in *Uranographie Chinoise*, "is the fourth asterism of the grand northern constellation of the Black Warrior."[99] The Black or Dark Warrior is described as the nature of Hei Hou 黑侯, the Black Ruler, one of the Five Celestial Rulers and a figure who appears in the "You Guan" chapter of the *Guanzi* 管子 and in the *Zhou li* 周禮. He is linked with the north, winter, and the musical note *zhi* 徵.[100]

All these mythic pieces constitute an imaginative dramatization of the winter solstice, which is believed by the Chinese to occupy the metaphorical position of an orphan before the tomb of his parents, "an idea represented by the characters 'orphan mound' (*guxu* 孤虛),"[101] and symbolically re-enacted by Kongzi's followers Ziyou, Zigong, Zixia, and others, discussed above. When we think of the raised earth mounds marking burial in northern China, it is not difficult to recognize the *qiu* of Kong's given name as such a mound, much as the gloss from the *Explanation of Pattern, Elucidation of Graphs* implies. And when we consider the natural confluence of death and fertility common in any agricultural society and pronounced in the burial rites of the Chinese wherein the body of the deceased is fetally entombed in the golden urn (*jindou* 金斗) and then placed in a hole in the earth, it is possible to recognize that there is no more appropriately concave and convex object as the womb.[102] We are reminded of this, too, in the language of the Kongzi myths where, as noted above, *gan* describes human incipience in the womb as well as the affective ties that bind ancestors and descendants in the cult of the dead. The intricate binding of memory and forgetting, the living and the dead, assumes in this instance a fuller significance.

Beyond the organic apprehension of tomb as womb in Chinese ancestral cult, the movements of the stars are imagined and represented by the cycle of birth and decay. "Orphan mound" is also understood as "the gate of heaven

---

98. Xu Shen, *Shuowen*, 169.1.

99. Schlegel, *Uranographie chinoise*, p. 214.

100. *Guanzi jiaozheng*, 39; *Zhou li zhushu*, 34.2.

101. Schlegel, *Uranographie chinoise*, p. 217.

102. Gary Seaman's 1974 film *Blood, Bones, and Spirits* provides vivid documentation of death's metaphorical representation as birth in the re-interment of the exhumed remains of a male who died without heirs. On the generative power of the tomb, see Thompson, "Death, Food, and Fertility," pp. 102–8. Victor Mair has suggested to me that the protuberance on Kongzi's head may well be a womb or a collapsed funeral mound.

and the door of earth" and is related to the denary and duodenary signs and is also associated with the future in divination.[103] The winter solstice signifies the birth of new light, the beginning of creation, and the marriage of light and dark and so it is that the "mound" asterism becomes the tomb of the sun, "the northern mound of perpetual repose." It is said that with the inception of the solstice the sun thus goes into "a dark hollow" (*xuanxiao* 玄枵) from which it will emerge after its winter rest.

The deep darkness of the double eclipses of the commentaries on the *Spring and Autumn Annals* and the mythic frontal protuberance of Kongzi take on a different meaning in this context. The Black Lord (Hei di) appears as a localization of the dark bird (*xuanniao*), perhaps even a northern subcult reaction with emphasis on the winter solstice rather than the spring equinox. Black is the color of the north; *qiu* is "a northern mound" that contains the sun. Lastly, the *yisi* day in which the Black Lord beckons Zhengzai to join him in the marsh is yet another metaphor for the dark, being double six in the stems and branches, perfect *yin* 陰. The mother's role in this fatherless astral drama is to do the bidding of the season to come. We may read the *zheng* of her name as *zhi*, the fourth of the five notes of the pentatonic scale, and that one which responds to the heat of the sun and is associated with Hei Hou in the *Guanzi*. In so doing, we are reminded of the coincidence of the sun's residence in the murky hollow and Zhengzai's giving birth to *qiu* in the center of the hollow mulberry. The coincidence is explicit connection in the brief birth account of Zhongni in the *Collected Anecdotes of the Taiping Era*. Here it is not the Black Lord (Hei di) but the "Ascendant Lord" (Tian di) to whom Jiang Yuan performed the *yin* and *si* sacrifices and who now comes to Zhengzai in the dark of night through spiritual intermediaries; conception occurs musically:

In the night there were two female spirits. Zhengzai was bathed by an arising fragrant dew. The Ascendant Lord descended and harmonized the ascendant music. From the middle of the hollow there were words, saying "The Ascendant [Tian] yearns to give birth to a sage.[104]

The names of the astral protagonists have been altered, but the narrative is structurally identical and achieves the same effect as the dreamlike accounts

---

103. David W. Pankenier, pers. comm., 1995.
104. Li Fang, *Taiping guangji*, 558.1.

of birth by heavenly intercession: they yield a man transmuted into a god, in other words, "euhemerized."

The normative narratives and apocrypha, when juxtaposed in this manner, reveal the fugal quality of the early accounts and make it virtually impossible to determine the earliest source of the story of Kongzi. Evidence of this sort undermines any effort at coherent recollection. The entanglement of the apocryphal (*wei* 緯) and canonical (*jing* 經) accounts, much like the coincidence of memory and forgetting, suggests that there is no origin, only a relationship of supplementarity.[105] The genealogical, biographic, philological, phonological, and mythic material assembled above, all suggesting links among Kongzi, Zhengzai, and Shuliang He, links with the Shang and Zhou and planetary movement, must be treated as fragments of competing forms of representation among elites in the pre-Qin and early Han still extant in the citations of the many auguries implicit in the events of the normative accounts of Kongzi's birth. The record, when reassembled by us, appears as a kind of miraculous thick description in which layer after layer of significance was produced in the recollection of this remote history.

CONCLUSION: GODS, ANCESTORS

At the close of this tracing of the many families that make up the branches of the story of Kongzi, we are returned to the matter of legacy with which we began. Remember his final lamentation "no one can ancestor me" (*mo neng zong yu*) and recall the ethnopoetics of the cult of the dead wherein gods are formed from the souls of the descendantless dead;[106] Kongzi's ritually intestate passing made him a god, not an ancestor. His association with fertility cult and seasonal sacrifice seems perfectly apposite in this light. Thus, unbound by local worship by agnates, Kongzi was a salient figure in the landscape of ancient China. Moreover, given his diverse presence in the received texts of the *Analects*, *Mozi* 墨子, *Zhuangzi* 莊子, *Han Feizi* 翰非子, *Huainan zi* 淮南子, and *Mr. Lü's Springs and Autumns*, among others, he should be considered a free-floating signifier. In these texts, as much as in the *Zuo Commentary*, he appears as a tropic presence or plot device, a narra-

---

105. See Jacques Derrida's discussion in *Of Grammatology*, p. 243, of "the supplement" in his critique of Rousseau and Lévi-Strauss in which he asserts that an origin is "nothing but a point situated within a system of supplementarity."

106. Wolf, "Gods, Ghosts, and Ancestors," p. 144.

tive voice for anecdotes pertaining to ritual meticulousness and the sanctions of traditional authority.[107] Much like Athena in Greek legend, the Kongzi of the pre-Qin era is full-grown, embodied, and, above all, outside history. This history-less quality no doubt underwrote the popular view of Kongzi in the Han as an exalted, transcendent omniscience who, alas, lived as a prophet without honor in his own time, an uncrowned king (*suwang* 素王).

In the early twentieth-first century, we think of him less as a meta-historical incarnation than as a man of earthly omniscience with a comprehending eye for much of what we hold dear in daily life—virtue, friendship, family, love of scholarship—all conveyed in the finely phrased imaginings of service that make up the *Analects*. Our own view of Kongzi as the philosopher of public practice, or that of the Qufu Kongs as their ancestral, historical deity, or that of our Han forebears as an unrecognized sage-king, or even that of the apocrypha as an astral deity, make of him an artifact of respective longings. Although such fanciful appropriation delivers him from history, it returns him to the place of his invention—the imagination. This is perhaps how it should be with legend, but there is good reason, as I have shown, to examine the conditions of this legend's making for what it may tell us of a particular worldview of ancient Chinese, of the pluralist constitution of the figure known as Kongzi, and of differing mythic constellations in which the stars of this symbol and its diverse communities were arrayed.

He was essentially fatherless, and considering the late appearance of an official biography offering equivocal details of his conception and birth, Kongzi may be understood as a symbolic rather than historic artifact. Moreover, the diverse imaginings of Kongzi uncovered through a selected study of texts and lore suggests that there may be other myths, histories, and legends according to which this figure conjured a very different kind of sense. To acknowledge this, then, is to recognize the diverse authorities governing the literary and mythic communities of Chinese antiquity and to realize that the official remembrance of Kongzi in Han texts and by the genealogical narrative of the Kong clan has encouraged a forgetting, not yet complete.

To overcome this forgetting requires us to view the cultural action encased in the texts and transmissions vouchsafed us as overdetermined and multivalent and to consider sound and sense, graph and text, as elements

---

107. The narrative of events of summer in the tenth year of Ding Gong provides an exemplary portrait of Kong Qiu as adjudicator of the proper conduct of the *meng* rite; see Yang Bojun, *Chunqiu Zuo zhuan zhu*, 4: 1578–79.

swirling about within a field coherent to the actors and yet analyzable only by us. In the end, we must allow ourselves a more evocative, less intellectual, more accidental, less intentional model for reading the past, a model in which visualization, wordplay, and magic names are constitutive of understanding. The diverse mythic geography from which Kongzi was spawned is mapped in the texts—genealogical, canonical, and apocryphal—we have inherited. It is our role as latter-day pilgrims, and avid questioners, to visit those sites of ancient imagination and endeavor with the earnestness and vulnerability of a child in the mulberry so that we may be raised among the clans and surnames, perhaps one day to be drawn up into the rite of seeking divine intercession in the name of a spirit we have heretofore known in another guise as ancestor, sage, and teacher.

WORKS CITED

Allan, Sarah. *The Shape of the Turtle: Myth, Art, and Cosmos in Early China.* Albany: State University of New York Press, 1991.

Baihu tong 白虎通. Congshu jicheng 叢書集成 ed.

Bilsky, Lester James. *The State Religion of Ancient China.* 2 vols. Taipei: Orient Cultural Service, 1975.

Birrell, Anne. *Chinese Mythology: An Introduction.* Baltimore: Johns Hopkins University Press, 1993.

Bodde, Derk. *Festivals in Classical China: New Year and Other Annual Observances During the Han Dynasty, 206 B.C–A.D. 220.* Princeton: Princeton University Press, 1975.

———. "Sexual Sympathetic Magic in Han China." In *Essays on Chinese Civilization,* ed. Charles Le Blanc and Dorothy Borei, pp. 373–80. Princeton: Princeton University Press, 1981.

Boltz, William G. "Kung Kung and the Flood: Reverse Euhemerism in the Yao Tien." *T'oung Pao* 67 (1981): 141–53.

Brooks, E. Bruce. "The Death of Confucius." Warring States Working Group Website, <http://www.umass.edu/wsp/method/confucius.html>, Summer 2000, pp. 1–2.

———. "The Life and Mentorship of Confucius." *Sino-Platonic Papers,* no. 72 (May 1996).

———. "Warring States Working Group: Queries and Notes, 1993–1997."

Brooks, E. Bruce, and A. Taeko Brooks. *The Original Analects: The Sayings of Confucius and His Successors.* New York: Columbia University Press, 1998.

Calasso, Roberto. *The Marriage of Cadmus and Harmony.* Trans. Tim Parks. New York: Alfred A. Knopf, 1993.

Chavannes, Edouard. *Mission archéologique dans la Chine septentrionale,* vol. 2. Paris: Imprimerie Nationale, 1913.

Chen Zhi. "A Study of the Bird Cult of the Shang People." *Monumenta Serica* 47 (1999): 127–47.

Chow Tse-tsung. "The Childbirth Myth and Ancient Chinese Medicine: A Study of Aspects of the Wu Tradition." In *Ancient China: Studies in Early Civilization,* ed. David T. Roy and Tsuen-hsuin Tsien, pp. 43–89. Hong Kong: Chinese University of Hong Kong Press, 1978.

Chun, Allen J. "Kinship and Kingship in Classical Chou China." *T'oung Pao* 76 (1990): 19–22.

Chunqiu Gongyang zhuan zhushu 春秋公羊傳注疏. *Shisanjing zhushu* 十三經注疏 ed. Reprinted—Shanghai: Guji chubanshe, 1990.

Chunqiu Guliang zhuan zhushu 春秋穀梁傳注疏. *Shisanjing zhushu* 十三經注疏 ed. Reprinted—Shanghai: Guji chubanshe, 1990.

Chunqiuwei Yan Kong tu 春秋緯演孔圖. In *Yuhan shanfang jiyishu* 玉函山房輯佚書, ed. Ma Guohan 馬國翰, 56/6.1a–12a.

Dalby, Michael. "The King's Two Fathers in Imperial China." A paper presented before the Department of History, University of California, Berkeley, Spring 1983.

Derrida, Jacques. *Of Grammatology*. Trans. Gayatri Chakravorty Spivak. Baltimore: Johns Hopkins University Press, 1976.

Di Ziqi 狄子奇. *Kongzi biannian* 孔子編年. Zhejiang shuju, 1887.

Du Zhengsheng 杜正勝. *Zhoudai chengbang* 周代城邦. Taipei: Lianjing chubanshe, 1979.

Dubs, Homer H. "The Date of Confucius's Birth." *Asia Major*, n.s. 1, no. 2 (1949): 139–46.

Eberhard, Wolfram. "The Leading Families of Ancient Tunhuang." In idem, *Settlement and Social Change in Asia*, pp. 102–29. Hong Kong: Hong Kong University Press, 1967.

————. *The Local Cultures of South and East China*. Leiden: E. J. Brill, 1968.

Eno, Robert. "The Social Background of the Kong Family of Lu and the Origins of Ruism." MS. Apr. 2000.

Erya zhushu 爾雅注疏. *Shisanjing zhushu* 十三經注疏 ed. Reprinted—Shanghai: Guji chubanshe, 1990.

Falkenhausen, Lothar von. "The Concept of *Wen* in the Ancient Chinese Ancestral Cult." *Chinese Literature: Essays, Articles, Reviews* 18 (1996): 1–22.

Granet, Marcel. *Danses et légendes de la Chine ancienne*. 2 vols. Reprinted—Paris: Editions d'aujourd'hui, 1982.

Guanzi xiaozheng 管子校正. *Zhuzi jicheng* 諸子集成 ed. Reprinted—Beijing: Zhonghua shuju, 1990.

Guo yu 國語. 2 vols. Reprinted—Shanghai: Guji chubanshe, 1990.

Han Ying 韓嬰. *Hanshi waizhuan* 韓詩外傳. Sibu congkan 四部叢刊 ed.

Hanshu buzhu 漢書補注. Taipei: Shangwu yinshuguan, 1968.

Harper, Donald J. *Early Chinese Medical Literature: The Mawangdui Medical Manuscripts*. London: Kegan Paul International, 1998.

Henricks, Robert G. "The Hero Pattern and the Life of Confucius." *Journal of Chinese Studies* 1, no. 3 (1984): 241–60.

————. "On the Whereabouts and Identity of the Place Called 'K'ung-sang' (Hollow Mulberry) in Early Chinese Mythology." *Bulletin of the School of Oriental and African Studies* 58, pt. 1 (1995): 69–90.

Hu Pu'an 胡樸安. *Zhonghua quanguo fengsu zhi* 中華全國風俗志, vol. 1. Shanghai: Dada chubanshe, 1935.

Jensen, Lionel M. *Manufacturing Confucianism: Chinese Traditions and Universal Civilization.* Durham, N.C.: Duke University Press, 1997.

———. "Wise Man of the Wilds: Fatherlessness, Fertility, and the Mythic Exemplar, Kongzi." *Early China* 20 (1995): 407–37.

Jiang Yong 江永. *Kongzi nianpu* 孔子年譜. In Huang Dingyi 黃定宜, *Kongzi nianpu jizhu* 孔子年譜輯註. Pingxiang, Jiangxi, 1847.

Jing, Jun. *The Temple of Memories: History, Power, and Morality in a Chinese Village.* Stanford: Stanford University Press, 1996.

Kalinowski, Marc. "Les traités de Shuihudi et l'hémérologie chinoise a la fin des Royaumes-Combattants." *T'oung Pao* 72 (1986): 175–228.

Karlgren, Bernhard, trans. *The Book of Odes.* Stockholm: Museum of Far Eastern Antiquities, 1950.

Kinney, Anne Behnke. "Infant Abandonment in Early Imperial China." *Early China* 18 (1993): 107–38.

Kong congzi 孔叢子. Reprinted—Shanghai: Guji chubanshe, 1990.

Kong Demao 孔德懋 and Ke Lan 柯蘭. *In the Mansion of Confucius' Descendants: An Oral History by Kong Demao and Ke Lan.* Beijing: New World Press, 1984.

———. *Kongfu neizhai yishi—Kongzi houyi de huiyi* 孔府內宅軼事—孔子後裔的回憶. Beijing: Xin shijie chubanshe, 1984.

Kongzi wenhua da dian 孔子文化大典. Beijing: Zhongguo shushe, 1994.

Li Fang 李昉, ed. *Taiping guangji* 太平廣記. Huang Xiaofeng ed. of 1753. Reprinted—Taipei: Xinxing shuju, 1962.

———. *Taiping yulan* 太平禦覽. Sibu congkan 四部叢刊 ed.

Li ji zhengyi 禮記正義. *Shisanjing zhushu* 十三經注疏 ed. 2 vols. Reprinted—Shanghai: Guji chubanshe, 1990.

Lunyu zhushu 論語注疏. *Shisanjing zhushu* 十三經注疏 ed. Reprinted—Shanghai: Guji chubanshe, 1990.

Lüshi chunqiu 呂氏春秋. Zhuzi jicheng edition. Reprinted—Beijing: Zhonghua shuju, 1990.

Ma Guohan 馬國翰, ed. *Yuhan shanfang jiyishu* 玉函山房輯佚書, vol. 4. Reprinted—Taipei: Wenhai chubanshe, 1967.

Mair, Victor H. "Old Sinitic MyAG, Old Persian Magus and English 'Magician.'" *Early China* 15 (1990): 27–47.

Maoshi zhengjian 毛氏正箋. Sibu beiyao 四部備要 ed.

Mawangdui Hanmu boshu 馬王堆漢墓帛書, vol. 4. Beijing: Wenwu chubanshe, 1985.

Mengzi zhushu 孟子注疏. *Shisanjing zhushu* 十三經注疏 ed. Reprinted—Shanghai: Guji chubanshe, 1990.

Pankenier, David W. "On the Cosmo-Political Background of Heaven's Mandate." *Early China* 20 (1995): 121–36.

Raglan, F. R. R. S. *The Hero: A Study in Tradition, Myth, and Drama*. New York: Oxford University Press, 1937.

Rank, Otto. *The Myth of the Birth of the Hero: and Other Writings*. New York: Vintage Books, 1964.

Savage, William. "In the Tradition of Kings: The Gentleman in the *Analects* of Confucius." Ph.D. diss., University of Michigan, 1984.

Schafer, Edward H. *The Divine Woman: Dragon Ladies and Rain Maidens*. San Francisco: North Point Press, 1980.

Schlegel, Gustave. *Urnagraphie chinoise*. Leiden: E. J. Brill, 1875.

Shirakawa Shizuka 白川靜. *Kōshi den* 孔子伝. Tokyo: Chūō kōronsha, 1972.

Shisan jing zhushu 十三經注疏. 1816. Ed Ruan Yuan 阮元. Reprinted—Shanghai: Guji chubanshe, 1990.

Sima Qian 司馬遷. *Shi ji* 史記. 10 vols. Reprinted—Beijing: Zhonghua shuju, 1975.

Su Yu 蘇輿, ed. *Chunqiu fanlu yizheng* 春秋繁錄義正. Reprinted—Taipei: Hele tushu, 1973.

Taichan shu 胎産書. In *Mawangdui Hanmu boshu* 馬王堆漢墓帛書, vol. 4. Beijing: Wenwu chubanshe, 1985.

Tan Qixiang 譚其驤. *Zhongguo lishi ditu ji* 中國歷史地圖集, vol. 1. Shanghai: Tudi chubanshe, 1982.

Thompson, Stuart E. "Death, Food, and Fertility." In *Death Ritual in Late Imperial and Modern China*, ed. James L. Watson and Evelyn S. Rawski, pp. 71–108. Berkeley: University of California Press, 1988.

Tjan Tjoe Som. *Po Hu T'ung*. 2 vols. Leiden: E. J. Brill, 1949.

Waley, Arthur, trans. *The Analects of Confucius*. New York: Vintage Books, 1938.

Wang Jia 王嘉, ed. *Shiyi ji* 拾遺記. Hanwei congshu 漢魏叢書 ed.

Wang Su 王肅, ed. *Kongzi jiayu* 孔子家語. Reprinted—Shanghai: Guji chubanshe, 1990.

Wang Xianqian 王先謙. *Hanshu buzhu* 漢書補注. Reprinted—Taipei: Shangwu yinshuguan, 1968.

Wilson, Thomas A. "The Ritual Formation of Confucian Orthodoxy and the Descendants of the Sage." *Journal of Asian Studies* 55 (1996): 559–84.

Wolf, Arthur P. "Gods, Ghosts, and Ancestors." In idem, ed. *Religion and Ritual in Chinese Society*, pp. 131–82. Stanford: Stanford University Press, 1974.

Wu Yue chunqiu 吳越春秋. Sibu beiyao 四部備要 ed.

Xiao Zhihan 蕭智漢, ed. *Yueri jigu* 月日紀古. Sibu congkan 四部叢刊 ed.

Xu Shen 許慎. *Shuowen jiezi* 說文解字. Reprinted—Beijing: Zhonghua shuju, 1963.

Xunzi 荀子. Sibu beiyao 四部備要 ed.

Yang Bojun 楊伯峻, ed. *Chunqiu Zuo zhuan zhu* 春秋左傳注. 4 vols. Beijing: Zhonghua shuju, 1981.

Yang Kuan 楊寬. *Gushi xintan* 古史新探. Beijing: Zhonghua shuju, 1965.

Yiwen leiju 藝文類聚. Reprinted—Beijing: Zhonghua shuju, 1965.

Zhou li zhushu 周 禮 注 疏. *Shisanjing zhushu* 十三經注疏 ed. Reprinted— Shanghai: Guji chubanshe, 1990.

Zhu Xi 朱熹. *Hui'an xiansheng Zhu wengong wenji* 晦庵先生朱文公文集. Sibu congkan chubian jibu 四部叢刊初編集部 ed. Reprinted—Shanghai: Shang-wu chubanshe, n.d.

FIVE

Varied Views of the Sage

Illustrated Narratives of the Life of Confucius

Julia K. Murray

As the prestige and importance of Confucius[1] became firmly established in the Han period, the sage himself began to be represented in visual images. The creation of such images was undoubtedly stimulated by the institution of regular sacrifices to Confucius and the official adoption of a modified version of his teachings. Idealized portraits of Confucius were probably included in murals of exemplary figures,[2] and they may also have played a role in sacrificial rituals. Depictions of Confucius are mentioned in Han texts, and some survive from sites in Shandong, typically in the form of incised stone slabs, such as those at the well-known offering shrines of the Wu family in Jiaxiang.[3]

---

1. For the convenience of readers of English, I use the designation "Confucius" rather than "Kongzi."

2. Confucius was surely among the images portrayed on the walls of the Lingguangdian 靈光殿, built by the Han prince Liu Yu 劉餘 (fl. 154–129 BCE) between 154 and 129 BCE and located near the ancestral temple of Confucius. According to the Lingguangdian fu 靈光殿賦 (Rhapsody on the Hall of Numinous Light) by the Eastern Han poet Wang Yanshou 王延壽 (ca. 124–ca. 148), all manner of beings from cosmic deities to recent historical figures were represented in the murals. The text is fully translated by David Knechtges in Xiao Tong, Wen Xuan, 2: 262–77.

3. See reproductions in Chavannes, La Sculpture sur pierre, pls. 8, 12, 22, and 26; and in Wu Hung, Wu Liang Shrine, pp. 43–44. Wu (p. 364) also calls attention to Kongzi turen tufa 孔子徒人圖法 (Method of painting Confucius and his disciples), a two-scroll work in the Han imperial library, recorded in Ban Gu, Han shu 30.1717. Fan Ye, Hou Han shu 60 xia.1998, re-

Even with these early images it is useful to distinguish two major kinds of representation. One category consists of idealized or iconic portraits of Confucius alone or accompanied by disciples, which evoke no specific occasion (see frontispiece).[4] The other comprises narrative illustrations that present Confucius in the context of some particular event, performing some action (e.g., playing a set of chime stones; Fig. 5.1 [all illustrations follow p. 254]) or interacting with other people (Fig. 5.2). In the Tang through early Ming periods, iconic portraits of the sage and his followers were made in great numbers, in part to supply the needs of an extensive network of temples in the imperially sponsored cult of Confucius (see the Introduction to this volume, pp. 1–2). In contrast, there was little demand for narrative representations of Confucius, which had no role to play in the sacrificial cult. Moreover, the surviving examples and documentary evidence suggest that only about seven events were illustrated, of which the best known was Confucius's purported meeting with the Daoist sage, Laozi 老子 (Fig. 5.2).[5] Il-

cords a painting by Cai Yong 蔡邕 of Confucius and 72 disciples in the Hongdumen 鴻都門 school in 178 CE.

4. I discuss such representations in "Portraits of Confucius: Icons and Iconoclasm."

5. The seven episodes that I have found to date are as follows:

I. *Confucius meets Laozi*. Han depictions show two men of equal dignity bowing in greeting (e.g., Fig. 5.2). An anonymous middle Ming handscroll painted in the Ma-Xia 馬夏 style also shows the two men as equals, seated on rocks; see *Zhongguo gudai shuhua tumu*, 6, Su 18–12 (Nanjing University Museum). The Daoist master is portrayed as a figure of higher status in the representation that eventually became part of the multiple-scene pictorial biography called *Pictures of the Sage's Traces* (*Shengji tu*), discussed in the present chapter (e.g. Fig. 5.5). This scene shows Confucius seated lower than Laozi, whose dais is backed by a grand screen. The composition was influenced by illustrations of another subject, *Laozi Transmitting the Dao de jing* 道德經, of which Ming and Qing examples with false attributions to Li Gonglin 李公麟 (ca. 1049–1106) survive in the National Palace Museum and Freer Gallery of Art. The textual basis for the meeting of the two sages is Sima Qian, *Shi ji* 47.1909.

II. *Confucius asks about the rites*. A painting entitled *Zhongni wen li tu* 仲尼問禮圖 is recorded under the name of Zhou Fang 周昉 (fl. 8th c.) by Zhu Jingxuan in *Tangchao ming hua lu*, p. 77 (translated in Acker, *Some T'ang and Pre-T'ang Texts on Painting*, p. 292). It is unclear from the title whether the painting depicted Confucius asking Laozi about the rites (and if so, depicting the same event as in I, above), or his inquiry about rituals while visiting the ancestral temple of the Duke of Zhou 周公 in Lu, a scene incorporated only into long versions of the *Shengji tu*. The textual basis is *Lunyu*, book 3, chap. 15 (trans. Legge, *Four Books*, p. 160).

III. *Confucius meets the boy-sage Xiangtuo* 項橐. Three examples from Han tablets reproduced in Powers, *Art and Political Expression*, pp. 44, 149, and 167, are based on *Huainanzi*; see *Huainanzi zhuzi suoyin* 19.208.11. Mentioned only in passing by Sima Qian (*Shi ji* 71.2319), the encounter does not appear in any version of the *Shengji tu*, perhaps because popular later ac-

lustrations of these episodes appear to have been independent and self-contained, rather than excerpts from a more extensive pictorial biography, which was created much later. When these illustrations of single events were juxtaposed with other pictures, as at the Wu family shrines, the adjoining scenes depicted different subjects in a similar rhetorical vein, rather than additional stories about Confucius.[6]

---

counts made fun of Confucius as a pedant who was easily outwitted by a child; see examples analyzed in Soymié, "L'Entrevue de Confucius et de Hiang T'o."

IV. *Confucius plays the chime stones.* This incident was depicted at the Wu family shrine (Fig. 5.1) and was later included in the *Shengji tu* (Fig. 5.7). The event is recounted in *Lunyu*, book 14, chap. 42 (trans. Legge, *Four Books*, 290–91), and Sima Qian, *Shi ji* 47.1925. The *Lunyu* version makes it clear that the encounter underscored Confucius's stubborn determination to continue seeking employment after repeated failure to gain it.

V. *Confucius encounters the happy Daoist recluse Rong Qiqi* 榮啓期. This event was invoked to decorate Tang mirrors, two of which are reproduced in Laufer, "Confucius and His Portraits," 156–57. A painting of the subject by Lu Tanwei 陸探微 (ca. 440–ca. 500) was extant in the late Tang and recorded in 847 by Zhang Yanyuan in *Li dai ming hua ji* (6.77). An anonymous Southern Song fan in the Boston Museum of Fine Arts has recently been identified as illustrating the encounter; see Tung Wu, *Tales from the Land of Dragons*, pp. 156–57. The episode was not adopted into the *Shengji tu*. The story comes from *Liezi* 1.9 (trans. Laufer, pp. 157–58).

VI. *Confucius sees a tilting vessel.* While visiting the ancestral temple of Duke Huan of Lu, Confucius discoursed on an analogy between human conduct and the effect of varying amounts of water in a suspended vessel: when there is too little water, the vessel tilts; too much, and it overturns; just the right amount, and it stands upright. The text for the episode is transcribed from "Three Ways of Reciprocity" ("Sanshu di jiu" 三恕第九), *Kongzi jiayu* 2.9 (p. 19). An anonymous Ming hanging scroll of the theme is reproduced in *Kongzi xiang*, p. 2; a Yuan example is recorded in Chen Lü (1288–1343), *Anyatang ji* 13.4b–5a (pp. 164–65). The Korean *Veritable Records* for the year 1433 mention such a painting on the wall of the imperial palace; see An Hwi-jun, *Chosŏn wangjo sillok ŭi sŏhwa saryo*, p. 36. The theme entered the *Shengji tu* in the sixteenth century; see note 41 to this chapter, p. 238.

VII. *Confucius weeps over the dead qilin.* A colophon for a painting of this title, by the Yuan court artist He Cheng 何澄 (ca. 1223–ca. 1312), is recorded but not described in the collected writings of Liu Yueshen 劉岳申 (fl. fourteenth c.); see *Shenzhai Liu xiansheng wenji* 14.1 (pp. 583–84). The episode occurred shortly before Confucius died and is included in all versions of the *Shengji tu* (e.g., Fig. 5.8).

6. These contexts usually involve presenting the patron or recipient as a person of lofty morality and conduct; see exhaustive discussions in Wu Hung, *Wu Liang Shrine*, and Powers, *Art and Political Expression*.

NARRATIVE PICTURES OF THE SAGE

A comprehensive series of narrative pictures of the life of Confucius, entitled *Pictures of the Sage's Traces* (*Shengji tu* 聖蹟圖), first appeared in the mid-Ming. Over the course of subsequent centuries, it underwent several major changes to serve the diverse purposes of its various patrons.[7] The initial compilation was based on thirty-odd events selected from Sima Qian's 司馬遷 (ca. 145–ca. 86 BCE) normative biography of Confucius in the "Master Kong's Hereditary Household" ("Kongzi shijia" 孔子世家) chapter of the *Records of History* (*Shi ji* 史記).[8] The episodes were chosen by a censor named Zhang Kai 張楷 (1398–1460; *jinshi* 1424), who then had pictures made for them by an anonymous illustrator, for which he composed poetic eulogies.[9] As an introduction to the sequence of annotated pictures, Zhang transcribed Zhu Xi's 朱熹 (1130–1200) preface to the *Analects* (*Lunyu*),[10] which had become an authoritative summary of Sima Qian's biography when Zhu's editions of the Four Books were promulgated as the official texts for the civil service examinations. Probably soon after writing his concluding colophon in 1444, and in any case before his death in 1460, Zhang had the entire compendium of texts and pictures carved onto stone tablets, which were installed in a courtyard of his home in Siming (modern Ningbo).[11] Rubbings from these tablets could be made to disseminate the *Pictures of the Sage's Traces* and fulfill Zhang's desire "to make the correct path

---

7. I discuss the contents, sources, patrons, and purposes of the pictorial biography of Confucius in much greater detail in "The Temple of Confucius" and "Illustrations of the Life of Confucius."

8. Sima Qian, *Shi ji* 47.1905–47. For detailed discussion of this biography, see Lionel Jensen's chapter in the present volume, pp. 189–95; and also Durrant, *The Cloudy Mirror*, chap. 2.

9. Zhang Kai's actions are noted in his colophon of 1444. Although Zhang's original compilation and the stone tablets are no longer extant, I have been able to reconstruct most of his *Pictures of the Sage's Traces* from later versions; see my "Illustrations of the Life of Confucius."

10. Zhu Xi, *Si shu ji zhu*, pp. 29–31. Zhu's account omitted certain awkward details of Confucius's family background, particularly references to his humble origin, in order to present him as a more perfect sage. The tension among Sima Qian's account, Zhu Xi's summary, and Zhang Kai's interpretation of Confucius's life surfaces in Zhang's colophon. Zhang thought that some of the events reported by Sima and Zhu strained credulity; see Murray, "Illustrations of the Life of Confucius," p. 85n53.

11. Yang Shouchen 楊守陳, "Nanjing you qian du yushi Zhanggong xingzhuang" 南京右僉都御史張公行狀 (Career summary of Mr. Zhang, the Nanjing assistant censor-in-chief of the right), in *Siming congshu*, ser. 7, 25.609.

be followed more widely, in order to avoid the delusion of heterodox ideas."[12]

Although Zhang Kai's *Pictures of the Sage's Traces* is no longer extant, its contents can largely be reconstructed from later compilations that it inspired.[13] The pictorial narrative begins by depicting Confucius's mother offering a sacrifice on a mountaintop to obtain a son (Fig. 5.3), an event discussed by Lionel Jensen elsewhere in this volume (pp. 194–202). In the following illustration, Confucius is shown as a young boy, wearing a ceremonial robe and leading several playmates in a mock performance of the rites (Fig. 5.4). His young adulthood is summarized in two compositions that depict him as a local administrator and in a third that portrays his meeting with the aged Laozi to inquire about Zhou rituals (Fig. 5.5).[14] The following scenes variously present Confucius in the service of an array of local rulers, on his travels between states in an ox-drawn cart (Fig. 5.6), or as a retired scholar surrounded by books and disciples (Figs. 5.7 and 5.15). Two illustrations treat the last days of his life: one portrays him in great distress upon discovering a unicorn (*qilin* 麒麟)[15] killed by hunters in the countryside (Fig. 5.8); the other shows him sick and weak, leaning on a staff in the gateway of his home, as he tells his disciple Zigong 子貢 that he had dreamed of his own funeral (Fig. 5.9). The pictorial biography concludes with two posthumous scenes: his disciples lamenting at his grave mound, with Zigong in a mourning hut adjacent to it (Figs. 5.10 and 5.18); and, over two hundred years later, the sacrifice by the Han emperor Gaozu (r. 206–195 BCE) at what had become a temple to Confucius (Fig. 5.11).

As Lionel Jensen notes in his chapter in this volume (pp. 189–95), Sima Qian's biography of Confucius is a multilayered construction whose ele-

---

12. *Yi ju guang ju zun zheng lu, bu wei yi duan ta qi zhi huo* 以居廣居遵正路, 不爲異端他歧之惑; Zhang Kai, colophon.

13. For an extensive but not exhaustive list of various versions of the *Shengji tu*, see my "Illustrations of the Life of Confucius," appendix.

14. The *Shengji tu* rendition diverges from the portrayals of the theme in the Wu Liang Shrine 吳梁祠 (Fig. 5.2) and anonymous Ming handscroll (see note 5 to this chapter, p. 223, group I), which imply that the two men met as equals. Instead, a youthful Confucius is shown receiving wisdom from an aged Laozi. The scene probably was influenced by pictures of Laozi transmitting the *Dao de jing* (see note 5, group I).

15. I use "unicorn" as a convenient translation for *qilin*, even though the fabulous auspicious beast with a scaly body and one fleshy horn is not identical to the unicorn of Western lore.

ments were drawn from the disparate narratives of various groups that claimed Confucius. From it, Zhang Kai's pictorial biography extracted a relatively straightforward chronicle of the incidents or situations that epitomized Confucius's moral character, the vicissitudes of his career as a statesman and teacher, and the inauguration of his official cult. This conception of the sage's life and its significance is fully consistent with Zhu Xi's representation of Confucius as an exemplary teacher and statesman in the preface to the *Analects*, which by the mid-fifteenth century was tantamount to an orthodox vision. But its transposition into pictures suggests something more than a routine affirmation of the widely professed ideals of self-cultivation and public service believed to be embodied in Confucius's life. By bringing the sage into the viewer's visual realm, Zhang's pictures showed these values in action and asserted them in novel and vivid ways.

It can hardly be coincidence that Zhang compiled the *Pictures of the Sage's Traces* in the aftermath of a major confrontation between scholar-officials and Wang Zhen 王振 (d. 1449), the first of the powerful Ming eunuchs.[16] The life of Confucius personified the moral ideals professed by scholar-officials, in contrast to the supposedly depraved opportunism of eunuchs. The symbolic message of the pictorial biography is that only scholar-officials are morally fit to govern, but their desire to serve may be thwarted by circumstances. As an imperial censor, Zhang Kai may also have been particularly conscious of an implicit contrast between Confucius's uncompromising idealism and contemporary officials' expedient accommodations to the realities of power. In this respect, his *Pictures of the Sage's Traces* could even be construed as a protest intended to assert a lofty ideal under the cover of an unimpeachably orthodox theme.[17] If this was Zhang's motivation, it is understandable that the evidence is circumstantial, because it would have been dangerous for him to be more direct.

---

16. In 1443, Wang's arrest of Li Shimian 李時勉 (1374–1450), the libationer of the Imperial University (Guozijian 國子監), provoked a mass protest by the students. Although Li was soon released, this incident marked a serious escalation of tensions between scholar-officials and eunuchs. The incident is analyzed in depth in Mote and Goodman, *Research Manual*.

17. By the middle of the Ming dynasty, scholar painting had a long tradition of embedding political symbolism in the depiction of seemingly innocuous subjects; for a brief review of studies of various examples, see Silbergeld, "Chinese Painting Studies in the West," pp. 870–74, to which Bickford, "Stirring the Pot of State," and Murck, *Poetry and Painting in Song China*, can be added.

Additional insights may be drawn from Zhang Kai's decision to embody his representation of Confucius in a series of narrative pictures that were then carved in stone, a medium typically used for preserving and circulating faithful reproductions of important texts and model calligraphy. Zhang did not name the artisan who designed the pictures, nor did he comment on their artistic qualities. Later versions of the pictorial biography that evolved from Zhang's seminal series (discussed below) also were usually produced by anonymous artists who worked in media that allowed ready replication, although more often woodblock prints than incised stones. These circumstances suggest that patrons of the *Pictures of the Sage's Traces* were not concerned about impressing connoisseurs of art, who disdained even very skilled renditions of representational subject matter, no matter how venerable the theme. The highest esteem was reserved for cerebral landscape painting, whose disciplined brushwork purportedly revealed the cultivated personality of a distinguished artist.[18] The intent of the pictorial biographies of Confucius was not to make an artistic statement but to promote orthodox behavior.

It seems likely that Zhang Kai's choice of pictorial biography as a medium for his message was influenced by the appearance only a few years earlier of an important and widely distributed Buddhist work, *Shishi yuanliu* 釋氏源流 (Origins and evolution of the Sakya clan).[19] Chronologically arranged and encyclopedic in its detail, it covers not only the Buddha's last earthly life but also earlier and later events, including milestones in the evolution of the early Buddhist church. Published in Nanjing in the early fifteenth century, this woodblock-printed compendium was widely circulated and much reprinted, and its compositions were copied onto the walls of fif-

---

18. These preferences and their lingering effects on the study and practice of Chinese painting are forcefully discussed in Cahill, *Painter's Practice*.

19. Other variations of the title are *Shijiarulai chengdao yinghua shiji ji* 釋迦如來成道應化事蹟記 and *Shijiarulai yinghua shiji ji* 釋迦如來應化事蹟記 (Record of Sakyamuni Buddha's attainment of the way and transformation of his life-traces). It was compiled and published at the Baoensi 報恩寺, an important temple in Nanjing, by Baocheng 寶成, a monk from Siming (Ningbo), and the date 1425 follows a list of people who paid for the carving and printing. The Ming palace published a recarved edition in 1486, of which an example is in the Beijing Library (Rare Book no. 8987). An edition dated 1556 was reproduced in facsimile in 1993 by the Zhongguo shudian in Beijing. The compendium includes 208 pictures, each accompanied by a four-character title and a lengthy quotation from one of several sutras in the lower half of the page.

teenth-century Buddhist temples.[20] Besides offering a template for depicting events in the life of Confucius, the book implies that narrative pictures were an important instrument for transmitting the full range of an ancient sage's teachings and personal example to later generations. Indeed, by the mid-fifteenth century, pictorial biography had become a standard element in the cultic construction of a god or sage.[21]

Pictorial biography may be defined as a linked series of pictures, often based on textual sources, that portray the life of an individual through a sequence of significant events.[22] Although written biographical narratives are indigenous to China and first appeared during the Warring States period, the concept of *pictorial* biography seems to have entered China with Buddhism in the post-Han period. Narrative illustrations of events in the life of the historical Buddha (Gautama Siddhartha/Sakyamuni) and in his earlier incarnations had appeared in India by the first century BCE, and the genre continued to evolve in the ensuing centuries.[23] Through such representations, the earthly lives of the Buddha were commemorated and established as models for devotees. Incorporated into the decoration of an Indian stupa, the beneficial karma of these scenes was thought to be transferred to the worshippers who circumambulated the reliquary mound. Pictorial biographies (or hagiographies) also served to make concrete what was abstract or diffuse in the Buddha's teachings and to impress them more vividly on the consciousness of the beholder. In effect, the images visually asserted the transcendent or superhuman stature of the Buddha.

Brought to China and assimilated into Chinese religious art by the fifth century CE (Fig. 5.12), pictorial biographies of the Buddha may have helped to attract converts and to clarify Buddhist doctrines. The life of the Buddha

---

20. Examples that have been reproduced include murals at the Duofusi 多福寺 in Taiyuan, Shanxi, dated 1458 (see *Shanxi siguan bihua*, pls. 231–38); at the Chongshansi 崇善寺, in Taiyuan, now preserved only in an album of meticulous copies made in 1483 (see *Taiyuan Chongshansi wenwu tulu*); and at the Jueyuansi 覺苑寺 in northern Sichuan, dated 1489 (see *Jian'ge Jueyuansi Mingdai Fozhuan bihua*, p. 2).

21. For an overview of its origins and conventions, see Murray, "The Evolution of Pictorial Hagiography in Chinese Art."

22. Ibid.; see also Kohara, "Illustration in the Handscroll Format," pp. 247–48.

23. Among the earliest extant examples are the scenes carved on the architraves of the gates of the Great Stupa at Sanchi; closer to the model found in China, however, are depictions dating to the second and third centuries CE, such as those from Amaravati. For the former, see Marshall and Foucher, *The Monuments of Sanchi*; for the latter, see Knox, *Amaravati*, esp. pls. 68–78.

took on a distinctly Chinese appearance as its motifs, styles, and thematic emphases were modified in response to Chinese cultural expectations. From the period of Northern and Southern Dynasties (265–589) virtually to the present, a great number of paintings and prints on the subject, sometimes called *Pictures of the Original Deeds* (*Benxing tu* 本性圖), were produced in China.[24] Besides being useful for popularizing Buddhist doctrine, hagiographical pictures may have helped Buddhist monasteries attract interest and financial support from the local population or even encourage pilgrimage to temples whose precincts contained a hall with murals on the theme.[25] In addition, an individual or group might obtain religious merit by sponsoring, making, or even just contemplating pictures of the life of the Buddha.

The concept of representing the significant stages in the life of the Buddha provided an inspiration and model for commemorating other transcendent beings in China. The practice of serial pictorial biography was adopted by Daoists and popular cults that worshipped various types of deities and deified individuals.[26] The range of figures whose lives eventually came to be pictorialized includes Mencius (Mengzi 孟子), Laozi, Lü Dongbin 呂洞賓, Guan Yu 關羽, and Mazu 媽祖 / Tianhou 天后.[27] Although the details of each hagiography reflect circumstances specific to the life of its protagonist, the works display some common themes. For example, miraculous events are associated with the individual's conception and/or birth; he or she exhibits extraordinary conduct as a child; adulthood brings hardships and obstacles that are successfully overcome; and the individual acquires some degree of preternatural power or wisdom.

The genre of pictorial biography is ideal for expounding a vivid and authoritative interpretation of the life of the great personage. Pictures have an

---

24. See Uyeno, "Tonkō-bon banga"; Shinbo and Kaneko, *Butsuden zu*; Weidner, *Latter Days of the Law*; and Murray, "The Evolution of Pictorial Hagiography in Chinese Art."

25. Well-published surviving examples include the twelfth-century Yanshansi 岩山寺 in Shanxi (see *Fanzhi Yanshansi*) and the fifteenth-century Jueyuansi 覺苑寺 in Sichuan (see *Jian'ge Jueyuansi Mingdai Fozhuan bihua*).

26. Late Yuan murals depicting the life of Lü Dongbin in 52 scenes still survive on the walls of the Chunyangdian 純陽殿, a building at the Daoist temple Yonglegong 永樂宮 in Ruicheng 芮城, Shanxi; see Anning Jing, "A Pictorial Hagiography of Lü Dongbin"; Katz, "The Function of Temple Murals in Imperial China"; idem, *Images of the Immortal*; and *Yonglegong*.

27. Further discussed in Murray, "The Evolution of Pictorial Hagiography in Chinese Art," pp. 89–91.

immediacy and impact that reach a different part of the psyche than do verbal or written texts, facilitating recognition and readily becoming indelible mental images.[28] Although outstanding artistic quality or exquisite craftsmanship might well enhance a particular presentation and make it more memorable than a routine production on the same theme, aesthetic contemplation is not the main purpose. In fact, for spreading an idea, it is more effective to make many prosaic examples of the same thing than to create a one-of-a-kind masterpiece. Pictorial biographies are essentially functional art and provide a material means by which ideas can be disseminated, affirmed, or inculcated.

Even though the episodes in the *Pictures of the Sage's Traces* are based on Sima Qian's *Records of History*, a text that predates Buddhist activity in China, pictorial biographies of Confucius clearly owe their visual form to the genre that evolved from illustrations of the life of the Buddha. Following the major conventions of this genre, the life of Confucius displays the pattern associated with extraordinary individuals. Throughout the various editions of the *Pictures of the Sage's Traces*, his figure is readily distinguished from others by its dignity and slightly greater size. Each illustration is accompanied by an inscription that identifies and confirms its place in a catechism of significant events. Although Confucius was not exactly a god, his constructed persona was awe-inspiring and profoundly venerated. Moreover, the regular sacrifices offered to him in temples and schools throughout China made Confucius analogous to beings worshipped by other cults. Ordinary people certainly seem to have regarded him as a deity, as indicated by persistent attempts to worship sculptural images of Confucius even after the 1530 ritual reform, which required temples to replace statues with inscribed tablets (see the chapters by Deborah Sommer, p. 126, and Huang Chin-shing, pp. 267–82, in this volume).[29]

---

28. The separate storage of visual and verbal information is vividly described in Goleman, "Studies Point to Flaws in Lineups of Suspects," C1, C7. Freedberg, *Power of Images*, also usefully discusses human responses to visual images.

29. Even at present, some people regard Confucius as a deity. For his transformation from ancestor to deity among an enclave of Kongs in Gansu, see Jun Jing, *Temple of Memories*, pp. 152–53. The editors of a 1994 facsimile reproduction of a late Ming *Shengji tu* describe how local people in modern Hubei have continued to believe in Confucius as a god, even after several decades of Communist attempts to stamp out traditional beliefs; see *Shengji tu* (Wuhan, 1994), endnote.

Whereas Buddhist and Daoist groups may have created pictorial biographies in order to proselytize or to secure financial and social support from the general populace, pictorial biographies of Confucius were usually directed to a more restricted elite. The sponsors of the various editions of the *Pictures of the Sage's Traces* used them to claim possession of the true meaning of Confucian ideals, as well as to promote solidarity among men who served as officials or were qualified to do so.

POPULARIZING THE SAGE:
THE EVOLUTION OF CONFUCIUS'S
PICTORIAL BIOGRAPHY

Like early textual constructions of Confucius, his pictorial biography was not an unchanging entity; rather, it was (and continues to be) subject to revision. Its configuration and meaning were transformed time and again in the centuries between Zhang Kai's *Pictures of the Sage's Traces* of 1444 and a set of biographical pictures authorized by the Chinese Communist government in the late 1980s (cf. Fig. 5.31). The addition or deletion of episodes served as the primary means for changing the character of the pictorial biography. In addition, the treatment of the same event may vary from one version to another, creating a subtle shift of emphasis or interpretation. Even the choice of medium may be significant, as an indication of the intended audience of the work. Illustrated narratives of the life of Confucius served a variety of purposes, including instruction, pious affirmation, even entertainment. They could be vehicles of argument, like written commentaries and essays on the Classics or debates about which Confucians to canonize in the temple (see the chapter by Thomas Wilson in this volume, pp. 79–85). Accordingly, editions that furthered competing intentions often coexisted. In order to focus the present discussion on the multivocality of the pictorial biography of Confucius, and in particular, on what the variations suggest about the preoccupations of certain people at particular times, I refer to the major versions of the *Pictures of the Sage's Traces* that appeared between 1444 and 1989 (see Table 5.1 on pp. 234–35), whose filiations I have reconstructed in a separate study.[30]

---

30. For a chronological presentation and detailed discussion, as well as an annotated bibliography of editions, see Murray, "Illustrations of the Life of Confucius."

As discussed above, Zhang Kai's *Pictures of the Sage's Traces* of 1444 presented Confucius as the merely human teacher and transmitter of ancient wisdom, an image in accord with the orthodox "ancient text" sources.[31] Except for his encounter with the dead unicorn, his life is unmarked by prodigious events. However, starting with an expanded version of the pictorial biography compiled by He Tingrui 賀廷瑞 (fl. late fifteenth c.) and published in 1497, supernatural omens and demonstrations of preternatural wisdom were introduced into later representations of Confucius's life. These additions fundamentally transformed the character and appeal of the pictorial biography, as well as its protagonist. According to the colophon of the 1497 edition,[32] He Tingrui thought that Zhang Kai had "left out" important events in his pictorial account of Confucius; so he selected nine additional episodes from various sources and commissioned illustrations for them.[33] When He died suddenly, his colleagues raised the funds to have the expanded compendium carved onto woodblocks in order to fulfill He's desire to circulate the pictorial biography more widely as an album of printed pictures.

Among He Tingrui's additions to Zhang Kai's core group of biographical scenes are three pictures pertaining to the conception and birth of Confucius. Now treated in detail, these events are replete with heavenly manifestations that mark Confucius as an extraordinary being. Inserted after the tableau of his mother's prayer on Mount Ni 尼山 is a scene in which she learns of her pregnancy: an inscribed jade tablet is brought to her by a unicorn, the harbinger of a sage-king (Fig. 5.13). A host of paranormal phenomena accompany the birth itself, including apparitions in the sky on the night

---

31. Texts of the Confucian classics, written in pre-Qin script, were reputedly hidden inside a wall during Qin Shihuangdi's persecution of scholars and were rediscovered by Kong Anguo 孔安國, a twelfth-generation descendant of Confucius. They were called "ancient text" or "ancient script" (*guwen* 古文) because the pre-Qin script was considered archaic in r¹ Han period. For the discovery of the texts, see Kong Yuancuo, *Kongshi zuting guan⁻¨* 6.1b.

32. The colophon was written in 1497 by a group of He's colleagues, who saw ι ⌐ject to completion after He died. It is preserved in editions based on He Tingrui's revision, such as one in the Harvard University Art Museum (85.536.MI.24.1971). To my knowledge, no example of the original edition survives.

33. The new material was taken from the third-century compilation *Kongzi jiayu* (discussed by Jensen in this volume, pp. 194–95) and Kong Yuancuo's *Kongshi zuting guangji*, in addition to Sima Qian's biography of Confucius in *Shi ji*.

Table 5.1 Major Versions of the *Shengji tu*

Date	Compiler/publisher	Place	No. of pictures	Medium	Collection
1444	Zhang Kai	Ningbo?	29 or 34	handscroll; later incised stone tablets	not extant?
1497	He Tingrui	Hengyang, Hunan	39	woodblock-printed album	not extant?
before 1506[a]	Zhu Jianjun (Prince of Ji)	Changsha, Hunan	41	woodblock-printed album	Beijing Library; Harvard Univ. Art Museums (later impression)
1548	Zhu Yinyi (Prince of Shen)	Changzhi, Shanxi	39	woodblock-printed album	Beijing Library
mid-late 16th c.	unknown	unknown	36	painted album	Qufu Cultural Relics Commission
1570s–1580s[b]	unknown	Qufu, Shandong?	over 70	woodblock-printed book	not extant? (later edition in Harvard-Yenching Library, et al.)
1589[c]	Wu Jiamo	Shexian, Anhui	41	woodblock-printed book	National Central Library, Taiwan, et al.

1592[d]	He Chuguang & Zhang Yingdeng	Qufu, Shandong	112	incised stone tablets	Shengjidian, Kongmiao, Qufu
1598[e]	Liu Shuang-song	Fujian	39	woodblock-printed book	Hōsa bunko, Nagoya
1599[f]	An Mengsong/Zheng Yunzhu	Zongwen shushe (Fujian?)	19	woodblock-printed book	Tōyō bunka kenkyūjo, Tokyo Univ.
17th c.[g]	"Huanyu xianshenggong"	probably Nanjing	19	woodblock-printed book	National Palace Museum Library, Taiwan
1874	Kong Xianlan	Qufu, Shandong	105	woodblock-printed album	Harvard-Yenching Library, et al.
1934[h]	Li Bingwei (Beiping minshe)	Beijing	104 or 105	woodblock-printed album	Capital Museum, Beijing; et al.
1989[i]	Cultural Relics Commission, Qufu	Qufu, Shandong	39	incised stone tablets	"Confucius's Former Residence" Qufu, Shandong

[a]Entitled *Kongzi Shengji zhi tu.*
[b]The title of the later edition based on it is *Shengji quantu.*
[c]Entitled *Kongsheng jiayu tu.*
[d]Entitled *Shengji zhi tu.*
[e]Entitled *Kong Meng xiang tuzan;* also called *Xiansheng xiaoxiang.*
[f]Entitled *Kongsheng quanshu.*
[g]Entitled *Xinbian Kongfuzi zhouyou lieguo dacheng qilin ji.*
[h]Entitled *Kongzi Shengji tu.*
[i]Entitled *Kongzi shiji tu.*

before and day of Confucius's birth and a portentous five-character inscription on the baby's chest (cf. Fig. 5.14).[34] These supernatural events bear obvious parallels with marvelous phenomena associated with the birth of the Buddha, who was conceived when his mother dreamed of a visitation by a white elephant and was born with 32 unusual signs on his body. Comparable claims concerning Confucius's conception and birth originating in Kong family oral accounts of the Warring States period were published in family histories from at least the Song period onward, and He Tingrui's text quotes directly from them.[35]

He Tingrui's representation of Confucius also built upon Han "modern text" interpretations of Confucius's life as foreshadowing an ideal political order.[36] Despite his failure to create a utopia in his own lifetime or even to exert much influence on the powerful lords of the day, Confucius succeeded in compiling and editing the wisdom of ancient sages, and his efforts had long-lasting and far-reaching effects. He Tingrui's revised pictorial biography includes a scene in which Heaven's approval of Confucius's editorial labors is memorably portrayed (cf. Fig. 5.15). As the aged sage kneels before an altar, flanked by the books that he is presenting to Heaven, the constellation of the Big Dipper sends down an extraordinary beam of light. According to the accompanying text, this "red rainbow" (chi hong 赤紅) then turned into an inscribed tablet of yellow jade, although the transformation is not shown in the illustration.[37] Other images added by He Tingrui depict Confucius as an official who was able to establish exemplary order within his jurisdiction. For example, when he was the administrator of the central district (zhong-

---

34. The mysterious inscription might be translated "Sign [of the one who will] create the regulations to order the world" (zhi zuo ding shi fu 制作定世符).

35. E.g., Kong Yuancuo, Kongshi zuting guangji 8.2a–b; see also Shiyi ji (3.4b), an Eastern Jin anthology of anomalies (zhiguai 志怪). Jensen argues for Warring States origins elsewhere in this volume. The continuing importance of such stories in Kong family oral history is discussed by Jun Jing, Temple of Memories, p. 30.

36. Led by Dong Zhongshu 董仲舒 (ca. 179–ca. 104 BCE), the Han "modern text" school paid great attention to portents and read heavenly correlations even into seemingly mundane events mentioned in the Classics. Advocates believed that only a sage could have a true understanding of the workings of the cosmos and had a responsibility to educate ordinary people; see Indiana Companion to Traditional Chinese Literature, pp. 834–36; also the much more extensive discussion in Elman, Classicism, Politics, and Kinship, esp. introduction and 205–13, 240 ff.

37. This occurrence is noted with greater embellishment of details in the Eastern Jin zhiguai anthology Soushen ji, 8.68 (translated in In Search of the Supernatural, p. 108 [8.232]), but He's account quotes directly from Kong Yuancuo, 9.10b.

duzai 中都宰) in Lu 魯, "the four quarters took him as their model."[38] The respect accorded him by enlightened rulers is suggested in a scene in which Duke Zhao of Lu 魯昭公 presents a carp to celebrate the birth of Confucius's son, who was named "Carp" (Li 鯉) after the gift (cf. Figs. 5.16 and 5.30). He Tingrui's representation of Confucius thus offered both a more heroic model to scholar-officials and a deity-like being who more closely resembled the gods of Buddhism, Daoism, and popular religion. This Confucius held appeal for a more diverse constituency than the one presented in Zhang Kai's original pictorial biography.

Both privately and commercially printed versions of the *Pictures of the Sage's Traces* proliferated in the sixteenth century. Some editions are closely based on He Tingrui's compilation and are actually called *Pictures of the Sage's Traces* (*Shengji tu*) or a variation of that title. For example, Zhu Yinyi 朱胤栘, the Prince of Shen 瀋王 (d. 1549), published a sumptuous edition in 1548 in order to enhance his reputation as a cultivated Confucian who deserved his princely title (Fig. 5.15).[39] Although it includes the same episodes as He's pictorial biography, all the pictures were redesigned. As befits a regal production, the compositions were embellished with elaborate architectural and landscape settings, and the carving and printing are of high quality. Another edition whose revisions of He's compilation are minor was published in Hunan around 1506 by Zhu Jianjun 朱見浚, the Prince of Ji 吉王 (ca. 1455–ca. 1512; e.g., Figs. 5.3, 5.6–7, 5.16–17).[40] In this edition, the compositions follow He's more faithfully, but two pictures were added to the core group. The new scenes both relate to a single event, Confucius's visit to the

---

38. *Sifang ze zhi* 四方則之; see Sima Qian, *Shi ji* 47.1915.

39. This may be surmised from comments in Zhu Yinyi's colophon (Beijing Library, Rare Book no. 16646); see also *Ming shi* 118.3606 and *Mingren zhuanji ziliao suoyin*, 134. A sixth-generation descendant of Taizu 太祖, Zhu Yinyi's accession had been controversial because the rightful heir in his generation had died in 1530 without a son (see the chapter by Huang Chin-shing in this volume, pp. 268–69), and the Jiajing emperor had made him the acting administrator of the realm (*shefu* 攝府). However, two other princes joined forces to protest the appointment, and it was another ten years before the emperor punished them and formally invested Zhu with the princely title. In the spring of 1548, a local scholar presented an old copy of *Shengji tu*, and the prince took the opportunity to make a public display of his Confucian piety by having the work beautifully recarved for wider distribution. His principality was in Luzhou 潞州 (modern Changzhi 長治), Shanxi.

40. For a brief biographical entry, see *Gujin tushu jicheng* (1934 reprint), 346.72.24a, upper.

ancestral temple of Duke Huan of Lu 魯桓公, where he discoursed on morality, using the metaphor of water in a suspended bucket (Fig. 5.17).[41]

Other sets of biographical pictures, based to varying degrees on He Tingrui's 1497 version, appeared under other titles and made additional connections. The life of Confucius was combined with a similar series of pictures on the life of Mencius in a small, two-volume work entitled *Pictures and Eulogies for the Images of Confucius and Mencius* (*Kong Meng xiang tuzan* 孔孟像圖讚).[42] Published in 1598 by Liu Shuangsong 劉雙松 of the Anzhengtang 安正堂, a Fujian commercial house, the work is an inspirational guide to the lives of the founders of Confucianism. Both sets of illustrations emphasize human interactions in each scene by presenting just a few large figures, with virtually no background (Fig. 5.18). Not only were such closeup pictures easier, quicker, and cheaper to carve, they also engaged the viewer's interest and helped to popularize the subject at a time when a flourishing "floating world" culture emphasized visuality in various forms.[43] Nonetheless, the utility and reliability of pictures as a primary source of knowledge had intermittently been disputed since the Han period, and pictures were

---

41. I do not have a satisfactory reason for its addition to the pictorial biography in the early sixteenth century. Duke Huan of Lu was a hegemon who had gained power by murdering his predecessor in 711 BCE.

In the Prince of Ji's edition, one illustration shows Confucius talking with the caretaker of the temple as four disciples listen (Fig. 5.17); the other is a closeup view of three buckets hanging from wooden frames, with the upright vessel in the center flanked by vessels that slant or face downward. The latter picture may have been based on a very similar illustration in the *Zuantu huzhu Xunzi* 纂圖互注荀子 (The illustrated and annotated *Xunzi*), published in Fujian in the early thirteenth century; reproduced in Zhou Wu, *Zhongguo banhua shi tulu*, 1, no. 76.

Later versions of the *Shengji tu* retain the theme but reduce its depiction to a single illustration. The initial conflation shows the men looking at a rack on which three suspended vessels are in the different positions (e.g. *Shengji quantu* 聖蹟全圖 [mid-sixteenth c.] and *Kongsheng jiayu tu* [1589]; discussed below). In the 1590s, the composition became streamlined, with only one upright bucket on the rack (e.g., *Shengji zhi tu* 聖蹟之圖 [1592]). A very similar picture is also included in *Yangzheng tushuo* 養正圖說 (1594), an illustrated guide to self-cultivation, prepared for the heir-apparent by Jiao Hong 焦竑 (1541–1620; jinshi 1589). As discussed in note 5 to this chapter (p. 224), illustrations of this encounter originated independently of and earlier than the complete pictorial biography.

42. A complete copy exists in the Hōsa bunko, Nagoya (no. 161/10), and a fragmentary one in the National Central Library, Taipei, under the title *Xiansheng xiaoxiang* 先聖小像 (Rare Book no. 02667).

43. For extended discussions, see Clunas, *Pictures and Visuality*; and Hegel, *Reading Illustrated Fiction*.

particularly controversial in the late sixteenth century.[44] Conservative critics believed that knowledge gained from pictures was superficial and focused on trivia. Both critics and advocates assumed that pictures were more accessible than writings.

Excerpts from the pictorial biography of Confucius were also exploited to embellish a variety of texts, sometimes just to make them more attractive. Wu Jiamo 吳嘉謨 (*jinshi* 1607) of Hangzhou added a version of the pictorial biography to his lavish reproduction of a Song edition of the *Family Sayings of Confucius* (*Kongzi jiayu* 孔子家語), which he published in 1589 under the title *Illustrated Family Sayings of the Sage Confucius* (*Kongsheng jiayu tu* 孔聖家語圖). Attempting to establish himself as a learned man of exquisite taste, he had the pictures made by the renowned Huang workshop of southern Anhui, which represented the highest artistic and technical standards of the day (e.g., Fig. 5.14) and whose designers and carvers had sufficient prestige to sign their names on their work.[45] Wu's handsome book was reprinted almost immediately (probably pirated) much more cheaply by several commercial houses, who circulated it to a wider public.[46] A little farther down the scale of scholarly respectability and more popular in its approach is another work that was commercially published, in 1599, entitled *The Complete Writings of the Sage Confucius* (*Kongsheng quanshu* 孔聖全書).[47] This handy compendium of texts about or associated with Confucius was made more attractive by the inclusion of nineteen biographical illustrations in its opening section (see Fig. 5.13).

---

44. See Wang Chong (27–ca. 97), *Lun heng*, chapter 13, *bie tong pian* 別通篇 section. The issue is further discussed in the present chapter in connection with a set of stone tablets exhibited at the Temple of Confucius in Qufu; see below.

45. Examples of the original edition are held in the National Central Library, Taipei (Rare Book no. 5326), and Beijing Library (Rare Book no. 11054). Signatures on the work indicate that the pictures were designed by Cheng Qilong 程起龍 of Xindu 新都, and the blocks were carved by Huang Zu 黃組 of Shexian 歙縣, Anhui. For Wu Jiamo's biography, see *Gujin tushu jicheng* (1934 reprint), 347.82.6b, middle.

46. Many copies of various commercial reprints survive, only some of which identify their publishers; see Murray, "Illustrations of the Life of Confucius," appendix D-3–D-9.

47. Edited by An Mengsong 安夢松, the work was published by Zheng Yunzhu 鄭雲竹 (AKA Zheng Shihao 鄭世毫) of the Zongwen shushe 宗文書舍. A copy exists in the Tōyō bunka kenkyūjo, Tokyo University (call no. 2348); later impressions with only seventeen pictures can be found in the Beijing Library (Rare Book no. 14508) and Hōsa bunko, Nagoya (no. 156/52).

An unambiguously popular and accessible version of Confucius's life is presented in an undated southern drama (*chuanqi* 傳奇) entitled *Newly Compiled Record of Confucius Making the Rounds of the States and Fulfilling the Unicorn* (*Xinbian Kongfuzi zhouyou lieguo dacheng qilin ji* 新編孔夫子周游列國大成麒麟記), probably published in Nanjing.[48] The script is prefaced with nineteen illustrations, which not only differ considerably from He Tingrui's but also include episodes that flatly contradict Sima Qian's account of Confucius's life. Moreover, the script itself contains numerous references to Daoist deities and popular beliefs of much later times. In the double-width opening scene, the prayer for a son (by both parents) is offered not on a barren hillside, but in a bustling temple before anthropomorphic cult images (Fig. 5.19), a familiar sight in the Ming urban landscape. The pictorial account makes Confucius's life more relevant to the late Ming viewer by placing it in a contemporary setting, and to a striking degree, the play embeds the life of Confucius amid the concerns of popular culture. Considerable attention is paid to the sage's flesh and blood: his mother appears in five of the nineteen pictures (see, e.g., Figs. 5.19–21); his wife and son are depicted in two scenes (Fig. 5.20), and even his son's wife and child are featured (Fig. 5.22). Confucius himself is presented as a prosperous late Ming paterfamilias and owner of a well-appointed garden villa, as in the picture of the feast for his parents (Fig. 5.20)—an imaginary event, because they died during his childhood. Family interests are also underscored in the last scene, in which Heaven rewards Confucius for editing the Six Classics by bestowing titles on the entire family: Confucius himself, his wife, his parents, his son, and his daughter-in-law.[49]

---

48. The author, perhaps a member of the Kong family in Qufu, is identified only by his pseudonym, "Huanyu xianshenggong" 寰宇顯聖公 (Illustrious Sage of the World), which plays off the title Yansheng gong 衍聖公 (Duke for Fulfilling the Sage) held by the senior member of each generation of Kong descendants. The blockcarver, who signed his name, is Liu Suming 劉素明, a Jianyang carver who also worked in Nanjing. The first illustration, reproduced here as Fig. 5.19, is twice as large as the others and occupies two folios. I have examined two examples of the late Ming edition, one in the National Palace Museum Library (Rare Book no. 02761), and the other in the Beijing Library (Rare Book 12606). The work has been reproduced in the series *Quan Ming chuanqi*.

49. It seems significant that the Beijing Library's example has an inner cover page in which the publisher asserts that it was "Recarved at the Changgengguan following original blocks in Queli [Qufu]" (*zunyi Queli yuanban Changgengguan chong zi* 遵依闕里原板長庚館重梓), suggesting a close connection indeed with Kong family interests. (The Taipei example has no front matter).

QUFU CONNECTIONS AND
MAJOR EXPANSIONS

Alongside the preceding examples, all of which are variations on a tightly focused pictorial biography of Confucius, a greatly enlarged set was also formulated in the mid- to late sixteenth century. If He Tingrui's expansion
may be taken as the second recension, stemming from but transforming
Zhang Kai's original *Pictures of the Sage's Traces*, then an anonymous and un-
titled 70-scene expansion may be considered the third recension.[50] With
this dramatic enlargement, the pictorial biography changed from a concise
sequence, which has a sustained narrative momentum, to a slow-moving,
discursive compendium. Like some of the later editions based on the second
recension, the third recension of the *Pictures of the Sage's Traces* has the format of a book for reading, rather than that of an album or portfolio for pe-
rusing. Each picture and its accompanying text occupy facing pages, and a
four-character descriptive title conveniently identifies the scene. Many illustrations reflect the ambiance of late Ming material culture, with the action
set amid garden pavilions, fine furnishings, decorated screens, and tables of
antiques.

Although the authorship of the third recension is unknown, circumstantial evidence indicates that it originated in Qufu.[51] Such an origin seems
borne out by the added scenes that call attention to Qufu as cult center, an
emphasis that served family-cult interests. Prominent in the greatly expanded compilation are new posthumous episodes involving the tomb, former residence, and ancestral temple of Confucius. One scene shows the tyrant Qin Shihuangdi 秦始皇帝 desecrating Confucius's grave and finding a
tablet inscribed with a rhymed prediction of his own imminent death (Fig.

---

50. A commercial reprint of this recension, called *Complete Pictures of the Sage's Traces*
(*Shengji quantu*), was published after 1684. I have examined a nearly complete copy of the reprint in the Beijing Library, Beihai branch (*zhuan* 傳 50/16.15), and a more fragmentary one in
the Harvard-Yenching Library (T1786.2/1346D). There is no title page or publication data;
and the title *Shengji quantu* appears only as a running head in the margin of each page. I discuss
the dating of this recension in "Illustrations of the Life of Confucius," pp. 92–94.

51. More specifically, it seems to have been the compilation brought back from Qufu in
the mid-1580s by Wu Jiamo's teacher, Yang Shijing 楊士經; see Wu's preface to *Kongsheng
jiayu tu*; also further discussion in Murray, "Illustrations of the Life of Confucius," pp. 95–96.

5.23).[52] Three compositions depict events of the Han period: the discovery of "ancient text" editions of the classics inside the wall of Confucius's house, heralded by music (Fig. 5.24); the unearthing of jade slabs and an urn (with another occult inscription) that had belonged to Confucius, during repairs to the temple; and the planting of a juniper tree on the temple grounds.[53] These four pictures emphasize the mystique of Qufu, Confucius's hometown, by asserting preternatural manifestations of heavenly powers in the area. The final scene shows the Song emperor Zhenzong sacrificing at the temple in 1008, an event that contributed to the rise in the prestige of the cult of Confucius.[54]

Some of the other additions or changes in the expanded set, as compared with He Tingrui's rendition, seem intended to polish the image of Confucius as an exemplary figure. His parentage is revised to give him a more conventionally acceptable family background. Instead of showing his mother praying alone on Mount Ni, both parents are present in the modified scene, and Confucius's father takes the lead in sacrificing to the spirits (Fig. 5.25). Moreover, the parents are depicted as a well-dressed middle-aged couple, even though Shuliang He 叔梁紇 was an elderly soldier and Yan Zhengzai 顏徵在 was a poor young woman who was not his first wife.[55] Other added pictures emphasize Confucius's superior wisdom, such as his identifying a strange clay sheep unearthed by workmen digging a well.[56] It is also worth noting the omission of one core scene from the earlier recension, the episode in which Confucius gives up eating meat for three months after hearing the Shao 韶 music. In its place is a different music-related scene, "Visiting

---

52. The desecration is referred to by Kong Yuancuo (*Kongshi zuting guangji* 9.13b), but he says that there was a white rabbit inside the tomb instead of an inscription.

53. For the discovery of the texts in the wall, see ibid., 6.1b. The tale of the jade slabs and urn comes from the same source (9.7a). The juniper scene is accompanied by a text that says that the present tree was planted in the Yüan period to replace the original one, which had been destroyed by fire.

54. The occasion is described in Kong Yuancuo (ibid., 4.2b–3a); it is more tersely recorded in *Song shi* 7.138–39.

55. According to Sima Qian, they married without proper rituals (*ye he* 野和), a comment that Zhu Xi deleted; compare Sima Qian, *Shi ji* 47.1905, and Zhu Xi, *Si shu ji zhu*, p. 29. Kong Yuancuo was the first to claim that both parents had prayed for a son; see *Kongshi zuting guangji* 9.9a. See also Jensen's discussion in this volume.

56. The episode is recounted in Sima Qian, *Shi ji* 47.1912 and *Kongzi jiayu*, 4.16 (p. 39); however, the text accompanying the picture is closest to (but more colloquial than) the account in *Soushen ji* 12.90; for English translation, see *In Search of the Supernatural*, p. 144 (12.301).

Chang Hong to study music" (*Fangyue Chang Hong* 訪樂萇弘). Giving up
meat may have suggested vegetarianism and by extension, Buddhism, in the
late Ming.[57]

Legends that assert Confucius's supernatural affiliations had long been
part of Kong family tradition.[58] However, the depiction of ancient texts being found inside the wall of Confucius's former residence (Fig. 5.24) not
only served Kong interests, drawing attention to their role in preserving
Confucius's textual legacy, it also endorsed the old texts themselves, which
were important to the orthodox formulations of Zhu Xi. In the late Ming,
the teachings of Wang Yangming 王陽明 (1472–1529) and his followers
presented a serious challenge to the ascendancy of Zhu's doctrines, even
though the latter were the required texts in the civil service examinations.
From the late sixteenth century until the end of the Ming dynasty, examination candidates sometimes included Wang's ideas in their answers and even
attacked Zhu's interpretations directly.[59] During the 1580s, the ancient- and
modern-text editions of the *Great Learning* (*Daxue* 大學) in particular figured in philosophical debates.[60] Although some people suspected the ancient texts to be Han forgeries, the illustration offers pictorial proof that
they really did come from Confucius's house. The pictorial endorsement
thus suggests that the sponsors of the third recension were staunch supporters of Cheng-Zhu orthodoxy.

In the early 1590s, a new building was constructed on the grounds of the
Temple of Confucius in Qufu to house a permanent and comprehensive
display of Confucius's life in pictures.[61] High officials posted to the area
took the initiative in erecting this Hall of the Sage's Traces (Shengjidian
聖蹟殿) by securing funds for its construction and for the preparation of
120 stone tablets, which included 112 for pictorial scenes and 8 for accompanying texts. The censor He Chuguang 何 出 光 (*jinshi* 1583) had con-

---

57. This was suggested to me by Benjamin Elman (pers. comm). The substitution also
appears in Wu Jiamo, *Kongsheng jiayu tu.*

58. E.g., Kong Chuan, *Dongjia zaji* 1.2a–3a; Kong Yuancuo, *Kongshi zuting guangji* 8.2a–b;
and Jensen's discussion in this volume, pp. 233–37, 242–43.

59. Chow, "Discourse, Examination, and Local Elite," p. 185. Useful background on the
Ming exams is given in Elman, "Changes in Confucian Civil Service Examinations from the
Ming to the Ch'ing Dynasty."

60. I am grateful to Benjamin Elman for this information. For general discussion, see Elman, *Classicism, Politics, and Kinship.*

61. For more detailed discussion, see Murray, "The Temple of Confucius."

ceived the project when he visited Qufu on an inspection tour, but its final configuration was determined by Zhang Yingdeng 張應鄧 (*jinshi* 1583, d. 1642), the surveillance vice-commissioner for Shandong (*Shandong ancha fushi* 山東按察副使).[62] The Kong family was also involved through the participation of Kong Hongfu 孔弘復, a descendant of Confucius in the sixty-first generation, who was the district magistrate of Qufu.

Like the third recension, which promoted Kong family and local Qufu interests as well as a more purely philosophical agenda, the pictures in the Hall of the Sage's Traces were directed to a number of political and philosophical concerns. Some of them are discussed in Zhang Yingdeng's inscription, "Record of the Hall of Pictures of the Sage" ("Shengtudian ji" 聖圖殿記), which was also carved on a stone tablet and displayed with the pictures. Zhang reveals a fundamentalist's heartfelt commitment to promoting the authentic values of Confucius in explaining his insistence on adding eight specific scenes to the set when he took over the project. Two of the pictures, "Transmitting (the Doctrines of) Subduing (self) and Returning (to Propriety) to Yan (Hui)" ("Ke fu chuan Yan" 克復傳彥) and "Transmitting the *Classic of Filial Piety* to Zeng(zi)" ("*Xiaojing* chuan Zeng" 孝經傳曾), affirm the true lineage of the transmission of Confucian principles.[63] Two others, "Burying Parents in the Same Mound" ("Hesang yufang" 合喪於防, Fig. 5.26) and "Crossing the Courtyard [and inquiring about the *Books of*] *Odes* and *Rites*" ("Guoting *Shi Li*" 過庭詩禮), exemplify the cardinal principles of filial piety and parental benevolence.[64] Further additions, "Planting a Juniper at the Apricot Altar" ("Xingtan zhi gui" 杏壇植檜) and "Planting a Mulberry Tree at the Three Mounds" ("Sanlong zhi kai" 三壟植楷), commemorate memorials to the Master within the temple and fam-

---

62. Information about the project is taken from Zhang Yingdeng's "Record of the Hall of Pictures of the Sage" of 1592, discussed below. My references to rubbings of the tablets use the order of the set in the Field Museum of Natural History, Chicago (acc. no. 244657a–h [texts] and 244658.1–112 [illustrations]). A brief biography of Zhang Yingdeng appears in *Gujin tushu jicheng*, 359.252.39b, lower.

63. In Zhang's words, *daotong zhengmai* 道統正脉. The two scenes are no. 92 and no. 93 (out of 112), respectively.

64. *Xiao ci da jie* 孝慈大節. The two scenes are no. 11 and no. 40, respectively. A scene in which Confucius questions his son about studying the *Odes* and the *Rites* appears in the third recension, however; so it is puzzling that Zhang claims to have added it. It is possible that the scene had been dropped (along with many others) before Zhang took charge of preparing the stone tablets.

ily cemetery, respectively.[65] The remaining two scenes show Confucius ever concerned with governance, even when he is out on an excursion.[66]

Similar concerns are also embedded in many of the episodes that had been added to the pictorial biography prior to Zhang Yingdeng's arrival.[67] A preoccupation with lines of transmission and particularly with teaching is evident from the numerous depictions of encounters between Confucius and an assortment of other people, including mentors, disciples, rulers, and petty aristocrats. In many of these meetings, Confucius is discussing or demonstrating the moral conduct appropriate to a particular situation, within the larger context of a hierarchically organized society. For example, in scene 27, "Duke Jing: Respect and Yielding" ("Jinggong zun rang" 景公 尊讓; Fig. 5.27), the reciprocity between Duke Jing's respect for Confucius and Confucius's deference to the duke exemplifies the ideal relationship between ruler and minister. Interest in principled admonition is highlighted in episodes that portray Confucius fearlessly advocating righteous action, as in scene 103, "Receiving Favor and Requesting Punishment" ("Muyu qingtao" 沐浴請討, cf. Fig. 5.28), where he demands that Duke Ai 魯哀公 mount an expedition to punish Chen Heng 陳恒 of Qi 齊, who had murdered his lord.[68] The addition of such scenes is suggestive as tacit commentary on late Ming political issues, such as the Wanli emperor's failure to discharge the responsibilities of a ruler and the factionalism that made denunciation the weapon of choice.

Zhang's "Record" also tells us what this monument to the life of Confucius meant to its sponsoring officials, whose names and titles he duly lists. Indeed, he claims to have written his "Record" with their assent and refers to them as "the sixtieth generation of the Sage's disciples" (*shengmen liushi chuan*

---

65. Scenes 111 and 107, respectively.

66. Zhang refers to the episodes as "Climbing the Eastern Mountains and Resting at Datong Ledge" ("Deng dongshan, qi datong yan" 登東山, 憩大同岩) and "Climbing Mt. Tai with Yanzi and Gazing at the Palace Gate of Wu" ("Deng Taishan, yu Yanzi wang Wu changmen" 登泰山, 與顏子望吳閶門). These correspond most closely with scenes 26 and 96, respectively, but the four-character titles on these pictures are "Inquiring about Governance at Taishan" ("Taishan wenzheng" 泰山問政) and "Looking at the Horse Outside Wu Gate" ("Wang Wumen ma" 望吳門馬).

67. Although they are not discussed in Zhang Yingdeng's "Record," they can be identified by comparing the 112 titles and pictures in the 1592 stone tablets with the 70 in the third recension. Because some of third-recension episodes were not included in the 1592 set, there are actually about 60 new scenes in the latter.

68. *Kongzi jiayu* 9.41 (p. 100).

聖門六十傳). They saw themselves as establishing an enduring archive of pictures not only to record the life of Confucius but, even more important, to ensure that present and future generations of officials could be inspired by viewing the sage in action. Nonetheless, the latter proposition was challenged by another member of the group, the military circuit intendant Shao Yiren 邵以仁 (*jinshi* 1580), who wrote a "Statement on the Hall of Pictures of the Sage" ("Shengtudian shuo" 聖圖殿說), the second inscription accompanying the tablets.[69] Shao intimates that pictures are irrelevant or even misleading for the truly important mission of assuring that the Dao would continue to be transmitted. He believed that it was more useful to study the Classics, which embodied Confucius more profoundly than pictures of his material "traces": "Confucius used his heart-mind and obtained the transmission of Yao and Shun. . . . This is how he made himself the model both for his own age and for transmission to later generations."[70] Nonetheless, although Shao was distrustful of representational imagery, it is clear that he shared Zhang's fervor for transmitting the authentic doctrines. In the late Ming political environment, this concern was typical of reformers who viewed contemporary politics as hopelessly corrupt and who conceived a return to ancient ideals as both a literal possibility and moral necessity.

Compared with the diverse emphases of the pictorial biographies produced by the late Ming publishing industry, the stone tablets in the Hall of the Sage's Traces affirm traditional values on matters of social change and hierarchical authority. By their very material, the stolid tablets implicitly reject the ephemeral pleasure-seeking values abetted by the late Ming book trade and hark back instead to the ancient tradition of didactic murals. They resist the growing discrepancy between the traditional ideal of a social hierarchy based on a self-sufficient agrarian society and the late Ming reality of more fluid social structures, which emerged with the development of a monetarized economy and the urban culture facilitated by it.[71] Moreover, the tablets' installation in the Hall of the Sage's Traces publicly affiliated the pictorial biography with the imperially sponsored sacrificial cult and with

---

69. Information about Shao Yiren (*zi* Ziren 子仁) comes from his inscription and from a brief biography in He Chuguang, *Lantai fajian lu* 20.26b. A censorial official from Puan 普安, Guizhou, Shao was posted to Qufu as a military circuit intendant in the winter of 1591.

70. *Kongzi de tong yu Yao Shun yi xin ye . . . shi Kongzi zhi suo yi fa dang shi er chuan hou shi zhe ye* 孔子得統於堯舜以心也 . . . 是孔子之所以法當時而傳後世者也.

71. Ko, *Teachers of the Inner Chambers*, pp. 20, 31–34.

the descendants of Confucius. Positioned on the main axis of the temple, the Hall of the Sage's Traces also functioned analogously to the buildings dedicated to the lives of cult deities or founding patriarchs in some Buddhist, Daoist, and popular-cult temples.[72] The enshrined pictorial biography offered a mode of visual rhetoric that was both powerful and familiar. Accordingly, the representation of Confucius's life carved on the 1592 tablets quickly became the most authoritative version. It was widely disseminated through rubbings and, in the early Qing, through a woodblock-printed reproduction containing 105 of the 112 scenes and Zhang Yingdeng's "Record" (Fig. 5.28).[73]

NATIONALIZING CONFUCIUS: RECENT EDITIONS OF THE "PICTURES OF THE SAGE'S TRACES"

Although space does not permit detailed discussion here, various versions of the illustrated life of Confucius continued to be made during the Qing period and throughout the twentieth century. Many of the later versions retained the basic conceptual structure of the pictorial narrative of the 1592 tablets, but their enframing prefaces and colophons suggest a new direction: to popularize and nationalize Confucius by identifying his teachings with Chinese civilization itself.

A large edition was published in 1874 by Kong Xianlan 孔憲蘭, a seventy-second-generation descendant of Confucius, who worried about continued support for the cult and the Kong family in a period of protracted

---

72. See discussion above and notes 25–26 to this chapter, p. 230.

73. Using the numbering of the Field Museum's rubbings, the seven scenes omitted are nos. 11 (Burial of the Parents), 48 (Duke Ai Asks About Governance), 49 (Discussing the Five Human Principles), 51 (Ancestors as Correlates in *jiao* 郊 Sacrifice), 53 (Revering the Lord and Refusing to Ride), 54 (Great Administration in the State of Lu), and 111 (Planting a Juniper at the Apricot Altar). All had entered the biography with the stone tablet recension, and nos. 11 and 111 had been added at Zhang Yingdeng's insistence. It is not clear why these particular episodes were dropped in the early Qing; however, the choices probably were not simply made at random to trim the compendium.

I have not seen a completely intact copy of the woodblock reproduction but can reconstruct it from several copies that are missing only a page or two each (Harvard-Yenching Library [T 1786.2/1346], Beijing Library [Rare Book no. 16825 and Beihai branch *zhuan* 50/16.11], and Tōhoku University Library [*bing* 丙 B 2–3/14]).

rebellions, foreign encroachment, and social chaos (Fig. 5.29).[74] In a tone that suggests an open-minded search for new patrons, Kong's preface proposes that any person, even a commoner, could be inspired by viewing pictures of Confucius's life. Making it clear that visitors are allowed and even encouraged in the Hall of the Sage's Traces, Kong wrote, "When [people] enter the hall, it seems that they can hear his voice, and when they go into the room, it seems that they can see him."[75] However, the images on the tablets had become effaced from repeated rubbing,[76] and Kong wanted "to preserve and renew the deeds of the Ultimate Sage and Foremost Teacher as they become more distant in time and space."[77] For convenience in producing his new edition of the *Pictures of the Sage's Traces*, Kong Xianlan took the 105-scene woodblock-printed reproduction of the tablets (e.g., Fig. 5.28) and had the pictures copied and recarved onto high-quality hardwood blocks. His publication introduced only minor variations in the style and compositional structure of the pictures.

A more finely detailed rendition of the same compositions was published in 1934 as part of a larger compilation on Qufu, entitled *Pictures of the Traces of the Sage Confucius* (*Kongzi Shengji tu* 孔子聖蹟圖), by the Nation Society of Beiping (Beiping minshe 北平民社), a nationalistic group concerned that modernization had eroded important traditional values.[78] At a time

---

74. Many copies of this edition are available, including one in the Harvard-Yenching Library (T 1786.2/1346C). The texts are fully translated in Lair and Wang's bilingual reprint of the edition, *An Illustrated Life of Confucius*.

75. *Deng tang huang wen qi sheng, ru tang ru jian qi ren* 登堂恍聞其聲, 入堂如見其人.

76. It did not take long for the tablets to become very worn, as Yu Zhaohui 俞兆會 noted in *Shengmiao tongji* 聖廟通記 (Comprehensive account of the Sacred Temple), dated 1687; quoted in *Queli wenxian kao*, 34.32a–b (pp. 891–92).

77. *Shu Zhishengxianshi zhi shiji yu jiu er yu xin, yi mi yuan er mi sheng* 庶至聖先師之事蹟愈久而愈新, 亦彌袁而彌盛.

78. In addition to reproducing a pictorial biography, the Beiping minshe's *Kongzi shengji tu* also contains a photographic survey of the Temple of Confucius, the Kong Family Cemetery, and Kong Family Mansion; plus a *nianpu* 年譜 chronology of Confucius's life and a chart of major events relating to Confucius in later periods, such as honors and titles bestowed on him. I have seen original editions of this publication at the Temple of Confucius in Beijing and Qufu; and modern reprints are widely available (e.g., Taipei 1984; Ji'nan 1988).

The pictorial biography reproduced by the Beiping minshe was not identified and its whereabouts is now unknown. However, the pictures are identical to those in an edition in the Changyangxian Library 長陽縣圖書館, Hubei, which has been authenticated as a high-quality late Ming Anhui publication (see *Shengji tu*, Wuhan, 1994). The texts on the Hubei version are not printed but handwritten, and they sometimes differ from those that appear on

when China's modern identity as a nation among nations was evolving, great anxieties were being raised by a host of social and political changes: the civil-service examinations had been abandoned as the primary route to elite status, which threatened to make irrelevant the Confucian learning on which they had been based; the old dynastic system had collapsed, and the former empire was fragmented in the hands of regional warlords; the government of the Republic was superficial and ineffectual and justified only by a thinly rooted political philosophy imported from the West; and the Japanese had invaded the continent, rationalizing their bid to dominate East Asia on the grounds that China was politically and morally in decay. Moreover, the government was trying to end its official support for the cult of Confucius, which was closely identified with dynastic rule, and in 1935 the seventy-sixth-generation titleholder was forced to relinquish his designation as official heir of Confucius's line.[79] In his preface to the *Pictures of the Traces of the Sage Confucius*, Jing Yaoyue 景耀月 (1881–after 1937) argues that Confucian values are central to a distinctive Chinese culture and the only basis on which the Great Unity (*datong* 大同) can emerge, implicitly rejecting other strategies for ensuring China's survival in the modern world.[80] Another preface by Li Bingwei 李炳衛, the general editor, explains why pictures were chosen for inculcating the desired values: "Although texts can affect people, they are not as satisfactory as pictures for moving the emotions and inspiring profound reflection."[81]

In recent years, the Nation Society's compilation has been republished several times in Taiwan (Fig. 5.30) and on the mainland. In Taiwan, the work continues to symbolize a strong advocacy of traditional Chinese val-

---

the pictures in the Beiping minshe compilation. It is possible that the edition reproduced by the Beiping minshe also had handwritten texts, which would not be obvious from its reproduction; another possibility is that the texts were printed with separate blocks.

79. Jun Jing, *Temple of Memories*, p. 39; Wilson (p. 72) in this volume.

80. Jing was an active participant in the 1911 revolution and prominent in educational circles under the Republic; see biographical sketches in *Who's Who in China*, pp. 202–3; and *Gendai Chūgoku Manshū teikoku jinmeikan*, p. 118.

81. *Suiran wenzi gan ren, jiu bu ruo tuhua zhi zu yi dong qingxu er fa shenxing* 雖然文字感人，究不若圖畫之足以動情緒而發深省. I have not found any biographies of Li, but he authored or compiled several works on geography. Li's preface says that he found a fine old edition of the pictorial biography of Confucius while collecting maps for publication, and he made special efforts to reprint it so that it could take its place beside such treasures as Maps from the Imperial Household (*Neifu ditu* 內府地圖), Map of the Sino-Russian Border (*Zhong E jiaojie tu* 中俄交界圖), and Map of the New Europe (*Xin Ouzhou tu* 新歐洲圖).

ues. The unsigned publisher's postscript to a 1984 facsimile reprint explains that the book should "gladden those who cherish Chinese culture and be sufficient for manifesting the perpetual renewal of Confucian unitary culture."[82] In dramatic detail, he describes how an "anonymous patriot" (buzhi xingming de aiguo zhi shi 不知姓名的愛國之士) risked his life to escape from China with a copy of the 1934 work, during the Cultural Revolution.[83] In Hong Kong, the book was entrusted to a monk named Old Dharma-Master Sage-Thoughts (Shenghuai lao fashi 聖懷老法師), who revered Confucius and treasured Chinese culture despite being a "disciple of the Buddha's way" (Fomen dizi 佛門弟子). When the publisher saw the book in 1983, he immediately recognized its importance to the survival of the traditional cultural heritage, which had been destroyed on the mainland by over thirty years of communism, especially the Cultural Revolution. Noting that President Chiang Kai-shek had established a special holiday for cultural revival in 1965, the publisher proclaims Taiwan the bastion for preserving Chinese values.

Mainland publications of the Pictures of the Sage's Traces, which resumed only in the late 1980s, embody a different attitude toward traditional culture. Because the Chinese Communist Party vilified Confucius and demythologized him for so many years, he no longer embodies core values to mainlanders. Although he has returned to favor since the late 1970s, he now is a lifeless relic of the past, useful primarily as a tourist attraction.[84] And indeed, Confucius has become the particularly prized possession of Shandong regional chauvinists, who regard his legacy as their cultural capital. The Shandong Provincial Press has issued an ambitious series, "The Great, Complete Culture of Confucius" (Kongzi wenhua daquan 孔子文化大全), which contains a large number of works associated in some way with Confucius. The series includes not only a reprint of the Nation Society's Pictures of the Traces of the Sage Confucius of 1934 but also the first publication of a late Ming album containing paintings based on He Tingrui's recension

---

82. Dang wei aixi Zhonghua wenhuazhe suo lewen, yi zu yi jian rujia datong wenhua zhi wangu changxin 當爲愛惜中華文化者所樂聞, 亦足以見儒家大同文化之萬古常新; see Kongzi shengji tu (1984 Wensi reprint).

83. For the Cultural Revolution and Confucius, see the chapters by Jun Jing, pp. 335–75, and Wang Liang, pp. 376–98, in this book.

84. There are some indications that mainland leaders are increasingly invoking Confucius as a symbol of Chineseness in their rhetoric of nationalism, which is replacing Marxist ideology as the basis for national unity; see the chapter by Jun Jing, pp. 335–75, in this volume.

of the pictorial biography (see Fig. 5.11).[85] The painted album has recently
been exhibited in Japan and Europe, shown in Japan on national television,
and fully reproduced in color in a Japanese publication.[86] Such activities,
carried out with the official blessing of the Cultural Relics Bureau, have
brought foreign funds to Qufu. For visitors to the Temple of Confucius itself, facsimile reproductions of the painted album leaves have sometimes
been displayed in a side building, as part of an exhibit on Confucius's life.
However, the scenes that portray supernatural elements are not included,
because they conflict not only with the "modern" outlook but also with a
deeply ingrained and longstanding Marxist prejudice against superstition.
Also at the Qufu temple, a new set of prints made from Qing woodblocks of
the pictorial biography is exhibited in a major building on the main axis, the
Pavilion of the Constellation of Learning (Kuiwen'ge 奎文閣).

In the late 1980s, a thoroughgoing revision of the pictorial biography was
newly created for exhibition in "Confucius's former residence" (*Kongzi gu
zhai* 孔子古宅) immediately adjacent to the Qufu temple (Fig. 5.31).[87] The
pictures are constructed from carved and polished black limestone squares
that fit together to form 31 large compositions, each depicting multiple
events. In contrast to the various replicas of earlier pictorial biographies, this
new series portrays Confucius as a great man from ancient history. Not surprisingly, the standard biographical episodes are drastically reconceptual-
ized, and there is no mention of supernatural events or powers. The preface
declares that Confucius was a great philosopher, statesman, and educator,
and his thought had a long-lasting and major influence on the evolution of
Chinese society, as well as on people of other countries. Guided by inscriptions that accompany each scene, the viewer is shown that Confucius was
extremely studious, filial, diligent, and correct in his behavior—a model citizen of a secular society. Literally larger than life, he towers over the other
figures in most of the pictures. The hagiography contains elements, both
verbal and pictorial, that are reminiscent of conventions used for presenting

---

85. See *Shengji zhi tu* (1988); and also Kaji, *Kōshi gaden*; and Murray, "Illustrations of the
Life of Confucius," esp. p. 118n145. The album now belongs to the Qufu Cultural Relics
Commission.

86. I.e., Kaji, *Kōshi gaden*.

87. The set is entitled *Pictures of the Deeds of Confucius* (*Kongzi shiji tu*). It is not exactly identical to the twenty-scene version of the same name that is reproduced by Shi Ke in *Kongzi shiji tu*.

communist heroes, such as Mao Zedong.[88] In style and technique, however, the set deliberately evokes the stone-carved pictures made in Shandong during the Eastern Han period (cf. Figs. 5.1 and 5.2), in order to underscore the links with ancient artistic and cultural traditions of the region.

THE CASE OF
THE VANISHING WOMEN

The preceding account should make it clear that the pictorial biography of Confucius has appeared in many contexts, symbolized various ideas, and served several different agendas. As a result, the compilations vary in their presentation of events in Confucius's life and in the themes that are emphasized. I conclude by drawing on the editions introduced above to examine a group of scenes whose alterations signify late Ming anxieties concerning women: episodes involving the women of Confucius's family. The pictures provide a channel for responding to the challenges that social changes of the late sixteenth and seventeenth centuries brought to traditionally prescribed gender roles.[89] As women gained opportunities to become educated and to come into contact with the world beyond their homes, prescriptive ideals for female comportment became more circumscribed. The perception that women were breaking out of their proper bounds helps to account for the sudden proliferation at this time of moralistic works directed to women, such as Lü Kun's 呂坤 (1536–1618) *Regulations for the Women's Quarters* (*Guifan* 閨範) and the numerous reissues of classics like *Biographies of Exemplary Women* (*Lienü zhuan* 列女傳) and *Ladies' Classic of Filial Piety* (*Nü xiao jing* 女孝經). In the pictorial biography of Confucius, the appearance or nonappearance of a woman (or women) in the illustration of appropriate events points to the notions of propriety that were at issue in the late Ming.

Confucius's mother, Yan Zhengzai, is depicted in the opening scene of Zhang Kai's first-recension *Pictures of the Sage's Traces* of 1444, in which she sacrifices to the spirits to obtain a son (cf. Fig. 5.3). However, Confucius's fa-

---

88. For some examples, see Stewart E. Fraser, *100 Great Chinese Posters* (New York: Images Graphiques, 1977), esp. pp. 18–19, 97, and 99.

89. For these social changes and their effects, see Carlitz, "Desire, Danger, and the Body"; idem, "Social Uses of Female Virtue"; Handlin, "Lü K'un's New Audience"; Ko, *Teachers of the Inner Chambers*; Shek, "Religion and Society in Late Ming"; and T'ien, *Male Anxiety and Female Chastity*.

ther, Shuliang He, is added to the scene in some of the late Ming pictorial biographies, such as in the anonymous third recension (ca. mid-sixteenth c.; Fig. 5.25), Wu Jiamo's *Kongsheng jiayu tu* (1589), and the play *Newly Compiled Record of Master Kong Making the Rounds of the States and Fulfilling the Unicorn* (ca. early seventeenth c.; Fig. 5.19). Although Sima Qian's account is ambiguous, the *Family Sayings of Confucius* clearly states that Confucius's mother offered the prayer alone.[90] Nonetheless, Wu Jiamo comments that Shuliang He must have been present, "on the principle that a wife would not do this on her own or roam alone outside of her domain."[91] His attitude reflects the strict construction of Confucian morality in the late Ming, which could not admit the possibility that the sage's mother had committed the impropriety of being in the wilderness unescorted. Late Ming moralists railed against women escaping their proper domestic sphere and engaging in loose conduct, particularly if it involved cult activity.[92] Nonetheless, this change in the opening illustration of Confucius's pictorial biography was not universally accepted, probably because it contradicted the *Family Sayings of Confucius*. The majority of later versions follow the influential stone tablets in the Hall of the Sage's Traces of 1592, which continued to portray Yan Zhengzai sacrificing alone.

He Tingrui's expansion of Zhang Kai's core compilation, which incorporated the supernatural lore connected with Confucius's birth from Kong family publications,[93] added two more depictions of Confucius's mother: receiving the tablet from the unicorn (cf. Fig. 5.13), and resting from childbirth while the infant is washed (cf. Fig. 5.14). In the Prince of Ji's edition of approximately 1506, the visitation scene shows her standing close and holding out a sash to the unicorn, whose mouth emits an aura that touches her. Some depictions, including the 1592 and Qing editions, place one end of the sash in the creature's mouth, tightly linking the two figures. A few renditions suggest an even more risqué interaction, with Ms. Yan fondling its horn, as seen in *Kongsheng quanshu* of 1599 (Fig. 5.13). The illustration for the popular play asserts propriety and patriarchal authority by having the crea-

---

90. Sima Qian, *Shi ji* 47.1905; *Kongzi jiayu* 9.39 (p. 93).

91. *Furen wu zhuan zhi, wu duyou jingwai zhi li* 夫人無專制, 無獨遊境外之理; see Wu Jiamo, *Kongsheng jiayu tu* 1.2b. Since his view was not supported by the text for which he was supplying illustrations, he may have felt compelled to explain his reason.

92. For relevant discussion, see Handlin, "Lü K'un's New Audience," pp. 17ff.

93. Particularly Kong Yuancuo, *Kongshi zuting guangji* 8.1b–2a.

ture deliver the tablet to Shuliang He (Fig. 5.21); nonetheless, his wife appears to be throwing her sash onto the creature as it passes by her.

Contending views of propriety are even more evident in the treatment of Confucius's nativity in various versions. The earliest illustration of the event portrays an intimate scene in the birthing chamber, in which the mysteriously inscribed infant is being washed as his mother rests on her bed (Fig. 5.14). Starting with the 1592 stone tablets, most later editions remove the mother and baby from sight. Instead, only the cloud-enshrouded roof of the building is visible, and the emphasis has shifted to the large figures of five deities hovering in the sky (Fig. 5.29).[94] A similar situation occurs with the scene in which Duke Zhao of Lu gives a fish to Confucius when the latter's son is born, an illustration also added by He Tingrui. The initial depiction includes the figures of mother and infant (Confucius's wife and baby), but they disappear in later editions, again beginning with the 1592 tablets (compare Figs. 5.16 and 5.30). Such deletions may reflect a belief that it was indecorous to expose the intimate life of a respectable woman to public gaze, suggesting again a protest against the looser social practices of the late Ming. It may also embody a moralistic reaction to the illustrated dramas, novels, and other publications of the late Ming period, which did gratify viewers with displays of private scenes, sometimes erotic ones, in the lives of historical, fictional, or divine women.[95] A close counterpart to the scene of Confucius's birth is readily found in this literature (Fig. 5.32).

From a somewhat different standpoint, the removal of mothers and babies from these scenes may also be interpreted as an implicit rejection of the growing tendency to "familize" the official cult of Confucius in the late Ming, as discussed by Thomas Wilson.[96] By elevating the ritual status of the fathers of Confucius and of his leading followers, the Jiajing emperor had in-

---

94. Some depictions show the entire building, tightly closed and curtained.

95. Indeed, it was all too easy to transform moralistic illustrations into titillating ones, as demonstrated by Katherine Carlitz in her study of links between late Ming editions of the illustrated *Lienü zhuan* and illustrated works of drama and fiction ("The Social Uses of Female Virtue"). Late Ming illustrated books made women available to public gaze, as also discussed by Ko, *Teachers of the Inner Chambers*, p. 65. Qing emperors attempted to suppress this hedonistic culture by banning improper works; see Naquin and Rawski, *Chinese Society in the Eighteenth Century*, p. 109.

96. Wilson, "The Ritual Formation of Confucian Orthodoxy and the Descendants of the Sage."

Fig. 5.1 Confucius plays the chime stones. Eastern Han period, second century. Rubbing of incised stone slab from the Wu Family Shrines, Jiaxiang, Shandong. Field Museum, Chicago (acc. no. 244572).

Fig. 5.2 Confucius meets Laozi. Eastern Han period, second century. Rubbing of incised stone slab from the Wu Family Shrines, Jiaxiang, Shandong. Field Museum, Chicago (acc. no. 241).

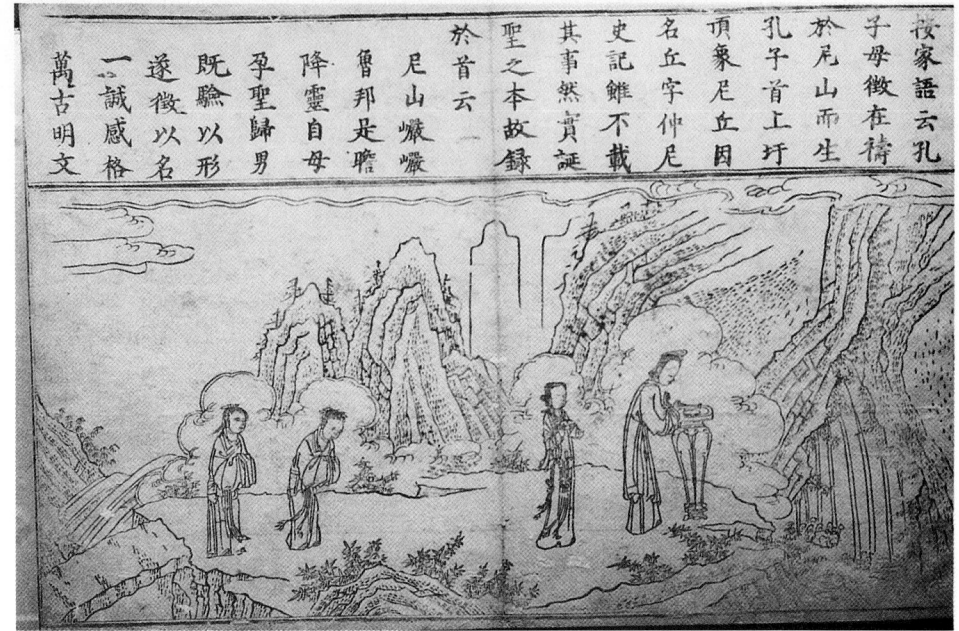

投家語云孔
子母徵在禱
於尼山而生
孔子首上圩
頂象尼丘因
名丘字仲尼
史記雖不載
其事然實証
聖之本故錄
於首云一
足山巉巉
魯邦是瞻
降靈自母
孕聖歸男
既驗以形
遂徵以名
一誠感格
萬古明文

Fig. 5.3 Confucius's mother prays on Mount Ni, *Kongzi Shengji tu*, scene 2. Late Ming impression of Zhu Jianjun's early sixteenth-century edition. Woodblock print, 39.4 x 61.25 cm. Harvard University Art Museums (85.536.MI.24.1971).

Fig. 5.4 Confucius plays at performing rites, *Shengji tu*, scene 6. Late Ming recut purporting to be 1444 original edition. Woodblock print, 25 x 56 cm. Beijing Library (Rare Book no. 16645). After *Zhongguo gudai banhua congkan*, p. 376.

Fig. 5.5 Confucius visiting Laozi, *Shengji tu*, scene 11. Late Ming recut purporting to be 1444 original edition. Woodblock print, 25 x 56 cm. Beijing Library (Rare Book no. 16645). After *Zhongguo gudai banhua congkan*, p. 378.

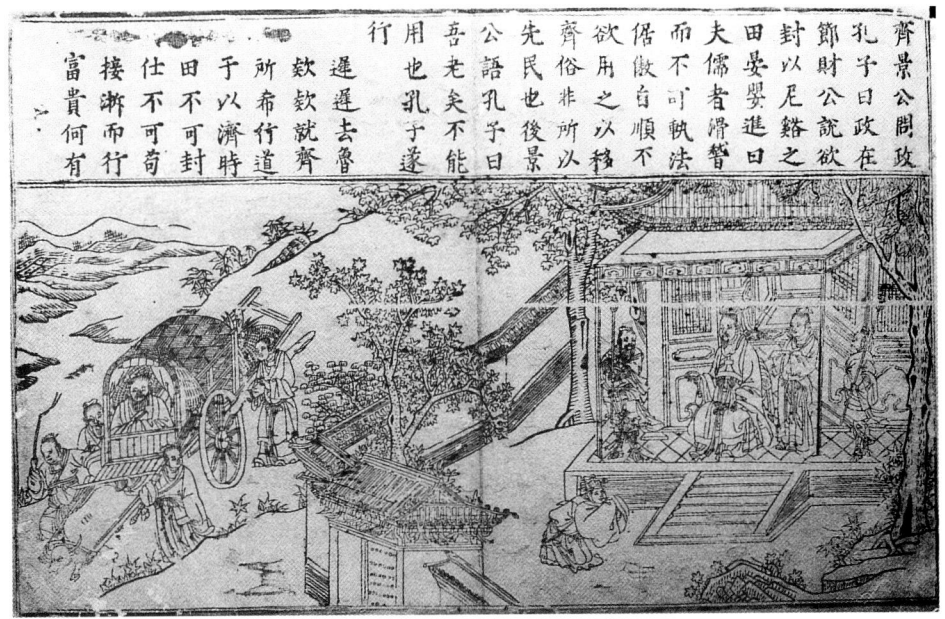

Fig. 5.6 Confucius leaves the state of Qi, *Kongzi Shengji tu*, scene 13. Late Ming impression of Zhu Jianjun's early sixteenth-century edition. Woodblock print, 39.4 x 61.25 cm. Harvard University Art Museums (85.536.MI.24.1971).

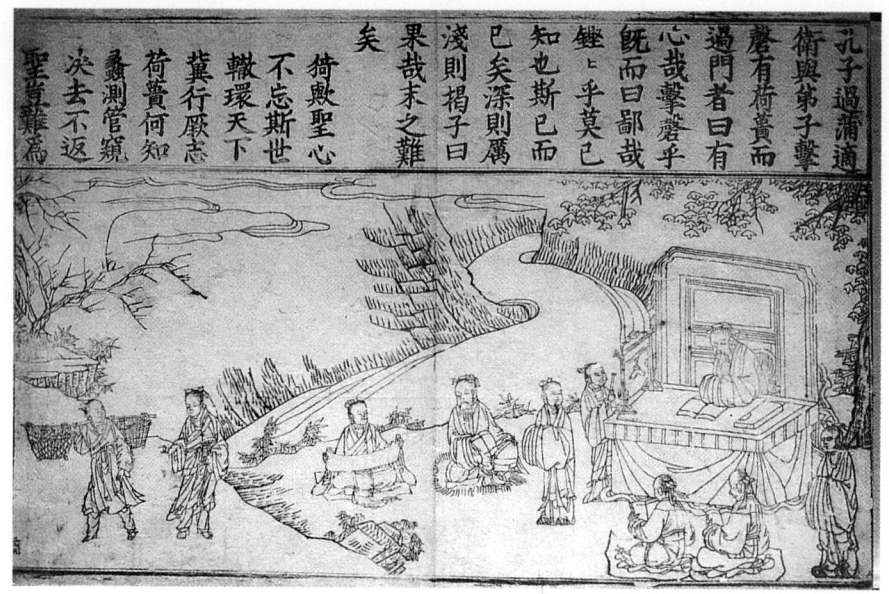

矣果哉末之難聖豈難為

孔子過蒲過門者曰有荷蕢而
衛與弟子擊心哉擊磬乎
磬有荷蕢而既而曰鄙哉
猶歟聖心知也斯已而
不忘斯世已矣深則厲
轍環天下淺則揭子曰
冀行厥志
蒭蕘何知
荷蕢管窺
決去不返

Fig. 5.7 Confucius plays the chime stones, *Kongzi Shengji zhi tu*, scene 29. Late Ming impression of Zhu Jianjun's early sixteenth-century edition. Woodblock print, 39.4 x 61.25 cm. Harvard University Art Museums (85.536.MI.24.1971).

Fig. 5.8 Confucius mourns the dead *qilin*, *Shengji tu*, scene 35. Late Ming recut purporting to be 1444 original edition. Woodblock print, 25 x 56 cm. Beijing Library (Rare Book no. 16645). After *Zhongguo gudai banhua congkan*, p. 388.

Fig. 5.9 A feeble Confucius stands in the gate and talks with Zigong, *Shengji tu*, scene 36. Late Ming recut purporting to be 1444 original edition. Woodblock print, 25 x 56 cm. Beijing Library (Rare Book no. 16645). After *Zhongguo gudai banhua congkan*, p. 388.

Fig. 5.10 The disciples mourn at Confucius's grave, *Shengji tu*, scene 38. Original 1548 edition of Zhu Yinyi. Woodblock print, 25 x 56 cm. After *Zhongguo gudai banhua congkan*, p. 389.

先聖著作既成齋戒向北斗告備忽有
赤虹自天而下化爲黃玉刻文先聖跪
而受之

Fig. 5.15 Confucius kneels to acknowledge the rainbow from the Big Dipper, *Shengji tu*, scene 35. Original 1548 edition of Zhu Yinyi. Woodblock print, 25 x 56 cm. After *Zhongguo gudai banhua congkan*, p. 387.

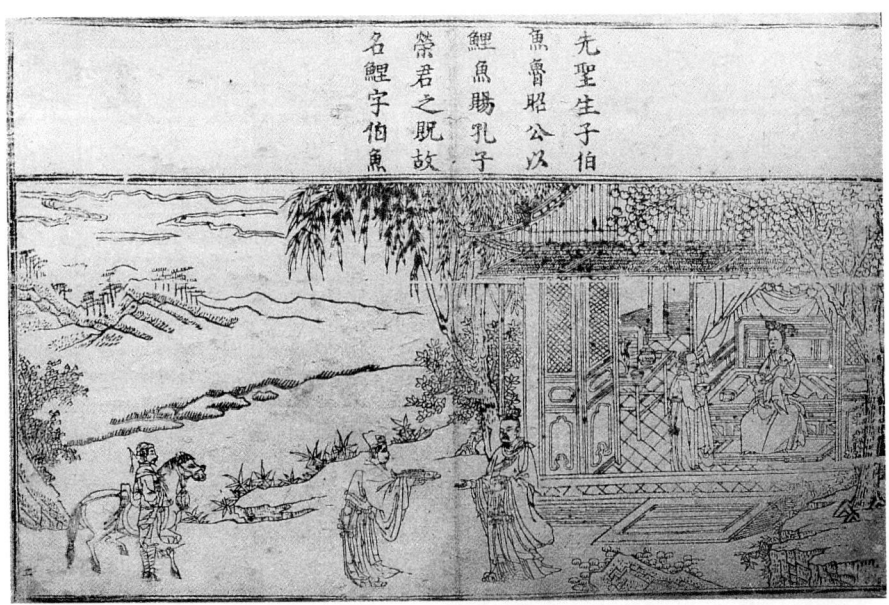

先聖生子伯
魚魯昭公以
鯉魚賜孔子
榮君之貺故
名鯉字伯魚

Fig. 5.16 The birth of Confucius's son and gift of a carp, *Kongzi Shengji zhi tu*, scene 9. Late Ming impression of Zhu Jianjun's early sixteenth-century edition. Woodblock print, 39.4 x 61.25 cm. Harvard University Art Museums (85.536.MI.24.1971).

孔子觀於魯桓公之廟，有欹器焉。問於守廟者曰：此謂何器。守廟者曰：此蓋為宥坐之器。孔子曰：吾聞宥坐之器，虛則欹，中則正，滿則覆。明君以為至誡，故常置之於坐側。顧謂弟子曰：試注水焉。乃注之水，中則正，滿則覆。夫子喟然歎曰：嗚呼，夫物惡有滿而不覆者哉。子路進曰：敢問持滿有道乎。子曰：聰明睿智，守之以愚；功被天下，守之以讓；力振世，守之以怯；富有四海，守之以謙。此所謂挹而損之之道也。

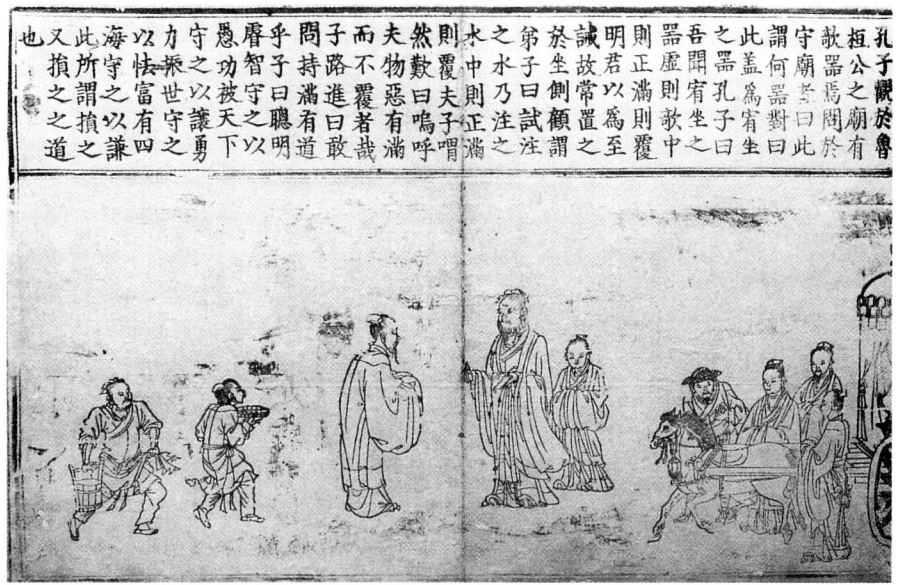

Fig. 5.17 Confucius at the ancestral temple of Duke Huan of Lu, *Kongzi Shengji zhi tu*, scene 16. Late Ming impression of Zhu Jianjun's early sixteenth-century edition. Woodblock print, 39.4 x 61.25 cm. Harvard University Art Museums (85.536.MI.24.1971).

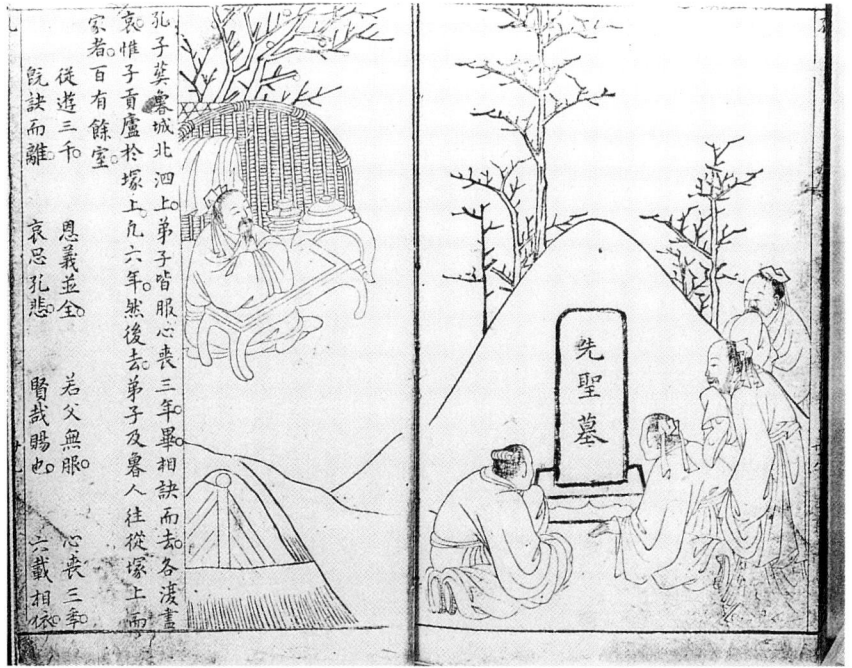

孔子葬魯城北泗上，弟子皆服心喪三年畢，相訣而去，各復盡哀，唯子貢廬於塚上，凡六年，然後去。弟子及魯人往從塚上而家者百有餘室。

從遊三千
恩義並全
若父無服
心喪三年
既訣而離
哀思孔悲
賢哉賜也
六載相依

先聖墓

Fig. 5.18 Disciples mourn at Confucius's grave, *Kong Meng xiang tuzan (Xiansheng xiaoxiang)*, scene 38. Late Ming, 1598. Woodblock print. H: 21.6 cm. National Central Library, Taipei

Fig. 5.19 Confucius's parents pray in temple to deity of Mount Ni, *Xinbian Kongfuzi zhouyou lieguo dacheng qilin ji*, scene 1 (recto and verso). Late Ming, early seventeenth century. Woodblock print, H: 22 cm. National Palace Museum, Taipei (Rare Book no. 2761).

Fig. 5.20 Confucius entertaining his parents at a feast, *Xinbian Kongfuzi zhouyou lieguo dacheng qilin ji*, scene 4. Late Ming, early seventeenth century. Woodblock print, 22 x 13.9 cm. National Palace Museum, Taipei (Rare Book no. 2761).

Fig. 5.21 Confucius's father receives the tablet from the *qilin*, *Xinbian Kongfuzi zhouyou lieguo dacheng qilin ji*, scene 2. Late Ming, early seventeenth century. Woodblock print, 22 x 13.9 cm. National Palace Museum, Taipei (Rare Book no. 2761).

Fig. 5.22 Birth of Confucius's grandson, *Xinbian Kongfuzi zhouyou lieguo dacheng qilin ji*, scene 16. Late Ming, early seventeenth century. Woodblock print, 22 x 13.9 cm. National Palace Museum, Taipei (Rare Book no. 2761).

Fig. 5.23 Qin Shihuangdi desecrates Confucius's grave, *Shengji quantu*, scene 65. Qing reprint of late Ming edition. Woodblock print, 20.5 x 14.5 cm. Harvard-Yenching Library (T1786.2/1346D).

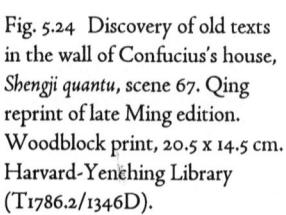

Fig. 5.24 Discovery of old texts in the wall of Confucius's house, *Shengji quantu*, scene 67. Qing reprint of late Ming edition. Woodblock print, 20.5 x 14.5 cm. Harvard-Yenching Library (T1786.2/1346D).

Fig. 5.25 Confucius's parents pray on Mount Ni, *Shengji quantu*, scene 2. Qing reprint of late Ming edition. Woodblock print, 20.5 x 14.5 cm. Harvard-Yenching Library (T1786.2/1346D).

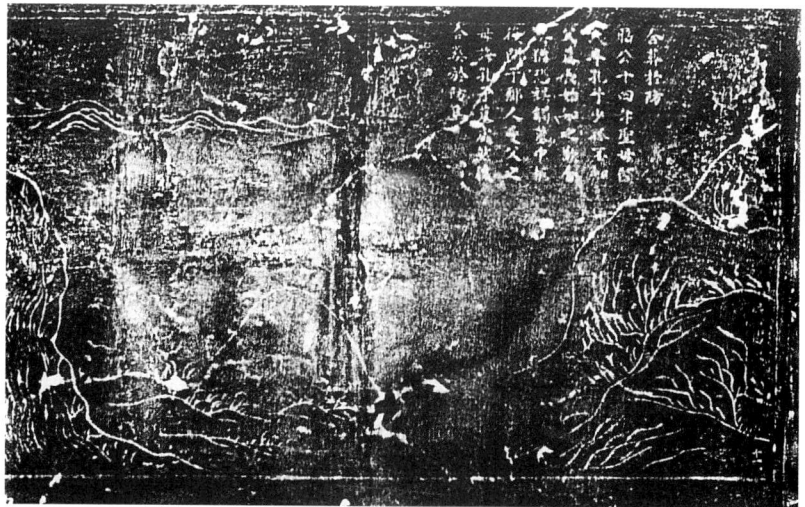

Fig. 5.26 Burying his parents in the same mound, *Shengji zhi tu*, scene 11. Late Ming, 1592. Rubbing of incised stone tablet, Shengjidian, Temple of Confucius, Qufu. 28.75 x 55.31 cm. Field Museum, Chicago.

Fig. 5.27 Respect and yielding: Duke Jing, *Shengji zhi tu*, scene 27. Late Ming, 1592. Rubbing of incised stone tablet, Shengjidian, Temple of Confucius, Qufu. 28.75 x 55.31 cm. Field Museum, Chicago.

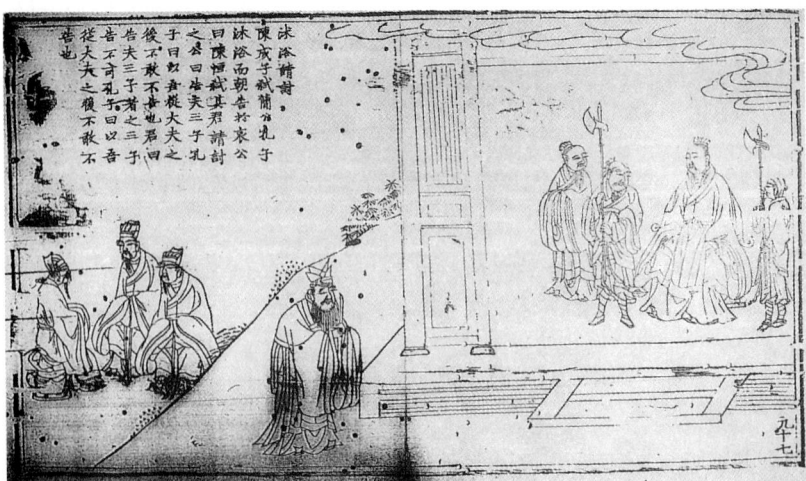

Fig. 5.28 Receiving favor and requesting punishment, *Shengji zhi tu*, scene 103. Early Qing, seventeenth century. Reproduction of 1592 stone tablets. Woodblock print, 28.5 x 51.5 cm. Harvard-Yenching Library, Rare Book no. T1786.2/1346 (from microfilm).

Fig. 5.29 The birth of Confucius, *Shengji tu*, scene 5. Late Qing reprint of Kong Xianlan's 1874 edition. Woodblock print, 22.5 x 38.75 cm. Freer-Sackler Library (920.052 C75f).

Fig. 5.30 Birth of Confucius's son, *Kongzi Shengji tu*, scene 9. 1984 Taipei reprint of 1934 Beiping minshe edition.

Fig. 5.31 Confucius sets his heart on study, *Kongzi shiji tu*, scene 3. 1989. Incised limestone tablets displayed in Confucius's Former Residence (*Kongzi guzhai* 孔子故宅), Qufu.

Fig. 5.32 Page from *Recorded Matters Concerning Divine Beauties, with Illustrations* (*Xianyuan jishi zhatu*). Original 1602 edition of Yang Erzeng. Woodblock print, H: 20.7 cm. National Central Library, Taipei (Rare Book no. 9217). After *Zhongguo banhua xuan* (Beijing: Rongbaozhai, 1958), pl. 119.

stitutionalized a conflation of the transmission of the sage's teachings with his flesh-and-blood genealogy. Although objections to this commingling were not clearly articulated until Liu Zongzhou's 劉宗周 (1578–1645) critique at the very end of the Ming dynasty, some sixteenth-century thinkers were already worried about the undesirable consequences of diverting attention away from the sage's doctrine. As Shao Yiren wrote in his 1592 "Statement on the Hall of Pictures of the Sage," Confucius was the model for his own age and later generations because he "obtained the transmission of Yao and Shun by using his heart-mind" not because of "the experiences of his body and things he did not talk about."[97] This thinking is reflected in the tablets in the Hall of the Traces of the Sage, which were the first to withdraw flesh and blood from the birth scenes, providing a precedent that was followed by most subsequent versions. Besides being encouraged by the Jiajing reforms, however, familization was also linked to popularization. Thus, familizing elements are rampant in the most popularized rendition of the pictorial biography, the illustrations to the play *Newly Compiled Record of Master Kong Making the Rounds of the States and Fulfilling the Unicorn*. As previously discussed, the major project of the play seems to be to both "familize" and "familiarize" the life of Confucius.

SUMMARY

For over 500 years, the pictorial biography of Confucius has served as a flexible medium for communicating beliefs and values, particularly concerning society and governance. Pictures are used to make a vivid impression on the viewer; at the same time, the ambiguity of pictorial images makes them safer than texts for expressing potentially dangerous ideas. The additions, deletions, and modifications of episodes in successive editions of the *Pictures of the Sage's Traces* reflect controversial issues in society at large and embody shifts in official and popular conceptions of Confucius and Confucian morality.

After the ritual reforms instituted by the Jiajing emperor in 1530, inscribed tablets replaced the figural icons in all temples of Confucius except the one in Qufu (see the chapter by Deborah Sommer in this volume, pp. 106–10). By no means universally welcomed, the iconoclasm removed the

---

97. *Shen zhi jingli yu qi suo bu yu zhe* 身之經歷與其所不語者. See note 70 to this chapter, p. 246, for preceding quote.

possibility of encountering a visual embodiment of Confucius in state temples around the empire. Since then, pictorial biographies of Confucius have been the primary vehicle for visual representations of the sage. To the extent that the presence of icons in the temple suggested influence from Buddhism, as the Jiajing emperor proclaimed, it is striking that the circulation of the equally Buddhist-influenced pictorial biographies of Confucius went unchallenged, enabling them to satisfy desires for visual imagery. Pictures of Confucius's life offered a means by which his cult could continue to compete with Buddhism and various deity cults as an outlet for the expression of veneration or even religious devotion, even though his cult no longer had icons.[98] Because the biographical illustrations were privately compiled and had nothing to do with the liturgy of the temple of Confucius, they escaped stricture.

Moreover, for the purposes of promoting or inspiring desirable behavior more broadly through society, pictorial biographies of Confucius had the potential to be much more effective than iconic images. The icon appears to be timeless and universal, imposing no particular interpretation on the viewer, but instead accommodating multiple values. By contrast, the sequential narrative portrays Confucius's responses to specific situations, suggesting and implicitly prescribing certain values and attitudes whose coherence is assured by the unifying framework of the "whole" story. Furthermore, whereas the sculptural icons were seen only by officials and other select individuals allowed access to the temples of Confucius, there was no restriction on the circulation of illustrated biographies, and they might potentially be viewed by a wide range of people. The production and distribution of printed editions of the pictorial biography were facilitated by the great expansion in the publishing industry that occurred in the decades following the destruction of icons, so that many people were exposed to the seductive appeal of the narrative pictures. Ming sponsors of various *Pictures of the Sage's Traces* typically expressed the hope that the pictures would inspire viewers to heightened moral cultivation, as the basis for more widespread improvement in social and political life. Later versions are more likely to affirm tra-

---

98. Moreover, it is worth noting that the connection was missed by late Ming Cheng-Zhu orthodox thinkers, who were trying to root out Buddhist influence (discussed by Elman, "Changes in Confucian Civil Service Examinations," p. 130). Not only did the pictorial biography of Confucius go unchallenged on these grounds, on the contrary, it was used as a vehicle for promoting conservative views.

ditional social and cultural values in the face of modernization, and most recently, to assert Chinese values over those associated with the West. The many transformations of the *Pictures of the Sage's Traces* have offered a flexible material means of reaffirming ancient values and ethical codes in times of political turbulence or social change.

WORKS CITED

Acker, William Reynolds Beal. *Some T'ang and Pre-T'ang Texts on Painting*, vol. 2, pt. I. Leiden: E. J. Brill, 1974.

An Hwi-jun 安輝濬. *Chosŏn wangjo sillok ŭi sŏhwa saryo* 朝鮮王朝實錄의 書畫史料. Seoul: Hanguk chongsin munhwa yonguwon, 1983.

Ban Gu 班固. *Han shu* 漢書 (Book of the Han). Beijing: Zhonghua shuju, 1962.

Bickford, Maggie. "Stirring the Pot of State." *Asia Major*, 3rd ser. 6, no. 2 (1993): 169–225.

Cahill, James F. *The Painter's Practice: How Artists Lived and Worked in Traditional China*. New York: Columbia University Press, 1994.

Carlitz, Katherine. "Desire, Danger, and the Body: Stories of Women's Virtue in Late Ming China." In *Engendering China: Women, Culture, and the State*, ed. Christina K. Gilmartin, Gail Hershatter, Lisa Rofel, and Tyrene White, pp. 101–24. Cambridge, Mass.: Harvard University Press, 1994.

————. "The Social Uses of Female Virtue in Late Ming Editions of *Lienü zhuan*." *Late Imperial China* 12, no. 2 (1991): 117–48.

Chavannes, Edouard. *La Sculpture sur pierre en Chine*. Paris: Ernest Leroux, 1893.

Chen Lü 陳旅 (1288–1343). *Anyatang ji* 安雅堂記. In *Jingyin Wenyuange Siku quanshu* 景印文淵閣四庫全書 (*jibu* 集部 152, *bieji lei* 別集類 1213), comp. Chen Yu 陳吁. Reprinted—Taipei: Taiwan Shangwu yinshuguan, 1983.

Chow, Kai-wing. "Discourse, Examination, and Local Elite." In *Ed ation and Society in Late Imperial China*, ed. Benjamin A. Elman and Alexander Woodside, pp. 183–219. Berkeley: University of California Press, 1994.

Clunas, Craig. *Pictures and Visuality in Early Modern China*. In the series *Picturing History*, ed. Peter Burke et al. London: Reaktion Press, 1997.

————. *Superfluous Things: Material Culture and Social Status in Early Modern China*. Cambridge, Eng: Polity Press; Urbana: University of Illinois Press, 1991.

Durrant, Stephen W. *The Cloudy Mirror: Tension and Conflict in the Writings of Sima Qian*. Albany: State University of New York Press, 1995.

Elman, Benjamin A. "Changes in Confucian Civil Service Examinations from the Ming to the Ch'ing Dynasty." In *Education and Society in Late Imperial China*, ed. idem and Alexander Woodside, pp. 111–49. Berkeley: University of California Press, 1994.

————. *Classicism, Politics, and Kinship: The Ch'ang-chou School of New Text Confucianism in Late Imperial China*. Berkeley: University of California Press, 1990.

Elvin, Mark. "Female Virtue and the State in China." *Past and Present* 104 (1984): 111–52.

Fan Ye 范曄 (398–446). *Hou Han shu* 後漢書 (Book of the Later Han). Beijing: Zhonghua shuju, 1965.

Fanzhi Yanshansi 繁峙岩山寺. Beijing: Wenwu chubanshe, 1990.

Freedberg, David. *The Power of Images*. Chicago: University of Chicago Press, 1989.

Gendai Chūgoku Manshūteikoku jinmeikan 現代中國滿洲帝國人名鑑 (Who's-who in contemporary China and Manchukuo). Tokyo: Gaimushō, 1937.

Goleman, Daniel. "Studies Point to Flaws in Lineups of Suspects." *New York Times*, Jan. 17, 1995.

Gujin tushu jicheng 古今圖書集成. Comp. Jiang Tingxi 蔣廷錫 et al. 1726. Reprinted—Shanghai: Zhonghua shuju, 1934.

Handlin, Joanna F. "Lü K'un's New Audience: The Influence of Women's Literacy on 16th-Century Thought." In *Women in Chinese Society*, ed. Margery Wolf and Roxane Witke, pp. 13–38. Stanford: Stanford University Press, 1975.

He Chuguang 何出光. *Lantai fajian lu* 蘭臺法監錄. 1597. Harvard-Yenching microfilm.

Hegel, Robert E. *Reading Illustrated Fiction in Late Imperial China*. Stanford: Stanford University Press, 1998.

Huainanzi zhuzi suoyin 淮南子諸子索引 (A concordance to the *Huainanzi*) ICS Ancient Chinese Text Concordance Series. Comp. Chinese University of Hong Kong, Institute of Chinese Studies. Hong Kong: Shangwu yinshuguan, 1992.

In Search of the Supernatural: The Written Record. Trans. Kenneth DeWoskin and J. I. Crump, Jr. Stanford: Stanford University Press, 1996.

Indiana Companion to Traditional Chinese Literature. Ed. William H. Nienhauser, Jr. 2nd rev. ed. Taipei: SMC Publishing, 1986.

Jian'ge Jueyuansi Mingdai Fozhuan bihua 劍閣覺苑祀明代佛傳壁畫. Comp. Mu Xueyong 母學勇. Beijing: Wenwu chubanshe, 1993.

Jing, Anning. "A Pictorial Hagiography of Lü Dongbin." Unpublished paper presented at the conference "State and Ritual in East Asia." Paris, 1995.

Jing, Jun. "Qufu: Confucius and His Charisma." Unpublished paper presented at the Harvard University Asia Center Workshop on Local Politics and Local Histories in Contemporary China. Cambridge, Mass., 2000.

————. *The Temple of Memories: History, Power, and Morality in a Chinese Village*. Stanford: Stanford University Press, 1996.

Kaji Nobuyuki 加地伸行. *Kōshi gaden* 孔子畫傳 (Pictorial biography of Confucius). Tokyo: Shūeisha, 1991.

Katz, Paul R. *Images of the Immortal: The Cult of Lü Dongbin at the Palace of Eternal Joy*. Honolulu: University of Hawai'i Press, 1999.

————. "The Function of Temple Murals in Imperial China: The Case of the Yung-lo Kung." *Journal of Chinese Religions* 21 (Fall 1993): 45–68.

Knox, Robert. *Amaravati: Buddhist Sculpture from the Great Stupa*. London: Trustees of the British Museum, 1992.

Ko, Dorothy. *Teachers of the Inner Chambers: Women and Culture in Seventeenth-Century China*. Stanford: Stanford University Press, 1994.

Kohara Hironobu. "Illustration in the Handscroll Format." In *Words and Images: Chinese Poetry, Calligraphy, and Painting*, ed. Alfreda J. Murck and Wen C. Fong, pp. 247–66. New York: Metropolitan Museum of Art, 1991.

Kong Chuan 孔傳. *Dongjia zaji* 東家雜記 (Miscellaneous records of the eastern house). 1134. In *Linlang bishi congshu* 琳琅秘室叢書. Reprinted—Baibu congshu 百部叢書, ser. 65. Taipei: Guangwen shuju, 1967.

Kongsheng quanshu 孔聖全書 (Complete writings of the sage Confucius). 1599. Comp. An Mengsong 安夢松. Jianyang, Fujian: Zongwen shushe.

Kong Yuancuo 孔元措. *Kongshi zuting guangji* 孔氏祖庭廣記 (An expanded record of the Kong lineage). 1227. In *Linlang bishi congshu* 琳琅秘室叢書. Reprinted—Baibu congshu 百部叢書, ser. 65. Taipei: Guangwen shuju, 1967.

Kongzi jia yu 孔子家語 (Family sayings of Confucius). 3rd c. Ed. Wang Su 王肅. Reprinted—Taipei: Shijie shuju, 1962.

Kongzi Shengji tu 孔子聖蹟圖 (Pictures of the traces of the sage Confucius). Beiping: Beiping minshe, 1934. Reprinted—Taipei: Wensi, 1984.

Kongzi Shengji tu 孔子聖蹟圖 (Pictures of the traces of the sage Confucius). In *Kongzi wenhua daquan* 孔子文化大全, ed. Miao Fenglin 苗楓林. Ji'nan: Shandong meishu chubanshe, 1988.

Kongzi Shengji zhi tu 孔子聖蹟之圖 (Pictures of the traces of the sage Confucius). Ed Zhu Jianjun 朱見浚. Changsha, Hunan, ca. 1506.

Kongzi xiang, Yanshenggong ji furen xiaoxiang 孔子像, 衍聖公及夫人肖像 (Portraits of Confucius, portraits of the Dukes of Yansheng and their wives). Comp. Shandongsheng Qufushi wenwu guanli weiyuanhui 山東省曲阜市文物管理委員會 (Qufu Administrative Commission of the Culture Relics of Shandong [*sic*]). Ji'nan, Shandong: Youyi shushe, 1987.

Lair, H. P., and L. C. Wang. *An Illustrated Life of Confucius*. Abridged reprint of Kong Xianlan's 1874 edition. N.p., n.d. (early 20th c.).

Laufer, Berthold. "Confucius and His Portraits." *Open Court* 26 (1912): 147–68, 202–18.

Legge, James. *The Four Books*. Reprinted—Taipei: Dashen, 1973.

Liu Yueshen 劉岳申. *Shenzhai Liu xiansheng wenji* 申齋劉先生文集. In *Yuandai zhenben wenji huikan* 元代珍本文集彙刊. Taipei: Guoli zhongyang tushuguan, 1970.

Lunyu (The *Analects* of Confucius). Text and annotated translation in James Legge, *The Four Books*. Reprinted—Taipei: Dashen, 1973.

Marshall, Sir John, and Alfred Foucher. *The Monuments of Sanchi*, vol. 2. London: Probsthain, 1940.

Mingren zhuanji ziliao suoyin 明人傳記資料索引 (Index to material for Ming biographies). Taipei: Guoli zhongyang tushuguan, 1965.

Ming shi 明史 (History of the Ming). Comp. Zhang Tingyu 張廷玉 et al. Beijing: Zhonghua shuju, 1974.

Mote, Frederick, and Howard L. Goodman. *A Research Manual for Ming History*. Research Manual Series. Princeton: East Asian Studies, 1985.

Murck, Alfreda J. *Poetry and Painting in Song China: The Subtle Art of Dissent*. Cambridge, Mass.: Harvard University Asia Center, 2000.

Murray, Julia K. "The Evolution of Pictorial Hagiography in Chinese Art: Common Themes and Forms." *Arts Asiatiques* 55 (2000): 81–97.

———. "The Hangzhou Portraits of Confucius and 72 Disciples (*Shengxian tu*): Art in the Service of Politics." *Art Bulletin* 74, no. 1 (Mar. 1992): 7–18.

———. "Illustrations of the Life of Confucius: Their Evolution, Functions, and Significance in Late Ming China." *Artibus Asiae* 57, no. 1–2 (1997): 73–134.

———. "Portraits of Confucius: Icons and Iconoclasm." *Oriental Art* 47, no. 3 (Autumn 2001): 17–28.

———. "The Temple of Confucius and Pictorial Biographies of the Sage." *Journal of Asian Studies* 55 (1996): 269–300.

Nagahiro Toshio 長廣敏雄. *Rikuchō jidai bijutsu no kenkyū* 六朝時代美術の研究 (The representational art of the Six Dynasties). Tokyo: Bijutsu shuppansha, 1969.

Naquin, Susan, and Evelyn Rawski. *Chinese Society in the Eighteenth Century*. New Haven: Yale University Press, 1987.

Powers, Martin J. *Art and Political Expression in Early China*. New Haven: Yale University Press, 1991.

Quan Ming chuanqi 全明傳奇. In *Zhongguo xiju yanjiu ziliao* 中國戲劇研究資料, ser. 1, no. 236. Taipei: Tianyi, 1983.

Queli wenxian kao 闕里文獻考 (An examination of the documents at Queli). 1762. Comp. Kong Jifen 孔繼汾. Reprinted—Taipei: Zhongguo wenxian chubanshe, 1966.

Qufu Kongmiao jianzhu 曲阜孔廟建築 (The architecture of the Temple of Confucius in Qufu). Comp. Nanjing gongxueyuan, jianzhu xi 南京工學院建築系 and Shandongsheng Qufushi wenwu guanli weiyuanhui 山東省曲阜市文物管理委員會. Nanjing: Zhongguo jianzhu gongye chubanshe. 1988.

Shanxi siguan bihua 山西寺觀壁畫. Comp. Chai Zejun 柴澤俊. Beijing: Wenwu chubanshe, 1997.

Shek, Richard Hon-chun. "Religion and Society in Late Ming: Sectarianism and Popular Thought in 16th and 17th Century China." Ph.D. diss., University of California at Berkeley, 1980.

Shengji tu 聖蹟圖 (Pictures of the Sage's traces). Ed. Zhu Yinyi 朱胤栘. Changzhi, Shanxi: 1548.

Shengji tu 聖蹟圖 (Pictures of the Sage's traces). Late Ming recut purporting to be 1444 edition, n.p., n.d. Reproduced in *Zhongguo gudai banhua congkan* 中國古代版畫叢刊. Comp. Zheng Zhenduo 鄭振鐸. Shanghai: Gudian wenxue chubanshe, 1958.

Shengji tu 聖蹟圖 (Pictures of the Sage's traces). Facsimile reprint. Ed. Gong Fada 龔發達 and Xiao Yu 肖玉. Wuhan: Hubei jiaoyu chubanshe, 1994.

Shengji tu 聖蹟圖 (Pictures of the Sage's traces). Incised stone tablets, Temple of Confucius, Qufu, 1592.

Shengji zhi tu 聖蹟之圖 (Pictures of the Sage's traces). Reproduction of 1592 stone tablets, Qufu, early Qing, 17th c.

Shengji zhi tu 聖蹟之圖 (Pictures of the Sage's traces). Reproduction of late Ming painted album. Comp. Shandongsheng Qufushi wenwu guanli weiyuanhui 山東省曲阜市文物管理委員會 (Qufu Administrative Commission of the Culture Relics of Shandong [*sic*]). Ji'nan: Shandong General Press, 1988.

Shi Ke 石可. *Kongzi shiji tu, Lunyu zhenyan yin* 孔子事蹟图, 論語真言印 (Pictures of the deeds of Confucius, and seal-impressions of true sayings from the *Analects*). Ji'nan, Qi Lu shushe, 1987.

Shinbo Tōru 真保亨 and Kaneko Keizō 金子桂三. *Butsuden zu* 佛傳圖 (Pictures of the life of the Buddha). Tokyo: Mainichi shinbunsha, 1978.

Shishi yuanliu 釋氏源流 (Origins and evolution of the Sakya clan); also called *Shijiarulai chengdao yinghua shiji ji* 釋迦如來成道應化事蹟記 (Record of Shakyamuni Buddha's attainment of the way and transformation of his life-traces) or *Shijiarulai chengdao yinghua shiji ji* 釋迦如來成道應化事蹟 (Record of Shakyamuni Buddha's attainment of the way and transformation of his life-traces). Comp. Baocheng 寶成. Nanjing: Baoensi 報恩寺, 1425 (and later reprints).

Shiyi ji 拾遺記 (Gathering remaining accounts). Comp. Wang Jia 王嘉 (4th c.). In *Gujin yishi* 古今遺事, ser. 1. Reprinted—Baibu congshu jicheng 百部叢書集成, ser. 9. Taipei: Yiwen, 1966.

Silbergeld, Jerome. "Chinese Painting Studies in the West: A State-of-the-Field Article." *Journal of Asian Studies* 46 (1987): 849–97.

Sima Qian 司馬遷 (145–86 BCE). *Shi ji* 史記 (Record of history). Beijing: Zhonghua shuju, 1962.

Siming congshu 四明叢書. Comp. Zhang Shouyong 張壽鏞. Reprinted—Taipei: Xinwenfeng chuban gongsi, 1988.

Song shi 宋史 (History of the Song). Comp. Toqto 脫脫. Beijing: Zhonghua shuju, 1977.

Soushen ji 搜神記. Comp. Gan Bao 干寶 (E. Jin). Reprinted—Taipei: Shijie shuju, 1962.

Soymié, Michel. "L'Entrevue de Confucius et de Hiang T'o." *Journal Asiatique* 242 (1954): 311–91.

Taiyuan Chongshansi wenwu tulu 太原崇善寺文物圖錄. Comp. Zhang Jizhong 張紀仲 and An Ji 安笈. Taiyuan: Shanxi renmin chubanshe, 1987.

T'ien Ju-k'ang. *Male Anxiety and Female Chastity: A Comparative Study of Chinese Ethical Values in Ming-Ch'ing Times*. Leiden: E. J. Brill, 1988.

Uyeno Aki 上野あき. "Tonkō-bon banga Butsuden zu kō" 敦煌本幡畫佛傳圖考 (Banner paintings from Dunhuang representing Buddha's life). *Bijutsu kenkyū* 美術研究, no. 269 (May 1970): 1–35; no. 283 (May 1973): 25–36.

Wang Chong 王充 (27–ca. 97). *Lun heng* 論衡. In *Lun heng suoyin* 論衡索引, comp. Cheng Xiangqing 程湘清 et al. Beijing: Zhonghua shuju, 1994.

Weidner, Marsha, ed. *Latter Days of the Law: Images of Chinese Buddhism, 850–1850*. Lawrence, Kans.: Spencer Museum of Art, in association with the University of Hawai'i Press, 1994.

Who's Who in China. 3rd ed. Shanghai: Chinese Weekly Review, 1925.

Wilson, Thomas A. "The Ritual Formation of Confucian Orthodoxy and the Descendants of the Sage." *Journal of Asian Studies* 55 (1996): 559–84.

Wu Hung. *The Wu Liang Shrine*. Stanford: Stanford University Press, 1989.

Wu Jiamo 吳嘉謨. *Kongsheng jiayu tu* 孔聖家語圖 (Illustrated sayings of the sage Confucius's family). Hangzhou, 1589.

Wu, Tung. *Tales from the Land of Dragons*. Boston: Museum of Fine Arts, 1997.

Xiao Tong. *Wen xuan*. Trans. David R. Knechtges. Vol. 2. Princeton: Princeton University Press, 1987.

Xinbian Kongfuzi zhouyou lieguo dacheng qilin ji 新編孔夫子周游列國大成麒麟記 (Newly compiled record of Master Kong making the rounds of the states and fulfilling the *qilin*). By Huanyu xianshenggong 寰宇顯聖公 (Illustrious sage of the world). N.p., early 17th c.

Yonglegong 永樂宮 (Palace of Eternal Joy). Beijing: Renmin meishu chubanshe, 1964.

Zhang Kai 張楷. Colophon to *Shengji tu* 聖記圖. 1444. Reprinted in *Zhongguo gudai banhua congkan* 中國古代版畫叢刊, comp. Zheng Zhenduo 鄭振鐸. Shanghai: Gudian wenxue chubanshe, 1958.

Zhang Yanyuan 張彥遠. *Lidai ming hua ji* 歷代名畫記. In *Huashi congshu* 畫史叢書, ed. Yu Anlan 于安蘭. Reprinted—Taipei, Wenshizhe chubanshe, 1974.

Zhongguo gudai banhua congkan 中國古代版畫叢刊 (Compendium of traditional Chinese printed pictures). Comp. Zheng Zhenduo 鄭振鐸. Shanghai: Gudian wenxue chubanshe, 1958.

Zhongguo gudai shuhua tumu 中國古代書畫圖目, vol. 6. Beijing: Wenwu chubanshe, 1988.

Zhou Wu 周蕪. *Zhongguo banhua shi tulu* 中國版畫史圖錄 (Illustrated catalogue of the history of Chinese printed pictures). Shanghai: Shanghai renmin meishu chubanshe, 1988.

Zhu Jingxuan 朱景玄. *Tangchao minghua lu* 唐朝名畫錄 (Record of famous painters of the Tang dynasty). Ca. 840. In *Huapin congshu* 畫品叢書, ed. Yu Anlan 于安蘭. Shanghai: Shanghai renmin meishu chubanshe, 1982.

Zhu Xi 朱熹 (1130-1200). *Si shu ji zhu* 四書集注 (Collected annotations on the Four Books). Reprinted—Taipei: Yiwen yinshuguan, 1959.

PART III
Politics and Society

Previous page: Altar to Confucius at the Confucius Temple, Beijing (photograph by Thomas A. Wilson, 1995).

SIX

The Cultural Politics of Autocracy

The Confucius Temple and Ming Despotism, 1368–1530

Huang Chin-shing

Translated by Curtis Dean Smith

and Thomas A. Wilson

In imperial times, the Confucius temple symbolized the tradition of the Way (*Daotong* 道統); it was also well integrated into the imperial tradition of legitimate governance (*zhitong* 治統). Both emperors and Confucian scholars continually manipulated the ritual practices of the temple to serve their own interests. Because of this, the Confucius temple has been in a perpetual process of becoming. From the Tang period, Confucius temples spread throughout China at a steady pace. Despite the growing influence of Confucius temple rites, the changes in ritual ordered by the Ming emperor Shizong (r. 1521–67) in 1530 ran counter to the main tenets of this liturgical tradition. This chapter is devoted to showing how Shizong drew on the political resources of the ruler to weaken the morale of the scholar-officials and thereby strengthen despotism.

THE CONFUCIUS TEMPLE
REFORMS OF 1530

When Emperor Wuzong (r. 1505–21) died in 1521 without leaving an heir, the Empress Dowager Cishou 慈壽 and Grand Secretary Yang Tinghe 楊廷和 (1459–1529) invited the deceased emperor's cousin and eldest son of Prince Xingxian, Zhu Houcong 朱厚熜 (1507–67), to take the throne, in accordance with Wuzong's posthumous decree. This new emperor was Emperor Shizong, also known as the Jiajing emperor. Shortly after taking the throne, Shizong announced his desire to worship his own natal father in the imperial ancestral shrine as a deceased sovereign rather than have himself adopted into his cousin's line, as precedent dictated. The resulting conflict with the court officials became known as the "Great Rites Controversy." At issue was Shizong's insistence on "continuing the imperial order" (*ji tong* 繼統) without "continuing the dynastic line" (*ji si* 繼嗣) of his predecessor. Court officials argued that the late emperor's line had to be continued if the imperial order were to continue. Neither side was willing to compromise.

Then, in 1524, Shizong removed the word "natal" (*bensheng* 本生) from the title of his natural mother, Lady Zhang, the Empress Dowager. When court officials demurred, the Imperial Guards beat sixteen of them to death on the spot and imprisoned another 143. The protest immediately subsided,[1] and the controversy temporarily ceased.

The Qing editors of the *Ming History* elaborated on the relationship of this debate to the principle of "serving one's lord according to the Dao":

Yang Tinghe promoted [Shizong's] "Great Rituals" and drew the court to speak out in one accord, basing his argument mostly on the Puyuan debates of Sima Guang 司馬光 [1019–86] and Cheng Yi 程頤 [1033–1107] of the Song.... Yet since Shizong inherited the throne by imperial decree, succeeding Wuzong, the situation was different. All the officials accepted the arguments of these wise scholars of the past as reliable. They attempted not to offend the world and later generations, yet did not help Shizong plan thoroughly or handle the situation with refinement. They did not help him reflect on his reasoning in order to obtain absolute appropriateness. The harder they struggled, the more they lost. What a pity![2]

---

1. Zhang Tingyu, *Mingshi* 17.219.
2. Ibid., 191.5078.

The Qing scholar Mao Qiling 毛奇齡 (1623–1716) attributed the disaster of the Great Rites Controversy to the failure of both sides to consider ancient rituals and to their shallow learning.[3] Mao's command of the sources was broad, and he was familiar with both recent and ancient developments. His views were truly unique, yet the controversy over Shizong's reforms cannot simply be explained as a matter of shallow learning. Rather, the debates were a test of autocratic authority and its legality.

For this reason, it is difficult to reach a judgment on whether Shizong's ritual changes did more good than harm. Although Shizong was not a direct natal descendent of the previous emperor, after succeeding to the throne, he was in complete control and was not swayed by his court officials. This is a good example of Ming autocracy. After the ritual debate of 1524, Shizong proceeded to overhaul all rituals in order to validate his actions. For example, in 1525 he had a comprehensive account of the ritual changes entitled *Collected Debates on the Great Rites Controversy* (*Dali jiyi* 大禮集議) distributed throughout the empire. After completion of the *Great Statutes of Ming Ethics* (*Minglun dadian* 明倫大典) in 1528, charges were brought against the officials who had opposed him in the debates; Yang Tinghe and others were demoted to commoners.[4] These actions prove not only that Shizong understood how to use power to accomplish his aims but also that he knew how to use principle (and ritual) to defend his actions. The editors of the *Ming History* made an acute observation on Shizong's behavior: "The Emperor [Shizong] personally charged the court to debate and determine the 'Great Rituals,' but he then used his authority to create the rites and music himself."[5] Shizong's interest in changing the rituals was not naturally inspired but grew out of the Great Rites Controversy.

Shizong made the most numerous revisions to the rituals in 1530. He created a rite in which the empress personally tended to silkworms in the northern suburbs, changed the enshrinement positions at the Altar of the Gods of Soils and Grains, re-established the four suburban sacrifices, and reinstituted separate sacrifices to Heaven and Earth.[6] In the eleventh month, he began to revise the liturgy for the Temple of Culture (*wenmiao*

---

3. Mao Qiling, "Bianding Jiajing daliyi."
4. Zhang Tingyu, *Mingshi* 17.220–22.
5. Ibid., 196.5178.
6. *Shizong shilu* 109–20.

文廟; AKA Confucius temple). It is clear that the Confucius temple reforms were an important link in this chain of ritual changes. The implications were indeed extraordinary. If Shizong was following a whim in revising the other rituals—merely exercising authoritarian fiat—then his Confucius temple reforms were a challenge to "institutionalized" orthodoxy and an intentional act of degradation.

Scholars have claimed that the revision of the Temple of Culture originated with Grand Secretary Zhang Cong's 張璁 (1475–1539) proposals,[7] yet full consideration of the sources shows that this is not the case. Before the temple changes of the tenth month of 1530, Shizong instructed Zhang Cong to "order and compile all sacrificial ceremonies for clouds, rain, wind, and lightning, and those of the late Sage and Master" in a compilation titled the *Established Precedents of Ritual Ceremonies* (*Siyi chengdian* 祀儀成典).[8] In a memorial to the throne, Zhang Cong reported:

> The sacrifices to clouds and lightning and the allocation of state spirit tablets have all been revised under your sagacious wisdom, but the liturgy of the late Sage and Master still requires revision. Shuliang He 叔梁紇 was the father of Confucius, and Yan Lu 顏路, Zeng Xi 曾晳, and Kong Li 孔鯉 were the fathers of Yan [Hui] 顏回, Zeng [Sen] 曾參, and Zisi 子思 [Kong Ji 孔伋], respectively. The three sons are enshrined in the main hall, but Shuliang He and the other fathers are all in the side cloisters. Could the original intentions of the sages have been thus? This ought to be urgently corrected. I, your subject, request that a new hall be erected behind the main hall to worship Shuliang He and that Yan Lu, Zeng Xi, and Kong Li receive secondary sacrifices.[9]

The enshrinement in the Temple of Culture was in accordance with established rankings. Yan Hui, Zeng Sen, and Kong Ji were enshrined in correlate positions; this much exceeded the position of their fathers in the two cloisters,[10] not to mention Confucius's status in relation to Shuliang He. This is why Zhang Cong found fault with the existing regulations.

---

7. E.g., Pang Zhonglu, *Wenmiao sidian kao* 4.11b–13b.

8. Zhang Cong, *Yudui lu* 22.1b; idem, *Luoshan zoushu* 6.1a.

9. *Shizong shilu* 119.3–4a. Due to the length of Zhang Cong's original memorial, I use the abstracted version found in the *Ming shilu*.

10. According to the order of sacrifices in the Confucius temple, beside Confucius as the supreme sage, the "four correlates" and "ten savants" were established in the main hall, and the "former worthies" and the "scholars," who received sacrifice in the side cloisters.

We can see that the reforms in the Confucius temple came from Shizong and that Zhang Cong perceptively used the model of the ritual debates on the emperor's status in relation to his natal parents—rooted in the immutable moral principle of father and son—to affirm the aims of Shizong's changes. The ultimate power was nonetheless held by Shizong himself. Clearly the phrase "Although the son be equal to a sage, he should not take precedence over his father" was appropriated from the Great Rites Controversy.[11] Shizong agreed.

Immediately after Zhang Cong presented his memorial, Shizong announced his judgment:

If We enshrine Confucius in the main hall and relegate his father to the side cloisters, the spirits will surely be very displeased. How could there be peace [if we did this]? If a person shows respect for his parents in this fashion, we can see how he respects Heaven. Using twelve sacrificial vessels and prepared sacrificial meat closely copies the Great Sacrifice. This reasoning cannot be doubted; the rites must be corrected to show respect for Heaven.[12]

Shizong then ordered Zhang Cong to "further apprehend Confucius's mind and elaborate on it."[13] We have no way of knowing whether Zhang Cong did "further apprehend Confucius's mind" before elaborating on it, but Zhang Cong's statement in his memorial in response that "I followed the Emperor's will" (*Cong yuan di yi* 璁缘帝意) in revising the regulations for the Temple of Culture shows there is evidence to support the view that the emperor initiated the changes. In his memorial, Zhang Cong wrote:

The rites to Confucius have been in chaos since the Tang and Song dynasties, and no one has been able to correct them. We should now call [Confucius] the "First Sage and Master" and not call him "king." In the sacrifice, it is better to refer to [the building as] "the temple" and not "the court." During the sacrifice, wooden spirit tablets should be used; the sculptures [of Confucius and the other honorees] should be destroyed. Ten sacrificial vessels [rather than twelve] should be used, and six rows of dancers [rather than eight]. Shu Lianghe should receive sacrifices in a separate temple, with the three [other fathers] as his correlates. The noble titles should be eliminated in favor of "wor-

---

11. The sentence "Even though the son is a sage, he must not eat before his father" originates in the *Zuo Commentary of the Spring and Autumn Annals* (see Hong Liangji, *Chunqiu Zuozhuan gu* 9.354) and was adopted by Fang Xianfu 方獻夫 as a metaphor for the lord/subject relationship in the Great Rites Controversy. Shizong took a liking to this phrase.

12. Zhang Cong, *Yudui lu* 22.15b.

13. Ibid., 22.17a.

thy" and "scholar." The sacrifices to Shen Dang 申黨, Gongbo Liao 公伯寮, Qin Ran 秦冉, Yan He 顏何, Xun Kuang 荀況, Dai Sheng 戴聖, Liu Xiang 劉向, Jia Kui 賈逵, Ma Rong 馬融, He Xiu 何休, Wang Su 王肅, Du Yu 杜預, and Wu Cheng 吳澄 should cease; Lin Fang 林放, Qu Yuan 蘧瑗, Lu Zhi 盧植, Zheng Xuan 鄭玄, Fu Qian 服虔, and Fan Ning 范甯 should receive sacrifices in regional [temples]. Hou Cang 后蒼, Wang Tong 王通, Ouyang Xiu 歐陽修, Hu Yuan 胡瑗, and Cai Yuanding 蔡淵定 should be added [to the temple].[14]

Zhang Cong's proposed reforms may be examined in four main areas:

(1) *Posthumous titles.* Confucius was not to be referred to as "king." Zhang Cong claimed to be continuing the business left unfinished by Wu Chen 吳沈 (d. 1386) of the early Ming. In "Disputing Confucius's Ennoblement as King" (*Kongzi feng wang bian* 孔子封王辯), Wu had argued that Confucius was only a minister and that conferring the title of king on one who was not born into the nobility was a transgression of ritual. According to Wu Chen, "It is permissible to say the Master [Confucius] possessed the way of a king, but not to say that the Master had the title of king."[15] Zhang Cong also used Qiu Jun's 丘濬 (1421–95) argument that the imperial worship of Confucius began during the reign of Emperor Ping of the Han (r. 1–6 CE), when the "traitorous followers of Wang Mang 王莽 (r. CE 9–23) appeared and falsely worshipped the teachings of the Confucians to elevate their own reputations."[16] Zhang Cong thus argued that later generations referred to Confucius as the "'First Master Confucius' to show that the reason the Sage was revered lay in the Dao, not in noble rank."

(2) *Substitution of wooden spirit tablets for sculptures and court robes and reduction in the number of ceremonial utensils.* Emperor Taizu (r. 1368–98) ordered that wooden tablets be used at the Imperial University in Nanjing. This precedent was invoked by Zhang Cong. In addition, Qiu Jun had argued that "China did not have the practice of installing sculptures until the arrival of Buddhism."[17] In fact, since the founding of the Ming dynasty, and even during the Song, there had been intermittent debates about removing the sculptures and installing tablets.[18] Zhang Cong proposed that this change be ordered. Once the sculptures were removed, there was no need for court

---

14. *Shizong shilu* 119.4a. For the original annotation, see Zhang Cong, *Yudui lu* 22.1b–15a.
15. Quoted in Zhang Cong, *Yudui lu* 22.3a.
16. Qiu Jun, *Daxue yanyi bu* 65.6b–7a.
17. Ibid., 65.11a–14a.
18. Shen Defu, *Wanli yehuo bian* 14.361.

robes. Initially Ming regulations called for six rows of ceremonial dancers and ten sacrificial vessels. In 1476, at the request of Chancellor Zhou Hong-mo 周洪謨 (1420–91), the number of ceremonial dancers had been increased to eight rows and the number of sacrificial vessels to twelve, thus using rites appropriate for the Son of Heaven.[19] Now, they were reduced to the original number.

(3) *Revision of the sacrificial regulations by removal of titles of nobility and reordering of the scholars.* Once Confucius no longer had a title of nobility, the other enshrinees did not need them either. Zhang Cong's reordering of the honorees was based on the writings of Cheng Minzheng 程敏政 (1445–99).[20] This change originated in the shift of scholarly fashion from an emphasis on transmitting the classics (*chuan jing zhi shi* 傳經之師) to an emphasis on transmitting the Way (*chuan Dao zhi shi* 傳道之師).[21] The enshrinement of Cai Yuanding (1135–98) drew on the arguments of the brothers Gui Hua 桂華 and Gui E 桂萼 (d. 1531)[22] that Ouyang Xiu was enshrined because of position during the Puyuan debates of 1063.[23] Wu Cheng (1249–1333) was removed from the temple because he had served in the Yuan court after originally serving in the Song court. He had been denounced previously by Xie Duo 謝鐸 (1435–1510).[24]

(4) *Renaming the Hall of Great Completion* (Dacheng dian 大成殿) *the "Confucius Temple" and adding the "Shrine of Giving Birth to the Sage"* (Qi sheng ci 啓聖祠). Since Confucius was no longer a king, the sacrifice had to take place in a temple (*miao* 廟) and not a court (*dian* 殿). The establishment of the Shrine of Giving Birth to the Sage had been discussed for a long time. Hong Mai 洪邁 (1123–1202) in the Song and Xiong He 熊鉌 (1253–1312) in the Yuan had noted the moral dilemma of "revering the son and

---

19. Zhang Tingyu, *Mingshi* 50.1297–98.

20. Cheng Minzheng, *Huangdun wenji* 10.4a–10b.

21. See my "Xueshu yu xinyang."

22. Gui E, *Gui Wenxiang gong zouyi* 8.17a–20b.

23. Ouyang Xiu, *Ouyang Xiu wenji*, pp. 977–95. Ouyang Xiu's opinions were counter to those of Sima Guang. For background on the Puyuan debate's connection with Ouyang Xiu's enshrinement in the Confucius temple, see Gu Yanwu, *Yuanchaoben Gu Tinglin Rizhi lu* 18.432. Much earlier Xu Xuemo (1522–94; *Shimiao shi yulu* 4.5a) had said that Shizong wished to enshrine Ouyang Xiu in the temple because his position in "the Puyuan debates was in accordance with the sages' thoughts." Shizong's mention of Ouyang Xiu shows that Xu's and Gu's claims are not baseless; see Zhang Cong, *Yudui lu* 22.26a.

24. This position first originated with Xie Duo and was used later by Zhang Cong; see Zhang Tingyu, *Mingshi* 163.4432, 50.1298–1300.

humbling the father" (*zi zun fu bei* 子尊夫卑) in the enshrinement of the sages and worthies in the Confucius temple.[25] During the Ming, Cheng Minzheng had even more emphatically attacked this contradiction.[26] Zhang Cong's advocacy of establishing the Shrine of Giving Birth to the Sage in order to emphasize the primacy of ethical relations neatly paralleled the deeper significance of the Great Rites Controversy of 1524.

The reforms in the Confucius temple proposed by Zhang Cong coincided with Shizong's intentions, but generations of scholars have considered them an insult to Confucianism.[27] According to a contemporary record, "The scholars of the time, whose eyes and ears had been polluted for a long time already, argued and debated vigorously, all with differing views."[28] In other words, the scholar-gentry had long been used to the old institutions and did not approve of the new institutions. The censor Li Guan 黎貫 (*jinshi* 1517) pointed out:

[If Confucius] is called "First Master" and not "King," . . . not only would eight rows of ceremonial dancers and twelve sacrificial vessels constitute a breach, using six rows of ceremonial dancers and ten sacrificial vessels would also be a breach. Not only should the sculptures be destroyed, but the multiple halls and double eaves as well.[29]

From the beginning, many people found fault with the Shrine of Giving Birth to the Sage, especially after the removal of Confucius's title of king. It was also considered highly unsuitable that Shuliang He retained a noble title.[30] At the conclusion of the debates, Shizong ordered the sculptures de-

---

25. Hong Mai, *Rongzhai bisui* 22.26a; Xiong He, *Xiong Wuxuan ji* 4.52.

26. Cheng Minzheng, *Huangdun wenji* 10.10b–12a.

27. Shen Defu, *Wanli yehuo bian*, "Buyi" (Supplement), 2.854; Jiao Hong, *Yutang congyu* 3.93.

28. Xu Xuemo, *Shimiao shi yulu* 6.19b.

29. Li Guan, "Lun Kongzi sidian shu," in *Guandong wenzheng* 6.19b.

30. Xu Xuemo, *Shimiao shi yulu* 6.19b–20a. Xu criticized Zhang Cong: "This is also just remnants of [his] ingratiating [himself] by debating over rituals." Erudites such as Qu Jiusi, when considering the reorganization of the institution of the Confucius temple in the Wanli era (1573–1619), were unable to make sense of the Shrine for Giving Birth to the Sage: "No one refers to the Duke who Gave Birth to the Sage. Shizong called the four correlates 'sages,' and the ten correlates in the side halls as 'worthies,' all of which are not noble titles. Only the Duke who Gave Birth to the Sage has noble status. Perhaps the emperor felt this statute to be too lofty and so did not discuss it. Perhaps this was not an omission" (Qu Jiusi, *Kongmiao liyue kao* 10.47b).

stroyed and tablets installed. Many local prefects could not bear to destroy the sculptures and hid them in walls.[31] The sculptures in Queli (Qufu) were preserved unharmed.[32] Destruction of the sculptures went against human conscience, and the officials could not do much to enforce the regulations.

At the time, Junior Compiler Xu Jie 徐階 (1503–83) submitted a memorial opposing the elimination of the noble titles and the destruction of the sculptures and went on to strongly criticize the emperor:

All of Your Highness's actions have been in accordance with the founding emperor, Taizu. Taizu demoted the rank of many spirits, but he spared Confucius's title as king. This was because he did not think lightly of this change. Even if the great mountains and rivers are made sacred and Confucius is humanized, there will still be some debate on the significance of these changes.[33]

Shizong and Zhang Cong had based their reform of the Confucius temple on the dynastic founder's decisions. Xu Jie challenged them using their own weapon.

The tradition of sacrificing to Confucius has been handed down throughout the empire for a long time. Scholars and students of the Classics have become accustomed to it, and peasants and commoners are extravagant in their worship. If it is decreed that the title of king be removed, the populace will be stupefied and become anxious and fearful, not understanding the reason behind Your Highness's actions. After some speculation, they may believe Your Highness has no regard for others and lightly robs Confucius of his nobility. It is difficult to predict people's fickle suspicions.[34]

On one hand, Xu Jie elevated Taizu and, on the other, he provoked Shizong by pointing out that people's emotional responses must be considered. An angry Shizong had Xu Jie exiled. Although Xu Jie gained a reputation for virtue throughout the empire,[35] he was not able to shake Shizong's determination.

In response to the doubts of other officials, Zhang Cong wrote a point-by-point rebuttal entitled "Inquiries on the Sacrifices to the First Teacher

---

31. Gu Yanwu, *Yuanchaoben Gu Tinglin Ri zhi lu* 18.429; see also Shao Changheng (1637–1713), *Qingmen lugao* 10.10a. Shao suggested reinstalling Confucius's sculpture in the early Qing.
32. Yu Zhengxie, *Guisi cungao* 9.256.
33. Xu Jie, *Shijingtang ji* 6.41a–41b.
34. Ibid., 6.41b.
35. Shen Defu, *Wanli yehuo bian* 14.361–62.

Confucius" (*Xianshi Kongzi sidian huoda* 先師孔子祀典或答). Two points are worthy of attention in this document. First, at the beginning of the dynasty, Song Lian 宋濂 (1310–81) had submitted a memorial entitled "Debate on the Confucius Temple Hall," whose main point was that "not to use the ancient rites in sacrificing to Confucius is to desecrate the sacrifice. A desecrated sacrifice is disrespectful; and, if one is disrespectful, one shall have bad luck."[36] A careful reading of Song Lian's text suggests his purpose was to persuade Taizu to respect Confucius and Confucianism. Zhang Cong, on the other hand, used it as a base for the reforms in the Confucius temple.[37]

Second, another question raised in Zhang's rebuttal is "If the reform of the Confucius temple sacrifice ceremony is enforced throughout the empire, what about Queli [the temple to Confucius in Qufu]?"[38] This question suggests that opponents of the reforms had retreated and were defending their second option, to shield the temple in Queli from the reforms. This sort of two-track policy had been apparent earlier in the Ming, although the situation was vastly different. In 1438, Pei Kan 裴侃 had noted the tendency toward "respecting the son over the father" in the Confucius temple rites and memorialized: "The Temples of Culture throughout the empire stress the transmission of the Way in the ordering of the tablets. The family temple in Queli must preserve [distinctions of] father and son to promote the cardinal human relationships."[39] The court established the Shrine of the King Who Gave Birth to the Sage (*qi sheng wang ci* 啓聖王祠), with the fathers of the four masters, Yan Hui, Zeng Sen, Kong Ji, and Mencius, as correlates.[40] This was done only in Queli. Zhang Cong evoked the words of Zisi as a basis for extending this practice throughout the empire: "Today, all vehicles of the empire use the same axle width and everyone writes with the same characters. Action is in accordance with ethics. This is called greater unification. How can this be doubted in Queli?"[41] According to Zhang, the Queli temple could not be an exception. As prime minister, Zhang Cong represented the court in demanding a unified position on education. After his memorial

---

36. See Li Zhizao, *Pan'gong liyue shu* 1.42a.

37. Zhang Cong, *Luoshan zoushu* 6.29a.

38. Ibid., 6.30a.

39. Zhang Tingyu, *Mingshi* 50.1297.

40. The title "King Who Gave Birth to the Sage" (*Qisheng wang* 啓聖王) had been bestowed on Shuliang He during the Yuan dynasty, in 1330 (Song Lian, *Yuan shi* 76.1892–93).

41. Zhang Cong, *Luoshan zoushu* 6.30b.

was submitted, the texts of the debates at the Ministry of Rites were collected. Most of the ritual treatises issued by the court were based on Zhang Cong's views.[42] Shizong ordered that ritual practice follow these treatises, which thus became the definitive statutes for the empire.

SHIZONG'S CONFUCIUS TEMPLE
REFORMS OF 1530

As noted above, when Shizong first assumed the throne, he got into a conflict with court officials over the Great Rituals. Just as the contention was at its peak, Senior Compiler Yang Shen 楊慎 (1488–1559) sighed: "This dynasty has nurtured scholars for 150 years. Now is the time to fight and die for ideals." Yang and over 200 other officials knelt outside a gate to the palace in the hope of persuading Shizong to rescind his order.[43] On the contrary, Shizong angrily had sixteen men beaten to death, and many more exiled. In 1525, Yu Shan 余珊 (*jinshi* 1508) submitted a statement on the event: "When officials speak of rituals today, if they disagree [with the throne] on one point, they are charged with treason. They are exiled or sentenced to death, so that the court is empty."[44]

Shizong thought himself knowledgeable about matters of ritual and considered himself a lover of antiquity. In fact, he was opinionated and often at odds with court officials. He attempted to awe his officials and establish an air of imposing authority. When Zhang Cong submitted his memorial on reforming the Confucius temple, Shizong ordered the Ministry of Rites to meet with the members of the Hanlin Academy to discuss it. Xu Jie objected to the reforms and was immediately demoted. Shizong personally drafted "Explanation of the Corrected Sacrifices to Confucius" (*Zheng Kongzi sidian shuo* 正孔子祀典說) and "Extensive Record of the Corrected Sacrifice to Confucius" (*Zheng Kongzi sidian shenji* 正孔子祀典申記), and ordered the Ministry of Rites to discuss these two essays.[45] In response, Xia Yan 夏言 (1482–1548), a favored minister of Shizong, praised Shizong for

---

42. On the urging of Senior Messenger Xue Kan 薛侃, Lu Jiuyuan 陸九淵 (1139–93) was included among those who received sacrifices (Zhang Tingyu, *Mingshi* 50.1300).

43. Ibid., 191.5068.

44. Ibid., 208.5499.

45. For complete versions of these essays, see Zhu Silan, *Jiajing sidian kao*; *Ming shilu* and *Gujin tushu jicheng* include edited versions of these sources on the temple.

"using a sage's mind to deduce the Sage's mind; the analysis is detailed and clear, and the inquiry precise and accurate." He followed this, however, by saying: "In the past few days, debate has been rampant. In all loyalty, I request that Your Highness . . . temporarily postpone Your ritual of sacrifice to Confucius."[46] Clearly, the opposition was enormous. The censor Li Guan even said that if Shizong insisted on reforming the Confucius temple, he would only "be criticized by contemporaries and laughed at by later generations."[47] Zhang Cong, however, seems to have been prepared for this response, for after he recited Shizong's essays, he said:

The difficulties in changing customs cannot be understood by the average fool, who will defend himself by claiming to "respect Confucius." They are directed by profit and never have been directed by righteousness. It is only the Emperor who is justly righteous. Acting on authority of his own heart is what is what is meant by "only a sage can understand a sage."[48]

Shizong wished to confer further with other court officials and perhaps divine an oracle from the imperial ancestors.[49] Because of Shizong's resolve, Zhang Cong was able to unite his supporters and attack his opponents, thus realizing Shizong's demand.[50] This imperceptibly helped advance Shizong's authoritarian power. By advising Shizong to reform the Confucius temple "on authority of his own heart," Zhang Cong was in fact handing over the "creation of rites and music" (the authority of cultural creation) to an autocratic ruler.

The two essays by Shizong are useful for understanding the emperor's reforms of the Confucius temple. In the first month of 1525, Shizong stubbornly insisted on creating the Rite of the Empress Personally Tending the Silkworms over the strong objections of many officials. The emperor announced: "The institutions of rites and music originate from the Son of Heaven. This is purely the way of antiquity. Thus, Confucius wrote this saying in order to inform all later generations."[51] The passage from the Analects reads: "When all under Heaven is in accordance with the Way, rites,

---

46. *Shizong shilu* 119.6a.
47. Li Guan, "Lun Kongzi sidian shu," 6.209.
48. Zhang Cong, *Luoshan zoushu* 6.24b–25a.
49. Zhang Cong, *Yudui lu* 22.26b.
50. Ibid., 22.26b–27a.
51. *Shizong shilu* 109.4a.

music, and military action originate from the Son of Heaven."[52] Shizong's selective quotation of this passage was meant to use the name of Confucius to oppress Confucian officials. Ironically, Shizong's target was Confucius himself.

In the introduction to the "Extensive Record of the Corrected Sacrifice to Confucius," Shizong wrote: "It is Our view that the Way of Confucius was the Way of a king, his virtue was the virtue of a king, his accomplishments were the same as a king's, and his work was the same as a king's. It is only that his position was never that of a king."[53] Confucius "had the virtue without the position" and hence ought not receive the rites of a king. Shizong criticized the "conferring of the title of king" on Confucius, an error repeated from the time of Tang Xuanzong (r. 846–73) to that of Yuan Wuzong (r. 1307–11). He pointed out that in the *Spring and Autumn Annals* Confucius had reprimanded all those in his own day who had usurped the title of king. Some might call misunderstanding the intentions of the Sage and recklessly conferring the title of king on him reverence, but in fact it "villainously inflicts extreme harm on the Sage."[54]

In his "Extensive Record of the Corrected Sacrifice to Confucius," Shizong elucidated—in great detail—the meaning of the word "king" (*wang* 王). "King" as used as Confucius's posthumous title is not the same as the "heavenly king" (*tianwang* 天王) of the Zhou institution, "the king who rules over all under Heaven." Rather, it is the later noble title of king "as conferred on the [feudal] ruler" (*zhuhou wang* 諸侯王). Rulers throughout history have posthumously conferred the title of king on Confucius and have not elevated him to the position of emperor, "not wishing him to be of equal status [with themselves]." The title of king thus confers on Confucius the position of subject. How can this be considered a sign of reverence?[55] Shizong used this argument not only to refute Xu Jie's argument but also to rebut the arguments of earlier scholars, such as Zhou Hongmo,[56] who wished to elevate Confucius to the status of the Zhou dynasty's Heavenly King. If Confucius retained the title of king yet received the rites due an emperor, he could not escape allegations of transgression and usurpation.

---

52. *Lunyu* 16.2.
53. Shizong, "Zheng Kongzi sidian shuo," 5, n.p.
54. Shizong, "Zheng Kongzi sidian shuo."
55. Shizong, "Zheng Kongzi sidian shenji."
56. Kong Zhencong, *Queli zhi* 11.17a–18a.

Scholars such as Zhu Yizun 朱彝尊 (1629–1709) would later disagree with Shizong's opinion. As Zhu delicately explained: "The emperor rules over the Imperial University. The rites of the emperor are administered in accordance with the learning of the emperor, performing the music of the emperor, sacrificing with twelve vessels, and dancing in eight rows."[57]

Shizong put unprecedented stress on a sacrifice's rank in the ritual hierarchy. When in the second month of 1530, he objected to Song Taizu's (r. 960–78) and Taizong's (r. 978–97) rankings on the Altar of the Gods of Soils and Grains, he stated very clearly: "Every time We sacrificed to the gods of Soils and Grains and presented offerings to Taizu and Taizong as correlates, We had doubts. Heaven and Earth are the most highly respected, followed by the imperial ancestral temple, and only then the Altar of Soils and Grains. This is the underlying principle of the order of ritual sacrifices."[58] Thus Shizong permitted only the principle of "respecting the ancestor who attended Heaven," and not "offering to the ancestor who attended the Earth."[59] In Shizong's view, there was no comparison between the importance of "country" and that of the "ancestral temple." The ritual of the Confucius Temple can thus be imagined.

Shen Defu's 沈德符 (1578–1642) subtle analysis of Shizong's reform of the Confucius temple is quite astute: "Replacing the statues with tablets and the title of 'king' with that of 'master' can be justified. As for replacing eight rows of dancers with six and reducing the sacrificial vessels, this was because the emperor [Shizong] did not want the Master to be on the same level as the ruler."[60] Shen Defu's conclusions are supported by the events of the time. As the court was debating the Confucius temple reforms, Li Guan led a group of thirteen censors in jointly submitting a strong memorial of objection. This memorial said that Shizong's rituals honoring Heaven and ancestors had been grand indeed. Why then did he call into question only Confucius's title of king? This criticism struck a sensitive nerve, and Shizong had Li Guan and the others arrested. Shizong said: "Rectifying the sacrificial ceremony arises from My respect for the Master and the Way. Li Guan has absurdly brought up ancestral worship ceremonies, with the intent of slandering the Great Ritual. He collaborated with others and insolently har-

---

57. Zhu Yizun, *Pushuting ji* 60.697.
58. *Shizong shilu* 109.11a.
59. Ibid., 109.11b.
60. Shen Defu, *Wanli yehuo bian* 14.360.

assed the court with petitions. Let him be stripped of his office and title." At Censor-in-chief Wang Hong's (*jinshi* 1496) request, Shizong disciplined only Li Guan.[61]

Shizong's continuing anger over the Great Rites Controversy unmistakably revealed itself in the reformed rituals of the Confucius temple. In speaking of the issue of "respecting the son and humbling the father" in the Northern Song rites for the Confucius temple, Shizong could not help placing blame on the Confucian officials involved in the Puyuan debates.[62]

How can the son sit in the main hall while the father eats below? This is called unrectified names. Once the standards were muddled, all details were destroyed as well. By the time of the Song, Cheng Yi claimed to have received the tradition of the Way and advised Song Yingzong [r. 1063–67] against recognizing King Pu 濮王 as his father. If this can be endured, what cannot be endured![63]

The extent of Shizong's anger is apparent.

Shizong claimed time and again that he had no intention of using his position to oppress the Former Master. He also said that if the Confucius temple rituals were not reformed, "sons would not treat fathers as fathers, subjects would not treat rulers as rulers, families would break down and rebels would revolt, and much more." "We cannot but defend Ourselves and Our official [Zhang] Cong. What he is doing is for the sake of obligation (*mingfen* 名分) and principle, not so as to flatter Us, not to demote the Master. This is the way We, too, would correct matters."[64] What is surprising is that Shizong boldly criticized Xianzong (r. 1465–87) for accepting the Ministry of Rites' argument that to "increase the dancers to eight rows, use twelve sacrificial vessels, use prepared meat and follow the rituals of serving Heaven" is "without problems."[65] Throughout history, it has been truly rare for a ruler to criticize a predecessor.

Shizong often made himself responsible for continuing in the footsteps of Taizu, and the Confucius temple reforms were no exception. When Taizu first took control of the empire, he ordered that the sacrifices to Confucius in Nanjing use tablets rather than statues, six rows of dancers, and ten sacrificial vessels. Shizong felt that this was respectful to an extreme and

---

61. Zhang Tingyu, *Mingshi* 208.5502; see also *Shizong shilu* 119.8b.
62. *Song shi jishi benmo* 1: 248–57.
63. Shizong, "Zheng Kongzi sidian shuo," 5.
64. Ibid.
65. Ibid.

so did not add to it. As to why Taizu still retained Confucius's title of nobility, Shizong explained: "How could he not have expected this of a later generation?"[66] The implication is that Shizong himself is the "later generation" that would remove the noble title.

Strictly speaking, Shizong did not blindly accept all rituals set by Taizu. In fact, he made many amendments to the rituals established by Taizu in his later years. Shizong was very conscious of this, and in the third month of 1530, he expressed his position very clearly.

The world created by Taizu was vast and open; the number of exemplary virtues that could be retained and emulated were many. But as for rites and music, there could not but be some matters to be left to later generations. As for upholding and expanding these, despite the sagacious mind of Our Ancestor [Taizu], how could there not have been matters left to sagely sons and spirited descendants? These are the matters now at hand. How can we sink into the view that Our Founding Ancestor is indubitably correct, daring not to change a thing?[67]

In 1533, a student of Puzhou 蒲州 named Qin Tang 秦鐘 (1463–1541) submitted a petition saying the separate suburban rites and the revision of the Confucius temple "are not consonant with the intentions of the sagely Founder. Please return them to their original states."[68] Qin Tang may have understood how to use ancestral precedent to limit the whims of Shizong, but he ignored Shizong's self-image. Besides being condemned to death for his improper petition, Qin was not able to change what had already been done. As it turned out, in Shizong's point of view, the "son of heaven" in the passage from the *Doctrine of the Mean* "None but the son of heaven determines rites, sets measures, and defines the forms of written characters" meant not only "the dynastic founder Taizu" but also successive rulers.[69] This is why, in the "Extensive Record of the Corrected Sacrifice to Confucius," Shizong said the ritual of the Confucius temple "must be appropriate to the times. When it comes to maintaining social order, [error] must be speedily corrected."[70]

---

66. Ibid.
67. Ibid.
68. Zhang Tingyu, *Mingshi* 197.5223.
69. Shizong, "Fen jiao huiyi diyi shu," 1.
70. Shizong, "Zheng Kongzi sidian shenshuo," 5.

THE STATE TEACHINGS OF
MING TAIZU

Upon close examination, it is evident that although Shizong did not leave the rituals as set by Taizu untouched, he retained their general spirit. It is not difficult to recognize a similarity between the attitudes of Taizu and those of Shizong toward the Confucius temple and other sacrificial rites. In the second month of 1368, Taizu followed precedent in establishing a new dynasty and offered a great sacrifice to Confucius at the National University; he also sent a representative to Confucius's home in Qufu to hold a sacrifice. On this occasion, he said:

Zhongni's Way is as broad and ancient as Heaven and Earth. Therefore, no one who has since taken possession of the empire has not shown reverence and exhausted the rites by maintaining the sacrifices to him. Now that We rule the empire, [Our] hopes lie in the brilliant transformation of the realm through the propagation of the Master's Dao.[71]

This passage clearly expresses Taizu's understanding that the sacrifice to Confucius was an indispensable symbol of the dynastic founder's resolve to continue the imperial order. The following year, however, his attitude changed precipitously. He suddenly announced that the spring and autumn sacrifices at the Confucius temple would be held in Qufu only, and no longer throughout the empire.[72]

Since the time of the Han dynasty, [Confucius's] spirit has been sacrificed to throughout the land. We have unified the people in the name of the earlier kings. While going through Confucius's writings, We saw such teachings as: "To sacrifice to spirits not of one's own ancestor is flattery" [*Analects* 2.24]; "Respect spirits but keep them at a distance" [6.22]; "Sacrifice according to the rites" [2.5]. If the sages and worthies had not clearly stated this, how could he say it? Therefore, We dare

---

71. *Taizu shilu* 30.5b–6a.

72. The discontinuation of sacrifices to Confucius throughout the empire in 1369 is not mentioned in the "Treatise on Rites" ("Lizhi" 禮志) or "Taizu's Basic Annals" ("Taizu benji" 太祖本纪) in the *Ming History*, nor is it mentioned in the *Ming Veritable Records*, probably because later official historians concealed these facts for Taizu's sake. This information can be found only in Qian Tang's biography in the *Ming History* (39.3981). Qin Huitian (1702–1764) mistakenly quotes Wang Qi's *Xu wenxian tongkao*, which dates this edict to May 29, 1369 (Hongwu 2/4/23). In fact, it should be on June 5, 1382 (15/4/23); see *Taizu shilu* 144.2a; Qin Huitian, *Wuli tongkao* 120.1b–2a; and Wang Qi, *Xu wenxian tongkao* 57.7b–8a.

not sacrifice [to Confucius] throughout the land and exhaust resources to burden the sagely virtue of [Confucius's] spirit.[73]

The founding of the Ming dynasty was a time of reconstruction. Taizu often ordered officials to reform rites.[74] In the same year, he ordered that the city god, Chenghuang 城隍, should receive sacrifices throughout the land. It was inconceivable that Confucius was not receiving sacrifices in official temples throughout the empire. Both Minister Qian Tang 錢唐 and Vice Minister Cheng Xu 程徐 submitted petitions strongly protesting this. Cheng wrote:

Of all the sacrifices of ancient and present times, only those to the Soils and Grains, the Three August Ones, and Confucius are held throughout the land. If the people throughout the realm do not sacrifice to Soils and Grains, then the Three August Ones would have no means to thrive; if they do not follow Confucius's Way, then they would have no means on which to establish themselves. . . . Confucius established his teachings based on the Way, and so all under Heaven sacrifice to him. They do not sacrifice to the man, but to his teachings and to his Way. To have all people read his books, follow his teachings, practice his Way, and yet not be allowed to sacrifice to him is not the way to secure the hearts of the people and uphold the teachings of the world.[75]

Taizu would not listen. In 1371, Song Lian submitted "On the Confucius temple," in which he spoke of the advantages of sacrificing to Confucius throughout the empire. Surprisingly enough, he was banished and exiled.[76]

---

73. Xu Yikui, *DaMing jili* 16.20a. *DaMing jili* was completed in the third month of 1370, and it includes "Zhiji Qufu Kongzi yuzhi zhuwen" 致祭曲阜孔子禦制祝文 of 1369.

74. *Taizu shilu* 30.1a–4b, 38.1a–10a.

75. Zhang Tingyu, *Mingshi* 139.3981–82. The three August Ones (*san huang* 三皇) refers to cultural heroes of remote antiquity whose legendary accomplishments at the beginning of the mythological era are credited with the foundation of Chinese civilization. Fuxi apprehended the patterns of the heavens and earth, drew the eight trigrams, domesticated the animals, and ruled as the Son of Heaven with the power of wood; Shennong, the Divine Farmer, taught the people how to domesticate the five grains and ruled with the power of fire; and Huangdi, the Yellow Emperor, ruled with the power of earth.

76. *Taizu shilu* 67.7a; see also Deng Qiu, *Huangming yonghua leibian* 72.12b. Song Lian's treatise can be found in Li Zhizao, *Pan'gong liyue shu* 1.42a–44b. Yu Zhengxie (*Guisi cungao* 9.256) and Shao Changheng (*Qingmen lugao* 10.9b) say Song Lian was exiled due to his request to destroy the statues. The histories are inaccurate. In "DaMing chijian taixue bei" (Plaque for the building of the National University by imperial order), Song Na clearly records: "From the time of Confucius, statues were not made for [the imperial temple; rather] spirit tablets were

It is evident that, on the one hand, Taizu understood the importance of the sacrifices to Confucius in the founding of a dynasty, but on the other hand, he discontinued the sacrifices in state temples throughout the empire for the sake of minor sacrificial quibbles. There must have been a deeper reason for this. Indeed, when Taizu's general Xu Da (1332–85) advanced into Jining in the third month of 1368, the Yansheng Duke 衍聖公, Kong Kejian 孔克堅 (1316–70), who had been ennobled in 1335 by the Mongols, pleaded illness and sent his son Xixue 希學 (1336–81) to the capital to have an audience with Taizu. Taizu was upset over this and personally wrote to Duke Kong Kejian:

I hear you are ill. Is this truly so? Yet you, Sir Kong, are an extraordinary person. Your ancestor's teachings have spread throughout the land. For many generations, all [of your family] have received noble titles from the court. Not even barbarian Mongol rulers dissolved them. Only today is this different. I have led the people of the central land in driving out the Mongols, bringing peace to the central kingdom. Although I may be a commoner, the ancients chose their emperors from the people, such as [the founder of the] Han dynasty, Gaozong. If you plead illness but are not ill, to treat my kingdom with disrespect, I will not allow it![77]

Taizu obviously was well aware of the importance of Confucius's ancestral line to the legitimation of his political power. Kong Kejian's hesitation to respond to Taizu's summons may have been a sign that the combat in the north was not yet over, and the victor not yet clear. Later, when Kong Kejian did come to court, Taizu broke precedent and did not confer an office on him. Taizu held an audience with him in court but said: "Although your age is not advanced, illness plagues you. Thus, I will not trouble you with an office."[78] Taizu explained to his officials: "The reason I did not confer an office on Kong Kejian was because he is the descendant of the late Sage. To be especially polite to him, I am giving him a salary, but not burdening him with work."[79] The same month, Taizu nonetheless conferred the title of Yansheng Duke on Kong Kejian's son, Xixue. Taizu's displeasure could not be veiled.

---

used in the sacrifice. This changed after many centuries of barbarian customs" (Song Na, *Xiyin wen'gao* 7.388). Obviously, Taizu had no objections to eliminating the statues.

77. *Kongfu dang'an xuanbian* 1:17.

78. Ye Sheng, *Shuitong riji* 19.188. These two records are more colloquial and are certainly original documents. *Taizu shilu* 31.8b.

79. *Taizu shilu* 31.8b.

When reading *Mencius* in 1372, Taizu came upon the passage: "If the ruler views his ministers as dirt and grass, then his ministers will view him as a bandit and villain" (4B.3). Taizu felt this was inappropriate reading matter for his subjects and banned Mencius from receiving sacrifices as correlate in the Confucius temple. He also announced that any remonstration would be regarded as treason. Qian Tang still objected, saying: "If I die for Mencius's sake, I will die with great honor."[80] The official histories say "the emperor appreciated his sincerity and so did not punish him."[81] Qian Tang's willingness to sacrifice his life for his ideals exemplifies the conflict between political authority and cultural belief; the price of this conflict was too high for an autocratic ruler to bear. In 1373, Taizu reinstated Mencius in the sacrifices.[82] Only in 1382 did he restore the sacrifice to Confucius in state temples throughout the empire. The edict said: "Confucius understood the Dao of the sovereign and taught it to the world, allowing rulers to be rulers, subjects to be subjects, fathers to be fathers, and sons to be sons, setting standards and ordering ethics. His accomplishments are equal to Heaven and Earth."[83]

"Allowing rulers to be rulers, subjects to be subjects, fathers to be fathers, and sons to be sons" is truly a Confucian teaching, but in this context, Taizu's emphasis is worth some consideration. In 1380 Taizu had executed his prime minister, Hu Weiyong 胡惟庸, on suspicion of treason, and the repercussions were wide and long lasting.[84] Taizu may have wished to make use of Confucius's teachings to dissolve the political strife then rampant at court. During the Wanli era (1573–1619), while explaining that sacrificing to Confucius throughout the empire was not blasphemous, Qu Jiusi 瞿九思 (*juren* 1573) said something interesting:

Looking over the lands of the empire, our Emperor on High feared there were those who were not loyal and so intended to use the spirit of the great sage to pacify them. He thus had no choice but to make use of Confucius's importance. . . . Once this had been completed, Confucius received sacrifices throughout the empire. It is precisely because he relied upon the Sage that he cannot be criticized.[85]

---

80. Zhang Tingyu, *Mingshi* 139.3982.
81. Ibid.
82. Wang Qi, *Xu wenxian tongkao* 57.11b; see also Sun Chengze, *Chunmingmeng yulu* 21.36b.
83. *Taizu shilu* 144.2a.
84. For more on the Hu Weiyong case, see Zhang Tingyu, *Mingshi* 308.7906.
85. Qu Jiusi, *Kongmiao liyue kao* 1.20a.

Qu Jiusi was renowned as a pure Confucian, and his defending of Confucianism is not unusual. This passage, however, has other implications about which the histories say nothing. What these implications may be, we may never know.

In 1370, Taizu revoked the titles of nobility of all spirits except Confucius. Since the Tang dynasty, the spirits of mountains and rivers had been honored with such titles as "emperor" and "king." Taizu explained his action by saying that "for the relations between spirits and humans to be appropriate, titles must be correct and appropriate to the Rites."[86]

In 1371, Taizu proclaimed that the Three August Ones could not receive sacrifices in the provinces and counties. In 1295, the Yuan emperor Chengzong (r. 1295–1307) had ordered the establishment of temples to the Three August Ones in the provinces. Sacrifices were to be held in the spring and autumn, to be led by a pharmaceutical master.[87] Taizu felt this was an improper rite and forbade the provinces from conducting such sacrifices.[88] The unintentional result of this was that there were no sacrifices to the Three August Ones; in 1373, a Temple of Kings and Emperors (Lidai diwang miao 歷代帝王廟) was built in the capital for the sacrifices to the Three August Ones and the Five Emperors and the founding emperors of the Han, Tang, Song, and Yuan dynasties.[89] In 1388, 37 eminent officials throughout history were included as correlates in the Temple of Kings and Emperors.[90] The temple's form and regulations imitated those of the Confucius temple's, but the offerings and ceremonies exceeded those of the Confucius temple. Every spring and autumn, the emperor conducted the ceremonies in person, to emphasize the glory of imperial legitimacy. There was a strong suggestion of competition with the Confucius temple.[91]

In 1387, Taizu eliminated the Temple of the King of Military Accomplishment (Wucheng wangmiao 武成王廟). This temple, originally called the Taigong 太公 Temple, had been established in 731, during the Tang dynasty, for sacrifices to the Taigong Wang 太公望. In 760, Taigong Wang was given the title of King Wucheng, with a liturgy comparable to

---

86. *Taizu shilu* 53.1b–2a.
87. Song Lian, *Yuanshi* 76.1902.
88. *Taizu shilu* 62.3b–4a.
89. Ibid., 64.2b–3b.
90. Ibid., 188.5b–6a.
91. Li Dongyang, *DaMing huidian* 91.1a–11a.

that of the Confucius, King of Exalted Culture. In imitation of the Confucius temple, there were ten correlates, all great military generals of old.[92] Later generations also added 72 worthies as correlates. The original intention was to build two peaks of Exalted Culture and Military Accomplishment, with equal status. Because of the civil service examination system, Confucianism had subsequently become the basis of official learning. As the literati gained confidence, there was a tendency to value the literary over the martial. In 788, Attendant to the Ministry of Military Affairs Li Shu 李紓 suggested that the sacrificial ceremonies of the Confucius temple and the Wucheng temple ought not be equal:

Exalted Culture has been passed down, and a hundred generations revere the Master [Confucius]. Without his teachings, the five constant virtues [i.e., humanity, righteousness, propriety, wisdom, and faithfulness] and three bonds [i.e., ruler-minister, father-son, husband-wife] would not be clear; if not for his regulations, countries and families could not be established; this is why Mencius said that since the birth of the people, there has been this one man [Confucius]. Therefore, the regulations of the uncrowned king were rectified; the title of "First Sage" (xian sheng 先聖) was added; for music, court instruments were used; for the sacrifice, the protector-in-chief was sent. The Master is revered, and the Dao is worshipped; all is refined and proper. Taigong wrote only "Six Stratagems," and his achievements were evident for only one generation. How can his virtues deserve such ceremony?[93]

Li Shu's petition is representative of the attitude of civil officials. For this reason, although the sacrificial ceremonies of the Wucheng temple were grand, they could not compare with those of the Temple of Culture.[94]

In any case, Taizu did not eliminate the sacrifice at the Temple of King Wucheng solely because he emphasized the Temple of Culture. He had other intentions. The Qing scholar Qin Huitian 秦蕙田 (1702–64) misunderstood Taizu's reason for eliminating the Martial Temple and wrote: "How can Taigong's accomplishments be compared with those of Confucius?"[95] He even praised Taizu's actions for "breaking from a millennium of blasphemous sacrificial rites." Taizu's reasons are clear: "Taigong was ennobled as a lord of the Zhou. If he receives the sacrifices of a king, he would be

---

92. Ouyang Xiu, *Xin Tangshu* 15.377.

93. Du You, *Tongdian* 53.307.

94. For more on the evolution of the differences between the Temple of Culture and the Martial Temple, see Tao Xisheng, "Wumiao zhi zhengzhi shehui de yanbian."

95. Qin Huitian, *Wuli tongkao* 120.18a.

equal to the Zhou Son of Heaven. If he is given a false title, he shall surely not receive the sacrifice."[96] For this reason, Taizu eliminated Taigong's title of king, closed his temple, and ordered that he receive sacrifices as a correlate in the temple of Kings and Emperors.

Shizong eliminated Confucius's title of king for the same reason. Shizong's intention was clear: a subject must not receive an emperor's rites. To do so infringes on the emperor's privileges. In the policy question for the palace examinations in 1388, Taizu expressed his opinion concerning ritual: "The way of serving spirits is no different from that of leading the people. All sacrifices, from the beginning of time to the present, have been instituted for a reason, but the ritual regulations of the sages and worthies have distinctions. From the Son of Heaven to the common people, the sacrificial titles and the distinctions have deep roots."[97]

Taizu's revoking of the feudal titles of the spirits reflects his attitude. But despite Taizu's strict adherence to the order of the sacrifices, when Wu Chen argued that "Confucius should not be called king,"[98] Taizu still refused to deny Confucius his royal title. Perhaps he remembered the enormous protest that had arisen when he ended the empire-wide sacrifices to Confucius in 1369 and wanted to avoid aggravating the scholar-officials.

THE CULTURAL LEGITIMATION
OF AUTOCRACY

Shizong's reign began over a century after the founding of the dynasty. Autocratic government was already accepted; the ruler's power consolidated. Shizong shared none of Taizu's concerns. Indeed he had higher praise for Taizu than he did for Confucius:

Of the rulers of later generations who have been in the position of king, although many have been similar to Confucius, there have been none whose virtue could equal Confucius's. As for my lofty ancestor [Taizu], although he followed Confucius's

---

96. *Taizu shilu* 183.3a.

97. Ibid., 189.1a.

98. Wu Chen, "Kongzi feng wang bian," 11.63a–b. Wu Chen entered government service in 1379 as a Confucian scholar and was liked by Taizu. "Kongzi feng wang bian" may have been written because Taizu retained Confucius's title of king, whereas the titles of all other spirits were stripped in 1370. For more about Wu Chen, see Fu Weilin, *Mingshu* 17.6b–7b; and Guo Tingxun, *Ben chao fensheng renwu kao* 52.23a–25a.

Dao, his sagely benevolence, martial prowess, and literary virtues were equal to those of Yao and Shun. I fear Confucius could not compare.[99]

Thus, Shizong believed that "the title of a king ought not be falsely used, and the virtue of a king ought not be falsely imitated."[100]

In the early years of the Hongwu era, Wu Chen said: "The two emperors and three kings [of archaic times] filled their roles as rulers and teachers. Since Confucius was not able to be ruler, he was a teacher."[101] Once put in Shizong's hands, this attitude became even more amplified. In rebutting Li Guan, Shizong said:

The ruler concurrently holds the role of teacher, but a teacher must never feign the title of ruler. Confucius was originally a subject of the Zhou dynasty, no different from Taigong Wang. The teachings he transmitted were originally the teachings of [Fu]xi and [Shen]nong [who were both rulers]. He only expounded them.[102]

In the second month of 1520, Shizong decided to establish the sacrifice to the "Sagely Masters." The nine sage-rulers, Fuxi 伏羲; Shennong 神農; the Yellow Emperor 黃帝, Xuanyuan 軒轅; Yao 堯; Shun 舜; the founder of the Xia dynasty, Yu 禹; the founder of the Shang dynasty, Tang 湯; and the founders of the Zhou dynasty, Kings Wen 文 and Wu 武, were placed in the ruling position facing south. The Sage Duke of Zhou was placed in the left correlate position and Master Confucius on the right.[103]

In 1371, Song Lian had suggested following the argument of Xiong He of the early Yuan dynasty and considering Fuxi as the founding ancestor of the tradition of the Way, followed by Shennong, the Yellow Emperor, Yao, Shun, Yu, Tang, Wen, and Wu, with Gao Yao 皋陶, Yi Yin 伊尹, Taigong Wang, the Duke of Zhou, Ji 稷, Xie 契, Yi 夷, Yi 益, Fu Yue 傅說, and Jizi 箕子 as correlates. The emperor and court officials, Song Lian said, should take these persons as models. If sacrifices to these persons are ordered, the tradition of the Way will be all the more respected.[104] Taizu did

---

99. Shizong, "Zheng Kongzi sidian shuo," 5.

100. Ibid.

101. Kong Zhencong, *Queli zhi* 11.63a.

102. *Shizong shilu* 119.8a.

103. Ibid., 120.6b; Li Dongyang, *DaMing huidian* 91.16a–18b. The Qing emperor Kangxi (r. 1662–1722) based the Hall of the Transmission of the Mind/Heart (Chuan xin dian 傳心殿) on this, but the ideas behind these two temples were completely different. See my "Qingchu zhengquan yishi xingtai zhi tanjiu."

104. Xiong He, *Xiong Wuxuan ji* 4.55; Song Lian, "Kongzi miaotang yi," 1.44a–b.

not follow this advice. Since Xiong He and Song Lian were in favor of increased respect for Confucius, it is significant that they advocated having everyone from the emperor to the common people sacrifice to Confucius separately rather than as a correlate of the sage-rulers throughout history.[105] Shizong implemented this model, but he replaced Gao Yao and the others with the Duke of Zhou as the "Sage" (*xiansheng* 先聖) and Confucius as "Master" (*xianshi* 先師). This was in accordance with Shizong's statement: "The Dao that [Confucius] transmitted was based on the transmission of [Fu] Xi and [Shen]nong. It is just that he greatly illuminated them."

In Shizong's sacrifice to the Sagely Masters, Confucius was returned to his early Tang status as correlate of the Duke of Zhou. Although he was not the correlate of the Duke of Zhou as sage, the implication is the same. Fei Mi 費密 (1599–1671) felt Confucius's demotion from sage to master was very unjust:

The titles "sage" and "master" are different. In the *Rites of Zhou*, there are many kinds of masters. Later generations called anyone who taught disciples a "master" but did not dare call him a "sage." Thus, "sage" is respectful, and "master" is subordinate. Now, a "sage" has been demoted to a "master" for no reason. . . . I do not know on which canonical source this is based.[106]

Such was Fei Mi's displeasure with Confucius's designation as master, let alone Confucius's demotion to the position of correlate. For Confucians, Shizong's actions amounted to a nightmare. No wonder that even Zhang Cong, who so strongly supported the Confucius temple reforms, tried to prevent Shizong from going through with his plan of the sacrifice to Sagely Masters by saying "the world of the Three August Ones was chaotic, and many matters were mysterious."[107] But Shizong was obstinate, and this sacrifice was implemented. Confucius, revered in the "tradition of the Way," became subservient to "political legitimacy" in the imperial register of sacrifices.

---

105. Xiong added: "If Confucius did indeed actually unite the laws and regulations of the ancestors, complete the great accomplishments of the sages, and is then offered sacrifices by everyone throughout all the ages, from the Son of Heaven down to the villages, at the spring and autumn sacrifices, the Son of Heaven must personally bow and complete all matters" (*Xiong Wuxuan ji* 4.55).

106. Fei Mi, *Hongdao shu* 2.7a. Fei also said that for Shizong to change Confucius's title to "Great Sage and Former Master" was incongruous and extremely defaming (ibid., 23.9a–b).

107. Zhang Cong, *Yudui lu* 23.9a–10b.

In the context of Chinese political history, the combination of the tradition of the Way (*Daotong*) and tradition of legitimate governance was the last step in the growth of autocracy. Full autocracy implies a ruler with absolute and unrestrained political power. In history, the tradition of the Way symbolized the cultural power of Confucianism and was political in that it was used as the criterion for judging the legitimacy and the competence of a government. The independence of the Way from the political establishment served as a check on political power and so blocked autocracy. No one understood this better than Lü Kun 呂坤 (1536–1618) in his reflections on the relation between power and truth:

Although ministers dispute one another at court, after the issuance of an edict from the emperor, no one dares to defy it and speak out against it; although scholars argue with one another in school, when someone invokes the words of Confucius, everyone agrees and keeps silent. Therefore, in the world only principle (*li* 理) and political power (*shi* 勢) are the most respected; but principle is supreme. The emperor cannot suppress principle with his power at court. Even if he did so, principle nevertheless would exist in the world forever. In fact, political power lies within the realm of emperors, whereas principle lies within the realm of the sages. If the reign of an emperor is not legitimated by the principle of the sages, it will decline. Thus political power needs principle for the justification of its existence.[108]

To be sure, just because a political ruler claims absolute power does not necessarily mean that he has identified with the tradition of the Way, nor does it necessarily mean that political and cultural authority are united in the ruler. The ruler might attempt to challenge or even destroy the tradition of the Way and the power of the Confucian authorities as a means of expanding his power over that tradition. Such were the measures adopted by the founder of the Ming dynasty, Taizu, and followed by Shizong.

Undermining an independent tradition of the Way is a perfectly logical step in the process of strengthening autocracy. The methods used to do this vary, however, as is clear from the differences between the tactics of Ming Taizu and Ming Shizong, on the one hand, and those of the Qing emperor Kangxi, on the other. In retrospect, the Qing emperor, although an alien ruler, was much more successful. Unlike the Ming founder, the Kangxi emperor did not directly confront the tradition of the Way as the symbol of cultural authority. The Kangxi emperor was more sensitive to, and more

---

108. Lü Kun, *Shenyin yu* 1.4–12a.

conscious of, the subtle influence of Confucian symbols on Chinese politics and society.[109] His promotion of the Confucius temple rituals was only one of many demonstrations of this sensitivity. The Qing emperor used the Confucian cultural heritage as a means of reinforcing his political legitimacy. Through his restructuring of the relationship between the tradition of the Way and the tradition of imperial governance, the Kangxi emperor assumed the leadership of both, an ideal that had never been realized by the Ming rulers.

---

109. As Qian Mu observed on his visit to the Confucius temple in Qufu, most of the steles dedicated to Confucius were set up by alien rulers (see Qian Mu, "Shiyou zayi'" [Recollections of teachers and friends], *China Monthly* 2 [May 1980] 4: 59). According to Kong Jifen's *Queli wenxian kao* (12.1b), there are thirteen stele pavilions (*beiting*) in the Confucius temple; nine were built by three Qing rulers. Kong Jifen also confirms that no new buildings "could be added since our [Qing] dynasty has enlarged [the temple] to such an extent" (ibid., 11.1a).

WORKS CITED

Cheng Minzheng 程敏政. *Huangdun wenji* 篁墩文集. Wenyuange siku quanshu 文淵閣四庫全書 ed.

Deng Qiu 鄧球. *Huangming yonghua leibian* 皇明咏化類編. Longqing ed.

Du You 杜佑. *Tongdian* 通典. Taipei: Xinxing shuju, 1963.

Fei Mi (Jingyu) 費密 (經虞). *Hongdao shu* 弘道書. Yilan tang 怡蘭堂 ed., 1919.

Fu Weilin 傅維鱗. *Mingshu* 明書. Taipei: Huazheng, 1974.

Gu Yanwu 顧炎武. *Yuanchaoben Gu Tinglin Rizhilu* 原抄本顧亭林日知錄. Taipei: Wenshizhe chubanshe, 1979.

Gui E 桂萼. *Gui Wenxiang gong zouyi* 桂文襄公奏議. Qianlong (1762) ed.

Gujin tushu jicheng 古今圖書集成.

Guo Tingxun 過庭訓. *Ben chao fensheng renwu kao* 本朝分省人物考. Taipei: Chengwen chubanshe, 1971.

Hong Liangji 洪亮吉. *Chunchiu Zuozhuan gu* 春秋左傳詁.

Hong Mai 洪邁. *Rongzhai bisui* 容齋筆隨. Shanghai: Guji chubanshe, 1978.

Huang Chin-shing 黃進興. "Qingchu zhengquan yishi xingtai zhi tanjiu: zhengzhihua de daotong guan" 清初政權意識形態之探究: 政治化的道統觀. *Lishi yuyan yanjiusuo jikan* 58 (1987): 105–32.

———. "Xueshu yu xinyang: lun kongmiao cong sizhi yu rujia daotong yishi" 學術與信仰: 論孔廟從祀制與儒家道統意識. In idem, *Yuru shengyu* 優入聖域, pp. 218–312. Taipei: Yunchen wenhua, 1994.

Jiao Hong 焦竑. *Yutang congyu* 玉堂叢語. Beijing: Zhonghua shuju, 1981.

Kong Jifen 孔繼汾. *Queli wenxian kao* 闕里文獻考.

Kong Zhencong 孔貞叢. *Queli zhi* 闕里志. Wanli ed.

Kongfu dang'an xuanbian 孔府檔案選編. Beijing: Zhonghua shuju, 1982.

Li Dongyang 李東陽. *DaMing huidian* 大明會典. Taipei: Xinwenfeng chuban, 1976.

Li Guan 黎貫. "Lun Kongzi sidian shu" 論孔子祀典疏. In *Guangdong wenzheng* 廣東文徵, vol. 6. Guofeng chubanshe, 1965.

Li Zhizao 李之藻. *Pan'gong liyue shu* 頖宮禮樂疏. Wenyuange siku quanshu 文淵閣四庫全書 ed.

Lü Kun 呂坤. *Shenyin yu* 呻吟語. Taipei: Hanjing wenhua shiye, 1981.

Mao Qiling 毛奇齡. "Bianding Jiajing daliyi" 辨定嘉靖大禮議. In idem, *Xihe quanji* 西河全集 2. *Longwei mishu* 龍威秘書.

Ouyang Xiu 歐陽修. *Ouyang Xiu wenji* 歐陽修文集. Taipei: Shijie shuju, 1961.

———. *Xin Tangshu* 新唐書. Beijing: Zhonghua shuju, 1976.

Pang Zhonglu 龐鍾璐. *Wenmiao sidian kao* 文廟祀典考. Taipei: Zhongguo liyue xuehui, 1977.

Qin Huitian 秦蕙田. *Wuli tongkao* 五禮通考. Wenyuange siku quanshu 文淵閣四庫全書 ed.

Qiu Jun 丘濬. *Daxue yanyi bu* 大學衍義補. Wenyuange siku quanshu 文淵閣四庫全書 ed.

Qu Jiusi 瞿九思. *Kongmiao liyue kao* 孔廟禮樂考. Wanli ed.

Shao Changheng 邵長蘅. *Qingmen lugao* 青門簏稿. In *Changzhou xianzhe yishu* 常州先哲遺書.

Shen Defu 沈德符. *Wanli yehuo bian* 萬曆野獲編. Beijing: Zhonghua shuju, 1980.

Shizong 世宗. "Fen jiao huiyi diyi shu" 分郊會議第一疏. In *Jiajing sidian kao* 嘉靖祀典考, ed. Zhu Silan 朱絲欄. Nangang, Taiwan: Zhongyang yanjiu yuan, Fu Sinian tushuguan, n.d.

———. "Zheng Kongzi sidian shenji" 正孔子祀典申記. In *Jiajing sidian kao* 嘉靖祀典考, ed. Zhu Silan 朱絲欄. Nangang, Taiwan: Zhongyang yanjiu yuan, Fu Sinian tushuguan, n.d.

———. "Zheng Kongzi sidian shuo" 正孔子祀典說. In *Jiajing sidian kao* 嘉靖祀典考, ed. Zhu Silan 朱絲欄. Nangang, Taiwan: Zhongyang yanjiu yuan, Fu Sinian tushuguan, n.d.

Shizong shilu 世宗實錄. In *Ming shilu* 明實錄. Nangang, Taiwan: Zhongyang yanjiuyuan, Lishi yuyan yanjiusuo, 1962.

Song Lian 宋濂. "Kongzi miaotang yi" 孔子廟堂議. In Li Zhizao 李之藻, *Pangong liyue shu* 頖宮禮樂疏 1.44b–45a. Wenyuange siku quanshu 文淵閣四庫全書 ed.

———. *Yuanshi* 元史. Beijing: Zhonghua shuju, 1980.

Song Na 宋訥. *Xiyin wen'gao* 西隱文稿. Taipei: Wenhai chubanshe, 1970.

Songshi jishi benmo 宋史紀事本末. 1605. Ed. Feng Qi 馮琦, Chen Bangzhan 陳邦瞻, et al. Beijing: Zhonghua shuju, 1955.

Sun Chengze 孫承澤. *Chunmingmeng yulu* 春明夢餘錄. Hongkong, 1965.

Taizu shilu 太祖實錄. In *Ming shilu* 明實錄. Nangang, Taiwan: Zhongyang yanjiuyuan, Lishi yuyan yanjiusuo, 1962.

Tao Xisheng 陶希聖. "Wumiao zhi zhengzhi shehui de yanbian" 武廟之政治社會的演變. *Shihuo yuekan* 2, no. 5 (Aug. 1972): 1–19

Wang Qi 王圻. *Xu wenxian tongkao* 續文獻通考. Wanli (1603) ed.

Wu Chen 吳沈. "Kongzi feng wang bian" 孔子封王辯. In Kong Zhencong 孔貞叢, *Queli zhi* 闕里志 11.63a–b. Wanli ed.

Xiong He 熊鈇. *Xiong Wuxuan ji* 熊勿軒集. Shanghai: Shangwu yinshuguan, 1936.

Xu Jie 徐階. *Shijingtang ji* 世經堂集. Kangxi (1681) ed.

Xu Xuemo 徐學謨. *Shimiao shi yulu* 世廟識餘錄. Taipei: Guofeng chubanshe, 1965.

Xu Yikui 徐一夔. *DaMing jili* 大明集禮. Wenyuange siku quanshu 文淵閣四庫全書 ed.

Ye Sheng 葉盛. *Shuitong riji* 水東日記. Beijing: Zhonghua shuju, 1980.

Yu Zhengxie 俞正燮. *Guisi cungao* 癸巳存稿. Taipei: Shangwu yinshuguan, 1971.

Zhang Cong 張璁. *Luoshan zoushu* 羅山奏疏. Wanli (1577) ed.

————. *Yudui lu* 諭對錄. Wanli (1607) ed.

Zhang Tingyu 張廷玉. *Mingshi* 明史. Beijing: Zhonghua shuju, 1980.

Zhu Silan 朱絲欄, ed. *Jiajing sidian kao* 嘉靖祀典考. Nangang, Taiwan: Zhongyang yanjiu yuan, Fu Sinian tushuguan, n.d.

Zhu Yizun 朱彝遵. *Pushuting ji* 曝書亭集. Taipei: Shijie shuju, 1964.

SEVEN

The Kongs of Qufu

Power and Privilege in Late Imperial China

Abigail Lamberton

From the beginning of official recognition of Confucianism in the Han period (206 BCE–220 CE) through the Neo-Confucianism of the Song (960–1126) to the doctrinaire orthodoxy of the Qing (1644–1912), the growth of the state sponsorship of Confucianism is well documented in Imperial China. With the establishment of an official temple of culture (*wen miao* 文廟) in every prefectural school in 630[1] and the use of the Confucian classics in the civil service examination system, the imperial court asserted its authority over the interpretation of the teachings of Confucius. By the late imperial period, Confucianism, with its emphasis on orderly relations within a hierarchical structure, was uniquely adaptable as a political theory by the rulers of Imperial China.[2] Proper behavior within society was premised on all members knowing, accepting, and acting according to their place as defined by the correct interpretation of the Confucian canon. With the general acceptance of the civil examination system as a valid means of determining entry into the government service, imperial rulers and high officials at court could use bureaucratic instruments to influence, if not determine, the curriculum of Confucian education.[3]

---

1. Wilson, *Genealogy of the Way*, p. 33.

2. James Liu ("How Did a Neo-Confucian School," p. 484) points out that during the Song period, the growth of a civil bureaucracy was advantageous to rulers because it minimized the threats of separatists and militarists.

3. Elman, "Political, Social, and Cultural Reproduction."

The elite section of imperial society agreed that Confucianism offered an ethical blueprint for a moral and stable society. The emperor and his officials shared the conviction that the improvement of Chinese society depended on the proper behavior of its members. The teachings of Confucius gave behavioral guidelines for all members of society. John Dardess has demonstrated that the founder of the Ming dynasty (1368–1644) used Confucianism as an authoritarian tool to shape governmental policies, and James Polachek has discussed attempts by scholar-officials to use the imperial system to create a better, more moral society.[4] In addition, Victor Mair has shown how local literati disseminated the emperor's views on Confucian morality to the general population through privately printed handbooks based on sacred edicts.[5] Although elite scholars played a crucial role in the interpretation of Confucian doctrine through the construction of lineages of orthodoxy, particularly when the court endorsed these genealogies,[6] the emperor remained a key figure in the promulgation of orthodox views on proper Confucian behavior. Certainly, some rulers were not intellectually capable of issuing Confucian dogma, but several Ming-Qing emperors—Hongwu (r. 1368–98) and Jiajing (r. 1521–66) of the Ming, and Kangxi (r. 1661–1722) and Qianlong (r. 1735–96) of the Qing—left unmistakable marks on state orthodoxy. What remains unexplored is the methods by which emperors gained the moral right to play such a prominent role in the interpretation of the teachings of Confucius. One such method was their close association with the descendants of the First Sage, Confucius.

This chapter seeks to explore one facet of the imperial association with Confucius; namely, the forging of a close relationship between the Kong lineage, the direct descendants of Confucius (Kongzi, 551–479 BCE), and the imperial house in the seventeenth and eighteenth centuries. Although the Kongs were not considered transmitters of Confucius's teachings, they were the one living link with the First Sage. They used this link as a strategy to enhance their social status, wealth, and political influence throughout the imperial period. By establishing strong connections with Confucius's living descendants and the sacred environs of Qufu 曲阜, where Confucius had lived, was buried, and his descendants still remained, emperors such as Kangxi and Qianlong could portray themselves as sagely rulers who both re-

---

4. Dardess, *Confucianism and Autocracy*; Polachek, *The Inner Opium War*.
5. Mair, "Language and Ideology."
6. Wilson, *Genealogy of the Way*.

spected and, through his living descendants, were associated with Confucius himself. For ruling emperors, maintaining this stance required a close link with the Kongs and the burial site of Confucius and led to occasional imperial processions to Qufu and the granting of imperial audiences to Kong lineage members. For the Kongs, maintaining their status as a privileged family required translating the symbolic capital of their sagely descent into power, wealth, and influence.

From the beginning of the imperial period, the Kongs received titles, wealth, lands, and signs of imperial favor that elevated them above others. The Kongs themselves were rarely involved with interpreting the words and teachings of their ancestor and left such pursuits to other, more common men. Instead they concentrated on following the way of the Sage by emphasizing their correct behavior among living men, which arose from their ability to trace an ordered path from antiquity. In the preface to the 1684 Kong genealogy, Kong Yuqi 孔毓圻 (1653–1723), the then-head of the lineage, asserted that having a genealogy grounded in historical records not only "restricts false men, deepens family ties, [and] lengthens harmonious virtues," but also has cosmological significance. Continuing his analogy between the affairs of the Kong family and the state of the universe, Kong Yuqi expanded on the contents to be found in the Kong genealogy:

Taking this one step further, the vast space between heaven and earth, the vicissitudes of fate, the forces controlling entropy, the residence of the Dao, the discovery of talented men, the cyclical nature of civilization, all these are here. If the way of Confucius has not ceased for even one day, it is because the descendants of Confucius have continued in an unbroken line. . . . The annals of the lineage are in fact the way of orthodoxy (*jia sheng ye shi daotong ye* 家乘也實道統也).[7]

In addition to living the way of the Sage, the Kongs worked to maintain their wealth and status by carefully controlling and recording the names and circumstances of all who could legitimately claim to be descendants of Confucius. Pursuing their own interests, they played a quiet role in imperial history: overthrowing no emperor, proposing no long-lasting reforms, making no earth-shattering expositions of philosophy.[8] To most observers, they

---

7. See the preface written by Kong Yuqi in Kong Shangren, *Kongzi shi jiapu*, "xu," 9b–10a.

8. An exception to this statement can be found in the life of Kong Guang. For an account of his role in the brief reformist movement immediately before the Wang Mang interregnum (9–23 CE), see Loewe, "The Former Han Dynasty," esp. pp. 198–222.

were a lineage of considerable local wealth and power but with little or no impact at the national level. Yet a closer examination of the Kong lineage reveals that this assessment leaves much of the story untold.

Although the Kongs could boast of few high officials or successful examination candidates over the course of the imperial period, they still achieved a national presence that belied their modest record of government service. The Kongs possessed their name, the favor of the reigning emperor, and control of the temple to Confucius at Qufu. Due to their name, they were granted imperial favors that gave them special powers within their home province of Shandong. They received preferential treatment within the civil service system and the privilege of memorializing the emperor directly.[9] The special treatment given the Kongs is also unprecedented in its duration. No other lineage was as celebrated dynasty after dynasty, nor was any other allowed to escape the opprobrium of having prominent members serve two dynastic houses without pause. Nor did any other lineage live in an imposing mansion that was the site of sacrifices to the First Sage.

The Kongs were neither statesmen nor scholars; indeed when Kong Shangren 孔尚任 (1648–1718) was selected to present a lecture before the Kangxi emperor on his tour to Qufu in 1684, his lecture was first commented on by the chancellor of the Hanlin Academy, a reader of the Hanlin Academy, the governor of Shandong province, and the Duke for Fulfilling the Sage (Yansheng gong 衍聖公, hereafter the Yansheng Duke), the head of the Kong lineage.[10] The benevolence shown them can only be explained through their close relationships with emperors, from whom they received material gifts and concrete powers. The emperors in return gained political and philosophical capital through their imperial patronage of the descendants of the First Sage.

In the following pages, I situate the Kongs at the temple in Qufu, the source of much of their influence. I then turn to the Kongs' exploitation of the benefits received from the state to further their dominance of their local region, with remarkably little interference from the central state. In addi-

---

9. For the Kong exemption from the triennial review of serving officials, see *Mingdai dang'an shiliao*, doc. #0011.2, 1: 60–61. Although the privilege of directly memorializing the throne is not stated explicitly, the Kong archive documents have many such memorials from the heads of the lineage during the Ming and Qing as well as records of personal interviews with the emperor in the capital.

10. Strassberg, *The World of K'ung Shangren*, 75–78.

tion, the Kongs used their descent from Confucius and their hereditary titles to develop personal relationships with reigning emperors and to secure marriage alliances with gentry families of national status. Through their wealth and political influence, they maintained their local dominance and national presence for much of the history of imperial China. I conclude with a brief consideration of the benefits that accrued to Ming and Qing dynasts through their support of a sagely lineage with more ancient and venerable antecedents than their own.

THE TEMPLE AT QUFU

The founder of the Han dynasty was the first of many emperors to travel to the Shandong peninsula to honor Confucius at the site of his tomb.[11] According to the Kong records, Han Gaozu (r. 206–195 BCE) himself "entered the temple (*wen miao*) and, after bowing, performed a great sacrifice."[12] Confucius's descendants and disciples had jointly established the temple shortly after his death to store his ritual clothing, caps, musical instruments, utensils, and books.[13] By the time of Han Gaozu's visit, more than two hundred years later, it had evolved from a small hall (*tang* 堂) into a three-room temple (*miao* 廟). The eastern area was dedicated to Kongzi, the middle area to his mother née Yan 顏氏, and the western area to his wife.[14]

Although not every emperor, nor even an emperor from every succeeding dynasty, made a pilgrimage to the temple in Qufu, Han Gaozu's visit set a precedent for the honors due the First Sage and his descendants. Emperors in succeeding dynasties followed Han Gaozu's actions and enfeoffed Kongzi's descendants with hereditary honors and grants of land and periodically assigned revenues for temple renovations. The token of favor in this first imperial visit was the ennobling of the ninth-generation descendant of the First Sage as lord sacrificer (*fengsi jun* 奉祀君),[15] a title about which there is very little information.

The growth of the temple and its outbuildings in Qufu in many ways mirrored the growth of the wealth and privileges of the Kongs themselves.

---

11. Kong Jifen, *Queli wenxian kao* 18.1a.

12. *Kongfu dang'an xuanbian*, #1114, 1: 1.

13. Liang, *Qufu Kongmiao*, p. 6.

14. Ibid., p. 71.

15. Unless otherwise noted, all translations of titles are taken from Hucker, *A Dictionary of Official Titles*. For more about this ninth-generation descendant, see below, pp. 304–6.

From its beginnings as a simple hall to warehouse Confucius's effects,[16] it grew throughout the imperial period. By the Song, it was a large complex, with palaces (*dian* 殿), halls (*ting* 亭), covered verandahs (*lang* 廊), and verandah rooms (*wu* 廡), totaling 316 separately delineated spaces.[17] By the eighteenth century, the main building of the complex, the Hall of Great Completion (Dacheng dian 大成殿), consisted of nine areas, and measured more than 85 feet tall and approximately 155 feet across by 91 feet deep.[18] This was a far cry from the simple building to store Confucius's effects. According to the eighteenth-century gazetteer, the front displayed

stone pillars [carved] with coiled dragons; to the sides and back were stone pillars surmounted by eaves carved with flowers. Amid [the eaves] were cedar wood overhangs ornamented with 486 polished gold dragons. Between [the pillars and the building] were sandalwood crossbeams of five colors with gold interspersed, while yellow tiles covered the [plain uncarved pillars of] stone. Before [the building] was an open space encircled by stone balustrades of two courses, in the center of which was two sets of stairs each having twelve steps.[19]

Although no significant new buildings were added to the temple grounds after the Song, each succeeding dynasty demonstrated support for the temple complex through gifts and occasional imperial processions to the site. The pattern for imperial gifts to the temple was set by the Song period and was followed with additional embellishments by all succeeding dynasties.

As a concrete measure of respect for Confucius, each new dynasty after the Song renovated parts of the complex soon after its founding. This expressed in material form the tradition of a close link between the imperial house and the Kongs.[20] Maintaining the relationship beyond the initial conquest period, the various dynasties continued to support the complex financially, periodically sending funds for upkeep and, more important, for re-

---

16. Pan, *Qufu xianzhi* 5.10b, quotes the *Shiji* to this effect.

17. I am defining *jian* here at this point as "spaces." This particular measure word can either mean spaces, bays, or rooms, depending on the context. For a mid-eighteenth-century description, see Pan, *Qufu xianzhi* 5.9b–14b. For an early twentieth-century description of the complex, see Liang, *Qufu Kongmiao*, p. 74.

18. These measurements are based on multiplying the figures provided by Pan, *Qufu xianzhi* 5.10b, of 78 feet 6 inches tall, and 142 feet 7 inches broad by 84 feet deep by 1.094 as suggested in Saunders, *The Right Word*, p. 255.

19. Pan, *Qufu xianzhi* 5.10b.

20. The Jin renovated the temple in 1142, the Yuan in 1233, the Ming in 1374, the Qing in 1656, and the Republic of China in 1933. See Liang, *Qufu Kongmiao*, pp. 71–85.

building whenever a fire or other disaster damaged the buildings.[21] This financial support could on occasion be considerable. For example, the renovations ordered by the Kangxi emperor in 1691 (Kangxi 30) and carried out by the Board of Works over the next two years cost 86,500 taels to rebuild the 54 bays (*jian* 間) of the Hall of Great Completion, the 61 bays of the gates associated with the hall, the 88 bays of the connected covered verandahs, and the stelae garden.[22] In 1730 (Yongzheng 8), this work was redone after a calamitous fire at a total cost of 157,000 taels.[23] A memorial from the Yansheng Duke, Kong Zhuanze 孔傳澤 (1671–1735), gave a full account of the disaster:

On the late afternoon of the ninth day of the sixth month of this year [1724, or Yongzheng 2] an ill wind and sudden rain with alternating thunder and lightning sprang out, a fire suddenly emerged from the dragon ridge roof of the Hall of Great Completion. The ridge is very steep, it was not possible to extinguish [the fire] . . . it spread to the Hall of Repose (Qin dian 寢殿),[24] its two covered verandahs, the Hall of Great Completion gates, the two stelae gardens of the Kangxi emperor to the east and west, to the old Hall of the King Who Gave Birth to the Sage (Qisheng wang dian 啓聖王殿), and the Hall of Musical Tones (Jin si tang 金絲堂).[25] [All] these places were obliterated by the early morning hours.[26]

Not all these rooms and palaces were set aside for the private use of the Kongs. The heart of the complex, the Hall of Great Completion, housed a central altar to Confucius, and side altars to Mencius, Zeng Sen, Yan Hui, and Kong Ji (Confucius's grandson), as well as smaller shrines to 33 other worthies.[27] Other areas housed records, shrines to lesser worthies, offices of the temple, and repositories of imperial gifts, books, and ritual instruments,

---

21. For a brief account of the major renovations of the complex, see ibid., pp. 5–13. A more detailed account can be found in Kong Jifen, *Queli wenxian kao* 12.4a–11b.

22. Kong Jifen, *Queli wenxian kao* 12.9a.

23. Ibid., 12.10b.

24. According to Pan, *Qufu xianzhi* 5.14a, this hall contains the ancestral tablet of Confucius's mother.

25. According to *Shandong shengzhi* (p. 333), when an old wall of Confucius's dwelling was demolished, the sound of percussion and stringed instruments (*jinshi sizhu zhi sheng* 金石絲竹之聲) was heard, and ancient manuscripts were discovered within; hence the name of the hall.

26. The Yansheng Duke Kong Zhuanze's memorial is quoted in Liang, *Qufu Kongmiao*, p. 12.

27. Pan, *Qufu xianzhi* 5.10b–11a.

as well as side temples for descendants of Confucius's disciples.[28] Still, within the temple complex, the Kongs had their own private ancestral hall, dedicated to the ancestral worship of the senior descent line (dazong 大宗) of the Kong lineage. Originally called the Family Temple (Jia miao 家廟), in 1723 it was combined with the larger Temple for Venerating the Sage (Chongsheng ci 崇聖祠)[29] and incorporated ancestral tablets of Kong descendants of the senior descent line.[30]

Government support of the Family Temple, and the later Temple for Venerating the Sage, distinguished the Kong senior descent line above all other lineages, except the imperial family. The family shrines for Confucius's disciples at the temple in Qufu were not housed in separate buildings, and the worship of the disciples as ancestors occupied a secondary place to their status as Confucius's disciples. Various dynasties allowed tax exemptions for other lineages engaged in charitable works, but seldom were imperial coffers used for building and maintaining a private shrine.[31] That it occurred in Qufu is a result of the confluence of the Kong family's ancestral worship of Confucius and the central role of the temple to Confucius in the state's efforts to maintain its legitimacy.

The initial visit to Qufu by Han Gaozu resulted in the nebulous title of lord sacrificer, which carried more prestige at the national level than economic or political power. However, the emperor's visit started the Kongs' climb to prominence. During the Han dynasty, various Kongs were ennobled and held high offices within the government. For example, at the start of the Han period, Kong Fu 孔鮒 (264–208 BCE), the head of the lineage in the ninth generation, had served as grand mentor for the Qin heir[32] before serving and dying with one of the many contestants trying to succeed to the Qin, Chen She 陳涉.[33] Fu's brother, variously known as Kong Teng 孔騰 or Kong Xiang 孔襄,[34] was first made a general and then lord sacrificer, be-

---

28. For a description of these buildings, see ibid., 5.9b–27a; and Kong Jifen, *Queli wenxian kao* 12:1a–4a.

29. *Shandong shengzhi*, pp. 331–332.

30. Pan, *Qufu xianzhi* 5.13b–14a.

31. See Twitchett, "The Fan Clan's Charitable Estate," pp. 114–30, for the tax-exempt status of a charitable estate.

32. Kong Yuancuo, *Kongshi* 1.5b.

33. Ban Gu, *Han shu* 81.3352.

34. The *Han shu* refers to him as Kong Rang, but Kong Shangren (*Kongzi shi jiapu* 3.7b–8a) lists him as Kong Sheng.

fore being transferred to the new capital of Chang'an as grand mentor (*tai fu* 太傅).[35] The thirteenth-generation descendant, Kong Ba 孔霸, was enfeoffed as Guannei Marquis (關內侯) by the emperor Yuandi (48–32 BCE) on his ascendance to the throne since Ba had served as his tutor while he was the heir apparent.[36]

The political prominence of the Kongs continued until the end of the Former Han dynasty (202 BCE–9 CE). Kong Guang 孔光, a fourteenth-generation descendant, reached the position of imperial counselor but was demoted for advocating the half-brother of the Chengdi emperor as heir to the throne.[37] In the Later Han dynasty (25–220 CE), the Kongs continued to be enfeoffed as Guannei Marquises but did not reach the exalted political prominence of earlier times.[38]

After the Han period, imperial attention to the descendants of the First Sage focused mainly on the site of Qufu; emperors gave the Kongs the localized political power of sinecured appointments in their own county and the economic benefits of a large estate but only the ephemeral power of prestige titles at the national level. Although this was no doubt due in part to the decline of the eastern area of the north macroregion of China,[39] the Kongs nevertheless slowly faded from the national scene until the start of the conquest dynasties at the end of the northern Song, when they once again became feted as living links to Confucius.

Hosting imperial processions was the most visible sign of prestige that the Kong lineage of Qufu received as a result of its reputedly unbroken descent from the First Sage.[40] Other more tangible signs, whether titles, land grants, or special privileges, evolved over time and became more substantial

---

35. For Kong Rang's career as an erudite and grand mentor see Ban Gu, *Han shu* 81.3352.

36. Ibid. Kong Ba is listed in the *Han shu* as the direct descendant of Kong Rang; however, in the Yuan period, Kong Yuancuo (*Kongshi* 1.5b–6b) listed him as the direct descendant of Rang's elder brother, Kong Fu. Finally, Kong Shangren (*Kongzi shi jiapu* 3.7a–9b) followed the *Han shu* without explanation for the change.

37. For details of Kong Guang's dismissal, see Loewe, *Crisis and Conflict*, pp. 264–65. For other details of his career, see Ban Gu, *Han shu* 81.3352–65.

38. For example, Kong Fen 孔奮, a sixteenth-generation descendant, was made a marquis but served only as a commandery aide. For his biography, see Fan Ye, *Hou Han shu* 31.1098–99.

39. See Hartwell, "Demographic, Political, and Social Transformations," pp. 374–89.

40. Kong Shangren, *Kongzi shi jiapu*, "xu," 9b. The claim of unbroken descent is found in the sixty-seventh-generation Yansheng Duke Kong Yuqi's preface to the genealogy.

over the centuries.[41] By the Ming and Qing dynasties, the head of the Kong lineage was a titled duke as a result of centuries of imperial gifts. The Yansheng Duke controlled the rents and tax revenues of a very large estate and was able to claim exemptions from corvée labor for fellow lineage members and from the grain tax on most of his own lands. He could also memorialize the throne directly and have personal interviews with the emperor whenever he traveled to the capital. Both of these invaluable privileges were often used to defend the Kong lineage from the investigating censors. Finally, the duke was allowed to recommend officials to fill various positions within the county government of Qufu and surrounding areas. The first imperial visit by the founder of the Han dynasty to the Kong temple in Qufu had longlasting effects. It set the pattern that had by the late imperial period transformed the Kongs from a family of local repute to a lineage that combined a prestigious descent line with the economic and political power to protect its own interests and members at the national level.

THE STRATEGY OF DESCENT

Various strategies were available to a family in imperial China to preserve or enhance its social position. A common method was identification with the national elite through landownership and participation in the civil service, as demonstrated in Hilary Beattie's study of a Ming-period Anhui lineage, which preserved its status through resource management and education.[42] Another common means was alliances with the local elite through marriage or business ventures, as Robert Hymes points out for Song-period lineages during a chaotic time in Jiangxi.[43] A third possible strategy was to combine the localist strategy with the strategy of identification with the national elite. In a study of Sichuan diaspora elites of the early Yuan (1264–1368), Paul J. Smith found that lineages that successfully re-established themselves within new areas did indeed combine these two strategies. Dispossessed members

---

41. The first reliable record of title the Kongs received was to the thirteenth-generation Ba, in the Han Yuandi era (48–32 BCE). Ba was granted a fief, the rank of Guannei Marquis and the title of Lord Praised for Fulfillment (*baocheng jun* 褒成君) in recognition of his tutoring of the new emperor. See Ban Gu, *Han shu* 81.3352–54. The rank of Guannei Marquis would have exempted Ba from labor service; see Ch'ü, *Han Social Structure*, p. 16. For other land grants starting in the Han, see Kong Yuancuo, *Kongshi juan* 3.

42. Beattie, *Land and Lineage*.

43. Hymes, "Marriage, Descent Groups, and the Localist Strategy."

of Sichuan elite society gained new alliances by transforming their status as part of a supra-local educated elite into patronage networks leading to public office. From public office they then used their positions to amass new landholdings and associate themselves with the elites of their new locality.[44]

The method a particular family chose often depended on a combination of its status, location, and individual circumstances. During times of dynastic upheaval, such as the Song to Yuan transition (1127–1264) or the late Ming, localist strategies were often more effective in maintaining a family's status. During periods of strong central government, such as after the founding of a dynasty, owning land and educating promising youngsters for the civil service examinations were better long-term tactics. Families dispossessed of their landholdings and forced to start over in a new locale often found it best to combine localist strategies with education for the civil service examinations. On the whole, the strategies developed by lineages enabled families to better manage scarce resources and husband them against future times of uncertainty. These strategies also provided an entry into the elite of a new locale if disaster overtook the family. Most lineages in late imperial China were aware of the possible downward mobility awaiting those who lacked talented heirs armed with higher examination degrees. Landholding combined with patronage networks often provided the best guarantee for a lineage's continued examination success.[45]

Although prominent landholders, few Kongs entered government service through the civil service examinations. Of the 25 men named Kong from Shandong's Yanzhou prefecture who attained the highest examination degree (*jinshi* 進士) in the Qing,[46] few attained exalted posts. Of the ten Kongs with *jinshi* degrees who have biographies in the Shandong provincial gazetteer, most had unremarkable careers. Two were unranked secretaries or scholars (*zhushi* 主事 or *xueshi* 學士),[47] two were county magistrates

---

44. Smith, "Family, Landsmann, and Status-Group Affiliation."

45. Ho, *The Ladder of Success.*

46. This figure is from Sun, *Shandong tongzhi, juan* 94–96, on *jinshi* degrees during the Qing. There were a total of 121 *jinshi* degree–earning scholars, of whom 25 have the surname Kong. It is impossible to tell from these lists whether all these men are lineage members or not.

47. Kong Jihan 孔繼涵 (1739–83), son of the sixty-eighth-generation Yansheng Duke, became a secretary for the Ministry of Personnel in Henan, before retiring home to Qufu (Sun, *Shandong tongzhi,* p. 4967). Kong Xianglin 孔祥霖 (1852–1917) was appointed to the

(*zhixian* 知縣),[48] one was an examining editor of the Hanlin Academy (*jiantao* 檢討),[49] two became prefects (*zhifu* 知府),[50] and two were surveillance commissioners (*ancha shi* 按察使).[51] Only one became a provincial-level official, Kong Zhaoqian 孔昭虔 (1775–1835), son of the Hanlin editor mentioned above and great-grandson of a Yansheng Duke. After starting his career at the Hanlin Academy following his 1811 (Jiaqing 6) *jinshi* degree,[52] Zhaoqian became a Jiangxi circuit censor (*dao yushi* 道禦史) before being promoted to provincial administration commissioner (*bu zhengshi* 布政使).[53]

These were respectable careers, but the majority of Kongs from Qufu with long careers in the civil service attained posts solely through the recommendation of the head of the Kong lineage, the Yansheng Duke. The most exalted career belonged to Kong Yuxun 孔毓珣 (d. 1730), a lineage member without an examination degree. He achieved the highly ranked post of Guangxi governor-general in 1723 (Yongzheng 1) after entry into the civil service as a tribute student (*gong sheng* 貢生), a position to which he had been recommended by the duke.[54] One consequence of this ability to at-

---

Hanlin Academy as a bachelor, then traveled as an examiner before retiring to Qufu (*Shandong shengzhi*, p. 224).

48. Kong Qingquan 孔慶銓 (d. 1853), a *jinshi* of 1838 (Daoguang 18) was appointed to Jiaowen county in Zhili, before losing his life in the uprisings of the early Xianfeng reign. Kong Xianzeng 孔憲曾, a *jinshi* of 1877 (Guangxu 3), was appointed as a magistrate in Zhili (Sun, *Shandong tongzhi*, p. 4970).

49. Kong Guangsen 孔廣森 (1752–86), the grandson of the sixty-eighth Yansheng Duke and son of Kong Jifen, was a prodigy who attained a *jinshi* in 1771 (Qianlong 36) at age 20, was appointed to the Hanlin Academy, and retired to travel and study (Sun, *Shandong tongzhi*, p. 4968; Hummel, *Eminent Chinese*, p. 434).

50. Kong Zhuantang 孔傳堂 was a *jinshi* of 1724 (Yongzheng 2), who became the prefect of Zhen'an in Guangxi. He took his duties seriously enough that the people sacrificed to him after his departure (Sun, *Shandong tongzhi*, p. 4965). Kong Zhaoci 孔昭慈 was an 1835 (Daoguang 15) *jinshi*, became a Hanlin bachelor, and then a magistrate in Guangdong before becoming a prefect in Taiwan (ibid., p. 4970).

51. Kong Zhuanke 孔傳柯 was a *jinshi* of 1739 (Qianlong 4) and served as commissioner in Jiangsu (ibid., pp. 4965–966). Kong Qinghu 孔慶瑚 (d. 1854) was an 1836 (Daoguang 16) *jinshi*, appointed as a Hanlin bachelor. He served as a commissioner in Shanxi and Guizhou before retiring in 1854 (Xianfeng 4), five years before his death (ibid., pp. 4966–67).

52. Kong Zhaoqian was appointed a Hanlin bachelor and then assigned as a junior compiler (ibid., p. 4968).

53. Ibid.

54. See biography of Kong Yuxun, in ibid., p. 4961.

tain office through family connections was that there was no reason for Qufu lineage members, whether of the senior descent line or lesser branches, to spend resources forming relationships with higher officials in the civil service. It was easier to attain a civil service appointment through the recommendation of a relative than through an unrelated patron in officialdom.

Nor did the Kongs in government service depend on the bonds commonly formed among the successful participants of particular examinations to build networks of influence and protection to shelter them in their later careers.[55] Their kinship with the reigning Yansheng Duke was a more effective shield than the fellowship of their brother-officials. Even the value of attaining an advanced degree was occasionally overshadowed by the importance of close kinship to the Yansheng Duke. In 1757 (Qianlong 22), the emperor granted Kong Jihan 孔繼涵 (1739–83), a younger son of the sixty-eighth generation Yansheng Duke, the prestige title of Grand Master for Court Discussion after Kong spoke with Qianlong on his southern tour.[56] Fourteen years later, Jihan attained his *jinshi* degree, but was appointed only to the low-ranking post of unrated academician. The highest-ranked official with a *jinshi* degree was the provincial administration commissioner, Kong Zhaoqian, who, perhaps only coincidentally, was a great-grandson of a Duke.

The Kong lineage also did not need to focus on a narrow localist strategy. The Kongs did indeed have considerable local power in the counties surrounding Qufu, but this power was maintained through hereditary landholdings, position, and the influence of officials who were members of the lineage. In 1723 (Yongzheng 1), the Ministry of Rites, after consulting with Kong Yuxun, the governor-general of Guangxi mentioned above, recommended that questions on the Kong family household registration for corvée labor and the tax status of lands should be resolved by the governor of Shandong and the Yansheng Duke in consultation.[57] This removed the de-

---

55. For examples of these types of networks in the collection of works for the *Siku quanshu* and in efforts to promote reform within government, see Guy, *The Emperor's Four Treasures*, pp. 38–67; and Polachek, *The Inner Opium War*, pp. 63–105, respectively.

56. *Shandong shengzhi*, pp. 217–18. In his biography in this modern compilation, he is listed as the son of Kong Zhuanzheng 孔傳鉦. Elsewhere, he is listed as the younger brother of Kong Jihan, which would make him a son of the Yansheng Duke. See Sun, *Shandong tongzhi*, p. 4967.

57. *Qingdai dang'an shiliao*, #4993, 3: 12–19.

cision from the local magistrate's court.[58] Memorials as early as the Shunzhi period (1644–62) bemoaned the difficulties of documenting the tax status of Kong fields or households, since the Kong registers presented to investigating censors did not always distinguish the various tax categories of their landholdings.[59]

In one case, Kong Jifen 孔繼汾 (1721–86), the author of the *Queli wenxian kao*, impeached fellow lineage member Kong Xingshu 孔興抒 for selling land to an outsider without changing the tax status of the land. Kong Jifen was surprised to discover that the land had been registered under his name at the time of the transaction for taxation purposes. Kong Jifen protested this situation because he "believed that the light taxes of the Kongs arose from the dynasty's honor toward the descendants of the Sage," and if abuses were not corrected, "not only will the Kong lineage suffer and gain an empty reputation, but also crafty false men will increasingly use the [tax] regulations to do harm, taking advantage of our lineage members."[60] This case was resolved when the Yansheng Duke reported the situation as an honest bureaucratic mistake on the part of the Kongs. The duke then suggested that since the trouble arose from the county's negligence in preventing the outsider Wang from claiming tax-exempt status on land, greater attention on the county's part "to avoid yamen secretaries from manipulating the facts will be to our mutual benefit."[61]

The Kongs also differed from other landholding families in that the Kong lands were largely grants from the government. The lands were

---

58. In all other areas, the secretary of taxation for each county was responsible for drawing up the tax rolls and corvée registration for the magistrate. If the taxes were not forthcoming, a deadline hearing would be held by the magistrate (see Ch'ü, *Local Government*, pp. 131–39). If the amount or registration was disputed, it was to be investigated thoroughly by the magistrate of the area (see Huang, *A Complete Book*, pp. 232, 235 on taxation, and p. 544 on land registration).

59. An investigating censor sent to Qufu in 1661 concluded that "I sincerely and tremblingly investigate and examine without dependable [results]," due in part to the fact that the Kong tax registers presented were missing the official seal of the household, making them suspect. The other difficulties the censor faced were sworn statements of nonlineage members charging their lands had been seized or purchased by the Kongs and reported to the central government as tax-exempt lands. What made the situation worse, the censor plaintively noted, was that "the Kongs complain of unfair treatment, and adamantly insist [that they have] never at any time [done this]" (*Qingdai dang'an shiliao*, #4086, 6: 9–10).

60. Ibid., #1558.1, 3: 521–22.

61. Ibid., #1558.2, 3: 523–24.

mostly sacrificial fields for the maintenance of rites to the First Sage or lands to be used for the support of needy lineage members and thus were exempt from all corvée taxes.[62] Over the course of the Qing dynasty, there were numerous futile impeachments of the Kongs over the merging of their privately owned fields with sacrificial fields in order to exempt more of their lands from taxes or over their claims that seized lands were wasteland and therefore exempt from taxation.[63] The tax-exempt status of much of their land and the privilege of maintaining that status even after selling the land, combined with the Yansheng Duke's status as the person responsible for investigating irregularities, made the Kong landholdings secure.[64]

Finally, in case of disaster or relocation, the Kongs did not have to trust to luck and innate ability to gain the patronage of officeholders in new locales. They were often feted for their name and imperial connections. After Kong Shangren gave a lecture to the Kangxi emperor, he was received by the Grand Secretary Wang Xi 王熙 (1628–1703), and appointed to the post of erudite by the Ministry of Personnel.[65] When he reached the capital, Kong Shangren attended a banquet with other Kongs given by the Ministry of Rites, and hosted by Zhang Shizhen 張士甄, the minister of rites.[66] Even after the immediate excitement of having given a lecture to the emperor was over, Kong Shangren still gained entry into rarefied social circles wherever he traveled. Within his first year in Yangzhou in 1686, Kong Shangren was hosting poetry parties that attracted the luminaries of that city,[67] and when he returned to Beijing a few years later, still as an erudite, Kong Shangren became intimate with Wang Shizhen 王士禎 (1634–1711), vice minister of the Censorate and the Ministry of War, and Tian Wen 田雯 (1635–1704), vice minister of the Ministries of Revenue and Justice.[68] Since he had not yet written his famous

---

62. For tax-exempt sacrificial lands, see Guo, "Qufu Kongfu yu Ming Qing guizu dizhu," p. 283. For land used as charitable support, see the Board of Rites report of 1723 in *Qingdai dang'an shiliao*, #4993, 3: 12–19.

63. In 1681 another censor reported that Kong Yinfang 孔印方, "who presumes on the Kong surname," had forcibly removed tenants from Pingyin 平陰 county, burning their fields and houses, and then registering the land as wasteland. The censor foresaw no way to force the Kong household to investigate (ibid., #3904, 6: 11–13; see also note 59 to this chapter).

64. *Qingdai dang'an shiliao*, #1558.2, 3: 523–24.

65. Strassberg, *The World of K'ung Shangren*, pp. 114–15.

66. Ibid., p. 116.

67. Ibid., p. 135; for a list of the attendees, see ibid., pp. 363–64n50.

68. Ibid., pp. 217–23.

play, *The Peach Blossom Fan* (1699), Kong Shangren's entry into these high literary and official circles likely owed more to his name than to his own fame.

By the Song period, the Kongs of Qufu were not haunted by fear of future reversals that often dictated the family survival strategies outlined above. According to the eighteenth-century Qufu county gazetteer, the Kongs had already faced the worst during the period of the Five Dynasties (907–60). In Pan Xiang's colorful account, which echoes the information given in the Kongs' 1684 genealogy,[69] Kong Guangsi 孔光嗣, the senior descent line heir and lineage head was assassinated in 912, and his positions and titles were usurped by the descendant of a corvée laborer named Kong Mo 孔末 (see the chapter by Thomas Wilson in this volume, pp. 64–65). The usurpation and assassination were possible because many lineage members had fled the disorder in Qufu during the fall of the Tang dynasty (618–905). At this time, the entire Kong lineage was destroyed, leaving only Kong Guangsi's infant son alive, hidden by his mother at her parents' house. Most ordinary lineages, with their members scattered and their lands lost, would have been unable to recoup their position and faded back into the obscurity from which they emerged. However, due to the special nature of the Kong lineage and its direct connection to Confucius, the ordinary people of Qufu petitioned the officials of the Latter Tang dynasty (923–34) to restore the true descendant of the Sage, Kong Guangsi's son, Renyu 仁玉, and execute the usurper Kong Mo. This was speedily done in 930, resolving the worst crisis the Kongs ever confronted in the history of their lineage.[70]

This detailed account cannot be fully confirmed by contemporary sources. Two Yuan sources, the *Songshi* 宋史 and Kong Yuancuo's 孔元措 *Kongshi zuting guangji* 孔氏祖庭廣記, fail to mention either Guangsi's assassination or Kong Mo's usurpation. The *Songshi* merely mentions that Guangsi became an assistant magistrate (*zhu bu* 主簿) in 905 and performed sacrifices to Confucius. His son Renyu then became assistant magistrate of Qufu in 930. The twenty-five years between the two appointments is passed over without comment, despite the hagiographic details of Renyu's early erudition.[71] Kong Yuancuo also passes over any details, although he clearly intimates that there was some trouble when he obliquely mentions in Kong

---

69. Kong Shangren, *Kongzi shi jiapu* 4.1b–2b.

70. Pan, *Qufu xianzhi* 60.4b–5a.

71. Kong Renyu could understand the *Spring and Autumn Annals* at age nine, and his manner and general appearance were stately (Tuotuo, *Songshi* 431.12814).

Renyu's biography that "for a short time the matter was cut off."[72] Even in the Ming period, the details of Kong Renyu's escape remain obscured. Kong Gonghuang 孔公璜, writing in 1501, mentioned merely that "Renyu survived the adversity of the five seasons of chaos."[73] Whatever the truth of Renyu's miraculous escape or of the request of the people of Qufu to replace the usurper Kong Mo with a "true" Kong, the acquiescence of the Latter Tang dynasty to the request was probably more a result of Kong Mo's inability to collect taxes for the new dynasty rather than the dynasty's recognition of an innate lack within his character. When the Latter Tang gained control of Qufu in 923, they forgave the people's debts and taxes in both 924 and 927, an action that reflected badly on the current officeholder of the area, Kong Mo. The Latter Tang then imposed a special grain excise tax the following year, which was not fulfilled until 931, by the newly appointed assistant magistrate, Kong Renyu. Shortly thereafter, the Latter Tang dynasty renovated the temple to Confucius and promoted Kong Renyu to magistrate (*ling* 令).[74]

The family history of the circumstances surrounding the restoration of Kong Renyu and the proper descent line of the lineage had several lasting effects. It underlined the importance of keeping accurate lineage records of descendants in order to separate the "false" from the true. Significantly, it was an appeal to the ruling dynasty to preserve the purity of the Kong lineage that resolved the crisis, not an appeal to powerful in-laws. The restoration demonstrated that the imperial court would step in and support the rightful duke under certain conditions; this willingness to intercede made the granting of the title of duke a joint decision between the Kongs and the court. The restoration of Kong Renyu and the true lineage by the court demonstrated that the Kongs did not need to align themselves with other families within local elite society for protection.

How, then, are we to characterize the strategy of the Kong lineage? Basically, Kongs depended on their unique status to preserve their social position. They did not earn honors and titles for being a lineage of sages; rather, they rested on the laurels of being the lineage descended directly from the First Sage. Their significant landholdings were due to imperial generosity rather than innate talent. They did not seek official positions or patrons

---

72. Or, "the sacrifices were temporarily discontinued." Kong Yuancuo, *Kongshi* 1.9b.
73. Kong Shangren, *Kongzi shi jiapu*, "Di yi kao" 嫡裔考, 1a.
74. Pan, *Qufu xianzhi* 23:11a–b.

from within their own class, but depended on imperially granted official sinecures. In a supposed meritocracy, with positions open to all based on individual merit, the Kongs did not need to compete. They could guarantee
official positions for their members without recourse to the examination
system. No other lineage retained unrestricted hereditary titles and honors
over more than one dynasty.[75] Unlike other lineages, the Kongs followed
neither a localist nor a national strategy. They were not dependent on patrons from their own class to help them in times of disaster. Instead, their
strategy was to rely on the common blood they shared with Confucius, presenting themselves as the living link to the golden age of the past. In the last
three dynasties of the imperial period, the reigning Yansheng Duke traveled
to the capital to present himself to the new emperor. Kong Yuancuo traveled to Bianjing and confirmed the Kongs' privileges at the beginning of the
Yuan,[76] and both Kong Kejian 孔克堅 (1316–70) and his son Xixue
希學 (d. 1381) met with the Hongwu emperor during the first year of the
Ming for the same purpose.[77] Following the example of his predecessors,
the sixty-fifth Yansheng Duke, Kong Yanzhi 孔衍植 (1592–1647), attended the first Qing emperor in the company of his son Kong Xingxie
孔興燮 (1636–72).[78]

Thus, the Kongs stood alone among the class of educated elite. They
were the only lineage whose members never had to present proof of their
ability, only of their birth. They depended on a special relationship with the
ruling dynasty that was based on their descent from the First Sage, Kongzi.
The imperial house recognized the Kongs as the epitome of the Confucian
order and thus granted the Kongs their lands and sinecures in recognition of
their unique position in Chinese society.[79] Every dynasty in the late imperial

---

75. A limited exception to this statement is the eldest descendant of the Mengs 孟, Yans
顏, Zengs 曾, Zhongs 仲, and Quzhou Kongs, who were granted the title of erudite of the
Five Classics during the Ming dynasty, a sinecure reconfirmed by the Qing dynasty. Their
erudite status, however, depended on a qualifying examination of the candidate, a requirement never demanded of the Qufu Kongs (Kong Jifen, *Queli wenxian kao* 18.3b–4a).

76. For a description of a Yuan stele commemorating this event, see Xiao, "Da Menggu,"
p. 268.

77. *Mingdai dang'an shiliao*, #0006.1, 1: 5.

78. *Qingdai dang'an shiliao*, #6308.6, 3: 58–59.

79. Xiao Minqing ("Da Menggu," pp. 268–72) places this development at the beginning of
the Yuan period as part of the strategy of reassurance by the Mongol conquerors to the Han
people that the new dynasty would support Confucian orthodoxy and hence the culture of
the central plains.

period upheld the previous honors given to Confucius's descendants. The Kongs capitalized on the respect shown to their ancestor and the precedents of earlier times to maintain their status nationally and to uphold their position in local society.

WEALTH AND DESCENT

All members of the Kong lineage shared in the benefits of belonging to a wealthy family, but the bulk of the wealth was concentrated in the senior descent line of the northern branch of the Kongs. The lineage had been split into two parts when the forty-eighth-generation Yansheng Duke retreated with the Song dynasty to the south before the Jin (1115–1234) invaders. The younger brother of the duke, Kong Duancao 孔端操, who was left behind in Qufu to meet the invaders, was honored by the Jin as the temporary Yansheng Duke.[80] From the forty-ninth generation on, the northern branch, which resided in the ancestral home and descended from the younger brother of a duke who fled, was granted the titles and lands that had always gone to the eldest son of the senior descent line.[81] The southern branch, established in the Quzhou 衢州 area of Zhejiang province during the Southern Song period (1127–1279) by the forty-eighth-generation Duke, Kong Duanyou 孔端友, finally renounced its claims to titles and lands during the Yuan dynasty.[82] The northern branch retained the dukedom and the lands, and in 1506 (Zhengde 1), the Ming dynasty granted the eldest in the southern senior descent line the hereditary title of erudite of the Five Classics (*wujing boshi* 五經博士).[83] Previously, this title had been reserved for the second son of the Yansheng Duke or for selected descendants of the Worthies, the disciples of Confucius, who lived in the Qufu area. The imperial awarding of a hereditary erudite position to the southern branch clarified the descent line of the Sage by giving priority to the northern branch. From the Ming period on, senior heirs of the southern branch were the recipients of an erudite position that clearly labeled them as the cadet line. The title of Yansheng Duke was no longer contested, yet the situation also raised the is-

---

80. Kong Shangren, *Kongzi shi jiapu* 4.9a–b.
81. Tuotuo, *Jinshi* 105.2311.
82. Strassberg, *The World of K'ung Shangren*, 22.
83. Kong Jifen, *Queli wenxian kao* 18.3a.

sue of how a descent line was drawn up and to how many ancestors it was proper to sacrifice.

Normally the senior descent line (*dazong* 大宗) is calculated strictly by genealogical descent. Starting in the Song period, ritualists suggested following the descent-line system of the ancient Zhou period (1122–255 BCE) by having the eldest son, the descent line heir, carry out rites to the ancestors stretching back into the past, whereas younger sons were to sacrifice only to the previous four generations.[84] Because of Zhu Xi's 朱熹 (1130–1200) promotion of this system, it became widely accepted after his death with the publication of his book on family rituals.[85] However, even though the system received imperial sanction from the Yuan to the Qing periods, Zhu Xi's insistence on limiting sacrifices to only the four previous generations was seldom followed.[86] Most lineages, besides the Kong family, followed the practice of sacrificing to a focal ancestor far removed from the prescribed four generations. In this regard, the Kong's senior descent line heir's sacrifice to a distant ancestor was not unusual.

The splitting of the lineage during the Southern Song (1126–1279) made the northern Kong branch the cadet line, according to the rules of genealogical descent. Yet from the Yuan period on, the northern Kongs were acknowledged as the possessors of the titles and land previously held by the senior descent line.[87] In the early Qing genealogy, the northern branch of the Kongs brushed aside the entire question of seniority in the brief biography of the forty-eighth-generation duke, Kong Duanyou. An abrupt statement relates that Duanyou established his family in Zhejiang province after joining the Song emperor's retinue in the south and "hereafter [his record] is not set down."[88] What makes this entry more telling is that the editor, Kong Shangren of the northern Kongs, did not state whether Duanyou had sons, a departure from every other important entry. Furthermore, Kong Shangren included in this 1684 genealogy a treatise originally written in 1501 by a fellow lineage member Kong Gonghuang. The treatise, entitled *Record of the Legal Descendants*, demonstrates in a few brief pages that the senior descent line of the southern branch had died out within a few generations of the

---

84. Ebrey, *Confucianism and Family Rituals*, pp. 45–67.
85. Ibid., pp. 104–8.
86. Ibid., pp. 150–54.
87. See Guo, "Kong xing zongpu," pp. 200–201.
88. Kong Shangren, *Kongzi shi jiapu* 4.9a.

north-south split with the death of Kong Zhu 孔洙 (d. 1316), the fifty-third-generation descendant in the line of Duanyou, who, the treatise asserts, had no heirs, despite spurious claims by the southern branch in the fifteenth century; Kong Zhu's death made the problem of seniority a moot question. To the late Ming author Kong Gonghuang and the later Qing editor Kong Shangren, the true descent line of the Kong lineage had reverted to the northern branch by the beginning of the Yuan.[89]

Although the northern branch was demonstrably not the senior descent line of the lineage, by virtue of being in the right place at the right time it secured recognition as the senior descent line. Regardless of Kong Gonghuang's accusation that the southern branch had attempted to alter the ancestral temple and "usurp" the genuine (north) senior descent line's place,[90] the northern branch's assumption of seniority remained an act of faith, not proof. Still, the northern branch's assertion that it was the senior descent line shows that although the northern Kongs may have emphasized their right as the direct descendants of Confucius to their various honors, their rhetoric, like that of their southern cousins, cannot withstand strict scrutiny. The answer to this genealogical anomaly may lie in the possession of the ancestral mansion and its environs.

The Kong manor, situated directly to the east of the Qufu temple complex, was started in the early Ming. Previously Kong descendants had lived in an attached building on the temple grounds.[91] As the family grew, space became limited, until in 1377 (Hongwu 10) a mansion was built by imperial order for the Yansheng Duke.[92] The mansion was originally intended for the family of the Yansheng Duke, but it was enlarged in 1504 (Hongzhi 16) to include offices for the lineage and living quarters for members of the senior descent line after a disastrous fire in 1499 (Hongzhi 12/6/16) destroyed much of the temple grounds.[93] From the Ming on, the mansion was

89. Ibid., "Di yi kao" 1a–3b; Wilson, "The Ritual Formation of Confucian Orthodoxy," pp. 571–77; and pp. 70–71 of this volume.

90. Kong Shangren, *Kongzi shi jiapu*, "Di yi kao" 3a.

91. *Shandong shengzhi*, pp. 483–85.

92. Pan, *Qufu xianzhi* 28.5b.

93. This fire, like the one in 1730, according to the grand coordinator of Shandong (the Ming equivalent of governor-general) was also started by a summer thunderstorm. The damage from this fire was repaired in 1503 (Hongzhi 17) at a total cost of 52,600 taels (see ibid., 29.5b–7a).

enlarged, rebuilt, and embellished until it encompassed over thirteen acres (80 *mu* 畝) of land and more than five hundred delineated spaces.[94]

Before construction of the Yansheng Duke's mansion, the Kongs were differentiated from all other lineages by being housed within a temple complex. They lived at government expense and were clearly connected to the worship of Confucius through their blood relationship. After the separation of the Kong living space from the temple, the Kongs were further set apart. They remained connected with the religious aspects of the worship of Confucius, but they also now lived in a mansion adjoining the complex maintained at government expense for the noble descendants of non-imperial dukes. The possessors of such exalted living arrangements could not be taken lightly by new dynasties.

By legitimizing the residents of the Kong manor, new dynasties avoided complications. It was at once an assertion of imperial will and a reward for the Kongs' future support. If a reigning duke fled and could not easily be brought back, the new dynasty simply enfeoffed a duke from among the available candidates. This situation occurred in 1133 with the enfeoffment of Kong Fan 孔璠 (d. 1140), the nephew of Duanyou, by both the short-lived client state of the Jin, the Qi, and in 1140, by the Jin themselves.[95] The Jin choice of the residents of the manor, rather than installing the true scion of the senior descent line, tied the new duke to the new dynasty and eliminated whatever advantage to the Southern Song dynasty of having the support of the only surviving Yansheng Duke. The advantage to the Kongs was to have, in effect, a foot in every dynastic camp. If fortune turned against the invaders, the original duke could return home unsullied by association with rebellious would-be usurpers. Alternatively, if found in the wrong camp, like the forty-ninth-generation duke, Kong Fan, who had accepted a title from the Qi dynasty, the duke could depend on his descendants to ignore the incident. According to Kong Fan's biography in the 1684 genealogy, although "the false dynasty of Qi 偽齊 [founder] Liu Yu 劉豫 wanted to enfeoff him as the Yansheng Duke, he did not accept this temporary management of affairs."[96]

---

94. *Shandong shengzhi*, p. 485. For calculations of relative value, one *da* 大 or great *qing* 頃 is equal to three *guanqing* 官頃, or official *qing*. There are 100 *mu* per *qing*. Since the mu is equal to 0.164 acres, this would be approximately 13 acres. For these measurements, see Saunders, *The Right Word*, p. 255.

95. Tuotuo, *Jinshi* 105.2311.

96. Kong Shangren, *Kongzi shi jiapu* 4.10b.

If, for future dynasts, the prospect of assuring the goodwill of the Kongs was not sufficient in itself to prevent pillage, there was the daunting prospect of becoming known as the desecrators of the First Sage's grave and the murderers of his direct descendants. Even bandits could be leery of treading on the sacred grounds of Qufu. In 1641, for example, the sixty-fifth-generation Yansheng Duke, Kong Yanzhi, climbed the city walls and exhorted "bandits" from the Zhili border to break off their siege of the town by "making public the advantages and disadvantages, reciting on loyalty and virtue, whereupon the people bowed down like a net, cried with emotion and dispersed."[97]

The northern branch's hereditary titles were more than a matter of prestige. Considerable economic power accompanied the titles through land grants and tax benefits added by various emperors. Kong family tradition places the receipt of their first title and lands from Han Gaozu on his visit to Qufu,[98] although evidence would suggest that the hereditary titles originated later in the Han period when the title of Guannei Marquis was granted to thirteenth-generation Kong Ba in the Yuandi era.[99] This first inheritable title of Praising Perfection Marquis (Baocheng hou 褒成侯), bestowed on the sixteenth generation of Kongs, was accompanied by a grant of 2,000 households (hu 戶) to support sacrifices to the First Sage.[100] These lands and households were added to previous grants of lands and 1,800 households.[101] Thus, by the middle of the Han, the Kongs were the owners of a considerable estate, with at least 3,800 imperially granted households providing financial support for sacrifices to Confucius in the Kong temple.

Wealth and land grants continued to roll into the coffers of the Kong lineage over succeeding centuries. Although the Kongs' fortunes and numbers fluctuated over time, every reversal due to chaotic conditions of dynastic decline was usually offset by the succeeding dynasty's generosity to the heirs of the First Sage. The most spectacular example of this was Ming Taizu's grant in 1368 (Hongwu 1) to the Kongs of 98,400 acres (or 2,000 *da*

---

97. Kong Yanzhi was also known by the name Kong Yinzhi 孔胤植 (ibid., 5.13a).
98. *Kongfu dang'an xuanbian*, #1114, 1: 1.
99. See Ban Gu, *Han shu* 81,3353.
100. Kong Jifen, *Queli wenxian kao* 18.2b.
101. Ibid., 18.1a–2b.

qing 大頃, or 6,000 *qing* of lands).[102] In 1644 (Shunzhi 1), the first emperor of the Qing reconfirmed this grant.[103] Generosity of this magnitude allowed the Kongs to amass over 164,000 acres, or approximately 256 square miles of land by the middle of the Qing dynasty.[104] At the same time, the Kongs also maintained imperially granted households as tenants. This privilege gave the Kongs a large pool of able-bodied men exempt from both grain taxes and government corvée work to serve the ancestral temple[105] and to perform work for the Kongs themselves.[106]

As a result of the imperially granted lands amounting to nearly 100,000 acres during the Qing period, along with other privately accumulated lands, the Kongs were safe from the rapid changes in fortunes that other families of considerable wealth had to fear. The only concern of the Kongs was to maintain their special status as the descendants of the First Sage, through their possession of the Kong manor and lands. This was, after all, the well-spring of their wealth, security, and social position.

GUARANTORS OF WEALTH
AND STATUS

For maintaining the special position of the Kongs during the Ming and Qing periods, the Yansheng Duke was the Kongs' advocate to the world outside Qufu. The title Yansheng Duke was first granted in the Song dynasty,[107] and holders of the title did not have significant powers outside the locale of Qufu until the Ming dynasty. Starting in the Hongwu period of the Ming, the duke was accorded privileges as a high official on a national scale. Previously the Yansheng Duke was often treated as a prestige title, but, from the first year of the Hongwu reign, the emperor ordered that newly granted prestige titles were not to be considered on par with the enfeoffment and that the Yansheng Duke was to "stand in court audiences in

---

102. Ibid., 18.2b. The grant by Ming Taizu, reconfirmed by Qing Shunzhi, was for 98,400 acres, or approximately 154 square miles of land at 640 acres per square mile. For conversion rates, see note 94 to this chapter.

103. *Da Qing Shizu zhang huangdi shi lu* 9.6b (dated Shunzhi 1/10/2).

104. Guo, "Qufu Kongfu yu Ming Qing guizu dizhu," p. 284.

105. Ibid., p. 286.

106. Ibid., p. 291.

107. Kong Jifen, *Queli wenxian kao* 18.1b. The senior descent line had been ennobled with various titles from the Han period on, starting in 1 CE (ibid., 18.1a–2b).

the second row to [the rear of] the Grand Secretaries, ... in the row before various civil officials."[108] The duke attended audiences standing behind the highest-ranking officials in the land but before all others. At the same time, the duke was presented with clothing, "thereupon making it the custom that court clothes, ducal clothes, and ordinary clothes were all of the first rank."[109] Thus, by the beginning of the Ming, the Yansheng Duke ranked with the highest officials in the land, both in imperial audiences and in everyday life.

The privileges granted to the Yansheng Duke also extended to his sons. In the Ming, the duke enjoyed the hereditary protection privilege (yin 蔭) of an official of the second degree. In 1645 (Shunzhi 2), the Qing gave the duke the same protection privilege of an official of the first rank.[110] The duke's *yin* privilege exceeded the usual privilege of qualifying one or more sons for official position; his first three sons were appointed to hereditary positions upon their fifteenth year.[111]

The hereditary positions of the first three sons of the Yansheng Duke were clearly specified. The eldest son was recognized as the next Yansheng Duke and granted the rank of 2a at age fifteen or at his ascension as duke.[112] The second son was given the title of Hanlin erudite of the Five Classics

---

108. Ibid., 18.2a.

109. Ibid.

110. Ibid., 18.3a.

111. Pan Xiang, Kong Shangren, and Kong Jifen are unclear about the exact parameters of the *yin* privilege. The biography of the sixty-second-generation Kong Wenshi 孔聞詩 in the 1684 genealogy (Kong Shangren, *Kongzi shi jiapu* 5.9a) states that his father, Kong Hongtai 孔弘泰, was made Hanlin erudite of the Five Classics due to the *yin* privilege. Since his father was the second son of the sixtieth-generation Yansheng Duke, this implies the *yin* privilege was used for the position of Hanlin erudite of the Five Classics, erudite of the Court of Imperial Sacrifice, and either an unnamed post, or the position of Yansheng Duke. However, since no biography of a Hanlin erudite of the Five Classics, including that of Kong Hongtai himself (Kong Shangren, *Kongzi shi jiapu* 5.7a–b), states that their position was due to the Yansheng Duke's *yin* privilege, the granting of the *yin* privilege remains slightly ambiguous. Furthermore, since no Yansheng Duke of the Qing period as reported by Kong Shangren's genealogy had four sons, the exact number of sons who could be sheltered under the *yin* privilege remains unclear. However, it is entirely possible that other arrangements could be made for additional sons. The above-mentioned *jinshi* Kong Jihan was the younger son of a duke and received a prestige title from the emperor after an interview. His younger brother Kong Jisu 孔繼涑, the fifth son, was engaged to the daughter of a prominent official at an early age. See note 135 to this chapter and associated text.

112. *Mingdai dang'an shiliao*, #0001, 2: 30; Kong Jifen, *Queli wenxian kao* 18.3a.

(*Hanlin wujing boshi* 翰林五經博士) and performed sacrifices in the Middle Path Academy (Zhongtang shuyuan 中堂書院) with a rank of 8a.[113] The Middle Path Academy was located in Zou 鄒 county, directly south of Qufu, and held sacrifices four times a year in a small temple to both the grandson of Confucius, Zisi, and the Second Sage, Mencius.[114] The Duke's third son lived in the neighboring county of Wenshang 汶上 and performed sacrifices at the Sagely Graced Academy (Shengze shuyuan 聖澤書院),[115] with the rank of 7a[116] and the title of erudite of the Court of Imperial Sacrifice (*taichang boshi* 太常博士).[117] Wenshang county was located east northeast of Qufu and held sacrifices four times a year to the First Sage and his disciples Yan Hui and Zeng Sen.[118] Furthermore, sons of the Duke's concubines were eligible for the post of erudite of the Five Classics in the absence of a second son of the legal wife. If no concubine's son was available, a close relation of the Duke could be substituted.[119] No other holders of hereditary erudite status enjoyed such favors.[120]

The Yansheng Duke's first three sons were thus exempt from the pressures faced by most children of high officials. They were born to a sinecure, purely through their descent from Confucius. As the sons of the Yansheng Duke, they were also exempt from the qualifying examination given all other hereditary erudites in their fifteenth year by the Ministry of Rites.[121] They grew up in a magnificent mansion, with over 500 rooms, that housed the Duke's immediate family and the offices and officials necessary to run a large estate.[122] From their earliest days, the sons of the Yansheng Duke knew exactly what position they would occupy in the world. Most important, in their respective capacities as the next Yansheng Duke, Hanlin erudite of the Five Classics, and the erudite of the Court of Imperial Sacrifice, the three eldest sons of the Duke were accustomed to traveling to court and

---

113. Kong Jifen, *Queli wenxian kao* 18.3a.

114. Ibid., 13.2b–3a.

115. *Qingdai dang'an shiliao*, #0079.3, 3: 2.

116. Marta Hanson has questioned the ambiguity of having the third son outrank the second son; this is obviously a point that needs further research.

117. Kong Jifen, *Queli wenxian kao* 18.4b–5a.

118. Ibid., 13.2a–b.

119. *Qingdai dang'an shiliao*, #0064.4, 3: 9.

120. Kong Jifen, *Queli wenxian kao* 18.4b.

121. Ibid., 18.3b–4a.

122. *Shandong shengzhi*, p. 146.

attending imperial interviews and rites performed at the capital. Of course, other members of the Kong lineage did not have the same security or exalted privileges, yet they still had the knowledge that they belonged to a powerful lineage with a recognized close tie to the imperial court.[123]

GUARANTORS OF LOCAL DOMINANCE

In addition to their hereditary titles and lands, the Kongs also controlled a number of official posts that were set aside for the benefit of the descendants of the First Sage. The Yansheng Duke recommended candidates for the posts of four different instructors (*xuelu* 學錄) at separate schools; over 80 official positions to supervise sacrifices and incense at the Temple of the Sage under the heading of temple functionaries; the positions of lineage elder; archivist (*dianji* 典籍); music director (*ciyue* 祠樂); state farms clerk (*tuntian guan'gou* 屯田管句); seal keeper (*zhiyin* 知印); Hall of Books copyist (*shuxie* 書寫); agent (*zouchai* 奏差); and miscellaneous other postings, such as the 100 householders who maintained the cemetary temple.[124] The qualifications of these officeholders did not include passing an examination, nor were they subject to the usual triennial review by the Ministry of Personnel.[125] These positions ensured that the Kongs maintained an imposing presence in Qufu county, and the posting of the Duke's younger sons to neighboring counties spread their influence farther afield in Shandong province. The only necessary qualification for these posts was the Kong surname or the recommendation of the Yansheng Duke.

The final post recommended by the duke in Qufu was that of the district magistrate. In the Tang this position was held originally by the Duke for the Propagation of Culture (*wenxuan gong* 文宣公), a forerunner to the title of Yansheng Duke. By Song times, the custom was to fill this post with the third son of the Yansheng Duke, the erudite of the Court of Imperial Sacrifice. Finally, by the Ming dynasty the office was made into a hereditary posting for members of the lineage on the recommendation of the Yansheng

---

123. Again, Kong Shangren's experience at Yangzhou and Beijing, mentioned above, is telling. Although Shangren was no doubt charming, to imagine that a lowly erudite could easily be accepted into the homes and entertainments of the most senior officials of the realm is doubtful.

124. Kong Jifen, *Queli wenxian kao* 18.3a–7a.

125. *Mingdai dang'an shiliao*, #0011.2, 0011.8, 1: 60–64.

Duke.[126] Despite instances of considerable malfeasance, including, but not limited to, accusations of murder by hire, seduction, extortion, and gambling,[127] the Kongs served as the Qufu magistrate until the middle of the Qing period.

In 1756 (Qianlong 21) the post of Qufu magistrate was stripped from the Kongs and turned into an appointment granted by the central government. The precipitating factor was not the direct result of misuse of the post, but a dispute between the seventieth-generation Yansheng Duke, Kong Guangqi 孔廣棨, and a neighboring magistrate over the corvée duty assessed to the Kong temple households of Zou county. Because of this quarrel, the Kongs lost the hereditary post of magistrate for Qufu county, the duke had his salary cut in half for nine years, and the imperial court ordered an investigation into the registration of Kongs in the Kong lineage.[128] This left the Kongs with only the lament that their privilege of appointing the magistrate "has been done away with and is not being carried out, thereby not using [the ancient customs] honoring the First Sage."[129]

The loss of the appointment was a blow to the duke's control of Qufu but not a lasting one. As Bai Zhongshan 百鍾山, the governor-general of Shandong, pointed out in 1756 (Qianlong 21), "Every time [the recommendation of the duke's candidate] was considered, it was for [the duke's] personal gain. If the candidate was timid and weak, he would submit to influence and pressure; if the candidate was competent, then all matters would be obstructed."[130] Bai's recommendation that the post be changed to a regularly appointed official did nothing to ameliorate the underlying problem; namely, the influence of the Yansheng Duke. Any magistrate appointed to Qufu county was cognizant of the wealth of the Kong lineage. In addition, the Kongs' frequent trips to the capital and the occasional imperial procession to Qufu soon laid to rest any doubts about their political influence.

---

126. Kong Jifen, *Queli wenxian kao* 18.7a–b.

127. Magistrate Kong Hongyi 孔弘毅 was removed from office in 1636 by request of the Yansheng Duke for official malfeasance and murder (see *Mingdai dang'an shiliao*, #0004.1, 2, 3, and 5, 1: 46–52). In 1741, Magistrate Kong Yuju 孔毓琚 was impeached by the seventieth Yansheng Duke for nine crimes (*Qingdai dang'an shiliao*, #0309.1, 3: 137–39). For other communications on this last troubled magistrate, see "Qianlong liunian Yansheng gong yu Qufu zhixian hujie an."

128. He et al., *Fengjian guizu*, pp. 26–28.

129. Kong Jifen, *Queli wenxian kao* 18.7b.

130. *Qingdai dang'an shiliao*, #0311.1, 3: 48.

Any chance of maintaining the Qufu magistracy as an impartial appointment, responsible only to the central government and above all possible local influence, was permanently lost in 1773 (Qianlong 37) by the spectacular marriage of Kong Xianpei 孔憲培, the heir of the seventieth-generation Yansheng Duke, to the daughter of Yü Minzhong 于敏中 in Beijing. The engagement and ensuing matrimonials were so infused with signs of special imperial favor that it gave rise to the rumor, which lingers even today, of a Yansheng Duke contracting a marriage with a Qing imperial princess.[131] Although not of imperial blood, Yü Minzhong was a grand secretary,[132] and thus this marriage demonstrated the influential relationship the Kongs could claim with both the emperor and his highest officials.

The marriage of the future Yansheng Duke to the daughter of a grand secretary was neither the first nor the last impressive marriage the Kongs were to contract during the late imperial period. During the Ming, the Kongs' record had been even more impressive: three Kongs of the sixty-second generation had married into the imperial family itself; one married the granddaughter of an emperor, and two married great-granddaughters.[133] The Yansheng Duke of that generation also married an imperial relative, the daughter of Li Dongyang 李東陽 (1447–16) and his third wife, who was herself the daughter of Zhu Yi 朱儀 (1427–96), the third Duke of Chengguo (Chengguo gong 成國公).[134]

Because of the Qing's ban on Han-Manchu intermarriages, the marriage alliances of the Kongs were more often to other well-connected national officeholders than to the imperial family. The fifth son of the sixty-eighth-generation Yansheng Duke was engaged to the daughter of the future president of the Ministry of Punishments, Zhang Zhao 張照, at an early age.[135] The poetess Kong Luhua 孔 椔華,[136] the granddaughter of Kong Xianpei,

---

131. Du, "Qianlong zi nü."

132. Hummel, *Eminent Chinese*, pp. 942–44.

133. See the biographies of Kong Wenhan 孔聞翰, Wenpin 聞聘, and Wenru 聞儒, in Kong Shangren, *Kongzi shi jiapu* 5.9b.

134. For Li Dongyang's biography, see Goodrich and Fang, *Dictionary of Ming Biography*, pp. 877–81. I owe this glimpse of an imperial marriage to the Kong family to Julia Murray's paper "The Temple of Confucius" presented at the 1995 Association for Asian Studies, p. 59.

135. For Kong Jisu 孔繼涑, see Sun, *Shandong tongzhi*, p. 4969; for Zhang Zhao, see Hummel, *Eminent Chinese*, pp. 24–25.

136. For a sketch of the life of Kong Luhua, see Mann, "Learned Women," pp. 27–46.

herself married another grand secretary, Ruan Yuan 阮元 (1764–1849).[137]
The seventy-fifth-generation Yansheng Duke married the granddaughter of
Peng Yunzhang 彭蘊章, minister of the Ministry of War.[138] Their son,
Kong Lingyi 孔令貽, the seventy-sixth-generation Yansheng Duke, married the daughter of a grand minister of state (junji dachen 軍機大臣), Sun
Yuwen 孫毓汶.[139] These marriage alliances demonstrate that the Kongs
were considered part of the national elite. They did not formulate political
policy, but they married the daughters and granddaughters of those who
did.

However, in the Ming and Qing period, the naming of the local magistrate was still the most visible means of preserving the Kongs' power. From
1368 (Hongwu 1) until 1756 (Qianlong 21), as both the Ministry of Rites and
the Ministry of Personnel pointed out, "all the departments [zhou 州] and
districts [xian 縣] under heaven have centrally appointed Magistrates, only
Qufu uses the Kong lineage to lead the people."[140] Only in Qufu was the
magistrate not held to the law of avoidance in imperial China, a measure designed to prevent an official from serving in his native province and thereby
limit possible conflicts of interest.[141] In Qufu, the magistrate was definitely
related to most of the people under his charge, and furthermore, he was a
junior relation of the head of the most prominent local family, the Yansheng
Duke. By having the Yansheng Duke select the candidate for the post until
1756, Qufu county was governed almost as a private preserve of the duke and
his family. Even after the abolition of this hereditary office, the centrally appointed magistrate of Qufu county was definitely an interloper in what had
been a private sinecure for over 800 years. As such, the chances for an independent magistrate nurturing the emperor's subjects against all private and
local interests were slim even before the 1773 marriage in the capital of the
future Yansheng Duke to the daughter of one of the most powerful officials

---

137. For Ruan Yuan's distinguished career, see Hummel, Eminent Chinese, pp. 399–402.

138. Qingdai dang'an shiliao, #5476.9, 3: 35–40. For Peng Yunzhang's biography, see Hummel, Eminent Chinese, pp. 620–21.

139. Qingdai dang'an shiliao, #6316.1, 3: 61–62. For Sun Yuwen's biography, see Hummel,
Eminent Chinese, pp. 683–85.

140. This discussion is reported in a Ministry of Personnel discussion of Shandong governor-general Fang Daxian's 方大獻 memorial on respecting Ming institutions regarding the
Kongs in order to pacify Shandong (see Qingdai dang'an shiliao, #0079.3, 3: 2). This phrase is
also used in a Yongzheng document from the Ministry of Rites (see ibid., #4993, 3: 12–19).

141. Watt, The District Magistrate, 20.

in the land under the eyes of a fond emperor. The duke was in effect the most visible and prominent government official in his own home county.

This combination of vast landholdings, hereditary titles, and the power to name the local magistrate, along with the steady stream of imperial favor, gave the Kongs immeasurable security. The Kongs had little reason to fear the fall of their lineage into abject poverty through a reversal of fortune or a weakening of the moral fiber of their line.

CONCLUSION

Through the prerogatives of the Yansheng Duke and the compliance of the Qufu magistrate, the Kong lineage was able to maintain its position in late imperial China. The duke's privilege of memorializing the emperor directly and his frequent travel to the capital for ceremonial visits ensured the Kong lineage of a powerful advocate with personal ties with the emperor and the highest officials of the central state. The personal relationship with the emperor developed in the late Ming and early Qing through the Yansheng Duke's appointment as tutor to the heir apparent.[142] The most striking example of this relationship was the Yongzheng emperor, who sent his personal physician with a supply of ginseng to Kong Yuqi upon learning that his old tutor, the sixty-seventh Yansheng Duke, was ailing.[143] (Unfortunately, the attentions of the physician and the ginseng were ineffective, and Yuqi died shortly thereafter.) With the addition of marriage alliances to various grand secretaries, the reigning Kong duke could easily maintain the peculiar status of his lineage.

In terms of local dominance, the official government posts at the disposal of the Yansheng Duke as the head of the Kong lineage made Qufu a county that owed more to a powerful local family than it did to the state. With these advantages, there was good reason for the Kongs to call themselves

---

142. Starting with the sixty-fifth-generation descendant, Kong Yanzhi, in 1627, the Yansheng Dukes were appointed as tutors to the heir apparent (*taizi taibao* 太子太保, *taizi taifu* 太傅, *taizi shaobao* 少保, *taizi shaofu* 少傅) until the death of the sixty-seventh Yansheng Duke Kong Yuqi in 1723. Although the post was no doubt largely ceremonial in nature, it still brought the Kongs into personal contact with the last two emperors of the Ming and the first four emperors of the Qing period. For a brief biography of these Yansheng Dukes and details of their entitlement as tutors see Pan, *Qufu xianzhi* 60.12a–13b.

143. *Qingdai dang'an shiliao*, #0064.4, 3: 7–9.

"the First Family of China,"[144] a feeling reflected in the common saying "Under heaven there are two-and-one-half rich and noble families; one family being the Zhang Daoist teachers, one family being the Kong sagely men, and one-half being the dynastic emperor."[145] The Kong lineage maintained its status during the late imperial period by capitalizing on the privileges it received as descendants of the First Sage.

The question remains why the various dynasties allowed and even encouraged the growth of the Kong lineage's local sphere of influence. One possible answer is that the southeastern portion of Shandong, where Qufu is located, was historically a troublesome area,[146] plagued by frequent flooding, roving bandits, and crop failures. Allowing a local family to keep control may have been less costly than exerting a direct imperial presence. This cannot be the complete answer, however, since many places in imperial China suffered from these same conditions, and the imperium did not allow a local family to exercise such uncontested dominance.

Another issue raised by the uncontested power and prestige of the Kongs is the surprising lack of imperial concern about this influential lineage. This contrasts with the Qing emperors' concern with the growth of powerful lineages in the south of China. The answer, lies, I believe, in the tight connection of the Kongs with the imperial state. As the descendants of Confucius, the Kongs were committed to living in an ordered world. The idea of an ordered world was based on Kongzi's notion of the five important relationships: ruler and minister, father and son, older brother and younger brother, husband and wife, friends. Throughout imperial times, the Kongs served as loyal ministers who rectified the world through their behavior. By supporting the ruling dynasty, the Kongs demonstrated their belief in the imperial system, if not a particular ruler. Their ambitions remained safely confined to the role of loyal ministers. In return, they received unprecedented honors and wealth from the ruling dynasty. For the imperial dynasts, this transaction symbolized and simultaneously proved their right to the Mandate of Heaven.

---

144. See Kong Demao and Ke Lan, *In the Mansion.*
145. Luo, "Kongfu dang'an zai yanjiu," p. 290.
146. Perry, *Rebels and Revolutionaries.*

WORKS CITED

Ban Gu 班固. *Han shu* 漢書. Beijing: Zhonghua shuju, 1962.

Beattie, Hilary J. *Land and Lineage in China: A Study of T'ung-ch'eng County, Anhwei, in the Ming and Ch'ing Dynasties*. Cambridge, Eng.: Cambridge University Press, 1979.

Ch'ü, T'ung-tsu. *Han Social Structure*. Ed. Jack L. Dull. Seattle: University of Washington, 1972.

————. *Local Government Under the Ch'ing*. Cambridge, Mass.: Harvard University Press, 1962.

Da Qing Shizu zhang (Shunzhi) huangdi shilu 大清世祖章[順 治]皇帝實錄. Beijing: Huawen shuju, 1964.

Dardess, John W. *Confucianism and Autocracy: Professional Elites in the Founding of the Ming Dynasty*. Berkeley: University of California Press, 1983.

Du Jiaji 杜家驥. "Qianlong zi nü jia Kongfu ji xiangguan wenti zhi kaobian" 乾隆子女嫁孔府及相關問題之考辨. *Lishi dang'an* 歷史檔案 47, no. 3 (1992): 98–101.

Ebrey, Patricia Buckley. *Confucianism and Family Rituals in Imperial China: A Social History of Writing About Rites*. Princeton: Princeton University Press, 1991.

Elman, Benjamin A. "Political, Social, and Cultural Reproduction via Civil Service Examinations in Late Imperial China." *Journal of Asian Studies* 50 (1991): 7–28.

Fan Ye 范曄. *Hou Han shu* 後漢書. Beijing: Zhonghua shuju, 1965.

Goodrich, L. Carrington, and Chaoyang Fang. *Dictionary of Ming Biography*. 2 vols. New York: Columbia University Press, 1976.

Guo Songyi 郭松義. "Kong xing zongpu he Kong shijiazu zuzhi: jieshao Qufu Kongfu suo zang jiapu ziliao" 孔姓宗譜和孔氏家族組織介紹曲阜孔府所藏家譜資料. In idem, *Pudie xue yanjiu* 譜牒學研究, 1: 195–208. Beijing: Shuwen xian, 1989.

————. "Qufu Kongfu yu Ming Qing guizu dizhu" 曲阜孔府與明清貴族地主. In *Ming Qing dang'an yu lishi yanjiu: Zhongguo diyilishi dang'an guan liushi zhou nian ji'nian lunwenji* 明清檔案與歷史研究: 中國第一歷史檔案館六十周年紀念論文集, ed. Zhongguo diyi lishi dang'an guan 中國第一歷史檔案館, 1: 283–97. Beijing: Zhonghua shuju, 1988.

Guy, R. Kent. *The Emperor's Four Treasures: Scholars and the State in the Late Qianlong Era*. Cambridge, Mass.: Harvard University, Council on East Asian Studies, 1987.

Hartwell, Robert M. "Demographic, Political, and Social Transformations of China, 750–1550." *Harvard Journal of Asiatic Studies* 42, no. 2 (Dec. 1982): 365–442.

He Lingxiu 何齡修, Liu Zhongri 劉重日, Guo Songyi 郭松義, Hu Yiya 胡一雅, Zhong Zunxian 鍾遵先, and Zhang Zhaolin 張兆麟. *Fengjian guizu da dizhu de dianxing: Kongfu yanjiu* 封建貴族大地主的典型: 孔府研究. Beijing: Zhongguo shehui, 1981.

Ho, Ping-ti. *The Ladder of Success in Imperial China: Aspects of Social Mobility, 1368–1911*. New York: John Wiley & Sons, 1964.

Huang Liu-hung. *A Complete Book Concerning Happiness and Benevolence: A Manual for Local Magistrates in Seventeenth-Century China*. Trans. and ed. Djang Chu. Tucson: University of Arizona Press, 1985.

Hucker, Charles O. *A Dictionary of Official Titles in Imperial China*. Stanford: Stanford University Press, 1985.

Hummel, Arthur W. *Eminent Chinese of the Ch'ing Period*. Washington D.C.: U.S. Government Printing Office, 1944.

Hymes, Robert. "Marriage, Descent Groups, and Localist Strategy in Sung and Yuan Fu-chou." *In Kinship Organization in Late Imperial China, 1000–1940*, ed. Patricia Buckley Ebrey and James L. Watson, pp. 95–136. Berkeley: University of California Press, 1986.

Kong Demao and Ke Lan. *In the Mansion of Confucius' Descendants: An Oral History*. Trans. Rosemary Roberts. Beijing: New World Press, 1984.

Kong Jifen 孔繼汾. *Queli wenxian kao* 闕里文獻考. 1762. Reprinted—Taipei: Zhong ding wenhua, 1967.

Kong Shangren 孔尙任. *Kongzi shi jiapu* 孔子氏家譜. Reprint of *Kong da sheng zang Kangxi ershisan* 孔達生藏康熙二十三. 1684. Taipei: Guoli zhongyang tu-shuguan, 1969.

Kong Yuancuo 孔元措. *Kongshi zuting guangji* 孔氏祖庭廣記. 1312. Taipei: Guangwen shuju, 1970.

Kongfu dang'an xuanbian 孔府檔案選編. 2 vols. Ed. Zhongguo shehui kexueyuan, Jindaishi yanjiusuo, Zhonghua minguo shi yanjiushi 中國社會科學院近代史研究所中華民國史研究室. Beijing: Zhonghua shuju, 1982.

Liang Sicheng 梁思成. *Qufu Kongmiao zhi jianzhu ji qi xiuqi jihua* 曲阜孔廟之建築及其修葺計劃. Beiping: Zhongguo gonggao xueshe, 1935.

Liu, James T. C. "How Did a Neo-Confucian School Become the State Ortho-doxy?" *Philosophy East and West* 23, no. 4 (Oct. 1973): 483–505.

Loewe, Michael. *Crisis and Conflict in Han China, 104 BC to AD 9*. London: George Allen & Unwin, 1974.

———. "The Former Han Dynasty." In *The Cambridge History of China*, vol. 1, *The Ch'in and Han Empires 221 BC–AD 220*, ed. Denis Twitchett and Michael Loewe, pp. 103–222. Cambridge, Mass.: Cambridge University Press, 1986.

Luo Chenglie 駱承烈. "Kongfu dang'an zai yanjiu zuquan wenti shang de jiazhi" 孔府檔案在研究族權問題上的價值. In *Quanguo di'er ci dang'an xueshu taolunhui lunwen xuanji* 全國第二次檔案學術討論會論文選集, pp. 290–96. Beijing: Dang'an chubanshe, 1985.

Mair, Victor H. "Language and Ideology in the Written Popularizations of the Sa-cred Edict." In *Popular Culture in Late Imperial China*, ed. David Johnson, Andrew

J. Nathan, and Evelyn S. Rawski, pp. 325-59. Berkeley: University of California Press, 1987.

Mann, Susan. "Learned Women in the 18th Century." In *Engendering China: Women, Culture, and the State,* ed. Christina K. Gilmartin, Gail Hershatter, Lisa Rofel, and Tyrene White, pp. 27-46. Cambridge, Mass.: Harvard University Press, 1994.

Mingdai dang'an shiliao 明代檔案史料. Ed. Zhong Zunxian 鍾遵先 et al. Qufu Kongfu dang'an shiliao xuanji 曲阜孔府檔案史料選集, Series 2. Ji'nan: Qi Lu shushe, 1980.

Murray, Julia K. "The Temple of Confucius and Pictorial Biographies of the Sage." Paper presented at the Annual Meeting of the Association for Asian Studies, Washington, D.C., 1995.

Pan Xiang 潘相. *Qufu xianzhi* 曲阜縣志. 1774. Reprinted—Taipei: Taibei xuesheng shuju, 1968.

Perry, Elizabeth J. *Rebels and Revolutionaries in North China, 1845-1945.* Stanford: Stanford University Press, 1980.

Polachek, James W. *The Inner Opium War.* Cambridge, Mass.: Harvard University Press, 1992.

"Qianlong liunian Yansheng gong yu Qufu zhixian hu jie'an" 乾隆六年 [1741] 衍聖公與曲阜知縣互訐案. *Lishi dang'an* 歷史檔案 (Zhongguo diyi lishi dang'an guan 中國第一歷史檔案館) 3 (1995): 20-25.

Qingdai dang'an shiliao 清代檔案史料. Ed. Luo Chenglie 駱承烈 et al. Qufu Kongfu dang'an shiliao xuanji 曲阜檔案史料選集, Series 3. Ji'nan: Qi Lu shushe, 1980.

Qufu Kongfu dang'an shiliao xuanbian 曲阜孔府檔案史料選編. Ed. Qufu xian wen guanhui 曲阜縣文館會. Ji'nan: Jilu chubanshe, 1981- .

Qufu: Kongzi de guxiang 曲阜孔子的故鄉. Ed. Shandongsheng Qufushi wenwu guanli weiyuanhui 山東省曲阜市文物管理委員會. Beijing: Wenwu chubanshe, 1990.

Saunders, Irene. *The Right Word in Chinese.* Hong Kong: Commercial Press, 1972.

Shandong shengzhi: Kongzi gulizhi 山東省志孔子故里志. Comp. Shandongsheng difang shizhi bianzuan weiyuanhui 山東省地方史志編纂委員會. Beijing: Zhonghua shuju, 1994.

Smith, Paul J. "Family, Landsmann, and Status-Group Affiliation in Refugee Mobility Strategies: The Mongol Invasions and the Diaspora of Sichuanese Elites, 1230-1330." *Harvard Journal of Asiatic Studies* 52, no. 2 (1992): 665-708.

Strassberg, Richard E. *The World of K'ung Shangren: A Man of Learning in Early Ch'ing China.* New York: Columbia University Press, 1983.

Sun Baotian 孫葆田. *Shandong tongzhi* 山東通志. 1915. Reprinted—Taibei: Zhonghua shuju, 1969.

Tuotuo 脫脫. *Jinshi* 金史. Beijing: Zhonghua shuju, 1975.

———. *Songshi* 宋史. Beijing: Zhonghua shuju, 1977.

Twitchett, Denis. "The Fan Clan's Charitable Estate, 1050–1760." In *Confucianism in Action*, ed. David S. Nivison and Arthur F. Wright, pp. 97–133. Stanford: Stanford University Press, 1959.

Watt, John R. *The District Magistrate in Late Imperial China*. New York: Columbia University Press, 1971.

Wilson, Thomas A. *Genealogy of the Way: The Construction and Uses of the Confucian Tradition in Late Imperial China*. Stanford: Stanford University Press, 1995.

———. "The Ritual Formation of Confucian Orthodoxy and the Descendants of the Sage." *Journal of Asian Studies* 55 (1996): 559–84.

Xiao Minqing 簫敏慶. "Da Menggu guo shidai Yansheng gong fu jue kaoshi" 大蒙古國時代衍聖公復爵考事. *Dalu zazhi* 大陸雜誌 85, no. 6 (1992): 268–72.

PART IV

The Past in the Present

EIGHT

Knowledge, Organization, and Symbolic Capital
Two Temples to Confucius in Gansu

Jun Jing

This chapter examines the role of knowledge in the reconstruction of two local temples to Confucius in the northwestern province of Gansu. Rebuilt by a multi-village lineage in the early 1990s, these temples are the ceremonial sites for the combined worship of Confucius, famous Confucian scholars, and the founding ancestors of the local lineages of the Kong family. The material presented here was collected during eight months of fieldwork in 1992 and through summer research from 1989 to 1995.

Since the early 1980s, an upsurge of religious activism has transformed China's social landscape. In rural areas especially, an "intensified ritual landscape"[1] has emerged as community temples, ancestor halls, and even pilgrimage sites in holy mountains have been rebuilt.[2] In many cases, the struc-

My field research in northwest China was funded in part by the National Science Foundation and the Wenner-Gren Foundation for Anthropological Research. I thank Thomas Wilson of Hamilton College for offering insightful comments on a draft version of this article.

1. Siu, "Recycling Rituals," p. 126.

2. Among the best and most detailed studies of religious revival and temple reconstruction is Kenneth Dean's *Taoist Ritual*. Dean's work is based on extensive fieldwork in Fujian province in 1985–87, following a year of similar work in Taiwan. For other studies, see Luo, *Religion Under Socialism*; MacInnis, *Religion in China Today*; and the collection of translated articles in Seymour and Wehrli, "Religion in China." Most of the articles included in Seymour and Wehrli deal with the restoration of sacred sites in Gansu. See also Wang Huning, *Dangdai Zhongguo cunliao*, a fifteen-village survey that covers, among other things, ancestor worship and ancestor-hall restoration (see esp. pp. 291–568). For the influence of Hong Kong's reli-

tures at these sacred places had been seriously damaged, converted to secular uses, or completely dismantled under the harsh anti-religious policy of
the Maoist era (1949–76). As Prasenjit Duara and C. K. Yang have reminded us, however, temples in China were the targets of organized destruction long before the Maoist regime came to power.[3] In the environment
of what Myron Cohen calls the "iconoclastic nationalism" in the post-Qing
period, hostility toward popular religion intensified among China's new
elites—officials, educators, social reformers, and urban scholars—who had
been educated in the modern school system based on Western models and
curricula introduced at the end of the nineteenth century.[4] In a survey-study
of Dingxian 定縣, a rural county in north China, Li Jinghan systematically
documented the impact of this movement. According to Li, iconoclasm
peaked in Dingxian in 1914–15 when a new county magistrate had the clay
statues in 245 temples smashed and the temple buildings converted into
classrooms. His actions had little lasting effect, however. In 1930, Dingxian
still had 879 functioning temples in 453 villages.[5]

A key difference between the iconoclasts of the Republican period and
those of the Maoist era is that the Communists espoused a long-term and
intransigent policy of crushing the rituals and ideologies of all religious traditions. This policy resulted in the closure of temples and other religious
structures on a much larger scale. Gansu province, for example, had 1,054
functioning Taoist temples in 1949. Many of these were dismantled at the
onset of the Great Leap Forward (1958–60). In the Cultural Revolution
(1966–76), Gansu's most famous Taoist temple—the Altar of Thunder—
was vandalized by Red Guards.

Official attitudes toward religion began to change in 1979. In that year,
the government adopted a policy of allowing religious sites to be repaired
and reopened. By 1985–86, however, only 27 Taoist temples in Gansu had
been restored sufficiently to permit reopening.[6] The state-sanctioned reconstruction of these temples as well as other religious sites such as mosques,

---

gious societies on the reconstruction of temples for the worship of a particular deity in southern China, see Lang and Ragvald, *The Rise of a Refugee God*, pp. 126–48.

3. Duara, "Knowledge and Power"; C. K. Yang, *Religion in Chinese Society*, pp. 367–71.
4. Cohen, "Religion in a State Society," p. 28.
5. Li, *Dingxian shehui zhuangkuang diaocha*, pp. 416–46.
6. Seymour and Werhli, "Religion in China," p. 14.

churches, and Buddhist monasteries stimulated the community-based temple restorations in Gansu begun in the early 1980s.

As a key catalyst in the formation of religious networks,[7] the reconstruction of community-based temples in rural China can be explored from a variety of analytical approaches. One is to pinpoint its causes by determining whether it is a response to what Richard Madsen terms "the general failure of the Chinese party-state to provide any satisfying experience of moral community or any plausible sense of transcendent meaning."[8] Another is to consider the impact of economic reforms by investigating, as Mayfair Yang has done in a study of rural Wenzhou 溫州, whether "economic privatism has paradoxically produced, not so much individualism, as a great deal of community participation in the rebuilding of local infrastructure and traditional culture."[9] Yet another approach is Helen Siu's argument that religious life in China is still at the stage of "recycling cultural fragments" from within a social environment that has been penetrated by a highly intrusive state power.[10] In one way or another, these approaches are all deeply concerned with the problem of state-society relations in the sphere of religion.

This chapter is also concerned with state-society relations, but it focuses on the problem of knowledge in light of Pierre Bourdieu's concept of symbolic capital. In interpreting fieldwork findings from rural Nigeria, Bourdieu used the term "symbolic capital" to refer to social prestige and special knowledge.[11] Then, in an analysis of the French education system, Bourdieu developed this concept by identifying a set of cultural dispositions—lifestyles, socialization skills, scopes of knowledge, aesthetic tastes, choices of reading material, bodily characteristics, and linguistic markers of social status—that people use with more or less dexterity to distinguish themselves from other members of their society.[12] The elements of symbolic capital are derived from and can be converted into three vital resources: "cultural capital" (academic knowledge, education degrees, and types of schooling);

---

7. On the development of religious networks in local communities, see Cai, "Shangfang shan jie yinzhai"; Hu, "Hugong dadi xinyang"; and Shen and Le, "Lingfeng shan gexian weng." These studies cover the rebuilding of some rather large temples in the rural areas around Shanghai, Suzhou, and Hangzhou, respectively.

8. Madsen, in MacInnis, *Religion in China Today*, p. xvi.

9. Mayfair Yang, "Tradition," p. 2.

10. Siu, "Recycling Rituals," p. 121–37.

11. Bourdieu, *Outline of a Theory*, pp. 171–83.

12. Bourdieu, *Distinction*, see esp., pp. 13–29, 125–131.

"economic capital" (money, property, and control of productive materials); and "social capital" (occupational prestige, social status, interpersonal networks, and group solidarity). For instance, French schools, according to Bourdieu, routinely reward the symbolic capital of the dominant class and devalue that of the working class. The French education system operates within a system of class interests, ideologies, and social hierarchies to favor children of upper-class origin, who inherit a set of cultural, social, and economic capital that differs substantially from that found among working-class children.[13]

Central to Bourdieu's views is his argument that symbolic capital functions within a structured system of ideas through which the objective reality of society is perceived, interpreted, and justified. This subjectified system of social reality is the foundation for the transformation of symbolic capital into "symbolic power," that is, the power to impose on others a vision of social distinctions and divisions within a society's overall structure of hierarchical relations.[14] Given the place of education and knowledge (cultural capital) in Bourdieu's treatment of the relationship of symbolic capital and symbolic power, the question then becomes Why are the bearers of certain types of knowledge honored and privileged in a particular society? In Bourdieu's view, this question must be addressed by inspecting the institutionalization of knowledge, which is grounded in such social structures as schools, religious organizations, professional associations, kinship groups, state apparatuses, and the mass media, to name just a few. These are the mechanisms of both practice and cognition, where, to use Bourdieu's own words, "the objects of knowledge are constructed."[15]

In relating Bourdieu's work to my analysis of the role of knowledge in the reconstruction of Chinese temples, I ask several questions: What kind of knowledge is valued in the rebuilding of sacred landmarks in villages and small towns? Who are the retainers of such knowledge? What influence do these individuals wield in the mobilization of money, labor, and materials for temple reconstruction? And how do they deal with local politics and government policies? I address these questions by linking them to my own fieldwork findings and singling out four specific categories: (1) ritual knowl-

---

13. Bourdieu, "Cultural Reproduction."
14. Bourdieu, "Social Space," p. 23.
15. Bourdieu, *Outline of a Theory*, p. 96.

edge, (2) literary knowledge, (3) historical knowledge, and (4) political knowledge. My central argument is that they are as indispensable to temple reconstruction as economic and organizational resources. The management of these knowledge-based resources is determined both by patterns of social organization and by strategies of particular individuals operating within organizational confines. One major implication of this dialectical relationship is the merging of institutional power and personal prestige. In other words, temple reconstruction is a domain of social organization in which existing interpersonal networks can be transformed into powerful institutions and effective providers of the needed knowledge rewarded in terms of honor, prestige, and deference. To substantiate this argument, the historical dimension is introduced first, followed by a "thick description" of the two temples to Confucius in Gansu. In this discussion, I focus on symbolic capital by examining the role of ritual, literary, historical, and political knowledge in temple reconstruction.

A GENEALOGICAL CORNERSTONE
OF COLLECTIVE IDENTITY

The two temples to Confucius are found in the villages of Dachuan 大川 ("Big Valley") and Xiaochuan 小川 ("Small Valley"), located on a section of the Yellow River that zigzags through the heartland of Yongjing 永靖 county in Gansu. The recent reconstruction of these temples illustrates the distinctive form of symbolic capital that Bourdieu identifies as "the prestige and renown attached to a family and a name."[16] In both Dachuan and Xiaochuan, the majority of local villagers are surnamed Kong. These Kongs make the grand claim that they are descendants of Confucius (Kong Fuzi 孔夫子 in Chinese). This claim is certainly extraordinary and even fantastic, but it is not without culturally grounded justifications. A case in point is a 108-fascicle genealogy published in 1937 by the Kong clan in Qufu 曲阜, Confucius's birthplace in Shandong.[17] This genealogy meticulously documents the history of emigration of Kongs from Qufu in a nationwide diaspora. Organized into ten major "branches" (*pai* 派), the Kong diaspora con-

16. Ibid., p. 179.

17. This genealogy was published under the name of Kong Decheng, who headed the Kong clan in Qufu until 1948.

tained by the late 1930s hundreds of smaller segments (*zhi* 支) throughout China.[18]

Earlier editions of the Kong clan's official genealogy mentioned the existence of Kong lineages outside Qufu but did not contain descent charts for them.[19] The failure to include this information was neither an oversight nor a reflection of the difficulties of communication between Qufu and the Kongs living elsewhere. For under the imperial policy of granting special favors to the "sage's descendants" (*sheng yi* 聖裔), those Kongs in Qufu who were registered in the clan genealogy were able to enjoy, among a great many privileges, reductions in taxes and exemptions from corvée. Kongs in other parts of China could also enjoy such privileges, but only after local genealogies containing their descent claims were submitted to Qufu, verified as legitimate by the clan's genealogical office, and stamped with a special seal.[20] As a means of safeguarding the interests of the Kongs in Qufu, genealogies from the Kong diaspora were fastidiously examined at the clan's genealogical office in order to restrict the number of those eligible for official favors.[21]

Although these privileges were not officially abolished after the collapse of the imperial polity in 1912, local bureaucrats and regional warlords ignored them. By the late 1920s, they were totally worthless.[22] The ending of official favors undermined the economic rationale for excluding the Kong diaspora from the clan genealogy, and in 1930, when the council of elders heading the Kong clan announced a plan to compile a new genealogy, it decided to incorporate Kong lineages outside Qufu. In response to a letter from the clan council, the Kongs in Yongjing sent a genealogical registry to Qufu in 1930,[23] and this registry was incorporated into the 1937 edition of the clan genealogy. I know of no written documents that verify contact between the Kongs in Yongjing and the Kong council of elders in Qufu before 1930.

---

18. Judging by the place-names in the 1937 edition of the clan genealogy, the Kong diaspora was widely distributed, ranging from the border with the former Soviet Union in the northeast to the Pearl River Delta in south China, and from the affluent coastal regions in the east to the Qinghai-Tibet plateau in the northwest.

19. Two earlier Kong clan genealogies were compiled by Kong Shangren in 1685 and by Kong Jifen in 1744.

20. He, *Fengjian guizu*, pp. 31–61; Qi, *Kongshi dizhu zhuangyang*, pp. 138–43. See Lamberton (pp. 297–328) in this volume.

21. *Kongfu dang'an xuanbian*, pp. 66–74.

22. Ibid., pp. 705–9.

23. Kong Qinghui, *Qufu lingpu jixing*, p. 22.

The 1937 edition of the clan genealogy identifies the "Guangdong branch" (*Lingnan pai* 嶺南派) as one of the Kong diaspora's ten major branches. It is said to have been founded by Kong Changbi 孔昌弼, a scholar-official who went to Guangdong on a military assignment in 990 and continued to live in this southern province after retiring from his official duties. In an unspecified year during the period of Mongol rule (1271–1368), Kong Jiaxing 孔嘉興, one of Kong Changbi's descendants in Guangdong, embarked on a long journey to Lanzhou, the provincial capital of Gansu. The 1937 genealogy dates the origin of the Kongs in Gansu to Jiaxing's arrival in Lanzhou. Seven generations later, four brothers descended from Kong Jiaxing settled in Dachuan, about seventy kilometers south of Lanzhou. In 1585, a small segment of the Kongs moved from Dachuan to the nearby village of Xiaochuan.

Nor was this the end of emigration of Kongs from Dachuan. Because of population pressures, Kongs settled elsewhere in the Yongjing valley. More recently, construction of a hydroelectric dam and a large reservoir in Yongjing, begun at the height of the Great Leap Forward in 1958 and completed in 1961, forced half of Dachuan's residents to resettle in other local communities. As a result, the Kongs of Yongjing now live in 23 different villages. In 1992, county officials estimated the number of Kongs at over 20,000.

Kong Qinghui 孔慶蕙, a resourceful merchant from Xiaochuan, visited Qufu in 1948 and brought a copy of the Qufu genealogy to Lanzhou. Even though this copy was burned by Red Guards from a local college in 1966, the legitimacy conferred by the Qufu genealogy has not been forgotten by the Kongs in Yongjing. Qufu's formal recognition of their genealogical status has remained a matter of collective pride, especially among those Kongs in Qinghui's home village, who can still recall that he sent the local genealogy to Qufu and then brought the clan genealogy to Lanzhou. Since Kong Qinghui's visit in 1948, only two Kongs from Yongjing have traveled to Qufu again. One was a middle-aged man, who visited Qufu in 1974 while serving with an army unit stationed near Ji'nan, the provincial capital of Shandong. The other was an elderly man, whose trip to Qufu in 1984 was funded by a successful son. Otherwise, the Kongs in Yongjing have seen Qufu only on television and in magazine pictures.

RITUAL AUTHORITY
AND SACRED LANDMARKS

Another distinctive form of symbolic capital possessed by the Kongs of Yongjing is their awareness of an age-old ritual tradition for the commemoration of Confucius. Long before their claim of descent was recognized by Qufu in 1930, the Kongs in Yongjing had identified themselves with the Confucian heritage through three important means: a carefully guarded collection of local genealogies, a ritual cycle of ancestor worship, and, above all, two local temples to Confucius. Before taking a closer look at these ceremonial sites, we need to address the question of why they can be identified as "temples."

The Chinese term for "temple" is *si* 寺 in the Buddhist tradition and *guan* 觀 in the Taoist tradition. Neither is ordinarily applied to the buildings erected in memory of great men or ancestors, which are called *ci* 祠 and *citang* 祠堂, respectively. In Chinese popular religion, the temples enshrining medicine gods, fertility goddesses, flood-control deities, and other supernatural beings are usually called *miao* 廟. Interestingly, the architectural complexes once found in every seat of government across China for the combined worship of Confucius and prominent Confucian scholars were also called *miao*. During the Tang dynasty (618–906), for instance, these structures were called *xiansheng miao* 先聖廟, or "temples to the First Sage." The two most popular terms, which remained in use into the twentieth century, are *wenmiao* 文廟, literally "temples of culture," and *Kongzi miao* 孔子廟, sometimes simply *Kong miao* 孔廟, "temple to Confucius" or "temple of Master Kong." In all existing temples to Confucius, the central halls are called *dacheng dian* 大成殿, or "halls of great accomplishment." In Dachuan and Xiaochuan, this is the most frequently used term for the two local temples to Confucius.[24]

---

24. How these temples were named is an interesting subject. The Kongs of Dachuan and Xiaochuan seldom used the term *Kong miao* in reference to the Confucius temples. In addition to the popular name "Hall of Great Accomplishment," an alternative term frequently used was *shengren dian* 聖人殿, or "Hall of the Sage" in English. However, Kong Decheng, the last Yansheng Duke, who lived in Taiwan, sent Dachuan and Xiaochuan, in 1995, two horizontal scrolls after he received a letter containing photographs of the temple from the Kongs in Yongjing. On the scrolls he wrote in black ink and with a brush four large Chinese characters—*yuan yuan zhu si* 淵源洙泗—which can be translated as "The origin (of Kongs)

No written records have been found that clarify when these temples were constructed. The earliest documented reference to the Dachuan temple is a register of sheep sacrificed from 1643 to 1664 preserved in a local genealogy.[25] As for Xiaochuan's temple, oral accounts point to a founding date of around the turn of the twentieth century. After the Communists took control of Yongjing in the summer of 1949, individual visits to these temples continued but large-scale ceremonies came to a stop. Formal rites in memory of Confucius and local ancestors were ended by a Communist campaign to outlaw Yongjing's major religious societies, the two largest of which—the Society of Morality (Daode hui 道德會) and the Dao of Conscience (Liangxin dao 良心道)—had been formed and were tightly controlled by the Kongs in Dachuan and Xiaochuan.[26] In 1958, the temples to Confucius in Dachuan and Xiaochuan were sealed by government decree. Xiaochuan's temple was leveled in 1961 to clear space for the construction of the hydroelectric power station. Dachuan's temple, which was seriously damaged during the construction of the station—was dismantled in 1974 at the onset of the Campaign Against Lin Biao and Confucius.[27] In 1985, plans to rebuild the tem-

---

is the Zhu and Si Rivers." Of the two rivers Kong Decheng mentioned, one runs through Qufu, and the other is located to the north of Qufu. In a row of smaller Chinese characters on the horizontal scrolls, Kong Decheng identified these calligraphic gifts as his tributes to the "temples to Confucius" (*Kongzi miao*) of Dachuan and Xiaochuan.

25. This local genealogy was compiled in 1905 by Kong Xianmin. He was the father of Kong Qinghui, the merchant who brought the clan genealogy from Qufu to Lanzhou.

26. Before these organizations were crushed by the newly established Communist government in 1951, more than 8,000 people were affiliated with the Society of Morality and the Dao of Conscience (Yongjingxian xianzhi bianji weiyuanhui, *Yongjing xianzhi*, 3: 28; 14: 79). The Dao of Conscience was also known as the Society of Confucius and Mencius (Kong Meng hui 孔孟會).

27. At a conference in March 1973, Mao said it was necessary to criticize Lin Biao and Confucius. Lin had been Mao's designated successor but later clashed with him and reportedly died in an airplane crash while attempting to flee to the Soviet Union after the failure of an assassination plot against Mao. The curious inclusion of Confucius as a target in this campaign, formally launched in early 1974, is now generally interpreted as an attack on Premier Zhou Enlai, who, following Lin Biao's death, attempted to rehabilitate senior officials sacked by Mao at the onset of the Cultural Revolution. During this campaign, Confucius was denounced for having urged the restoration of the political institutions and rituals of the Zhou dynasty by reviving the noble families whose lines of succession had been interrupted. "This was an oblique but unmistakable critique of Zhou's rehabilitation of senior cadres, particularly clear to those who knew that this passage referred to the actions of Zhou's namesake, the great twelfth century B.C. statesman, the Duke of Zhou" (MacFarquhar, "The Succession to Mao," pp. 550–51). With its bizarre linkage of Confucius, Lin Biao, and Zhou Enlai, this

ples were made. In 1991, Dachuan's temple was restored, and a year later, Xiaochuan's temple was rebuilt. Needless to say, the central figure of enshrinement at each temple is Confucius, known among the Kongs in Yongjing as the "sage ancestor" (*sheng zu* 聖祖).

But which new temple is the central site of ancestor worship for the Kongs scattered through the villages of Yongjing county? This question of the ritual leadership of the ancestor cult of the Kongs was carefully addressed by the organizers of Dachuan's temple-rebuilding project. They made it clear that their temple, not the one to be built in Xiaochuan, was to be regarded as the ceremonial center of the Kongs. This point was repeatedly stressed in the village-by-village drive to raise funds and construction materials. When the fundraisers from Dachuan visited the other Kong settlements, they emphasized a ritual tradition that had been suspended for more than thirty years. The social organization of the Kongs in Yongjing prior to 1949 constituted "a higher-order lineage," which by definition is a multi-locality lineage.[28] A variety of social, economic, and political factors explain why Dachuan was the nucleus of the Kong lineage in the pre-Communist era, but the most decisive factor was perhaps Dachuan's ritual authority on three important ceremonial occasions.

First, the Spring Equinox (*chun fen* 春分) was the occasion for the lineage's four branches to perform separate rites to commemorate their early ancestors, centered on the tombs of the four Kong brothers who were the first of the line to settle in Dachuan from the village of Yanjiawan near Lanzhou. Each of the lineage's four branches traces its descent from one of the four brothers. The tombs of these local founding ancestors were in Dachuan, but they were ruined in the early 1960s by the dam and reservoir construction.

Second, on the day before the Clear and Bright Festival (Qing ming jie 清明節), a select group of people from Dachuan visited the village of Yanjiawan, where they would sweep the tomb of Kong Gongyou 孔公佑, the father of the four Kong brothers who settled in Dachuan. A local tale has it that Kong Gongyou sent his sons to Dachuan because of its favorable geo-

---

campaign involved millions of people, from schoolchildren, officials, and intellectuals to workers, farmers, and soldiers. At the village level, perhaps the most affected were those who bore the surname of Confucius, Kong. Certainly that was the case in Yongjing.

28. Baker, *Inventing the French Revolution*, pp. 67–70; Freedman, *Chinese Lineage and Society*, pp. 19–21; Watson, "Chinese Kinship Reconsidered," pp. 608–9.

mancy. The village lay in an S-shaped valley, which to him symbolized a flying phoenix, and was in front of a mountain range whose structure resembled, to his eyes, the writhing shape of a dragon. With these auspicious signs, he decided on Dachuan for his sons' new home.

Third, on the day of the Clear and Bright Festival itself, a lineage-based ceremony was performed at Dachuan's Confucius temple, which enshrined the spirit tablets of Confucius and six early ancestors: Kong Gongyou, his four sons, and Kong Jiaxing.[29] Jiaxing's tomb, in the southern suburbs of Lanzhou, was cared for by those Kongs who remained in or returned to that city. The Kongs in Yongjing sacrificed not at his tomb, but to his spirit tablet inside Dachuan's temple.

After their descent claim was acknowledged by Qufu in 1930, the Kongs in Yongjing learned about and then began to follow the Kong clan's practice of commemorating Confucius's birthday on the twenty-seventh day of the eighth lunar month. In Yongjing, the ceremonial center for the birthday commemoration was Dachuan's temple. But even in Qufu, the commemoration of the Sage's birthday was a rather late cultural invention that grew out of attempts by the authorities of the new Republic of China to distinguish themselves from their imperial predecessors by celebrating Confucius's birthday instead of adhering to the imperial tradition of seasonal sacrifices.[30]

The ritual tradition of sacrificing to the local lineages' founding ancestors early in the year and then celebrating Confucius's birthday in late autumn

---

29. "Spirit tablets," *shenwei* 神位 or *lingpai* 靈牌 in Chinese (sometimes also translated as "soul tablets"), are made of wood. They are bigger along the vertical axis and come in various sizes. On the front are written the names of the deceased, his or her family's status, and any official titles. The words are written from top to bottom. If known, the hour, day, month, and year of the birth and death of the deceased are noted on the back. When used as the objects of ancestor worship, they are either installed in a communal hall all year around or displayed in the central room of a residence on important ritual days such as the Lunar New Year and the Clear and Bright Festival.

30. In a conscious attempt at identity assertion, a delegation of government officials converged on Qufu in 1913, the second year of the Republic, to celebrate Confucius's birthday anniversary. Then in 1914 the government decreed that the sage's birthday be celebrated as a national holiday with a government-financed sacrificial ceremony in Qufu. This newly created ritual was called *guo ji* 國祭, or "state-organized sacrificial ceremony." Its participants included representatives of the Yuan Shikai regime, officials of the Nationalist government, provincial governors, and county magistrates (Kong Fanyin, *Yansheng gongfu jianwen*, pp. 185–89; Kong Zhaozeng, *Qufu xianzhi*, 2: 6–7; Sun and Kong, *Kongfu dang'an xuanbian*, pp. 30–42).

became a subject of conversation during Dachuan's drive to gather money and materials to rebuild its temple. As some of the fundraisers related in interviews, their talks with Kongs in other villages dwelled on Dachuan's status as the "old settlement" (*lao zhuang* 老庄) where the Kong lineage's four principal founders had lived and were buried. Dachuan's effort to establish its ritual authority over Xiaochuan were based on arguments surprisingly similar to those that Thomas Wilson has identified in his study of the tensions between the northern (Qufu) and the southern (Quzhou) lineages of the Kong clan.[31] The rivalry between the two lineages over ritual leadership, according to Wilson, revolved around discussions of migration from an original site of settlement, notions of lineage segmentation, different lines of descent, and, above all, ancestral tombs.

The assertion of ritual leadership by the fundraisers from Dachuan was an institutionalized effort, symbolized by a pair of documents hanging at Dachuan's new temple to Confucius. Flanking the entrance to the temple's offering hall are two placards notable for their great size and fine calligraphy. The text on the placard on the right reviews the temple's history, its original location, destruction, and latest incarnation. At the end of this text are listed the names of the fourteen men in charge of the temple-rebuilding project and the fundraising drive. These men became the temple's managers when its reconstruction was completed. The placard on the left lists the names of the people in a total of 25 villages who contributed money or materials for the temple's reconstruction. These documents arguably enact what James Scott would call a "public declaration of the hidden transcript."[32] The "hidden transcript" here is the reassertion of Dachuan's status as the ceremonial center for the Kongs not just in Dachuan but in other local villages as well. This message is conveyed in two ways. The temple managers named in the placard on the right are five Dachuan residents and nine people from the villages of Sigou 四沟, Huangci 黄刺, and Zhongzhuang 中莊, which contain a concentrated number of Kong households. In the other document, the donors list names of people from every Kong settlement in Yongjing and two villages in Qinghai province long ago settled by Kongs from Dachuan.

31. Wilson, "Ritualization." See also Wilson (pp. 67–71) in this volume.

32. Scott, *Domination and the Arts of Resistance*, p. 202.

CLASSICAL EDUCATION
AND GENERATIONAL COHORTS

What kind of individuals manage Dachuan's new temple to Confucius, particularly in terms of their educational background? Dachuan's old temple had, on the eve of the Communist takeover of Yongjing, three large halls and a primary school with more than twenty classrooms. Rents from 40 *mu* 畝 (one *mu* is about one-sixth acre) of high-quality farmland under the temple's control provided for ritual expenses, building maintenance, and salaries for teachers. In 1953, a team of three county officials stopped the temple's supervision of the primary school and parceled its farmland out to land-reform activists.

Interestingly, nine of the fourteen managers of the new temple graduated from the old temple's primary school. One went on to attend a prestigious senior high school in Lanzhou, two attended a teachers college, also in Lanzhou, and three attended junior high schools closer to home but dropped out before finishing their studies. This means that a significant number of the people in charge of the new temple had received a rudimentary or higher level of "classical education" featuring the learning of Confucian texts and the ability to use classical Chinese in composition. Their classical education, especially at the rudimentary level, was characterized by long hours of recitation and repeated calligraphy drills.

These men also had been trained to be "ritual performers" (*li sheng* 禮生) as students and then, for three of them, as teachers at the old primary school. They had been taught the principles and procedures of temple rituals by an older generation of educated Kongs in the hope that they would one day be able to carry on the tradition of offering sacrifices to Confucius and local founding ancestors. Four of these men were young assistants at a temple ceremony in 1949. Thereafter, no lineage-wide ceremony was performed until a simple three-room house in Dachuan was turned, in 1984, into a provisional altar for the enshrinement of spirit tablets in memory of Confucius and local founding ancestors.

Until the formal temple could be built, the provisional altar was used as the site for the ceremony of five rites performed every year in the past. The men most responsible for the revival of this ceremony were the fourteen who later became managers of Dachuan's new temple. These temple managers are locally known as "vow-takers" (*yuan zhu* 願主). Here "vow" refers to a ritualized promise to rebuild the temple and to manage it well thereafter. At a meeting in 1985, each vow-taker placed his right hand over his chest and uttered a pledge of personal commitment and responsibility. All the vow-takers were in their late sixties and early seventies, except the "chief vow-taker" (*da yuan zhu* 大願主) who was in his late thirties at the time of the meeting. From 1986 to 1988, he was Dachuan's village head (*cunzhang* 村長), a key position that allowed him to readjust residential space and vegetable fields in order to find a spot in an already crowded village to build the new temple.

The vow-takers ran into many problems in trying to revive the five-rite ceremony. Since no ceremonies had been held for over three decades, many technicalities had to be worked out and rehearsed to reach perfection. The temple managers sought out whatever written materials might be relevant. This search was limited to the Dachuan area. Because they were not affiliated with an academic institution, they did not have access to the provincial library's rare-book depository. If they had, they would have found highly useful materials there. Three complete sets of ritual texts and moral teachings on the worship of Confucius can be found in local gazetteers and other official records stored at the library.

Unable to make use of the provincial archives, the managers of Dachuan's Confucius temple turned to a source that some of them knew best: local genealogies. They studied two genealogies in particular. One was compiled in 1905 by Kong Xianmin 孔憲敏, who lived in Xiaochuan. The other was completed in 1989 by an elderly man in a village settled by some of the Kongs displaced from Dachuan in 1961.[33] The second genealogy was compiled on the basis of the 1905 genealogy, and this is why the two genealogies share some striking similarities and contain, in each case, more than 1,000 pages. These voluminous genealogies record past practices of ancestor worship, but they do not have technical information on ritual performance. A trip to Qufu to secure a ritual handbook was out of the question because the temple managers in Dachuan did not know whom they should contact in order to get official permission to use Qufu's rare-book library, where the Kong clan's documents and ritual texts are preserved.

To solve the problem of ritual performance, the vow-takers asked more than thirty elderly men in other villages to attend a meeting. For three days,

---

33. The genealogy was compiled by Kong Lingshu.

these elderly men and the vow-takers discussed their memories of the ceremony. Many of those at the meeting had performed specific ritual duties at Dachuan's temple in their early adulthood. Among them was a former ceremonial flute player and a butcher of sacrificial animals. Another man had been responsible for carrying incense sticks and yellow paper to lineage elders when prompted by the ceremony's chief liturgist and by the leading liturgists in charge of the ceremony's individual rites. The leaders of the ceremony, all of whom had belonged to an older generation, had passed away by the mid-1980s. Since nobody at the meeting had a thorough knowledge of the complete ceremony, the attendants concentrated on recalling their own duties and physically demonstrated how individual ritual acts had been performed and what words had been uttered by the leaders of the ceremony.

One outcome of this rehearsal-like gathering was a written outline of the ceremony's five rites. In the first stage, called "Greeting the Sacrifices" (*ying sheng li* 迎聖禮), food and drink are transported to the temple. The sacrifices are prepared in a residential compound and then carried to the temple in a ceremonial procession through the main streets of the community. The second rite, called "Greeting the Arrival of the Holy Spirits" (*ying sheng jia li* 迎聖駕禮), is performed in the temple's courtyard. The central act of this rite is to chant a written prayer appealing to the spirits of the ancestors to descend to the temple and enjoy the sacrificial food. The next three rites are a sequence of "presenting sacrifices" (*xian li* 獻禮) to the spirit tablets inside the temple's offering hall. These rites include the pouring of liquor onto the ground, the presentation of cooked meat, fruits, and other delicacies, the chanting of ritual speeches, the burning of incense, and the ritualized demonstration of gratitude by bows and kowtows.

In interviews with the temple managers, they said that another problem they had encountered in reconstituting this five-rite ceremony was the necessity of refining the "sacrificial texts" (*ji wen* 祭文) to be read in front of the enshrined spirit tablets as a way of extolling the heroic deeds and upright characters of the dead. The very acts of reading and then burning these sacrificial texts are crucial steps in calling on the dead to accept the food offerings in the hope that they shall reciprocate by rendering protection to the living in this world. Through rehearsals in private homes, textual revisions at small meetings, and actual performances at the provisional altar, the sacrificial texts were polished every year; an example of the gradual enrichment of their contents can be found in the written speech to honor the four Kong brothers who pioneered the Kong lineage in Yongjing. In 1985, this text had only a few dozen words; by 1991 it was expanded to more than 300 characters.

In the spring of 1991, Dachuan's temple entered its final phase of construction with the installation of the ridgepole of the offering hall. Unlike the old temple, which had three large halls in a row and a primary school with more than twenty classrooms, the new temple had only one large hall, a single-room house for the temple's watchman, and two classrooms for a preschool. With these buildings in place, the work on the ritual ceremony also entered a crucial phase. Over the next four months, the temple managers held another round of intensive rehearsals to finalize the sacrificial texts and ritual procedures they had worked out. The result was the appearance of a ritual handbook, which, in September 1991, guided the first ceremony of ancestor worship at the new temple.[34]

This ritual handbook was written in "full-form characters" (*fanti zi* 繁體字) and "classical Chinese" (*wenyan* 文言), rather than "simplified characters" (*jianti zi* 簡體字) and "vernacular language" (*baihua* 白話). Since only a small number of Kongs, mostly elderly men who had received a traditional education, could write the full-form characters and use classical Chinese to compose, revise, or copy religious texts, this ritual handbook should be viewed as a reincarnation of two traditional styles of communication in opposition to the dominant trends of using everyday language since the 1920s and the simpler form of characters since the 1960s.

As a general practice in the recent reconstruction of religious structures, full-form characters and classical Chinese have served as the standard vehicles for writing the boards with temple names, ritual documents, poetic couplets, donation registers, and temple histories. And as is the case with the ritual handbook written by Dachuan's temple managers, simplified characters and vernacular language are avoided in composing writings for the temples. The ability to write the full-form characters and to compose in classical Chinese is becoming a highly valued body of cultural knowledge in an increasingly active sphere of life in rural areas. In religious activities, the use of full-form characters and classical Chinese appears to function as a traditionalizing instrument, a symbolic device that encourages the belief in

---

34. This ritual handbook was collectively compiled but its cover has the name of the temple's resident ritualist, Kong Xiangguo, as the author.

the holiness of inscribed religious texts and ritual objects.[35] Given their familiarity with this symbolic device, the managers of Dachuan's temple were able to establish a claim to a source of symbolic power in an increasingly important aspect of rural life.

AN INSTITUTIONAL BASIS FOR
CULTURAL INVENTION

Although Dachuan's new temple is clearly a monument to Kong ancestors, its managers insisted in interviews that it is more than an ancestral hall, that it is a place where the broader public can honor the founders of Chinese culture. One iconographic presentation of this claim is the temple's enshrinement of five spirit tablets. As explained below, cultural inventions, based on memories of political persecution, played a key role in the making and arranging of the spirit tablets.

Made of willow wood, these tablets are painted blue, framed in black, and inscribed in gold. The tablet in the center, three meters high and less than a meter wide, is devoted to Confucius. Placed on a brick platform, it is veiled by colorful silk screens and surrounded by vases of paper flowers. In front of the central tablet is an offering table, flanked by two wooden pillars bearing the lines of a couplet in fine calligraphy. The tablet to the right of the offering table is devoted to Yan Hui, Zeng Sen, Zisi, and Meng Ke, collectively known as the "four correlates" (*si pei* 四配) in the worship of Confucius. The tablet on the left is devoted to seventy-two "former worthies," eminent men of the Confucian tradition. Against the side walls are two plain tables. On one is displayed the "Spirit Tablet of the Fifty-Second-Generation Ancestor Xin Ke Gong, Who Came to Gansu"; on the other is the "Spirit Tablet of the Fifty-Eighth-Generation Ancestor Yu Hou Gong, and His Four Sons: Yanzheng, Yankui, Yanbin, and Yanrong, Who Came to Dachuan."

These spirit tablets bring together two different categories of people—ancestors of the Kongs and ancient scholars unrelated to the Kongs—in an arrangement that breaks sharply with tradition. The tablet of Confucius in

---

35. In parts of mainland China, especially coastal regions that have attracted large investments from Hong Kong and Taiwan, it was no longer rare by the late 1980s to see billboards, tourist maps, commercial catalogues, or business cards written and printed in full-form characters.

the old temple was, for example, surrounded by the spirit tablets for the founders of the Kong lineages in Gansu and Dachuan. But in the new temple, these tablets have been relegated to the side walls. The central tablet is now flanked by the tablets of Confucius's disciples. Only one of them, Confucius's grandson Zisi, or Kong Ji, is a Kong. Also extremely noteworthy is that in the old temple the Chinese characters meaning "sage ancestor" were inscribed on Confucius's spirit tablet. But on his new tablet, this phrase is omitted, and only his honorary titles—"great accomplisher, supreme sage, ultimate teacher, and culture-propagating king"—appear.

The reasons why the temple managers chose to integrate spirit tablets for outsiders with those for their own ancestors and to give these ancestors second billing, and why they found it necessary, in public at least, to redefine the temple's nature arose from their attempts to reconstruct the temple's history, to recover whatever remained from the old temple, and to devise appropriate rituals. At the outset, the temple managers' fundraising strategy emphasized the temple's importance to the Kong lineage. But this changed when, as part of their preparations, they examined surviving genealogies in the Dachuan area. In the genealogy compiled by Kong Xianmin in 1905, they found accounts of the temple's destruction in 1785, its reconstruction in 1792, and the ethnic violence that led to its torching in 1864. Through discussions in meetings and private conversations, the managers developed clear ideas about who had been in charge of a temple-rebuilding project in 1934 and who had been behind the confiscation of the temple's farmland in 1953, its forced closure in 1958, and, finally, its demolition in 1974.

This review of the temple's history served to make Dachuan's troubled past apparent to the organizers of the fundraising drive. The political complications of their task were brought home to them when they started to recover objects once owned by the temple. These fell into three categories: ritual objects, ordinary furniture, and building materials. The ritual objects included a large iron bell, incense burners, offering tables, and small oil lamps. These items had fallen into private hands in 1953 when the temple lands were lost to land-reform activists and, above all, when those in charge of the temple became too intimidated to defend it. The furniture included the temple school's desks and chairs. Some of these became office furnishings when a production brigade and eight subsidiary production teams were set up in Dachuan in 1958. The building materials included bricks, tiles, stones, beams, windows, and gates. Initially kept at a local carpenter's workshop after the temple's destruction in 1974, these materials were distributed to individual households when Dachuan's collectively held property was privatized in 1981.

To track down these things, the temple managers questioned the cadres who had been in charge of Dachuan at different times from the onset of the land reform to the early 1980s. Their pursuit of the temple's furnishings literally placed the entire history of radical socialism under review. Retired village cadres were asked who had benefited from the distribution of temple property and why. Since the building materials were considered the most important items to retrieve, the particular circumstances of the old temple's destruction in the "Campaign Against Lin Biao and Confucius" of 1974 were closely examined. Account books were checked, witnesses consulted, an itemized list of temple property drawn up, and a notice posted asking individuals to return the temple's belongings voluntarily. In the end, over half of the construction materials used in the new temple came from the old temple.

In their efforts to review the temple's history and to recover its property, the temple mangers were unavoidably reminded of many graphic details of the Maoist era, particularly the closure of the temple during "the Big Manhunt of 1958." From mid-August to late September that year, police and militia rounded up 855 people in Yongjing, mostly former landlords, leaders of secret societies, and people with Guomindang ties. Of the arrested, 21 were executed immediately. The others were detained in the offices of the county and district (commune) governments and not released until the people's commune system was in place.

The massive arrests and summary killings in Yongjing were accompanied by an "anti–feudal privilege campaign." The term "feudal privileges" refers to what county officials regarded as undesirable remnants of the old society, especially in the realm of religion. In the first few years of Communist rule, the larger religious societies in Yongjing were eradicated, but the smaller ones were spared and continued to operate quietly despite official warnings. County officials considered the religious structures that survived a possible threat to collectivization, and the "anti-feudal privilege campaign" led to the near-total destruction of the county's major temples. Only one Buddhist pilgrimage site was spared, because the central government has determined that it had archeological value. Materials from the dismantled temples were used to construct bridges, schools, and irrigation facilities. The campaign also led to the closing of smaller shrines and ances-

tor halls in rural settlements.[36] Dachuan's temple to Confucius was sealed
at this time, but it was not dismantled until the 1974 Campaign Against
Lin Biao and Confucius.

The Dachuan temple was dismantled by the Kongs themselves. In February 1974, government officials held a series of meetings in Yongjing at
which they planned mass rallies to criticize Lin Biao and Confucius in all the
county's communes. A work team of fourteen cadres from the county's Department of People's Armed Forces (Wuzhuang bu 武裝部) was sent to
the commune to which Dachuan belonged. Upon their arrival at commune
headquarters, said my informants in Dachuan, the county officials decided
that the temple was to be leveled to remove the last material evidence of
Confucianism from public sight. They also decreed that what was left of the
temple should be taken to the commune seat and used to build a warehouse.
When this news reached Dachuan, a group of elderly men and Dachuan's
village cadres mobilized the Kongs to tear down the temple first so they
could at least keep the building materials for themselves. In interviews, the
managers of Dachuan's new temple recalled that Dachuan's refusal to sur-
render the temple materials to the commune exasperated commune leaders
and the delegation of county officials. In retaliation, they brought middle-
school students to the site of the ruined temple and instructed them to build
a grave-like mound from the rubble. The children were then led in the
shouting of political slogans against this substitute symbol of Confucianism.
Many of the students who participated in this public ritual of humiliation
were themselves Kongs. Dachuan's village cadres were required to attend,
and many inhabitants of Dachuan witnessed it. My informants said that
nobody from Dachuan dared utter a word because the work team and
commune officials, backed up by a hundred armed militiamen at commune
headquarters a kilometer away, were being deliberately provocative and
looking for any excuse to take harsher action.

After reviewing local history, the planners of the new temple began to realize, they said, that they had to convince government and party authorities

36. The closings of religious structures throughout Yongjing in 1958 were in part a response to an armed uprising in nearby Dongxiang 東鄉 county. In mid-August 1958, the
Muslim imams of local mosques organized their followers to resist the total collectivization of
farmland during the Great Leap Forward. An unknown number of government officials were
killed, including the Dongxiang county magistrate. The rebellion was put down by a People's
Liberation Army brigade.

in the county and township seats that their project did not represent the revival of an illicit, superstitious cult or a secret society. In particular, they said, they assured the officials in charge of the county's offices of public security and religious affairs that the temple would be an educational center to instill an appreciation of the cultural legacy of Confucius, not a cover for suspect activities.

This attempt to defuse official suspicion was precipitated by personal experiences of political persecution. The majority of the temple managers had suffered greatly during the Maoist era for a variety of political reasons. One of the five Dachuan-based temple managers was a former government official and veteran Communist. He was forced to return to Dachuan in 1961 when a team of famine inspectors from Lanzhou and Beijing discovered that some 300 people had starved to death in a rural district under his control. He was spared the death penalty, he said in an interview, only after he disclosed at a public rally that he had been totally helpless in the face of shortages of food and medicine during the Great Leap Forward and that his wife, his son, his brother, and his brother's wife and children had died of starvation. Following his return to Dachuan, his disgrace left him a peripheral member of the village's local party organization even though he was one of this organization's founders. Another temple manager in Dachuan had been branded a "historical counter-revolutionary" in 1954 because of his previous membership in a Guomindang youth organization. He lost his position as a primary school principal, was sent back to Dachuan to work in a thought-reform team, and experienced many years of humiliation until he was officially rehabilitated in 1984. Even the chief vow-taker, the only young member of the temple organization, grew up in the shadow of political stigma. His family was repeatedly denounced by village cadres during the early phases of the Cultural Revolution because his grandfather had headed the village's defense corps in the pre-Communist era and because his classically educated father could not break his opium-smoking habit despite publicly announced fines by village cadres for his addiction. In a rather absurd case of political persecution, one temple manager was singled out for struggle at a communal meeting because he had told his neighbors' children ghost stories. The only temple manager living in Dachuan who had not had "political problems" was a former "model chef" who had served county officials.

Interviews and government documents in Yongjing county archives revealed that at least ten Kongs in Dachuan were executed or hounded to death between 1950 and 1958. During these eight years, 121 people in Dachuan were classified as "bad elements" and "class enemies." These included two former lineage chiefs (*zhu zhang* 主長), two schoolteachers, four low-ranking Guomindang officers and officials, five practitioners of "feudal superstition," nine local security chiefs (*baozhang* 保長), 48 adults from "landlord" and "rich-peasant households," and 51 members of "counter-revolutionary religious societies" (*fandonghui daomen* 反動會道門). The penalties against these people, mostly male Kongs and their wives, ranged from forced labor, lengthy imprisonment, and police surveillance to loss of property, prohibitions on travel, and public rituals of humiliation during each major Maoist campaign.

Because of these deeply painful memories of the village's terrifying history in the Maoist era, the temple managers felt it absolutely necessary to cultivate an image of their organization that promoted Dachuan's new temple to Confucius as a place for the general public to honor the founders of Chinese culture. To this end, they embarked on cultural invention by installing spirit tablets for the non-Kong disciples of Confucius together with tablets for their local founding ancestors. Then they worked out another cultural invention by designing a double liturgy. They kept the traditional practice of staging a midnight ceremony, during which male representatives of the Kong lineage played carefully defined roles and kowtowed to all the tablets in the temple. Women surnamed Kong or married to Kongs were allowed to attend the ceremony but excluded from such important ritual assignments as offering sacrificial food and reading texts in front of the enshrined tablets.[37] The midnight ceremony was followed by a newly created daytime ceremony for the lineage's ordinary members, affinal relatives, and even total strangers from other villages and nearby factories. These people were encouraged to pay their respects, by bows and kowtows, to the spirit tablets of Confucius and his disciples, but, unless they were Kongs or married to Kongs, not to the enshrined Kong ancestors. The daytime ceremony was accompanied by a feast, with special dishes offered to all visitors who brought gifts or made cash donations to the temple. In essence, a pub-

---

37. At the end of the midnight liturgy, two men stay behind the temple's closed gates to eat a portion of the sacrificial meat. To symbolize the continuity of the bloodline, one is a representative of the most senior generation and the other a member of the most junior generation of adults.

lic festival was established at a site whose original function had been the private worship of ancestors.

SYMBOLS UNITED, SYMBOLS DIVIDED

The new temple to Confucius in Xiaochuan contains a cluster of sacred symbols that can be decoded as representing Xiaochuan's cultural agreements with Dachuan. For example, the temples in both villages were reopened on the Sage's birthday. In the offering halls of both temples, the enshrined spirit tablets of Confucius and local founding ancestors are arranged in the same order. Each temple contains two spirit tablets collectively dedicated to the famous disciples of Confucius. In imitation of what had been done in Dachuan the previous year, a five-rite ceremony was performed at Xiaochuan's temple in 1992, also beginning at midnight. In line with Dachuan's precedent, Xiaochuan organized a public festival by opening its temple to outsiders. And in each temple festival, two sacrificial tables were set up, one for Kongs and one for non-Kongs, to present offerings.

These ritually manifested similarities, however, become dramatically less significant in light of what Victor Turner calls the "multivocality" of ritual symbolism.[38] That is to say, the symbolism of ritual actions speaks not in one but many voices. To be more specific, the two temples embody what Pierre Bourdieu would describe as "conflicts between symbolic powers that aim at imposing the vision of legitimate divisions."[39] For example, only spirit tablets were enshrined in Dachuan's temple, but a larger-than-life-sized statue of Confucius was installed in Xiaochuan's temple. Molded of clay by a craftsman from Lanzhou, the statue is more than three meters high, taller than any religious statues in Yongjing except the stone figures at Binglingsi 炳靈寺, a government-controlled complex of Buddhist temples.

At the beginning, neither the craftsman from Lanzhou nor the Kongs themselves knew what a statue of Confucius should look like and what should be inside it. A color photograph of the Confucius statue in Qufu's Hall of Great Accomplishment was cut out of a magazine to serve as a model. The question of what should be inside the statue was resolved by appealing to local custom. According to this custom, the internal parts of statues of supernatural beings must approximate the anatomy of a real person in order to ac-

---

38. Turner, *Dramas, Fields, and Metaphors*, pp. 23–59.
39. Bourdieu, "Social Space," p. 22.

tivate the deity's ability to respond to human supplications. Modeled after the internal structure of statues for flood-control gods and fertility goddesses, the heart of Confucius's statue was represented by a ruby. The intestines were made with artificial pearls, the spine was a pole fashioned from a pine tree, the arteries were red threads, and the kidneys and liver were silk bags of twelve ingredients used in Chinese herbal medicines.

The making of this giant Confucius statue had a "de-ancestralizing" effect. In popular perception, a statue set up for worship is the effigy of a god or goddess who protects everyone, irrespective of descent line, family origin, and social background. The people of Yongjing had never heard of statues of ancestors. In their experience, religious statues depicted Buddhist, Taoist, or local deities.[40] In other words, the decision by Xiaochuan's temple managers to make the statue of Confucius may have transformed their ancestor into a patron god who could be worshipped by all and who must respond to appeals for protection and good fortune from non-Kongs as well as from Kongs. Furthermore, Xiaochuan's refusal to disclose to outsiders how much the statue cost and what items were secreted inside only served to lend credence to the widely circulated rumor that the statue contained gold, real pearls, and rare gemstones. This rumor fueled curiosity about the statue and was a major reason why some 10,000 people from 40 or so villages attended Xiaochuan's temple festival in 1992.

The Confucius temple in Xiaochuan also differs greatly from the one in Dachuan in its aesthetic and functional uses of space. For example, the Dachuan temple is rather plain. Its beams, eaves, columns, and bracketings are not painted but varnished to keep the timber's original color. The entrance gate to the temple courtyard is solemn but not elaborately decorated. The moral explanation for the aesthetic style of this temple is that Confucius preferred simplicity over elaborateness. Within the temple, a preschool offers classes for six-year-olds to prepare them for enrollment in the village's primary school. The township government saw this preschool as a place that exposed young children to "feudal superstition." Despite repeated official demands that it be relocated to the village's regular, government-controlled primary school, however, the preschool was in operation at least as late as 1995.

---

40. The ubiquitous statues of Mao were icons of a personality cult involving no ritual acts of praying, prostration, and burning incense.

By contrast, Xiaochuan's Confucius temple is heavily painted, with crimson being the dominant hue. Instead of providing schooling for young children, Xiaochuan has tried to turn its temple into a sightseeing spot by joining the county government's promotion of local tourist attractions. For this purpose, Xiaochuan's temple managers raised 30,000 yuan to build a towering wooden archway at the entrance to the temple's courtyard; they used another 10,000 yuan to make life-sized clay statues of the Four Correlates and 72 palm-sized clay figures for the enshrined disciples of Confucius. After the temple was rebuilt, its managers asked an urban journalist to write articles to promote it as a major historical sightseeing place in this part of Gansu. And in summer 1995, the idea of charging admission fees was considered. Xiaochuan's temple may appear to be motivated by crass commercialism, but a closer look reveals that it is not entirely materialistic. These characteristics of the temple derive from the efforts of its managers to distinguish their temple from the one in Dachuan both socially and symbolically.

SEPARATION, WEALTH, AND RIVALRY

Dachuan contains members from all four of the lineage's major branches, but the Kong settlements in other parts of Yongjing tend to be composed of people from one or perhaps two of the lineage's branches. As one of the breakaway Kong settlements, Xiaochuan was founded by a group descending from the third of the four brothers who established the Kong lineage in Dachuan. In the eyes of the Dachuan Kongs, Xiaochuan is only a branch of the tree rooted in Dachuan. But this small branch has always been unique.

Xiaochuan became the Kong lineage's wealthiest branch during the first half of the twentieth century. Starting in the late 1910s, foreign and domestic demand for sheep wool from Tibet and Qinghai rose sharply, and Xiaochuan prospered because it is next to a gorge where the Tao, Daxia, and Yellow Rivers merge. To avoid capsizing in this narrow and extremely dangerous gorge, the bulky rafts and their cargoes of logs, animal pelts, and wool from the upstream grasslands had to be disassembled, portaged around the obstacle, and then reassembled so that they could continue their journey to Lanzhou. Since some of the Kongs living in Xiaochuan owned the fields surrounding this gorge, they served as foremen and recruiters of workers. The hired workers were from Xiaochuan too.

The combination of landownership and labor monopoly at the gorge gave Xiaochuan an enviable position in the local logging industry and water-borne transportation. The most powerful commercial organization in Yongjing, the "log-hauling union" (*laomu gonghui* 撈木工會), was dominated by Xiaochuan. Although the war between China and Japan dealt a heavy blow to the wool trade in the late 1930s, those Xiaochuan Kongs who controlled the narrow gorge were able to expand into other profitable businesses, especially long-distance transportation and the local marketing of cloth and tobacco from other regions. Kong Qinghui, who brought the Qufu genealogy to Lanzhou in 1948, was from one of the wealthiest merchant families in Xiaochuan. Even when air travel was still extremely expensive, he could afford to fly between Lanzhou and major cities in north China on his business trips.

When Xiaochuan's temple was being constructed, Kong Qinghui's trips to Qufu were enthusiastically remembered by the temple managers. According to them, it was Kong Qinghui who had received the letter from Qufu in 1930 calling for a local registry to be included in the Kong clan's new genealogy. After the local registry was completed, Kong Qinghui had it revised by scholars in Lanzhou, for it had not been written in the style stipulated by the genealogical office in Qufu. In 1937, on one of his business trips, Kong Qinghui stopped in Qufu to see if he could acquire a copy of the clan genealogy to take back to Gansu. But it was still being printed. By the time he had completed his business trip, war had broken out between China and Japan, forcing him to return home empty-handed. In 1948, Kong Qinghui traveled to Qufu again and was able to obtain a copy of the clan genealogy.

Kong Qinghui's written account of his efforts to bring the Qufu genealogy to Gansu relates that he was warmly received by six clan elders during his second trip to Qufu. The day after his arrival, a banquet was given in his honor. Toward the end of the banquet, a messenger came in to report that Communist troops had advanced into the adjacent Sishui county. After hurriedly visiting Qufu's Confucius temple, he left the next day, just hours before Qufu was besieged by Communist troops.[41] The banquet Kong Qinghui attended may well have been the clan council's last supper. He was probably the last person to acquire a copy of the Qufu genealogy before the clan council was abolished.[42]

---

41. Kong Qinghui, *Qufu lingpu jixing*, pp. 10–15.

42. A unit of Nationalist soldiers besieged in Qufu was allowed to leave by Qufu's south gate but was suddenly gunned down in an open field by the Communist troops. As soon as

Although the managers of the Xiaochuan temple see Kong Qinghui's second trip to Qufu as a great contribution to the whole Kong lineage, this trip caused a deep rift between Xiaochuan and Dachuan. In his published memoir, Kong Qinghui says Dachuan reneged on its promise to cover half the expenses of his 1948 trip to Qufu. In reaction, the board of directors of the log-hauling union decided to finance Kong Qinghui's trip. Even so, Kong Qinghui had to spend a large sum of his own money to escape from Qufu and return home.

Elderly villagers in Dachuan flatly deny Kong Qinghui's allegations. They insist that since Kong Qinghui wanted to honor only himself and his home village, he added the accusation against Dachuan to his account after it had been reviewed by representatives of the Kong lineage who gathered in Lanzhou to greet the arrival of the clan genealogy. Whatever the truth of the matter is, Kong Qinghui's praise of Xiaochuan greatly pleased his village's commercial elites, but the Kongs of Dachuan were outraged. Kong Lingshu 孔令述, an elderly genealogist and a former resident of Dachuan now living in the village of Huangci, said during an interview in 1992 that, following publication of his memoir, Kong Qinghui never dared visit Dachuan again because of rumors that the young men of Dachuan wanted to break his legs in revenge.

The tensions between Dachuan and Xiaochuan reflect the historical economic disparities and social distance between the two villages. Xiaochuan's rebuilding of its temple to Confucius rekindled this tension. In early 1992, three fundraisers from Xiaochuan visited Dachuan and were received by a gathering of elderly Kongs, including five Dachuan temple managers. After a long exchange of pleasantries, the most senior of the visitors presented his hosts with a fundraising booklet. As it was passed around, a statement of purpose at the front of the booklet was singled out for criticism for its literary style and terminology. The critics lectured the visitors, concentrating on one of them who was in his early fifties and a generational junior. Referring to Xiaochuan's temple as a *ga miao* 尕廟, or "minor temple,"[43] they told him that

---

Qufu fell to the Communists on June 11, 1948, the council of clan elders was disbanded and a work team of Communist officials entered the Yansheng Duke's residence to inventory its property and the cultural relics in the nearby Confucius temple (Kong Fanyin, *Yansheng gongfu jianwen*, pp. 388–89).

43. In the local dialect, *ga* means small in size, low in social position, and generally unimportant.

historically it had served only one segment of the Kongs whereas Dachuan's temple was the main temple for the entire Kong lineage. They also tried to impress on the visitors that no one in Xiaochuan had a solid command of ritual knowledge. One of Dachuan's temple managers wrote down four pairs of Chinese characters and then asked the youngest fundraiser from Xiaochuan whether he knew what they meant. When he shook his head, it was explained to him that these words were ritual terms for four sacrificial animals used in the temple ceremony: *gang lie* 剛烈, the "hot-tempered one," for the pig; *rou mao* 柔毛, the "soft-haired one," for the sheep; *han yin* 翰音, the "clear-voiced one," for the chicken; and *ming shi* 明視, the "sharp-eyed one," for the rabbit.

The Dachuan temple managers also learned that day of Xiaochuan's plan to make a clay statue of Confucius. Interpreted as an obvious bid to outdo Dachuan, the statue provoked another burst of disparaging remarks. The watchman at Dachuan's temple said somberly that Xiaochuan was embarking on a dangerous path. He explained that Confucius had been exceptionally ugly at birth: the front of his head was concave, his eyes bulged, his teeth protruded, and his nostrils turned upward. Thinking she had given birth to a monster, his mother abandoned him in a mountain cave. A tiger and an eagle discovered the baby and fed and protected him. When his mother heard of these wonders, she realized that her child must have been sent from heaven. She retrieved him from the cave and thereafter devoted herself to his education.[44] The watchman asked whether Xiaochuan was planning to make a realistic statue of Confucius or portray him as a good-looking man. Before a reply could be offered, he declared that it would be best for Xiaochuan to follow Dachuan's practice of using only Confucius's spirit tablet.[45] The visitors failed to be convinced.

---

44. This story also can be found in Kong Demao, *In the Mansion of Confucius*, p. 18.

45. The controversy over the use of statues in the worship of Confucius was new to Yongjing but not to the history of ritual politics. Deborah Sommer's chapter in this book (pp. 118–27) captures the iconographic changes in the temple to Confucius at the Imperial University in Beijing when the clay statues of Confucius and other scholars were ordered destroyed by the Ming court in 1530. According to Sommer, the decision to destroy the statues reflected literati concepts of the body, of spiritual beings, and of images used in sacrifices. The Kongs in Dachuan were not aware of the Ming's iconoclastic directive, but they knew that the temple to Confucius in Qufu had statues during the Qing dynasty and the Republican period. They also learned from television newscasts of the new statues in Qufu's refurbished Confucius temple. The original statues in Qufu has been destroyed by a group of Red Guards from

SELF, COMMUNITY, AND STATE

Unlike Dachuan's temple, which was rebuilt with support from the entire multi-village Kong lineage, Xiaochuan's temple was rebuilt with money and materials raised by and from Xiaochuan itself. Also unlike Dachuan's temple, which was controlled by one middle-aged man and thirteen elders from four major Kong villages, Xiaochuan's temple was managed by ten local residents, with a very different repertoire of cultural (educational) capital, primarily because of age. Only three of these men were over the age of sixty; the others were in their early fifties and mid-forties. The leader of this group was a retired construction foreman who had learned how to read and write through an "illiteracy eradication" program in the 1950s. Of the other two elderly temple managers, one worked as a primary school teacher, and the other was a semi-literate tobacco seller.

On the surface, the three elderly temple managers ran everything. In reality, the temple management in Xiaochuan was controlled by the seven middle-aged men. All had been educated after the founding of the Communist regime, but none of them finished junior high school. Moreover, all of these middle-aged men had either served as village cadres or worked in low-ranking capacities at government agencies and state-run industrial enterprises. These younger temple managers were so assertive that as early as 1992 the elderly leader of Xiaochuan's temple project threatened to resign. Although he kept his nominal position, his leadership role was assumed in 1995 by a middle-aged man, an amateur photographer and owner of a photo-developing shop.

In contrast to the managers of Dachuan's temple, the majority of whom were comfortably off but hardly wealthy by local standards, Xiaochuan's temple managers belonged to a group of individuals who became noticeably wealthy after rural economic reforms were introduced in Yongjing in the early 1980s. But despite their enviable occupational backgrounds and their

---

Beijing during the Cultural Revolution (see the chapter by Wang Liang, pp. 390–93, in this volume). Although the temple managers in Dachuan disapproved of Xiaochuan's plan to make a statue of Confucius, they approved of the installation of new statues in Qufu. They explained that Qufu occupies the highest place in the worship of Confucius and that its supremacy is rightly distinguished by the use of statues for the worship of the ancient sage and his esteemed disciples. For more on Confucius's birth and appearance, see pp. 196–201, 233–34, and 253–54 of this volume.

material wealth, only the schoolteacher could read the ritual handbook borrowed from Dachuan in preparation for Xiaochuan's temple-opening festival. Yet even he did not feel confident enough to take charge of the planned festival. After a round of intense discussions, it was decided that the three classically educated people in charge of Dachuan's temple would be asked to supervise the festival.

Xiaochuan's temple managers, as explained above, did not follow every step Dachuan had taken. In considerable measure, these men became temple managers on the strength of their previous careers as village cadres, industrial workers, low-ranking government employees, and, more recently for some of them, successful private entrepreneurs. Pivotal to their control of the temple was their ability to manipulate government policies to favor themselves and their home village. This ability is an extremely potent form of symbolic capital and social authority in Xiaochuan. Whereas Dachuan remained a primarily agricultural community with one-third of its local households living below the official poverty line in 1991–92, Xiaochuan had by then become a thriving community of vendors and long-distance traders. Its commercial bent is traceable to the construction of the hydroelectric dam, which resulted in the flooding of nearly 70 percent of Xiaochuan's arable land. There is no doubt that Xiaochuan's economic loss was enormous. But during the construction, the county government moved its headquarters to Xiaochuan, and a railway was built nearby, bringing into Xiaochuan and its environs hundreds of bureaucrats, three major industrial enterprises, and thousands of urban workers. Other benefits were two high schools and two modern hospitals. The influx of government agencies and industrial enterprises helped establish a growing base of wholesalers and retailers and other commercial services. The Xiaochuan Kongs found themselves living within a hundred yards of the county government's office buildings. Dachuan also was severely affected by the dam, but it was not geographically positioned to take advantage of the benefits engendered by the influx of government agencies, industrial facilities, and educational and medical institutions.

Even before rural collectives were abolished in Xiaochuan in 1981, many local residents had found jobs in government or factories, thanks to the village's location in an administrative, urbanized, and industrialized environment. Whereas only a handful of people in Dachuan possess an insider's knowledge of how government agencies and urban work units function, a considerable number of male adults in Xiaochuan are perceptive observers of the bureaucratic system because of their direct involvement in the operations of the county government and state-owned industries. These men's knowledge of how national policies are implemented in the county government's different agencies and in local industrial enterprises has enabled them to develop a better understanding of those government policies that directly affect their hometown and themselves.

In the economic reforms following decollectivization, many of the Xiaochuan Kongs began renting sidewalks or street corners in the county seat to set up fruit stalls, grocery stores, and small food stands to service government officials, industrial workers, and their families. By 1992, the Kongs of Xiaochuan were ubiquitous along the county seat's main road, a busy street filled with noodle shops, small hostels, grocery stores, clothing boutiques, newsstands, ice-cream parlors, and shoe-repair services. Some Kongs even became involved in key sectors of local commerce. One Kong household signed a responsibility contract with the county government to take over the county seat's second largest department store and within two years turned it into a profitable business. In another major business venture, three Kongs established a company running mini-buses along a paved road between Xiaochuan and an industrial town. And about twenty households in Xiaochuan pooled their money to transport local produce, especially fruits and vegetables, to the city of Lanzhou and smaller cities in Gansu.

The managers of Xiaochuan's temple were not at the top of their hometown's economic ladder, but they were active participants in the commercial development of the county seat and in the transportation of local produce to city dwellers. Six members of the temple organization controlled small private businesses in 1992. The others had at least one immediate family member working in state-run enterprises or government agencies. In many respects, economic reforms created the environment that allowed Xiaochuan's temple managers to thrive. In 1992, none of them still held an official position or industrial job, although their prior occupations and knowledge of government policies enabled them to continue serving as intermediaries between Xiaochuan and local government agencies. Especially in land, water, and pollution disputes, they worked together with village cadres to represent their community in negotiations to demand compensation from nearby factories and construction companies. In 1995, when negotiations to get a higher rate of compensation failed, at least half the temple managers were

involved in organizing local villagers to form a human wall to stop the
county government's construction of a new road that would cut through
Xiaochuan and destroy about twenty courtyards. After local police knocked
three Kongs unconscious in breaking up the blockade, the head of
Xiaochuan's temple went into hiding for about twenty days. He had mas-
terminded the blockade and openly demanded that the county magistrate be
indicted for ordering the police to use violence and wave pistols to intimi-
date the protestors. With the help of friends and kinsmen in the county and
prefectural governments, the police warrant for his arrest was revoked, and a
new round of negotiations began.

The temple managers in Xiaochuan had not, however, banded together
to form an anti-government organization. On the contrary, they were willing to cooperate with government officials on most occasions of importance.
A case in point is their decision to emulate the state-sponsored refurbish-
ment of Confucius's hometown and to embrace the county government's
promotion of local tourism.

At the national level, the official reopening of Qufu as a historic town in
1979 was followed by a series of national and international conferences to assess Confucius's legacy positively. The sage's life and his hometown gradually became a frequent topic in newspapers and on television. The temple
managers in Xiaochuan closely followed the official attitude toward Confucius and his hometown as expressed in the mass media's coverage of these
conferences and the frequent visits by national leaders and foreign dignitaries to Qufu. One conclusion they reached, they said, was to model their
style of temple management on that found in Qufu, which had since the
early 1980s assertively tapped regional, national, and overseas funding to re-
furbish the buildings in the splendid Confucius temple complex (Kongmiao
孔廟), the multi-courtyard residence of the Kong family mansion (Kongfu
孔府), and the Kong clan's immense cemetery (Konglin 孔林).[46] With investments pouring into the rapid expansion of tourist facilities in a small city
of no more than 60,000 local residents, Qufu was able to receive, in 1992
alone, 1,300,000 domestic tourists and 14,600 overseas visitors.

The success of tourism in Qufu has been enthusiastically promoted by national news agencies as an exemplary case of utilizing historically renowned
landmarks to boost the local economy. This official message did not go unno-

---

46. The temple and the residential compound occupy a total of 40 acres of land today,
and the cemetery occupies about 450 acres of afforested fields within its walls.

ticed by the temple managers in Xiaochuan. But they did not embark on the temple-rebuilding project until they learned from their contacts in the county seat and in the city of Lanzhou that a Hong Kong investor and a provincial tourist agency wanted to build a park at the nearby reservoir. The waterfront park's potential visitors were well-to-do urban families headed by younger couples in Lanzhou who could afford to spend weekends and holidays away from the provincial capital. The temple managers in Xiaochuan also learned that the county government was drawing up a plan to link the proposed park with a newly created "cultural festival" (*wenhua jie* 文化節) to coincide with the annual arrival of thousands of pilgrims at the Binglingsi, a Buddhist complex located on a mountain at the middle of the reservoir and accessible only by boats from a pier near Xiaochuan.

This knowledge galvanized Xiaochuan's temple-rebuilding project. Unlike Dachuan's temple, which received no official support, the reconstruction of Xiaochuan's temple was encouraged by the county government with the intention of attracting domestic and overseas investment by setting up a new tourist site in the name of Confucius. As one of its temple managers vividly put it, Xiaochuan received a "double indemnity" (*shuang baoxian* 雙保險). On the one hand, the state-approved conversion of Qufu's historic sites into tourist attractions provided an archetype of political legitimacy; on the other, the county government's decision to attract investment from outside was an ideal opportunity to build the temple and form a temple organization without taking political risks, at least for the time being. Compared with the temple managers in Dachuan who deeply feared and actively evaded official intervention, the managers of Xiaochuan's temple took full advantage of the central government's treatment of Confucius's hometown and, more crucially, aligned themselves with the county government. The sophistication of Xiaochuan's temple managers in dealing with officials arose from their intimate knowledge of how government policies could be adjusted in an expedient fashion to serve their own and their home community's interests.

CONCLUSION

At the beginning of this chapter, I argued that four distinctive categories of knowledge—ritual expertise, literary skills, informed notions of history, and political awareness—are among the vital resources that must be considered in analyzing the religious revival in rural China. To situate my case study within the mainstream of social theory, I have drawn on Bourdieu's concept of symbolic capital by treating these four categories as pivotal to the rebuilding and, thereafter, the managing of the temples in Dachuan and Xiaochuan. I have argued in particular that the mobilization of knowledge-based resources involves the accumulation of symbolic capital through the institutionalization of personal knowledge and the appropriation of social authority by individual retainers of the needed knowledge. As Bourdieu has noted:

Symbolic capital is a credit; it is the power granted to those who have obtained sufficient recognition to be in a position to impose recognition. In this way, the power of constitution, a power to make a new group, through mobilization, or to make it exist by proxy, by speaking on its behalf as an authorized spokesperson, can be obtained only as the outcome of a long process of institutionalization, at the end of which a representative is instituted, who receives from the group the power to make the group.[47]

In addition, I would single out social change and generational differences as two factors with an impact on the reconstruction of the two temples.

Xiaochuan's temple was dominated by a group that benefited from industrial development and bureaucratic buildup under Mao's rule. These people continued to thrive in the post-Mao era by tapping into the opportunities engendered by the economic reforms and other policy changes. A crucial source of these men's symbolic power came from the political knowledge they accumulated through their work in government agencies or state-run enterprises. Their continuing access to vital information about government policies was maintained in the reform era by their cultivation of official connections. More important, their ability to acquire, interpret, and make effective use of the official information allowed them to take full advantage of many policy changes. As a knowledge-based resource, their political awareness, characterized by their intimate knowledge of the bureaucratic system and their readiness to cooperate with government officials, was crucial to the maintenance of their social status and to their control of Xiaochuan's temple.

By contrast, the men in charge of Dachuan's temple were primarily political victims during the Maoist era. Their knowledge of politics grew out of the attacks on themselves and their families, and their behavior was charac-

---

47. Bourdieu, "Social Space," p. 23.

terized by the fear that this violence might be repeated. In the post-Mao era, however, these men experienced a drastic reversal of status and once again became respected villagers. Closely linked with ancestor worship at Dachuan's temporary shrine before the village's new temple was built, this turn in personal fortunes must be viewed from a historical perspective. Up to 1949, the social organization of the Kongs of Yongjing revolved around (1) a lineage organization based on the shared ideas of common descent and the celebrations of ritual unity through ancestor worship; (2) a body of corporate property; and (3) a government-regulated but locally selected group of administrators in each Kong village in charge of community security, military recruitment, collection of agricultural taxes, and public works. With the Communist takeover of Yongjing in 1949, the first two parts of this threefold system began losing their importance and the third part was quickly reshuffled, giving rise to a new rural bureaucracy. At the village level, the new system of social organization was dominated by rural cadres, especially those low-ranking cadres belonging to the village-based party sub-committees (*dang zhi bu* 党支部). With the launching of the Great Leap Forward, the power of the local party and administrative organs escalated in scope and intensity because of the change from small-scale collectives to total collectivization of both agricultural work and everyday life.[48]

The resumption of household production in 1981 ended the collective system in Yongjing. Consequently, many of the village-based party organizations and administrative cadres (who are not necessarily party members) lost a fundamental source of power and authority. This can be seen in the decline of village militia groups, Communist youth leagues, and women's associations. These organization began to disintegrate after decollectivization and, by 1992, existed in name only. A major reason for the erosion in the power of these organizations and village cadres was the lack of collectively owned industries in rural Yongjing. Had such industries been significant, they might have prevented the decline of the party-state's administrative or-

---

48. Back in 1956, the majority of villagers in Yongjing joined "high-level cooperatives." These were collective units of agricultural production, but the villagers were still allowed to keep a small number of cultivated fields and draft animals under private ownership. Once the people's commune system was established in 1958, however, only tiny vegetable plots were retained for private use, and they were treated as collective property and allocated by village cadres to individual households. Meanwhile, the administrative power of village cadres expanded quickly, touching nearly every aspect of the individual's life from birth to marriage to death.

gans at the village level.[49] With the weakening of government-sponsored organizations in Yongjing villages, networks of personal contacts gained
greater importance.

One such network was a group of about 30 elderly Kongs who called
themselves "old schoolmates" (*laotongxue* 老同學). These people had attended the primary school at Dachuan's old temple, and some had even received a further education in county seats, market towns, and the city of
Lanzhou before returning to Yongjing between the late 1940s and the late
1950s. Nine of the managers of Dachuan's new temple came from this
group. In social gatherings I observed from 1989 to 1995, the members of this
group often spoke emotionally of their pride, nostalgia, and mutual respect.
Although they lived in different settlements throughout the Yellow River
valley of Yongjing, their personal ties were maintained by visits and especially through invitations to banquets to celebrate marriages, the construction of new houses, and the birth of grandsons. Most of all, many of them
had acted since the early 1980s as consultants and experts in the production
of "ancestor charts" (*shen zhu* 神主) and "segmentary genealogies" (*fen pu*
分譜).[50] By offering advice to fellow villagers on these genealogical records,
the elderly Kongs succeeded in gaining a considerable measure of respect in
their home villages and in the greater Kong community in Yongjing.

In the reconstruction of Dachuan's temple, these people, already loosely
organized and linked by a desire to vindicate their traditional educations, either became temple managers or offered staunch support for the fundraising
drive. As if desperately trying to revive a lost tradition by educating a new
generation, they insisted that a preschool be founded at the temple proper
and that the preschool teachers be selected by the temple organization.
They also urged the temple's watchman, an experienced ritualist, to provide
special instruction for the parents of schoolchildren in offering money,
burning incense, and lighting oil lamps before the examinations that would

---

49. A similar argument has been made in Yan, "Everyday Power Relations." See Huang,
The Spiral Road, pp. 136–91, for the administrative power of village cadres in a Fujian village in
which rural industries and commercial enterprises remained under collective ownership.

50. The ancestor charts are wall-sized paintings made of canvas, decorated with drawings
of auspicious symbols and covered with the names of dead ancestors, usually within ten generations, to be displayed during death rituals. Also usually covering ten generations, the segmentary genealogies are book-sized documents about the dead and the exact locations of their
tombs.

determine whether their children could attend senior high schools, technical schools, or regular four-year colleges.

The second factor, generational difference, was clearly a considerable barrier between the temple managers in Dachuan and their counterparts in Xiaochuan. Their varying educational backgrounds profoundly affected their managerial strategies. In the social sciences, the idea that each generation receives a distinctive imprint from the social or political events of its own life-course is often associated with the work of Karl Mannheim.[51] Although Mannheim emphasized that a generation is a social creation rather than a biological necessity, he suggested, as almost all later writers have done, that it is during late adolescence and early adulthood that a distinctive personal outlook emerges to exert "an important, even decisive, influence upon the later attitudes and actions of its members."[52] Perhaps the most striking example of generational differences in Yongjing is "the consequence of literacy," to borrow a phrase from Jack Goody and Ian Watt.[53] As shown above, a significant number of the managers of Dachuan's new temple had at least some basic literary skills. Two of them were college graduates, another was a graduate of a prestigious high school, and six others had received an education at the primary school at Dachuan's old Confucius temple; the management of the new temple was dominated by those who were ritually experienced and classically educated. Their social authority was rooted in their exposure to a now-outmoded educational system and a lineage-organized program of ritual training in the pre-Communist era.

The majority of Xiaochuan's temple managers, however, grew up and were educated at a time when the Chinese party-state was trying to create a socialist culture, which led to radical reforms of the education system and the Chinese script. Xiaochuan's predominantly younger temple managers were seriously challenged by the need to apply the literary skills they had acquired in the new educational system to a religious undertaking that demanded special literary knowledge to underscore cultural continuity and historical authenticity. A more serious challenge was ritual performance, especially the delivery of ritual speeches in a culturally acceptable manner. Since they lacked both the needed literary and ritual skills, they had to invite

---

51. See esp. Mannheim's *On the Sociology of Knowledge*.
52. Schuman and Scott, "Generations and Collective Memory," p. 359.
53. Goody and Watt, "The Consequences of Literacy," p. 27.

three elderly men from Dachuan to supervise opening ceremonies for the Xiaochuan temple in 1992.

At the time, there were at least four men in their seventies in Xiaochuan who could have advised the temple managers. But these people recommended that ritualists from Dachuan be invited, because they had "a better understanding of ritual propriety" (*geng dong li* 更懂禮). This recommendation highlights the advantage that accrued to Dachuan of enlisting the help of classically educated and ritually experienced individuals not from just one Kong village but from the greater Kong community of Yongjing. In the process, a critical mass of ritual knowledge was accumulated that rendered Dachuan's ritualists credible and authoritative.

The temple managers in Dachuan and Xiaochuan had at their disposal different forms of symbolic capital, characterized by noticeable variations in knowledge. Differences in knowledge affected all their major decisions. None of their choices could be fully understood had we failed to probe the specific contexts in which personal knowledge was put into practice and institutionalized. This chapter, I hope, has demonstrated the centrality of institutionalized knowledge in the rise of religious activism during the post-Mao era. As a whole, community efforts in rural China to rebuild local religious landmarks have brought many people together and tapped numerous social networks. Such collective efforts are carving out a domain of local autonomy and resulting in a growing number of relatively independent religious organizations in the Chinese countryside. Pivotal to the emergence of these organizations and their religious pursuits are the social organization of symbolic capital and the institutionalization of symbolic power, including ritual, literary, historical, and political knowledge.

WORKS CITED

Baker, Keith. *Inventing the French Revolution*. Cambridge, Eng.: Cambridge University, 1990.

Bourdieu, Pierre. "Cultural Reproduction and Social Reproduction." In *Power and Ideology in Education*, ed. Jerome Karabel and A. H. Halsey, pp. 487–511. New York: Oxford University Press, 1977.

———. *Distinction: A Social Critique of the Judgement of Taste*. Cambridge, Mass.: Harvard University Press, 1984.

———. *Outline of a Theory of Practice*. Cambridge, Mass.: Harvard University, 1977.

———. "Social Space and Symbolic Power." *Sociological Theory* 7 (1989) 1: 14–25.

Cai Limin 蔡利民. "Shangfang shan jie yinzhai" 上方山偕陰債 (Borrowing spirit money at Shangfang Mountain). *Zhongguo minjian wenhua* 6 (1992): 239–56.

Cohen, Myron. "Religion in a State Society: China." In *Asia: Case Studies in Social Sciences*, ed. Myron Cohen, pp. 17–31. Columbia Project on Asia in the Core Curriculum, pt. 1. Armonk, N.Y.: M. E. Sharpe, 1992.

Dean, Kenneth. *Taoist Ritual and Popular Cults in Southeast China*. Princeton: Princeton University Press, 1993.

Duara, Prasenjit. "Knowledge and Power in the Discourse of Modernity: The Campaigns Against Popular Religion in Early Twentieth-Century China." *Journal of Asian Studies* 50 (1991) 1: 67–83.

Freedman, Maurice. *Chinese Lineage and Society: Fukien and Kwangtung*. London: Athlone, 1966.

Goody, Jack, and Ian Watt. "The Consequences of Literacy." In *Literacy in Traditional Societies*, ed. Jack Goody, pp. 27–84. Cambridge, Eng.: Cambridge University Press, 1968.

He Lingxiu 何凌修, ed. *Fengjian guizu dadizhu de dianxing* 封建貴族大地主的典型 (The archetype of feudal landlords). Beijing: Zhongguo shehui kexue yanjiuyuan, 1981.

Hu Guojun 胡國均. "Hugong dadi xinyang yu fangyan miaohui" 胡公大帝信仰于方岩廟會 (Faith in Hugong, the Supreme King, and temple festivals at Fangyan). *Zhongguo minjian wenhua* 4 (1991): 184–221.

Huang, Shu-min. *The Spiral Road: Changes in a Chinese Village Through the Eyes of a Communist Party Leader*. Boulder: Westview, 1989.

Kong Decheng 孔德成. *Kongzi shijia pu* 孔子世家譜 (Genealogy of the Kongs). 1937.

Kong Demao. *In the Mansion of Confucius: An Oral History*. Beijing: New World Press, 1984.

Kong Fanyin 孔繁銀. *Yansheng gongfu jianwen* 衍聖公府見聞 (Anecdotes about the Dukes of Yansheng). Ji'nan: Qi Lu shushe, 1992.

Kong Jifen 孔繼汾. *Kongzi shijia pu* 孔子世家譜 (Genealogy of the Kongs). 1744 ed.

Kong Lingshu 孔令述. *Kongshi jiapu* 孔氏家譜 (Genealogy of the Kongs). Manuscript, 1989.

Kong Qinghui 孔慶蕙. *Qufu lingpu jixing* 曲阜領譜記行 (My trip to Qufu to get the clan genealogy). N.p., 1948.

Kong Shangren 孔尚任. *Kongzi shijia pu* 孔子世家譜 (Genealogy of the Kongs). 1684.

Kong Xiangguo 孔祥國, ed. *Ji shengzu yishi* 祭聖祖儀式 (Rites of offering sacrifices to our holy ancestor). Manuscript, 1991.

Kong Xianmin 孔憲敏. *Jincheng Kongshi zupu* 金城孔氏族谱 (Genealogy of the Kongs at Jincheng). 1905 ed.

Kong Zhaozeng 孔昭增. *Qufu xianzhi* 曲阜縣志 (Qufu county gazetteer). 1934 ed.

Kongfu dang'an xuanbian 孔府檔案選編 (Selection of documents from the Kong Mansion archives). 2 vols. Comp. Zhongguo shehui kexueyuan, Jindaishi yanjiusuo 中國社會科學院近代史研究所 and Shandongsheng Qufu wenwu guanli weiyuanhui 山東省曲阜文物管理委員會. Beijing: Zhonghua shuju, 1982.

Li Jinghan 李景漢. *Dingxian shehui zhuangkuang diaocha* 定縣社會狀況調查 (Dingxian: a survey of social conditions). Dingxian, Hebei: Zhonghua pingmin jiaoyu cujinhui, 1933; Reprinted—Beijing: Renmin daxue chubanshe, 1985.

Lang, Graeme, and Lars Ragvald. *The Rise of a Refugee God: Hong Kong's Wong Tai Sin.* Hong Kong: Oxford University, 1993.

Luo, Zhufeng, ed. *Religion Under Socialism in China.* Armonk, N.Y.: M. E. Sharpe, 1991.

MacFarquhar, Roderick. "The Succession to Mao and End of Maoism." In *Cambridge History of China*, vol. 15, *People's Republic*, pt. II, ed. Roderick MacFarquhar and John King Fairbank, pp. 496–620. Cambridge, Eng.: Cambridge University Press.

MacInnis, Donald. *Religion in China Today: Policy & Practice.* Maryknoll, N.Y.: Orbis Books, 1989.

Mannheim, Karl. *Essays on the Sociology of Knowledge.* London: Routledge & Kegan Paul, 1952.

Qi Wu 齊武. *Kongshi dizhu zhuang yuan* 孔氏地主莊園 (The manor of the Kong landlords). Beijing: Zhonghua shehui kexue chubanshe, 1982.

Schuman, Howard, and Jacqueline Scott. "Generations and Collective Memory." *American Sociological Review* 54 (June 1989): 359–83.

Scott, James. *Domination and the Arts of Resistance: Hidden Transcripts.* New Haven: Yale University, 1990.

Seymour, James, and Eugene Werhli, eds. and trans. "Religion in China." *Chinese Sociology and Anthropology* 26, no. 3 (1994): 1–96.

Shen Zhiyuan 沈志遠 and Le Bingcheng 樂炳成. "Lingfeng shan gexian weng pusa xinyang diaocha" 靈峰山葛仙菩薩翁信仰調查 (Investigating the worship of Ge Xian Weng Bodhisattva at Lingfeng Mountain). *Zhongguo minjian wenhua* 3 (1991): 172–83.

Siu, Helen. "Recycling Rituals: Politics and Popular Culture in Contemporary Rural China." In *Unofficial China: Popular Culture and Thought in the People's Republic*, ed. Perry Link, Richard Madsen, and Paul Pickowicz, pp. 121–37. Boulder: Westview, 1989.

Turner, Victor. *Dramas, Fields, and Metaphors*. Ithaca, N.Y.: Cornell University, 1974.

Wang Huning 王滬寧, ed. *Dangdai Zhongguo cunluo jiazu wenhua* 當代中國村落家族文化 (Villages, family groups, and culture in contemporary China). Shanghai: Shanghai renmin chubanshe, 1991.

Watson, James. "Chinese Kinship Reconsidered: Anthropological Analysis of Historical Research." *China Quarterly* 92 (1982): 589–622.

Wilson, Thomas. "The Ritualization of Confucian Orthodoxy and the Descendants of the Sage." Paper presented at the Neo-Confucian Seminar, Columbia University, May 5, 1995.

Yan Yunxiang. "Everyday Power Relations: Changes in a North China Village." In *The Waning of the Communist State: Economic Origins of Political Decline in China and Hungary*, ed. Andrew G. Walder, pp. 215–41. Berkeley: University of California Press, 1995.

Yang, C. K. *Religion in Chinese Society*. Berkeley: University of California Press, 1961.

Yang, Mayfair. "Tradition, Travelling Anthropology, and the Discourse of Modernity in China." Paper presented at the Fourth Decennial Association of Social Anthropology Conference, Oxford University, England, July 1993.

Yongjingxian xianzhi bianji weiyuanhui 永靖縣縣志編輯委員會. *Yongjing xianzhi* 永靖縣志 (Yongjing county gazetteer). 1992.

NINE

The Confucius Temple Tragedy of the Cultural Revolution

Wang Liang

Translated by Curtis Dean Smith

THE AUGUST 26 INCIDENT

In August 1966, anything was possible. The destruction of the "Four Olds" (*si-jiu* 四旧) was growing ever increasingly fierce.[1] The leaders of Qufu County felt an enormous threat because their county was the home of Confucius, symbol of ancient Chinese culture. Located on this ancient land were such cultural relics as the Three Kong Sites (san Kong 三孔)—the Temple to Confucius (Kongmiao 孔庙), the Kong Mansion (Kongfu 孔府), and the Kong Cemetery (Konglin 孔林)—the Temple to Yan Hui 颜回, and the Temple to the Duke of Zhou 周公. According to the logic of the Red Guards, all of these were examples of the Four Olds and should be destroyed. The Qufu County Communist Party decided to appoint Deputy County Chief Cui Xuyi, who was also secretary of the Party Support Section attached to the Cultural Relics Management Committee, and Deputy County Magis-

My thanks to Jing Jun, who edited the original Chinese version of this essay, and to Judy Wolf, who edited the English translation.

1. The campaign against the Four Olds (old ideology, culture, customs, and habits) was launched in the summer of 1966 and was later criticized as insufficiently radical after the Red Guards began their attack on the Party apparatus.

trate Wang Huatian to sit on the Cultural Relics Management Committee, in order to strengthen the leadership of the committee and prevent the Red Guards from damaging cultural relics such as the Three Kong Sites.

Late at night on August 23, news came that the Tai'an Naval Academy Red Guards had stormed the peak of nearby Mount Tai, destroying stelae and engravings on the cliffs, and were threatening to destroy the Four Olds of Qufu next. At approximately the same moment, Qufu County Committee Secretary Li Xiu received a telephone call from the party committee secretary of Yao Village Commune, which lay along the Tianjin–Pukou railroad line, reporting that the Tai'an Naval Academy Red Guards were advancing on Qufu with the intent of destroying the Three Kong Sites.

The leaders of the Qufu County Committee and Qufu County People's Committee were woken from their sleep and sent to all units and schools to prepare defensive measures. That night, students of Qufu First Middle School posted banners on the main gate of the Temple to Confucius with slogans such as:

"Long live the proletarian Cultural Revolution!"
"Long live the dictatorship of the Proletariat!"
"Emergency brigades arise, prevent all destructive activities of the class enemies!"

The students also blocked the eastern and western gates to the temple grounds. Students of Qufu Normal University covered the ground before the front gate of the Kong Mansion with banners, leaving only a narrow passage and threatening to punish anyone who stepped on their banners.

Some local Red Guards also stood watch at the south, north, and west gates. The agricultural organization of the municipal commune guarded the entrance to the Kong Mansion. They did not have time to make Red Guard armbands; instead, they hung pieces of red cloth on their chests with "We are poor farmers" written on them.

In an instant, all of Qufu was roaring as if a great enemy were approaching.

On August 24, the Qufu County Committee called a meeting of the municipal commune representatives, the supervisor of security, and the supervisors of the county organizations and enterprise units. County Committee Secretary Li Xiu said: "According to the State Council, the Temple to Confucius, the Kong Mansion, and the Kong Cemetery are national property, listed as the nation's protected cultural units. These sites are truly invaluable not only in China, but in the world. No person may casually destroy them. To destroy the Three Kong Sites is to destroy national property. All units must obey the orders of the County Committee and keep up their guard so that no delinquents find an opportunity to do damage. When the Red Guards come, we must do our best not to have a conflict with them. We must reason with them, engage them in revolutionary debate, and send them safely on their way."

Twenty-four years later, Li Xiu told me that at the time it was thought that it would take centuries to recover from a few days' destruction. "Old Kong 孔老二 is a symbol of feudalism, but the Three Kong Sites are national property. We weren't protecting Old Kong; we were protecting national relics."[2] For Li, Old Kong was a symbol of feudalism, an abstract ideological symbol, but the actual concrete Three Kong Sites were a political truth—an estate under the administration of national political authority. They were national property, and so they had to be protected. This suggests that protecting the Three Kong Sites is the same as preventing the destruction of national power, even though Confucius can and ought to be criticized.

On August 24, the leaders of the Qufu Normal University Mao Zedong's Thought Red Guards met. The news that the Tai'an Naval Academy Red Guards were coming to destroy the Four Olds at the Three Kong Sites made them feel ashamed and guilty. At this moment, the whole country was busy destroying the Four Olds, and they—sitting in the homeland of the Four Olds—had to wait for Red Guards to come from outside. It was a disgrace! They decided that they would go to the Kong Mansion the next day and rebel.[3]

On the morning of August 25, the Qufu Normal University Mao Zedong's Thought Red Guards, the East-Is-Red Red Guards, and some of the Normal University–Affiliated Middle School Red Guards marched to the front gate of the Kong Mansion, shouting slogans on the way. They pasted big character posters on the front gates of the Temple and Mansion. Staff members of the Cultural Relics Management Committee blocked the students from entering the Mansion and began to debate with them. Both sides held fast to their positions, and neither side could sway the other.

---

2. Interview with Li Xiu, Dec. 9, 1990.
3. "Bei 'Dongfang hong' diandao de lishi."

Deputy County Magistrate Wang Huatian tried to persuade the Red Guards to disperse and return to their schools. He said the Temple and Mansion were national property: they were nationally protected units. He pointed to the stone plaque on the western side of the main gate to the Kong Mansion, on which was written "Key cultural relics under protection of the State Council," and said, "The plaque of the State Council is right over there. Whoever tries to destroy anything here is violating the law."[4]

The Red Guards did not know who Wang was. One Red Guard pointed a finger at Wang and asked, "What do you do for a living?"

Wang replied, "I'm Wang Huatian, the county magistrate!"

The Red Guards immediately began shouting, "Topple Wang Huatian! Topple Old Kong's watchdog!"[5]

A group of construction workers employed by the Cultural Relics Management Committee came to the magistrate's defense. The maintenance of the Three Kong Sites was in the hands of this group of workers, whose ancestors had done the same work. This superior proletarian pedigree gave them an advantage and power. An old artisan said to the noisy Red Guards, "Chairman Mao didn't say the Kong Mansion was one of the Four Olds. I don't understand anything about feudal relics, but if you want to wreck anything, show us the papers!"[6] The Red Guards could boss government officials, but they were helpless against these workers. They could do nothing but leave.

On the afternoon of August 26, the Tai'an Naval Academy Red Guards finally arrived. Over twenty of them, wearing green military uniforms and carrying red flags, marched to the gate of the Kong Mansion and demanded entry to destroy the Four Olds. Members of the southern group of the municipal commune rushed to the Mansion. They surrounded the Red Guards and started to debate with them. The students of the Tai'an Naval Academy were outnumbered and retreated to Qufu Normal University to look for allies.

In the evening, the Qufu Normal University Red Guards again came to the Kong Mansion. They shouted slogans like "Revolution is faultless, rebellion is reasonable," "Topple Old Kong," and "The Qufu County Committee will never succeed in suppressing the student movement!" The People's

---

4. Interview with Fan Xueqin, Mar. 1990.
5. Ibid.
6. Interview with Gao Jinghong, Mar. 20, 1990.

Army of the municipal commune and a unit of the Peasant Red Guard moved in to divide the student Red Guards. They surrounded them and then proceeded to debate and attack. The farmers of Qufu were angered by the actions of the Red Guards. These residents of Qufu had always viewed the Three Kong Sites as a source of pride and stature. They fought to preserve their self-esteem. Deep into the night, the Red Guards were pushed around, and some students were even pulled into the Kong Mansion and beaten. Around one o'clock in the morning of August 27, Deputy Secretary to the County Committee Zhang Yumei ordered the farmers to release the students immediately, stating that it would be inconvenient if things got out of hand. Only then did groups of students straggle back to their school.

On August 26, five members of the Qufu Normal University Red Guards arrived at the office of the Ministry of Culture in Beijing, where they discussed how to handle the problem of ancient cultural sites with officials in the Bureau of Cultural Relics. The following is an extract from the pamphlet on this discussion printed by the Qufu Normal University Hawk Squad Red Guards:

On August 26, five members of our squad conferred with the head of the Bureau of Cultural Relics, Central Ministry of Culture, on how the Great Cultural Revolution ought to handle the problem of ancient cultural sites. After our classmates expressed their opinions, they discussed some guidelines, the main points of which are listed below:

... Concerning how to deal with artifacts, it is our [the Bureau of Relics] opinion that they ought not be demolished at the very outset of the movement. They can be closed off, and a public debate may be held. Raise the issues of the units concerned, and allow the people to express their opinions about which artifacts ought to be criticized, which ought to be demolished, which ought to be closed off, which ought to be used, and how they ought to be used. As for which should be preserved, used, and demolished, we and all administrative units do not have the authority to set regulations. Let the lower and middle peasants discuss this. Everyone knows what should be done. Use great debates as the foundation for unifying thought, then reform old, and renew. This is how the Beijing "Palace of Blood and Tears" (formerly the Imperial Palace) handles things. For now, it is preferable to close the sites.[7]

---

7. "He Zhongyang wenhuabu tubowenwuju fuze tongzhi tanhua jiyao."

PROTECTIVE MEASURES OF
THE QUFU COUNTY COMMITTEE

In early September, the County Committee received notice from the Secretarial Office of the State Council that the Qufu County Party Committee should send one secretary, and Qufu Normal University should send one student representative, to Beijing for a meeting to discuss the Three Kong Sites. On September 5, Deputy Secretary and County Magistrate Gao Keming and one student representative arrived in the capital. A representative from the Ministry of Culture listened in private to Gao's report on the "August 26 incident" and the Qufu County Committee's plan, devised in 1965, to reform the Three Kong Sites and then discussed with Gao how to deal with the student representative. After some excited discussion, the three parties finally agreed to follow the 1965 reform plan temporarily; to gradually reform the Kong Mansion, the Kong Temple, and the Kong Cemetery; and to open them to the public.[8] By the time Gao Keming returned to Qufu, the fall harvest and fall planting had begun. The County Committee decided to wait until after the harvest to commence work on the Three Kong Sites.

At the same time, the students began a wave of destruction of the Four Olds within the city, tearing down plaques, destroying decorations on houses, and changing all store signs. The County Committee leaders were worried that the Three Kong Sites would soon be targeted. In late September, as the entire country was being inundated in a sea of red, the County Committee encased the two stone lions at the entrance to the Kong Mansion in wooden boxes and wrote two sayings of Chairman Mao in red paint on the boxes: "We must believe in the masses; we must believe in the Party; these are two fundamental principles." "To know if a youth is part of the revolution, you must first see whether or not he is in unison with the proletariat masses."

The stone lions became billboards for the sayings of Chairman Mao. It was as if they were under the protection of the highest authority. Leaders of

---

8. In 1981, Gao Keming was interviewed by Kong Xiangmin, the chief cultural historian in the Qufu County government, who wished to write an article on the destruction of the Three Kong Sites during the Cultural Revolution. The article was never finished. By the time I began writing about this period of history, Gao had already passed away; I thank Mr. Kong for permitting me to use his interview notes.

the County Committee thought that such methods would protect the statues of Confucius, the four correlates, and the twelve savants in the main hall of the Temple to Confucius. Similar reasoning was behind their decision to move the Qufu County Agricultural Accomplishments Exhibit from the Kong Mansion to the main hall of the temple. The leaders imagined that the record of seventeen years of agricultural accomplishments could protect the temple from the Red Guards, who were about to storm it at any moment.

Deputy County Magistrate Ban Shouzheng ordered the workers to place large sacrificial tables in front of the statues of Confucius, the four correlates, and the twelve savants, and then to put display boards over them. Cultural Relics Management Committee artists worked day and night, painting, cutting, and pasting a variety of pictures displaying the agricultural accomplishments of Qufu onto these boards. Bright and colorful pictures covered the majestic and mysterious statues of sages. The once august and awesome temple hall was suddenly transformed with a brilliant array of colors. Above Confucius's statue hung a board with a saying of Chairman Mao written on it: "All problems of ideology, all disagreements among the people, can be solved only through democratic methods; can be solved only through discussion, criticism, and persuasion; but they must not be solved through force and oppression."[9] The leaders of the exhibition committee carefully selected this saying to remind marauding Red Guards of the methods expounded by the Great Helmsman.

Two months later, all these measures would become incriminating evidence in charges that the County Committee had conspired to protect the Temple to Confucius.

THE STATE COUNCIL PLAQUE
IS SMASHED

On November 9, 1966, one of the four main leaders of the Beijing Red Guards, Tan Houlan, led over 200 members of the Beijing Normal University Mao Zedong's Thought Red Guard's Mount Jinggang Brigade to Qufu. The suggestion that Tan go to Qufu to destroy the "Kong Family Shop" (*Kong jiadian* 孔家店) came from Lin Jie, editor of *Red Flag*, close friend of Guan Feng and Qi Benyu of the Central Cultural Revolution Leadership

---

9. Interview with Ban Shouzheng, Mar. 23, 1990.

Committee, and famous proponent of the radical leftists of the Cultural Revolution.[10] Before leaving for Qufu, Tan Houlan made appropriate preparations. At the advice of Lin Jie, she wrote "Burn Down the Kong Family Shop—Declaration to Rebuke Confucius (*tao Kong* 讨孔)" and "Notice to the People of the Nation," which she printed as a pamphlet, and later published in the founding issue of *Tao Kong zhanbao* (讨孔战报; Report on the battle to rebuke Confucius). At about 9:00 A.M. on the second day after arriving in Qufu, Tan led the Beijing Normal University Red Guards and some of the Qufu Normal University Red Guards to the County Committee headquarters. The County Committee had anticipated trouble and was prepared. When Tan and the Red Guards arrived, Deputy Secretaries Gao Keming and Zhang Yumei led the members of the Committee Executive Office to the front door to welcome them.

In a simple welcoming ceremony, Gao Keming gave a short speech, welcoming the Beijing Normal University Red Guards to Qufu.[11] Tan read her two pamphlets. After listing all of Confucius's crimes, she roared:

Today, we raise the great red banner of Mao Zedong's thought and herald the revolution against the Kong Family Shop! Topple the Kong Family Shop! Burn the Kong Family Shop! Pull the "uncrowned king" Kong (Kong suwang 孔素王) off his horse and smash him to a pulp! We're going to destroy every symbol of the authorities of the Four Olds! Your dukes of Zhou and Lu, your revered sage, your sagely doctrines, and your imperial gifts; to hell with them all!

We want to establish the ultimate authority of Mao Zedong's thought and topple the Kong Family Shop to its foundations! Burn the Confucian scholars, flatten the Kongs' graves, haul out the Kong sycophants and the reactionary "authorities" who worship Confucius, and parade them in the streets! Let those capitalist pigs chatter with their backs turned!

Just as Tan Houlan's voice started to go hoarse, the Red Guards started to yell: "Topple Old Kong!" and "Burn the Kong Family Shop!"

At this point, the County Committee Executive Office members, as planned, calmly began to recite three of Mao's articles: "Serving the People," "In Memory of Norman Benthume," and "The Foolish Old Man Who

---

10. In the early 1970s, during the investigation of the May Sixteenth movement, this action was said to be a revolt against the State Council, with the final purpose of overthrowing Zhou Enlai. To this day, however, no substantial evidence of this accusation has been found.

11. "Beishida hongweibing lai Qu hou shijian jilu."

Moved a Mountain."[12] The protestors were caught off guard. They were unable to recite works of the great leader in response. In this unique battle, both of the two opposing camps used the writings of Mao. Mao's words became the weapons of both sides.

After this short encounter, Tan Houlan led the Red Guards, under the direction of the County Committee Executive Office, to view the Three Kong Sites. In the Kong Mansion, they turned up flags of the Nationalist Party and of Manchukuo; in a pile of clothing, they found an ancient sword and a Japanese samurai sword, wedding gifts from Han Fuqu (warlord and governor of Shandong) and Kong Xiangxi[13] to the seventy-seventh direct male descendant of Confucius, Kong Decheng. They also uncovered items such as a photograph of Yuan Shikai,[14] a Nationalist Party manual for its extermination campaign against the Communist Party, and photographs and letters exchanged between the inhabitants of the Kong Mansion, the traitor Wang Jingwei,[15] and the invading forces of the Japanese army.[16] If Tan was initially at a loss for where to begin to topple the Kong Family Shop, she certainly knew where to start when she saw these items.

Turning up these items was a victory for the Red Guards and caused the County Committee considerable guilt and frustration. In the political environment of the time, there was no way to explain the historical value of these items to the Red Guards. The leaders of the County Committee and the County Cultural Relics Management Committee fell into a panic. Cui Xuyi, director of both committees, felt as if he were up against a wall. He was worried that the Red Guards might soon destroy such relics as the "Ten Shang-Zhou gifts" (Shang Zhou shi gong 商周十供)[17] as one of the Four Olds. These ten sacrificial vessels had been a gift from the Qianlong emperor (r. 1736–96) when he held the sacrificial rite for Confucius in Qufu in 1772. The Kong Mansion considered this gift a glorious honor and had kept the relics a close secret. Cui and County Magistrate Gao Keming discussed the matter and, late that night, had the vessels buried in the ground and hid other valu-

---

12. Interview with Hu Yuan, Mar. 2, 1990.

13. AKA H. H. Kung (1881–1967) served as minister of finance in the 1930s and briefly served as president during Jiang's military campaign against Japan in 1938.

14. President of the Republic from 1912 to 1916.

15. Left-wing rival to Jiang Kaishek in the Nationalist Party.

16. Interview with Kong Fanyin, May 21, 1990.

17. The ten ritual utensils include Shang wine vessels, Zhou bowls, a boiling pot;. see Shandong shengzhi, pp. 507–8.

able relics, such as paintings and calligraphy. At the same time, they sank such sensitive statues as Buddhas, wooden carvings, and other sculptures in a well in the back gardens, and burned large numbers of photographs of Republican politicians and warlords at the Kong Mansion.[18]

While Tan Houlan was viewing the Three Kong Sites, she sent people into town to post "Burn Down the Kong Family Shop—Declaration to Rebuke Confucius" and "Notice to the People of the Nation" throughout the streets. The fierce language that filled the articles alarmed the people of Qufu. Within one night, the bad news of an impending strike against the Three Kong Sites spread like wildfire.

The committee leaders were still unsettled by the discovery of the swords and flags. At this moment, anything might happen. The County Committee decided to notify the State Council immediately. On the morning of November 11, Deputy Director of the County Committee Office Zhang Yongnian contacted the State Council by telephone. The answer was short: the State Council would reply after consulting with central leadership comrades.[19]

At 1:30 A.M. on November 12, the County Committee received a telephone call from the Shandong Provincial Communist Party reporting orders from Communist Party Central Cultural Revolution Leadership Committee members Qi Benyu and Chen Boda: "Do not destroy the mansion, temple, or the cemetery. Leave them as museums of the Kong family feudal landowners, just like the 'Rent Collection Court.' Confucius's grave may be dug up."[20] According to another source, the Leadership Committee said, "The Han stelae must be spared. All stelae dating up through the Ming dynasty must be spared. The Qing stelae may be smashed. The Temple to Confucius may be renovated, like the 'Rent Collection Court.' Confucius's grave may be dug up. Have an archeological expert inspect it."[21]

Holding these messages in his hand, County Magistrate Gao Keming felt he had been abandoned. It seemed undeniable that Tan had the support of the Central Cultural Revolutionary Committee, and that the Qufu County Committee had been set up to be criticized. At 11:00 P.M. on the same day, Tan Houlan received a telegram and a telephone call from two high-ranking Central Cultural Revolutionary Committee members. She immediately real-

---

18. Ibid.
19. Interview with Zhang Yongnian, Dec. 10, 1990.
20. Telephone message from Chen Boda, Nov. 12, 1990.
21. Telephone message from Qi Benyu, Nov. 12, 1990.

ized that the Qufu County Committee had contacted the central government, but she was also sensitive enough to understand that the Central Cultural Revolutionary Committee supported her actions. Thus the Qufu County Committee had become the accused, and Qi Banyu and Chen Boda conveyed this information directly to Tan.[22]

As soon as Tan Houlan received the orders from Chen and Qi, she called a meeting of all brigade leaders. After reporting these orders, she decided to immediately establish the "National Red Guard Revolutionary Rebellion Contact Station for the Utter Crushing of the Kong Family Shop and Establishment of the Absolute Authority of Mao Zedong's Thought" (Quanguo Hongwei bing chedi zalan Kong jiadian shuli Mao Zedong sixiang juedui quanwei geming zaofan lianluo zhan 全国红卫兵彻底砸烂孔家店树立毛泽東思想绝对权威革命造反联络站) to encourage Red Guards from all over the nation who were in Qufu, those who had not yet arrived, as well as local Qufu Red Guard organizations, to participate in the action.[23]

At 7:00 A.M. on November 12, County Magistrate Gao Keming and Deputy Secretary Zhang Yumei arrived at Qufu Normal University to consult with Tan Houlan on how to carry out Chen's and Qi's orders. They were instantly encircled by Red Guards accusing them of making accusations against them with the central government. Gao and Zhang were unable to defend themselves. Tan said that they absolutely must smash the State Council plaque stating that the Three Kong Sites were nationally protected cultural relics. Gao insisted that this plaque had been put up by the People's Government of Shandong Province, with the intention of protecting the Three Kong Sites, which were national property. If they were to be destroyed, the group would have to consult higher authorities. Gao stated that if they had to destroy the sites, he did not support the action, nor did he understand it. Tan charged that Gao was a relic of feudalism and the Three Kong Sites were beds of demons and had to be destroyed. Protecting the Three Kong Sites was equivalent to protecting a den of demons. The Red Guards who were present all joined in the attack, shouting out slogans, until the meeting finally came to an unsatisfactory ending.[24]

---

22. Investigation testimony of Zhang Daoying, 1971.
23. Ibid.
24. Kong Xiangmin's 1981 interview of Gao Keming; interview with Zhang Daoying during a 1971 investigation.

That afternoon, the Beijing Normal University Rebuke Confucius Headquarters called a meeting of representatives of all Qufu Red Guard organizations, announcing the establishment of the "National Red Guard Revolutionary Rebellion Contact Station for the Utter Crushing of the Kong Family Shop and Establishment of the Absolute Authority of Mao Zedong's Thought," abbreviated as the "Rebuke Confucius Contact Station" (Tao Kong lianluo zhan 讨孔联络站). The establishment of the Rebuke Confucius Contact Station ended the conflict among the different Red Guard organizations. The Rebuke Confucius Contact Station brought together all the disparate groups under the undisputed leadership of the Beijing Normal University Mount Jinggang Brigade. A whole series of destructive activities would be conducted under this name.

On the morning of November 13, the Kong Mansion and the Temple to Confucius were opened to the public. The covering over one of the two stone lions by the gate to the Kong Mansion was removed; the other was left as it was as evidence of the County Committee's plot to use Mao's sayings to shield the Kong Family Shop. On one side was a fierce and ferocious stone lion, and, on the other, a stone lion packaged in boards with the saying "Our responsibility is to care for the people. Every word, every action, must comply with the good of the people."

The eastern and western doors of the temple complex were broken open. The posters of the Qufu County Agricultural Accomplishments Exhibit were torn down, the tables were pulled to the ground, and the statues were plastered with slogans. An especially striking poster on the statue of Confucius read "Number one hooligan!"

Upon receiving the orders from Chen Boda and Qi Benyu, the Shandong Provincial Committee sent Committee Head Secretary Zhou Haizhou to Qufu, along with two experts in relics, Yang Zifan and Jiang Yingju. They were to carry out Chen's and Qi's orders that all pre-Qing stelae were to be preserved.

After arriving in Qufu, Zhou moved into the County Committee guest accommodations, just next to the Kong Mansion. He never appeared in public; rather, he acted as a secret agent for the Provincial Committee. He reported every day's happenings to the Provincial Committee but was unable to influence the situation. Zhou called in Guan Qisheng of the County Cultural Relics Management Committee and told Yang Zifan, Jiang Yingju, and Guan Qisheng: "I am unable to do anything. The Red Guards will not listen to me. Anything I say will only backfire. You are experts, and they will still listen to you. You must do your best to persuade them. Save any relics that can be saved, but don't get into a conflict with them, and don't excite them."[25]

Yang, Jiang, Guan, and some of the Red Guards constituted the Relics Judgment Team. Following Qi Benyu's orders, they appraised whether relics and stelae were from the Ming dynasty or before. Any stelae from the Ming and before were marked with the word "Spare" in red paint.

Guan Qisheng told this author, "The Red Guards still listened to us. We told them which stelae should be spared, and they wrote 'Spare' on them. At the time, we strictly differentiated between Ming and Qing. Some of the more valuable stelae were turned over to prevent them from being destroyed in the confusion. The Han stone carvings at the Temple to Confucius and the handwritten 'Fortune' and 'Longevity' tablets from the Empress Dowager Cixi in the Kong Mansion were saved in this way. Later, even the stelae with 'Spare' written on them were destroyed. That was done by local Qufu rebels, after the Beijing Normal University Red Guards left."

On the afternoon of November 14, Deputy Commander of the Beijing Normal University Rebuke Confucius Headquarters Zhang Daoying rushed into the County Cultural Relics Management Committee office and solemnly announced:

Tomorrow morning, we are going to hold an "Establish the Absolute Authority of Mao Zedong's Thought and Utterly Crush the Kong Family Shop Inauguration Ceremony" in front of the main gate of the Kong Mansion. At the ceremony, we are going to smash the State Council's imperialist plaque [i.e., the Cultural Relics Protection Plaque]! The County Committee secretary, magistrate, and Executive Office must attend the ceremony. The County Committee must notify the peasant farmers in all communes to attend the ceremony; the County Committee must see that the ceremony goes smoothly; if anyone ruins the ceremony, the County Committee will be held responsible.[26]

On the evening of November 14, Qufu County Committee Secretary Li Xiu, who was at a meeting in the provincial capital of Ji'nan, received a telephone call from the Qufu County Committee office. When Deputy Director Zhang Yongnian reported to Li Xiu that the Beijing Normal University

25. Interview with Guan Qisheng, Nov. 1990.
26. "Beishida hongweibing lai Qu hou shijian jilu."

Red Guards were going to destroy the State Council plaque, Li told Zhang not to hang up and to wait for him to talk to the Provincial Committee leaders before making a response. After reporting the situation to Provincial Committee Secretary Bai Rubing, Li said that they must report this to the central government. Bai suggested that they not report the incident, since the results would be the same as last time, and they would hurt only themselves. The Provincial Committee notified Gao Keming and Zhang Yumei that they must do their best to see that the State Council plaque not be destroyed, the statue of Confucius not be toppled, and that there be no conflict with the Red Guards.[27]

At 7:00 in the morning on November 15, Gao and Zhang went to Qufu Normal University to speak with Tan Houlan. They hoped that Tan would change her mind and felt that it was their duty to make a final effort. Gao told Tan that 90 commune members were protecting the State Council plaque that morning, and they opposed destroying it. If the Red Guards insisted on destroying it, there would most likely be a conflict. As soon as the words came out of his mouth, he was surrounded by Red Guards. Tan responded, "We are smashing the State Council's imperialist plaque today! If there are problems, the County Committee will be held responsible. The ceremony will begin at 11:00. The County Committee secretary must come to the ceremony to speak in support of our revolutionary actions." Gao informed her that the County Committee had decided that it would not countenance destroying the plaque, it would not participate in the ceremony, it would not speak, and it would not make any comments.[28]

The State Council's plaque protecting the Three Kong Sites held great significance for both sides of the struggle. The County Committee saw the plaque as their strongest weapon in defending the Three Kong Sites. The plaque was an enormous source of psychological, spiritual, and moral support. At the same time, it was a symbol of authority and order that held back the Qufu Red Guard organizations and the general public.

For Tan and the Beijing Normal University Red Guards she led, this plaque was also an enormous symbol of authority and order, but a stagnant and conservative authority and order. It was a shield of demons and the Four Olds. The plaque stood between them and their goal of toppling the

---

27. Interview with Li Xiu, Dec. 9, 1990.
28. Notes of Kong Xiangmin's 1981 interview with Gao Keming.

Kong Family Shop, burning Confucius's statue, and leveling the Sage's grave. Only by smashing this plaque could toppling the Kong Family Shop become feasible. They first had to overcome this modern authority before they could overcome Confucius, cultural relic of the past.

At 9:00 A.M. on November 15, Red Guards began gathering in front of the gate of the Kong Mansion. A thick rope had already been tied around the stone plaque, and hoards of onlookers filled the streets. Everyone waited with mixed emotions for the plaque to be destroyed.

Gao Keming and Zhang Yumei entered the front gate of the Kong Mansion with an escort of Red Guards. Shortly after, Zhang quietly sneaked out and found a County Committee secretary. She told the secretary to immediately notify the clerks of all party units of the Municipal Commune to meet in the theater next to the Temple to Confucius. Zhang told the clerks that the Red Guards were going to destroy the State Council's stone plaque, and that an uproar would probably ensue. She told them to spread out and control their people. There could be no conflicts with the Red Guards, or things would get serious. The clerks carried out Zhang's orders.[29]

In the County Cultural Relics Management Committee office, the Red Guards who were to preside over the ceremony were negotiating with Gao Keming. They wanted Gao to preside over the ceremony and to express his support of the revolutionary act of destroying the plaque. Gao held fast and refused to express an opinion or participate in the ceremony. That morning, Gao had asked the secretary to contact the Provincial Committee. When Gao left the office to find out if new orders had arrived, the Red Guards sent two people to accompany him so he could not escape. When Gao reached the second gate of the Kong Mansion, he met the secretary, who had been searching for him. The secretary told him that Bai Rubing said to give up and not persist any longer. Gao felt as if he had lost the strength to stand. At that moment, he felt more alone than ever and dared not think about what would happen next. He sat numbly on the front stage. In 1981, Gao would look back and say, "I understood this was to prevent greater opposition between the masses, which could have led to something unfortunate. So I sat to one side of the stage and watched blankly as something unfolded that I had never imagined possible."[30]

---

29. Interview with Zhang Yumei, Nov. 17, 1990.
30. Notes of Kong Xiangmin's 1981 interview of Gao Keming.

At 11:00, the ceremony began punctually. "Burn Down the Kong Family Shop—Declaration to Rebuke Confucius," "Letter of Protest to the State Council," "Notice to the Fellow Revolutionaries of Shandong," and "Notice to the People of the Nation" were read. Speeches by representatives of Beijing Normal University, Qufu Normal University, and Qufu Number One Middle School Red Guard organizations followed.

Zhang Daoying led the Red Guards in reading "Oath to Smashing the Plaque." Then Zhang announced: "Let the smashing of the plaque begin!" Red Guard plaque-smashing teams, already organized, used the rope to pull down the symbol of national authority, the State Council stone plaque protecting the Three Kong Sites. Red Guards with hammers in hand rushed up to the plaque, and the solid stone plaque was quickly reduced to a pile of rubble.

The Red Guards then split into two groups. The first group rushed into the Temple to Confucius and smashed the heads off all the statues. All the statues—with the exception of the one of Confucius, for it was to be paraded in the streets and burned—were pulled down. In minutes, the once solemn, beautifully decorated main hall became filthy. Ancient editions of the *Book of Change*, the *Documents*, the *Record of Rites*, the *Analects*, and the *Spring and Autumn Annals* were pulled out of the bellies of the statues. Qufu residents began to enter. According to one contemporary account:

At this point, a thirty-some-year-old person noticed a hole in the belly of Old Kong, and stuck his hand in. As he used his strength to make a hollow in Old Kong's belly, others joined in. From within the hole, they pulled out a bunch of cotton, books, and the lousy guts of Old Kong (made of bronze mirrors and pieces of bronze). The Sage's throat was slit, and the four sagely disciples were split open, thrown to the ground, and stamped on! The peasant farmers slit the throat of Old Kong in the Confucius Temple.[31]

The seventeen sets of priceless books, silver internal organs, and bronze mirrors from the insides of Confucius, the four correlates, and the twelve savants were destroyed without a trace. The other group of Red Guards went to the Temple of the Duke of Zhou, smashed the State Council's protective stone plaque in front of the temple, and pulled down the statue of the Duke of Zhou. They then went to the Kong Cemetery, pulled down the plaque with the words saying "Tomb of the Supreme Sage" above the gate, and

---

31. "Pinxia zhongnong kaile Kong Laoer de tang."

smashed it.[32] The Red Guard plaque-smashing teams spent the next few days tearing down most of the Qing stelae in the Confucius and Duke of Zhou temples, and gravestones in the Kong Cemetery, smashing some of them into pieces.

THE COUNTY COMMITTEE RETREATS
ON ALL POINTS

The smashing of the State Council's stone plaque destroyed the County Committee's support, and the Red Guards reduced the County Committee to a rubberstamp. On November 19, the County Committee held a meeting of the Executive Office. Gao spoke, demanding that the Executive Office support the revolutionary actions of the Red Guard. Beijing Normal University representative Zhang Daoying spoke at the meeting, criticizing the earlier performance of the County Committee, and called upon the Executive Office to mobilize immediately and join the Rebuke Confucius Brigade.

On November 22, the County Committee called a high-level Executive Office meeting encouraging the Executive Office to support the Beijing Normal University students' revolutionary actions. The County Committee issued the following orders:

1. Actively support the revolutionary activities of Beijing Normal University.
2. Organize the peasant farmers to view the Three Kong Sites.
3. Call for wide-ranging criticism meetings.
4. Actively prepare a Rebuke Confucius Ceremony to be attended by 50,000 people.[33]

In 1981, Gao Keming would recall that "after the Red Guards smashed the plaque, the County Committee retreated on all points."

On November 23, the Beijing Normal University Rebuke Confucius Headquarters decided to call all residents of the county to a two-day meeting, to be held on November 28 and 29 and attended by 100,000 people. The plans for the meeting were to be as follows:

---

32. "Chedi daohui Kongjiadian de youxing shiwei."
33. Zhang Daoying's testimony during a 1971 investigation.

1. Zhang Daoying, local leader of the revolutionaries, would deal with the County Committee, which would notify the entire county to stop production on those days. All commune organizations were to attend the meeting, with commune executives leading the way.

2. The statue of Confucius would be put on the back of a truck, and accompanied by leading reactionary scholars, it would be paraded through the streets.

3. After the parade, the statue would be burned, and Confucius's grave would be leveled.[34]

By this point, the Qufu County Committee had lost all control over the situation. Since the State Council plaque had been destroyed and the Provincial Committee's attitude was unclear, all decisions were made by the Beijing Normal University Rebuke Confucius Headquarters and then ratified by the County Committee. The committee had lost the power to protect the Three Kong Sites. Committee leaders felt extremely frustrated. On one hand, they sincerely wished to protect the Three Kong Sites, but on the other, they were afraid of being labeled imperialists and left behind by the Cultural Revolution. At the time, the Cultural Revolution was synonymous with the direction of Chairman Mao's revolution. To be left behind by the Cultural Revolution was to be politically blacklisted. In short, they had no choice but to cooperate with the Red Guards. Out of fear of coming into conflict with the Red Guards, they even, on occasion, actively expressed their support for the revolutionary activities.

BURNING THE STATUE OF CONFUCIUS
AND LEVELING HIS GRAVE

On November 26, Qufu County Committee Secretary Li Xiu, who had been in Ji'nan for over half a month meeting with the Provincial Committee, returned to Qufu. After receiving a telephone call, Zhang Yumei went to the train station to meet Li. The two left the bus from the train station before it reached Qufu. They did not dare enter the town, since "Topple Li Xiu!" and "Topple Gao Keming!" banners were everywhere. Full of anticipation and anxiety, they wandered in the countryside, waiting for the sun to set. Once it

---

34. "Beishida hongweibing lai Qu hou shijian jilu."

was dark, Zhang silently led Li to the city wall. They crawled into the city through a drainage hole and snuck back to the County Committee.[35]

Interestingly enough, although the County Committee was absolutely powerless to stop Tan Houlan, rather than dissolve the County Committee, Tan had it voice its support at all major activities. Tan may have wished to bring down the existing authorities, but she also relied on these authorities to prove the reasonableness of her own actions. On November 28, the first day of the Utterly Smash the Kong Family Shop Ceremony, the participants in a conference on Confucius scholarship that had been held in Ji'nan in 1962 became targets of attack.[36] Signs were hung around their necks, and they were criticized. At the meeting, Provincial Committee Secretary Ye Zaiwen represented the Provincial Committee, and Li Xiu represented the County Committee. In self-criticism, they admitted the errors of their attitudes toward the Red Guards.[37]

After the meeting, the Red Guards put the statue of Confucius on a truck. On its head was placed a paper hat with "Topple the number one hooligan, Old Kong!" written on it. "Old Kong" was crossed out in red paint, and the statue's face was smeared over. Yu Xiu and other known sympathizers of Confucianism were made to stand on both sides of the Supreme Sage and First Master and were paraded through the streets. The truck circled the town to the sound of chants and finally stopped on a small bridge west of the Kong Cemetery. Below the bridge, a fierce bonfire was already burning. Amid chants from the Red Guards, the statue of Confucius was thrown into the flames. The giant wooden "Teacher and Paragon of the Ten-thousand Generations" tablet was also thrown into the raging flames, along with many other relics, such as paintings, calligraphy, books, and wooden plaques.[38] On November 30, the gravestone before Confucius's grave was pulled down and smashed. The grave was dug up, but the Red Guards found only an empty tomb.

---

35. Interview with Li Xiu, Dec. 9, 1990.

36. Held in Ji'nan in November 1962 in commemoration of the 2440th anniversary of Confucius's death, the Conference on Confucius Scholarship 孔子学术讨论会 was attended by more than 150 scholars, including Fung Yu-lan 馮友兰 (1895–1990), Lü Zhenyu 呂振羽 (1901–80), Zhu Qianzhi 朱谦之 (1899–1972), Zhou Yutong 周予同 (1898–), Cai Shangsi 蔡尙思 (1905–), and Yang Rongguo 杨荣国 .

37. "Chedi daohui Kongjiadian dahui shengli zhaokai."

38. Ibid.

In early December, Tan Houlan led the leaders of the Beijing Normal University Red Guards back to Beijing. The Rebuke Kong Contact Station was turned over to Qufu Normal University Mao Zedong's Thought Red Guards, run by Wang Zhengxi. In January 1967, a detachment of the Rebuke Kong Contact Station Red Guards "patrolled the battle grounds," pulling down all remaining Qing dynasty stelae and even some Yuan and Ming dynasty stelae marked "Spare" by the Beijing Normal University Red Guards. Included in this list were the famous large stelae of the Chenghua (1464–87) and Hongzhi (1487–1505) eras. Two Jin dynasty (1115–1234) stelae also disappeared.

The east and west sides of the Hall of Great Completion in the temple had been the sites at which the four correlates and twelve savants received sacrifices. In the side cloisters a total of 156 worthies and scholars were represented by name tablets rather than statues. These tablets were completely dismantled and destroyed. In our interviews and research, it never became clear which organization was responsible for this. Watchman and craftsman Zhang Jinshan recalled, "The destruction of the altars of the Hall of Great Completion and the side cloisters occurred in the winter, after Tan Houlan left. The altars were extremely large and high. It could not have been done without sledgehammers and saws. Laborers were called in to smash the wood and move it to the court behind the temple. Even the altar platforms were removed. Only one platform, in the main hall, remained."[39]

In August 1968, the Qufu Normal University Revolutionary Committee and the Qufu Revolutionary Committee established the Preparatory Team for Renovating the Three Kong Sites Office, with Wang Zhengxi and a deputy director of the Qufu Normal University Revolutionary Committee as team director and vice director, respectively. In late August, the Preparatory Team drafted a "Proposal for Renovating the Three Kong Sites." On September 6, Shandong Province Revolutionary Committee Director Wang Xiaoyu came to Qufu to hear a report on the renovation. When it was reported that the Provincial Revolutionary Committee Propaganda Team did not approve the plowing up and planting over of the Kong Cemetery, Wang said: "Who has to give approval? Just rebel!"[40]

In accordance with Wang's orders, in late September, the team drew up a second draft of the proposal. This draft outlined plans for demolishing the

---

39. Interview with Zhang Jinshan, Apr. 25, 1990.
40. Interrogation testimony of Sun Zihui, 1971.

entire front portion of the Temple to Confucius and erecting a Long Live the Victory of Mao Zedong's Thought Exhibition Hall: "This structure must be tall and large, grand, majestic, and extensive. Even in its form, it must oppress the old nest of Confucius." The rear portion of the Temple to Confucius was to be made into a hall commemorating the struggles between anti-Confucians and pro-Confucians since 1949.[41]

For political and economic reasons, this proposal came to naught. Had it been implemented, not only would it have meant the loss of the Temple to Confucius, but it would also have been a great tragedy in the history of human civilization. The Cultural Revolution saw the greatest destruction of Confucian temples in Chinese history. At the time, this destruction was a rallying point for proponents of Marxism and Maoism. On the surface, this was merely a political incident, but, in fact, it was a great cultural tragedy.

---

41. "Gaige Sankong."

WORKS CITED

"Bei 'Dongfang hong' diandao de lishi, bixu zai diandao guolai—ba, erliu shijian zhenxiang" 被〈東方红〉颠倒的历史必须再颠倒过來八二六事件真相. Hongweibing Shandong zhihuibu Qushiyuan Mao Zedong sixiang hongweibing wuli fendui 红卫兵山东指挥部曲师院毛泽东思想红卫兵物理分队. Aug. 27, 1967.

"Beishida hongweibing lai Qu hou shijian jilu" 北师大红卫兵来曲后事件记录. Nov. 4–Dec. 1, 1966. Qufu County Committee office document.

"Chedi daohui Kongjiadian dahui shengli zhaokai" 彻底捣毁孔家店大会胜利召开. *Tao Kong zhanbao* 讨孔战报, Nov. 30, 1966.

"Chedi daohui Kongjiadian de youxing shiwei he shishi dahui longzhong juxing" 彻底捣毁孔家店的遊行示威和誓师大会隆重举行. *Tao Kong zhanbao* 讨孔战报, no. 2 (mimeograph), Nov. 17, 1966.

"Gaige Sankong [Kongfu, Kongmiao, Konglin] fang'an (chugao)" 改革三孔孔府孔庙孔林方案初稿. Qufu County Three Kong Sites Renovation Office 曲阜县三孔改革办公室. Sept. 30, 1968.

"He Zhongyang wenhuabu tubowenwuju fuze tongzhi tanhua jiyao" 和中央文化部图博文物局负责同志谈话记要 (Notes on a discussion with comrades at the Central Archive of the Culture Section). Qufu Archive (uncatalogued document).

Interview: Ban Shouzheng 班守正, former Qufu deputy magistrate 曲阜副县长. Mar. 23, 1990.

Interview: Fan Xueqin 范学勤, retired carpenter for Qufu Cultural Relics Management Committee 曲阜文管会. Mar. 1990.

Interview: Gao Jinghong 高景洪, former cadre of the Qufu Cultural Relics Management Committee 曲阜文管会. Mar. 20, 1990.

Interview: Guan Qisheng 关啓生, deputy director of the Qufu County Cultural Relics Management Committee 曲阜文管会副局长. Nov. 1990.

Interview: Hu Yuan 胡远, director, Qufu Party Committee Office 曲阜市党委办公室主任. Mar. 2, 1990.

Interview: Kong Fanyin 孔凡银, deputy director of the Qufu Cultural Relics Management Committee 曲阜文管会副局长. May 21, 1990.

Interview: Li Xiu 李秀, former secretary, Qufu County Committee 曲阜县委会书记. Dec. 9, 1990.

Interview: Zhang Jinshan 张金山, temple watchman and craftsman, Qufu County Relics Management Committee 曲阜文管会. April 25, 1990.

Interview: Zhang Yongnian 张永年, former deputy director, Qufu County Committee Offices 曲阜县委办公室主任. Dec. 10, 1990.

Interview: Zhang Yumei 张玉美, deputy secretary, Qufu County Committee 曲阜县副书记. Nov. 17, 1990.

Investigation testimony: Sun Zihui 孫梓辉, former deputy director, Qufu Normal University Revolutionary Committee 曲师院革委会副主任. 1971.

Investigation testimony: Zhang Daoying 张道英, deputy commander, Beijing Normal University Rebuke Kong Headquarters 北师大讨孔指挥部副总指挥. 1971. Qufu Archive.

Kong Xiangmin 孔祥民. Interview: Gao Keming 高克明, deputy secretary 副书记 and county magistrate 县长. 1981.

"Pinxia zhongnong kaile Kong Lao'er de tang" 贫下中农开了孔老二的趟. *Tao Kong zhanbao* 讨孔战报, no. 2 (mimeograph), Nov. 17, 1966.

Shandong shengzhi: Kongzi guli zhi 山东省志孔子故里志. Beijing: Zhonghua shuju, 1994.

Telephone message from Chen Boda 陈伯达, former member, CCP Central Cultural Revolution Leadership Committee 中共中央文革领导小组成员, to Qufu County Committee Office 曲阜县委办公室. 1:30 A.M., Nov. 12, 1966. Qufu Archive (uncataloged document).

Telephone message from Qi Benyu 戚本禺, former member, CCP Central Cultural Revolution Leadership Committee 中共中央文革领导小成员, to Qufu County Committee Office 曲阜县委办公室. 1:30 A.M., Nov. 12, 1966. Qufu Archive (uncataloged document).

Index

Index

In this index an "f" after a number indicates a separate reference on the next page, and an "ff" indicates separate references on the next two pages. A continuous discussion of two or more pages is indicated by a span of page numbers, e.g., "57–59." *Passim* is used for a cluster of references in close but not necessarily consecutive sequence.

abstinence (ritual fasting), 78, 78n121
agnosticism, Confucian, 7–13; juxta-
   posed to primitive superstition, 7–8
Altar of Heaven (*tiantan*), 1, 7
Altar of Thunder, 336
Amherst, Lord William Pitt, 47
An Mengsong, 235, 239n47
Analects (*Lunyu*), 17, 176, 180, 186, 189,
   215, 391; exegetes of, 62; modern
   scholars' reliance on, 12–13; on
   Kongzi, 3, 44, 45–46, 49, 181–82; on
   Kongzi's agnosticism, 5, 9–11; on
   Kongzi's disciples, 79, 184; on ritual
   music, 134, 145–46; on sacrifice, 9–
   10, 31, 283, 102; on the Son of
   Heaven, 278–79; teachings, 45; use
   of, 4, 13, 18; Zhu Xi's preface on
   Kongzi to, 225, 227
ancestor charts (*shen zhu*), 370, 370n50
ancestral teacher (*zongshi*), 176
ancient script (*guwen*), *see* Ancient
   Text

Ancient Text, 30, 56, 80ff, 233, 233n31,
   243; discovery in wall of Kongzi's
   house, 242f, Fig. 5.24
aniconism, 26, 106, 115–19 *passim*
anti-feudal privilege campaign, 353
anti-Lin Biao / anti-Confucius campaign (1974), 343–44, 344n27, 353,
   354
antireligious policy under socialism,
   336, 343, 353–56
apocryphal texts (*weishu*), 47–48, 176,
   202–9
appearance: vs. virtue, 112; *mao*, 113
Apricot Altar (*xingtan*), 73, 244, 247n73
Asad, Talal, 11
august axial standard (*huang ji*), 116
August Earth (*huangdiqi*), 2
autocracy, 30, 267, 278, 289, 292

Bai Rubing, 389f
Bai Zhongshan, 324
Ban Shouzheng, 382

Baocheng, 228n19
baocheng xuan Ni gong, 50
Beattie, Hilary, 306
Beijing Normal University Rebuke
    Confucius Headquarters, 387f, 392–
    93
Beiping minshe, see Nation Society of
    Beiping
bell-chimes (zhong), 148
benevolence (ren), see humanity
bidding farewell to the spirits (song-
    shen), 140
Big Dipper, 30, 236, Fig. 5.15
Binglingsi, 357, 367
Biographies of Exemplary Women (Lienü
    zhuan), 252
black bird (yuanniao), 199–204 pas-
    sim
black god (hei di), 47f, 51
Black Lord (Hei Di), 206, 213
Black Warrior (Hei hou), 212f
Bodde, Derk, 9–10
Book of Rites, see Record of Rites
Boone, William J., 6
Bourdieu, Pierre, 337–39, 357, 368
Boxia, 192
Boyu, 181f, 185n22
Brooks, E. Bruce, and A. Taeko
    Brooks, 182n16
Buddha, see Sakyamuni
Buddhism, 82, 243, 250, 272; effect on
    Confucianism, 105, 108, 118–20, 256;
    gods of, 237, 247; monasteries of, 1,
    342; pictorial biographies in, 29,
    228–30

Cai Shangsi, 394n36
Cai Yong, 222n3
Cai Yuanding, 155–56, 272f
Cai Yuanpei, 72

Calendric Etymology of Customs and Festi-
    vals (Yueri jigu), 200
Campaign Against Lin Biao and Con-
    fucius, 343–44, 344n27, 353, 354
Cang Jie, 44n2
canonical exegetes, 75, 77, 79ff, 141
canonical vs. non-canonical figure of
    Kongzi, see under Kongzi
Cao Bo, 187
Ceremonial Records (Yili), 77
Chang Hong, 243
Change, Book of, 22, 109, 391
Chen Boda, 385ff
Chen Chun, 101
Chen Hao, 65
Chen Heng, 245
Chen Huanzhang, 86
Chen She, 304
Chen Shou, 75n111
Chen Yang, 148
Chen Yaofei, 156
Chen Yingyuan, 155
Cheng Hao, enshrinement of, 83
Cheng Minzheng, 273f
Cheng Tang, 211
Cheng Xu, 284
Cheng Yi, 5n12, 268, 281; enshrinement
    of, 83; on ancestral portraits, 112–14
Cheng-Zhu orthodoxy, see orthodoxy
Chi You, 201
Chiang Kai-shek, 250
chime stones, 223, 224n5, Fig. 5.1, Fig.
    5.7
Christianity, see missionaries on Chi-
    nese religion
chuanqi, 29, 240
Chuci, 9n24
Chun, Allen, 59n57
Chunmingmeng yulu, 125
Cishou, 268

city god, 284
civil examinations, 82, 84, 289
Cixi, 388
Clear and Bright Festival (*qing ming jie*), 344–45
Cohen, Myron, 336
Collected Anecdotes of the Taiping Era (*Taiping guangji*), 205, 213
Collected Debate on Ritual Reform (*Dali jiyi*), 269
Collected Statutes of the Eastern Han, 74
community temples, 345n29
Complete Pictures of the Sage's Traces (*Shengji quantu*), 235, 241–43; as third recension of *Shengji tu*, 241nn50–51, 245n67, 253
Complete Writings of the Sage Confucius (*Kongsheng quanshu*), 235, 239, 253
Conference on Confucius Scholarship, 394
Confucian/Ru, 21–25, 45
Confucian canon, imperial regulation of, 84, 297
Confucian Society (Kong jiao hui), 86
Confucius, 2n3; as pagan philosopher, 3–5. *See also* Kongzi
Confucius, Chinese Philosopher (*Confucius Sinarum Philosophus*), 4
Confucius, the Man and the Myth, 11–12
Continuing Auspice Marquis of Yin (*Yin shaojia hou*), 61
continuing the dynastic line (*ji si*) vs. the imperial order (*ji tong*), 268
Correct Meaning of the Five Classics (*Wujing zhengyi*), 80
correlates (*pei*), 52, 351, 382
County Cultural Relics Management Committee, 376, 378, 388, 390
County People's Committee, 384–94 passim

Court of Imperial Sacrifice, 21, 67, 78
court robes, 272–73
Creel, Herrlee, 8–12; on James Legge, 9
Cui Xuyi, 376, 384
cult, agricultural, 2n2
cult, ancestor, 344, 348
cult liturgy, ancestral, 344, 348, 351–52; public, 351–52, 356ff; multivocality of, 357; reconstruction of, 348–51, 366
cult of Kongzi, 2, 20–22, 52, 72–87, 95–128 passim, 223, 227, 242, 246f, 249, 256; equal to Heaven and Earth, 49, 49n25, 85; familization of, 254–55; flesh-and-blood man vs. his Dao, 57, 272, 284; in Qufu, 73; impact of modernization on, 248–50; imperial and ancestral 74–76; liturgy of, 25f, 72–79; music of, 74ff; temple rank as sage, 52–53, 73; under the Republic, 85–87; vs. Duke of Zhou, 72–73, 80f; worship of, 44. *See also* Kongzi Temple; sacrifice; spirit image
cult of silk worms, 269, 278
cultural capital, 337, 367
cultural festival (*wenhua jie*), 367
Cultural Relics Management Committee, 382
Cultural Revolution (1966–76), 34, 250, 336, 355, 376–96 passim

Dacheng dian, *see* Hall of Great Completion
Dacheng liyue ji (Collection of the great completion rites and music), 154
Dacheng yuewu tupu (Musical scores and dance illustrations for the Confucian ceremonial), 143, 150f, 154

Dachuan: temple managers, 346–48, 355–56, 361, 369, 370–71; vow-takers (*yuan zhu*), 347–48, 355

Dachuan Kongs, 32–33; compared with Xiaochuan Kongs, 367–72; Kongzi temple of, 343, 346, 352–55, 358, 363; local lineage primacy of, 344–46, 361–62, 364; persecution under socialism, 352–56 *passim*, 368–69; worship of Kongzi, 347, 350

Dai Sheng, 272

Dalby, Michael, 208*n*86

dance (*wu*), 134, 140, 154, 157, 161–62, 164

dancers (ritual), choreography of, 27, 149f, 161–62, 164–65; costumes of, 157; rows of, 54f, 75f, 144, 164–65, 273f, 280f

Daoist deities, 230, 237, 240, 247; temple (*guan*), 1, 336, 342

Dao Learning, *see* Dao School

Dao of Conscience (*liangxin dao*), 343

Dao School (*Daoxue*), 23–24; and enshrinement, 82–85

daotong (transmission/genealogy of the Way), 23, 244ff, 298; conflation with Kong lineal descent, 299; and enshrinement, 83–84, 273, 276; Kongzi's role in, 43; and political legitimacy, 115f, 267, 291–92; and *Shengji tu*, 255

Dardess, John, 298

dark bird (*xuanniao*), 201, 203, 213. *See also* black bird (*yuanniao*)

Dark Sage (*xuansheng*), 48, 51–52, 52*n*35

datong, 249

Daxue, *see* Great Learning

Daxue yanyibu, 118–25

Dazai Kongzi (Great is Confucius), 149f, 153f, 161

de-ancestralization, 358

deceased, envisioning of, 99–101

decollectivization, 364f

Department of People's Armed Forces (*wu zhuang bu*), 354

Derrida, Jacques, 214*n*105

despotism, *see* autocracy

Dewey, John, 7*n*19

Di, *see* Shangdi

Di Yi, 58, 178, 194, 202f

Dictionary of the Chinese Language, A, 5

Didactic Use of the Book of Odes (*Hanshi waizhuan*), 196

Diku, 58*n*53

Dingji liyue beikao (Complete study of the rites and music of the Confucian sacrifices), 143, 161–64

Discourses of the Kingdoms (*Guo yu*), 193

"Disputing Confucius's Ennoblement as King" (*Kongzi feng wang pien*), 272

district magistrate (*zhixian*), 323–27

Divine Farmer (Shennong), 58*n*53

Dizi Qi, 188*n*31

Doctrine of the Mean (*Zhongyong*), 111f, 114; and Confucian religiousness, 14; Kong Ji's authorship of, 62, 83, 182; on the sage, 49*n*25; on the Son of Heaven, 282

Documents, Book of, 5, 22, 62, 73, 75, 80, 100, 112, 115, 391

Dong Zhongshu, 81, 202, 209, 236*n*36

Du You, 2*n*1

Du Yu, 189f, 272

Duara, Prasenjit, 20, 336

Dubs, Homer, 188

ducal mansion, *see* Kong mansion

Duke Ai of Lu, 44, 245, 247*n*73

Duke for Fulfilling the Sage (*Yansheng gong*), 67, 177, 177*n*4, 240*n*48, 249. *See also* Yansheng Duke

Duke for the Propagation of Culture, *see wenxuan gong*

Duke Huan of Lu, ancestral temple of, 224n5, 238, Fig. 5.17

Duke Jing of Qi, 245

Duke Mu of Lu, 185, 190

Duke of Accomplished Propagation, *see* Wenxuan gong

Duke of Exalted Culture, *see wenxuan gong*

Duke of Overflowing Sageliness (*Yansheng gong*), *see* Duke for Fulfilling the Sage

Duke of Song (*Song gong*), 61n68

Duke of the State of Zou (*Zouguo gong*), 50

Duke of Zhou: ancestral temple of, 223n5; and Kongzi cult, 55, 290; and rites, 156; and sacrifice, 2n1; and the *Odes*, 111. *See also under* cult of Kongzi

Duke Xuanni of Baocheng (*baocheng xuan Ni gong*), 140

Duke Zhao of Lu, 237, 254

dummy-people of clay and wood (*ou ren*), 111

earl (*bo*), 77

Eberhard, Wolfram, 180n8, 205n81, 209

Ebrey, Patricia, 11n31, 16

economic capital, 338

economic reforms, 363, 365

education, 338, 347, 371

eight types of materials (*bayin*), 146

Elman, Benjamin, 12n33

Empress of Heaven, 19

Encyclopedia of Illustrations and Documents from Ancient and Modern Times (*Gujin tushu jicheng*), 126–27

enfeoffment, *see under* Kongzi's descendants

enshrinement (*congsi*): of canonical masters, 79–82, 272; of Kongzi's disciples, 74, 77, 79–85, 351, 356; of local ancestors, 351, 356; of the sages' and worthies' fathers, 270; of transmitters of the Dao, 82–85, 273, 276

Erudite of the Court of Imperial Sacrifice (*taichang boshi*), 322

Erudite of the Five Classics, 314n75, 315

Established Precedents of Ritual Ceremonies (*Siyi chengdian*), 270

ethics vs. ritual, 11

eunuchs, 227

Exalted Culture (*wenxuan*), 288

Exalted Ni, Duke of Consummate Perfection (*baocheng xuan Ni gong*), 50

exorcism, 119

Expanded Record of the Kong Family's Ancestral Court (*Kongshi zuting guangji*), 61, 67

Explanation of Pattern, Elucidation of Graphs (*Shuowen jiezi*), 15, 196–204 passim, 212

"Explanation of the Corrected Sacrifices to Confucius," 277, 279

"Extensive Record of the Corrected Sacrifices to Confucius," 277, 279, 282

Family Sayings of Kongzi (*Kongzi jiayu*), 176; and the *Shengji tu*, 239, 253; and the *Shiji*, 195, 200; authorship of, 61n66; on Kongzi's ancestry, 28, 60–61, 190, 193–94, 202–3; on Kongzi's birth, 205, 211, 253; on Kongzi's de-

scendants, 180; on Kongzi's disciples, 79
family temple (*jia miao*), 304
Fan Ning, 272
Fan Xuan, 54
Fang Daxian, 326*n*140
Fang Xianfu, 271*n*11
Fang Xuanling, 75*n*111
Fei Mi, 291
fertility cult, 197–201, 203, 209, 342, 358; and agricultural cycle, 208–9
filial piety, 19, 244; and relations with deceased, 104
Filial Piety (*Xiaojing*), 62, 244
Fingarette, Herbert, 16–18
First Family of China, 328
first master (*xianshi*), 55, 75, 125
First Sage (*xiansheng*), 175, 271f. See also Kongzi
Five Classics (*wu jing*), 22–23, 63
Five Emperors, 2*n*2; cult of, 287
five phases (*wuxing*), 48
flood-control gods, 342, 358
Four Books, 23, 82ff
Four Olds, 34–35, 376, 376*n*1, 377, 383f, 389
Freedberg, David, 118–19
Fu Fu He, 178
Fu He, 59f
Fu Qian, 272
Fu Yue, 290f
Fung Yu-lan, 9–10, 394*n*36
Fuxi, 44*n*2, 109, 290f
Fuzi (master), 22. *See also* Kongzi

ga miao, 361
gan (fecund arousal, concinnity), 207*n*84
gang lie (hot-tempered one, pig), 362
Gansu Kongs, 180

Gao Keming, 380, 384–92 *passim*
Gao Xin, 203
Gao Yao, 290f
Gautama Siddhartha, *see* Sakyamuni
genealogy of Kongs, 61, 64–71 *passim*, 69*n*92, 70*n*94, 299, 313, 315–17, 339–40
Genealogy of Kongzi's Hereditary Household (*Kongzi shijia pu*), 61
Gong Gong, 201
Gongbo Liao, 272
Gongyang Commentary on the *Spring and Autumn Annals*, 47f, 187–88, 193
Goody, Jack, 371
governance and self-cultivation, 134
Granet, Marcel, 200, 213
Great Accomplisher, Supreme Sage, Ultimate Teacher, and Culture Propagating King, 352
Great Accomplishment (*da cheng*), 125
Great Completer, Supreme Sage, First Master of Exalted Culture (*dacheng zhisheng wenxuan xianshi*), 57
Great Leap Forward (1958–60), 336, 341, 355, 369
Great Learning (*Daxue*), 4, 127, 243; Zeng Sen's authorship of, 83
Great Rites Controversy, 268–69, 271, 274, 281
Great Sacrifice (*da si*), 1, 78, 271, 283, 301
Great Star (i.e., Jupiter), 76*n*113
Great Statutes of Ming Ethics (*Minglun dadian*), 269
Great Unity (*datong*), 249
Gu Jiegang, 87
Gu Yanwu, 126
Guan Feng, 382
Guan Qisheng, 387–88
Guan Yu, *see* Guandi

Guandi, 20, 230

Guangdong branch (Lingnan pai), 341

Guannei Marquis (*Guannei hou*), 63, 305*n*41, 319

Guanyin, statue of, 105

Guanzi, 212f

Gui E, 273

Gui Hua, 273

Guifan, 252

Guliang Commentary on the *Spring and Autumn Annals*, 60f, 187–88, 193

Guliang Shu (or Chi), 60*n*63

Guodian texts, 185

Guoxue liyue lu (Record of rites and music at the imperial university), 156–57, 160

Hall of Great Accomplishment, *see* Hall of Great Completion

Hall of Great Completion (Dacheng dian), 166, 273–74, 302, 342

Hall of Musical Tones (Jin si tang), 303, 303*n*25

Hall of Repose (Qin dian), 303, 303*n*24

Hall of the King Who Gave Birth to the Sage (Qisheng wang dian), 303

Hall of the Sage (Shengren dian), 342*n*24

Hall of the Sage's Traces (Shengjidian), 243–48 passim, 253, 255

Hall of the Transmission of the Mind/Heart (Chuanxin dian), 290*n*103

halls for shades (*ying tang*), 112

Han Bangqi, 156

Han Fuqu, 384

Han Gaozu, 48, 73, 226, Fig. 5.11, 301

Han Huidi, 62

Han Pingdi, 272

Han Wudi, 200

han yin (clear-voiced one, chicken), 362

Han Yuandi, 61, 177, 187, 305

Han Zhaodi, 62

Hanlin Academy, 277

Hanlin Erudite of the Five Classics (*Hanlin wujing boshi*), 69, 321*n*14

He Cheng, 224*n*5

He Chuguang, 234, 243–44

He Tingrui, 233–37, 240ff, 250, 253f

He Xiu, 272

heart/mind (*xin*), 27; and musical creativity, 134, 136, 145f, 152, 165, 167; and personal meaning in rites, 135f, 142–44, 150–65 passim

heathen, 6

Heaven, cult of, 1, 3, 8, 21, 271; and Christian monotheism, 6; and human nature, 15–16; and Kongzi's religiousness, 9–12; missionaries on, 5–8, 17; and Shangdi, 6*n*15, 7*n*18

Heaven, response to Kongzi, 30, 48–49, 236, 240, 242

Heaven and Earth, cults of, 269, 280, 283; and Kongzi cult, 286

heavenly inscriptions, 233, 236, 241–42, Fig. 5.14, Fig. 5.23

heavenly king (*tianwang*) vs. feudal king (*zhuhou wang*), 279

historical knowledge, 339, 368

Historical Records (*Shiji*), and *Kongzi jiayu*, 193ff; and *Shengji tu*, 225, 231, 233*n*33, 240, 242*n*56; on Kongfu Jia, 59*n*58; on Kongzi as a seer, 60; on Kongzi's ancestry, 202; on Kongzi's birth, 187f, 192, 200, 205, 211; on Kongzi's death, 184; on Kongzi's descendants, 180, 182f, 186; on Kongzi's disciples, 176; on Kongzi's disciples, 79; on Kongzi's parents, 208, 242*n*55, 253

History of the Former Han (Hanshu), 176

hollow mulberry (*kongsang*), 207

Holy Rite, *see* Fingarette, Herbert

Hong Kong investment, 367

Hong Mai, 273

Hongdumen school, 222*n*3

Hongwu emperor, *see* Ming Taizu

Hou Cang, 272

Hou Ji, 198, 207, 210–11

Hu Pan'an, 210

Hu Shi, 7–8, 86

Hu Weiyong, 31, 286

Hu Yuan, 272

Hua Du, 59*n*58, 191

Huang Di, 204

Huang E, 204

Huang Gan, 109

Huang workshop of woodblock publishing, 239

Huang Zongxi, 36

Huang Zuo, 148, 157

huangzhong, 147, 152ff

humanity (*ren*), 14–17 passim, 45, 145, 150

hydropower station, 341, 343, 364

Hymes, Robert, 306

iconic images, 223, 256; vs. narrative representation, 223; vs. pictorial biographies, 256

iconoclasm, 26, 97, 97*n*3, 103, 105, 118–27, 255–56, 336, 362*n*45; defined, 97

iconoclastic nationalism, 336

iconodule, 104, 126

iconography, 96, 107, 112

iconolatry, 97, 117, 127; defined, 97

iconomachy, 97

iconophile, 103, 107, 127

idolatry, 13, 104, 125

Illustrated Family Sayings of the Sage Confucius (Kongsheng jiayu tu), *see* Wu Jiamo

illustrations 223–24; vs. (classical) writing, 232, 238–39, 246, 255. *See also* pictorial biography

Illustrious Sage of the World ("Huanyu xianshenggong"), 235, 240*n*48. *See also Newly Compiled Record of Confucius Making the Rounds of the States*

image, *see* spirit image

images of Kongzi, 222–24, 231, 246, 255–57; and his cult, 222–23, 255–56; distrust of, 246, 255; earliest, 222; major types of, 223; removal of, 255–56. *See also Pictures of the Sage's Traces*

immemorial construction, 178–80

imperial ancestral shrine, 268

imperial cult of Kongzi, 52, 72–79. *See also* cult of Kongzi; orthodoxy; sacrifice

imperial pantheon, 14, 21, 52*n*37; temple cults of, 1–3; Kongzi cult in, 25, 76–77

Imperial Survey of the Taiping Era (Taiping yulan), 205ff

Imperial University (Biyong), 141, 156f, 362*n*45; cult sacrifice at, 74, 110, 115–18 passim, 121; emperor's rule of, 280. *See also* Nanjing Imperial University

"Inquiries on the Sacrifices to the First Teacher Confucius," 275–76

Jade Box Collection of Lost Books (Yuhang shanfang jiyishu), 206

jade chimes and bronze bells, 54, 75

jade tablet (from Heaven/unicorn), 233, 236, 253f, Fig. 5.13, Fig. 5.21

Jesuits, 3–5, 25, 27

Ji, 290f
Ji clan, 210f
Jia Kui, 272
Jiajing emperor: and autocracy, 30, 289,
  292–93; and court officials, 277–78,
  282; on images of Kongzi, 231, 255–
  56; and Kong temple reforms, 26,
  56–57, 96, 126, 231, 255–56, 270–82;
  and orthodoxy, 298; and posthumous titles, 274–75, 290f; and
  Zhang Cong's proposal, 271–74;
  compared with Ming Taizu, 281–83,
  289; essays on temple reforms, 26,
  254–56, 279–80; Great Rites Controversy, 268–69, 281; on sacrifice to
  gods, 290–91; on Taizu, 283; temple
  reforms, 269–70
Jian Di, 203
Jiang Yingju, 387–88
Jiang Yong, 188n31
Jiang Yuan, 198, 210, 213
Jiao Hong, 238n41
Jing Yaoyue, 249
Jizi, 290f
Jocham, Christian, 8n21

Kalinowski, Marc, 209
Kang Youwei, 49, 86
Kangxi emperor, 290n103, 292–93, 298,
  300, 303, 311
King of Exalted Culture (*Wenxuan
  wang*), 51, 77, 287–88
King Qi of Wei, 141
King Wen, 2n2, 111–12, 116, 290
"King Wen's tune" ("Wenwang cao"),
  137
King Who Gave Birth to the Sage
  (*Qisheng wang*), 276n40
King Wu, 2n2, 116, 290
King Xiaowen of Wei, 141

Kong An, 62n69
Kong Anguo, 10, 61n66, 62, 233n31
Kong Ba, 62, 187, 305, 306n41, 319
Kong cemetery (*Kong lin*), 65, 366,
  391ff
Kong Changbi, 341
Kong Chuan, 67, 67n88, 69n94, 70
Kong Clan Anthology (*Kong congzi*), 184
Kong cult under Republic (*Kong jiao*),
  86
Kong Decheng, 342–43n24, 384
Kong Demao, 176
Kong Duancao, 178, 315
Kong Duanchao, 64
Kong Duanyou, 66, 178, 315ff
Kong Family Shop, 382–91 *passim*, 394
Kong Fan, 318
Kong Fang, 61
Kong Fangshu, 192
Kong Fen, 305n38
Kong Fu, 62f, 304
Kong Fuzi (Master Kong), 2, 22, 339.
  See also Kongzi
Kong Gonghuang, 70–71, 313, 316–17
Kong Gongyou, 344–45
Kong Guang, 99n8, 305
Kong Guangqi, 324
Kong Guangsen, 308n49
Kong Guangsi, 64, 312
Kong Heqi, 61
Kong Hongfu, 244
Kong Honggan, 69n92
Kong Honghao, 69n92
Kong Hongtai, 321n14
Kong Hongyi, 324n127
Kong Ji, 62, 83, 270, 276; altar of, 303
Kong Jiaxing, 341, 345
Kong Jie, 70n94
Kong Jifen, 143, 293n109, 310, 321n111
Kong Jihan, 307n47, 309, 321n111

Kong Jing, 68
Kong Jingjin, 68
Kong Kejian, 285, 314
Kong Li, 270; gift of carp, 237, Fig. 5.16,
    Fig. 5.30
Kong Lingshu, 348n33, 361
Kong Lingyi, 326
Kong Lü, 70n94
Kong mansion (*Kong fu*), 64, 285, 366;
    building of, 317–18; Red Guard as-
    sault on, 377f, 384–90 *passim*
Kong Masters' Anthology, The (*Kong-
    congzi*), 62
Kong Meng xiang tu zan, see *Pictures and
    Eulogies for the Images of Confucius and
    Mencius*
Kong miao, see Kongzi Temple
Kong Mo, 64–65, 65n82, 68, 70, 312–13
Kong Qinghu, 308n51
Kong Qinghui, 341, 360–61
Kong Qingquan, 308n47
Kong Qiu, 22, 44, 190. See also Kongzi
Kong Renyu, 64–65, 177, 312–13
Kong Rong, 63n73
Kong Ruoyu, 70
Kong Shangren: and elite circles, 311–12,
    323n123; on hereditary privilege,
    321n111; and Kangxi emperor, 300;
    on Kong genealogy, 61, 69n92,
    70n94, 316f
Kong Sihui, 64, 68–69
Kong Sixu, 70n94
Kong Sizhe, 63
Kong Suizhi, 63
Kong surname, 300; origin of, 59–60,
    178
Kong Teng (aka Rang), 62, 304
Kong Wenhan, 325n133
Kong Wenping, 325n133
Kong Wenru, 325n133

Kong Wenshi, 321n111
Kong Xiang, 304–5
Kong Xiangguo, 350n34
Kong Xianglin, 307n47
Kong Xiangmin, 381n8
Kong Xiangxi, 384
Kong Xianlan, 235, 247–48, Fig.
    5.29
Kong Xianmin, 348, 352
Kong Xianpei, 325
Kong Xianzeng, 308n48
Kong Xingshu, 310
Kong Xixue, 285, 314
Kong Yanbin, 351
Kong Yankui, 351
Kong Yanrong, 351
Kong Yansheng, 69–70, 69–70n94
Kong Yanzheng, 351
Kong Yanzhi, 314, 319, 327n142
Kong Yinfang, 311n63
Kong Yingda, 63, 189
Kong Yuancuo: on Kong genealogy, 61,
    61n67, 67–68, 236n37, 312; as Yan-
    sheng duke, 67, 314
Kong Yuqi, 299, 327, 327n142
Kong Yuxun, 308f
Kong Zhaoci, 308n50
Kong Zhaoqian, 308f
Kong Zhaozhen, 70n94
Kong Zhen, 68
Kong Zhi, 68
Kong Zhu, 66, 69n94, 70, 317
Kong Zhuanke, 308n51
Kong Zhuantang, 308n50
Kong Zhuanze, 303
Kong Zhuanzheng, 309n56
Kong Zonghan, 69n92
Kongfu Jia, 59f, 61n67, 178, 190
Kongfu neizhai yishi–Kongzi houyi de huiyi
    (Anecdotes from the Inner Quar-

ters of the Kong Residence—The Reminiscences of Kongzi's Descendant), 176

Kongs of the outer court (*wai yuan*), 65, 68

Kongsheng quanshu, see Complete Writings of the Sage Confucius

Kongshi zuting guangji, see Kong Yuancuo

Kongzi jiayu, see Family Sayings of Kongzi

Kongzi miao, see Kongzi Temple

Kongzi shengji tu, see Pictures of the Traces of the Sage Confucius

Kongzi/Confucius: and modernization, 248–50; and the rites, 223n5, 226; as a boy, 226, Fig. 5.4; as a god, 231, 231n29, 237; as a model for scholar-officials, 225–29 *passim*, 236f, 245–46, 255; as a teacher, 230, 233, 245, 251; as a tourist attraction, 250–51; as seer, 60; birthday celebration of, 345n30; body inscription of, 49, 236, 254, Fig. 5.14; body of, 26, 196–97, 211, 362; canonical and non-canonical figure of, 25, 28, 30, 43–49, 51–52, 176, 189–202 *passim*, 202–14; as commoner, 53–55; Communist views of, 231n29, 232, 250–52; conception and birth, 198–201, 206, 233–34, 236, 253–55, Fig. 5.14, Fig. 5.29, 362; death of, 226; disciples of, 223, 226, 244–45, 251, Fig. 5.24; father of, *see* Shuliang He; flesh-and-blood man vs. his Dao, 53, 57, 254–55; grave of, 226, 241, Fig. 5.10, Fig. 5.18, Fig. 5.23; identification with Chinese civilization, 86, 247, 249–50, 251, 376; images of, 222–24, 231, 246, 255–57; life events of, 225, 231,

233, 237–38, 240, 244–45; miraculous tales of, 46–49, 60, 233–37, 242–43, 253, Figs. 5.13–15, Fig. 5.21, Fig. 5.29; modern uses of, 30, 249–51, 256–57; mother of, *see* Zhengzai; sagehood of, 46, 49; on music, 134, 136–37, 145–46; on the five relationships, 328; ornithilogical lore and, 203–5, 211; parents of, 240, 242, 244, Figs. 5.19–20, Figs. 5.25–26; pictorial biography of, 224–27, 243, 255–57 (see also *Pictures of the Sage's Traces*); popularization of, 232, 237–40, 255; wife of, 240, Fig. 5.20; transcendence of history, 55–56

Kongzi's ancestry, 178, 189–95; descent from Shang royal house, 58–62, 202–3; father, 189–91; absence of, 208, 211, 213, 215; mother, 191–95, 206–8. *See also* Shuliang He; Zhengzai

Kongzi's descendants: adoption among, 70n94; and imperial house, 298–300, 302, 327f; bureaucratic appointments of, 307–9; direct memorializing to the emperor, 300; enfeoffment of, 61, 301, 304–6; examination degree holders, 63, 297, 307–8, 314; genealogical disputes among, 64–66, 67–71, 346; genealogies of, 64–69 *passim*; hereditary noble titles of, 63, 66, 69, 177, 249; inner Kongs (*nei Kong*), 65; landholding of, 310–11, 319–20; lineage disputes among, 62–72, 299, 312–13, 315–17; local dominance of, 71–72, 323–27; malfeasance, 310, 324; marriages of, 325–26; northern and southern branches of, 66–71, 178, 315–17; persecution under socialism, 352–

56; tax exemptions of, 319; taxation,
309–10, 310n58, 311, 313; triennial
review exemption, 300n9; uncertain
legacy of, 180–86, 214–15; under
Republic, 72. *See also* individual list-
ings under Kong; Yansheng duke
Kongzi Temple (*Kongzi miao*), 2, 4, 342;
description of, 301–4; liturgy of, 25f,
72–79; memorial tree in, 242, 244,
247n73; music of, 74ff; names of,
342n24; rank as sage, 52–53, 73; Red
Guard assault on, 32–33, 387, 391–92;
reconstruction of, 336–37, 344, 352–
57; renovations of, 301, 302n20, 303;
sacrificial vessels, 75n110; spirit images in, 74; Temple of Culture
(*wenmiao*), 22, 297, 342; Zhongni
temple, 73, 76n114. *See also* cult of
Kongzi
Kongzi Temple, Ilan (Taiwan), 127
Kongzi Temple, Tainan, 144
Kongzi Temple, Taipei, 168
Kongzi turen tufa (Method of painting
Kongzi and his disciples), 222n3
Korean images of Kongzi, 224n5
Kuaiji Kongs, 51
Kuiwen'ge, *see* Pavilion of the Constel-
lation of Learning

Ladies' Classic of Filial Piety (*Nü xiao jing*),
252
Lady Zhang, 268
landownership, 319–20
Lanzhou Kongs, 32–33
Laozi, 52n35, 120; Kongzi's meeting
with, 223, 223n5, 223n5, 226, 226n14,
Fig. 5.2, Fig. 5.5; pictorial biography
of, 230
large beast sacrifice (*tailao*), 73–75,
75n109, 140, 201

learning of the Dao (*Daoxue*), see Dao
School
Legge, James, 5–11 *passim*
Leng Qian, 156–57
Lévi-Strauss, Claude, 195
Li Bingwei, 235, 249
Li Dongyang, 325
Li Gonglin, 223n5.I
Li Guan, 274, 278, 280–82, 290
Li Jinghan, 336
Li Shimian, 227n16
Li Shu, 288
Li Weizhen, 155
Li Xiu, 377f, 388f, 393–94
Li Yuan'guan, 104
Li Zhizao, 27, 76n114, 77, 152–54, 159
Li Zhouwang, 156–57, 160
libations (*shidian*), 75
Lienü zhuan, 252
Liji, see *Record of Rites*
Lin Biao, 343n27
Lin Fang, 272
Lin Jie, 382f
lineage: higher order, 344; multivillage,
335
lineage branch (*pai*), 339, 341
lineage segment (*zhi*), 330n50, 340, 370
Lingguangdian, 222n2
Literary Expositor (*Erya*), 198f
literary knowledge, 339, 368
*Literary Writings Grouped According to
Categories* (*Yiwen leiju*), 205f
Liu Bang, *see* Han Gaozu
Liu Shuangsong, 235, 238
Liu Suming, 240n48
Liu Xiang, 176, 272
Liu Xin, 176
Liu Yu, 222n2
Liu Yu of Qi, 318
Liu Zongzhou, 255

Liu, James, 297n2
logging industry, 359–61
Lord Millet (Hou Ji), 111
Lord Praised for Fulfillment (*baocheng
    jun*), 306n41
Lord Sacrificer (*fengsi jun*), 301, 304
Lü Dongbin, 230, 230n26
Lu Jia, 60n63
Lu Jiuyuan, 77n42
Lü Kun, 252, 292
Lü Nan, 150, 156
Lu Tanwei, 224n5
Lü Zhenyu, 394n36
Lu Zhi, 272
Lülü jingyi, 153
Lülü xinshu, 155–56
Lülü zhengyi houbian, 142f, 161–62, 163
Lunyu, see *Analects*
*Luxuriant Dew of the Spring and Autumn
    (Chunqiu fanlu)*, 209
Lüyin huikao, 163–64

Ma Duanlin, 148
Ma Guohan, 206
Ma Rong, 2n1, 272
Ma Yuan, 197n55
Madsen, Richard, 337
mage, 199–200. *See also* Zhengzai
Mair, Victor, 298
Mannheim, Karl, 371
Mao Heng, 203, 211
Mao Qiling, 269
Mao Zedong, 30, 34, 256, 379–93 *passim*
marquis (*hou*), 63, 77, 80
Marquis of the Consummate Sage (*bao
    sheng hou*), 63
Martial Temple, 287–89
"Master Kong's Hereditary House-
    hold" (*Kongzi shijia*), 225

May Fourth Movement, 86
Mazu, 230
Medhurst, Walter, 5
Mei Fu, 61
Mencius, *see* Mengzi
Meng clan (Mengzi's descendants),
    314n75
Meng Ke, *see* Mengzi
Meng Pi, 194, 196
Meng Xianzi, 190
Meng Xizi, 190
Mengzi/Menciu: altar of, 303, 322; and
    Daotong, 83–84; enshrinement, 82,
    276, 286, 351; on Confucius, 46–47,
    125, 184, 202; pictorial biography of,
    230, 238; teachings, 45; and Xunzi,
    16. *See also* Four Books
metallic sounds and jade vibrations
    (*jinsheng yuzheng*), 147, 168
middle-level sacrifice, 2
Middle Path Academy (*Zhongtang
    shuyuan*), 322
Milne, William, 5
Ming History (Mingshi), 150, 268f
ming shi (sharp-eyed one, rabbit), 362
Ming Shizong, *see* Jiajing emperor
Ming Taizu, 30, 272, 275; and Mengzi,
    286–87; and orthodoxy, 298, 314;
    and Song Lian, 284; and the Yan-
    sheng duke, 285, 314, 319; compared
    with Jiajing emperor, 283, 293;
    iconoclasm of, 109–10, 117; on rela-
    tion between military and civil cults,
    287–88; on sacrifice to gods, 287–
    89; on sacrifices to Kongzi, 53f, 57,
    283; on spirit images, 109, 115; sus-
    pension of sacrifice to Kongzi, 31,
    283–85
Ming Wuzong, 268
Ming Xianzong, 281

Mingtang, 1n1
Ministry of Culture, 380f
Ministry of Personnel, 323, 326
Ministry of Rites, 1, 21, 52, 65, 77f, 277, 281, 309, 311, 322, 326
minor temple (ga miao), 361
Miscellaneous Record of the Eastern Household, 67
missionaries on Chinese religion, 3–7, 13f, 25, 27
Mo Ti, 8
modern script, see Modern Text
Modern Text (jinwen), 48n24, 48–49, 80f, 86, 202, 236, 236n36, 243
monotheism, 3–4, 6, 8, 13f
Monthly Ordinances (Yue ling), 201
Morrison, Robert, 5
mountains and rivers, cult of, 275, 287
Mount Ni, 29, 44n7, 233, 242, Fig. 5.3, Fig. 5.19, Fig. 5.25
Mount Tai, 245n66, 377
mourning, 182–84 passim
Mr. Lü's Springs and Autumns Chronicle (Lüshi chunqiu), 191, 214
mulberry, 206n83
Mungello, David E., 4
murals, 222, 222n2, 246
music, 242f; and dance, 134f, 140, 161–63; ceremonial songs, singing of, 144, 149–51, 152f, 156–57, 161, 164; drum calls (sangu), 144, 147f, 155; harmony, 149, 153–54, 157; improper, 142, 145f; of Shao, 134, 242; performance/practice of, 140, 150, 152; pitch, 27, 146–47, 152ff, 157, 163f; popular, 164; production and consumption, 134, 136–37; proper, 135–36, 145, 146–47, 157, 165; theory vs. practice of, 136, 143–43, 148, 166–68; westernization of, 167; vulgar, 145

musical modes, 144, 147–48, 153
musical instruments, 135, 143f, 147f, 150, 152, 155f, 161

Nanjing Imperial University, 272; cult sacrifice at, 115–18 passim
Nanyong zhi, 148–49, 157
narrative illustration, 223, 225, 228f, 232, 256. See also pictorial biography
natal parents: sacrifices to, 268, 271; descent from, 268–69
nationalism: and Kongzi, 248–51
National Red Guard Revolutionary Rebellion Contact Station, 386f, 393ff
Nation Society of Beiping (Beiping minshe), 235, 248–50, Fig. 5.30
New Life Movement, 30
Newly Compiled Record of Confucius Making the Rounds of the States and Fulfilling the Unicorn, 235, 240, 253–55, Figs. 5.19–22
New Script, see Modern Script
Nicephorus the Patriarch, 107–8
Niqiu, 194–95, 204, 208
noble titles, see posthumous names and titles
noble type of orchestra (xuanxuan), 144

Odes, Book of (Shijing, Maoshi), 5, 12, 62, 75, 80, 111–12, 114, 154, 164, 244
Old Dharma-Master Sage-Thoughts (Shenghuai lao fashi), 250
Old Kong (Kong lao'er), 378
ornamental tones (yuyun), 164
orthodoxy, 19, 66, 243; and enshrinement in the imperial temple, 79–87; emperor and, 297–98
orthopraxy, 19
Otsuki Nobuyoshi, 5n12

outer Kongs (*wai Kong*), 65, 68
Ouyang Xiu, 272

painted portraits (*xiao xiang*), 117
Palace of Blood and Tears (AKA Imperial Palace), 380
Pan Xiang, 312, 321*n*111
Pang Zhonglu, 151
Pangong liyue shu (Proposal on rites and music in schools), 152–54, 159
pantheon, *see* imperial pantheon
patriline, 102
Pavilion of the Constellation of Learning (Kuiwen'ge), 251
Peach Blossom Fan, 312
Pei Kan, 276
Peng Yunzhang, 326
Peony Pavilion (*Mudan ting*), 113
people of clay (*ni ren*), 111
people of copper (*tong ren*), 111
People's Army, 379–80
People's Liberation Army brigade, 354n36
Perfected Sage Premier Teacher Confucius (*zhisheng xianshi Kongzi*), 126
personators (*shi*), 97, 99, 101–2
pictorial biography, 228–32, 241, 255–57; of Buddha, 228–30, Fig. 5.12; Buddhist roots of, 229–32, 256; conventions of, 230–31, 251–52; and cult deities, 229–30; of Kongzi, *see Pictures of the Sage's Traces*; and popularization, 232, 238; and proselytizing, 229–31, 256; uses of, 229–32, 246, 247, 255–57; vs. iconic images, 223, 256; vs. textual biography, 227, 231
pictures, ambiguity of, 255; efficacy of, 227, 231, 238, 246, 255–56; misgivings about, 238–39, 246

Pictures and Eulogies for the Images of Confucius and Mencius (Kong Meng xiang tu zan), 238, Fig. 5.18
Pictures of the Sage's Traces (Shengji tu), 49, 225–28, 232–38, 241–52; anonymity of illustrators of, 225, 228, 241; artistic vs. pedagogical aims of, 228, 231; authoritative version of, 247; Buddhist pictorial biographies and, 229–30, 236; circulation of, 228, 232, 233, 237, 239, 247–48, 256; court politics and, 227, 245f; creation of, 224–25, 231; criticisms of, 239, 246; English translation of, 248n74; evolution of, 226, 232, 241–45, 251, 255; handwritten texts in, 248–49n78; inspirational purposes of, 225–26, 228, 232, 237–38, 246, 248f, 251, 256; and late Ming book trade, 237–40, 246, 254, 256; and late Ming culture, 238–41, 246, 252–54; long vs. short versions of, 241; media used for, 228, 232f, 241, 247; as a medium for communicating ideas, 232, 243f, 249–50, 252, 255, 257; modernization and, 249, 251–52, 257; orthodoxy and, 243; Qufu in, 241–42; patronage of, 225, 228, 232, 237, 239, 245, 248; popularization of Kongzi and, 232, 237–40, 255; preternatural events in, 233–37, 242–43; preternatural events removed from, 251; recensions of, 232, 234–35, 237, 239, 241f, 251–55; recensions of, first, *see under* Zhang Kai; second, *see* He Tingrui; third, *see under Complete Pictures of the Sage's Traces*; reproductions from various versions, Figs. 5.3–31; and *Shiji*, 225, 226–27, 231, 240, 253; stone tablet recension in

Qufu temple, 244–47, 253, 255; and traditional cultural heritage, 246, 249–50, 256–57; under other titles, 235, 238–40; versions of, 226n13, 234–35, 241; women in, 252–55; woodblock-printed versions, 233–39, 248, 250–51. See also Hall of the Sage's Traces; He Tingrui; Zhang Kai; Zhu Jianjun; Zhu Yinyi

Pictures of the Traces of the Sage Confucius (Kongzi Shengji tu), 235, 248–49

pilgrimage, 230, 248

Pingyao, 47

Polachek, James, 298

political knowledge, 339, 363–68 *passim*

polytheism, 5–7, 13

popular religion, 13, 29, 230, 237, 240, 247

portraits, *see* images; spirit image

posthumous names and titles of Kongzi, 25, 50–57, 75, 124–25, 272f, 287–89; as duke, 50–51, 54, 71; as king, 51–56 *passim*, 73, 75, 271–75 *passim*, 279f, 288f; as emperor, 53, 56; and relationship with the throne, 53–54, 57

power (cosmic, *de*), 48

power (political) vs. Principle (*li*), 292

Praising Perfection Marquis (*baocheng hou*), 319

privilege, *see under* Kongzi's descendants

Progenitor of the Revived Lineage, 64

Protestants, 5–7

Puyuan debates, 268, 273n23, 281

qi (vital energy), 2n1, 101; use in musical pitch, 163

Qi Benyu, 382, 385–88 *passim*

Qian Mu, 93n109

Qian Tang, 283n72, 284, 286

Qianlong emperor, and orthodoxy, 298; and Kongzi's descendents, 309

Qin Huitian, 125, 148, 288

Qin Jinfu, 190

Qin Pici, 190

Qin Ran, 272

Qin Shihuang, 233n31, 241–42, Fig. 5.23

Qin Tang, 282

Qing huidian, 142

Qingbai leichao, 162–63

Qiu Jun, 118, 272; aniconism of, 26, 118f; anti-Buddhism of, 118, 119–20; iconoclasm of, 121, 123f; influence of, 125–26; on images, 119–24 *passim*; on posthumous titles, 57, 124–25; on spirit tablets, 118; on spirits, 121–22

Qiu Zhilu, 143, 161–64

Qu Jiusi, 74n30, 286–87

Qu Yuan, 272

Queli, *see* Qufu

Queli wenxian kao, 310

Qufu, 35, 44, 50, 177f, 234f, 241–44, 248, 251; bandits and, 319; fall to CCP, 360–61n42; imperial processions to, 301, 305; imperial sacrifices at, 73–74; Kongzi cult in, 73; post-Mao economic development of, 366; temple, 275f, 283, 300, 301–6, 366

Qufu County Committee, 377–94 *passim*

Qufu County Communist Party, 376

Qufu Kongs, 31–32, 68–72; estate narrative of the Kong lineage, 176–86 *pasim*; local dominance, 71

Quzhou Kongs, 66–68, 314n75, 315–17

rainbow (*chi hong*) from the Big Dipper, 30, 49, 236, Fig. 5.15

Rawski, Evelyn, 19, 27, 33, 71

Rebuke Confucius (*tao Kong*), 383, 385, 392

Record of Music (*yueji*), 145

Record of Rites (*Liji*), 12, 22, 60, 74f, 99–100, 244, 391

"Record of the Hall of Pictures of the Sage," 244–45, 247

Record of the Legal Descendants (*Diyi kao*), 316

"Record of the Queli Genealogy," 65

Red Flag, 382f

Red Guard, 34f, 336, 341

Red Guard brigades: Beijing Normal University Mao Zedong's Thought Red Guard's Mt. Jinggang Brigade, 382, 387–95 *passim*; East-Is-Red Red Guard, 378; Mt. Tai Normal University Affiliated Middle School Red Guard, 378; Qufu Normal University [Hawk Squad] Red Guard, 378–91 *passim*; Qufu Normal University Mao Zedong's Thought Red Guard, 378, 394; Qufu Number One Middle School Red Guard, 391; Peasant Red Guard, 380; Tai'an Naval Academy Red Guard, 377, 379

"Register of Sacrifices" (*sidian*), 50, 52n37

"Register of the Disciples" (*Dizi ji*), 182n16, 185

Regulations for the Women's Quarters (*Guifan*), 252

religiousness (Confucian), 1–18

religious revivalism in post-Mao era, 335, 335–36n2, 350

"revering the son and humbling the father," 273–74, 276, 281

Ricci, Matteo, 3, 4n8, 27

rites, 2n2

Rites, see *Record of Rites*

Rites of the Kaiyuan Era (*Kaiyuan li*), 108

Rites of Zhou (*Zhouli*), 1n1, 73f, 115, 153f, 212, 291

ritual (*li*), 15, 134; vs. ethics, 11

ritual chamber charter (*zongfa*), 177

ritual knowledge, 339, 344, 347–51, 362, 364, 367, 371–72

ritual performers (*li sheng*), 347

ritual procedures (*yizhu*), 143, 154

ritual symbolism, multivocality of, 357

ritual theory (Confucian), 14–20

Rong Qiqi, 224n5

rou mao (soft-haired one, sheep), 362

Ru (Confucian, literatus, scholar, classicist), see Confucian/Ru; Weakling fellowship

ru (suckle), 204

Ruan Yuan, 326

rubbings, 225, 244n62, 247f, Figs. 5.1–2, Fig. 5.12, Fig. 5.27

sacrifice: as communication with spirits, 98, 102; and dance, 27; depicted in *Shengji tu*, 226, 242, Fig. 5.11; Kongzi on, 10–11; *Li* and, 15; liturgy of, 72–79, 138–39, 349; offerings, 78, 139; open air sacrifice (*yin*), 198, 209ff; prayer to obtain a son (*qi*), 195, 200, 226, 233, 240, 242, 252–53, Fig. 5.3, Fig. 5.19, Fig. 5.25; revival under socialism, 348; suburban (*jiao*), 198; to divine intermediary (*jiaomei/gaomei*), 199–204 *passim*, 208, 211; to Kongzi, 3, 74–75, 77–78, 226, 231, 242; to Kongzi suspended, 31, 283–85; types of, 198–201; wanton (*yin si*), 102. See also under cult of Kongzi

sacrificial texts (*ji wen*), 349–50

sacrificial vessels, number of, 271, 273f,
    280f
Sacrificing Official for the Supreme
    Sage and First Master of Great
    Completion (*dacheng zhisheng xianshi
    fengsi guan*), 72
sage ancestor (*sheng zu*), 344, 352
sagehood, 15, 46, 82
Sagely Graced Academy (Shengze
    shuyuan), 322
Sage of Culture Venerable Ni (*wen-
    sheng Nifu*), 50
sage's descendants (*sheng yi*), 340. *See
    also* Kongzi's descendants
Sakyamuni (Buddha), 120; pictorial bi-
    ographies of, 228–30, 231, Fig. 5.12
savant (*zhe*), 77–80 *passim*, 104, 382
Schafer, Edward, 200n66
Schlegel, Gustave, 196, 212
schools, state, 52, 74f, 77
Schwartz, Benjamin, 16–18
Scott, James, 346
scribe characters, 80
seal characters, 80
Second Sage, *see* Mengzi
self-cultivation, 134, 146
senior descent line (*dazong*), 304, 315
seven-string zither (*qin*), 135, 148, 155
shade (*ying*), 112–13
Shakyamuni, *see* Sakyamuni
shamanism, *see* mage
Shang Wei, 20
shangdi, cult of, 1–2n1; and Christian
    God, 5–6; vs. "Shin" (*shen*), 6
Shang origin myth, 203
Shao Changheng, 275n31, 284n76
Shao Hao, 204–5
Shao Yiren, 246, 255
Sheji, *see* Soils and Grains
Shen Dang, 272

Shen Defu, 274
Shengji quantu, see *Complete Pictures of the
    Sage's Traces*
Shengji tu, see *Pictures of the Sage's Traces*
Shengjidian, see Hall of the Sage's
    Traces
Shengren dian, *see* Hall of the Sage
Shennong (Divine Farmer), 2n2,
    284n75, 290f
shen wei, see spirit tablet
shen zuo, see spirit tablet
Shi Jishi, 154–56
Shi Xiang, 136–37
Shiji, see *Historical Records*
Shijiarulai yinghua shiji ji, 228n19
Shijing, see *Odes*
Shirakawa Shizuka, 199–202 *passim*
Shishi yuanliu (Origins and evolution of
    the Sakya clan), 228
Shizi Sheng, 178
Shrine of Giving Birth to the Sage (Qi
    sheng ci), 273–76
Shu He, *see* Shuliang He
Shuliang He: enshrinement of, 270f,
    274; and Kong lineage, 59, 189, 193–
    94; and Zhengzai, 197, 199; as
    Kongzi's father, 190, 192; death of,
    192, 195, 208; in *Shengji tu*, 242, 254,
    Fig. 5.21; prayers at Mt. Ni, 200;
    Shu He, 191. *See also* Hall of the
    King Who Gave Birth to the Sage;
    King Who Gave Birth to the Sage;
    Kongzi's ancestry; Shrine of Giving
    Birth to the Sage;
Shun, 2n2, 47, 55, 100–101, 116, 255
Shuowen, 15
Sima Guang, 268, 273n23
Sima Qian, 28, 60, 73, 182, 186f, 192f,
    196, 200, 202. See also *Historical Re-
    cords*

Sima Tan, 187

"Single Victim Feast" (*tesheng kuishi*), 77

sitting: of spirit, 108; in meditation (*zuo chan*), 108

Siu, Helen, 337

Smith, Paul J., 306–7

social capital, 338

Society of Confucius and Mencius (Kong Meng hui), 343n26

Society of Morality (Daode hui), 343

Soils and Grains, altar/cult of, 2, 75, 269, 280, 284

Song Gaozong, 49n25, 66, 178

Song Lian, 53n41, 109, 115, 276, 284, 290f; aniconism of, 106; on Buddhist images, 105–6

Song Na: aniconism of, 26, 110, 115–17, 284–85n76; on iconographic representation, 111–12; on spirit tablets, 110–11, 114–15; on spirits, 112–14; on temples to walls and moats, 110

Song Renzong, 177

Song shi, 312

Song Taizong, 280

Song Taizu, 280

Song Yingzong, 281

Song Zhenzong, 242

Songfu Zhou, 178

Songs of the South (*Chuci*), 9n24

Soothill, William E., 5n12, 10n28

southern drama (*chuanqi*), 29, 240

Southern Lineage Sacrificing Official for the Supreme Sage and First Master (*zhisheng xianshi nanzong fengsi guan*), 72

spirit image (*xiang*), 47, 74, 100, 271f, 280, 357–58, 362; connection to spirit, 106–7, 108, 121–23; destruction of, 26, 109–10, 119–26, 271, 274–

75, 284n76, 380, 390–93 *passim*; and garb, 54, 75n110; as incarnation, 101, 103; internal parts of, 357–58; as medium between living and spirits, 26, 101f, 117, 121; verisimilitude of, 26, 96, 112–13, 122–23; vs. spirit tablet, 106–10 *passim*, 124

spirits, 98, 114, 121–22

spirit statue, *see* spirit image

spirit tablet (*lingpai, shenwei, zhu*): and ineffability of spirits, 26, 95, 99, 107, 114–15; described, 345n29, 351; in Jiajing reforms, 272–73, 280f; precedent for, 106, 110–11, 118; spirit seat (*shen zuo*), 108; use in modern temples, 347

spirit world (hidden, invisible world) 97–98, 101, 114; and visible world, 101

spirit writing, 120

Spiro, Audrey, 103–4

Spring and Autumn Annals, 22, 28, 76, 279, 391; Kongzi's authorship of, 47ff, 53, 56

Spring Equinox (*chun fen*), 344

"Springs and Autumns Apocrypha Explanatory Kong Chart" (*Chunqiuwei Yan Kong tu*), 176n2, 206

standardized music vs. individual expression, 27, 142, 144–45, 151–52

State Council, 377–91 *passim*

"Statement on the Hall of Pictures of the Sage," 246, 255

statue, *see* spirit image

status strategies: descent, 308–15; Kongs' non-use of local, 306, 309–10

stone tablets of Kongzi's picture, in the Han period, 222, 225, 228, 252, Fig. 5.1, Fig. 5.2; in the Ming period, 225,

228, 244–47, 248, 248n76, 253ff, Fig.
5.27; in the 20th century, 251–52,
Fig. 5.31
strict abstinence (*zhi zhai*), 78n121
Su Shi, on spirit images, 106–8; on
spirit tablets, 107; on offerings,
106–7
Sun Chengze, 125
Sun Yuwen, 326
supernatural events, *see* "miraculous
tales" *under* Kongzi
*Supplement to the Extended Meaning of the
Great Learning (Daxue yanyibu)*, 118–
25
Supreme Emperor of Mysterious
Heaven (Xuan Tian shangdi), 1
Supreme Sage (*zhi sheng*), 44, 51, 52n35
Supreme Sage and First Master
(*zhisheng xianshi*), 3, 394
Supreme Sage, Exalted King of Culture (*zhisheng wenxuan wang*), 57
swallow (*ya*), 199, 201, 203
symbolic capital, 337–38, 342, 362, 364,
368, 372
symbolic power, 338

Taibo, 20
Taigong Temple, 287–89
Taigong Wang, 287–90
tailao, see large beast sacrifice
Taiyi, 2n1
Tan Houlan, 35, 382–85 passim, 389,
394–95
Tang (Shang founder), 2n2, 116, 203,
290; cult of, 61
Tang Kaiyuan li, 142
Tang Taizong, 71n99
Tang Xianzu, 113
Tang Xuanzong, 279
Tao Yuanming, 113

Taylor, Rodney, 14–15
Teacher and Paragon of the Ten-
thousand Generations, 394
temple closure, 336, 343
temple court (*dian*), 271, 273
temple cult, *see* cult of Kongzi
Temple for Venerating the Sage
(Chongsheng ci), 304
temple hierarchy, 50, 77; and posthumous titles, 52–53
Temple of Culture (Wenmiao), *see*
Kongzi Temple
Temple of Kings and Emperors (Lidai
diwang miao), 287
Temple of the King of Military Accomplishment (Wucheng wang
miao), 287–89
temple reform, *see under* Jiajing emperor; Ming Taizu
Temple to Confucius, *see* Kongzi
Temple
Temple to the Duke of Zhou, 376,
391–92
Temple to Yan Hui, 376
temple watchman, 395
ten pitches, 157
"Ten Shang-Zhou gifts" (*Shang Zhou
shi gong*), 384
Ten Wise Ones, *see* savant
Three August Ones (*san huang*), 2n2,
284, 287, 291
Three Kong Sites (*san Kong*), 376–82
passim, 384–86, 389, 393
Tian Wen, 311
Tianhou, 230
Tomb of the Supreme Sage, 391
tourism, 166, 250–51, 359, 366
tradition and invention, 178–80
tradition of legitimate governance (*zhitong*), 267, 291–92

transmission of the Way, see *daotong*

transmitting the classics, 273

Treatise on Music (*Yueshu*), 148

trigrams, 152, 163

Tu Wei-ming, 14–18 *passim*

tuning, 146–47, 168

Turner, Victor, 357

twelve absolute pitches (*shi'er lü*), 146–47, 152ff

twenty-five string zither, 148

twenty-two masters, *see* canonical exegetes

Tzu Lu, *see* Zilu

uncrowned king (*su wang*), 47, 52n35, 383

unicorn (*lin, qilin*), 47, 196, 224n5, 226, 226n15, 233, 253–54, Fig. 5.8, Figs. 5.13–14, Fig. 5.21

Unofficial History of the Scholars (*Rulin waishi*), 19–20

Ushnishashitatapattra, 119

Venerable Kong Temple (Kongfu miao), 76. *See also* Kongzi Temple

Venerable Ni (Nifu), 44

vermillion regulations, 48f

village cadre, 368–69

village head (*cunzhang*), 348

Waley, Arthur, 9n24

Wang Anshi, enshrinement of, 82f; ritual image of, 105

Wang Chong, 239n44

Wang Hong, 281

Wang Huatian, 376–77, 379

Wang Jingwei, 384

Wang Mang, 124–25, 272, 299n8

Wang Shizhen, 311

Wang Sixun, 156

Wang Su, 61n66, 194f, 200, 208, 272

Wang Tong, 272

Wang Xi, 311

Wang Xiaoyu, 395

Wang Yangming, 243

Wang Yanshou, 222n2

Wang Yun, 117

Wang Zhen, 227

Wang Zhengxi, 394f

Wanli emperor, 245

water in a suspended vessel, 224n5, 238n41, Fig. 5.17

Watson, James, 19

Watt, Ian, 371

Weakling fellowship (*ru*), 175, 179, 184. *See also* Confucian

Weizi Qi, 58, 178, 194

wen (accomplished), 177n4

Wen Weng, 103

Wenmiao sidian kao, 151

Wenxian tongkao, 148

wenxuan gong, 63, 177, 323

"When King Wen Was Heir Apparent," 75

White Lord (Bai Di), 204

White Tiger Hall Disquisitions (*Baihu tong*), 184

Williams, E. T., 8

women, 252–55

woodblock editions, *see under Pictures of the Sage's Traces*

working abstinence (*san zhai*), 78n121

Worshipping the Sage Code (*Chong sheng dianli*), 72

worthies (*xian*), 104

Wu Chen, 53, 55ff, 272, 289f

Wu Cheng, 272f

Wu Daozi, 4

Wu Hung, 222n3

Wu Jiamo, 234, 239, 241n51, 253

Wu Jingzi, 19–20
Wu Liang Shrine, 197, 222, 222n3, 224, 224n5, 226n14
Wu Tang, see Tang (Shang founder)
Wuli tongkao, see Qin Huitian

Xia Yan, 277–78
Xiangtuo, 223n5
Xiao Minqing, 314n79
Xiaochuan Kongs, 32–33, 359–67; commercial development and, 363–65; compared with Dachuan Kongs, 367–72; Dachuan Kongs and, 346, 359–62; founders of, 343; government contacts and, 365, 367f; Kongzi temple of, 343, 357–59, 362, 367; temple managers, 363–67, 371
Xie (Kongzi's ancestor), 58, 203, 209, 290f
Xie Duo, 273
Xie Lüzhong, 156–57, 160
Xin (King Zhou of Shang), 58f
Xin Ke Gong, 351
Xingtan, see Apricot Altar
Xiong He, 273, 290f
Xu Da, 285
Xu Ji, 155
Xu Jie, 275, 277, 279
Xu Ke, 162–63
Xu Shen, 196, 204, 210
Xu Xuemo, 274n30
xuan (propagator, eminent, exalted), 50n28
Xuanxiao, 58n53
Xuanyuan, 290
Xue Kan, 77n42
Xun Kuang, 272. See also Xunzi
Xunzi, 16, 45, 61n66, 121, 196
Yan clan (Yan Hui's descendants), 314n75

Yan He, 272
Yan Hui, 181, 244, 270, 276, 351; altar of 303, 322; cult of, 73–79 *passim*, 83n132; spirit image of, 104
Yan Lu, 270
Yan Yuan, see Yan Hui
Yan Zhengzai, see Zhengzai
Yang, C. K., 336
Yang, Mayfair, 337
Yang Rongguo, 394n36
Yang Shen, 277
Yang Shi, 105
Yang Shijing, 241n51
Yang Shouchen, 55ff
Yang Shusen, 143, 164–65
Yang Tinghe, 268f
Yang Zifan, 387–88
Yansheng Duke, 342n24; and imperial court, 314, 318; as guarantor of Kong status, 306, 309f, 319; as lineage head, 300, 308; control of local bureaucracy, 323–27; court's appointment of, 317; hereditary status of, 312, 321–22; promotion under the Ming, 320–21; status in imperial bureaucracy, 320–21; temporary appointment under Jin, 315. *See also* Duke for Fulfilling the Sage
Yao, 2n2, 46, 55, 100f, 116, 255, 290
Ye Zaiwen, 394
Yellow Emperor, 2n2, 58n53, 61n67, 290
Yi 益, 290f
Yi 夷, 290f
Yi Yin, 211, 290f
yin privilege, 321–24 *passim*
ying, 112–13
Yongjing Kongs, 32–33, ancestral worship of 344f; four brothers of, 341, 344; genealogies of, 340–41ff, 348, 360; local founding ancestors tem-

ples, 335; origins of, 339, 341, 351; Qufu Kongs and, 340f, 342n24, 345, 360–61; sacrifices of, 342; Kongzi temple of, 342f. *See also* Dachuan Kongs; Xiaochuan Kongs

Yongle emperor, 49

Yongzheng emperor, 327

You, 182

Yu, 2n2, 116, 207, 290

Yu Hou Gong, 351

Yü Minzhong, 325

Yu Shan, 277

Yu Xiu, 394

Yu Zhengxie, 284n76

Yuan Chengzong, 287

Yuan Shikai, 85–86, 345n30, 384

Yuan Wuzong, 49n25, 279

Yue Hesheng, 150f

Yueji, 145

Yueshu, 148

Yuyi, 59n58

Zeng clan (Zeng Sen's descendants), 314n75

Zeng Sen (Zengzi), 83, 184, 244, 270, 276, 351; altar of, 302, 322

Zeng Xi, 270

Zengzi, *see* Zeng Sen

Zhang Binlin, 86

Zhang Cong: and Jiajing emperor, 271, 274f, 278, 281; influences on, 57, 126; on enshrinement of sages' fathers, 271, 274, 276; on enshrinement of worthies and scholars, 271–72, 273; on posthumous titles, 56–57, 272, 291; on Qufu temple, 276; on sacrifice, 270; on spirit tablets and images, 272; on temple court, 273

Zhang Daoist teachers, 328

Zhang Daoying, 388, 391ff

Zhang E, 143, 150f, 154

Zhang Ertian, 86n124

Zhang Fujing, *see* Zhang Cong

Zhang Jinshan, 395

Zhang Kai, 29, 225–28, 233f, 241, 252, 253; on aims of *Shengji tu*, 225–26; creation of *Shengji tu*, 225–28; on Kongzi's moral character, 227, 233; eulogies of, 225

Zhang Shizhen, 311

Zhang Yingdeng, 234, 244–47

Zhang Yongnian, 385, 388f

Zhang Yuesheng, 143

Zhang Yumei, 380, 383, 386, 389f, 393–94

Zhang Zai, 156; enshrinement of, 83

Zhang Zhao, 325

Zheng Xuan, 211, 272

Zheng Yunzhu, 235, 239n47

Zhengxing yayue yi (Proposal for revitalizing proper music), 143, 164–65

Zhengzai: and Shuliang He, 194; and unicorn, 49, 226, Fig. 5.13; as mage, 199–200, 206–9, 213; dreams of, 236; illicit union, 197–99; prayers at Mt. Ni for son, 44, 226, 233, 242, 252–55, Fig. 5.3; temple for, 301. *See also* Kongzi's ancestry

zhonglü, 148–49, 153

Zhongni (Second son Ni), 22, 44. *See also* Kongzi

Zhongni temple, *see* Kongzi Temple

Zhongs (descendants of Zhou You, *zi* Zilu), 314n75

Zhongsi Yan (Weizhong, or Wei the Second), 58, 61

Zhongxing lishu (Compilation of ceremonials of the Southern Song), 142

Zhou Dunyi: enshrinement of, 83; spirit image of, 109

Zhou Enlai, 343n27, 383n10
Zhou Fang, 223n5
Zhou Haizhou, 387
Zhou Hongmo, 54–55, 273, 279
Zhou Yutong, 394n36
Zhouli, see Rites of Zhou
Zhu Houcong, 268
Zhu Jianjun, 234, 237, 238n41, 253, Fig.
   5.3, Figs. 5.6–7, Fig. 5.17
Zhu Qianzhi, 394n36
Zhu Xi, 192n42, 316; and Four Books,
   82; enshrinement of, 83, 85; Explana-
   tions of the Yili, 164; on Kongzi, 225,
   227; on Kongzi's parents, 242n55; on
   sacrifice, 5n12; on spirit images, 101n9,
   103, 108–9; on Great Learning, 243
Zhu Yi, 325
Zhu Yinyi, the Prince of Shen, 234,
   237, Fig. 5.10

Zhu Yizun, 280
Zhu Zaiyu, 153
Zhuangzi, 52n35
Zi clan, 202f
Zigong, 183, 212, 226, Fig. 5.9
Zilu, 5n12, 182
Zisi, 182, 184f, 182, 351. See also
   Kong Ji
Zito, Angel, 18n58
Zixia, 212
Ziyou, 212
Zou Gan, 117–18
Zou He, 189f
Zu Wuze, 67n87
Zuo Commentary on the Spring and Au-
   tumn Annals (Zuo zhuan), 26, 47,
   71n11, 114, 189f, 193, 197, 204, 214;
   quoted, 59f

Harvard East Asian Monographs

(* out-of-print)

*1. Liang Fang-chung, *The Single-Whip Method of Taxation in China*

*2. Harold C. Hinton, *The Grain Tribute System of China, 1845–1911*

3. Ellsworth C. Carlson, *The Kaiping Mines, 1877–1912*

*4. Chao Kuo-chün, *Agrarian Policies of Mainland China: A Documentary Study, 1949–1956*

*5. Edgar Snow, *Random Notes on Red China, 1936–1945*

*6. Edwin George Beal, Jr., *The Origin of Likin, 1835–1864*

7. Chao Kuo-chün, *Economic Planning and Organization in Mainland China: A Documentary Study, 1949–1957*

*8. John K. Fairbank, *Ching Documents: An Introductory Syllabus*

*9. Helen Yin and Yi-chang Yin, *Economic Statistics of Mainland China, 1949–1957*

*10. Wolfgang Franke, *The Reform and Abolition of the Traditional Chinese Examination System*

11. Albert Feuerwerker and S. Cheng, *Chinese Communist Studies of Modern Chinese History*

12. C. John Stanley, *Late Ching Finance: Hu Kuang-yung as an Innovator*

13. S. M. Meng, *The Tsungli Yamen: Its Organization and Functions*

*14. Ssu-yü Teng, *Historiography of the Taiping Rebellion*

15. Chun-Jo Liu, *Controversies in Modern Chinese Intellectual History: An Analytic Bibliography of Periodical Articles, Mainly of the May Fourth and Post–May Fourth Era*

*16. Edward J. M. Rhoads, *The Chinese Red Army, 1927–1963: An Annotated Bibliography*

17. Andrew J. Nathan, *A History of the China International Famine Relief Commission*

*18. Frank H. H. King (ed.) and Prescott Clarke, *A Research Guide to China-Coast Newspapers, 1822–1911*

19. Ellis Joffe, *Party and Army: Professionalism and Political Control in the Chinese Officer Corps, 1949–1964*

*20. Toshio G. Tsukahira, *Feudal Control in Tokugawa Japan: The Sankin Kōtai System*

21. Kwang-Ching Liu, ed., *American Missionaries in China: Papers from Harvard Seminars*

22. George Moseley, *A Sino-Soviet Cultural Frontier: The Ili Kazakh Autonomous Chou*

23. Carl F. Nathan, *Plague Prevention and Politics in Manchuria, 1910–1931*

*24. Adrian Arthur Bennett, *John Fryer: The Introduction of Western Science and Technology into Nineteenth-Century China*

25. Donald J. Friedman, *The Road from Isolation: The Campaign of the American Committee for Non-Participation in Japanese Aggression, 1938–1941*

*26. Edward LeFevour, *Western Enterprise in Late Ching China: A Selective Survey of Jardine, Matheson and Company's Operations, 1842–1895*

27. Charles Neuhauser, *Third World Politics: China and the Afro-Asian People's Solidarity Organization, 1957–1967*

28. Kungtu C. Sun, assisted by Ralph W. Huenemann, *The Economic Development of Manchuria in the First Half of the Twentieth Century*

*29. Shahid Javed Burki, *A Study of Chinese Communes, 1965*

30. John Carter Vincent, *The Extraterritorial System in China: Final Phase*

31. Madeleine Chi, *China Diplomacy, 1914–1918*

*32. Clifton Jackson Phillips, *Protestant America and the Pagan World: The First Half Century of the American Board of Commissioners for Foreign Missions, 1810–1860*

33. James Pusey, *Wu Han: Attacking the Present through the Past*

34. Ying-wan Cheng, *Postal Communication in China and Its Modernization, 1860–1896*

35. Tuvia Blumenthal, *Saving in Postwar Japan*

36. Peter Frost, *The Bakumatsu Currency Crisis*

37. Stephen C. Lockwood, *Augustine Heard and Company, 1858–1862*

38. Robert R. Campbell, *James Duncan Campbell: A Memoir by His Son*

39. Jerome Alan Cohen, ed., *The Dynamics of China's Foreign Relations*

40. V. V. Vishnyakova-Akimova, *Two Years in Revolutionary China, 1925–1927*, tr. Steven L. Levine

*41. Meron Medzini, *French Policy in Japan during the Closing Years of the Tokugawa Regime*

42. Ezra Vogel, Margie Sargent, Vivienne B. Shue, Thomas Jay Mathews, and Deborah S. Davis, *The Cultural Revolution in the Provinces*

*43. Sidney A. Forsythe, *An American Missionary Community in China, 1895–1905*

*44. Benjamin I. Schwartz, ed., *Reflections on the May Fourth Movement.: A Symposium*

*45. Ching Young Choe, *The Rule of the Taewŏngun, 1864–1873: Restoration in Yi Korea*

46. W. P. J. Hall, *A Bibliographical Guide to Japanese Research on the Chinese Economy, 1958–1970*

47. Jack J. Gerson, *Horatio Nelson Lay and Sino-British Relations, 1854–1864*

48. Paul Richard Bohr, *Famine and the Missionary: Timothy Richard as Relief Administrator and Advocate of National Reform*

49. Endymion Wilkinson, *The History of Imperial China: A Research Guide*

50. Britten Dean, *China and Great Britain: The Diplomacy of Commercial Relations, 1860–1864*

51. Ellsworth C. Carlson, *The Foochow Missionaries, 1847–1880*

52. Yeh-chien Wang, *An Estimate of the Land-Tax Collection in China, 1753 and 1908*

53. Richard M. Pfeffer, *Understanding Business Contracts in China, 1949–1963*

54. Han-sheng Chuan and Richard Kraus, *Mid-Ching Rice Markets and Trade: An Essay in Price History*

55. Ranbir Vohra, *Lao She and the Chinese Revolution*

56. Liang-lin Hsiao, *China's Foreign Trade Statistics, 1864–1949*

*57. Lee-hsia Hsu Ting, *Government Control of the Press in Modern China, 1900–1949*

58. Edward W. Wagner, *The Literati Purges: Political Conflict in Early Yi Korea*

*59. Joungwon A. Kim, *Divided Korea: The Politics of Development, 1945–1972*

*60. Noriko Kamachi, John K. Fairbank, and Chūzō Ichiko, *Japanese Studies of Modern China Since 1953: A Bibliographical Guide to Historical and Social-Science Research on the Nineteenth and Twentieth Centuries, Supplementary Volume for 1953–1969*

61. Donald A. Gibbs and Yun-chen Li, *A Bibliography of Studies and Translations of Modern Chinese Literature, 1918–1942*

62. Robert H. Silin, *Leadership and Values: The Organization of Large-Scale Taiwanese Enterprises*

63. David Pong, *A Critical Guide to the Kwangtung Provincial Archives Deposited at the Public Record Office of London*

*64. Fred W. Drake, *China Charts the World: Hsu Chi-yü and His Geography of 1848*

*65. William A. Brown and Urgrunge Onon, translators and annotators, *History of the Mongolian People's Republic*

66. Edward L. Farmer, *Early Ming Government: The Evolution of Dual Capitals*

*67. Ralph C. Croizier, *Koxinga and Chinese Nationalism: History, Myth, and the Hero*

*68. William J. Tyler, tr., *The Psychological World of Natsume Sōseki*, by Doi Takeo

69. Eric Widmer, *The Russian Ecclesiastical Mission in Peking during the Eighteenth Century*

*70. Charlton M. Lewis, *Prologue to the Chinese Revolution: The Transformation of Ideas and Institutions in Hunan Province, 1891–1907*

71. Preston Torbert, *The Ching Imperial Household Department: A Study of Its Organization and Principal Functions, 1662–1796*

72. Paul A. Cohen and John E. Schrecker, eds., *Reform in Nineteenth-Century China*

73. Jon Sigurdson, *Rural Industrialism in China*

74. Kang Chao, *The Development of Cotton Textile Production in China*

75. Valentin Rabe, *The Home Base of American China Missions, 1880–1920*

*76. Sarasin Viraphol, *Tribute and Profit: Sino-Siamese Trade, 1652–1853*

77. Ch'i-ch'ing Hsiao, *The Military Establishment of the Yuan Dynasty*

78. Meishi Tsai, *Contemporary Chinese Novels and Short Stories, 1949–1974: An Annotated Bibliography*

*79. Wellington K. K. Chan, *Merchants, Mandarins and Modern Enterprise in Late Ching China*

80. Endymion Wilkinson, *Landlord and Labor in Late Imperial China: Case Studies from Shandong by Jing Su and Luo Lun*

Harvard East Asian Monographs

*81. Barry Keenan, *The Dewey Experiment in China: Educational Reform and Political Power in the Early Republic*

*82. George A. Hayden, *Crime and Punishment in Medieval Chinese Drama: Three Judge Pao Plays*

*83. Sang-Chul Suh, *Growth and Structural Changes in the Korean Economy, 1910–1940*

84. J. W. Dower, *Empire and Aftermath: Yoshida Shigeru and the Japanese Experience, 1878–1954*

85. Martin Collcutt, *Five Mountains: The Rinzai Zen Monastic Institution in Medieval Japan*

86. Kwang Suk Kim and Michael Roemer, *Growth and Structural Transformation*

87. Anne O. Krueger, *The Developmental Role of the Foreign Sector and Aid*

*88. Edwin S. Mills and Byung-Nak Song, *Urbanization and Urban Problems*

89. Sung Hwan Ban, Pal Yong Moon, and Dwight H. Perkins, *Rural Development*

*90. Noel F. McGinn, Donald R. Snodgrass, Yung Bong Kim, Shin-Bok Kim, and Quee-Young Kim, *Education and Development in Korea*

91. Leroy P. Jones and Il SaKong, *Government, Business, and Entrepreneurship in Economic Development: The Korean Case*

92. Edward S. Mason, Dwight H. Perkins, Kwang Suk Kim, David C. Cole, Mahn Je Kim et al., *The Economic and Social Modernization of the Republic of Korea*

93. Robert Repetto, Tai Hwan Kwon, Son-Ung Kim, Dae Young Kim, John E. Sloboda, and Peter J. Donaldson, *Economic Development, Population Policy, and Demographic Transition in the Republic of Korea*

94. Parks M. Coble, Jr., *The Shanghai Capitalists and the Nationalist Government, 1927–1937*

95. Noriko Kamachi, *Reform in China: Huang Tsun-hsien and the Japanese Model*

96. Richard Wich, *Sino-Soviet Crisis Politics: A Study of Political Change and Communication*

97. Lillian M. Li, *China's Silk Trade: Traditional Industry in the Modern World, 1842–1937*

98. R. David Arkush, *Fei Xiaotong and Sociology in Revolutionary China*

*99. Kenneth Alan Grossberg, *Japan's Renaissance: The Politics of the Muromachi Bakufu*

100. James Reeve Pusey, *China and Charles Darwin*

101. Hoyt Cleveland Tillman, *Utilitarian Confucianism: Chen Liang's Challenge to Chu Hsi*

102. Thomas A. Stanley, *Ōsugi Sakae, Anarchist in Taishō Japan: The Creativity of the Ego*

103. Jonathan K. Ocko, *Bureaucratic Reform in Provincial China: Ting Jih-ch'ang in Restoration Kiangsu, 1867–1870*

104. James Reed, *The Missionary Mind and American East Asia Policy, 1911–1915*

105. Neil L. Waters, *Japan's Local Pragmatists: The Transition from Bakumatsu to Meiji in the Kawasaki Region*

106. David C. Cole and Yung Chul Park, *Financial Development in Korea, 1945–1978*

107. Roy Bahl, Chuk Kyo Kim, and Chong Kee Park, *Public Finances during the Korean Modernization Process*

108. William D. Wray, *Mitsubishi and the N.Y.K, 1870–1914: Business Strategy in the Japanese Shipping Industry*

Harvard East Asian Monographs

109. Ralph William Huenemann, *The Dragon and the Iron Horse: The Economics of Railroads in China, 1876–1937*

110. Benjamin A. Elman, *From Philosophy to Philology: Intellectual and Social Aspects of Change in Late Imperial China*

111. Jane Kate Leonard, *Wei Yüan and China's Rediscovery of the Maritime World*

112. Luke S. K. Kwong, *A Mosaic of the Hundred Days:. Personalities, Politics, and Ideas of 1898*

113. John E. Wills, Jr., *Embassies and Illusions: Dutch and Portuguese Envoys to K'ang-hsi, 1666–1687*

114. Joshua A. Fogel, *Politics and Sinology: The Case of Naitō Konan (1866–1934)*

*115. Jeffrey C. Kinkley, ed., *After Mao: Chinese Literature and Society, 1978– 1981*

116. C. Andrew Gerstle, *Circles of Fantasy: Convention in the Plays of Chikamatsu*

117. Andrew Gordon, *The Evolution of Labor Relations in Japan: Heavy Industry, 1853–1955*

*118. Daniel K. Gardner, *Chu Hsi and the "Ta Hsueh": Neo-Confucian Reflection on the Confucian Canon*

119. Christine Guth Kanda, *Shinzō: Hachiman Imagery and Its Development*

*120. Robert Borgen, *Sugawara no Michizane and the Early Heian Court*

121. Chang-tai Hung, *Going to the People: Chinese Intellectual and Folk Literature, 1918–1937*

* 122. Michael A. Cusumano, *The Japanese Automobile Industry: Technology and Management at Nissan and Toyota*

123. Richard von Glahn, *The Country of Streams and Grottoes: Expansion, Settlement, and the Civilizing of the Sichuan Frontier in Song Times*

124. Steven D. Carter, *The Road to Komatsubara: A Classical Reading of the Renga Hyakuin*

125. Katherine F. Bruner, John K. Fairbank, and Richard T. Smith, *Entering China's Service: Robert Hart's Journals, 1854–1863*

126. Bob Tadashi Wakabayashi, *Anti-Foreignism and Western Learning in Early-Modern Japan: The "New Theses" of 1825*

127. Atsuko Hirai, *Individualism and Socialism: The Life and Thought of Kawai Eijirō (1891–1944)*

128. Ellen Widmer, *The Margins of Utopia: "Shui-hu hou-chuan" and the Literature of Ming Loyalism*

129. R. Kent Guy, *The Emperor's Four Treasuries: Scholars and the State in the Late Chien-lung Era*

130. Peter C. Perdue, *Exhausting the Earth: State and Peasant in Hunan, 1500–1850*

131. Susan Chan Egan, *A Latterday Confucian: Reminiscences of William Hung (1893–1980)*

132. James T. C. Liu, *China Turning Inward: Intellectual-Political Changes in the Early Twelfth Century*

133. Paul A. Cohen, *Between Tradition and Modernity: Wang T'ao and Reform in Late Ching China*

134. Kate Wildman Nakai, *Shogunal Politics: Arai Hakuseki and the Premises of Tokugawa Rule*

135. Parks M. Coble, *Facing Japan: Chinese Politics and Japanese Imperialism, 1931–1937*

136. Jon L. Saari, *Legacies of Childhood: Growing Up Chinese in a Time of Crisis, 1890–1920*

137. Susan Downing Videen, *Tales of Heichū*

138. Heinz Morioka and Miyoko Sasaki, *Rakugo: The Popular Narrative Art of Japan*

139. Joshua A. Fogel, *Nakae Ushikichi in China: The Mourning of Spirit*

140. Alexander Barton Woodside, *Vietnam and the Chinese Model: A Comparative Study of Vietnamese and Chinese Government in the First Half of the Nineteenth Century*

141. George Elision, *Deus Destroyed: The Image of Christianity in Early Modern Japan*

142. William D. Wray, ed., *Managing Industrial Enterprise: Cases from Japan's Prewar Experience*

143. T'ung-tsu Ch'ü, *Local Government in China under the Ching*

144. Marie Anchordoguy, *Computers, Inc.: Japan's Challenge to IBM*

145. Barbara Molony, *Technology and Investment: The Prewar Japanese Chemical Industry*

146. Mary Elizabeth Berry, *Hideyoshi*

147. Laura E. Hein, *Fueling Growth: The Energy Revolution and Economic Policy in Postwar Japan*

148. Wen-hsin Yeh, *The Alienated Academy: Culture and Politics in Republican China, 1919–1937*

149. Dru C. Gladney, *Muslim Chinese: Ethnic Nationalism in the People's Republic*

150. Merle Goldman and Paul A. Cohen, eds., *Ideas Across Cultures: Essays on Chinese Thought in Honor of Benjamin L Schwartz*

151. James Polachek, *The Inner Opium War*

152. Gail Lee Bernstein, *Japanese Marxist: A Portrait of Kawakami Hajime, 1879–1946*

153. Lloyd E. Eastman, *The Abortive Revolution: China under Nationalist Rule, 1927–1937*

154. Mark Mason, *American Multinationals and Japan: The Political Economy of Japanese Capital Controls, 1899–1980*

155. Richard J. Smith, John K. Fairbank, and Katherine F. Bruner, *Robert Hart and China's Early Modernization: His Journals, 1863–1866*

156. George J. Tanabe, Jr., *Myōe the Dreamkeeper: Fantasy and Knowledge in Kamakura Buddhism*

157. William Wayne Farris, *Heavenly Warriors: The Evolution of Japan's Military, 500–1300*

158. Yu-ming Shaw, *An American Missionary in China: John Leighton Stuart and Chinese-American Relations*

159. James B. Palais, *Politics and Policy in Traditional Korea*

160. Douglas Reynolds, *China, 1898–1912: The Xinzheng Revolution and Japan*

161. Roger Thompson, *China's Local Councils in the Age of Constitutional Reform*

162. William Johnston, *The Modern Epidemic: History of Tuberculosis in Japan*

163. Constantine Nomikos Vaporis, *Breaking Barriers: Travel and the State in Early Modern Japan*

164. Irmela Hijiya-Kirschnereit, *Rituals of Self-Revelation: Shishōsetsu as Literary Genre and Socio-Cultural Phenomenon*

165. James C. Baxter, *The Meiji Unification through the Lens of Ishikawa Prefecture*

Harvard East Asian Monographs

166. Thomas R. H. Havens, *Architects of Affluence: The Tsutsumi Family and the Seibu-Saison Enterprises in Twentieth-Century Japan*

167. Anthony Hood Chambers, *The Secret Window: Ideal Worlds in Tanizaki's Fiction*

168. Steven J. Ericson, *The Sound of the Whistle: Railroads and the State in Meiji Japan*

169. Andrew Edmund Goble, *Kenmu: Go-Daigo's Revolution*

170. Denise Potrzeba Lett, *In Pursuit of Status: The Making of South Korea's "New" Urban Middle Class*

171. Mimi Hall Yiengpruksawan, *Hiraizumi: Buddhist Art and Regional Politics in Twelfth-Century Japan*

172. Charles Shirō Inouye, *The Similitude of Blossoms: A Critical Biography of Izumi Kyōka (1873–1939), Japanese Novelist and Playwright*

173. Aviad E. Raz, *Riding the Black Ship: Japan and Tokyo Disneyland*

174. Deborah J. Milly, *Poverty, Equality, and Growth: The Politics of Economic Need in Postwar Japan*

175. See Heng Teow, *Japan's Cultural Policy Toward China, 1918–1931: A Comparative Perspective*

176. Michael A. Fuller, *An Introduction to Literary Chinese*

177. Frederick R. Dickinson, *War and National Reinvention: Japan in the Great War, 1914–1919*

178. John Solt, *Shredding the Tapestry of Meaning: The Poetry and Poetics of Kitasono Katue (1902–1978)*

179. Edward Pratt, *Japan's Protoindustrial Elite: The Economic Foundations of the Gōnō*

180. Atsuko Sakaki, *Recontextualizing Texts: Narrative Performance in Modern Japanese Fiction*

181. Soon-Won Park, *Colonial Industrialization and Labor in Korea: The Onoda Cement Factory*

182. JaHyun Kim Haboush and Martina Deuchler, *Culture and the State in Late Chosŏn Korea*

183. John W. Chaffee, *Branches of Heaven: A History of the Imperial Clan of Sung China*

184. Gi-Wook Shin and Michael Robinson, eds., *Colonial Modernity in Korea*

185. Nam-lin Hur, *Prayer and Play in Late Tokugawa Japan: Asakusa Sensōji and Edo Society*

186. Kristin Stapleton, *Civilizing Chengdu: Chinese Urban Reform, 1895–1937*

187. Hyung Il Pai, *Constructing "Korean" Origins: A Critical Review of Archaeology, Historiography, and Racial Myth in Korean State-Formation Theories*

188. Brian D. Ruppert, *Jewel in the Ashes: Buddha Relics and Power in Early Medieval Japan*

189. Susan Daruvala, *Zhou Zuoren and an Alternative Chinese Response to Modernity*

190. James Z. Lee, *The Political Economy of a Frontier: Southwest China, 1250–1850*

191. Kerry Smith, *A Time of Crisis: Japan, the Great Depression, and Rural Revitalization*

192. Michael Lewis, *Becoming Apart: National Power and Local Politics in Toyama, 1868–1945*

193. William C. Kirby, Man-houng Lin, James Chin Shih, and David A. Pietz, eds., *State and Economy in Republican China: A Handbook for Scholars*

194. Timothy S. George, *Minamata: Pollution and the Struggle for Democracy in Postwar Japan*

Harvard East Asian Monographs

195. Billy K. L. So, *Prosperity, Region, and Institutions in Maritime China: The South Fukien Pattern, 946–1368*

196. Yoshihisa Tak Matsusaka, *The Making of Japanese Manchuria, 1904–1932*

197. Maram Epstein, *Competing Discourses: Orthodoxy, Authenticity, and Engendered Meanings in Late Imperial Chinese Fiction*

198. Curtis J. Milhaupt, J. Mark Ramseyer, and Michael K. Young, eds. and comps., *Japanese Law in Context: Readings in Society, the Economy, and Politics*

199. Haruo Iguchi, *Unfinished Business: Ayukawa Yoshisuke and U.S.-Japan Relations, 1937–1952*

200. Scott Pearce, Audrey Spiro, and Patricia Ebrey, *Culture and Power in the Reconstitution of the Chinese Realm, 200–600*

201. Terry Kawashima, *Writing Margins: The Textual Construction of Gender in Heian and Kamakura Japan*

202. Martin W. Huang, *Desire and Fictional Narrative in Late Imperial China*

203. Robert S. Ross and Jiang Changbin, eds., *Re-examining the Cold War: U.S.-China Diplomacy, 1954–1973*

204. Guanhua Wang, *In Search of Justice: The 1905–1906 Chinese Anti-American Boycott*

205. David Schaberg, *A Patterned Past: Form and Thought in Early Chinese Historiography*

206. Christine Yano, *Tears of Longing: Nostalgia and the Nation in Japanese Popular Song*

207. Milena Doleželová-Velingerová and Oldřich Král, with Graham Sanders, eds., *The Appropriation of Cultural Capital: China's May Fourth Project*

208. Robert N. Huey, *The Making of 'Shinkokinshū'*

209. Lee Butler, *Emperor and Aristocracy in Japan, 1467–1680: Resilience and Renewal*

210. Suzanne Ogden, *Inklings of Democracy in China*

211. Kenneth J. Ruoff, *The People's Emperor: Democracy and the Japanese Monarchy, 1945–1995*

212. Haun Saussy, *Great Walls of Discourse and Other Adventures in Cultural China*

213. Aviad E. Raz, *Emotions at Work: Normative Control, Organizations, and Culture in Japan and America*

214. Rebecca E. Karl and Peter Zarrow, eds., *Rethinking the 1898 Reform Period: Political and Cultural Change in Late Qing China*

215. Kevin O'Rourke, *The Book of Korean Shijo*

216. Ezra F. Vogel, Yuan Ming, and Tanaka Akihiko, *The Golden Age of the U.S.-China-Japan Triangle, 1972–1989*

217. Thomas A Wilson, ed., *On Sacred Grounds: Culture, Society, Politics, and the Formation of the Cult of Confucius*